ECONOMICS

To Linda and Barbara

CONTENTS

FOREWORD

At last! Beginning economics students have for too long been denied a thoroughly critical analysis of the society in which they live. Hunt and Sherman have now provided them with such a critique, and at the same time they have supplied professional expositions of traditional economic theory. Other authors of elementary textbooks have presented this aspect or that of traditional theory as well as or even better or more fully than Hunt and Sherman have, good as their treatment generally is, but no authors, to my knowledge, have given elementary economics students a truer picture of modern capitalism in its national and world dimensions. There are many ways to present traditional economic theory, and each instructor undoubtedly has his or her favorites, but the theory presented in this book is by social critics rather than by apologists for the system, and that should make all the difference to students who truly wish to gain a deeper understanding of what is going on in the world today.

Radical economists are dissatisfied, to put the point gently, with the conventional approach to economics, which takes the capitalist system for granted, considering it more or less eternal, and so skimps on the history of both the system and its ideology. Accordingly, conventional textbooks serve capitalism to the students on a platter, as though there was nothing else in the kitchen or ever would be. Hunt and Sherman break with that approach, right off the bat, by devoting Part One of their book to the evolution of economic institutions and ideologies. Joseph Schumpeter once wrote that "nobody can hope to understand the economic phenomena of any, including the present, epoch who has not an adequate command of historical facts and an adequate amount of historical sense. . . ." The authors of this book have taken those words seriously.

There is another reason for discontent with the conventional approach. It distorts reality by assuming harmonies of interest throughout society, ignoring the deep class conflicts that prevail in our society. Such sweetness and light enable conventional economists to refer to "the general interest," "the public welfare," "the common good," and other equally soothing expressions and to assume that the State represents everyone's interests. Hunt and Sherman, I am pleased to say, look upon their discipline as "political economics" rather than economics in the narrow sense, and so throughout the book they study economic problems within the context of ruler-subject relations—always sensitive to the fact that there are pervasive relationships of domination and servitude throughout our society. That this makes a difference can easily be seen by comparing their analyses of income distribution, discrimination, economic waste, international finance, and development of poor countries with corresponding treatments in other textbooks. Hunt and Sherman come out on top because their conception of the world—which includes power, conflict, and disruptive change within a historical setting—is more accurate than the paradigms used by bourgeois economists.

Do we have to put up with the misinformation in the thin and slanted chapters in one elementary textbook after another, which are supposed to pass for serious analyses of socialism, communism, and Marxism? Not any longer. I do not mean that Hunt and Sherman have given us glowing accounts of the supreme joy of living in the Soviet Union and China, for they have not. What I mean is that we now have a serious discussion of alternative economic systems by experts who have more than their share of critical faculties. The five chapters that make up the last part of the book will inform and stimulate a large number of beginning economics students.

Radical economics still has a long way to go, as Hunt and Sherman well know, before it can sweep away most of the rubbish in present-day bourgeois economics. This book is an excellent contribution toward that end.

John G. Gurley

PREFACE

This book is very different from the traditional elementary economics text.

We do present the traditional economic theory. In addition, we present radical critiques and radical theories. In the traditional economics category we include economists who are generally classified as liberal as well as those generally considered conservative. The traditional view rests on Adam Smith's notion that in a market economy the forces of supply and demand act as an "invisible hand" to guide resources into their most efficient uses and to distribute the proceeds of the productive process in a reasonably fair manner.

Most economists realize that the forces of supply and demand do not always maximize social welfare. In some circumstances they might even be pernicious. In these instances it is necessary for the government to intervene in the market to ensure a socially acceptable outcome. Varying assessments of the extent and significance of these "special cases" differentiate liberals and conservatives. Liberals believe that promoting the society's welfare requires relatively frequent government intervention into market processes. Conservatives believe that these interventions should be relatively less frequent. Neither liberals nor conservatives seriously question the basic institutional framework of the private property, market capitalist economy within which the forces of supply and demand operate.

Radicals, however, subject these institutions to critical scrutiny. In this book we shall use the term *radical* in its traditional meaning. Traditionally, the adjective *radical* has referred to "leftist" or "socialist" criticisms or actions, and the noun *radical* has referred to these leftists and socialists. In recent times, particularly since the 1964 American presidential election, references have been made to the *radical right*. Included in the radical right have been various political conservatives, reactionaries, and assorted cranks. We do not refer to these right-wing radicals when we use the term. We mean only radicals of the left.

Thus, in this book we shall be concerned with radical criticism of the fundamental institutions of capitalism as well as the orthodox views on how the market capitalist system functions.

A HISTORICAL APPROACH

In Part One we introduce economics by way of a history of the great economists (some of them wild and wonderful). We present their ideas as set within the context of the institutions of their times, and therefore we sketch an economic history.

There is no easier and more pleasant way of learning economics than to follow the evolution of the main ideas of the great thinkers in the field. This will also impress upon the reader, as nothing else could, that there are at least two (and usually more) views on every subject in economics.

It is interesting to see how our modern economic institutions slowly evolved from feudal times. The usual textbooks start off cold from the present situation. We believe it is much more meaningful to witness all of the curious zigzags and the fighting that occurred in the development of our present institutions. How things developed in the past gives us a key to understanding the present and, hopefully, the future.

The history of economic ideas and the history of economic institutions are not totally independent of each other. In reality, they are very closely related, each affecting the other at all times. Thus, we shall see that the specific problems and interests of various groups gave rise to very specific economic ideologies and that these ideologies served as an excuse for the status quo or as a call for drastic change. For example, we shall see in the first few chapters that the dominant ideology in the medieval period fully supported the feudal economic system as just and correct and eternal. Eventually, however, the contrary ideas of the new groups of merchants and industrialists were reflected in new economic ideologies, which then helped overturn the old restrictive feudal order.

TEACHING ECONOMIC THEORY

The traditional approach concentrates on explaining how the consumer may maximize his satisfaction from spending, how the businessman may maximize his profits, and how the government may aid private business to maximize growth. This approach is often dull and mechanical. We include these usual and somewhat mechanical subjects, but to a lesser degree, focusing on the more exciting present-day social and political issues. In fact, ours is more of a political economics textbook than a purely economics textbook.

Thus, in Part Two we discuss the traditional microeconomic problems of the individual consumer and the individual business firm. We also investigate often neglected problems—for example, poverty, racism, sexual discrimination, monopoly power, unequal education opportunities, and tax loopholes.

Similarly, in Part Three we discussed the usual macroeconomic problems of the economy as a whole, including the basic questions of inflation and unemployment. In addition, we examine such problems as pollution and waste, population, war spending, the less developed countries, and imperialism.

OBJECTIVITY

Some traditional economists will complain that we do not present the conservative or traditional views completely enough. We do try, especially in the historical presentations of Part One, to state both the traditional and radical views as impartially as possible. Of course no one is impartial, so we undoubtedly state the radical view somewhat more effectively. In Parts Two and Three we again state the traditional views first, before giving the radical view, but our sympathy with the radical view will be quite apparent.

Some radical economists who have read this book before publication have complained of the opposite. They said that we sound too impartial between the conservative and radical views, especially in their historical presentation.

Other radicals have complained that it is not necessary to state the orthodox views at all because they are wrong. We believe, first, that students should be acquainted with all views. Second, present radical views can be understood only in their historical context, which definitely includes the traditional theories, criticism of which led to the radical theories. Third, we do not like a know-nothing radicalism of the type that says, Poverty and racism are bad, so we should just go out and demonstrate against them and toss tomatoes at their defenders. On the contrary, we believe one must put some hard study into political economics in order to understand the causes of poverty and racism and other evils and their possible cures.

A COMPARATIVE APPROACH

In Part Four we take the reader on an excursion through some of the countries that call themselves socialist, particularly Russia, China, and Yugoslavia. Various chapters examine their historical development, current institutions, and current problems. Their development and institutions are compared with those of the Western capitalist countries. This does not merely give us an idea of what the rest of the world looks like. It is also important because the comparisons bring out more clearly many of the features of the Western capitalist countries. For example, in studying the market process of the United States, it is very interesting and helpful to compare it with the planned nonmarket economies of eastern Europe.

SOME OTHER SPECIAL FEATURES

The usual elementary economics text is filled with nothing but graphs and mathematics. We have used graphs only where necessary to illustrate a point, but we have always explained them first in ordinary English and have kept the graphs as simple as possible.

For the convenience of students, summaries are provided at the end of each chapter. *Warning:* No summary can explain a chapter; it may merely remind you of the most important points. *Another warning:* No summary can be very accurate because it is too short to include all the necessary qualifications.

For instructors accustomed to standard textbooks, we have presented most theory in its usual order and covered the usual topics. In a few places that is not so. For example, international trade is sometimes placed in the microeconomics part, even though it always contains many macroeconomic observations. Because we found that the macroeconomic issues in international trade are the most interesting, we have emphasized them and put the discussion in that part. (It is independent enough of the surrounding chapters so that it can be used at a different point.) Also, we have omitted production functions, a traditional topic, because we approach the subject differently and believe recent theory has shown this approach to be based on indefensible assumptions.

HOW TO USE THIS BOOK

This book has been designed so that it may be used as the main text for a one-year course, but with plentiful use of supplements. Many good collections of readings are available. It may also be used for a one-semester or one-quarter course if one wishes to cover the material somewhat lightly or emphasize particular areas.

Most instructors prefer to teach macroeconomics before microeconomics. That is understandable because microeconomic theory is usually especially dull and lifeless in most texts. This book is so arranged that the instructor may, if he or she wishes, teach the macroeconomics first, even though it comes second. In other words, the two parts are sufficiently independent, even though they refer to each other at the appropriate points.

After some heated discussion between the authors, we decided to put the microeconomics part first. For one, we believe our microeconomics section is much more interesting than the average. We go through the usual supply and demand graphs, although as simply as possible. But the section also emphasizes the radical views on poverty, government behavior, and racial and sexual discrimination—all of which, we believe, the reader will find exciting. We also present the usual graphs on monopoly theory but give a great deal more attention than most books to the history and facts of monopoly in the United States. We believe the material on income distribution and monopoly is particularly important in understanding the later macro material on waste and cyclical unemployment in the United States. (But again, we emphasize that the instructor could conceivably teach Part Three ahead of Part Two if he or she so desired.)

Finally, the book may be used in special ways in one-quarter or one-semester courses emphasizing only one aspect of economics. First, in a macroeconomics course we suggest that Part One on history be assigned so as to be read lightly in the first few weeks. (Chapter 11 on Keynes could be emphasized.) Then jump to Part Three on macroeconomics; this is a lengthy part and will give plenty of meat, although a supplement could certainly be used as well.

Second, in a course on microeconomics we would again suggest beginning with Part One so that the student sees how microeconomics developed through the history of thought (particularly emphasizing the chapters on the neoclassical economists and on Marx). Part Two will then follow naturally. Since Part Two is fairly short, you may have time for the comparative material of Part Four, which examines several microproblems in the context of economic planning. You should also have time to include a supplement.

Third, some courses emphasize history and institutions and deemphasize theory. We believe our book is better suited for such a course than any other available complete textbook. All of Part One could be emphasized. In Part Two most of Chapters 14, 15, and 19 could be omitted. On the other hand, Chapters 16, 17, 18, 20, and 21 are mainly institutional. In Part Three Chapters 24 and 25 could be omitted. The other chapters are mainly institutional, although certain sections might be omitted. In Part Four all of the chapters are heavily historical and institutional.

ACKNOWLEDGMENTS

We are profoundly grateful to those whose teaching or direct help made this book possible: Professors Sidney Coontz, William Davisson, Douglas Dowd, Robert Edminster, David Felix, John Gurley, J. W. Hanks, Kiyotoshi Iwamoto, Robert Lekachman, Lawrence Nabors, Andreas Papandreou, Lynn Turgeon, Benjamin Ward, Thomas Weisskopf, and Stephen Worland. Extensive research help, for which we express our thanks, was furnished by Maryanna Boynton, Kathleen Pulling, Faris Bingaradi, Brian Bock, William Harnett, and Michael Sheehan.

We also wish to thank various publishers for giving us permission to use certain materials from our previous books: Hunt, *Property and Prophets* (Harper & Row, 1978); Sherman, *Elementary Aggregate Economics* (Appleton, 1966); Sherman, *The Soviet Economy* (Little, Brown, 1969); Sherman, *Profit Rates in the United States* (Cornell University Press, 1968); Sherman, *Radical Political Economy* (Basic Books, 1972); and Sherman, *Stagflation* (Harper & Row, 1976).

For later editions we gratefully acknowledge the extensive but constructive criticism of several reviewers: Professors Norris Clement, James Cypher, Clint Jencks, John Pool, Ross La Roe, Larry Sawyers, Jim Starkey, and Rick Wolff. We warmly appreciate the typing and clerical help of Poinka Pastucha, Susan Bradley, and Shirlee Pigeon.

For the future we invite any useful ideas for improvements in the book. Please write to us and we will take your suggestions very seriously.

E. K. Hunt
Howard J. Sherman

INTRODUCTION

This book is about traditional and radical economics. It may surprise you to learn that there is no single *truth* in economics but, rather, two or more conflicting approaches to it. That is, however, the sad fact in economics and in all the other social sciences. In studying society there is no important point that is noncontroversial; on every important issue there are a range of opinions from the most conservative to the most radical. Certainly there are some facts that most economists agree on, and there are some tools that most economists use—but we differ over what the important problems are, how to approach them, and how to interpret the findings.

One basic area of disagreement concerns the possibility of changing things. Radicals contend that society can and should be drastically changed. Conservatives contend that nothing can ever change because our behavior is rooted in an unchanging human nature. This basic difference is shown in an amusing imaginary dialogue between an old, conservative cannibal named Wowsy and his young, idealistic, and radical friend, another cannibal, named Bongo:

BONGO: Human beings should not eat each other.
WOWSY: Good Gooey Gow! You can't dictate to people what they're going to eat and what they're not going to eat. Men have always eaten each other and always will. It's natural. You can't change human nature.
BONGO: I love my fellow men.
WOWSY: So do I—with gravy on them.[1]

The conservative economists, like Wowsy, argue that people are born with certain ideas—such as eating people, or holding slaves, or being a competitive capitalist—and that there is no way to change those ideas. Since these ideas are held by everyone, our behavior is determined by these ideas and cannot be changed. Where do they come from? Some conservatives say God gives us our ideas. Others claim that certain ways of living are just "natural" and obvious, so everyone naturally knows they are best. Others, like Freud, simply say we are born with innate, inherited drives—for example, all men are aggressive and domineering; all women are passive and like to be dominated.

Similarly, conservatives in the South before the Civil War said that slavery was natural, that the blacks were happy only as slaves, and that the whites were natural slave owners. The clergy added that slavery was divinely ordained by God, that keeping slaves so that they would be happy—and whipping them occasionally for their own good—was the Christian white man's burden.

In the Middle Ages conservative religious leaders and social thinkers held that serfdom was natural and reflected human nature. The serfs were happy working

[1] From a newspaper column by the radical satirist, Mike Quinn, in the *Daily Peoples World*, 1938.

for landlords because that was a serf's nature. The landlords were happy directing serfs, judging them, and even executing them (but only when necessary)
because that was a landlord's nature. Thomas Aquinas contended that some
prices are normal and natural and that it is a sin to buy or sell at more or less than
these prices. Chapter 1 will explore medieval economic views more fully.

During the Industrial Revolution, a school of economists known as the classical school preached that capitalism is natural and eternal, earlier economic systems being "unnatural." They claimed that it is the natural proclivity of every
person to be greedy, to compete relentlessly, to calculate rationally every purchase and every other economic activity. These views are further explored in
Chapter 4 of this book.

Finally, most traditional economists of today (called neoclassical economists)
take as given at birth all the preferences of individual consumers. They seem to
think that we are born with a certain order of preferences for Cadillacs or TV
sets. In Chapter 7 we shall see that these natural consumer preferences constitute the heart of their economics.

THE RADICAL VIEW

By contrast with conservatives, radical economists believe that all ideas and preferences—such as our desire for Cadillacs—are shaped by the society in which
we live. Consumers are influenced not only by obvious means like advertising but
also by more subtle and pervasive means like family upbringing, religion, education, and the mass media. Similarly, it is no coincidence that the dominant view or
ideology under slavery supports slavery, that under serfdom supports serfdom,
and that under capitalism supports capitalism. Social scientists are human beings like everyone else and thus have their own ideas and preconceptions
shaped by society.

Since our ideology is determined by our social environment, radical economists contend that a change in our socioeconomic structure will eventually
change the dominant ideology. For example, before the Civil War most Southerners (including their social scientists) declared that slavery was natural and good;
but after 100 years of capitalist socioeconomic institutions, most Southerners
(including their social scientists) declare that capitalism is natural and good. So
the dominant ideas are not given by human nature but are shaped by socioeconomic relations and can be changed by changes in the underlying relationships.
There is thus hope for a completely new and better society with new and better
views by most people.

This does not mean that ideas are unimportant in the process of social
change. The ideas of at least a large number of people must change before a
revolutionary social change is possible. The point is only that our ideological
views are not God-given and do not change at random. New views—such as the
revolutionary ideology of liberty, equality, and fraternity—appeared and caused
the French and U.S. revolutions only because they reflected underlying social
conflicts. The needs of most people (farmers and workers and industrialists)
came into conflict with the old socioeconomic relationships (the French feudal
monarchy, British colonialism). These conflicts caused social thinkers, such as
Voltaire and Tom Paine, to present new ideologies. The new ideologies caught
on because they reflected most people's needs and desires. This led to political

revolutions, which changed socioeconomic structures. The new structures reinforced the new ideas and made their ideological conquest complete. This circular process is charted in the figure below.

Economic forces are defined here to include all the labor that workers do, the
tools and machinery with which they work, use of known natural resources, and
use of the available level of technology. *Economic relations* are the relations
among people doing economic activity—for example, the relations between
slaves and slaveowners, workers and capitalists, debtors and creditors. In Chapter 6 we shall find that Karl Marx said that economic activity and relations, defined in this broad matter, from the *base* or foundation of society; on this base is
built a *superstructure* consisting of institutions and ideologies. The social and
political *institutions* include the family, government, organized religions, all the
laws, the educational system, and the media of communication. *Ideologies* include philosophy, much of the social sciences, religion, and all folk customs and
biases (such as white or male supremacy).

In any nonrevolutionary period, all the elements of this system reinforce each
other. Suppose the economic forces consist of a fairly low level of technology in
isolated agricultural estates, while the economic relations are those of feudalism,
of landlords ruling over serfs. The political institutions reflect feudal relations in a
hierarchy of power up the largest landlord, the king. The ideology reflects this
hierarchy, claiming that the whole system—especially the king—is divinely ordained. So the ideology reinforces the existing institutions, which reinforce the
existing economic relations.

In the rare revolutionary situations, conflicts (which are always there to some
extent) suddenly become very evident among the elements of the system. For
example, over a long period in feudal Europe commerce and industry slowly
replaced agricultural economic activity. As a result, a new economic class of
capitalists and merchants appeared. There was conflict because the old feudal
lords had control of the political institutions and did not want to surrender any
power to the upstart capitalists. Eventually, these conflicts led to revolutionary
new ideologies, new institutions, and new relations.

Ideas and Economics

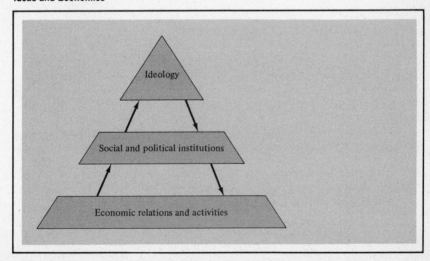

PRIMITIVE ECONOMIES

As an example of the various economies that have existed, let us examine the so-called *primitive* type. One British archaeologist lists the characteristics of most areas of human settlement in our first half-million years or so as follows: (1) very small communities; (2) communities quite isolated, self-sufficient, with little or no trade; (3) no writing; (4) a homogeneous group of people; (5) no full-time specialists; (6) the economic unit is the family or extended family of kinsmen; (7) relationships personal and status hereditary rather than economic; and (8) little or no political institutions.[2] There is one still-existing primitive community where even today "there is no private property in productive goods, and whatever the hunting band manages to kill is shared out among the members of the group."[3] In general, the most primitive societies have no market exchange, no money, and no economic competition in the modern sense. It is true that even the most primitive peoples known to anthropologists usually own their weapons, tools, and ornaments as individual private property; but the basic means of production at this stage are the hunting grounds, and these are owned collectively.

The point cannot be overstressed that in primitive societies men are not hired for jobs; they are not paid money; and purely economic relations do not prevail in any area (nor is force used in most cases). Rather, "men work together because they are related to each other, or have social obligations to one another."[4] Furthermore, work is done collectively and the results shared collectively. Or, as another anthropologist writes, "with qualifications such as the special shares locally awarded for special contributions to the group endeavor—the principle remains . . . 'goods collectively produced are distributed through the collectivity.'"[5]

The striking thing about such primitive societies from our present view is that everyone is on about the same plane of economic and political power. There is no ruling class, such as the ancient Roman or Greek or Egyptian slave owners, and no ruled class, such as the slaves in those societies. How did some collectivist, primitive societies evolve into class-divided societies—as in Greece, Rome, and Egypt?

THE TRANSITION TO CLASS SOCIETY

When "civilization" became established in the Middle East in the Bronze and Iron Ages, it was marked by large communities, taxes, public works, writing, use of mathematics and astronomy, internal and foreign trade, full-time specialists like farmers and metallurgists, political organization beyond family or kinship, a privileged ruling class, and an exploited class of workers, whether slaves or feudal serfs or peasants paying tribute. The key revolution, however, is the earlier transformation from hunting and gathering food to animal herding and agriculture.

[2] V. Gordon Childe, *Social Evolution* (London: Watts, 1951), passim.
[3] Manning Nash, in George Dalton, ed., *Tribal and Peasant Economies* (Garden City, N.Y.: Natural History Press, 1967), p. 3.
[4] Daryll Forde and Mary Douglas, in ibid., p. 17.
[5] Marshall Sahlins, "On the Sociology of Primitive Exchange," in Michael Barton, ed., *The Relevance of Models for Social Anthropology* (New York: Praeger, 1965), p. 142.

How did the agricultural revolution occur, and how did it end the primitive classless societies of these areas and bring about class rule? We know there was a slow expansion of technical knowledge and improvement of tools over hundreds of thousands of years. Then, in a few particularly fertile areas—perhaps more or less independently in China, Mesopotamia, Egypt, Mexico, and Peru— people discovered how to tame and breed animals and how to grow the most edible plants. This "revolution" did not occur in a momentary flash of insight to some individual. Rather, it seems to have been a very gradual process over thousands of years.

Recent work presents a detailed picture of this process in Mesopotamia and the Aztec areas of Mexico.[6] First, communities became more permanently settled, intensively collected food, and hunted in a smaller given area than previously. Second, the New Stone Age saw better tools being produced, including improved bows, drills, digging tools, and even boats and nets. Third, some crop—wheat, for example—that was already growing in the area might be moved to different areas as desired, protected by such means as removing any weeds, and eventually selected so as to obtain the desired food characteristics. Similarly, hunters of goats or cows might begin to follow one particular herd, protect it against its other enemies and finally feed and shelter it at times. All these changes could take thousands of years.

Once the pastoral-agricultural revolution is well under way, several important changes occur as a direct result. Obviously the level of productivity per worker increases. The first consequence of this fact is a much higher population density; herding and agriculture can support many people per square mile, whereas hunting and gathering require several square miles per person. At the same time, agriculture means that the population must settle in one place rather than moving here and there around the country. Such large, settled agglomerations mean the founding of permanent villages and, eventually, towns and cities in the most favored places.

There is enough economic surplus over immediate needs so that the economy may support various specialists, such as carpenters, shoemakers, and the like. Specialization, in turn, calls for exchange of products between individuals and between groups. Moreover, the higher productivity makes available wealth in the form of cattle and gold as well as consumer durables. Then the specialization and exchange slowly destroy the collective use and possession of property, so some individuals come to own more wealth than others.

With this increase of private property and larger, more permanently located groups of people, there is a need for a broader and stronger political structure to replace the family unit. At first, in both possession of private property and control of political power, the families or clans retain the semblance of unity and direction. Individuals slowly accumulate private property as there is more of it; so, too, do individuals slowly accumulate more political power as politics grows more complex.

A war chief may be elected from time to time as a result of small tribal conflicts; the post is likely to become a lifetime one or even hereditary as larger armies come into being. The area and intensity of wars increase at this time because wars for economic motives are used by advanced agricultural societies

---

[6] See Robert Adams, *The Evolution of Urban Society* (Chicago: Aldine, 1965), pp. 39–43.

for the acquisition of cattle or slaves. Most large-scale introductions of slavery seem to follow as the effect of a war of conquest. Yet such wars seem to occur only as the effect of a new technology high enough so that it is profitable to keep a slave (because he can produce a surplus). Slavery and wars of conquest are thus intertwined as cause and effect at a certain level of economic evolution.

To oversimplify a bit: Better technology following the agricultural revolution led to higher productivity per worker. The higher productivity, in turn, meant that a society could for the first time "afford" to have some nonworking individuals (such as slave owners, landlords, priests, full-time warriors). Conversely, until product per worker passed the point at which one worker could just keep himself alive, there could have been no surplus left for the ruling classes. Before that point, slavery or serfdom could not pay—hence prisoners were simply killed or eaten.

A similar increase of power may accrue to those in charge of public works. A director of irrigation for a small tribe may be appointed for a short time in one season; a director of irrigation for a large agricultural area along the Nile must be given more power for a lengthy period. Thus, in Egypt the government separates from and rises above family or clan for two different kinds of reasons: (1) to carry through public projects, including irrigation and warfare, and (2) to guard private property, including slaves (and to prevent slave revolt).

TYPES OF ECONOMIES

There have been many different types of economy in the world. We have examined in detail the *primitive* type, in which people worked in collective groups and shared the fruits of their labors. Another type is the *slave* economy, in which one class, the slaves, does all the work. The class of slave owners legally owns both the slaves and their whole product. They give the slaves barely enough to live on, keeping the surplus for themselves.

Still another economic system is *feudalism,* varieties of which appeared at different times in Europe, Asia, and Africa. Under feudalism the serf is bound to the land of some estate. The serf owes to the landlord—by tradition, but by force if necessary—150 to 200 days a year of service on the landlord's land. Yet the serf is better off than a slave, since he is not owned in body by the landlord and may work his own tiny plot of land when he finishes his chores on the landlord's land. In Chapters 1 and 2 we discuss the transition from feudalism to capitalism in Western Europe.

Most of this book discusses *capitalism,* the system existing at present in the United States. In this system capitalists are the class of people who own all factories and equipment. Capitalists employ workers, paying them a wage. Workers are not forced to work by physical coercion, as are slaves and serfs, but are "free" to work for a capitalist or not to work and hence to starve. Capitalists own the entire product beyond wages and material costs; they produce only if they expect to make a profit.

Part Four of this book discusses *socialist* economies. *Socialism* means ownership and control of the economy by the entire working population. Production is carried on for the benefit of society. Many countries, such as Cuba, the Soviet Union, and China, claim to have socialist economies.

PART ONE

PROPERTY AND PROPHETS: The Evolution of Economic Institutions and Ideologies

CHAPTER 1

THE IDEOLOGY OF PRECAPITALIST EUROPE

Human beings must exist in societies in order to survive. Unlike some species of animals, whose individual members can exist fairly adequately in relative isolation, human beings are not equipped by nature with the physical prowess to provide the material requisites of life by themselves. Humans survive and indeed prosper because by living in groups they have learned to subdivide tasks and use tools. It was this division of labor and the accumulation of more and better tools (or capital) that made possible the impressive increases in humankind's control over nature, or increases in our potential to produce the material necessities of life.

This division of labor also resulted, of necessity, in a differentiation of the roles that the different members of a society occupy. This differentiation was probably purely functional in earliest times; that is, when productivity was low, all members of a society lived near the subsistence level and social class, or hierarchical differentiation, was absent. Increasingly elaborate divisions of tasks, combined with more sophisticated tools, however, led to higher productivity, which made possible an escape from the drudgery of everyday toil for at least a small part of society.

A small leisure class could be supported because with higher per capita productivity the labor of a smaller number of people could support the entire society at its customary standard of living or at an even higher standard. When this occurred, societies began to differentiate among their members according to social class. This hierarchical class differentiation was generally economic in nature. Those who worked were usually assigned to the lowest classes; those who escaped the burdens of ordinary labor were of higher class standing. Although these higher-class people were no longer directly connected with the production of everyday necessities, they often performed rites, rituals, or extensive duties, some of which were undoubtedly beneficial to the society.

Such a system could not continue to exist for long if the majority of its members did not share common feelings about the proper way of conducting economic and social affairs. These common feelings and values, which generally stemmed from a common world view, or system of metaphysics, justified both the division of productive tasks and the class differentiation that existed. These common feelings and values were expressed in ideologies.

An *ideology*, as the term is used in this book, refers to ideas and beliefs that tend to justify morally a society's social and economic relationships. Most members of a society internalize the ideology and thus believe their functional role as

3

well as those of others are morally correct and that the method by which society divides its produce is fair. This common belief gives society its cohesiveness and viability. Lack of it creates turmoil and strife—and ultimately revolution, if the differences are deep enough.

This book is concerned primarily with our present economic system, capitalism. We sketch the broad outlines of the evolution of this system. In doing so we focus on conflicts and social antagonisms and examine the ideologies with which the capitalist system attempted to mitigate these conflicts and to promote social cohesiveness. By way of background we begin with the economic systems and ideologies of precapitalist Europe.

ANCIENT GREEK AND ROMAN SLAVERY

In ancient Greece and Rome as many as 80 percent of the people were slaves. The slaves did all the manual work and even much of the clerical, bureaucratic, and artistic work of these societies. They were given just enough food and clothing for bare subsistence. The slave owners owned and utilized the entire surplus produced by the slaves above their own subsistence. Most of the economy was agricultural, aside from a few cities where the central government was located. On each agricultural plantation the slave owner was king and lived in splendid luxury—though he might also have a villa in Athens or Rome. In addition to his wife, who was treated as a valuable piece of property, he sexually exploited his slave women.

What sort of economic ideology existed? There were a few treatises, especially in the Roman period, on the best ways to plant crops, the best agricultural implements to use, and the best ways to supervise, control, and punish slaves. In addition, there were a large number of justifications of slavery. Even such brilliant philosophers as Plato and Aristotle argued that slavery was "natural," was the only possible system, and would exist forever; they argued that some men and women were born to be slaves and were inherently inferior, while others were born superior and were meant to be slave owners. Plato and Aristotle were not verbal apologists; this was the dominant ideology and they simply took it for granted.

Slavery had many limitations, though it did result in many great public works and the advance of science and culture. One limitation was the fact that slaves could not be given complex or delicate machinery of any sort; they would break it up and would often use it for weapons to revolt. Moreover, agricultural organization had to be very simple, usually limited to one crop tilled with crude implements. As a result, much land was totally ruined and the agricultural product limited. Another effect of slavery was the view that all work was demeaning. This attitude spread even to invention, so the Roman period saw little technological advance and the economy stagnated.

Its economic weaknesses—and accompanying political and social weaknesses—made the Roman Empire vulnerable to attack by the primitive Germanic and Slav tribes. The Empire collapsed in the West, and out of the chaos eventually arose the system of feudalism. The kings of the feudal states were mostly former chiefs of the primitive tribes that invaded the area.

FEUDALISM

The decline of the western part of the old Roman Empire left Europe without the laws and protection the empire had provided. The vacuum was filled by the creation of a feudal hierarchy. In this hierarchy, the serf, or peasant, was protected by the lord of the manor, who, in turn, owed allegiance to and was protected by a higher overlord. And so the system went, ending eventually with the king. The strong protected the weak, but they did so at a high price. In return for payments of money, food, labor, or military allegiance, overlords granted the fief, or feudum—a hereditary right to use land—to their vassals. At the bottom was the serf, a peasant who tilled the land. The vast majority of the population raised crops for food or clothing or tended sheep for wool and clothing.[1]

Custom and tradition are the key to understanding medieval relationships. In place of laws as we know them today, the *custom of the manor* governed. There was no strong central authority in the Middle Ages that could have enforced a system of laws. The entire medieval organization was based on a system of mutual obligations and services up and down the hierarchy. Possession or use of the land obligated one to certain customary services or payments in return for protection. The lord was as obligated to protect the serf as the serf was to turn over a portion of the crop to or perform extensive labor for the lord.

Customs were broken, of course; no system always operates in fact as it is designed to operate in theory. One should not, however, underestimate the strength of custom and tradition in determining the lives and ideas of medieval people. Disputes between serfs were decided in the lord's court according to both the special circumstances of each case and the general customs of the manor for such cases. Of course, a dispute between a serf and a lord would usually be decided in his own favor by the lord. Even in this circumstance, however, especially in England, an overlord would impose sanctions or punishments on a lord who, as his vassal, had persistently violated the customs in his treatment of serfs. This rule by the custom of the manor stands in sharp contrast to the legal and judicial system of capitalism. The capitalist system is based on the enforcement of contracts and universally binding laws, which are softened only rarely by the possible mitigating circumstances and customs that often swayed the lord's judgment in medieval times.

The extent to which the lords could enforce their "rights" varied greatly from time to time and from place to place. It was the strengthening of these obligations and the nobleman's ability to enforce them through a long hierarchy of vassals and over a wide area that eventually led to the emergence of the modern nation-states. This process occurred during the period of transition from feudalism to capitalism. Throughout most of the Middle Ages, however, many of these claims were very weak because political control was fragmented.

The basic economic institution of medieval rural life was the manor, which contained within it two separate and distinct classes: noblemen, or lords of the manors, and serfs (from the Latin word *servus*, "slave"). Serfs were not really

[1] For a more complete discussion of the medieval economic and social system, see J. H. Claphan and Eileen E. Power, eds., *The Agrarian Life of the Middle Ages*, 2d ed, The Cambridge Economic History of Europe, vol. I (London: Cambridge University Press, 1966).

slaves. Unlike slaves, who were simply property to be bought and sold at will, serfs could not be parted from either their families or their land. If their lord transferred possession of the manor to another nobleman, the serfs simply had another lord. In varying degrees, however, obligations were placed upon the serfs that were sometimes very onerous and from which there was often no escape. Usually, they were far from being "free."

The lord lived off the labor of the serfs who farmed his fields and paid taxes in kind and money according to the custom of the manor. Similarly, the lord gave protection, supervision, and administration of justice according to the custom of the manor. It must be added that although the system did rest on reciprocal obligations, the concentration of economic and political power in the hands of the lord led to a system in which, by any standard, the serf was exploited in the extreme.

The Catholic church was by far the largest owner of land during the Middle Ages. While bishops and abbots occupied much the same place as counts and dukes in the feudal hierarchy, there was one important difference between the religious and secular lords. Dukes and counts might shift their loyalty from one overlord to another, depending on the circumstances and the balance of power involved, but the bishops and abbots always had (in principle at least) a primary loyalty to the church in Rome. This was also an age during which the religious teaching of the church had a very strong and pervasive influence throughout western Europe. These factors combined to make the church the closest thing to a strong central government throughout this period.

Thus the manor might be secular or religious (many times secular lords had religious overlords and vice versa), but the essential relationships between lord and serfs were not significantly affected by this distinction. There is little evidence that serfs were treated any less harshly by religious lords than by secular ones. The religious lords and the secular nobility were the joint ruling classes; they controlled the land and the power that went with it. In return for very onerous appropriations of the serf's labor, produce, and money, the nobility provided military protection and the church provided spiritual aid.

In addition to manors, medieval Europe had many towns, which were important centers of manufacturing. Manufactured goods were sold to manors and, sometimes, traded in long-distance commerce. The dominant economic institutions in the towns were the guilds—craft, professional, and trade associations that had existed as far back as the Roman Empire. If anyone wanted to produce or sell any good or service, it was necessary to join a guild.

The guilds were as involved with social and religious questions as with economic ones. They regulated their members' conduct in all their activities: personal, social, religious, and economic. Although the guilds did regulate very carefully the production and sale of commodities, they were less concerned with making profits than with saving their members' souls. Salvation demanded that the individual lead an orderly life based on church teachings and custom. Thus the guilds exerted a powerful influence as conservators of the status quo in the medieval towns.

THE CHRISTIAN PATERNALIST ETHIC

The feudal lords, secular as well as religious, needed an ideology that would reflect and justify the feudal status quo. This ideology, which provided the moral cement holding feudal Europe together and protecting its rulers, was the medieval version of the Judeo-Christian tradition. This tradition evolved a moral code sometimes called the Christian corporate ethic, reflecting the fact that all of society was considered a single entity or corporation. To emphasize another feature of it, the Judeo-Christian moral code, as interpreted in the medieval period, will be called the *Christian paternalist ethic* in this book. It can be understood most easily by comparing society with a family. Those with positions of power and wealth can be likened to the father or keeper of the family. They have strong paternalistic obligations toward the common people—the poor or, in our analogy, the children. The common person, however, is expected to accept his or her place in the society and to be willingly subordinate to the leadership of the wealthy and the powerful in much the same way that a child accepts the authority of his or her father.

The Old Testament Jews[2] quite literally regarded themselves as the children of one God. This relationship meant that all Jews were brothers; the Mosaic law was intended to maintain this feeling of membership in one big family. This brotherhood was one of grown children who acknowledged their mutual obligations, even though they no longer shared possessions.

From the confused mass of duties and regulations governing the early Jews, the most salient feature is the large number of provisions made for the prevention and relief of poverty. Their humane treatment of debtors was also notable. Each Jew was to be his brother's keeper; indeed, his obligations extended to caring for his neighbor's animals should they wander his way.[3] The first duty of all, however, and particularly of the wealthy, was to care for the poor: "Thou shalt open thine hand wide unto thy brother, to the poor, and to the needy, in the land."[4] An important element in this paternalistic code was the sanction against taking a worker's tools as a means of satisfying a debt: "No man shall take the nether or the upper millstone to pledge: for he taketh a man's life to pledge."[5] The same point was made elsewhere in the Old Testament: "He that taketh away his neighbor's living slayeth him."[6]

All Jews did not, of course, live up to these lofty professions. Great extremes of wealth and poverty existed that would have been impossible had the Mosaic law been strictly observed. Many of the prophets, who were often radical champions of the poor, eloquently denounced the rich for their abuse of their wealth, for their wicked, slothful luxury and general unrighteousness. The important point is not that they failed to live up to the code but that the moral code of this small tribe left so important an imprint on much of the subsequent history.

The teachings of Christ in the New Testament carry on part of the Mosaic tradition relevant to economic ideology. He taught the necessity of being con-

---

[2] This account relies on Alexander Gray, *The Socialist Tradition* (London: Longmans, 1963), chap. 2.
[3] Deut., 22:1–4.
[4] Deut., 15:7–11.
[5] Deut., 24:6.
[6] Eccles., 34:22.

cerned with the welfare of one's brother, the importance of charity and alms-giving, and the evil of selfish acquisitiveness and covetousness. His emphasis on the special responsibilities and obligations of the rich is even more pronounced than that of the earlier Jewish writers. In fact, on the basis of a reading of the Gospel of Luke, one might conclude that Christ condemned the rich simply because they were rich and praised the poor simply because they were poor: "Woe unto you that are rich! . . . Woe unto you that are full! for ye shall hunger. Woe unto you that laugh now! for ye shall mourn and weep."[7] However, on examining the other gospels, it must be concluded that this is probably Luke speaking, not Christ. Luke must be seen as the radical "leveller among the apostles."[8]

In the other gospels there are warnings that wealth may be a stumbling block in getting to heaven, but there is no condemnation of wealth as such. The most important passages in this regard deal with the wealthy young man who wants to know what he must do to attain eternal life.[9] Christ's first answer amounts to nothing more than a brief statement of the Ten Commandments. It is only after being pressed further that Christ goes beyond the binding, universal moral requirements to a counsel of perfection. "If thou wilt be perfect"[10] begins the statement in which he tells the young man to sell whatever he has and give to the poor.

The Christian paternalist ethic, with its parental obligations of the wealthy toward the poor, was developed more specifically and elaborately by most of the later Christian fathers. The writings of Clement of Alexandria are a reasonably good reflection of the traditional attitudes of the early church. He emphasized the dangers of greed, love of material things, and acquisition of wealth. Those who had wealth were under a special obligation to treat it as a gift of God and to use it wisely in the promotion of the general well-being of others.

Clement's *The Rich Man's Salvation* was written in order to free the rich of the "unfounded despair" they might have acquired from reading passages in the gospels like those found in Luke. Clement began by asserting that, contrary to anything one might find in Luke, "it is no great or enviable thing to be simply without riches." Those who were poor would not for that reason alone find God's blessedness. In order to seek salvation, the rich man need not renounce his wealth but need merely "banish from the soul its opinions about riches, its attachment to them, its excessive desire, its morbid excitement over them, its anxious cares, the thorns of our earthly existence which choke the seed of the true life."[11]

Not the possession of wealth but the way in which it was used was important to Clement. The wealthy were given the responsibility of administering their wealth, on God's behalf, to alleviate the suffering and promote the general welfare of their brothers. In decreeing that the hungry should be fed and the naked clothed, God certainly had not willed a situation in which no one could carry out these commandments for lack of sufficient material prerequisites. It followed, thus, that God had willed that some men should have wealth but had given them

---

[7] Quoted in Gray, op. cit., p. 41.
[8] Ibid., p. 42.
[9] Matt., 19:16–26; Mark, 10:17–27; Luke, 18.
[10] Matt., 19.
[11] Quoted in Gray, op. cit., p. 48.

the important functions of paternalistically caring for the well-being of the rest of society.

In a similar vein, Ambrose wrote that "riches themselves are not blamable" as long as they are used righteously. In order to use wealth righteously, "we ought to be of mutual help one to the other, and to vie with each other in doing duties, to lay all advantages . . . before all, and . . . to bring help one to the other."[12]

The list of Christian fathers who wrote lengthy passages to the same effect could be expanded greatly. Suffice it to say that by the early feudal period the Christian paternalist ethic was thoroughly entrenched in western European culture. Greed, avarice, materialistic self-seeking, the desire to accumulate wealth—all such individualistic and materialistic motives—were sharply condemned. The acquisitive, individualistic person was considered the very antithesis of the good man, who concerned himself with the well-being of all his brothers. The wealthy man had the potential to do either great good or great evil with his wealth and power, and the worst evil resulted when wealth was used either exclusively for self-gratification or as a means of continually acquiring more wealth for its own sake. The righteously wealthy were those who realized that their wealth and power were God's gift, that they were morally obligated to act as paternalistic stewards, and that they were to administrate their wordly affairs in order to promote the welfare of all.

THE ANTICAPITALIST NATURE OF FEUDAL IDEOLOGY

The philosophical and religious assumptions on which medieval people acted were extensions of the Christian paternalist ethic. The many particular additions to the ethic were profoundly conservative in purpose and content. Both the continuity in and conservative modifications of the ethic can be seen in the writings of Thomas Aquinas, the preeminent spokesman of the Middle Ages.

Tradition was upheld in his insistence that private property could be justified morally only because it was a necessary condition for almsgiving. The rich, he asserted, must always be "ready to distribute, . . . [and] willing to communicate."[13] Aquinas believed, with the earlier fathers, that "the rich man, if he does not give alms, is a thief."[14] The rich man held wealth and power for God and for all society. He administered his wealth for God and for the common good of mankind. Without proper use and administration of this wealth, it could no longer be religiously and morally justified, in which case the wealthy man was to be considered a common thief.

Aquinas' and, indeed, most of the medieval church fathers' profoundly conservative addition to the Christian paternalistic ethic was their insistence that the economic and social relationships of the medieval manorial system reflected a natural and eternal ordering of these relationships—indeed, that these relationships were ordained by God. They stressed the importance of a division of labor and effort, with different tasks assigned to the different classes, and insisted that

[12] Ibid., p. 49.
[13] Ibid., p. 57.
[14] Ibid.

the social and economic distinctions between the classes were necessary to accommodate this specialization.

If one was in the position of a lord, secular or religious, it was necessary to have an abundance of material wealth in order to do well the tasks providence had assigned. Of course, it took little wealth to perform the tasks expected of a serf. It was every person's duty to labor unquestioningly at the task providence had assigned, to accept the station into which one was born, and to accept the rights of others to have and do the things appropriate to their stations in life. Thus the Christian paternalist ethic could be, and was, used to defend as natural and just the great inequities and intense exploitation that flowed from the concentration of wealth and power in the hands of the Church and nobility.

Any account of medieval social and economic thought must also stress the great disdain with which people viewed trade and commerce and the commercial spirit. The medieval way of life was based on custom and tradition; its viability depended on the acceptance by the members of society of that tradition and their place within it. Where the capitalist commercial ethic prevails, greed, selfishness, covetousness, and the desire to better oneself materially or socially are accepted by most people as innate qualities. Yet they were uniformly denounced and reviled in the Middle Ages. The serfs (and sometimes the lower nobility) tended to be dissatisfied with the traditions and customs of medieval society and thus threatened the stability of the feudal system. It is not surprising, therefore, to find pervasive moral sanctions designed to repress or to mitigate the effects of these motives.

One of the most important of such sanctions, repeated over and over throughout this period, was the insistence that it was the moral duty of merchants and traders to transact all trade or exchanges at the just price. This notion illustrates the role played by paternalistic social control in the feudal era. A *just price* was one that would compensate the seller for his efforts in transporting the good and in finding the buyer at a rate that was just sufficient to maintain the seller at his *customary* or *traditional* station in life. Prices above the just price would, of course, lead to profits, which would be accumulated as material wealth.

It was the lust for wealth that the Christian paternalist ethic consistently condemned. Thus the doctrine of the just price was intended as a curb on such acquisitive and socially disruptive behavior. Then as now, accumulation of material wealth was a passport to greater power and upward social mobility. This social mobility was eventually to prove totally destructive of the medieval system because it put an end to the status relationships that were the backbone of medieval society.

Another example of this condemnation of acquisitive behavior was the prohibition of usury, or the lending of money at interest. A "bill against usury" passed in England reflected the attitudes of most of the people of those times. It read in part,

> But forasmuch as usury is by the word of God utterly prohibited, as a vice most odious and detestable . . . which thing, by no godly teachings and persuasions can sink in to the hearts of divers greedy, uncharitable and covetous persons of this Realm . . . be it enacted . . . that . . . no person or persons of what Estate, degree, quality or condition so ever he or they be, by any corrupt, colorable or deceitful conveyance, sleight or engine, or by any way or mean, shall lend, give, set out, deliver or forbear any sum or sums of money . . . to or

for any manner of usury, increase, lucre, gain or interest to be had, received or hoped for, over and above the sum or sums so lent . . . as also of the usury . . . upon pain of imprisonment. [15]

The church believed usury was the worst sort of acquisitive behavior because most loans on which interest was charged were granted to poor farmers or peasants after a bad crop or some other tragedy had befallen them. Thus, interest was a gain made at the expense of one's brother at a time when he was most in need of help and charity. Of course, the Christian ethic strongly condemned such rapacious exploitation of a needy brother.

Many historians have pointed out that bishops and abbots as well as dukes, counts, and kings often flagrantly violated these sanctions. They themselves granted loans at interest, even while they were punishing others for doing so. We are more interested, however, in the values and motives of the period than in the sins and infractions of the rules. The values of the feudal system stand in stark, antithetical contrast to those that were shortly to prevail under a capitalist system. The desire to maximize monetary gain, accumulate material wealth, and advance oneself socially and economically through acquisitive behavior was to become the dominant motive force in the capitalist system.

The sins that were most strongly denounced within the context of the Christian paternalist ethic were to become the behavioral assumptions on which the entire capitalist market economy was to be based. It is obvious that such a radical change would render the Christian ethic, at least in its medieval version, inadequate as the basis of a moral justification of the new capitalist system. The ethic would have to be modified drastically or rejected completely in order to elaborate a defense for the new system. Attempts to do both are explored in later chapters.

SUMMARY

Economic systems organize human effort to transform the resources given in nature into usable articles, or economic goods. Ideologies are systems of ideas and beliefs that are used to justify morally the economic and social relationships within an economic system.

The Christian paternalist ethic was used to justify the feudal economy and its attendant social and economic relationships. This ideology contained elements that were antithetical to the functioning of a capitalist market system. In later chapters we shall examine the ways in which men attempted to substitute new ideologies for the older Christian paternalist ethic or to modify this ethic in such a way that it could be used to provide a moral justification of a capitalist market economic system.

[15] Quoted in Leo Huberman, *Man's Worldly Goods* (New York: Monthly Review Press, 1961), p. 39.

CHAPTER 2

THE TRANSITION TO EARLY CAPITALISM AND THE BEGINNINGS OF THE MERCANTILIST VIEW

The medieval society was an agrarian society. The social hierarchy was based on individuals' ties to the land, and the entire social system rested on an agricultural base. Yet, ironically, increases in agricultural productivity were the original impetus to a series of profound changes. These changes, occurring over several centuries, resulted in the dissolution of medieval feudalism and the beginnings of capitalism.

CHANGES IN TECHNOLOGY

The most important technological advance in the Middle Ages was the replacement of the two-field system of crop rotation with the three-field system. Although there is evidence that the three-field system was introduced into Europe as early as the eighth century, its use was probably not widespread until around the eleventh century.

Yearly sowing of the same land would deplete the land and eventually make it unusable. Consequently, in the two-field system half of the land was always allowed to lie fallow in order to recover from the previous year's planting.

With the three-field system, arable land was divided into three equal fields. Rye or winter wheat would be planted in the fall in the first field. Oats, beans, or peas would be planted in the spring in the second, and the third would lie fallow. In each subsequent year there was a rotation of these positions. Any given piece of land would have a fall planting one year, a spring planting the next year, and none the third year.

A dramatic increase in agricultural output resulted from this seemingly simple change in agricultural technology. With the same amount of arable land, the three-field system could increase the amount under cultivation at any particular time by as much as 50 percent.[1]

The three-field system led to other important changes. Spring sowing of oats

---

[1] Lynn White, Jr., *Medieval Technology and Social Change* (Oxford: Clarendon, 1962), pp. 71-72.

and other fodder crops enabled the people to support more horses, which began to replace oxen as the principal source of power in agriculture. Horses were much faster than oxen, and consequently the region under cultivation could be extended. Larger cultivated areas enabled the countryside to support more concentrated population centers. Transportation of people, commodities, and equipment was much more efficient with horses. Greater efficiency was also attained in plowing: A team of oxen required three people to do the plowing; a horse-drawn plow could be operated by one person. The costs of transporting agricultural products were substantially reduced in the thirteenth century, when the four-wheeled wagon with a pivoted front axle replaced the two-wheeled cart.

These improvements in agriculture and transportation contributed to two important and far-reaching changes. First, they made possible a rapid increase in population growth. The best historical estimates show that the population of Europe doubled between 1000 and 1300.[2] Second, closely related to the expansion of population was a rapid increase in urban concentration. Before the year 1000, most of Europe, except for a few Mediterranean trade centers, consisted of only manors, villages, and a few small towns. By 1300, there were many thriving cities and larger towns.

The growth of towns and cities led to a growth of rural-urban specialization. With urban workers severing all ties to the soil, the output of manufactured goods increased impressively. Along with increased manufacturing and increased economic specialization came many additional gains in human productivity. Interregional, long-distance trade and commerce was another very important result of this increased specialization.

THE INCREASE IN LONG-DISTANCE TRADE

Many historians have argued that the spread of trade and commerce was the single most important force leading to the disintegration of medieval trade and customs. The importance of trade cannot be doubted, but it must be emphasized that this trade did not arise by accident or by factors completely external to the European economy, such as increased contact with the Arabs. On the contrary, it was shown in the previous section that this upsurge in trade was prepared for by the internal economic evolution of Europe itself. The growth of agricultural productivity meant that a surplus of food and handicrafts was available for local and international markets. The improvements in power and transportation meant that it was possible and profitable to concentrate industry in towns, to produce on a mass scale, and to sell the goods in a widespread, long-distance market. Thus, the basic agricultural and industrial developments were necessary prerequisites for the spread of trade and commerce—which then further encouraged industry and town expansion.

The expansion of trade, particularly long-distance trade in the early period, led to the establishment of commercial and industrial towns that serviced this trade. And the growth of these cities and towns, as well as their increased domination by merchant capitalists, led to important changes in both industry and agriculture. Each of these areas of change, particularly the latter, brought about

---

[2] Harry A. Miskimin, *The Economy of Early Renaissance Europe, 1300–1460* (Englewood Cliffs, N.J.: Prentice-Hall, 1969), p. 20.

a weakening and ultimately a complete dissolving of the traditional ties that held together the feudal economic and social structure.

From the earliest part of the medieval period, some long-distance trade had been carried on throughout many parts of Europe. This trade was very important in southern Europe, on the Mediterranean and Adriatic seas, and in northern Europe, on the North and Baltic seas. Between these two centers of commercialism, however, the feudal manorial system in most of the rest of Europe was relatively unaffected by commerce and trade until the later Middle Ages.

From about the eleventh century onward, the Christian Crusades gave the impetus to a marked expansion of commerce. Yet the Crusades themselves cannot be viewed as an accidental or external factor to European development. The Crusades were not undertaken for religious reasons, nor were they the result of Turkish molestation of pilgrims, for the Turks continued the Moslem policy of tolerance. Developments on the Moslem side did lead to increased attacks on Byzantium, but the West would normally have sent only token aid, since it had no great love for Byzantium. The basic reasons for the Crusades may be seen in the internal developments of France, where they had their most powerful backing. France had been growing stronger; it had more trade relations with and interest in the East; and it needed an outlet for social unrest at home. Additional propaganda for the Crusades came from the oligarchy of Venice, which wanted to expand its own Eastern trade and influence.

The development of trade with the Arabs—and with the Vikings in the North—led to increased production for export and to the great trade fairs that flourished from the twelfth through the late fourteenth centuries. Held annually in the principal European trading cities, these fairs usually lasted for one to several weeks. Northern European merchants exchanged their grain, fish, wool, cloth, timber, pitch, tar, salt, and iron for the spices, silks, brocades, wines, fruits, and gold and silver that were the dominant items in southern European commerce.[3]

By the fifteenth century the fairs were being replaced by commercial cities where year-round markets thrived. The trade and commerce of these cities was incompatible with restrictive feudal customs and traditions. Generally the cities were successful in gaining independence from church and feudal lords. Within these commercial centers there arose complex systems of currency exchange, debt-clearing, and credit facilities, and modern business instruments like bills of exchange came into widespread use. New systems of commercial law developed. Unlike the system of paternalistic adjudication based on custom and tradition that prevailed in the manor, the commercial law was fixed by precise code. Hence it became the basis of the modern capitalistic law of contracts, negotiable instruments, agency sales, and auctions.

In the manorial handicraft industry, the producer (the master craftsman) was also the seller. The industries that burgeoned in the new cities, however, were primarily export industries in which the producer was distant from the final buyer. Craftsmen sold their goods wholesale to merchants, who, in turn, transported and resold them. Another important difference was that the manorial craftsman was also generally a farmer. The new city craftsman gave up farming and became devoted to a craft, with which money was obtained to satisfy other needs.

---

[3] For a more complete discussion of the rise of trade and commerce, see Dudley Dillard, *Economic Development of the North Atlantic Community* (Englewood Cliffs, N.J.: Prentice-Hall, 1967), pp. 3–178.

THE PUTTING-OUT SYSTEM
AND THE BIRTH OF CAPITALIST INDUSTRY

As trade and commerce thrived and expanded, the need for more manufactured goods and greater reliability of supply led to increasing control of the productive process by the merchant-capitalist. By the sixteenth century the handicraft type of industry, in which the craftsman owned his workshop, tools, and raw materials and functioned as an independent, small-scale entrepreneur, had been largely replaced in the exporting industries by the *putting-out system*. In the earliest period of the putting-out system, the merchant-capitalist would furnish an independent craftsman with raw materials and pay a fee to work the materials into finished products. In this way the capitalist owned the product throughout all stages of production, although the work was done in independent workshops. In the later period of the putting-out system, the merchant-capitalist owned the tools and machinery and often the building in which the production took place. The merchant-capitalist hired workers to use these tools, furnished them with the raw materials, and took the finished products.

The worker no longer sold a finished product to the merchant. Rather, the worker sold only the worker's own labor power. The textile industries were among the first in which the putting-out system developed. Weavers, spinners, fullers, and dyers found themselves in a situation where their employment, and hence their ability to support themselves and their families, depended on the merchant-capitalists, who had to sell what the workers produced at a price that was high enough to pay wages and other costs and still make a profit.

Capitalist control was, then, extended into the process of production. At the same time, a labor force was created that owned little or no capital and had nothing to sell but its labor power. These two features mark the appearance of the economic system of capitalism. Some writers and historians have defined capitalism as existing when trade, commerce, and the commercial spirit expanded and became more important in Europe. Trade and commerce, however, had existed throughout the feudal era. Yet as long as feudal tradition remained the organizing principle in production, trade and commerce were really outside the social and economic system. The market and the search for money profits replaced custom and tradition in determining who would perform what task, how the task would be performed, and whether a given worker could find work to support himself. When this occurred, the capitalist system was created.[4]

Capitalism became dominant with the extension to most lines of production of the relationship that existed between capitalists and workers in the sixteenth-century export industries. For such a system to evolve, the economic self-sufficiency of the feudal manor had to be broken down and manorial customs and traditions undermined or destroyed. Agriculture had to become a capitalistic venture in which workers would sell their labor power to capitalists, and capitalists would buy labor only if they expected to make a profit in the process.

A capitalist textile industry existed in Flanders in the thirteenth century. When for various reasons its prosperity began to decline, the wealth and poverty it had created led to a long series of violent class wars, starting around 1280, that

[4] See Maurice H. Dobb, *Studies in the Development of Capitalism* (London: Routledge & Kegan Paul, 1946), particularly chap. 4.

almost completely destroyed the industry. In the fourteenth century a capitalist textile industry flourished in Florence. There, as in Flanders, adverse business conditions led to tensions between a poverty-stricken working class and their affluent capitalist employers. The results of these tensions were violent rebellions in 1379 and 1382. Failure to resolve these class antagonisms significantly worsened the precipitous decline in the Florentine textile industry, as it had earlier in Flanders.

In the fifteenth century England dominated the world textile market. Its capitalist textile industry solved the problem of class conflict by ruralizing the industry. Whereas the earlier capitalist textile industries of Flanders and Florence had been centered in the densely populated cities, where the workers were thrown together and organized resistance was easy to initiate, the English fulling mills were scattered about the countryside. This meant that the workers were isolated from all but a small handful of other workers, and effective organized resistance did not develop.

The later system, however, in which wealthy owners of capital employed propertyless craftsmen, was usually a phenomenon of the city rather than of the countryside. From the beginning, these capitalistic enterprises sought monopolistic positions from which to exploit the demand for their products. The rise of livery guilds, or associations of merchant-capitalist employers, created a host of barriers to protect their position. Different types of apprenticeships, with special privileges and exemptions for the sons of the wealthy, excessively high membership fees, and other barriers, prevented ambitious poorer craftsmen from competing with or entering the new capitalist class. Indeed, these barriers generally resulted in the transformation of poorer craftsmen and their sons into a new urban working class that lived exclusively by selling its labor power.

THE DECLINE OF THE MANORIAL SYSTEM

Before a complete system of capitalism could emerge, however, the force of capitalist market relations had to invade the rural manor, the bastion of feudalism. This was accomplished as a result of the vast increase of population in the new trading cities. Large urban populations depended on the rural countryside for food and much of the raw materials for export industries. These needs fostered a rural-urban specialization and a large flow of trade between the rural manor and the city. The lords of the manors began to depend on the cities for manufactured goods and increasingly came to desire luxury goods that merchants could sell to them.

The peasants on the manor also found that they could exchange surpluses for money at the local grain markets; the money could be used by the peasants to purchase commutation of their labor services.[5] Commutation often resulted in a situation in which the peasant became very nearly an independent small businessman. He might rent the land from the lord, sell the produce to cover the rents, and retain the remaining revenues himself. This system gave peasants a higher incentive to produce and thereby increased their surplus marketings, which led to more commutations, more subsequent marketings, and so forth.

---

[5] Commutation involved the substitution of money rents for the labor services required of the serf.

The cumulative effect was a very gradual breaking down of the traditional ties of the manor and a substitution of the market and the search for profits as the organizing principle of production. By the middle of the fourteenth century, money rents exceeded the value of labor services in many parts of Europe.

Another force that brought the market into the countryside and was closely related to commutation was the alienation of the lords' demesnes. The lords who needed cash to exchange for manufactured goods and luxuries began to rent their own lands to peasant farmers rather than having them farmed directly with labor service obligations. This process led increasingly to a situation in which the lord of the manor was simply a landlord in the modern sense of that term. In fact, he very often became an absentee landlord, as many lords chose to move to the cities or were away fighting battles.

The breakup of the manorial system, however, stemmed more directly from a series of catastrophies in the late fourteenth and fifteenth centuries. The Hundred Years' War between France and England (1337–1453) created general disorder and unrest in those countries. The Black Death was even more devastating. On the eve of the plague of 1348–1349, England's population stood at 4 million. By the early fifteenth century, after the effects of the wars and the plague, England had a scant 2.5-million population. This was fairly typical of trends in other European countries. The depopulation led to a desperate labor shortage, and wages for all types of labor rose abruptly. Land, now relatively more plentiful, began to rent for less.

These facts led the feudal nobility to attempt to revoke the commutations they had granted and to reestablish the labor service obligations of the serfs and peasants (peasants were former serfs who had attained some degree of independence and freedom from feudal restrictions). They found, however, that the clock could not be turned back. The market had been extended into the countryside, and with it had come greater freedom, independence, and prosperity for the peasants. They bitterly resisted efforts to reinstate the old obligations, and their resistance did not go unchallenged.

The result was the famous peasant revolts that broke out all over Europe from the late fourteenth through the early sixteenth centuries. These rebellions were extreme in their cruelty and ferocity. A contemporary French writer described a band of peasants who killed a "knight and putting him on a broach, roasted him over a fire in the sight of his wife and children. Ten or twelve of them ravished the wife and then forced her to eat of her husband's flesh. Then they killed her and her children. Wherever these ungracious people went they destroyed good houses and strong castles."[6] Rebellious peasants were ultimately slaughtered with equal or greater cruelty and ferocity by the nobility.

England experienced a series of such revolts in the late fourteenth and fifteenth centuries. But the revolts that occurred in Germany in the early sixteenth century were probably the bloodiest of all. The peasant rebellion in 1524–1525 was crushed by the Imperial troops of the Holy Roman emperor, who slaughtered peasants by the tens of thousands. Over 100,000 persons probably were killed in Germany alone.

These revolts are mentioned here to illustrate the fact that fundamental changes in the economic and political structure of a social system are often

[6] N. S. B. Gras, *A History of Agriculture in Europe and America* (New York: Appleton, 1940), p. 108.

achieved only after traumatic and violent social conflict. Any economic system generates a class or classes whose privileges are dependent on the continuation of that system. Quite naturally, these classes go to great lengths to resist change and to protect their positions. The feudal nobility fought a savage rearguard action against the emerging capitalist market system, but the forces of change ultimately swept them aside. Although the important changes were brought about by aspiring merchants and minor noblemen, the peasants were the pathetic victims of the consequent social upheavals. Ironically, they were usually struggling to protect the status quo.

OTHER FORCES IN THE TRANSITION TO CAPITALISM

The early sixteenth century is a watershed in European history. It vaguely marks the dividing line between the old, decaying feudal order and the rising capitalist system. After 1500, important social and economic changes began to occur with increasing frequency, each reinforcing the other and together having the cumulative effect of ushering in the system of capitalism. The population of western Europe, which had been relatively stagnant for a century and a half, increased by nearly one-third in the sixteenth century and stood at about 70 million in 1600.

The increase in population was accompanied by the *enclosure movement,* which had begun in England as early as the thirteenth century. The feudal nobility, in ever-increasing need of cash, fenced off, or enclosed, lands that had formerly been used for communal grazing. Enclosed lands were used to graze sheep to satisfy the booming English wool and textile industries' demand for wool. The sheep brought good prices, and a minimal amount of labor was needed to herd them.

The enclosure movement reached its peak in the late fifteenth and sixteenth centuries, when in some areas as many as three-fourths to nine-tenths of the tenants were forced out of the countryside and into the cities to try to support themselves. The enclosures and the increasing population further destroyed the remaining feudal ties, creating a large new labor force—a labor force without land, without any tools or instruments of production, and with only labor power to sell. This migration to the cities meant more labor for the capitalist industries, more men for the armies and navies, more men to colonize new lands, and more potential consumers, or buyers of products.

Another important source of change was the intellectual awakening of the sixteenth century, which fostered scientific progress that was promptly put to practical use in navigation. The telescope and the compass enabled men to navigate much more accurately for much greater distances. Hence the "age of exploration." Within a short period, Europeans had charted sea routes to India, Africa, and the Americas. These discoveries had a twofold importance. First, they resulted in a rapid and large flow of precious metals into Europe, and second, they ushered in a period of colonization.

Between 1300 and 1500, European gold and silver production had stagnated. The rapidly expanding capitalist trade and the extension of the market system into city and countryside had led to an acute shortage of money. Because money consisted primarily of gold and silver coin, the need for these metals was critical. Beginning around 1450, this situation was alleviated somewhat when the Portuguese began extracting metals from the African Gold Coast, but the general shortage continued until the middle of the sixteenth century. After that date there occurred such a large inflow of gold and silver from the Americas that Europe experienced the most rapid and long-lasting inflation in history.

During the sixteenth century prices rose in Europe between 150 and 400 percent, depending on the country or region chosen. Prices of manufactured goods rose much more rapidly than either rents or wages. In fact, the disparity between prices and wages continued until late in the seventeenth century. This meant that the landlord class (or feudal nobility) and the working class both suffered, because their income rose less rapidly than their expenses. The capitalist class was the great beneficiary of the price revolution. They received larger and larger profits as they paid lower real wages and bought materials that appreciated greatly as they held them as inventories.

These larger profits were accumulated as capital. *Capital* refers to the materials that are necessary for production, trade, and commerce. It consists of all tools, equipment, factories, raw materials and goods in process, means of transporting goods, and money. The essence of the capitalist system is the existence of a class of capitalists who own the capital stock. It is by virtue of their ownership of this capital that they derive their profits. These profits are then plowed back, or used to augment the capital stock. The further accumulation of capital leads to more profits, which leads to more accumulation, and the system continues in an upward spiral.

The term *capitalism* describes this sytem of profit-seeking and accumulation very well. Capital is the source of profits and hence the source of further accumulation of capital. But this chicken-egg process had to have a beginning. The substantial initial accumulation, or *primitive accumulation,* of capital took place in the period under consideration. The four most important sources of the initial accumulation of capital were (1) the rapidly growing volume of trade and commerce, (2) the putting-out system of industry, (3) the enclosure movement, and (4) the great price inflation. There were several other sources of initial accumulations, some of which were somewhat less respectable and often forgotten—for example, colonial plunder, piracy, and the slave trade.

During the sixteenth and seventeenth centuries the putting-out system was extended until it was common in most types of manufacturing. Although this was not yet the modern type of factory production, the system's increased degree of specialization led to significant increases in productivity. Technical improvements in shipbuilding and navigation also lowered transportation costs. Thus during this period capitalist production and trade and commerce thrived and grew very rapidly. The new capitalist class (or middle class or bourgeoisie) slowly but inexorably replaced the nobility as the class that dominated the economic and social system.

The emergence of the new nation-states signaled the beginning of the transition to a new dominant class. The new monarchs usually drew on the bourgeois capitalist class for support in their efforts to defeat feudal rivals and unify the state under one central power. This unification freed the merchants from the feudal maze of different rules, regulations, laws, weights and measures, and moneys; consolidated many markets; and provided military protection for commercial ventures. In return, the monarch relied on the capitalists for much-needed sources of revenues.

Although England was nominally unified much earlier, it was not until Henry VII (1485–1509) founded the line of Tudor monarchs that England was unified in fact. Henry VIII (1509–1547) and Elizabeth I (1558–1603) were able to complete the work of nation building only because they had the support of Parliament, which represented the middle classes of the shires and boroughs. In the revolutions of 1648 and 1688, the supremacy of Parliament, or of the bourgeois middle classes, was finally established.

The other important early capitalist nation-states also came into existence during this period. In France, Louis XI (1461–1483) was the first king to unify France effectively since the time of Charlemagne. The marriage in 1469 of Ferdinand of Aragon and Isabella of Castile, and their subsequent defeat of the Moors, led to the unification of Spain. The Dutch republic, the fourth of the important early nation-states, did not win its independence until 1690, when it finally expelled its Spanish oppressors.

By the late sixteenth and early seventeenth centuries, most of the large cities in England, France, Spain, and the Low Countries (Belgium and Holland) had been transformed into thriving capitalist economies dominated by the merchant-capitalists, who controlled not only commerce but also much of the manufacturing. In the modern nation-states, coalitions of monarchs and capitalists had wrested effective power from the feudal nobility in many important areas, especially those related to production and commerce. This period of early capitalism is generally referred to as *mercantilism*.

MERCANTILISM: FEUDAL PATERNALISM IN EARLY CAPITALISM

The earliest phase of mercantilism, usually called *bullionism*, originated in the period (discussed earlier) during which Europe was experiencing an acute shortage of gold and silver bullion and hence did not have enough money to service the rapidly expanding volume of trade. Bullionist policies were designed to attract a flow of gold and silver into a country and to keep them there by prohibiting their export. These restrictions lasted from the late Middle Ages into the sixteenth and seventeenth centuries.

Spain, the country into which most of the gold from the Americas flowed, applied bullionist restrictions over the longest period and imposed the most severe penalty for the export of gold and silver: death. Yet the needs of trade were so pressing and such large profits could be made by importing foreign commodities that even in Spain merchant-capitalists succeeded in bribing corrupt officials or in smuggling large quantities of bullion out of the country. Spanish bullion rapidly found its way all over Europe and was, to a large extent, responsible for the long period of inflation described above. Spain did not legalize the export of gold and silver until long after the bullionist restrictions had been removed in England and Holland in the middle of the sixteenth century.

After the bullionist period, the mercantilists' desire to maximize the gold and silver within a country took the form of attempts by the government to create a favorable balance of trade. To them a *favorable balance of trade* meant that money payments into the country would be greater than money flowing out of the country. Thus exports of goods as well as such things as shipping and insuring, when they were performed by compatriots and paid for by foreigners, were encouraged, and imports of goods and shipping and insurance charges paid to foreigners were discouraged. A favorable balance of trade would ensure the augmentation of the country's treasure. Even though some gold and silver would be paid out in the process, more would come in than would leave.

One of the most important types of policies designed to increase the value of exports and decrease that of imports was the creation of trade monopolies. A country like England could buy most cheaply (from a backward area, for example) if only one English merchant bargained with the foreigners involved rather than having several competing English merchants bidding the price up in an effort to capture the business. Similarly, English merchants could sell their goods to foreigners for much higher prices if there was only one seller rather than several sellers bidding the price down to attract each other's customers.

The English government could prohibit English merchants from competing in an area where such a monopoly had been established. It was much more difficult, however, to keep out French, Dutch, or Spanish merchants. Various governments attempted to exclude such rival foreign merchants by establishing colonial empires that could be controlled by the mother country to ensure a monopoly of trade. Colonial possessions could thereby furnish cheap raw materials to the mother country and purchase expensive manufactured goods in return.

In addition to the creation of monopolies, all the western European countries (with the exception of Holland) applied extensive regulations to the businesses of exporting and importing. These regulations were probably most comprehensive in England, where exporters who found it difficult to compete with foreigners were given tax refunds or, if that was not enough, subsidized. Export duties were placed on a long list of raw materials to keep them within England. Thus the price English merchant-manufacturers would have to pay for these raw materials would be minimized. Sometimes, when these items were in short supply for British manufacturers, the state would completely prohibit their export. The English textile industry received this type of protection. In the early eighteenth century it accounted for about half of England's exports. The English prohibited the export of most raw materials and semi-finished products, such as sheep, wool, yarn, and worsted, which were used by the textile industry.

Measures aimed at discouraging imports were also widespread. The importation of some commodities was prohibited, and other commodities had such high duties that they were nearly eliminated from trade. Special emphasis was placed on protecting England's principal export industries from foreign competitors attempting to cut into the export industries' domestic markets.

Of course these restrictions profited some capitalists and harmed others. As would be expected, coalitions of special interest groups were always working to maintain the restrictions or to extend them into different areas in different ways. Attempts such as the English Navigation Acts of 1651 and 1660 were made to promote the use of British ships (both British-made and British-manned) in both import and export trade. All these regulations of foreign trade and shipping were designed to augment the flow of money into the country while decreasing the outflow. Needless to say, many of the measures also stemmed from appeals and pressures by special interest groups.

In addition to these restrictions on foreign trade, there was a maze of restrictions and regulations aimed at controlling domestic production. Besides the tax exemptions, subsidies, and other privileges used to encourage larger output by industries that were important exporters, the state also engaged in extensive regulation of production methods and of the quality of produced goods. In France, the regime of Louis XIV codified, centralized, and extended the older decentralized guild controls. Specific techniques of production were made mandatory, and extensive quality control measures were enacted, with inspectors appointed in Paris charged with enforcing these laws at the local level. Jean Baptiste Colbert, Louis XIV's famous minister and economic advisor, was responsible for the establishment of extensive and minute regulations. In the textile industry, for example, the width of a piece of cloth and the precise number of threads contained within it were rigidly specified by the government.

In England the Statute of Artificers (1563) effectively transferred to the state the functions of the old craft guilds. It led to central control over the training of industrial workers, over conditions of employment, and over allocation of the labor force among different types of occupations. Regulation of wages, of the quality of many goods, and of other details of domestic production was also tried in England during this period.

What was the source of this extensive state control of trade, commerce, and domestic production? It might seem at first glance that the state was merely using its powers to promote the special interests of capitalists. This view is reinforced by the fact that most of the important writers of this period who dealt with economic issues were either merchants or employees of merchants. Undoubtedly many of the particular statutes and regulatory measures were backed by special interest groups that benefited handsomely from these measures.

However, the rising new middle class of merchant and industrial capitalists were often constrained in their pursuit of profits by the maze of state regulations. Therefore, throughout the period one finds extensive arguments advanced by these capitalists and their spokesmen for greater freedom from state controls. Economic regulation increasingly became anathema to the capitalists and their spokesmen. In fact, the mercantilist period represents an era in which an outdated economic ideology, the medieval version of the Christian corporate ethic, came into increasingly sharp conflict with a new social and economic order with which it was incompatible. Chapter 3 will be concerned with this conflict.

SUMMARY

A series of profound changes resulted in the decline of feudalism and the rise of a new, market-oriented economy. Perhaps the most important of these changes were the improvements in agricultural technology that occurred between the eleventh century and the end of the thirteenth century. These improvements in farming techniques were the original force that set into motion a centuries-long chain of events that ushered in capitalism.

Population grew rapidly and urban concentration increased, which led to a resurgence of long-distance trade. In the cities the putting-out system was created to produce items that were sold in this trade. This, in turn, led to an urban-rural specialization that could be accomplished only by the monetization of economic tasks and productive activities. The transformation of feudal social relationships into market cash relations destroyed the social base of feudalism. Attempts to preserve the feudal system resulted in bloody suppressions of peasant revolts.

The new capitalist market system was ushered in by the enclosure movement, the intellectual awakening, world exploration, the discovery of large quantities of precious metals, the price inflation of the sixteenth and seventeenth centuries, and the creation of the new nation-states.

In the early stages of capitalism mercantilist policies resulted in extensive government intervention into market processes, particularly those related to international commerce. These policies were generally aimed at securing high profits for the great merchant trading companies, raising revenues for national governments, and, more generally, bringing a maximum of precious metals into the country concerned.

CHAPTER 3

THE CONFLICT IN MERCANTILIST THOUGHT

The Christian paternalist ethic, with its condemnation of acquisitive behavior, conflicted with the interests of merchants throughout the feudal period. As the importance of trade and commerce grew, the intensity of the conflict grew. There were two principal themes underlying the development of English mercantilism.[1] "One was the biblical injunction to promote the general welfare and common good of God's corporate world and its creatures. The second was the growing propensity to define God's estate as the civil society in which the Christian resided."[2] During this period the state began to take over the role of the church in interpreting and enforcing the Christian paternalist ethic. The basic issue for the earliest formulators of mercantilist policies was whether the growing merchant class was to be allowed to pursue its profits recklessly, regardless of the social and economic consequences of that pursuit. The Christian ethic demanded that the activities of the merchants be checked and controlled in the interest of the welfare of the entire community.

THE MEDIEVAL ORIGINS OF MERCANTILIST POLICIES

The first indications of a mercantilistic type of economic policy can be traced to Edward I (1272–1307), who evicted several foreign economic enterprises from England, established the English wool trade in Antwerp, and made various attempts to control commerce within England. A short time later, Edward III significantly extended these policies of economic control. The long war with France (1333–1360) led him to attempt to mitigate the harsh effects of wartime inflation on the laborers. He did this by fixing wages and prices in a ratio that was more favorable to the laborers. In return for this aid, Edward required all men to work at whatever jobs were available. "As this *quid pro quo* indicates, mercantilism was grounded in the idea of a mutual, corporate responsibility. God's way was based on such reciprocal respect and obligation, and Jerusalem provided the example to be followed."[3]

Richard II (1377–1399) extended and systematized his predecessors' policies. The principal problems facing England during his reign were the social and

---

[1] We will concentrate primarily on English mercantilism in this chapter because industrial capitalism developed first in England and because most of the ideas in the capitalist ideology that we will discuss in Chapter 4 were developed in England.

[2] William Appleman Williams, *The Contours of American History* (New York: Quadrangle, 1966), p. 33.

[3] Williams, op. cit., p. 34. The following several pages draw heavily on Williams' excellent book.

economic conflict that led to the Peasants' Rebellion of 1381 (see Chapter 2) and the necessity of countering foreign competition more effectively. The latter led to the Navigation Act of 1381, which was designed to favor English shippers and traders and to bring gold and silver into England. This money was needed for his program of building England into a "well and rightly governed kingdom" in which greater economic security for all would mitigate the social tensions that existed.

Henry VII (1485–1509) renewed these policies. He commissioned numerous voyages of explorers and adventurers and attempted in various ways to secure legislation and negotiate treaties advantageous to English merchants. At the same time he subjected merchants to many controls and regulations imposed by the crown, for he believed that the unlimited pursuit of self-interest in the quest for profits was often harmful to general social interests and harmony.

Henry was still balancing feudal and capitalist interests; neither was dominant enough to persuade him to favor one over the other. The rapid growth of mining and wool raising during his reign led to an unfortunate neglect of food production. Moreover, the general excesses of the merchants had alienated both the peasants and the agrarian aristocracy. The merchants seemed to understand these problems and accepted a relationship in which, in return for Crown policies that would benefit them in foreign dealings, they submitted to domestic regulation of manufacturing and commerce.

THE SECULARIZATION OF CHURCH FUNCTIONS

During the reign of Henry VIII England broke with Roman Catholicism. This event was significant because it marked the final secularization (in England at least) of the functions of the medieval church. Under Henry, "the state in the form of God's monarchy assumed the role and the functions of the old universal church. What Henry had done in his own blunt way was to sanctify the processes of this world."[4] During his reign as well as those of Elizabeth I, James I, and Charles I (1558–1649), there was widespread social unrest. The cause of this unrest was poverty, and the cause of much of the poverty was unemployment.

The enclosure movements (discussed in Chapter 2) were responsible for much of the unemployment. Another factor, however, was the decline in the export of woolens in the second half of the sixteenth century, which created a great deal of unemployment in England's most important manufacturing industry. There were also frequent commercial crises similar to, but without the regularity of, the depression phase of later business cycles. In addition to these factors, seasonal unemployment put many workers out of work for as many as four months of the year.

The people could no longer look to the Catholic church for relief from widespread unemployment and poverty. Destruction of the power of the church had eliminated the organized system of charity. The state attempted to assume responsibility for the general welfare of society. In order to do this, "England's leaders undertook a general, coordinated program to reorganize and rationalize ... industry by establishing specifications of standards of production and market-

4 Ibid., p. 36.

ing."[5] All these measures were designed to stimulate English trade and alleviate the unemployment problem.

In fact, it appears that the desire to achieve full employment is the unifying theme of most policy measures advocated by mercantilist writers. The mercantilists preferred measures designed to stimulate foreign rather than domestic trade "because they believed it contributed more to employment, to the nation's wealth and to national power. The writers after 1600 stressed the inflationary effect of an excess of exports over imports and the consequent increase in employment which inflation produced."[6]

Among the other measures taken to encourage industry during this period was the issuance of patents of monopoly. The first important patent was granted in 1561, during the reign of Elizabeth I. Monopoly rights were given in order to encourage inventions and to establish new industries. These rights were severely abused, as might be expected. Moreover, they led to a complex system of special privileges and patronage and a host of other evils, which outraged most mercantilist writers every bit as much as similar abuses outraged late nineteenth-century American reformers. The evils of monopoly led to the Statute of Monopolies of 1624, which outlawed all monopolies except those that involved genuine inventions or would be instrumental in promoting a favorable balance of payments. Of course these loopholes were large, and abuses continued almost unchecked.

The Statute of Artificers (1563) specified conditions of employment and length of apprenticeships, provided for periodic wage assessments and established maximum rates that could be paid to laborers. The statute is important because it illustrates the fact that the Crown's paternalistic ethic never led to any attempt to elevate the status of the laboring classes. Monarchs of this period felt obliged to protect the working classes but, like their predecessors in the Middle Ages, believed those classes should be kept in their proper place. Maximum wage rates were designed to protect the capitalists, and furthermore, the justices who set these maximums and enforced the statute generally belonged to the employing class themselves. It is probable that these maximums reduced the real wages of laborers because prices generally rose faster than wages during the succeeding years.

Poor laws passed in 1531 and 1536 attempted to deal with the problems of unemployment, poverty, and misery then widespread in England. The first sought to distinguish between "deserving" and "undeserving" poor. Only the deserving poor were allowed to beg. The second decreed that each individual parish throughout England was responsible for its poor and that the parish should, through voluntary contributions, maintain a poor fund. This proved completely inadequate, and the "pauper problem" grew increasingly severe.

Finally, in 1572 the state accepted the principle that the poor would have to be supported by tax funds and enacted a compulsory "poor rate." And in 1576 "houses of correction" for "incorrigible vagrants" were authorized and provisions made for the parish to purchase raw materials to be worked up by the more tractable paupers and vagrants. Between that time and the close of the sixteenth century, several other poor law statutes were passed.

---

[5] Ibid., p. 40.

[6] William D. Grampp, *Economic Liberalism*, vol. 1 (New York: Random House, 1965), p. 59.

The Poor Law of 1601 was the Tudor attempt to integrate these laws into one consistent framework. Its main provisions included formal recognition of the right of the poor to receive relief, imposition of compulsory poor rates at the parish level, and provision for differential treatment for various classes of the poor. The aged and the sick could receive help in their homes; pauper children who were too young to be apprenticed in a trade were to be boarded out; the deserving poor and unemployed were to be given work as provided for in the act of 1576; and incorrigible vagrants were to be sent to houses of correction and prisons.[7]

From the preceding discussion it is possible to conclude that the period of English mercantilism was characterized by acceptance, in the spirit of the Christian paternalist ethic, of the idea that "the state had an obligation to serve society by accepting and discharging the responsibility for the general welfare."[8] The various statutes passed during this period "were predicated upon the idea that poverty, instead of being a personal sin, was a function of the economic system."[9] They acknowledged that those who were the victims of the deficiencies of the economic system should be cared for by those who benefited from the system.

THE RISE OF INDIVIDUALISM

After civil war of 1648 to 1660 and the Glorious Revolution of 1688, the English government was dominated by the gentry and the middle-class capitalists. The medieval world view that underlay the Christian paternalist ethic was eclipsed. A fundamental shift in the philosophy of the role of the State in society took place over the next 100 years. In 1776, with the publication of Adam Smith's *The Wealth of Nations,* a new individualistic philosophy—classical liberalism[10]—had definitely gained the ascendancy in England. This individualistic philosophy had existed throughout the mercantilist period, struggling to break the hold of the older paternalist world view. In the end the new classical liberalism prevailed because it—and not the older, essentially medieval world view—reflected the needs of the new capitalist order.

In condemning greed, acquisitive behavior, and the desire to accumulate wealth, the medieval Christian paternalist ethic condemned what had become the capitalist order's dominant motive force. The capitalist market economy, which had been extended by the late eighteenth century to almost every phase of production, demanded self-seeking, acquisitive behavior to function successfully. In this context new theories about human behavior began to emerge. Writers began to assert that selfish, egoistic motives were the primary if not the only ones that moved people to action.

This interpretation of humankind's behavior is expressed in the writings of many important thinkers of the period. Many philosophers and social theorists began to assert that every human act was related to self-preservation and hence

---

[7] For an extension of this discussion of the poor laws, see Arthur Birnie, *An Economic History of the British Isles* (London: Methuen, 1936), chaps. 12 and 18.

[8] Williams, op. cit., p. 41.

[9] Ibid., p. 44.

[10] We use the adjective *classical* to differentiate the traditional liberal world view from what is called liberalism in the twentieth century. This distinction is clarified further in Chapter 4.

was egoistic in the most fundamental sense. The English nobleman Sir Robert Filmer was greatly alarmed by the large number of people who spoke of "the natural freedom of mankind, a new, plausible and dangerous opinion" with anarchistic implications.[11] Thomas Hobbes' *Leviathan*, published in 1651, trenchantly articulated a widely held opinion—that all human motives stem from a desire for whatever promotes the "vital motion" of the human organism. Hobbes believed that everyone's motives, even compassion, were merely so many disguised species of self-interest: "Grief for the calamity of another is *pity*, and ariseth from the imagination that the like calamity may befall himself; and therefore is called . . . *compassion*, and . . . fellow-feeling. . . ."[12]

Except for the few special interest groups that benefited from the extensive restrictions and regulations of commerce and manufacturing during this period, most capitalists felt constrained and inhibited by state regulations in their quest for profits. The individualistic and egoistic doctrines were eagerly embraced by such people. This view began to dominate economic thinking, even among the mercantilists. One careful history asserts that "most of the mercantilist . . . policy assumed that self-interest governs individual conduct. . . ."[13]

The majority of mercantilist writers were either capitalists or employees of the great capitalist trading companies. It was quite natural for them to perceive the motives of the capitalists as universal. From the capitalists' views of the nature of humans, and their needs to be free from the extensive economic restrictions that inhibited them in the conduct of their everyday business, grew the philosophy of individualism that provided the basis of classical liberalism. Against the well-ordered, paternalistic view Europe had inherited from the feudal society, they asserted "the view that the human person ought to be independent, self-directing, autonomous, free—ought to be, that is, an individual, a unit distinguished from the social mass rather than submerged in it."[14]

PROTESTANTISM AND THE INDIVIDUALIST ETHIC

One of the most important examples of this individualistic and middle-class philosophy was the Protestant theology that emerged from the Reformation. The new middle-class capitalists wanted to be free not only from economic restrictions that encumbered manufacturing and commerce but also from the moral opprobrium the Catholic church had heaped upon their motives and activities. Protestantism not only freed them from religious condemnation but eventually made virtues of the selfish, egoistic, and acquisitive motives the medieval church had so despised.[15]

The principal originators of the Protestant movement were quite close to the Catholic position on such questions as usury and the just price. On most social

---

[11] Lee Cameron McDonald, *Western Political Theory: The Modern Age* (New York: Harcourt Brace Jovanovich, 1962), p. 29.

[12] Quoted in Harry K. Girvetz, *The Evolution of Liberalism* (New York: Colliers, 1963), pp. 28–29.

[13] Grampp, op. cit., p. 69.

[14] McDonald, op. cit., p. 16.

[15] The classic studies of the relationship between Protestantism and capitalism are Max Weber, *The Protestant Ethic and the Spirit of Capitalism* (New York: Scribner, 1958), and Richard H. Tawney, *Religion and the Rise of Capitalism* (New York: Mentor Books, 1954).

issues they were deeply conservative. During the German peasant revolt of 1524, Luther wrote a virulent pamphlet, *Against the Murdering Hordes of Peasants*, in which he said princes should "knock down, strangle and stab. . . . Such wonderful times are these that a prince can merit heaven better with bloodshed than another with prayer." His advice contributed to the general atmosphere in which the slaughter of over 100,000 peasants was carried out with an air of religious righteousness.

Yet despite the conservatism of the founders of Protestantism, this religious outlook contributed to the growing influence of the new individualistic philosophy. The basic tenet of Protestantism, which laid the groundwork for religious attitudes that were to sanction middle-class business practices, was the doctrine that human beings were justified by faith rather than by works. The Catholic church had taught that humans were justified by *works*, which generally meant ceremonies and rituals. In the Catholic view no one could be justified on merit alone. "Justification by works . . . did not mean that an individual could save himself: it meant that he could be saved through the Church. Hence the power of the clergy. Compulsory confession, the imposition of penance on the whole population . . . together with the possibility of withholding absolution, gave the priests a terrifying power."[16] These powers also created a situation in which the medieval doctrines of the Catholic church were not easily abandoned and in which the individual was still subordinated to society (as represented by the church).

The Protestant doctrine of justification by faith asserted that motives were more important than specific acts or rituals. Faith was "nothing else but the truth of the heart."[17] Each person had to search his or her own heart to discover if acts stemmed from a pure heart and faith in God. Each man and woman had to judge for himself and herself. This individualistic reliance on each person's private conscience appealed strongly to the new middle-class artisans and small merchants. "When the businessman of sixteenth and seventeenth century Geneva, Amsterdam or London looked into his inmost heart, he found that God had planted there a deep respect for the principle of private property. . . . Such men felt quite genuinely and strongly that their economic practices, though they might conflict with the traditional law of the old church, were not offensive to God. On the contrary: they glorified God."[18]

It was through this insistence on the individual's own interpretation of God's will that the "Puritans tried to spiritualize [the new] economic processes" and eventually came to believe that "God instituted the market and exchange."[19] However, it was only a matter of time before the Protestants expounded dogma that they expected everyone to accept. But the new dogma was radically different from medieval doctrines. The new doctrines stressed the necessity of doing well at one's earthly calling as the best way to please God, and emphasized diligence and hard work.

The older Christian distrust of riches was "translated" into a condemnation of extravagance and needless dissipation of wealth. Thus the Protestant ethic

[16] Christopher Hill, "Protestantism and the Rise of Capitalism," in D. S. Landes, ed., *The Rise of Capitalism* (New York: Macmillan, 1966), p. 43.
[17] Ibid.
[18] Ibid., pp. 46–47.
[19] Ibid., p. 49.

stressed the importance of asceticism and abstemious frugality. A theologian who has studied the connection between religion and capitalism sums up the relationship in this way: "The religious value set upon constant, systematic, efficient work in one's calling as the readiest means of securing the certainty of salvation and of glorifying God became a most powerful agency in economic expansion. The rigid limitations of consumption on the one hand and the methodical intensification of production on the other could have but one result— the accumulation of capital."[20] Thus, although neither Calvin nor Luther was a spokesman for the new middle-class capitalist, within the context of the new religious individualism the capitalists found a religion in which, over time, "profits . . . [came to be] looked upon as willed by God, as a mark of his favor and a proof of success in one's calling."[21]

THE ECONOMIC POLICIES OF INDIVIDUALISM

Throughout the mercantilist period this new individualism led to innumerable protests against the subordination of economic affairs to the will of the state. From the middle of the seventeenth century, almost all mercantilist writers condemned state-granted monopolies and other forms of protection and favoritism in the internal economy (as opposed to international commerce). Many believed that in a competitive market that pitted buyer against buyer, seller against seller, and buyer against seller, society would benefit most greatly if the price were left free to fluctuate and find its proper (market equilibrating) level. One of the earliest mercantilist writers of importance, John Hales, argued that agricultural productivity could best be improved if husbandmen were allowed to

> have more profit by it than they have, and liberty to sell it at all times, and to all places, as freely as men may do their other things. But then no doubt, the price of corn would rise, specially at the first more than at length; yet that price would evoke every man to set plough in the ground, to husband waste grounds, yes to turn the lands which be enclosed from pasture to arable land; for every man will gladder follow that wherein they see the more profit and gains, and thereby must need ensue both plenty of corn, and also much treasure should be brought into this realm by occasion thereof; and besides that plenty of other victuals increased among us.[22]

This belief—that restrictions on production and trade within a nation were harmful to the interests of everyone concerned—became increasingly widespread in the late seventeenth and early eighteenth centuries. Numerous statements of this view can be found in the works of such writers as Malynes, Petty, North, Law, and Child.[23] Of these men, perhaps Sir Dudley North (1641–1691) was the earliest clear spokesman for the individualistic ethic that was to become the basis for classical liberalism. North believed that all men were motivated primarily by self-interest and should be left alone to compete in a free market if

---

[20] Kemper Fullerton, "Calvinism and Capitalism; an Explanation of the Weber Thesis," in Robert W. Green, ed., *Protestantism and Capitalism: The Weber Thesis and Its Critics* (Lexington, Mass.: Heath, 1959), p. 19.

[21] Ibid., p. 18.

[22] Quoted in Grampp, op. cit., p. 78.

[23] Ibid., pp. 77–81.

the public welfare were to be maximized. He argued that whenever merchants or capitalists advocated special laws to regulate production or commerce, "they usually esteem the immediate interest of their own to be the common Measure of Good and Evil. And there are many, who to gain a little in their own Trades, care not how much others suffer; and each man strives that all others may be forced in their dealings to act subserviently for his Profit, but under the cover of the Publick."[24] The public welfare would best be served, North believed, if most of the restrictive laws that bestowed special privileges were entirely removed.

In 1714 Bernard Mandeville published *The Fable of the Bees: or Private Vices, Publick Benefits,* in which he put forth the seemingly strange paradox that the vices most despised in the older moral code, if practiced by all, would result in the greatest public good. Selfishness, greed, and acquisitive behavior, he maintained, all tended to contribute to industriousness and a thriving economy. The answer to the paradox was, of course, that what had been vices in the eyes of the medieval moralists were the very motive forces that propelled the new capitalist system. And in the view of the new religious, moral, and economic philosophies of the capitalist period these motives were no longer vices.

The capitalists had struggled throughout the mercantilist period to free themselves from all restrictions in their quest for profits. These restrictions had resulted from the paternalistic laws that were the remnants of the feudal version of the Christian paternalist ethic. Such an ethic simply was not compatible with the new economic system that functioned on the basis of strict contractual obligations between people rather than on traditional personal ties. Merchants and capitalists who invested large sums in market ventures could not depend on the forces of custom to protect their investments.

Profit seeking could be effective only in a society based on the protection of property rights and the enforcement of impersonal contractual commitments between individuals. The new ideology that was firmly taking root in the late seventeenth and eighteenth centuries justified these motives and relationships between individuals. It is to a consideration of this new individualistic philosophy of classical liberalism that we turn in Chapter 4.

SUMMARY

There is a basic continuity between medieval and mercantilist social thought. State intervention in economic processes was originally justified in terms of the medieval Christian notion that those to whom God had given power were obligated to use this power to promote the general welfare and common good of all society. In early capitalism the state began to assume many of the roles formerly held by the church.

The Christian paternalist ethic, however, had thoroughly condemned the acquisitive behavior that was to become the dominant motive force of the new capitalist system. It was therefore necessary to create a new philosophical and ideological point of view that morally justified individualization, greed, and profit seeking.

Protestantism and the new philosophies of individualism furnished the bases

[24] Quoted in Robert Lekachman, ed., *The Varieties of Economics,* vol. I (New York: Meridian, 1962), p. 185.

for the new ideology. The economic writings of the mercantilists reflected the new individualism. The new point of view emphasized the need for greater freedom for capitalists to seek profits and hence the need for less government intervention in the market. Thus the presence of two fundamentally different general points of view in mercantilist writings created an intellectual conflict that was not resolved until the classical liberal philosophy, including classical economics, effectively ferreted out all remnants of the medieval Christian paternalist ethic.

CHAPTER 4

CLASSICAL LIBERALISM AND THE TRIUMPH OF INDUSTRIAL CAPITALISM

A single theme runs through the works of the mercantilist writers (considered in the latter part of Chapter 3) that distinguishes them from the later classical liberal writers. They argued for a minimum of internal restriction and regulation, but they favored an active governmental policy designed to further England's commerce in the international trading markets. The classical liberals, however, advocated free trade internationally as well as domestically. In this chapter we examine the changes in England's commercial position that encouraged its economists to favor free trade.

THE INDUSTRIAL REVOLUTION

Between 1700 and 1770 the foreign markets for English goods grew much faster than did England's domestic markets. During the period 1700–1750, output of domestic industries increased by 7 percent, while that of export industries increased by 76 percent. For the period 1750–1770, the figures are 7 percent and 80 percent. This rapidly increasing foreign demand for English manufactures was the single most important cause of the most fundamental transformation of human life in history: the Industrial Revolution.

Eighteenth-century England was an economy with a well-developed market and one in which the traditional anticapitalist market bias in attitudes and ideology had been greatly weakened. In this England, larger outputs of manufactured goods produced at lower prices meant ever-increasing profits. Thus profit seeking was the motive that, stimulated by increasing foreign demand, accounted for the virtual explosion of technological innovations that occurred in the late eighteenth and early nineteenth centuries—and radically transformed all England and eventually most of the world.

The textile industry was the most important in the early Industrial Revolution. In 1700 the woolen industry had persuaded the government to ban the import of Indian-made "calicoes" (cotton) and thus had secured a protected home market for domestic producers. As outlined earlier, rising foreign demand spurred mechanization of the industry.

More specifically, an imbalance between the spinning and weaving processes led to many of the innovations. The spinning wheel was not as productive as the hand loom, especially after the 1730s, when the flying shuttle was invented and the weaving process was speeded up considerably. This imbalance led to three inventions that reversed it: the spinning jenny, developed in the 1760s, with which one person could spin several threads simultaneously; the water frame, invented in 1768, which improved spinning by using both rollers and spindles in the process; and the mule, developed in the 1780s, which combined features of the other two and permitted the application of steam power. These new inventions could be used most economically in factories located near sources of water power (and later steam power). Richard Arkwright, who claimed to be the inventor of the water frame, raised sufficient capital to put a great many factories into operation, each employing anywhere from 150 to 600 people. Others followed his example, and textile manufacturing in England was rapidly transformed from a cottage to a factory industry.

The iron industry was also very important in the early drive to mechanized factory production. In the early eighteenth century England's iron industry was quite inconsequential. Charcoal was still used for smelting and had been since prehistoric times. By this time, however, the forests surrounding the iron mines were almost completely depleted. England was forced to import pig iron from its colonies, as well as from Sweden, Germany, and Spain. In 1709 Abraham Darby developed a process for making coke from coal for use in the smelting process.

Despite the relative abundance of coal near the iron mines, it was not until the latter part of the eighteenth century (when the military demands on the arms and munitions industries were very great) that the iron industry began using coke extensively. This increased demand led to the development of the puddling process, which eliminated the excess carbon left by the coke. A whole series of innovations followed, including the rolling mill, the blast furnace, the steam hammer, and metal-turning lathes. All these inventions led to a very rapid expansion of the iron and coal-mining industries, which permitted the increasingly widespread use of machines made of iron in a great variety of industries.

Entrepreneurs in many other industries saw the possibilities for larger profits if they could increase output and lower costs. In this period there was a "veritable outburst of inventive activity":

> During the second half of the eighteenth century, interest in technical
> innovations became unusually intensive. For a hundred years prior to 1760, the
> number of patents issued during each decade had reached 102 only once, and
> had otherwise fluctuated between a low of 22 (1700–1709) and a high of 92
> (1750–1759). During the following thirty-year period (1760–1789), the average
> number of patents issued increased from 205 in the 1760's to 294 in the 1770's
> and 477 in the 1780's.[1]

Undoubtedly the most important of these innovations was the development of the steam engine. Industrial steam engines had been introduced in the early 1700s, but mechanical difficulties had limited their use to the pumping of water in mines. In 1769 James Watt designed an engine with such accurate specifications that the straight thrust of a piston could be translated into rotary motion. A Birmingham manufacturer named Boulton formed a partnership with Watt, and with Boulton's financial resources they were able to go into large-scale production of

[1] Reinhard Bendix, *Work and Authority in Industry* (New York: Harper & Row, Torchbooks, 1963), p. 27.

steam engines. By the turn of the century steam was rapidly replacing water as the chief source of power in manufacturing. The development of steam power led to profound economic and social changes.

> With this new great event, the invention of the steam engine, the final and most decisive stage of the industrial revolution opened. By liberating it from its last shackles, steam enabled the immense and rapid development of large-scale industry to take place. For the use of steam was not, like that of water, dependent on geographical position and local resources. Whenever coal could be bought at a reasonable price a steam engine could be erected. England had plenty of coal, and by the end of the eighteenth century it was already applied to many different uses, while a network of waterways, made on purpose, enabled it to be carried everywhere very cheaply; the whole country became a privileged land, suitable above all others for the growth of industry. Factories were now no longer bound to the valleys, where they had grown up in solitude by the side of rapid-flowing streams. It became possible to bring them nearer the markets where their raw materials were bought and their finished products sold, and nearer the centers of population where their labor was recruited. They sprang up near one another and thus, huddled together, gave rise to those huge black industrial cities which the steam engine surrounded with a perpetual cloud of smoke.[2]

The growth in the major manufacturing cities was truly spectacular. For example, the population of Manchester rose from 17,000 in 1760 to 237,000 in 1831 and 400,000 in 1851. Output of manufactured goods approximately-doubled in the second half of the eighteenth century and grew even more rapidly in the early nineteenth century. By 1801 nearly 30 percent of the English work force was employed in manufacturing and mining; by 1831 this figure had risen to over 40 percent. Thus the Industrial Revolution transformed England into a country of large urban manufacturing centers, where the factory system was dominant. The result was a very rapid growth of productivity that vaulted England into the position of the greatest economic and political power of the nineteenth century. The effects of the Industrial Revolution on the lives of the English people will be discussed in Chapter 5.

THE RISE OF CLASSICAL LIBERALISM

It was during this period of industrialization that the individualistic world view of classical liberalism became the dominant ideology of capitalism.[3] Many of the ideas of classical liberalism had taken root and even gained wide acceptance in the mercantilist period, but it was in the late eighteenth and nineteenth centuries that classical liberalism most completely dominated social, political, and economic thought in England. The Christian paternalist ethic was still advanced in the writings of many of the nobility and their allies as well as many socialists, but in this era these expressions were, by and large, dissident minority views.

---

[2] Paul Mantoux, *The Industrial Revolution in the Eighteenth Century* (New York: Harcourt Brace Jovanovich, 1927), pp. 344–345.

[3] This account of classical liberalism relies heavily on Harry K. Girvetz, *The Evolution of Liberalism* (New York: Collier, 1963), pp. 1–149.

THE PSYCHOLOGICAL CREED

Classical liberalism's psychological creed was based on four assumptions about human nature. People were believed to be egoistic, coldly calculating, essentially inert, and atomistic. (See Chapter 3 for a discussion of the egoistic theory of human nature.) The egoism argued by Hobbes furnished the basis for this view, and in the works of later liberals, especially Jeremy Bentham, it was blended with psychological hedonism: the view that all actions are motivated by the desire to achieve pleasure and avoid pain.

"Nature," Bentham wrote, "has placed mankind under the governance of two sovereign masters, *pain,* and *pleasure.* . . . They govern us in all we do, in all we say, in all we think."[4] Pleasures differed in intensity, Bentham believed, but there were no qualitative differences. He argued that "quantity of pleasure being equal, pushpin is as good as poetry." This theory of human motivation as purely selfish is found in the writings of many of the most eminent thinkers of the period, including John Locke, Bernard Mandeville, David Hartley, Abraham Tucker, and Adam Smith. Smith's ideas will be examined in some detail later in this chapter.

The rational intellect played a significant role in the classical liberal's scheme of things. Although all motives stemmed from pleasure and pain, the decisions people made about what pleasures or pains to seek or avoid were based on a cool, dispassionate, and rational assessment of the situation. Reason would dictate that all alternatives in a situation be weighed in order to choose that which would maximize pleasure or minimize pain. It is this emphasis on the importance of rational measurement of pleasures and pains (with a corresponding deemphasis of caprice, instinct, habit, custom, or convention) that forms the calculating, intellectual side of the classical liberal's theory of psychology.

The view that individuals were essentially inert stemmed from the notion that pleasure or the avoidance of pain were people's only motives. If people could see no activities leading to pleasurable conclusions or feared no pain, then they would be inert, motionless, or in simpler terms just plain lazy. Any kind of exertion or work was viewed as painful and therefore would not be undertaken without the promise of greater pleasure or the avoidance of greater pain. "Aversion," wrote Bentham, "is the emotion—the only emotion—which labor, taken by itself, is qualified to produce: of any such emotion as *love* or *desire, ease,* which is the *negative* or *absence* of *labor*—ease, not labor—is the object."[5]

The practical outcome of this doctrine (or perhaps the reason for it) was the widespread belief of the time that laborers were incurably lazy. Thus only a large reward or the fear of starvation and deprivation could force them to work. The Reverend Joseph Townsend put this view very succinctly: "Hunger is not only peaceable, silent and unremitted pressure, but, as the most natural motive to industry and labor, it calls forth the most powerful exertions." Townsend believed that "only the experience of hunger would goad them [laborers] to labor."[6]

This view differed radically from the older, paternalistic ethic that had led to the passage of the Elizabethan Poor Relief Act of 1601. The paternalistic concern

---

[4] Jeremy Bentham, "An Introduction to the Principles of Morals and Legislation," in A. I. Melden, ed., *Ethical Theories* (Englewood Cliffs, N.J.: Prentice-Hall, 1955), p. 341.

[5] Quoted in Girvetz, op. cit., p. 38.

[6] Bendix, op. cit., p. 74.

for the poor had lasted for two centuries and had culminated in 1795 in the *Speenhamland system,* which guaranteed everyone, able-bodied or not, working or not, a minimal subsistence to be paid by public taxes. It was against this system that the classical liberals railed. They eventually succeeded in passing the Poor Law of 1834, the object of which, according to Dicey, "was in reality to save the property of hard-working men from destruction by putting an end to the monstrous system under which laggards who would not toil for their support lived at the expense of their industrious neighbors. . . ."[7]

Classical liberals were persuaded, however, that the "higher ranks" of individuals were motivated by ambition. This differentiation of people into different ranks betrayed an implicit elitism in their individualistic doctrines. In order to ensure ample effort on the part of the "elite," the classical liberals believed the state should put the highest priority on the protection of private property. Although the argument began "as an argument for guaranteeing to the worker the fruits of his toil, it has become one of the chief apologies for the institution of private property in general."[8]

The last of the four tenets was atomism, which held that the individual was a more fundamental reality than the group or society. "Priority . . . [was] . . . assigned to the ultimate components out of which an aggregate or whole . . . [was] composed; they constituted the fundamental reality."[9] With this notion the classical liberals rejected the concept, implicit in the Christian paternalist ethic, that society was like a family and that the whole and the relationships that made up the whole were more important than any individual. The liberal's individualistic beliefs were inconsistent with the personal and human ties envisioned in the Christian paternalist ethic. The group was no more than the additive total of the individuals that constituted it. They believed that restrictions placed on the individual by society were generally evil and should be tolerated only when an even worse evil would result without them.

This atomistic psychology can be contrasted with a more socially oriented psychology that would lead to the conclusion that most of the characteristics, habits, ways of perceiving and thinking about life processes, and general personality patterns of the individual are significantly influenced, if not determined, by the social institutions and relationships of which he or she is a part. Atomistic psychology, however, sees the makeup of the individual as somehow independently given. It therefore regards social institutions as both tools for and the handiwork of these individuals. In this view society exists only because it is useful, and if it were not for this usefulness each individual could go his or her own way, discarding society much as he or she would discard a tool that no longer served its purpose.

THE ECONOMIC CREED

Several explanations are necessary for an understanding of why the classical liberals thought society so useful. For example, they talked about the "natural

[7] Albert V. Dicey, *Law and Public Opinion in England,* 2d ed. (London: Macmillan, 1926), p. 203.
[8] Girvetz, op. cit., p. 50.
[9] Ibid., p. 41.

gregariousness of men," the need for collective security, and the economic benefits of the division of labor, which society makes possible. The latter was the foundation of the economic creed of classical liberalism, and the creed was crucial to classical liberalism because this philosophy contained what appear to be two contradictory or conflicting assumptions.

On the one hand, the assumption of individual's innate egoism had led Hobbes to assert that, in the absence of restraints, people's selfish motives would lead to a "natural state" of war, with each individual pitted against all others. In this state of nature, Hobbes believed, the life of a person was "solitary, poor, nasty, brutish, and short." The only escape from brutal combat was the establishment of some source of absolute power—a central government—to which each individual submitted in return for protection from all other individuals.[10]

On the other hand, one of the cardinal tenets of classical liberalism was that individuals (or, more particularly, businessmen) should be free to give vent to their egoistic drives with a minimum of control or restraint imposed by society. This apparent contradiction was bridged by the liberal economic creed, which asserted that if the competitiveness and rivalry of unrestrained egoism existed in a capitalist market setting, then this competition would benefit the individuals involved and all society as well. This view was put forth in the most profound single intellectual achievement of classical liberalism: Adam Smith's *The Wealth of Nations*, published in 1776.

Smith believed that "every individual . . . [was] continually exerting himself to find out the most advantageous employment for whatever capital he can command."[11] Those without capital were always searching for the employment at which the monetary return for their labor would be maximized. If both capitalists and laborers were left alone, self-interest would guide them to use their capital and labor where they were most productive. The search for profits would ensure that what was produced would be what people wanted most and were willing to pay for. Thus Smith and classical liberals in general were opposed to having some authority or law determine what should be produced. "It is not from the benevolence of the butcher, the brewer, or the baker, that we expect our dinner, but from their regard to their own interest,"[12] wrote Smith. Producers of various goods must compete in the market for the dollars of consumers. The producer who offered a better-quality product would attract more consumers. Self-interest would, therefore, lead to constant improvement of the quality of the product. The producer could also increase profits by cutting the costs of production to a minimum.

Thus a *free market*, in which producers competed for consumers' money in an egoistic quest for more profits, would guarantee the direction of capital and labor to their most productive uses and ensure production of the goods consumers wanted and needed most (as measured by their ability and willingness to pay for them). Moreover, the market would lead to a constant striving to improve the quality of products and to organize production in the most efficient and least costly manner possible. All these beneficial actions would stem directly from the competition of egoistical individuals, each pursuing his or her self-interest.

[10] Hobbes, *Leviathan,* reprinted in Melden, op. cit., pp. 192–205.
[11] Adam Smith, *The Wealth of Nations* (New York: Modern Library, 1937), p. 421.
[12] Ibid., p. 14.

What a far cry from the "solitary, poor, nasty, brutish" world Hobbes thought would result from human competitiveness. The wonderful social institution that could make all this possible was the free and unrestrained market, the forces of supply and demand. The market, Smith believed, would act as an "invisible hand" channeling selfish, egoistic motives into mutually consistent and complementary activities that would best promote the welfare of all society. And the greatest beauty of it was the complete lack of any need for paternalistic guidance, direction, or restrictions. Freedom from coercion in a capitalist market economy was compatible with a natural orderliness in which the welfare of each, as well as the welfare of all society (which was, after all, only the aggregate of the individuals that constitute it), would be maximized. In Smith's words, each producer

> intends only his own security; and by directing that industry in such a manner as its produce may be of the greatest value, he intends only his own gain, and he is in this, as in many other cases, led by an invisible hand to promote an end which was no part of his intention. Nor is it always the worse for the society that it was not part of it. By pursuing his own interest he frequently promotes that of society more effectually than when he really intends to promote it. I have never known much good done by those who affected to trade for the public good. It is an affectation, indeed, not very common among merchants, and very few words need be employed in dissuading them from it.[13]

With this statement it is evident that Smith had a philosophy totally antithetical to the paternalism of the Christian paternalist ethic. The Christian notion of the rich promoting the security and well-being of the poor through paternalistic control and almsgiving contrasts sharply with Smith's picture of a capitalist who is concerned only with "his own advantage, indeed, and not that of the society. . . . But the study of his own advantage naturally, or rather necessarily leads him to prefer that employment which is most advantageous to the society."[14]

Not only would the free and unfettered market channel productive energies and resources into their most valuable uses, but it would also lead to continual economic progress. Economic well-being depended on the capacity of an economy to produce. Productive capacity depended, in turn, on accumulation of capital and division of labor. When one man produced everything he needed for himself and his family, production was very inefficient. But if men subdivided tasks, each producing only the commodity for which his own abilities best suited him, productivity increased. For such a subdivision of tasks a market was necessary in order to exchange goods. In the market each person could get all the items he needed but did not produce.

This increase in productivity could be extended further if the production of each commodity were broken down into many steps or stages. Each person would then work on only one stage of the production of one commodity. In order to achieve a division of labor of this degree, it was necessary to have many specialized tools and other equipment. It was also necessary that all the stages of production for a particular commodity be brought together and coordinated, as, for example, in a factory. Thus an increasingly fine division of labor required accumulation of capital in the form of tools, equipment, factories, and money.

13 Ibid., p. 423.
14 Ibid., p. 421.

This capital would also provide wages to maintain workers during the period of production before their coordinated efforts were brought to fruition and sold on the market.

The source of this capital accumulation was, of course, the profits of production. As long as demand was brisk and more could be sold than was being produced, capitalists would invest their profits in order to expand their capital, which would lead to an increasingly intricate division of labor. The increased division of labor would lead to greater productivity, higher wages, higher profits, more capital accumulation, and so forth in a never-ending, upward-moving escalator of social progress. The process would be brought to a halt only when there was no longer sufficient demand for the products to warrant further accumulation and more extensive division of labor. Government regulation of economic affairs, or any restriction on the freedom of market behavior, could only decrease the extent of demand and bring the beneficial process of capital accumulation to a halt before it would have ended otherwise. So here again there was no room for paternalistic government meddling in economic affairs.

THE THEORY OF POPULATION

Thomas Robert Malthus' population theory was an important and integral part of classical liberal economic and social doctrines. He believed most human beings were driven by an insatiable desire for sexual pleasure and that consequently natural rates of human reproduction, *when unchecked*, would lead to geometric increases in population—that is, population would increase each generation at the ratio of 1, 2, 4, 8, 16, and so forth. But food production, at the very best, increases at an arithmetic rate—that is, each generation it can increase only at a rate such as 1, 2, 3, 4, 5, and so on.

Obviously, something would have to hold the population in check. The food supply could not support a population that was growing at a geometric rate. Malthus believed there were two general kinds of checks that limited population growth: preventive checks and positive checks. Preventive checks reduced the birth rate, whereas positive checks increased the death rate.

Moral restraint, vice, and birth control were the primary preventive checks. Moral restraint was the means by which the higher ranks of humans limited their family size in order not to dissipate their wealth among larger and larger numbers of heirs. For the lower ranks of humans, vice and birth control were the preventive checks; but they were grossly insufficient to curb the vast numbers of the poor.

Famine, misery, plague, and war were the positive checks. The fact that preventive checks did not succeed in limiting the numbers of lower-class people made these positive checks inevitable. Finally, if the positive checks were somehow overcome, the growing population would press upon the food supply until starvation—the ultimate and unavoidable check—succeeded in holding the population down.

Before starvation set in, Malthus advised that steps be taken to help the positive checks do their work:

> It is an evident truth that, whatever may be the rate of increase in the means of subsistence, the increase in population must be limited by it, at least after the

food has once been divided into the smallest shares that will support life. All the children born, beyond what would be required to keep up the population to this level, must necessarily perish, unless room be made for them by the deaths of grown persons. . . . To act consistently therefore, we should facilitate, instead of foolishly and vainly endeavouring to impede, the operation of nature in producing this mortality; and if we dread the too frequent visitation of the horrid form of famine, we should sedulously encourage the other forms of destruction, which we compel nature to use. Instead of recommending cleanliness to the poor, we should encourage contrary habits. In our towns we should make the streets narrower, crowd more people into the houses, and court the return of the plague. In the country, we should build our villages near stagnant pools, and particularly encourage settlements in all marshy and unwholesome situations. But above all, we should reprobate specific remedies for ravaging diseases; and those benevolent, but much mistaken men, who have thought they were doing a service to mankind by projecting schemes for the total extirpation of particular disorders. If by these and similar means the annual mortality were increased . . . we might probably every one of us marry at the age of puberty, and yet few be absolutely starved. [15]

The masses, in Malthus' opinion, were incapable of exercising moral restraint, which was the only real remedy for the population problem. They were therefore doomed to live perpetually at a bare subsistence level. If all income and wealth were distributed among them, it would be totally dissipated within one generation because of profligate behavior and population growth, and they would be as poor and destitute as ever.

Paternalistic attempts to aid the poor were thus doomed to failure. Furthermore, they were a positive evil because they drained wealth and income from the higher (more moral) ranks of human beings. These higher-class individuals were responsible, either in person or by supporting others, for all the great achievements of society. Art, music, philosophy, literature, and the other splendid cultural attainments of Western civilization owed their existence to the good taste and generosity of the higher classes of men. Taking money from them would dry up the source of such achievement; using the money to alleviate the conditions of the poor was a futile, foredoomed exercise.

It is obvious that the Malthusian population theory and the liberal economic theories led to the same conclusion: Paternalistic government should avoid any attempt to intervene in the economy on behalf of the poor. Malthusian views— that poverty is the fault of the poor, who have too many babies, and that nothing can be done to end poverty—are still held by many people today.

THE POLITICAL CREED

The economic and population doctrines of classical liberalism gave rise quite naturally to a political creed that rejected the State, or government, as an evil to be tolerated only when it was the sole means of avoiding a worse evil. Much of this antipathy stemmed directly from the many corrupt, despotic, capricious, and tyrannical actions of several European kings, as well as from the actions of the English Parliament, which was notoriously unrepresentative and often despotic.

[15] Thomas Robert Malthus, *Essay on the Principle of Population*, vol. 2 (New York: Dutton, 1961), pp. 179–180.

The liberal creed was not put forward as an objection against particular governments, however, but against governments in general. Thomas Paine reflected the sentiment of classical liberals when he wrote: "Society in every state is a blessing, but government, even in its best state, is but a necessary evil; in its worst state an intolerable one. . . ."[16]

What were the functions that classical liberals thought should be given to governments? In *The Wealth of Nations* Adam Smith listed three: protection of the country against foreign invaders, protection of citizens against "injustices" suffered at the hands of other citizens, and the "duty . . . of erecting and maintaining those public institutions and those public works, which, though they may be in the highest degree advantageous to a great society, are, however, of such a nature, that the profit could never repay the expense to any individual or small number of individuals, and which it therefore cannot be expected that any individual or small number of individuals should erect and maintain."[17]

This list is very general, and almost any kind of government action could be justified under one of these three functions. In order to understand the specific functions the liberals believed government should have, it is necessary to deal first with an objection that is frequently raised when the writings of Adam Smith are said to comprise part of an ideology justifying capitalism. It is often pointed out not only that Smith was *not* a spokesman for the capitalists of his day but also that many of his passages show that he was in general suspicious and distrustful of capitalists.[18] This contention is certainly true. Nevertheless capitalists used the arguments put forward by Smith to justify their attempts to eliminate the last vestiges of paternalistic government when these stood in the way of their quest for profits. It was Smith's rationale that enabled them to quiet their consciences when their actions created widespread hardship and suffering. After all, they were only following his advice and pursuing their own profits; and this was the way they should act if they wished to be of the greatest service to society.

Finally, most classical liberals interpreted Smith's theory of the three general governmental functions in a way that showed they were not hesitant about endorsing a paternalistic government when they, the capitalists, were the beneficiaries of paternalism. Thus "the original doctrine of laissez faire . . . passed, for the most part, from the care of intellectuals like Adam Smith . . . into the custodianship of businessmen and industrialists and their hired spokesmen."[19]

First, the requirement that the government protect the country from external threats was often extended in the late nineteenth century to a protection or even enlargement of foreign markets through armed coercion. Second, protection of citizens against "injustices" committed by other citizens was usually defined to mean protection of private property, enforcement of contracts, and preservation of internal order. Protection of private property, especially ownership of factories and capital equipment, is of course tantamount to protection of the sine qua non

---

[16] Quoted in Girvetz, op. cit., p. 66.

[17] Smith, op. cit., p. 681.

[18] For a statement of this view, as well as a scholarly inquiry into classical economics from a viewpoint that differs from the one presented in this book, see Lionel Robbins, *The Theory of Economic Policy in English Classical Political Economy* (London: Macmillan, 1953).

[19] Girvetz, op. cit., p. 81.

of capitalism. It was their ownership of the means of production that gave the capitalists their economic and political power. Giving the government the function of protecting property relations meant giving the government the job of protecting the source of power of the economically and politically dominant class: the capitalists.

Contract enforcement was also essential for the successful functioning of capitalism. The complex division of labor and the necessity of complex organization and coordination in production, as well as the colossal capital investments necessary in many commercial ventures, meant that capitalists had to be able to depend on people to meet contractual commitments. The medieval notion that custom and the special circumstances of a case defined an individual's obligations was just not compatible with capitalism. Therefore the duty to enforce contracts amounted to governmental coercion of a type necessary for capitalism to function.

The preservation of internal order was (and is) always necessary. In the late eighteenth and early nineteenth centuries, however, it often meant brutally crushing labor union movements or the English Chartist movement, which capitalists considered threats to their profit-making activities.

Finally, the function of "erecting and maintaining those public institutions and those of public works" that were in the public interest generally was interpreted to mean the creation and maintenance of institutions that fostered profitable production and exchange. These included the provision of a stable and uniform currency, standard weights and measures, and the physical means necessary for conducting business. Roads, canals, harbors, railroads, the postal services, and other forms of communication were among the prerequisites of business. Although these were often privately owned, most capitalist governments were extensively involved in their erection and maintenance either through financial subsidies to private businesses or through the government's direct undertaking of these projects.

Thus it may be concluded that the classical liberals' philosophy of laissez-faire was opposed to government interference in economic affairs only if such interference was harmful to the interests of capitalists. They welcomed and even fought for any paternalistic interferences in economic affairs that stabilized business or made larger profits possible.[20]

CLASSICAL LIBERALISM AND INDUSTRIALIZATION

The Industrial Revolution and the triumph of the classical liberal capitalist ideology occurred together during the late eighteenth and early nineteenth centuries. Liberalism was the philosophy of the new industrial capitalism, and the new liberal ideas created a political and intellectual atmosphere in eighteenth-century England that fostered the growth of the factory system.

In its medieval version, the Christian paternalist ethic had led to a pervasive system of restrictions on the behavior of capitalists during the mercantilist pe-

[20] Considerable evidence for this assertion can be found in Warren J. Samuels, *The Classical Theory of Economic Policy* (New York: World Publishing, 1966).

riod. Capitalists and their spokesmen opposed most of these restrictions with a new individualistic philosophy that advocated greater freedom for the capitalist to seek profits in a market free of encumbrances and restrictions. It is not surprising that the triumph of this philosophy should coincide with the greatest achievement of the capitalist class: the Industrial Revolution. The Industrial Revolution vaulted the capitalist class into a position of economic and political dominance, and this fact goes far in explaining the triumph of classical liberalism as the ideology of the new age of industrial capitalism.

SUMMARY

The pressure of rapidly increasing demand and the prospect of larger profits led to a "veritable outburst of inventive activity" in the late eighteenth and early nineteenth centuries. This period of widespread innovation—the Industrial Revolution—transformed England (and later western Europe and North America) into urban societies dominated by great manufacturing cities in which large numbers of workers were subjected to the dehumanizing discipline of factory production.

During this period the classical liberal ideology of capitalism came to dominate social and economic thinking. The new ideology pictured individuals as egoistic, coldly calculating, lazy, and generally independent of the society of which they were a part. Adam Smith's analysis of the market as an "invisible hand" that channeled egoistic drives into the most socially useful activities supported a doctrine of laissez-faire. The only functions this philosophy assigned to the government were those that would support and encourage profit-making activites.

Finally, the Malthusian theory of population taught that social action designed to mitigate the suffering of the poor was not only useless but even had socially deleterious effects. Acceptance of this view necessitated complete abandonment of the Christian paternalist ethic.

CHAPTER 5

SOCIALIST PROTEST AMID THE INDUSTRIAL REVOLUTION

The Industrial Revolution brought about increases in human productivity without precedent in history. The widespread construction of factories and extensive use of machinery represented the mechanical basis of this increase. In order to channel the economy's productive capacity into the creation of capital goods, however, it was necessary to devote a relatively much smaller part of this capacity to the manufacture of consumer goods. Capital goods had to be purchased at a social cost of mass deprivation.

THE SOCIAL COSTS OF THE INDUSTRIAL REVOLUTION

Historically, in all cases in which society has had to force a bare subsistence existence on some of its members it has always been those with the least economic and political power who have made the sacrifices. And so it was in the Industrial Revolution in England. The working class lived near the subsistence level in 1750, and their standard of living (measured in terms of the purchasing power of wages) deteriorated during the second half of the eighteenth century. The trend of working class living standards in the first several decades of the nineteenth century is a subject of dispute among historians. The fact that many eminent scholars find sufficient evidence to argue that the living standard failed to increase, or even decreased, leads to the conclusion that any increase during this period was slight at best.

Throughout the period of the Industrial Revolution, there is no doubt that the standard of living of the poor fell precipitously in relative terms. A detailed analysis shows that "relatively the poor grew poorer, simply because the country, and its rich and middle class, so obviously grew wealthier. The very moment when the poor were at the end of their tether . . . was the moment when the middle class dripped with excess capital, to be wildly invested in railways and spent on the bulging opulent household furnishings displayed at the Great Exhibition of 1851, and on palatial municipal constructions . . . in the smoky northern cities."[1] There can be no doubt about which class paid the social costs in terms of the sacrificed consumption that was necessary for industrialization.

Yet the costs in terms of decreased consumption were by no means the only, and perhaps not even the worst, hardships forced upon the laboring class by the

---

[1] E. J. Hobsbawm, *Industry and Empire: An Economic History of Britain Since 1750* (London: Weidenfeld & Nicolson, 1968), p. 72. Several of Hobsbawm's ideas appear in this chapter.

Industrial Revolution. The new factory system completely destroyed the laborers' traditional way of life, throwing them into a nightmare world with which they were completely unprepared to cope. They lost the pride of workmanship and close personal relationships that had existed in handicraft industries. Under the new system their only relationship with their employer was through the impersonal market, or *cash nexus*. They lost direct access to the means of production and were reduced to mere sellers of labor power totally dependent on market conditions for their livelihood.

Perhaps worse than any of these was the monotonous, mechanical regularity imposed on the worker by the factory system. In pre-industrial Europe the worker's tasks were not so specialized. The worker went from one task to another, and the work was interrupted by variations in the seasons or the weather. When the worker felt like resting or playing or changing the pace of the work routine, there was a certain amount of freedom to do so. Factory employment brought the tyranny of the clock. Production was mechanized. Absolute regularity was necessary to coordinate the complex interaction of processes and to maximize the use of new, expensive machinery. The pace of work was no longer decided by the worker but by the machine.

The machine, which had formerly been an appendage to the worker, was now the focal point of the productive process. A worker became a mere appendage to the cold, implacable, pace-setting machine. During the late eighteenth and early nineteenth centuries, a spontaneous revolt against the new factory system saw bands of workers smashing and destroying machines and factories, which they believed were responsible for their plight. These revolts, called the Luddite revolts, ended in 1813 when large numbers of workers were hanged or deported for their activities.

The extensive division of labor in the factory made much of the work so routine and simple that untrained women and children could do it as well as men. Because women and children could be hired for much lower wages than men, and because in many cases entire families had to work in order to earn enough to eat, women and children were employed widely. Many factory owners preferred women and children because they could be reduced to a state of passive obedience more easily than men. The widespread ideology in this period that the only good woman is a submissive woman was a great help to their employers.

Children were bound to factories by indentures of apprenticeship for 7 years, or until they were 21. In these cases almost nothing was given the children in return for long hours of work under the most horrendous conditions. Poor-law authorities could indenture the children of paupers. This led to "regular bargains . . . [where] children . . . were dealt with as mere merchandise . . . between the spinners on the one hand and the Poor Law authorities on the other. Lots of fifty, eighty or a hundred children were supplied and sent like cattle to the factory, where they remained imprisoned for many years."[2]

These children endured the cruelest servitude. They were totally isolated from anyone who might take pity on them and were thus at the mercy of the capitalists or their hired managers, whose main concern was the challenge of competitive

[2] Paul Mantoux, *The Industrial Revolution in the Eighteenth Century* (New York: Harcourt Brace Jovanovich, 1927), pp. 410–411.

factories. The children's workday was from 14 to 18 hours, or until they dropped from complete exhaustion. The foremen were paid according to how much the children produced and therefore pushed them mercilessly. In most factories the children had hardly more than 20 minutes a day for their main (and often only) meal. "Accidents were very common, especially towards the end of the overlong day, when the exhausted children almost fell asleep at their work. The tale never ended of fingers cut off and limbs crushed in the wheels."[3] The children were disciplined in such savage and brutal ways that a recitation of the methods used would appear completely incredible to the reader of today.

Women were mistreated almost as badly. Work in a factory was long, arduous, and monotonous. Discipline was harsh. Many times the price of factory employment was submission to the sexual advances of employers and foremen.[4] Women in the mines toiled 14 to 16 hours a day, stripped naked to the waist, working with men and doing the work of men. There were reports of women who came out of the mines to bear children and were back in the mines within days after the birth. Many accounts have been written of the fantastically cruel and dehumanizing working conditions for women during this period. And of course the workingmen were not much better off than the women or the children. Industrialization was stern, harsh, and cruel in the extreme for men as well as for women and children.

Another important consideration in assessing the living standard of the working class during the period of capitalist industrialization was the rapid urbanization that took place at that time. In 1750, only 2 cities in Britain had populations over 50,000. In 1850, there were 29. By the latter date nearly one person in three lived in a city with over 50,000 inhabitants.

Conditions in the cities of this period were terrible:

> And what cities! It was not merely that smoke hung over them and filth impregnated them, that the elementary public services—water-supply, sanitation, street-cleaning, open spaces, etc.—could not keep pace with the mass migration of men into the cities, thus producing, especially after 1830, epidemics of cholera, typhoid and an appalling constant toll of the two great groups of nineteenth-century urban killers—air pollution and water pollution, or respiratory and intestinal disease. . . . The new city populations . . . [were] pressed into overcrowded and bleak slums, whose very sight froze the heart of the observer. "Civilization works its miracles" wrote the great French liberal de Tocqueville of Manchester, "and civilized man is turned back almost into a savage."[5]

Included in these slums was a district of Glasgow that, according to a report of a government commissioner, housed

> a fluctuating population of between 15,000 and 30,000 persons. This district is composed of many narrow streets and square courts and in the middle of each court there is a dunghill. Although the outward appearance of these places was revolting, I was nevertheless quite unprepared for the filth and misery that were to be found inside. In some bedrooms we visited at night, we found a whole mass of humanity stretched on the floor. There were often 15 to 20 men and

[3] Ibid., p. 413.
[4] Ibid., p. 416.
[5] Hobsbawm, op. cit., pp. 67–68.

women huddled together, some being clothed and others naked. There was hardly any furniture there and the only thing which gave these holes the appearance of a dwelling was fire burning on the hearth. Thieving and prostitution are the main sources of income of these people.[6]

The total destruction of the laborers' traditional way of life and the harsh discipline of the new factory system, combined with deplorable living conditions in the cities, generated social, economic, and political unrest. Chain reactions of social upheaval, riots, and rebellion occurred in the years 1811–1813, 1815–1817, 1819, 1826, 1829–1835, 1838–1842, 1843–1844, and 1846–1848. In many areas these were purely spontaneous and primarily economic in character. In 1816 one rioter from the Fens exclaimed: "Here I am between Earth and Sky, so help me God. I would sooner lose my life than go home as I am. Bread I want and bread I will have."[7] In 1845 an American named Colman reported that the working people of Manchester were "wretched, defrauded, oppressed, crushed human nature lying in bleeding fragments all over the face of society."[8]

There can be no doubt that industrial capitalism was erected on the base of the wretched suffering of a laboring class denied access to the fruits of the rapidly expanding economy and subjected to the most degrading of excesses to increase the capitalists' profits. The basic cause of the great evils of this period was "the absolute and uncontrolled power of the capitalist. In this, the heroic age of great undertakings, it was acknowledged, admitted and even proclaimed with brutal candor. It was the employer's own business, he did as he chose and did not consider that any other justification of his conduct was necessary. He owed his employees wages and once those were paid the men had no further claim on him."[9]

LIBERAL SOCIAL LEGISLATION

From the earliest introduction of factory production in the textile industries, worker's tried to band together to protect their interests collectively. In 1787, during a period of high unemployment, the Glasgow muslin manufacturers attempted to lower the piece rates they were paying. The workers resisted collectively, refused to work below a certain minimum rate, and organized a boycott of the manufacturers who would not pay the minimum rate. The struggle led to open rioting and shooting, but the worker's proved to have a strong and well-disciplined group, and they built a strong union. In 1792, a union of weavers forced a collective agreement upon Bolton and Bury Manufacturers.

Labor organizations spread rapidly in the 1790s. As a result of this and the concurrent growth of social and economic discontent, the upper classes became very uneasy. The memory of the French Revolution was fresh in their

---

[6] Quoted in F. Engels, *The Condition of the Working Class in England in 1844* (New York: Macmillan, 1958), p. 46.
[7] Quoted in Hobsbawm, op. cit., p. 74.
[8] Ibid., p. 75.
[9] Mantoux, op. cit., p. 417.

minds, and they feared the power of the united workers. The result was the Combination Act of 1799, which outlawed any combination of workers whose purpose was to obtain higher wages, shorter hours, or the introduction of any regulation constraining the free action of their employers. Proponents couched their arguments in terms of the necessity of free competition and the evils of monopoly—cardinal tenets of classical liberalism—but did not mention combinations of employers or monopolistic practices of capitalists. The effects of this legislation have been summarized as follows:

> The Combination Laws were considered as absolutely necessary to prevent ruinous extortions of workmen, which, if not thus restrained, would destroy the whole of the trade, manufactures, commerce and agriculture of the nation. . . . So thoroughly was this false notion entertained, that whenever men were prosecuted to conviction for having combined to regulate their wages or the hours of working, however heavy the sentence passed upon them was, and however rigorously it was inflicted, not the slightest feeling of compassion was manifested by anybody for the unfortunate sufferers. Justice was entirely out of the question: They could seldom obtain a hearing before a magistrate, never without impatience or insult . . . could an accurate account be given of proceedings, or hearings before magistrates, trials at sessions and in the Court of King's Bench, the gross injustice, the foul invective, and terrible punishments inflicted would not, after a few years have passed away, be credited to any but the best evidence.[10]

Another cause for which the classical liberals campaigned vigorously was the abolition of the Speenhamland system of poor relief that had come into existence in 1795. This system was (continuing in the tradition of the Elizabethan Statute of Artificers) the result of the Christian paternalist ethic. It held that unfortunates would be entitled to a certain minimum living standard whether employed or not. To be sure, the system had serious drawbacks: It actually depressed wages below the relief level in many cases (with the parish taxes making up the difference) and severely limited labor mobility at a time when greater mobility was needed.

The important issue, however, is not the deficiencies of the Speenhamland system but rather the type of legislation the liberals enacted in its place when they succeeded in abolishing it in 1834. The view of the classical liberals was that workers should accept any job the market offered, regardless of the conditions or pay involved. Any person who would not or could not do so should be given just enough to prevent physical starvation. His dole should be substantially lower than the lowest wage offered in the market, and his general situation should stigmatize him sufficiently to motivate him to seek gainful employment. Thus the new law

> was an engine of degradation and oppression more than a means of material relief. There have been few more inhuman statutes than the Poor Law Act of 1834, which made all relief "less eligible" than the lowest wage outside, confined it to the jail-like workhouse, forcibly separated husbands, wives and children in order to punish the poor for their destitution, and discourage them from the dangerous temptation of procreating further paupers.[11]

[10] Quoted in ibid., p. 449.
[11] Hobsbawm, op. cit., pp. 69–70.

THE PATERNALISM OF THE TORY RADICALS

It might seem from this discussion that the Christian paternalist ethic was completely eclipsed during the Industrial Revolution. This was not so. Among the landed or aristocratic wealthy, there were many Tory radicals, men who often had a "gentleman's disdain" for the "vulgar, money-grubbing" middle-class merchants and manufacturers. They asserted that it was the obligation of the "higher classes" to think for and protect the poor. Some of the most vivid descriptions and outspoken denunciations of the excesses of the factory managers came from the pens of Tory radicals.

The ideas of the traditionalist Tories were summarized by John Stuart Mill (who was critical of the point of view he was summarizing). According to Mill, the traditionalists believed that

> the lot of the poor, in all things which affect them collectively, should be regulated *for* them, not *by* them. They should not be required or encouraged to think for themselves, or give to their own reflection or forecast an influential voice in the determination of their destiny. It is supposed to be the duty of the higher classes to think for them, and to take the responsibility of their lot, as the commander and officers of an army take that of the soldiers composing it. This function, it is contended, the higher classes should prepare themselves to perform conscientiously, and their whole demeanour should impress the poor with a reliance on it, in order that, while yielding passive and active obedience to the rules prescribed for them, they may resign themselves in all other respects to a trustful *insouciance,* and repose under the shadow of their protectors. The relationship between the rich and poor, according to this theory, should be only partly authoritative; it should be amiable, moral and sentimental: affectionate tutelage on the one side, respectful and grateful deference on the other.[12]

Most of these traditionalists believed that the greedy profit seeking of the vulgar, unrefined, acquisitive middle classes was responsible for the social ills of the Industrial Revolution. Capitalism would function properly, in their opinion, only when capitalists functioned as gentlemen rather than moneygrubbers. These ideas were put into practice in several industrial enterprises owned either by the aristocracy or by humane middle-class capitalists with traditionalist views. Perhaps the most famous of the latter was Robert Owen.

Born in 1771, Owen served as a draper's apprentice from the age of 10. At 20 he was the manager of a large mill. Wise business decisions and good luck soon resulted in the acquisition of a considerable fortune. Owen was a perfect example of a benevolent autocrat. His factory at New Lanark became known throughout all England because he insisted on decent working conditions, livable wages, and education for working-class children. His workers received "affectionate tutelage" from him, and he thought of himself as their trustee and steward.

This paternalistic attitude did not interfere with Owen's very strict organizational discipline in his factory. Owen has described one of his methods of maintaining discipline:

[12] John Stuart Mill, *Principles of Political Economy* (Clifton, N.J.: Augustus M. Kelley, 1965 [first published in 1848]), p. 753.

that which I found to be the most efficient check upon inferior conduct was the contrivance of a silent monitor for each one employed in the establishment. This consisted of a four-sided piece of wood, about two inches long and one broad, each side colored—one side black, another blue, the third yellow, and the fourth white, tapered at the top, and finished with wire eyes, to hang upon a hook with either side to the front. One of these was suspended in a conspicuous place near to each of the persons employed, and the color at the front told the conduct of the individual during the preceding day, to four degrees of comparison. Bad, denoted by black and No. 4; indifferent by blue, and No. 3; good by yellow, and No. 2; and excellent by white, and No. 1. Then books of character were provided, for each department, in which the name of each one employed in it was inserted in the front of succeeding columns, which sufficed to mark by the number the daily conduct, day by day, for two months; and these books were changed six times a year, and were preserved; by which arrangement I had the conduct of each registered to four degrees of comparison during every day of the week, Sundays excepted, for every year they remained in my employment.[13]

So in his life and deeds, Owen, like other capitalists of his era, strove to maximize his profits. He believed his competitors' harsh treatment of their workers was stupid and shortsighted, and he based his life on the assumption that the Christian paternalist ethic was compatible with the capitalist system, at least at the factory level. In his own words, "My time, from early to late, and my mind, were continually occupied in devising measures and directing their execution, to improve the condition of the people, and to advance at the same time the works and the machinery as a manufacturing establishment."[14]

THE SOCIALIST VERSION
OF THE CHRISTIAN PATERNALIST ETHIC

Although Owen's life and actions did not differentiate him from many of the conservative Tory radicals of his time, some of his ideas did. He did not believe that any society in which one class was elevated to a position of power and used this power to exploit the lower classes could ultimately become a truly good society. Private ownership of the means of production (factories, machinery, tools) was the social institution by which one small class in the existing economic system gained immense power over the mass of farmers and workers. The profit motive was the force that drove this small class to use its power to exploit the workers and farmers in order to gain profits.

Owen believed that in an ideal society the people could most effectively control nature because they would reap the greatest collective benefit if they cooperated. This cooperation should take the form of self-governing industrial and agricultural communities. In such communities private ownership of the means of production would be abolished and the selfish quest for profits eliminated. He maintained that only when such a society was established would it be true that

---

[13] M. Beer, ed., *Life of Robert Owen* (New York: Knopf, 1920), p. 111.
[14] Ibid., p. 112.

One portion of mankind will not, as now, be trained and placed to oppress, by force or fraud, another portion, to the great disadvantage of both; neither will one portion be trained in idleness, to live in luxury on the industry of those whom they oppress, while the latter are made to labor daily and to live in poverty. Nor yet will some be trained to force falsehood into the human mind and be paid extravagantly for so doing while other parties are prevented from teaching the truth, or severely punished if they make the attempt.[15]

There was something in these writings that differed very radically from his description of the way in which he ran his own factory at New Lanark. The ideal society, for Owen, would be one in which the paternalism of the traditional Christian ethic would be expressed as a brotherhood of equals, a considerable shift from the parent–child type of subordination expressed in the medieval and Tory radical versions of the Christian paternalist ethic.

The feudal version of that ethic had accepted a hierarchical society. In this version those at the top lived lavishly (by the standards of the day, at least), and they did so by exploiting those at the bottom. Chaucer's parson's description of the medieval view is apt: "God has ordained that some folk should be more high in estate and degree and some folk more low, and that everyone should be served in his estate and his degree."[16] This traditional feudal ethic seemed to most capitalists to be incompatible with the capitalist order, and it was gradually replaced by the new individualist philosophy of classical liberalism.

Classical liberalism, however, was a two-edged sword. It became an ideology justifying the new capitalist order (see Chapter 4). But the individualistic assumptions of classical liberalism were very radical. If the old feudal aristocracy had no inherent superiority over the middle class and if any member of the middle class was to be freed of the old restraints, and if each individual should be the best judge in deciding his or her own affairs, then how could one stop short of asserting the same rights and advantages for the lowest classes? The ideal that each individual ought, in some abstract way, to be considered as important as any other individual was radical indeed.

If individualism seemed to imply equality in theory, however, it certainly did not lead to it in practice. The rugged battles for more profits led not only to the social misery described earlier but also to a new class division of society that was sharply defined and as exploitative in nature as the medieval class structure. Membership in the higher class of the new system depended not on genealogy but on ownership. Capitalists derived their income and their power from ownership of the means of production.

Socialism, then, was a protest against the inequalities of capitalism and the social evils resulting from these inequalities. The inequalities themselves, in the opinion of socialists from the earliest times to the present, resulted inevitably from the institution of private property in the means of production. Hence socialism asserted as its most cardinal tenet that social justice demanded the abolition of private ownership of capital.

Intellectually, socialism was a wedding of the liberal notion of the equality of all human beings to the notion inherent in the traditional Christian paternalist

[15] Robert Owen, "The Book of the New Moral World," reprinted in part in Carl Cohen, ed., *Communism, Fascism and Democracy* (New York: Random House, 1962), pp. 47–48.
[16] Quoted in J. L. and Barbara Hammond, *The Rise of Modern Industry* (New York: Harper & Row, Torchbooks, 1969), p. 215.

ethic that every man should be his brother's keeper. Incorporating the egalitarian elements of classical liberalism into the traditional Christian ethic made this a utopian ethic, and in comparison with it existing society was criticized. Without this egalitarian element the Christian ethic served well as an ideological justification of the hierarchical class system of the Middle Ages and was sometimes used to defend the capitalist system, particularly in the late nineteenth and twentieth centuries (of which more will be said later).

IMPORTANT PRE-MARXIST SOCIALISTS

When Owen asserted that in the ideal society private property and acquisitive profit seeking would be eliminated, he became part of a socialist tradition that was already firmly established by his time. One of the first voices of socialist protest against capitalist property relations was that of Gerrard Winstanley (1609–1652), a cloth merchant who had been bankrupted in the depression of 1643. He blamed his own misfortune as well as that of others on the "cheating art of buying and selling."[17] In 1649 he led a strange band of followers from London to Saint George's Hill, Surrey. There they occupied unused crown lands, which they cultivated in common and, in general, shared in a communal existence.

In the same year Winstanley published *The True Levellers Standard Advanced*, in which he rebuked "the powers of England" and "the powers of the world" for their failure to realize that "the great creator . . . made the Earth a common treasury for beasts and man."[18] He asserted that all who derived their incomes in part or in full from property ownership were violating God's commandment "Thou shalt not steal." "You pharaohs, you have rich clothing and full bellies, you have your honors and your ease; but know the day of judgment is begun and that it will reach you ere long. The poor people you oppress shall be the saviours of the land."[19]

Throughout the eighteenth and nineteenth centuries, a large number of writers argued that private property was the source of the inequities and exploitation that existed in the capitalist economy. In this chapter we can mention only a few of the better known among them. One of the most interesting was the Frenchman Gracchus Babeuf (1760–1797). Babeuf argued that nature had made all persons equal in rights and needs. Therefore the inequalities of wealth and power that had developed should be redressed by society. Unfortunately, most societies did the opposite: They set up a coercive mechanism to protect the interests of the property holders and the wealthy. For Babeuf the presence of inequality meant, of necessity, the presence of injustice. Capitalist commerce existed, he said, "for the purpose of pumping the sweat and blood of more or less everybody, in order to form lakes of gold for the benefit of the few."[20] The workers who created the wealth of society got the least; and until private property was eliminated, the inequalities in society could never be redressed.

Babeuf led the extreme left wing of the French revolutionary movement. After

---

[17] Quoted in Lee Cameron McDonald, *Western Political Theory: The Modern Age* (New York: Harcourt Brace Jovanovich, 1962), p. 63.
[18] Ibid.
[19] Ibid.
[20] Alexander Gray, *The Socialist Tradition* (London: Longmans, 1963), p. 105.

the fall of Robespierre he masterminded a conspiracy to destroy the French government and replace it with one dedicated to equality and brotherhood. The plot was betrayed by Georges Grisel, and its leaders were arrested. Babeuf and his lieutenant, Darthe, were executed on February 24, 1797.

Babeuf is important in the socialist tradition because he was the first to advance the notion that if an egalitarian socialist state is to be achieved, the existing government must be toppled by force. The issue of whether socialism can be achieved peacefully has divided socialists since Babeuf's time. Babeuf also believed that if his revolt were successful a period of dictatorship during the transition from capitalism to the communist democracy he envisioned would be necessary to extirpate the surviving remnants of the capitalist system. Thus in several important ways Babeuf was a precursor of the twentieth-century Russian Bolsheviks.

Other important ideas in the socialist critique of capitalism can be seen in the writings of the Englishman William Godwin (1756–1836). While the classical liberals were bemoaning the natural laziness and depravity of the lower classes, Godwin argued that the defects of the working class were attributable to corrupt and unjust social institutions. The capitalist society, in Godwin's opinion, made fraud and robbery inevitable: "If every man could with perfect facility obtain the necessaries of life . . . temptation would lose its power."[21] Men could not always obtain the necessities because the laws of private property created such great inequalities in society. Justice demanded that capitalist property relations be abolished and that property belong to that person whom it would benefit most:

> To whom does any article of property, suppose a loaf of bread, justly belong? To him who most wants it, or to whom the possession of it will be most beneficial. Here are six men famished with hunger, and the loaf is, absolutely considered, capable of satisfying the cravings of them all. Who is it that has a reasonable claim to benefit by the qualities with which the loaf is endowed? They are all brothers perhaps, and the law of primogeniture bestows it exclusively to the eldest. But does justice confirm this reward? The laws of different countries dispose of property in a thousand different ways; but there can be but one way which is most conformable to reason.[22]

That one way, of course, must be based on equality of all human beings. To whom could the poor turn to correct the injustices of the system? In Godwin's opinion it most certainly would not be the government. With economic power went political power. The rich are "directly or indirectly the legislators of the state; and of consequence are perpetually reducing oppression into a system."[23] The law, then, is the means by which the rich oppress the poor, for "legislation is in almost every country grossly the favorer of the rich against the poor."[24]

These two ideas of Godwin's were to be voiced again and again by nineteenth-century socialists: (1) that capitalist social and economic institutions, particularly private property relations, were the causes of the evils and suffering within the system and (2) that the government in a capitalist system would never redress these evils because it was controlled by the capitalist class. But Godwin

[21] William Godwin, *An Inquiry Concerning Political Justice*, pp. 33, 34. Quoted in Gray, op. cit., p. 119.
[22] Ibid., p. 131.
[23] Ibid., p. 119.
[24] Ibid.

had an answer to this seemingly impossible situation. He believed human reason would save society. Once people became educated about the evils of the situation, they would reason together and arrive at the only rational solution. As Godwin saw it, this solution entailed the abolition of government, the abolition of laws, and the abolition of private property. For this radical social transformation Godwin believed socialists could rely primarily on education and reason. Most subsequent socialists argued that education and reason alone were insufficient. Education, they believed, should be only a part of the larger objective of creating a mass socialist movement. The importance of education and intellectual persuasion in attaining socialist ends has remained a much-debated issue to this day.

Other important socialist ideas were advanced by Henri de Saint-Simon (1760–1825), who was actually closer to the Tory radicals than the socialists in many ways. He came from an impoverished family of nobility, and his writings show an aristocrat's disdain for the antisocial egoism of the rich capitalists.

He also condemned the idle rich who lived off the labor of the poor but contributed nothing to society's well-being:

> Suppose that France preserves all the men of genius that she possesses in the sciences, fine arts and professions, but has the misfortune to lose in the same day Monsieur the King's brother [and all of the other members of the royal household]. . . . Suppose that France loses at the same time all the great officers of the royal household, all the ministers . . . all the councillors of state, all the chief magistrates, marshals, cardinals, archbishops, bishops, vicars-general and canons, all the prefects and subprefects, all the civil servants, and judges, and, in addition, ten thousand of the richest proprietors who live in the style of nobles. This mischance would certainly distress the French, because they are kind-hearted, and could not see with indifference the sudden disappearance of such a large number of their compatriots. But this loss of thirty thousand individuals . . . would result in no political evil for the state.[25]

Saint-Simon was the first to emphasize the efficiency of huge industrial undertakings and argued that the government should actively intervene in production, distribution, and commerce in the interest of promoting the welfare of the masses. He sanctioned both private property and its privileges as long as they were used to promote the welfare of the masses.

Many of his followers were more radical. They wrote endless pamphlets and books exposing abuses of capitalism, attacking private property and inheritance, denouncing exploitation, and advocating government ownership and control of economic production in the interest of the general welfare. It was from Saint-Simon and his followers that socialism inherited the idea of the necessity of government administration of production and distribution in a socialist economy.

There were many other famous socialists in the first half of the nineteenth century. The Frenchman Charles Fourier popularized the idea of cooperatives (or *phalanxes,* as he called them). He attempted to change society by encouraging the formation of phalanxes. His failure proved to many socialists that capitalism could not be reformed by the mere setting of examples. He was also one of the first socialists to predict that competition among capitalists would lead inevitably to monopoly:

[25] F. M. H. Markham, ed., *Henri Comte de Saint-Simon, Selected Writings* (Oxford: Blackwell, 1952), pp. 72–73.

Among the influences tending to restrict man's industrial rights, I will mention a formation of privileged corporations which, monopolizing a given branch of industry, arbitrarily close the doors of labour against whomsoever they please. . . . Extremes meet, and the greater the extent to which anarchical competition is carried, the nearer the approach to *universal monopoly*, which is the opposite excess. . . . Monopolies, . . . operating in conjunction with the great landed interest, will reduce the middle and labouring classes to a state of commercial vassalage. . . . The small operators will be reduced to the position of mere agents, working for the mercantile coalition. We shall then see the reappearing of feudalism in an inverse order, founded on mercantile leagues, and answering to the Baronial Leagues of the Middle Ages.[26]

Fourier believed that in a capitalist economy only one-third of the people really did socially useful work. The other two-thirds were directed, by the corruption and distortion caused by the market system, into useless occupations or were useless, wealthy parasites. He divided these wastes into four categories:

First Waste: Useless or destructive labour. (1) the army (2) the idle rich (3) ne'er-do-wells (4) sharpers (5) prostitutes (6) magistrates (7) police (8) lawyers (9) philosophical cranks (10) bureaucrats (11) spies (12) priests and clergymen.

Second Waste: Misdirected work, since society makes it repellent, and not a vehicle of man's personality, attractive to him.
(a) Deflection of the passions into greed and morbidity, instead of being utilized as society's motors
(b) Scale of production too small to utilize labour properly.
(c) No co-operation.
(d) No control of production.
(e) No adjustment of supply to demand, except by the mechanism of the "blind" market.
(f) The family: this economic and educational unit is absurdly small.

Third Waste: Commerce dominated by middlemen. It takes a hundred men to do what society, with warehouses, distributed according to need, could do with one. A hundred men sit at counters, wasting hours waiting for someone to enter, a hundred people write inventories, etc., competitively. These hundred wasted merchants eat without producing.

Fourth Waste: Wage labour in indirect servitude; cost of class antagonisms. Since class interests are opposed, the costs of keeping men divided are greater than the gains in making them co-operate.[27]

Most socialists agreed that capitalism was irrational and wasteful and led to extreme inequalities, and hence was unjust and immoral. They disagreed, however, on the tactics they should use to achieve socialism. Many famous socialists, such as Louis Blanc (1811–1882), believed that the government could be used as an instrument of reform and that socialism could be achieved through gradual,

---

[26] Quoted in Sydney H. Coontz, *Productive Labor and Effective Demand* (Clifton, N.J.: Augustus M. Kelley, 1966), p. 54.
[27] Ibid., p. 55.

peacful, piecemeal reform. Others, such as Auguste Blanqui (1805–1881), the pupil of Babeuf, based his ideas on the assumption that capitalism involved a constant class war between capitalists and workers. He believed that as long as capitalists occupied the position of power that ownership of capital gave them, they would exploit the workers, and the government and laws would be weapons used in this exploitation. He therefore saw no hope through gradual political reform. Revolution was, for him, the only answer.

Pierre Joseph Proudhon (1809–1865), in his well-known book *What Is Property?*, answered the question posed in the title with a slogan that made him famous: "Property is theft." He believed property was "the mother of tyranny." The primary purpose of the state was the enforcement of property rights. Because property rights were simply sets of special privileges for the few and general restrictions and prohibitions for the masses, they involved coercion, of necessity, in their establishment and continued enforcement. Hence the primary function of the state was to coerce.

"Every state is a tyranny," declared Proudhon. The state was the coercive arm of the ruling class, and Proudhon advocated resistance rather than servitude: "Whoever lays a hand on me to govern me is a usurper and a tyrant. I declare him to be my enemy." There could be no justice until property relations were abolished and the state was made unnecessary:

> To be governed is to be watched over, inspected, spied on, directed, legislated, regimented, closed in, indoctrinated, preached at, controlled, assessed, evaluated, censored, commanded; all by creatures that have neither the right, nor wisdom, nor virtue. . . . To be governed means that at every move, operation, or transaction one is noted, registered, entered in a census, taxed, stamped, priced, assessed, patented, licensed, authorized, recommended, admonished, prevented, reformed, set right, corrected. Government means to be subjected to tribute, trained, ransomed, exploited, monopolized, extorted, pressured, mystified, robbed; all in the name of public utility and the general good. Then, at the first sign of resistance or word of complaint, one is repressed, fined, despised, vexed, pursued, hustled, beaten up, garroted, imprisoned, shot, machine-gunned, judged, sentenced, deported, sacrificed, sold, betrayed, and to cap it all ridiculed, mocked, outraged, and dishonored. That is government, that is its justice and its morality! . . . O human personality! How can it be that you have cowered in such subjection for sixty centuries?"[28]

Property rights were not only the source of tyranny and coercion, they were also the source of economic inequality. Whereas the amount of labor expended determined how much was produced in a capitalist society, ownership of property determined how that produce was divided. It was divided in such a way that those who produced got almost nothing of what they produced, whereas those who owned property used the laws of private ownership to "legally steal" from the workers. Proudhon's ideal state rejected not only capitalist property relations but industrialization as well. Like Thomas Jefferson, Proudhon envisioned a golden age of small-scale agriculture and handicraft production, in which each farmer and worker owned his or her own capital and no one lived through property ownership alone. The list could be continued, but we have included most of the important pre-Marxist socialist ideas and have introduced some of the most

[28] Quoted in Daniel Guerin, *Anarchism* (New York: Monthly Review Press, 1970), pp. 15–16; the quotations in the preceding paragraph are from the same source.

famous socialist thinkers. Unquestionably the most influential socialist thinker was Karl Marx, and it is to a summary of his ideas that we turn in Chapter 6.

SUMMARY

The workers bore the social costs of industrialization. The new factory system reduced most of them to poor, unhealthy, dehumanized wretches. Classical liberalism was not only impervious to their plight, it even taught that the desire to improve the conditions of the poor was quixotic and doomed to failure. Two groups of thinkers, the Tory radicals and the socialists, took strong exception to this view.

The Tory radicals had a gentleman's disdain for the vulgar, money-grubbing" middle-class merchants and manufacturers. They clung to an essentially reactionary version of the Christian paternalist ethic—reactionary because it seemed to assume that they could ignore industrialism and go back to an earlier agrarian way of life.

The socialists protested the inequalities of capitalism. They believed that by eliminating private ownership of capital they could create an industrial society in which every man and woman was treated with dignity and in which the fruits of production were equitably divided.

CHAPTER 6

SOCIALIST PROTEST: The Economics of Marx

Karl Marx (1818–1883) has been the most influential of all socialists. His writings have had, and continue to have, a profound impact not only on socialist thought but also on policy decisions that affect a large percentage of the world's population. Although he worked in close collaboration with Friedrich Engels (1820–1895) and was unquestionably deeply influenced by Engels, Marx was the intellectual leader in most matters of political economy, so no attempt is made in this chapter to distinguish Engels' separate contributions.

HISTORICAL MATERIALISM

Marx believed that most of the late eighteenth- and early nineteenth-century socialists were humanitarians who were rightly indignant about the harsh exploitation that accompanied early capitalism. Despite his admiration for many of them, he gave to them the derisive label "utopian socialists." He believed most of them to be quixotic utopians who hoped to transform society by appealing to the rationality and moral sensibilities of the educated class. In Marx's view, educated men were usually members of the upper classes, and thus they owed their position, prosperity, and superior knowledge and education to the privileges inherent in the capitalist system. Therefore they would generally do everything within their power to preserve that system. The few heretics and humanitarians among them would certainly never constitute the power base from which a transition from capitalism to socialism could be effected. Yet, Marx had an undying faith that such a social and economic transition would occur. This faith was not the result of his belief in the rationality and humanity of men but rather was based on an analysis of capitalism. He concluded that internal contradictions and antagonisms within the capitalist system would eventually destroy it.

Marx based his study of capitalist society on a historical approach that has been called *historical materialism*. When he looked at the mass of ideas, laws, religious beliefs, mores, moral codes, and economic and social institutions that were present in all social systems, he tried to simplify the complex cause-and-effect relationships among these many facets of social systems. Such a simplification, he believed, would enable him to focus his attention on the relationships that were most fundamental in determining a social system's overall direction of movement and change.

Although all social institutions and intellectual traditions were reciprocally related in a complex web of cause-and-effect relationships (each affecting and, in turn, affected by the other), he believed that a society's economic base, or mode of production, exerted the most powerful influence in determining the other social institutions as well as social and religious thought. The *mode of production* consisted of two elements: (1) the forces of production and (2) the relations of production. The *forces of production* included tools, factories, equipment, production skills and knowledge of the labor force, natural resources, and the general level of technology. The *relations of production* were the social relationships between humans, particularly the relationship of each class of humans to the means of production, which included the ownership of productive facilities and the division of the fruits of productive activity. The whole economic system, or mode of production, Marx called the *base*, or *substructure*. The religions, ethics, laws, mores, and institutions of society he called the *superstructure*.

Although the mode of production and the superstructure interacted reciprocally as both cause and effect, the mode of production was the base on which the superstructure was built. Therefore, the line of causation running from this economic base to the superstructure was much more powerful and important than the reverse line of causation. To argue that Marx believed the economic base determined, completely and rigidly, every aspect of the superstructure is grossly inaccurate (although it is often done). He did assert, however, that the mode of production was the most important single aspect in determining not only the present social superstructure but also the direction of social change.

When he referred to the relations of production, Marx meant the class structure of society, the most important single aspect of the mode of production. The antagonisms between social classes were, for Marx, the propelling force in history. "The history of all hitherto existing society is the history of class struggles,"[1] he proclaimed. The importance of the mode of production and the class antagonisms it engendered have been summarized by Marx in a famous passage:

> In the social production which men carry on they enter into definite relations that are indispensable and independent of their will; these relations of production correspond to a definite stage of development of their material powers of production. The sum total of these relations of production constitutes the economic structure of society—the real foundation, on which rise legal and political superstructures and to which correspond definite forms of social consciousness. The mode of production in material life determines the general character of the social, political, and spiritual processes of life. It is not the consciousness of men that determines their existence, but, on the contrary, their social existence determines their consciousness. At a certain stage of their development, the material forces of production in society come into conflict with the existing relations of production, or—what is but a legal expression for the same thing—with the property relations within which they had been at work before. From forms of development of the forces of production these relations turn into their fetters. Then comes the period of social revolution. With the change of economic foundation the entire immense superstructure is more or less rapidly transformed. In considering such transformations the distinction should always be made between the material transformation of the economic conditions of production which can be

[1] Karl Marx and Friedrich Engels, "The Communist Manifesto," in Arthur P. Mendel, ed., *Essential Works of Marxism* (New York: Bantam, 1965), p. 13.

determined with the precision of natural science, and the legal, political, religious, aesthetic, or philosophic—in short ideological forms in which men become conscious of this conflict and fight it out.[2]

Marx identified four separate economic systems, or modes of production, through which the European civilization had evolved: (1) primitive communal, (2) slave, (3) feudal, and (4) capitalist. In any one of these economic systems, there was a unique mode of production that included forces of production as well as a particular class structure, or relations of production. Increasing demands for more production inevitably led to changes in the forces of production, yet the relationships of production, or class positions, remained fixed and were fiercely defended. Therefore there were conflicts, tensions, and contradictions between the changing forces of production and the fixed social relations (and vested interests) of production. These conflicts and contradictions grew in intensity and importance until a series of violent social eruptions destroyed the old system and created a new system that would have new class relationships compatible (for a time at least) with the changed forces of production.

In each mode of production the contradictions that developed between the forces of production and the relations of production showed themselves in the form of a class struggle. The struggle raged between the class that controlled the means of production and received most of the benefits and privileges of the system (e.g., the Roman slaveholders) and the much larger class they controlled and exploited (e.g., the Roman slaves). In all economic systems prior to capitalism, this class struggle had destroyed one system only to create a new system based on exploitation of the masses by a new ruling class, and hence the beginning of a new class struggle. Capitalism, however, was, in Marx's opinion, the last mode of production that would be based on the existence of antagonistic classes. The capitalist class, which ruled by virtue of ownership of the means of production, would be overthrown by the proletariat, or working class, which would establish a classless society in which the means of production were owned in common by all. The transition from capitalism to socialism will be discussed in greater detail later. Before proceeding further, however, it is necessary to examine the basis of Marx's moral condemnation of capitalism.

MARX'S MORAL CRITIQUE OF CAPITALISM

According to Marx, two most important features define capitalism and distinguish it from other economic systems: (1) The separation of the worker from the means of production created a class of owners and a class of workers; (2) the market, or cash nexus, was extended into all human relationships involved in production and distribution. Like most socialists before him, Marx deplored the extremes of wealth and poverty this class relationship created.

His moral condemnation of capitalism, however, went beyond an ethical rejection of these great inequalities. His most important criticism of capitalism involved the idea that in a capitalist system people could not develop their poten-

---

[2] Karl Marx, *Critique of Political Economy*, reprinted in part in Howard Selsam and Harry Martel, eds., *Reader in Marxist Philosophy* (New York: International Publishers, 1963), pp. 186–187.

tialities. They could not become emotionally or intellectually fully developed human beings.

People differed from animals because in order to satisfy their needs they created tools and worked with them to shape and control their environment. An individual's senses and intellect were developed and refined through working. Through a person's relations with what he or she produced, an individual achieved both pleasure and self-realization. In precapitalist social systems like feudalism, people could achieve this self-realization through work despite an exploitative class structure. Because the exploitative social relations were also personal and paternalistic, work was not merely a means of making money.

This changed with capitalism, when, in Marx's opinion:

> the bourgeoisie, wherever it has got the upper hand, has put an end to all feudal patriarchal, idyllic relations. It has pitilessly torn asunder the motley feudal ties that bound man to his "natural superiors," and has left remaining no other nexus between man and man than naked self-interest, than callous "cash payment." It has drowned the most heavenly ecstasies of religious fervor, of chivalrous enthusiasm, of philistine sentimentalism, in the icy water of egotistical calculation. It has resolved personal worth into exchange value. . . .[3]

In a capitalist society the market separated and isolated "exchange value," or money price, from the qualities that shaped a person's relations with things as well as with other human beings. This was especially true in the work process. To the capitalist, wages were merely another expense of production to be added to the costs of raw materials and machinery in the profit calculation. Labor became a mere commodity to be bought if a profit could be made on the purchase. Whether the laborer could sell his or her labor power was completely beyond his or her control. It depended on the cold and totally impersonal conditions of the market. The product of this labor was likewise totally outside of the laborer's life, being the property of the capitalist.

Marx used the term *alienation* to describe the condition of individual's in this situation. They felt alienated or divorced from their work, from their institutional and cultural environment, and from their fellow humans. The conditions of work, the object produced, and indeed the very possibility of working were determined by the numerically small class of capitalists and their profit calculations, not by human need or aspirations. The effects of this alienation can best be summarized in Marx's own words:

> What, then, constitutes the alienation of labour? First, the fact that labour is external to the worker, i.e., it does not belong to his essential being; that in his work, therefore, he does not affirm himself but denies himself, does not feel content but unhappy, does not develop freely his physical and mental energy but mortifies his body and ruins his mind. The worker therefore only feels himself outside his work, and in his work feels outside himself. He is at home when he is not working, and when he is working he is not at home. His labour is therefore not voluntary but coerced; it is *forced labour*. It is therefore not the satisfaction of a need; it is merely a *means* to satisfy needs external to it. Its alien character emerges clearly in the fact that as soon as no physical or other compulsion exists, labour is shunned like the plague. External labour, labour in which man alienates himself, is a labour of self-sacrifice, or mortification. Lastly, the external character of labour for the worker appears in the fact that it is not

---

[3] Marx and Engels, "The Communist Manifesto," op. cit., p. 15.

his own, but someones else's, that it does not belong to him, that in it he belongs, not to himself, but to another. . . . As a result, therefore, man (the worker) no longer feels himself to be freely active in any but his animal functions—eating, drinking, procreating, or at most in his dwelling and in dressing up, etc.; and in his human functions he no longer feels himself to be anything but an animal. What is animal becomes human and what is human becomes animal.[4]

It was this degradation and total dehumanization of the working class, thwarting man's personal development and making an alien market commodity of man's life-sustaining activities, that Marx most thoroughly condemned in the capitalist system. Thus his moral critique went far beyond those of most of his socialist precursors. His faith in the possibility of a better future for the working class, however, was not based on the hope that ever-increasing numbers of people would share his moral indignation and therefore attempt to reform the system. Rather, he believed the capitalist mode of production and the class conflict inherent in it would lead to the destruction of capitalism. Capitalism, like all previous modes of production in which class conflicts were present, would destroy itself. In order to understand the basis for this faith, it is necessary to examine his economic theory, in which he attempted to analyze the "laws of motion" of capitalism.

THE LABOR THEORY OF VALUE AND SURPLUS VALUE

Because for Marx the capitalist mode of production was based on the opposition of labor and capital, he began by analyzing the capital-labor relationship. This relationship was essentially one of exchange. The worker sold his or her labor power to the capitalist for money, with which the worker bought the necessities of life. Thus this exchange relation was obviously merely a special case of the general problem of exchange values within a capitalist market economy. Marx therefore began volume 1 of *Capital* with a section entitled "Commodities," in which he defined *commodities* as objects that are usually intended for exchange rather than for the direct personal use of the producer. He then attempted to analyze the basic determinant of the exchange value of commodities. In other words, he analyzed the ratio in which commodities could be exchanged for other commodities, as opposed to use value, which was a measure of the usefulness of commodities to their possessor.

Like Adam Smith, David Ricardo, and most of the pre-Marxist classical economists, Marx believed the exchange value of a commodity was determined by the amount of labor time necessary for its production. His theory is therefore usually called the *labor theory of value*. He recognized that laborers differed in abilities, training, and motivation, but he believed skilled labor could be calculated as a multiple of unskilled labor. Thus all labor time could be reduced to a common denominator.

He also realized that labor time expended in the production of a useless commodity (one for which there was no demand) would not create a commodity with an exchange value equal to the labor time embodied in it. The desire of capital-

---

[4] Karl Marx, *Economic and Philosophic Manuscripts of 1844* (Moscow: Progress Publishers, 1959), p. 69.

ists to maximize their profits would, however, prevent the production of objects for which there was no demand. Capitalists would produce only commodities for which market demand would permit the realization of at least their costs of production. Market demand would determine not only what commodities were produced but also the relative quantities in which they were produced.

Marx began by describing how the capitalist buys the means of production and the labor power. Then, when the laborers complete the production process, the capitalist sells the commodities for more money. Thus the amount of money at the end of the production process is greater than that at the start. This difference is what Marx called *surplus value*. He considered it the source of capitalist profits.

Surplus value originated in the fact that capitalists bought one commodity—labor power—and sold a different commodity—that which labor produced in the production process. Profits were made because the value of labor power was less than the value of the commodities produced with the labor power. The value of labor power was "determined, as in the case of every other commodity, by the labor time necessary" for its maintenance and reproduction, which meant that "the value of labor power . . . [was] the value of the means of subsistence necessary for the maintenance of the laborer at a socially defined standard of living."[5] The fact was that the average length of the working day exceeded the time necessary for a laborer to produce the value equivalent of his or her subsistence wage, which enabled the capitalist to appropriate the surplus produced over and above this subsistence. Marx called this process the *exploitation* of workers by capitalists. If the worker works for 8 hours but uses only 6 hours to produce the value of his or her wage goods, then that worker is exploited because he or she works 2 surplus hours for the capitalist.

THE ACCUMULATION OF CAPITAL

Ownership of capital enabled the capitalist to gain profit. Most of these profits were plowed back to increase capital and hence increase future profits, which could then be plowed back into more capital, and so forth. This was the process of capital accumulation: Capital led to profits, which led to more capital. When and how did the process originate? Many classical economists and liberals, particularly the English economist Nassau Senior (1790–1864), had answered this question in a way favorable to the capitalist, arguing that through hard, diligent work and abstemious behavior a modest saving program was begun, which enabled the capitalist to accumulate slowly the fortunes many nineteenth-century capitalists owned. Laborers, on the contrary, rather than devoting themselves to working and living abstemiously, had profligately squandered their earnings.

Marx accused these defenders of the capitalist system of being totally ignorant of history. In a famous passage, which gives the flavor of some of his most colorful writing, Marx described the process of "primitive accumulation" by which the fortunes were originally made:

> This primitive accumulation plays in Political Economy about the same part as original sin in theology. Adam bit the apple, and thereupon sin fell on the

[5] Karl Marx, *Capital*, vol. 1 (Moscow: Foreign Language Publishing House, 1961), pp. 170–171.

human race. Its origin is supposed to be explained when it is told as an anecdote of the past. In times long gone by there were two sorts of people; one, the diligent, intelligent, and above all, frugal elite; the other, lazy rascals, spending their substance, and more, in riotous living. . . . Thus it came to pass that the former sort accumulated wealth, and the latter sort had nothing to sell except their own skins. And from this original sin dates the poverty of the great majority that, despite all its labour, has up to now nothing to sell but itself, and the wealth of the few that increases constantly although they have long ceased to work. Such insipid childishness is every day preached to us in the defence of property. . . . As soon as the question of property crops up, it becomes a sacred duty to proclaim the intellectual food of the infant as the one thing fit for all ages and for all stages of development. In actual history it is notorious that conquest, enslavement, robbery, murder, briefly force, play the great part. . . . The methods of primitive accumulation are anything but idyllic.[6]

Marx listed the important forms of primitive accumulation as the enclosure movement and the dislocation of the feudal agrarian population, the great price inflation, monopolies of trade, colonies, "the extirpation, enslavement and entombment in mines of the aboriginal population, the beginning of the conquest and looting of the East Indies, [and] the turning of Africa into a warren for the commercial hunting of black skins."[7]

Once this initial accumulation of capital had taken place, the drive to acquire more capital became the moving force of the capitalist system. The capitalist's social standing and prestige as well as his economic and political power depended on the size of the capital he controlled. He could not stand still; he was beset on every side by fierce competition. The system demanded that he accumulate and grow more powerful in order to outdo his competitors, or else his competitors would force him to the wall and take over his capital. Competitors were constantly developing new and better methods of production. Only by accumulating new and better capital equipment could this challenge be met. Thus Marx believed the capitalist

> shares with the miser the passion for wealth as wealth. But that which in the miser is a mere idiosyncrasy, is in the capitalist the effect of the social mechanism of which he is but one of the wheels. Moreover, the development of capitalist production makes it constantly necessary to keep increasing the amount of capital laid out in a given industrial undertaking, and competition makes the immanent laws of capitalist production to be felt by each individual capitalist as external coercive laws. It compels him to keep constantly extending his capital, in order to preserve it, but extend it he cannot except by means of progressive accumulation.[8]

SECTORAL IMBALANCES AND ECONOMIC CRISES

It was this ceaseless drive to accumulate more capital that created many of the contradictions to capitalist development. The capitalist would begin with the acquisition of more machines and tools of the types that were currently being used. This would require a proportional increase in the number of workers employed in

[6] Ibid., pp. 713–714.
[7] Ibid., p. 751.
[8] Ibid., p. 592.

order to operate the new equipment. But the capitalists had been able to keep the wage rate at the subsistence level only because there existed what Marx called an "industrial reserve army" of unemployed labor, which was living below the subsistence level and striving to take jobs that would pay a mere subsistence wage. Therefore, capitalists usually had no problem in keeping wage rates down. As the industrial expansion took place, however, the increasing demand for labor soon depleted the ranks of the reserve. When this happened, the capitalist began to find that he had to pay higher wages to get enough labor.

The individual capitalist took the wage level as given and beyond his power to change, so he attempted to make the best of the situation. The most profitable course of action seemed to be changing the techniques of production by introducing new labor-saving machinery so that each laborer would then be working with more capital, and output per laborer could be increased. This labor-saving investment would enable the capitalist to expand output with the same or an even smaller work force. When all or most of the capitalists, acting individually, did this, the problem of high wages was temporarily alleviated as the reserve army was replenished by workers displaced by the new productive techniques. The creation of technological unemployment saved the day. But not without introducing new problems and contradictions.

Labor-saving expansion permitted increases in total production without increasing the wages paid to workers. Therefore, while new goods were flooding the market, workers' wages were being restricted, with the result that consumer demand was limited. As Marx put it, the workers were still producing more profits in the form of goods, but the capitalists could not "realize" the profits by selling these goods in the market because of lack of consumer demand.

In order to clarify this process further, Marx divided the capitalist economy into two sectors, one producing consumer goods and the other producing capital goods. Lack of consumer demand meant that capitalists in the consumption goods sector would find that they could not sell their entire output and thus would lower their expectations of profits and would certainly not want to add to their productive facilities. They would therefore cancel any plans to add to their already excessively large capital stock. These decisions would, of course, significantly reduce the demand for capital goods, which would result in a decrease in production in the capital goods sector. Unlike the naïve underconsumptionist theories of the earlier socialists, Marx's view held that the first obvious sign of a depression might thus appear in the capital goods sector.

The actual decrease in capital goods production would mean that some workers in that sector would be fired, which would lower total wages, decrease national income, and reduce consumer demand. Thus there would be a cutback in consumer goods production, and layoffs of workers would spread to those industries. Wages and incomes would then be further reduced, causing a glut, or surfeit, of consumer goods. The entire process of successive repercussions in both sectors would then be one of economic collapse.

The resulting depression would more than restore the reserve army of unemployed and push labor's standard of living back to or below the subsistence level. Marx, however, was not a "stagnationist"—that is, he did not believe capitalism would suffer one long depression or that mass unemployment at high levels would last forever. In the depression workers' wages would fall, but not as rapidly as the output of goods. Thus eventually supply would be lower than consumer demand, and therefore recovery would occur. Marx believed that capitalism does grow, but jerkily, in cycles of boom and bust, with periodic high levels of unemployment for the workers.

ECONOMIC CONCENTRATION

Concentration of wealth and economic power in the hands of fewer and fewer capitalists was another important consequence of capital accumulation. This concentration was the result of two forces. First, competition between capitalists tended to create a situation in which the strong either crushed or absorbed the weak. "Here competition rages in direct proportion to the number, and in inverse proportion to the magnitudes, of the antagonistic capitals. It always ends in the ruin of many small capitalists, whose capitals partly pass into the hands of their conquerors, partly vanish."[9]

Second, as technology improved there was "an increase in the minimum amount of . . . capital necessary to carry on a business under its normal conditions." In order to remain competitive, a firm would constantly have to increase the productivity of its laborers. The "productiveness of labor . . . [depended] on the scale of production."[10] Thus changing technology as well as competition among capitalists created an inexorable movement of the capitalist system toward larger and larger firms owned by fewer and fewer capitalists. In this way the gulf between the small class of wealthy capitalists and the great majority of society, the proletariat, continually widened.

THE IMMISERIZATION OF THE PROLETARIAT

At the same time that this increasing concentration of capital was taking place, the misery of the proletariat grew constantly worse. In his famous "doctrine of increasing misery" (immiserization), Marx argued that the conditions of labor would worsen relative to the affluence of the capitalists until the laborers could stand no more. And then revolution was inevitable. Because Marx's doctrine of immiserization is very often misrepresented, we will quote his own writings on this point:

> Within the capitalist system all methods for raising the social productiveness of labour are brought about at the cost of the individual labourer; all means for the development of production transform themselves into means of domination over, and exploitation of, the producers; they multilate the labourer into a fragment of a man, degrade him to the level of an appendage of a machine, destroy every remnant of charm in his work and turn it into hated toil; they estrange from him the intellectual potentialities of the labour-process in the same proportion as science is incorporated in it as an independent power; they distort the conditions under which he works, subject him during the labour-process to a despotism the more hateful for its meanness; they transform his life time into working time, and drag his wife and child beneath the wheels of

[9] Ibid., p. 626.
[10] Ibid.

the Juggernaut of capital. But all methods for the production of surplus-value
are at the same time methods of accumulation; and every extension of
accumulation becomes again a means for the development of those methods. It
follows therefore that in proportion as capital accumulates, the lot of the
labourer, be his payment high or low, must grow worse. The law . . . establishes
an accumulation of misery, corresponding with accumulation of capital.
Accumulation of wealth at one pole is, therefore, at the same time
accumulation of misery, agony of toil, slavery, ignorance, brutality [and] mental
degradation at the opposite pole. . . .[11]

It should be noted that Marx asserted that the laborer would become worse off
even if his or her wages increased. There were two reasons for this. First, Marx
believed that even if workers' wages increased they would not increase by as
much as capitalists' profits increased. The worker would therefore become continuously worse off relative to the capitalist. Second, Marx correctly foresaw that
as the capitalist system progressed there was to be an increasingly minute division of labor.

A finer division of labor makes the worker's activities less varied, and his job
becomes more repetitious and tedious. Marx agreed with Adam Smith, who had
stated that "the man whose whole life is spent in performing a few simple operations . . . generally becomes as stupid and ignorant as it is possible for a human
creature to become."[12] Forced into a condition of stupor and increasingly severely alienated, "the lot of the labourer, *be his payment high or low*, must grow
worse."[13]

THE CAPITALIST STATE

Marx rejected the notion that socialism could be created through gradual, piecemeal reforms undertaken by the state. By *the state* Marx meant something more
than simply any government: ". . . we may speak of a state only where a special
public power of coercion exists which, in the form of an armed organization,
stands over and above the population."[14]

Many socialists believed the state was (or could be) an impartial arbiter in the
affairs of society, and they had faith in moral and intellectual appeals to the state.
Marx rejected this idea. "Political power," he declared in the *Communist Manifesto,* "is merely the organized power of one class for oppressing another."
During each period of history, or for each mode of production, the state is the
coercive instrument of the ruling class.

Friedrich Engels has summarized the Marxist argument:

Former society, moving in class antagonisms, had need of the state, that is, an
organization of the exploiting class at each period for the maintenance of
external conditions of production; that is, therefore, for the forcible holding
down of the exploited class in the conditions of oppression (slavery, villeinage
or serfdom, wage labor) determined by the existing mode of production. The
state was the official representative of society as a whole, its embodiment in a

[11] Ibid., p. 645.
[12] Adam Smith, *The Wealth of Nations,* ed. Andrew Skinner (London: Penguin Books, 1970), p. 80.
[13] Marx, *Capital,* op. cit., p. 645.
[14] Sidney Hook, *Towards the Understanding of Karl Marx* (New York: Day, 1933), p. 256.

visible corporation; but it was this only in so far as it was the state of that class which itself, in its epoch, represented society as a whole; in ancient times, the state of the slave-owning citizens; in the Middle Ages, of the feudal nobility; in our epoch, of the bourgeosie.[15]

Thus the state is simply a dictatorship of the ruling class over the remainder of society.

In the capitalist system the state has two functions. First, it has the traditional function of enforcing the dictatorship of the capitalists over the rest of society. The state achieves this primarily by enforcing property rights, the source of the capitalists' economic power. It also serves in innumerable other ways—for example, jailing or harassing critics of capitalism, fighting wars to extend capitalists' markets, and providing roads, railroads, canals, postal service, and hundreds of other prerequisites for profitable commerce. Second, the government acts as the arbiter of rivalries between capitalists. Each capitalist is interested only in his own profits, and therefore it is inevitable that the interests of capitalists will clash. If not resolved, many of these clashes would threaten the very existence of the system. Thus the government intervenes, and in doing so it protects the viability of the capitalist system. This is why it is sometimes possible to observe the government acting in a way that is contrary to the interests of some of the capitalists. But the government never acts in a way that is contrary to the interests of *all* capitalists taken as a class.

For these reasons Marx rejected the notion that socialists could rely on the government for help in bringing about the transition from capitalism to socialism. The establishment of socialism, in Marx's opinion, would require a revolution.

THE SOCIALIST REVOLUTION

In his overall view of capitalism Marx saw the process of capital accumulation as inevitably involving several steps. Business cycles or crises would occur regularly and with increasing severity as the capitalist economy developed. There would be a long-run tendency for the rate of profit to fall, and this would exacerbate the other problems of capitalism. Industrial power would become increasingly concentrated in fewer and fewer giant monopolistic and oligopolistic firms, and wealth would become concentrated in the hands of fewer and fewer capitalists. The plight of the laborer would steadily deteriorate.

Given these increasingly bad conditions, the system could not be perpetuated. Eventually life under capitalism would become so intolerable that workers would revolt, overthrow the whole system, and create a more rational socialist economy.

> Along with the constantly diminishing number of magnates of capital, who usurp and monopolize all advantages of this process of transformation, grows the mass of misery, oppression, slavery, degradation, exploitation; but with this too grows the revolt of the working-class, a class always increasing in numbers, and disciplined, united, organized by the very mechanism of the process of capitalist production itself. The monopoly of capital becomes a fetter upon the mode of production, which has sprung up and flourished along with, and under

[15] Friedrich Engels, "Anti-Duhring," in *Handbook of Marxism* (New York: Random House, 1935), p. 295.

it. Centralization of the means of production and socialization of labour at last reach a point where they become incompatible with their capitalist integument. This integument is burst asunder. The knell of capitalist private property sounds. The expropriators are expropriated.[16]

In subsequent chapters we shall examine the defenses of capitalism offered in opposition to Marx, as well as the further development of socialist thought after Marx.

SUMMARY

Karl Marx, the most influential of all socialists, based his economic analysis on a theory of history called historical materialism. Most social and political institutions, he believed, were significantly shaped by the economic base of society: the mode of production. Over time, conflicts developed between the forces of production and the relations of production. The working out of these conflicts was the most important element in the historical evolution of society.

Marx's economic writings were aimed at understanding the conflicts between the class system (or private property system) of capitalism and the methods of production and commodity exchange under capitalism. These conflicts, he believed, would ultimately lead to the overthrow of capitalism and its replacement by a classless, socialist society.

[16] Marx, *Capital*, op. cit., p. 763.

CHAPTER 7

THE RISE OF CORPORATE CAPITALISM AND THE DEFENSE OF LAISSEZ-FAIRE

The period from the mid-1840s to 1873 (the year that marked the beginning of the Long Depression in Europe) has been called the golden age of competitive capitalism.[1] These were years of rapid economic expansion throughout most of Europe. Industrialization was getting under way in the United States and continental Europe. The new capital goods necessary for industrialization were, to a large extent, imported from England. Between 1840 and 1860, England experienced an expansion of exports that was more rapid than ever before or since. Capital goods increased from 11 percent of English exports to 22 percent, and exports of coal, iron, and steel also rose sharply.

Between 1830 and 1850, England experienced a railroad-building boom in which some 6000 miles of railroads were constructed. This railroad building created a strong demand for iron, and iron production doubled between the mid-1830s and the mid-1840s. During the next 30 years the increases in industrial production were also very impressive. Between 1850 and 1880, the production of pig iron increased from 2,250,000 to 7,750,000 tons per year; steel production went from 49,000 to 1,440,000 tons; and coal increased by 300 percent, to 147,000,000 tons. The Bessemer converter (in the 1850s), the open-hearth furnace (in the 1860s), and the basic process (in the 1870s) completely revolutionized the steel industry, making large-scale production of high-quality steel possible at much lower costs. The capital goods industries also prospered in the second half of the nineteenth century. Production of machines, ships, chemicals, and other important capital goods employed twice as many men in 1881 as in 1851.

THE CONCENTRATION OF CORPORATE POWER

Just as competitive capitalism seemed to be achieving its greatest successes, the forces Marx had predicted would lead to the concentration of capital began

[1] Dudley Dillard, *Economic Development of the North Atlantic Community* (Englewood Cliffs, N.J.: Prentice-Hall, 1967), p. 363.

to show themselves. Improvements in technology were such that larger-sized plants were necessary to take advantage of more efficient methods of production. Competition became so aggressive and destructive that small competitors were eliminated. Large competitors, facing mutual destruction, often combined in cartels, trusts, or mergers in order to ensure their mutual survival. In the United States this competition was particularly intense. (It is described in greater detail in Chapter 8.)

A factor that Marx had nearly overlooked, the revolutionary changes in transportation and communication, led to ever-widening markets that could be efficiently supplied by single companies or corporations. The joint stock company, or corporation, became an effective means by which a single business organization could gain control over vast amounts of capital. And a large, well-organized money market evolved in Europe and North America that successfully channeled the smaller capital holdings of many thousands of individuals and small businesses into the hands of large corporations.

In the late nineteenth-century world of giant corporations, in which articles were mass produced for nationwide or worldwide markets, price competition (and indeed sometimes any kind of competition) proved so destructive that it was abandoned almost completely in the large and important industries. There was an inexorable trend toward monopoly power by a few corporations. Many business giants entered into voluntary combinations in which each firm remained somewhat autonomous (e.g., cartels and pools). Other combinations used a financial enterprise such as a trust or holding company to control the voting stock of the corporations involved. Still others used direct mergers and amalgamations from which a single unified corporation emerged.

The English Case

England, where the classical liberal laissez-faire philosophy had taken root most firmly, was perhaps least affected by this movement to corporate monopolies. Advances in technology led to a steel industry made of very large producers. Nevertheless, the fact that England had very few restrictions on imports prevented the industry from combining into an effectively coordinated group until after the trade restrictions of 1932. However, producers of some heavy steel products, such as ship and boiler plate, were able to create effective monopolies much earlier.

In other industries amalgamations led to heavy concentrations. English railroads were combined very early into four main companies. Banking was consolidated until five large commercial banks dominated the industry by the time of World War I. In 1896 the five rivals in the cotton sewing-thread industry had merged into a single monopoly (J. & P. Coats), which came to dominate the world market for that commodity and regularly made profits of 20 percent or more. The firm of Lever Brothers, through amalgamations, gained dominance over the soap business in England as well as in several other countries. Monopolies or closely coordinated oligopolies came to control the wallpaper, salt, petroleum, and rubber industries. Many other industries were either dominated or strongly influenced by a few large firms.

The German Case

In Germany the classical liberal ideology had never really taken root. During Germany's rapid rise to industrial power during the second half of the nineteenth century, there were neither philosophical nor ideological nor legal barriers to large-scale monopolistic industries. It is therefore not surprising that monopolies and combinations were more widespread in Germany than in any other country in Europe. The cartel was the main type of monopolistic business combination in Germany. There were approximately 16 cartels in 1879; the figure rose to 35 by 1885, 300 by 1900, 600 by 1911, 1000 by 1922, and 2100 by 1930.

Thus by the early twentieth century monopolistic cartels completely dominated almost all the important sectors of the German capitalist economy. (The legal and philosophical justifications of these monopolistic German cartels will be discussed in Chapter 8.)

The American Case

In the United States the Civil War gave a great stimulus to industrialization. The war not only increased the demand for industrially produced commodities but also led to the passage of laws that were beneficial to the newly emerging corporations that were soon to dominate American industry.

In an effort to provide civil and political rights for all Americans, Congress had passed the first Civil Rights Act in 1866. By 1868 the Fourteenth Amendment to the U.S. Constitution had been ratified by the states. The ostensible aim of these laws was to confer citizenship and equal rights on American blacks. The Civil Rights Act declared that citizens "of every race and color" were to have equal rights to make contracts, to sue, and enjoy "full and equal benefit of all laws and proceedings for the security of person and property."[2]

Most of the Civil Rights Act was incorporated into the Fourteenth Amendment. The Amendment also included the famous due process clause, which prohibited any state government from depriving "any person of life, liberty, or *property*, without due process of law."[3]

For decades after its ratification the Fourteenth Amendment had no effect at all on the civil rights of American blacks; many of them were thrust into situations worse than slavery. Rather, most court decisions based on the Fourteenth Amendment involved corporations. The courts ruled that corporations were persons and, as such, were protected under the due process clause.

Each time a state government attempted to curb the extravagant excesses of corporations by passing regulatory legislation, the federal courts would invalidate the legislation because it violated the due process clause of the amendment. State governments became powerless before the growing strength of large corporations.

Representative John A. Bingham, who had written the due process clause, later admitted that he had phrased it "word for word and syllable for syllable" to protect the rights of private property and corporations. Representative Roscoe Conkling, who had also helped frame the Amendment, later declared: "At the

---

[2] Quoted in Kenneth M. Stampp, *The Era of Reconstruction, 1865–1877* (New York: Random House, Vintage Books, 1967), p. 136.

[3] Ibid.; italics added.

time the Fourteenth Amendment was ratified, individuals and *joint stock companies* were appealing for congressional and administrative protection against invidious and discriminating state and local taxes. . . . [the Fourteenth amendment embodies] the Golden Rule, so entrenched as to curb the many who would do to the few as they would not have the few do to them."[4]

With the knowledge that they could go to almost any length in their pursuit of profits without fear of state government controls, the corporations thrived. They grew through internal expansion and, more important, by absorbing their competitors. As the giant corporations flourished, the entire American economy thrived and grew.

By the turn of the century, the United States had become the leading industrial power in the world. By 1913, when the American economy produced over one-third of the world's industrial output—more than double that of its closest competitor, Germany—most of the strategic industries (railroads, meatpacking, banking in the large cities, steel, copper, and aluminum) and important areas of manufacturing were dominated by a relatively small number of immensely powerful corporations.

With the exception of the railroads, most industries in the immediate post-Civil War years had been relatively atomistic by present-day standards. Although accurate statistics are not available for this early period, it has been estimated that the largest 200 nonfinancial enterprises would have controlled a very minor and inconsequential percentage of all business assets. By the end of the 1920s this had grown to 33 percent of all assets.[5]

The primary cause of this concentration was the wave of combinations and mergers that took place at an unprecedented rate during the last quarter of the nineteenth century. This merger movement was the outgrowth of the particularly severe competition that had ravaged and destroyed scores of businesses. During this period many people began to question seriously the liberal notion of the invisible hand. It seemed to them that unrestrained individualism had led to unrestrained warfare.

> As growing giant businesses locked horns, railroad against railroad, steel mill against steel mill, each sought to assure the coverage of its fixed expenses by gaining for itself as much of the market as it could. The outcome was the steady growth of cutthroat competition among massive producers. . . . On the Railroads for example, constant rate-wars were fought in the 1870's. In the oil fields, the coal fields, among the steel and copper producers, similar price-wars repeatedly broke out as producers sought to capture the markets.[6]

The outcome of such competition was the destruction or absorption of small competitors. Eventually only giants remained, and at this point further competition was immensely destructive to all competitors. The merger movement represented the means whereby the surviving firms could escape this competition.

> The scope of the merger movement was so great that by 1904 it had basically altered the structure of American industry. By the beginning of that year there were over three hundred large industrial combinations with a combined capitalization in excess of $7,000,000,000. They controlled more than two-fifths

[4] Ibid., p. 136.
[5] Joe S. Bain, *Industrial Organization* (New York: Wiley, 1959), pp. 191–192.
[6] Robert L. Heilbroner, *The Making of Economic Society* (Englewood Cliffs, N.J.: Prentice-Hall, 1962), p. 120.

of the manufacturing capital of the country and had affected about four-fifths of important American industries.[7]

THE CONCENTRATION OF INCOME

Accompanying this concentration of industry was an equally striking concentration of income in the hands of a small percentage of the population. Despite the fact that no accurate statistics for the early part of the period exist, it seems reasonably certain that the degree of concentration increased substantially between 1870 and 1929. By 1929 just 5 percent of the population received 34 percent of personal disposable income in the United States.[8] The degree of concentration had probably reached this extreme as early as 1913. By the end of the 1920s, the highest one-fifth of "families and unattached individuals" were receiving over 50 percent of all personal income.[9]

REEMERGENCE OF THE CLASSICAL LIBERAL IDEOLOGY

With this immense concentration of economic power in the hands of a small number of giant firms and a small percentage of the population, it would seem that the classical liberal ideology of capitalism would have been abandoned. The economic creed of classical liberalism, as developed by Adam Smith and refined by such well-known classical economists as David Ricardo, Nassau Senior, and J. B. Say, was based on an analysis of an economy composed of many small enterprises. In such an economy no individual enterprise could exercise a significant influence on the market price or on the total amount sold in the market. The actions of any firm were dictated to it by consumer tastes, as registered in the marketplace, and by the competition of innumerable other small firms, each vying for the consumer's dollars.

As wide as the gulf between classical economic theory and late nineteenth-century economic reality seems to have been, the economic creed of classical liberalism did not fall by the wayside in this later period. Rather, it was combined with Benthamite utilitarianism (which was already implicit in Adam Smith's normative model of the invisible hand) and refurbished within an elaborate and esoteric framework of algebra and calculus. This resurgence of the classical liberal economic creed was accomplished by a new school of economic thinkers known as *neoclassical* economists.

THE NEOCLASSICAL THEORY OF UTILITY AND CONSUMPTION

During the early 1870s, at precisely the time when the drive toward the economic concentration of corporate capitalism was taking place, three very famous eco-

---

[7] Joe S. Bain, "Industrial Concentration and Anti-Trust Policy," in Harold F. Williamson, ed., *Growth of the American Economy*, 2d ed. (Englewood Cliffs, N.J.: Prentice-Hall, 1951), p. 619.

[8] U.S. Department of Commerce, *Historical Statistics of the United States* (Washington, D.C.: GPO, 1961), p. 167.

[9] Ibid.; the data for 1913 do not give a figure for the income going to the top 5 percent. The amount going to the top 1 percent, however, was 14.98 percent in 1913 and 14.94 percent in 1928.

nomics texts were published. William Stanley Jevons' *The Theory of Political Economy*[10] and Karl Menger's *Grundsätze der Volkswirtschaftslehre*[11] both appeared in 1871, and three years later later Léon Walras's *Eléments d'économie politique pure* was published.[12] Athough there were many differences between the analyses of these men, the similarities in both approach and content of these books were striking.

Their theories pictured an economy made up of large numbers of small producers and consumers, each having insufficient power to influence the market significantly. The business firms hired or bought factors of production; they utilized the factors in the production process in such a way that their profits were maximized. Prices of the final products and factors of production were taken as given and beyond their control. The firms could control only the productive process chosen and the amount produced.

Households likewise sold their land and capital, as well as their labor, at prices determined in the market and used the receipts (their incomes) to buy goods and services. Consumers apportioned their income among the various commodities they wished to purchase in a way that maximized the utility they received from these commodities.

Commodities were the ultimate source of pleasure or utility, and the utility they yielded was assumed to be quantifiable. Jevons wrote, "A unit of pleasure or pain is difficult even to conceive; but it is the amount of these feelings which is continually prompting us to buying and selling, borrowing and lending, laboring and resting, producing and consuming; *and it is from the quantitative effects of the feelings that we must estimate their comparative amounts.*"[13]

Walras was less ambiguous in arguing that utility was quantifiable: "I shall, therefore, assume the existence of a standard measure of intensity of wants or intensive utility, which is applicable not only to similar units of the same kind of wealth but also to different units of various kinds of wealth."[14]

These economists, having presumably quantifiable magnitudes with which to work, next set up general mathematical formulas purporting to show a functional relationship between the utility a consumer received and the amounts of the various commodities he or she consumed. The problem then was to show how the consumer could get the maximum utility, given his or her income and the commodity prices prevailing in the market.

Consumers maximized utility when the increase in utility derived from the last unit consumed, expressed as a ratio over the price of that commodity, was an equal proportion for all other commodities. In other words, the last dollar spent on a commodity should yield the same increase in the utility derived by the consumer as the last dollar spent on any other commodity. Jevons explained the same thing in a different way, stating that the consumer maximized utility because he or she "procures such quantities of commodities that the final degrees of utility of any pair of commodities are inversely as the ratios of exchange [prices] of the commodities."[15]

[10] William Stanley Jevons, *The Theory of Political Economy*, 1st ed. (London: Macmillan, 1871).

[11] Karl Menger, *Grundsätze der Volkswirtschaftslehre* (Vienna: Braumuller, 1871), translated as *Principles of Economics* (New York: Free Press, 1950).

[12] Léon Walras, *Eléments d'économie politique pure* (Lausanne: Corbaz et Cie, 1874); translated as *Elements of Pure Economics* (Homewood, Ill.: Irwin, 1957).

[13] Jevons, op. cit., p. 11.

[14] Walras, op. cit., p. 117.

[15] Jevons, op. cit., p. 139.

Suppose there was a free market in which consumers could freely exchange their incomes for commodities. They would be led by their self-interest to maximize utility. Therefore it was concluded that consumers distributed their income among purchases of commodities in such a way that the welfare of all would be maximized, given the existing distribution of wealth and income.

THE NEOCLASSICAL THEORY OF PRODUCTION

In neoclassical production theory the analysis of the business firm was perfectly symmetrical with the analysis of consumer behavior. In order to maximize profits, the firm would operate at its highest efficiency and hence produce at the lowest possible cost. It purchased factors of production (such as labor) up to the point at which the amount added to production by the last unit of each factor of production, expressed as a ratio over the price of the factor, was an equal proportion for all factors. The last dollar spent on each factor should yield the same increase in production from all factors. In a free market firms would always attempt to maximize efficiency in order to maximize profits. Therefore this condition would always hold. Thus the factors of production would all be used in such a way that no possible reorganization of production (given the existing technology) could result in a more efficient use of the factors of production.

Neoclassical economists also believed that if an economy were characterized by a free market with many small competitive firms, then each commodity would be produced in such quantities and with such methods that it would be impossible to shift resources from the production of one commodity to the production of a different one without diminishing that total value of what was produced in the market economy.

LAISSEZ-FAIRE

Thus the neoclassical economists gave a very elaborate and esoteric analytical defense of Adam Smith's notion of the invisible hand of market competition and the economic policy of laissez-faire. They showed that, in a competitive market economy made up of innumerable small producers and consumers, the market would guide consumers in such a way that they would end up with an optimal mix of commodities, *given their original income and wealth.* Factors of production would be used in the most efficient way possible. Moreover, commodities would be produced in amounts that would maximize the value of society's production. This optimal result depended, however, on a minimum of interference by government in the processes of the free market.

They recognized that this result was optimal only if one accepted the existing distribution of income. Some (particularly the American economist John Bates Clark) tried to defend the distribution of income that obtained in a free-market economy. They argued that the principles of profit maximization would lead to a situation in which each category of productive factors would be paid an amount equal to the value of its marginal contribution to the productive process. This seemed to them a model of distributive justice, with each unit of the productive factors being paid an amount equal to what it produced. Critics were quick to point out, however, that units of productive factors were not people (at least as far as land, natural resources, and capital were concerned). In order for such a system to be fair, these critics insisted, an equitable distribution of ownership of the factors of production would be necessary.

Nevertheless, the neoclassical economists did succeed in erecting an impressive intellectual defense of the classical liberal policy of laissez-faire. But they did it by creating a giant chasm between economic theory and economic reality. From the 1870s until today, many economists in the neoclassical tradition have abandoned any real concern with existing economic institutions and problems. Instead, many of them have retired to the rarefied stratosphere of mathematical model building, constructing endless variations on esoteric trivia.

SUBSEQUENT MODIFICATIONS OF NEOCLASSICAL THEORY

Some economists in the second and third generations of neoclassical analysis recognized the need to make the theory more realistic. The economic system was *not* characterized by "perfect competition"; it had flaws. The principal admitted weaknesses were as follows: (1) Some buyers and sellers *were* large enough to affect prices; moreover the economies of large-scale production seemed to render this inevitable. (2) Some commodities should be "consumed socially," and their production and sale might never be profitable in a laissez-faire capitalist economy, even though they might be deemed highly desirable by most citizens (e.g., roads, schools, armies). (3) The costs to the producer of a commodity (such as automobiles) might differ significantly from the social costs (such as smog) of producing that commodity. In such a case it was possible that for society as a whole the costs of production might exceed the benefits of production for the commodity, even though the producer still profited from making and selling it. For example, consider the poisoning of the water and air by producers making profits but doing little or nothing about this evil, even though its side effects could endanger human life itself. (4) An unrestrained free-market capitalist system appeared to be quite unstable, being subject to recurring depressions that incurred enormous social waste.

It was generally agreed that such flaws did exist and did disrupt the otherwise beneficial workings of the capitalist system, but they could be corrected only by some amount of government intervention in the market system. Government antitrust actions, it was argued, could force giant firms to act as if they were competitive, and something called "workable competition" could be achieved. Roads, schools, armies, and other socially consumed commodities could be provided by the government. Extensive systems of special taxes and subsidies could be used to equate private and social costs in cases where they differed. Finally (especially after the 1930s), it was believed that through wise use of fiscal and monetary policy the government could eliminate the instability of the system. (This last point will be discussed in more detail in Chapter 11.)

The flaws in the system were thus seen as minor and ephemeral. An enlightened government could correct them and free the invisible hand once again to create the best of all possible worlds. There did develop, however, an inability to agree on the extent and significance of the flaws. Those who believe them to be fairly widespread and quite significant have, during the course of the twentieth century, become known as *liberals*. They have sometimes advocated fairly extensive government intervention in the economic system, but most have continued to use neoclassical economic theory as an ideology to defend the private ownership, capitalist market economic system.

Economists who see the flaws as minor and unimportant continue to advocate a minimum of government intervention in the market economy. Despite the fact that the laissez-faire policies advocated by these economists have been much closer to those advocated by the nineteenth-century classical liberals, they have become known in the twentieth century as *conservatives*. Both liberals and conservatives, as we have described them here, have used neoclassical economic theory to justify the capitalist system.

LAISSEZ-FAIRE AND THE SOCIAL DARWINISTS

Before leaving the topic of late nineteenth- and early twentieth-century advocates of laissez-faire capitalism, a brief discussion of *social Darwinism* is necessary. Social Darwinists believed the government should allow capitalists to compete freely in the marketplace with a minimum of government restrictions and, in general, favored as little government intervention as possible in all spheres of life. Therefore many people have imagined their defense of laissez-faire capitalism to be similar to that of the neoclassical economists. This is not so. Their policy recommendations were based on a substantially different theoretical framework.

The social Darwinists took Darwin's theory of evolution and extended it to a theory of social evolution (in a manner that Darwin himself strongly disapproved, it may be added). Competition, they believed, was a teleological process in which each succeeding generation was superior to the preceding one. This upward progress was made possible because those least fit to survive did not succeed in maintaining themselves and procreating. Greater ability to survive was equated with a biological as well as a moral superiority.

Herbert Spencer (1820–1903), the father of social Darwinism, based his evolutionary as well as his moral theory on what he called the *law of conduct and consequence*. He believed survival of the human species could be ensured only if society distributed its benefits in proportion to a persons' merit, measured by his or her power to be self-sustaining. A person ought to reap the benefits or suffer the evil results of his own actions. Thus the people most adapted to their environment would prosper, and those least adapted would be weeded out—provided that the laws of conduct and consequence were observed. If the government, wishing to mitigate the inequalities of wealth and income in society, took "from him who . . . [had] prospered to give to him who . . . [had] not, it [violated] its duty towards the one to do more than its duty towards the other."[16] This type of action slowed social progress and could, if carried to excess, destroy the human species. Survival and progress could be ensured only if the weak were weeded out and destroyed by the impersonal forces of social evolution.

In Spencer's opinion, "the poverty of the incapable, the distresses that come

[16] Quoted in Sidney Fine, *Laissez Faire and the General Welfare State* (Ann Arbor: University of Michigan Press, 1964), p. 38.

upon the imprudent, the starvation of the idle, and those shoulderings aside of the weak by the strong . . . are the decrees of a large, far-seeing benevolence."[17] Spencer categorically opposed any action by the government that interfered with trade, commerce, production, or the distribution of wealth or income. He rejected welfare payments of any kind, attempts to decrease the economic insecurity of workers, and government provision of schools, parks, or libraries as detrimental to human progress. His laissez-faire was thus much more extreme than that of the classical economists or most of the conservative neoclassical economists.

Social Darwinists accepted the large monopolistic and oligopolistic industries as the beneficient result of evolution. Neoclassical economists, if they did not simply define away or ignore the concentrations of economic power, believed government should attempt to create a more competitive and atomistic market situation. Thus in this very important respect the two theories were quite antagonistic.

LAISSEZ-FAIRE AND THE IDEOLOGY OF BUSINESSMEN

Most businessmen, however, were not very concerned with intellectual inconsistency. They feared radical and socialist reformers who wanted to use the government as a means of achieving greater equality and they welcomed any theory that concluded that the government should not intervene in the economic process. Even though they themselves used the government extensively to promote their own interests (through special tariffs, tax concessions, land grants, and a host of other special privileges), they relied on laissez-faire arguments when threatened with any social reform that might erode their status, wealth, or income. Thus in the ordinary businessman's ideology of the late nineteenth and early twentieth centuries there was a general attempt to combine neoclassical economics and social Darwinism.

In this ideology the accumulation of wealth was considered de facto proof of evolutionary superiority, whereas poverty was believed to be evidence of evolutionary inferiority. Success, asserted writer Benjamin Woods, was "nothing more or less than doing thoroughly what others did indifferently." Andrew Carnegie equated success with "honest work, ability and concentration"; another businessman argued that "wealth has always been the natural sequence to industry, temperance, and perseverance, and it will always so continue." At the same time, S. C. T. Dodd, solicitor for Standard Oil, maintained that poverty existed "because nature or the devil has made some men weak and imbecile and others lazy and worthless, and neither man nor God can do much for one who will do nothing for himself."[18]

The beneficial results of competition in neoclassical economic theory seemed to reinforce reliance on the "survival of the fittest" in the "struggle for survival." "Competition in economics," asserted Richard R. Bowker, "is the same as the law of . . . 'natural selection' in nature."[19]

[17] Ibid.
[18] All quotations in this paragraph are cited in Fine, op. cit., p. 98.
[19] Ibid., p. 100.

Although some businessmen and their spokesmen were trying to perpetuate the laissez-faire conclusions of the classical liberal ideology of capitalism, many defenders of the capitalist system believed that in the new age of mass production (with gigantic concentrations of wealth and power in the hands of so few corporations and capitalists) the older, individualistic, laissez-faire ideology was no longer appropriate. The late nineteenth century witnessed a rebirth of the older paternalistic ethic. In Chapter 8 we will examine a new ideology of capitalism that was based, in many essential respects, on a new version of the Christian paternalist ethic.

THE CRITIQUE OF THORSTEIN VEBLEN

At the turn of the twentieth century, neoclassical economics was subjected to a most searching (and often humorous) criticism by one of America's most original and enigmatic geniuses, Thorstein Veblen. He believed that the maximizing, utility-calculating "economic-man" of the neoclassical theory was a most unrealistic portrayal of actual human beings existing in early twentieth century capitalism. In describing the view of human nature implicit in neoclassical theory he wrote

> [This] conception of man is that of a lightning calculator of pleasures and pains, who oscillates like a homogeneous globule of desire of happiness under the impulse of stimuli that shift him about the area, but leave him intact. He has neither antecedent nor consequent. He is an isolated definitive human datum, in stable equilibrium except for the buffets of the impinging forces that displace him in one direction or another. Self-imposed in elemental space, he spins symmetrically about his own spiritual axis until the parallelogram of forces bears down upon him, whereupon he follows the line of the resultant. When the force of the impact is spent he comes to rest, a self-contained globule of desire as before.[20]

In a similar mocking tone, Veblen attacked the neoclassical view that utility maximization had a wider applicability than mere consumption theory. Many of the neoclassical economists argued (and many still argue) that all actions by all persons in all societies were the result of utility calculations. Veblen asserted that neoclassical economists would argue that

> a gang of Aleutian Islanders slushing about in the wrack and surf with rakes and magical incantations for the capture of shell-fish are held, in point of . . . reality, to be engaged on a feat of hedonistic equilibration in rent, wages and interest. And that is all there is to it.[21]

Veblen countered this simplistic neoclassical view of human behavior with his own theory of the structure of contemporary capitalism. Central to his theory was his distinction between "business" and "industry." By industry was meant all of the features which Veblen believed were important in modern technology. It included far more than the usual categories of land, labor, or physical capital. The

---

[20] Thorstein Veblen, "Why Economics Is Not an Evolutionary Science," in M. Lerner, ed., *The Portable Veblen* (New York: Viking Press, 1948), pp. 232–233.

[21] Thorstein Veblen, "Professor Clark's Economics," in E. K. Hunt and Jesse Schwartz, eds., *A Critique of Economic Theory* (Baltimore: Penguin Books, 1972), pp. 178–179.

most important element of industry was the whole complex of cultural, emotional, and intellectual traits that had slowly evolved into the "technological habits of thought" that made possible the enormous productivity of an industrial society. Industry, Veblen believed, was a socially progressive force which held the potential promise of material abundance and freedom from insecurity.

"Business," on the other hand, was a socially regressive force. It continuously thwarted the potential of industry. Veblen held that businessmen were essentially predators who received "unearned gain" by their ability to monopolize the funds necessary to acquire factories and machines. With this control of capital they were able to control industry. The purpose of business was profit making. The control of industry by business resulted in systematic repression of the naturally progressive tendencies of industry in several ways.

First, industry naturally tended to expand output and make more available to consumers. Businessmen, on the other hand, knew that if they could achieve a monopoly in an industry they could increase their profits by raising their prices. But the only way in which they could raise prices was to create artificial shortages in which consumers would bid up prices in an effort to obtain the commodities in short supply. In order to make profits, Veblen asserted, businessmen must sabotage industry. He defined "capitalistic sabotage" as "a system of industrial strategy or management" in which businessmen "resort to peaceable or surreptitious restriction, delay, withdrawal or obstruction."[22] In fact, Veblen argued that in a capitalist market system capitalistic sabotage is sometimes necessary to avoid a depression. "Without some . . . restraint in the way of sabotage on the productive use of the available industrial plant and workmen," he asserted, "it is altogether unlikely that prices could be maintained at a reasonably profitable figure for any appreciable time."[23]

Thus, the first contradiction between industry and business—the expansion of output versus the restriction of output—gave rise to a second contradiction: industry tended to increase efficiency and this would tend to lower prices. Business, however, was forced to resort to sabotage in order to raise prices and maintain profitability. These contradictions led to others. Business controlled industry and thereby subverted a naturally progressive force in such a way as to involve it in repressive imperialistic ventures, to subject it to recurring crises and depressions, and to create within it widespread waste and unemployment.

Furthermore, the acquisitive, "rational," maximizing side of human beings, which neoclassical theorists elevated to the defining feature of human nature, Veblen saw as one of the most absurd and least socially "serviceable" of all human attributes in modern society. What neoclassical theorists saw as maximizing behavior Veblen described as "pecuniary" and "predatory." Business or commercialism brought to the fore, accentuated, and developed the most socially destructive of all human motives. And this was inevitable in a business-oriented society because this behavior—which was destructive from a social point of view—was absolutely necessary for survival from a personal point of view for an individual functioning in modern capitalism. Veblen argued that many

---

[22] Thorstein Veblen, *The Engineers and the Price System* (New York: Augustus M. Kelley, 1967 [first published in 1919]), p. 4.
[23] *Ibid.*, pp. 7-8.

of the necessary mores and institutions of capitalism go "almost unequivocally in the direction of furthering a survival of the predatory temperament and habits."[24]

> The two barbarian traits, ferocity and astuteness, go to make up the predaceous temper or spiritual attitude. They are the expressions of a narrowly self-regarding habit of mind. Both are highly serviceable for individual expediency in a life looking for invidious success. . . . Both are fostered by the pecuniary culture. But both alike are of no use for the purposes of collective life.[25]

In each of the arguments touched in this brief account of Veblen's ideas, as well as in many other areas which we have not mentioned, Veblen developed in-depth, profound critiques of both neoclassical economic theory and of capitalist society. Nevertheless, his subsequent intellectual impact was to significantly influence only bits and pieces of various intellectual traditions. The diversity of his ideas can be seen by the fact that his influence has been felt among many socially and politically conservative theorists as well as among socialist and Marxist theorists. Veblen had relatively few disciples who shared both his critical spirit and his intellectually perceptive insights into the capitalist culture of his era. In the nearly one-half century since his death, however, no critics of neoclassical economic theory have surpassed the insightfulness and brilliance of his moral and intellectual critiques of capitalism and the neoclassical ideology that rationalized and defended capitalism.

SUMMARY

In the late nineteenth century capitalism was characterized by the growth of giant corporations. Control of most of the important industries became more and more concentrated. Accompanying this concentration of industry was an equally striking concentration of income in the hands of a small percentage of the population.

In view of these facts it would seem that the classical liberal ideology (which depended on an analysis of an economy based on many small, relatively powerless enterprises) would have to be abandoned. The gulf that separated the theory from reality had widened into a giant chasm. But the idea that the market economy channeled acquisitive profit seeking into socially benevolent practices was simply too elegant an apologia for unrestrained profit-making activity. So the classical liberal ideology of capitalism was even more assiduously disseminated in a new school of neoclassical economics.

An elaborate deductive theory permitted the neoclassical economists to defend the classical policy prescription of laissez-faire. Conservative neoclassical economists assigned to the government only the tasks that would directly or indirectly promote business profits. Liberal neoclassical economists also believed the government should enter a limited number of other areas in which the operation of the free market did not maximize the social welfare. Whether in the

---

[24] Thorstein Veblen, *The Theory of the Leisure Class* (New York: Augustus M. Kelley, 1965 [first published in 1899]), p. 271.
[25] Ibid., p. 275.

hands of the conservative or the liberal faction, neoclassical economics remained essentially an ideological defense for the status quo.

Finally, social Darwinist ideology and the ideology of most businessmen defended many of the neoclassical economists' conclusions. They did so, however, on entirely different grounds. They accepted the fact that corporate power, personal wealth, and personal income were highly concentrated. This, they believed, was evidence of the evolutionary superiority of the wealthy and, as such, was socially beneficial.

CHAPTER 8

THE CONSOLIDATION OF MONOPOLY POWER AND THE NEW CHRISTIAN PATERNALIST ETHIC

The process of industrialization in the United States after the Civil War involved, in its initial stages, a competition among industrial and financial capitalists that was unique in its ferocity. From 1860 until the early 1880s, the strongest and shrewdest businessmen built great empires with the fruits of economic conquest. The great improvements in transportation that occurred during this period, the rise of standardization in parts and finished products, and the increased efficiency in large-scale mass production created the possibility of nationwide markets. The stakes in the economic struggle were very large, and the participants neither asked for quarter nor received any.

COMPETITION AS INDUSTRIAL WARFARE

Examples of the industrial warfare of the time have filled many books.[1] In the oil industry, for example, John D. Rockefeller and Henry M. Flagler shipped so much oil that they were able to demand large concessions from the railroads. With this cost advantage they could undersell competitors. Their company, which was incorporated in 1870 under the name of Standard Oil Company of Ohio, was able to force many competitors to the wall and thus achieve regional monopolies, at which point the price could be substantially increased without fear of competition. After securing large rebates on transport costs, Standard Oil's share in the petroleum industry quickly increased from 10 to 20 percent. But the company did not stop there. Next it succeeded in forcing the railroads to give it rebates on its *competitors'* shipments as well as "all data relating to shipper, buyer, product, price and terms of payment," a scheme that "provided Rockefeller and his associates with rebates on all their own shipments, rebates on all shipments by their competitors, and in addition a complete spy system on their competitors."[2] With this power Rockefeller was able to smash most of his com-

---

[1] See, for example, Matthew Josephson, *The Robber Barons* (New York: Harcourt Brace Jovanovich, Harvest Books, 1962), for a fascinating account of the exploits of the capitalists of this era.
[2] Dudley Dillard, *Economic Development of the North Atlantic Community* (Englewood Cliffs, N.J.: Prentice-Hall, 1967), p. 410.

petitors. By 1879, only nine years after incorporation, Standard Oil controlled between 90 and 95 percent of the nation's output of refined petroleum. A sympathetic biographer of Rockefeller has written, "Of all the devices for the extinction of competition, this was the cruelest and most deadly yet conceived by any group of American industrialists."[3]

Competition among the railroad magnates was particularly intense. Rate wars were common, forcing weaker competitors out of business and giving stronger competitors monopoly power over large regions. The battles sometimes got so brutal that locomotives were crashed into each other and track was destroyed. The railroads also extorted money from towns along proposed railroad lines. A member of the California Constitutional Convention of 1878 described the technique.

> They start out their railroad track and survey their line near a thriving village. They go to the most prominent citizens of that village and say, "If you will give us so many thousand dollars we will run through here; if you do not we will run by." And in every instance where the subsidy was not granted this course was taken and the effect was just as they said, to kill off the little town.[4]

According to the same report, the railroad "blackmailed Los Angeles County for $230,000 as a condition of doing that which the law compelled them to do." The railroads also manipulated connections with politicians to get government handouts of public lands. It is estimated that these giveaways amounted to 158,293,-000 acres—a greater land area than that of some whole countries.[5] The railroads were certainly not in favor of a laissez-faire policy in practice.

The great entrepreneurs of that age were definitely not men of estimable social conscience. Many founded their fortunes on the Civil War. When shortages of supplies became desperate, they received high prices for selling to the army "shoddy blankets, so many doctored horses and useless rifles, [and] . . . stores of sickening beef."[6] In order to eliminate their competitors, they did not hesitate to use hired thugs, kidnaping, and dynamite. Likewise, they stopped at nothing as they mulcted the public of millions of dollars through stock frauds, schemes, and swindles. Some of these actions were legal and some were not, but the dominant mood of these capitalist entreprenuers was expressed by Cornelius Vanderbilt, who, when cautioned about the questionable legality of a desired course of action, exclaimed, "What do I care about the law? Hain't I got the power?"[7] Much the same idea was expressed by William Vanderbilt during a public outcry against one of his policy decisions: "The public be damned. I am working for my stockholders."[8]

BUSINESS COLLUSION AND GOVERNMENT REGULATION

After a few years of this type of competition, however, most of the remaining business firms were battle-tested giants. Continuing such competition would

---

[3] Allan Nevins, *John D. Rockefeller, The Heroic Age of American Enterprise,* vol. 1 (New York: Scribner, 1940), p. 325.
[4] Quoted in Josephson, op. cit., pp. 84–85.
[5] Ibid., p. 79.
[6] Ibid., p. 67
[7] Ibid., p. 72.
[8] Ibid.

have been ruinous for all. So, whereas competition was the road to large profits before 1880, after that date it became obvious that cooperative collusion would be more beneficial for the remaining firms. In that way they could exercise monopolistic power for their mutual benefit. Thus pools, trusts, and mergers (described in Chapter 7) were the consequence of the earlier competition. Increasingly as the turn of the century neared, the neoclassical vision of many small competing firms diverged from the reality of massive corporations acting cooperatively to maximize their joint profits.

With the rise of big corporations there was a parallel growth of grass-roots popular opposition to these companies and their blatant disregard for the public welfare. This popular antagonism became so widespread and intense that in the presidential campaign of 1888 both the Democrats and the Republicans advocated federal laws to curb the abuses of big corporations.

After the 1888 election both parties became extremely reluctant to take any such action. Many of the most important Republicans controlled the very corporations they had promised to curb, and the Democrats were only slightly less involved with big business. Only when public pressure reached incredible heights did Congress respond, in December 1889, by passing the Sherman Antitrust Act. The act, an obvious concession to aroused public opinion, passed both houses of Congress with only a single dissenting vote. But the wording of the law was so weak and vague that it appeared to be designed to ensure that it would be ineffective. Another proposal that recommended meaningful punishment of firms that violated the law was overwhelmingly defeated.

The law proscribed "every contract, combination in the form of a trust or otherwise, or conspiracy, in restraint of trade or commerce among the several states or with foreign nations. . . ." It also declared any person guilty of a misdemeanor who attempted "to monopolize, or combine or conspire with any other person . . . to monopolize any part of the trade or commerce among the several states, or with foreign nations. . . ."

The primary effect of the Sherman Act over the next few decades was to weaken labor unions. What had begun as a concession to the public's hatred of abuses by big business became an antilabor law. This effect followed because the courts ruled that many union strikes constituted constraints of trade. On this basis the government arrested numerous union leaders and broke up many unions.

While President McKinley was in office there were only five cases initiated under the Sherman Act, despite the fact that 146 major industrial combinations were formed between 1899 and 1901 alone. One of these was the massive United States Steel Corporation, which in 1901 controlled or acquired 785 plants worth a whopping $1,370,000,000.

Staggeringly high profits, graft, corruption, and discriminatory practices on the part of the nation's railroads led to the establishment of the first federal government regulatory agency. The Interstate Commerce Act of 1887 established the Interstate Commerce Commission (ICC), which was designed to regulate the railroads in order to protect the public interest.

Competition among the railroads had been so destructive that the railroads themselves were the leading advocates of extended federal regulation. A few years after the passage of the Interstate Commerce Act, U.S. Attorney General Olney wrote a letter to a railroad president that read, in part, "The Commission [ICC] . . . is, or can be made, of great use to the railroads. It satisfies the popular clamor for a government supervision of railroads, at the same time that supervision is almost entirely nominal. Further, the older such a commission gets to be, the more inclined it will be found to take the business and railroad view of things. . . ."[9]

The attorney general's prediction has certainly been borne out by the facts. In the years since the establishment of the ICC, many other federal regulatory agencies have been established. The Federal Communications Commission (FCC), the Civil Aeronautics Board (CAB), and the Securities and Exchange Commission (SEC) were among the federal agencies that joined the ICC as "protectors" of the public interest. Most serious students of government regulation would agree that "the outstanding political fact about the . . . regulatory commissions is that they have in general become promoters and protectors of the industries they have been established to regulate."[10] The agencies help the industries make extraordinary profits at the expense of the public.

Many oligopolistic industries seemed unable to cooperate and act collectively as a monopoly. For these industries there is a considerable body of evidence indicating that they turned to the government and to federal regulatory agencies as a means of achieving this monopolistic coordination.[11] Regulatory agencies have generally performed this function very effectively.

The collusive behavior of the oligopolistic businesses seemed to go unnoticed by neoclassical economists. They continued to frame their analyses in terms of innumerable small, competing business firms. In their advocacy of laissez-faire policies, they failed to see that it was primarily big business that supported active government intervention.

Neoclassical economists also continued to accept the classical economists' view that as long as free competition prevails the economy will tend toward full utilization of its productive capacity and full employment will be more or less continuous. During the second half of the nineteenth century, however, economic depressions became more frequent and more severe. During the first half of the nineteenth century, the United States had had two economic crises (in 1819 and 1837), and England had had four (in 1815, 1825, 1836, and 1847). During the second half of the century, the number increased to five in the United States (in 1854, 1857, 1873, 1884, and 1893), and six in England (in 1857, 1866, 1873, 1882, 1890, and 1900). Thus the neoclassical economic ideology was as poor a reflection of economic performances as it was of industrial concentration.

A NEW CHRISTIAN PATERNALIST ETHIC

The distance separating the neoclassical liberal ideology of capitalism and economic reality impressed itself on the minds of many academicians and businessmen. The result was a new ideology for the new age of corporate capitalism. Just as the new industrial and financial entrepreneurs came to resemble the feudal robber barons, so the new ideology resembled the feudal version of the Christian paternalist ethic. It emphasized the natural superiority of a small elite, the new

[9] Quoted in Grant McConnell, "Self-Regulation, the Politics of Business," in D. Mermelstein, ed., *Economics: Mainstream Readings and Radical Critiques* (New York: Random House, 1970), p. 197.

[10] Ibid., p. 199.

[11] The most thoroughly documented defense of this assertion can be found in Gabriel Kolko, *The Triumph of Conservatism* (New York: Free Press, 1963).

industrial and financial magnates, and the paternalistic functions of that elite in caring for the masses.

The new ideology reflected the fact that many of the wealthy capitalists of the era were becoming something of folk heroes among the general public. The last two decades of the nineteenth century and the first three of the twentieth were an age during which the businessman became the most admired social type. The success of businessmen was viewed as de facto proof that they possessed virtues superior to those of the ordinary person. This version of success was the theme of the biographies of William Makepeace Thackeray and the novels of Horatio Alger. These men and other writers created a cult of success that viewed the increase of industrial concentration as proof of Darwinian superiority on the part of the industrialists, glorified the self-made individual, and kept the Horatio Alger rags-to-riches myth constantly in the public mind.

The veneration of businessmen, added to the strong rejection of destructive competition by both businessmen and the general public, led to a new conservative version of the Christian paternalist ethic, which resembled the philosophy of the Tory radicals of the late eighteenth and early nineteenth centuries. The unfortunate plight of the poor received prominent mention in the new writings. This problem, as well as that of economic instability, could best be solved, according to the new ideology, by encouraging cooperation among the leaders of the giant corporations. Competition was viewed as antisocial. Through cooperation business cycles could be eliminated and the plight of the poor improved.

This new version of the Christian paternalist ethic received the support of Pope Leo XIII (1810–1903). Between 1878 and 1901 the pope sought to analyze the problems of corporate capitalism and to suggest remedies in a series of encyclicals. In *Rerum novarum* (1891) he argued that "a remedy must be found . . . for the misery and wretchedness which press so heavily at this moment on the large majority of the very poor." He continued with a condemnation of unrestrained laissez-faire competition:

> Working men have been given over, isolated and defenseless, to the callousness of employers and the greed of unrestrained competition. The evil has been increased by rapacious usury . . . still practiced by avaricious and grasping men. And to this must be added the custom of working by contract, and the concentration of so many branches of trade in the hands of a few individuals, so that a small number of very rich men have been able to lay upon the masses of the poor a yoke little better than slavery itself.[12]

This passage, which sounds so socialist in tone and content, was followed by a strong condemnation of socialism and a defense of private property. The pope hoped the problems could be corrected by rejection of competition and a return to the Christian virtues of love and brotherhood, with the leaders of business and industry leading the way to a new Christian paternalism within the context of a private property capitalist system.

The German Version

The new paternalistic ideology was probably strongest in Germany, where classical liberalism had never gained a good hold and industrial concentration

[12] Quoted in Daniel R. Fusfeld, *The Age of the Economist* (Glenview, Ill.: Scott, Foresman, 1966), p. 86.

was most pronounced. A famous German economist expressed the very widely held view that

> the proper kind of cartelization creates more or less a system of justice and equity. . . . The directors of the cartels are educators who wish to bring about the triumph of wide interests of a branch of industry over the egoistic interests of the individual. . . . The cartel system is, like a co-operative or merchant's association, an important element in the education of commercial and technical officials who want to make money but who have also learned to put themselves in the service of general interests and to administer the property of others in a loyal and honorable fashion. [13]

Cartels were also widely justified as means of eliminating economic crises. A German court decision, one of several that formed the legal justification of the cartel system in that country, stated that "Indeed the formation of syndicates and cartels . . . has repeatedly been considered a device especially useful for the economy as a whole, since they can prevent uneconomic overproduction and ensuing catastrophe." [14]

The American Version

In the United States, as mentioned earlier, the new ideology thrived in an atmosphere that venerated the successful businessman and was extremely weary of destructive competition. The view of many American industrial and financial magnates was expressed by Andrew Carnegie, one of the most successful of the magnates:

> Not evil, but good, has come to the race from the accumulation of wealth by those who have the ability and energy that produce it. . . . We have the true antidote for the temporary unequal distribution of wealth, the reconciliation of the rich and the poor—a reign of harmony—another ideal, differing, indeed, from that of the Communist in requiring only further evolution of existing conditions, nor the total overthrow of our civilization. . . . Under its sway we shall have an ideal state, in which the surplus wealth of the few will become in the best sense, the property of the many, because administered for the common good, this wealth passing through the hands of the few can be made a more potent force for the elevation of our race than if it were distributed in sums to the people themselves. [15]

Carnegie argued, and many businessmen and their spokesmen agreed, that the millionaire would be "a trustee for the poor, entrusted for a season with a great part of the increased wealth of the community, but administering it for the community far better than it could or would have done for itself" [16]

The Right Reverend William Lawrence gave the new elitist view the sanction of religion. "In the long run, it is only to the man of morality that wealth comes. . . . Godliness is in league with riches." [17] And railroad president George F. Baer had

---

[13] Gustave Schmoller, quoted in Koppel S. Pinson. *Modern Germany: Its History and Civilization* (New York: Macmillan, 1954), p. 236.

[14] Quoted in Dillard, op. cit., p. 396.

[15] Andrew Carnegie, "Wealth," in Gail Kennedy, ed., *Democracy and the Gospel of Wealth* (Lexington, Mass.: Raytheon/Heath, 1949), pp. 3, 5, 6.

[16] Cited in Kennedy, op. cit., p. xii.

[17] Ibid.

the same idea in mind when he tried to assure railroad workers that "the rights and the interests of the laboring man will be protected and cared for, not by the labor agitators, but by the Christian men to whom God in his infinite wisdom, has given control of the property interests of the country."[18]

SIMON PATTEN'S ECONOMIC BASIS FOR THE NEW ETHIC

Perhaps the most influential academic spokesman for the new corporate ideology was Dr. Simon N. Patten, professor of economics at the University of Pennsylvania from 1888 to 1917 and one of the founders of the American Economic Association.[19] In keeping with the paternalistic element of the new ideology, Patten denounced the poverty and economic exploitation of his era. The following passage could almost have been written by a Marxist of that era:

> There have flowed then, side by side, two streams of life, one bearing the working poor, who perpetuate themselves through qualities generated by the stress and mutual dependence of the primitive world, and the other bearing aristocracies, who dominate by means of the laws and traditions giving them control of the social surplus.[20]

In the same vein, 15 years late, he wrote,

> The glow of Fifth Avenue is but the reflection of a distant hell into which unwilling victims are cast. Some resource is misused, some town degraded, to create the flow of funds on which our magnates thrive. From Pennsylvania, rich in resources, trains go loaded and come back empty. For the better half no return is made except in literary tomes designed to convince the recipients that exploitation is not robbery. . . . But Nature revolts! Never does the rising sun see children yanked from bed to increase the great Strauss dividends, nor the veteran cripples of the steel mill tramping in their beggar garb, but that it shrivels, reddens, and would strike but for the sight of happier regions beyond.[21]

This poverty and exploitation were, in Patten's opinion, the last vestiges of an earlier age characterized by scarcity. In the economy of scarcity capitalists competed aggressively with each other, with the result that laborers as well as the general public suffered. The fierce competition of the robber barons, however, had marked a watershed in history. The merger movement that followed this competition was the beginning of a new era, an era of plenty rather than scarcity. Capitalists were becoming socialized. They were putting the public welfare ahead of their pursuit of profits, and in doing this they eschewed competition, recognizing that the public welfare could best be promoted by cooperation. (Of course we have seen that capitalists cooperated with each other mostly to squeeze more profit from the public.)

Evidence that the conditions of economic prosperity at the turn of the century were socializing capitalists could be seen in the fact that "hospitals . . . [were] established, schools . . . [were] made free, colleges . . . [were] endowed, muse-

---

18 Ibid.

19 For a more complete account of Patten's idea, see E. K. Hunt, "Simon N. Patten's Contribution to Economics," *Journal of Economic Issues*, December 1970, pp. 38–55.

20 Simon Nelson Patten, *The New Basis of Civilization* (New York: Macmillan, 1907), p. 39.

21 Simon Nelson Patten, *Mud Hollow* (Philadelphia: Dorrance, 1922), p. 226.

ums, libraries, and art galleries . . . [received] liberal support, church funds . . . [grew] and missions . . . [were] formed at home and abroad.[22] On almost every policy issue of his day, Patten took a strongly proindustrial capitalist position. He viewed the late nineteenth-century captains of industry as a paternally beneficient elite:

> The growth of large-scale capitalism has resulted in the elimination of the unsocial capitalist and the increasing control of each industry by the socialized groups. . . . At bottom altruistic sentiment is the feeling of a capitalist expressing itself in sympathy for the laborer. This desire of upper class men to improve the conditions of lower classes is a radically different phenomenon from the pressure exerted by the lower classes for their own betterment. The lower class movement stands for the control of the state by themselves in their own interests. The upper class movement directs itself against the bad environmental conditions preventing the expression of character.[23]

He believed competition should be discouraged by taxing competitive firms and exempting trusts and monopolies from these taxes. This would benefit all society by eliminating the extensive waste created by competition. In *The Stability of Prices* he argued that competition was largely responsible for the economic instability of the late nineteenth century. When the movement toward trusts and monopolies had been completed, production would be controlled and planned in such a way that this instability would be elimated.

Patten's paternalistic ideology was, like the liberal ideology of capitalism, ultimately a plea for a minimum of government interference with the actions of businessmen. The government was to interfere in the economy only by encouraging trusts and monopolies and discouraging competition. In Patten's scheme all important social and economic reforms were to be carried out voluntarily by the socialized capitalists in a system of cooperative corporate collectivism.

THE NEW PATERNALISM AND THE NEW DEAL[24]

Patten's version of the new ideology of corporate capitalism was to be very important historically. When the Great Depression of the 1930s struck, two of Patten's students and devotees, Rexford Guy Tugwell and Frances Perkins, had influential positions as members of Roosevelt's original cabinet. Tugwell had asserted that Patten's views "were the greatest single influence on my thought. Neither Veblen nor Dewey found their orientation to the future as completely and instinctively as did Patten. The magnificence of his conceptions and the basic rightness of his vision become clearer as time passes. I am eternally grateful to him."[25] Perkins believed her former teacher to be "one of the greatest men America has ever produced."[26]

---

[22] Simon Nelson Patten, *The Theory of Prosperity* (New York: Macmillan, 1902), p. 170.

[23] Simon Nelson Patten, "The Reconstruction of Economic Theory," reprinted in Simon Nelson Patten, *Essays in Economic Theory*, ed. Rexford Guy Tugwell (New York: Knopf, 1924), p. 292.

[24] For a more complete discussion of the material covered in this section, see E. K. Hunt, "A Neglected Aspect of the Economic Ideology of the Early New Deal," *Review of Social Economy*, September 1971, pp. 180–192.

[25] Quoted in Allan G. Gruchy, *Modern Economic Thought: The American Contribution* (Clifton, N.J.: Augustus M. Kelley, 1967), p. 408.

[26] Quoted in Arthur M. Schlesinger, Jr., *The Coming of the New Deal* (Boston: Houghton Mifflin, 1965), p. 229.

Through these two former students Patten exerted a considerable influence on the economic policies of the early phase of the New Deal. His ideas helped create the intellectual basis of the National Industrial Recovery Act of 1933 (NIRA).[27] Patten was not, of course, the only source of these ideas. During World War I, the War Industries Board had generated enthusiasm for corporate collectivism. Throughout the 1920s, trade associations prospered, and the doctrine of business self-government gained many adherents in the business world. In 1922, Franklin Roosevelt was president of one such association: the American Construction Council. However, Patten's teachings were unquestionably influential. His protégés, Tugwell and Perkins, were both instrumental in the actual framing of the NIRA.

The National Industrial Recovery Act proclaimed the intent of Congress "to promote the organization of industry for the purpose of cooperative action among trade groups."[28] The bill contained sections providing for codes of fair competition that permitted and even encouraged cooperative price fixing and market sharing and for virtually complete exemption from antitrust laws. Section 7A was designed to promote labor organization but was so diluted that very often it promoted the formation of company unions. "If it [the NIRA] worked, Tugwell thought, each industry would end with a government of its own under which it could promote its fundamental purpose ('production rather than competition'). NIRA could have been administered, Tugwell later wrote, so that a 'great collectivism' would have channeled American energy into a disciplined national effort to establish a secure basis for well-being."[29]

In explaining the bill to the National Association of Manufacturers, General Hugh S. Johnson, the first head of the National Recovery Administration (NRA), declared that "NRA is exactly what industry organized in trade associations makes it." He further asserted that before the NRA the trade associations had about as much effectiveness as an "Old Ladies' Knitting Society; now I am talking to a cluster of formerly emasculated trade associations about a law which proposes for the first time to give them power."[30]

Most of the economics literature that appeared in 1934 recognized that the early New Deal reforms had not significantly extended government control over business. On the contrary, it had given voluntary trade associations the support of the government in forcing the controls of trade associations on all industry.[31]

This experiment in business self-government proved disastrous. The distinguished historian Arthur M. Schlesinger, Jr., has assessed the success of this phase of the early New Deal. With Schlesinger we concur:

> And the result of business self-government? Restriction on production, chiseling of labor and of 7A, squeezing out of small business, savage personal criticism of the President, and the general tendency to trample down everyone in the rush for profits. Experience was teaching Roosevelt what instinct and doctrine had taught Jefferson and Jackson; that, to reform capitalism you must fight the capitalists tooth and nail.[32]

[27] Schlesinger, op. cit., p. 98.
[28] Quoted in ibid., pp. 98–99.
[29] Ibid., p. 108.
[30] Quoted in ibid., p. 110.
[31] See Leo Rogin, "The New Deal: A Survey of Literature," *Quarterly Journal of Economics,* May 1935, pp. 338, 346, 349–355. Typical of the comments of supporters of the early New Deal is this quotation from Tilly: "Here *industry* is setting up a legal and enforceable Golden Rule." Ibid., p. 351.
[32] Arthur M. Schlesinger, Jr., "The Broad Accomplishments of the New Deal," in Edwin C. Rozwenc, ed., *The New Deal: Revolution* (Lexington, Mass.: Raytheon/Heath, 1959), pp. 30–31.

The early New Deal philosophy underlying the NIRA was very quickly abandoned, and the NIRA was declared unconstitutional. The new paternalistic ideology of capitalism, however, was to receive more elaborate statements after World War II. (These statements and the later New Deal policies will be discussed in subsequent chapters.)

SUMMARY

The industrial warfare of the late nineteenth century led to an era of mergers and collusion among the giant corporations. Through collusion the few corporations that controlled an industry could act effectively as monopolists and maximize their joint profits. Where collusion was difficult, the corporations relied heavily on government regulatory agencies to help enforce mutual cooperation.

Within this economic and political context many ideologists of capitalism rejected classical liberalism because of its unrealistic assumptions. These thinkers created a new version of the Christian paternalist ethic that pictured the new industrial and financial magnates as beneficent, fatherly protectors of the public welfare.

The new ethic was to become particularly influential in the social and economic legislation of the early New Deal of the 1930s.

CHAPTER 9

ECONOMIC PROSPERITY AND EVOLUTIONARY SOCIALISM

In the late nineteenth and early twentieth centuries, the socialist analysis of capitalism was profoundly affected by two developments: (1) the economic and political gains made by the working class and (2) the imperialistic carving up of the economically less developed areas of the world by the major capitalist powers. These developments split the socialist movement into two camps. Some became convinced that governmental power could be peacefully acquired by socialists and used to promote economic and social reforms that would result in a gradual evolution to socialism. The more militant socialists, however, continued to accept the Marxist view of the class nature of capitalist governments and to insist on the necessity of revolution. This chapter considers the economic and political gains of the working class and the resultant conservative reformist tendency in the socialist movement. Imperialism and revolutionary socialism will be discussed in the next chapter.

THE ECONOMIC AND POLITICAL GAINS OF THE WORKING CLASS

During the second half of the nineteenth century, the real income of workers rose throughout the capitalist world. In England the average real wage increased rapidly throughout the 1860s and early 1870s. By 1875 it was 40 percent higher than it had been in 1862. After ten years in which wages sagged, they again rose sharply between 1885 and 1900. By 1900, the average real wage was 33 percent higher than in 1875 and 84 percent higher than in 1850. Most of the gains in real wages are attributable to the advent of mass production techniques that permitted the prices of many commodities consumed by laborers to be lowered. As a result of new methods of producing and labor's greater purchasing power, there was a fundamental change in patterns of consumption. Workers began to eat more meats, fruits, and sweets. Mass-produced shoes and clothing, furniture, newspapers, bicycles, and other new products came within the reach of many. Unquestionably, the average worker's lot improved substantially during the period.

It should be mentioned, however, that averages can be misleading. Two late nineteenth-century social surveys revealed that about 40 percent of the working class in London and York still lived in abject poverty. The fact that this could be so after a half-century of rapid increases in average real wages gives an indication of the truly pitiful conditions that must have existed in the early nineteenth century.

Similar gains were being made in western Europe and the United States during this period, and in most of these countries economic gains were accompanied by political gains. Most of the industrialized capitalist countries had nearly complete male suffrage by the early twentieth century. Political parties were created that were devoted to furthering the cause of workingmen. The most successful of these was the German Social Democratic Party, formed at a meeting in Gotha in 1875 between the followers of Marx, led by Wilhelm Leibknecht and August Bebel, and the followers of Ferdinand Lassalle. The program adopted in this first party congress was known as the *Gotha Programme*. It represented a compromise that was bitterly attacked by Marx.

Marx believed his followers had made too many concessions to the Lassallian outlook, which conceived of the government as a neutral instrument to be used by workers to achieve socialism through peaceful reform. Excessive concern with reformism could, he believed, divert workers from their task of overthrowing capitalism. The conflict between the revolutionary socialists and the reformers was to remain important in the Social Democratic Party for the next 40 years. Ultimately Marx's misgivings proved prophetic, however, and the reformists became dominant in the party.

In 1874 the two socialist groups had polled 340,000 votes. In the election of 1877 the newly formed party received more than 500,000 votes and had 12 representatives elected to the Reichstag. This show of strength frightened Bismarck, and in 1878 a series of infamous anti-socialist laws was passed. Many of the more militant socialist leaders were exiled, and the Social Democratic Party was prohibited from holding meetings or publishing newspapers.

In spite of this repression the party continued to grow. It received 549,000 votes in 1884 and 763,000 in 1887. By 1890 the Social Democratic Party polled 1,427,000 votes and had become the largest single party in the Reich. The repression had not worked; the anti-socialist laws were abandoned.

In both England and Germany, as well as several other western European countries, it appeared to many socialists that the capitalist system had provided the workers with an escalator on which they could steadily and peacefully advance in both economic well-being and political power.

THE FABIAN SOCIALISTS

In England, despite the brilliant achievements of individual Marxists like William Morris, the socialist movement was largely non-Marxist, the Fabian Society was the primary influence on English socialism, and it rejected Marx's analysis completely. In their economic analysis the Fabians used orthodox neoclassical utility theory. They believed labor received an amount equal to what it produced, and capitalists and landlords received the value of what was produced with their capital and land. The chief cause of injustice was not that labor's surplus value was appropriated by capitalists but rather that all the income from ownership accrued to a tiny percentage of the population. The only way to achieve an equitable society would be to divide the income from ownership equally, and this could be done only through government ownership of the means of production.

On the issue of the nature and role of the government, the Fabians differed radically from Marx. For Marx, the government was an instrument of coercion controlled and used by the ruling class to perpetuate the privileges inherent in the capitalist system. The Fabians believed that, in a parliamentary democracy based on universal suffrage, the State was a neutral agency that could be freely used by the majority to reform the social and economic system. Because the working class was the majority in a capitalist economy, they were confident that, step by step, piecemeal reforms would strip away the privileges of the owning class and result in socialism achieved by peaceful evolution rather than violent revolution.

The most influential of the Fabians were George Bernard Shaw, Sidney and Beatrice Webb, and Graham Wallas. For many years Shaw was the principal draftsman of Fabian publications and was widely known as the society's most lucid and forceful spokesman. The worst evil of capitalism was, in Shaw's opinion, the enormous inequality of wealth and icome that prevailed in every capitalist country. The cause of the most egregious inequity was the income that accrued from ownership of land and capital. Such unearned incomes, which Shaw combined under the label of "rents," created extremes of incredible wealth and power for a tiny minority while the majority of those who created the wealth lived in poverty. He also believed the capitalist system suffered from periods of chronic underproduction and incurred enormous wastes by devoting productive capacity to the creation of mountains of useless consumption goods for the rich. By expropriating these rents and eliminating the wastes and inefficiencies of capitalism, a socialist government could easily provide economic security and an ample livelihood for everyone.

The only ultimately just distribution of income was absolute equality. To achieve this, it would be necessary to sever any connection between productive services rendered and monetary remuneration. This, in turn, would require a reliance on noneconomic, or social, incentives to accomplish the necessary productive tasks. Shaw envisioned this equality not as an immediate possibility but only as a long-run goal.

Perhaps the least attractive aspect of Shaw's socialism was his extreme elitist bias. He had little faith in democracy. Rather, he believed an efficient and just organization of society required that policy making and administrative tasks be handled by experts. According to one eminent historian of socialism, Shaw "was apt to admire dictators, if only they would give the experts a free hand."[1]

Shaw's elitism was shown most clearly in his defense of British imperialism. He believed that

> no group or nation had any right to stand in the way of the full development in the interest of the whole world of any productive resource of which it stood possessed, and that accordingly higher civilizations had a complete right to work their will upon backward peoples and to override national or sectional claims, provided only that by doing so they increased the total wealth of the human race.[2]

---

[1] G. D. H. Cole, *A History of Socialist, Thought*, vol. III, pt. 1 (London: Macmillan, 1956), p. 211.
[2] Ibid., p. 219.

In view of these opinions, Shaw's leadership of the pro-imperialist faction of the Fabian Society is easily understandable.[3]

Among the general public Shaw was probably the most influential of the Fabians. Within the Fabian Society itself, however, the most influential theoreticians were Sidney and Beatrice Webb. The Webbs were probably the most serious scholars in the Fabian Society and undoubtedly among the most prolific writers in the history of socialism.

One of their first and most influential books, *Industrial Democracy*, rejected the notion that workers might democratically manage their own industries under socialism. They believed workers had neither the desire nor the capability to run their enterprises. Rather, industrial democracy under socialism was envisioned as a scheme in which industry was controlled by professional managers, who, in turn, were to be made accountable to the general population through supervision by a democratically elected parliament, local governments, and consumers' cooperatives.

They rejected the idea that socialism would involve ownership of all industry by the national government. Ownership should reside both in the national government and in any of a variety of smaller local or regional administrative units. The scope of an enterprise's activities and the portion of the population affected by these activities should, they believed, determine the nature of social ownership of any particular business firm.

In *A Constitution for the Socialist Commonwealth of Great Britain*, they proposed the creation of two separate, democratically elected parliaments. One was to handle political affairs and the other to preside over social and economic affairs. In addition, they advocated a system of local governments based on local units with fixed geographic boundaries. These local governments, however, were to be combined in various ways to form administrative units to supervise and control different economic and social services. The particular size, shape, and location of these administrative units was to depend on the nature of the service involved.

In general, it may be said that the Webbs wrote a lot about the nature of the socialist society they would have liked to have seen created at some future time but very little about specific tactics for transforming existing society into that future socialist system. They believed labor unions should confine their activities to representing the economic interests of their members in the collective bargaining process and should not act as insurgents. In fact, they seemed to see little hope for political change coming from a broadly based movement of workers. Rather, they assumed that an intellectual appeal might ultimately change the general public's opinions in a manner that would lead to the election of members of parliament who were sympathetic to socialist ideas.

The Fabian Society gradually succeeded in gaining influence in the parliamentary Labour Party. By 1918, the Labour Party had adopted a socialist program that reflected the Fabian Society's views and attitudes. By the 1920s the Labour Party had formed a government, and the cause of socialism via the voting booth seemed to many to be on the road to triumph.

The Fabians had never wanted to be a mass membership society. They were a small, select group, and most of their efforts were devoted to educating the middle class to accept socialism. They published innumerable tracts exposing

[3] See Chapter 10, p. 108.

the poverty and injustice they found in early twentieth-century England. Remedies for these evils would be forthcoming through paternalistic government actions and programs, they believed, once the government was made truly democratic and the people were made aware of these conditions.

However debatable their certainty that socialism could be achieved through education, it is undeniable that the Fabians offered an impressive group of teachers. Some of the most brilliant of the English intellectual elite were members of the society, including, in addition to the Webbs and Shaw, H. G. Wells, Sydney Olivier, and Graham Wallas. With such sponsorship the Fabians' reformist, evolutionary socialism became eminently respectable. One could espouse socialism and still remain completely secure in a comfortable middle-class niche in English capitalistic society.

THE GERMAN REVISIONISTS

The German counterparts of the English Fabians were the revisionists. At the turn of the century the Social Democratic Party was nominally a Marxist party. A large portion of the membership argued, however, that the course of history had proved Marx wrong on many issues, and that a "revision" of Marx's ideas was necessary to make them relevant to German economic and social life. The most famous of the revisionists was Eduard Bernstein, who presented a detailed critique of Marxist ideas in his best-known work, *Evolutionary Socialism,* published in 1899. Bernstein maintained that capitalism was not approaching any kind of crisis or collapse and, indeed, had never been more viable. Marx was also wrong, Bernstein declared, in predicting the concentration of all industries in the hands of a few giant firms. He argued that enterprises of all sizes thrived and would continue to do so (despite the fact that corporate concentration and the cartel movement were more extreme in Germany than in any other capitalist country). Even if large trusts did dominate the economy, Bernstein insisted, there would be a "splitting up of shares," making petty capitalists of a very large percentage of the population, including many workers. He believed the economy had already gone far in this direction: "The number of members of the possessing classes is today not smaller but larger. The enormous increase of social wealth is not accompanied by a decreasing number of large capitalists, but by an increasing number of capitalists of all degrees."[4]

Furthermore, even workers who received no profits, rents, interest, or dividends were rapidly becoming much better off. Improvements in the general standard of living and the democratization of the government had made revolution not only highly unlikely but also morally undesirable. The hopes of the working class lay more "in a steady advance than in the possibilities offered by a catastrophic crash."[5]

Bernstein's book contained much more than the simple substitution of "peaceful evolution" for "revolution": It was, in fact, a direct attack on nearly all of the intellectual foundations of Marxism. Capitalism was not, he asserted, characterized by two polarized, conflicting classes. Class struggle could hardly be

---

[4] Eduard Bernstein, *Evolutionary Socialism* (New York: Schocken Books, 1961 [first published in 1899]), p. xii.
[5] Ibid., p. xiv.

the moving force of history when class distinctions were rapidly breaking down and frequently nonexistent. Workers were far from being a homogeneous mass, he argued, and therefore "the feeling of solidarity between groups of workers . . . is only very moderate in amount."[6] Instead of two fundamentally antagonistic classes, Bernstein saw a multiplicity of interest groups that were often in conflict but even more often united in a collective "community."

From his rejection of the class nature of capitalist society, it follows that Bernstein would have to reject Marx's theory of historical materialism. He argued that as society developed, economic forces came to be less and less important and ideological and ethical forces became increasingly significant.

> Modern society is much richer than earlier societies in ideologies which are not determined by economics and by nature operating as an economic force. Science, the arts, a whole series of social relations are nowadays much less dependent on economics than formerly they were; or let us say, in order to leave no room for misunderstanding, the point of economic development that has now been reached leaves the ideological, and especially the ethical, factors greater scope for independent activity than used to be the case. Consequently, the interdependence of cause and effect between technological, economic evolution and the evolution of other social tendencies is becoming continually more indirect; and accordingly the necessities of the former are losing much of their power to dictate the form of the latter.[7]

He similarly rejected Marx's theory of surplus value. Marx had asserted that surplus value was created in the process of production by living labor alone. Bernstein simply dismissed this theory by stating that surplus value "can only be grasped as a concrete fact by thinking of the whole economy of society."[8] This, he believed, was a most damning criticism of Marx because the theory of surplus value was seen as the scientific basis for Marx's socialism. Henceforth, Bernstein averred, socialism would have to be based on ethical and not scientific foundations.

Perhaps the most fundamental difference between Marx and Bernstein was their difference concerning the nature of government in a capitalist society. Marx had asserted (and Bernstein's contemporary Marxist adversaries continued to assert) that capitalist governments were primarily instruments of class rule. Capitalists maintained their economic status and privileges through capitalistic property relations. They used their wealth, in turn, to control the political process in order to ensure the continuation of governments that were, above all else, committed to the defense of these property relations.

Bernstein dismissed the Marxist view of capitalist government as "political atavism." The Marxist notion may have once been valid, but contemporary extensions of suffrage had, he believed, invalidated it. Universal suffrage could make all people equally powerful in selecting the government and could thereby destroy class conflict by making each individual an "equal partner" in the community. "The right to vote," he wrote, "in a democracy makes its members virtually partners in the community, and this virtual partnership must in the end lead to real partnership."[9]

[6] Ibid., p. 120.
[7] Quoted in Cole, op. cit., p. 280.
[8] Bernstein, op. cit., p. 38.
[9] Ibid., p. 144.

Thus Bernstein, like the Fabians, rejected the notion that the government in a capitalist society had an inherent class bias. In a capitalist democracy each worker was seen as an equal partner with each capitalist, and they could all be induced, through moral appeals, to use peaceful political means to promote the general interests of the entire community.

THE FATE OF EVOLUTIONARY SOCIALISM

Throughout the period from the publication of *Evolutionary Socialism* until the outbreak of World War I, Bernstein's ideas evoked intense controversy in the Social Democratic Party and also throughout the entire worldwide socialist movement. The issue at stake was of the utmost significance.

The Fabians and the Revisionists argued that persistence in legislating reforms would ultimately achieve socialism. No single reform would, by itself, threaten the capitalist structure, but eventually the cumulative effect of many reforms would be the peaceful abdication of the capitalist class.

Marxists continued to believe, however, that as soon as any reforms seriously threatened the privileges and prerogatives of property rights, the capitalist class would resort to intimidation, repression, and ultimately abolition of the democratic rights of workers rather than seeing their economic power and social status eroded. When this happened, the working class would have to be prepared for revolution. If it were not, all of its hard-won concessions and advances would be lost.

By the beginning of World War I, it was obvious that the conservatives in the socialist movement had won at least a temporary victory over the revolutionaries. Capitalism in both England and Germany had passed through a period of prosperity in which the plight of workers had improved and a general feeling of optimism prevailed. In England the Fabian philosophy had come to dominate the Labour Party, and in Germany the Revisionists had gained control of the Social Democratic Party.

The subsequent history of those two parties was to illustrate the basic weakness of socialism that relied entirely on legislative reforms. Even though many party leaders continued to propound socialist ideas for some time, it was found that the pressure to attain an electoral majority continually forced party policies toward greater conservatism. In the 1950s both parties officially announced that they had given up the quest for social ownership of the means of production, distribution, and exchange. They asserted that ameliorative legislation to improve the living standards of the poor was all that remained to achieve a good and just society.

SUMMARY

In the late nineteenth and early twentieth centuries, improved working conditions, living standards, and political rights led to a split in the socialist movement. While the Marxist revolutionary socialists continued to affirm the necessity of a socialist revolution, a new school of reformist, evolutionary socialists argued that socialism could be achieved through gradual, peaceful legislative reforms.

In England, reformist socialism found its ablest leaders in George Bernard Shaw, Sidney and Beatrice Webb, and the other members of the Fabian Society. In Germany, it was Eduard Bernstein and the Revisionists who led the movement toward reformism. Both of these parties were ultimately pushed, by the pressures of achieving electoral majorities, to abandon the most fundamental tenet of socialism—socialization of the means of production.

CHAPTER 10

IMPERIALISM AND REVOLUTIONARY SOCIALISM

The idea that a democratic government in a capitalist country could be used to effect a gradual and peaceful transition from capitalism to socialism led to a controversy that split the European socialist movement.[1] However, the issue of imperialism was of equal if not greater significance in precipitating this division among socialists. During the late nineteenth and early twentieth centuries, European economic imperialism was most intensive. The nature and importance of an appropriate socialist response to imperialism were issues that created profound divisions among socialists—divisions that persist to this day.

EUROPEAN IMPERIALISM

India was one of the earliest and most dramatic cases of European imperialism. The East India Company had traded extensively in India for 150 years before the conquest of Bengal in 1757. During this period India was relatively advanced economically. Its methods of production and its industrial and commercial organization could definitely be compared with those prevailing in western Europe. In fact, India had been manufacturing and exporting the finest muslins and luxurious fabrics since the time when most western Europeans were backward primitive peoples.

But after the conquest the East India Company became the ruling power in much of India, and the trade of the previous 150 years turned to harsh exploitation. It has been estimated that between 1757 and 1815 the British took between £500 million and £1000 million of wealth out of India.[2] The incredible magnitude of this sum can be appreciated only when compared with the £36 million that represented the total capital investment of all the joint stock companies operating in India.[3]

The policy of the East India Company in the last decades of the eighteenth century and in the early nineteenth century reflected two objectives. First, in the short run the myriad of greedy officials sought personal fortunes overnight: "These officials were absolute, irresponsible and rapacious, and they emptied the private hoards. Their only thought was to wring some hundreds of thousands of pounds out of the natives as quickly as possible, and hurry home to display

---

[1] See Chapter 9.
[2] Paul A. Baran, *The Political Economy of Growth* (New York: Monthly Review Press, 1962), p. 145.
[3] Ibid.

their wealth. Enormous fortunes were thus rapidly accumulated at Calcutta, while thirty millions of human beings were reduced to the extremity of wretchedness."[4]

A British observer described this ruthless quest for wealth in similar terms: "No Mahratta raid ever devastated a countryside with the thoroughness with which both the Company [East India Company] and, above all, the Company's servants in their individual capacities, sucked dry the plain of Bengal. In fact, in their blind rage for enrichment they took more from the Bengali peasants than those peasants could furnish and live. And the peasants duly died."[5]

The second was a long-run goal: to discourage or eliminate Indian manufacturers and make India dependent on British industries by forcing the Indians to concentrate on raw materials and export them to supply the textile looms and other British manufacturers. The policy was brutally and methodically—and successfully—executed.

> The total effect of this was that the British administration of India systematically destroyed all the fibres and foundations of Indian economy and substituted for it the parasitic landowner and moneylender. Its commercial policy destroyed the Indian artisan and created the infamous slums of the Indian cities filled with millions of starving and diseased paupers. Its economic policy broke down whatever beginnings there were of an indigenous industrial development and promoted the proliferations of speculators, petty businessmen, agents, and sharks of all descriptions eking out a sterile and precarious livelihood in the meshes of a decaying society.[6]

It was only later, however, after the period of extensive railroad construction beginning in 1857, that the British thoroughly penetrated the interior of India. British investors who sank money into these railroads were guaranteed a 5 percent return by the government, which enforced a provision that if profits fell below 5 percent the Indian people would be taxed to make up the difference. Thus Indians were taxed to ensure that British investors would have adequate transport for further economic exploitation of the Indian interior.

Despite such harsh measures, the age of European imperialism really did not get under way on a broad, pervasive front until the last quarter of the nineteenth century. Between 1775 and 1875 the European countries had lost about as much colonial territory as they had won. The opinion was widely held that colonies were expensive luxuries.

All this changed suddenly and drastically after 1875. By 1900 Great Britain had grabbed 4,500,000 square miles, which she added to her empire; France had gobbled up 3,500,000; Germany, 1,000,000; Belgium, 900,000; Russia, 500,000; Italy, 185,000; and the United States, 125,000. Imperialism ran rampant as one-fourth of the world's population was subjugated and put under European and American domination.

Imperialism in Africa

By 1800 the Europeans had hardly penetrated beyond the coastal areas of Africa. By the early twentieth century, after a 100-year orgy of land grabbing and

---

[4] Brooks Adams, *The Law of Civilization and Decay, An Essay on History* (New York: 1896); quoted in Baran, op. cit., p. 146.

[5] John Strachey, "Famine in Bengal," in Robert Lekachman, ed., *The Varieties of Economics*, vol. 1 (New York: Meridian, 1962), p. 296.

[6] Baran, op. cit., p. 149.

empire building, they controlled over 10 million square miles, or about 93 percent of the continent. In that gigantic rape, various European powers sought to acquire the abundant minerals and agricultural commodities of the Dark Continent.

The brutality of the European exploitation of Africa was perhaps most severe in the Belgian Congo. Belgian King Leopold II had sent H. M. Stanley into central Africa in 1879. Serving a private, profit-seeking company headed by Leopold and some of his associates, Stanley had a network of trading posts constructed and also duped native chiefs into signing "treaties" that established a commercial empire stretching over 900,000 square miles. Leopold set himself up as sovereign ruler of the Congo Free State and proceeded to exploit the natural and human resources of the area for the profits of his company.

The exploitation was ruthless. Natives were forced, through outright physical coercion, to gather rubber from the wild rubber trees and ivory from the elephants. Leopold confiscated all land that was not directly cultivated by the natives and placed it under "government ownership." Atrocities of the worst sort were committed to force the natives to submit to a very burdensome tax system that included taxes payable in rubber and ivory as well as in labor obligations.

By the twentieth century the Congo had also become a rich source of diamonds, uranium, copper, cotton, palm oil, palm kernels, and coconuts. In general, it can be said that the Congo was one of the most profitable of European imperialistic exploits as well as one of the most scandalous.

The British grabbed the most populous and also the richest holdings in Africa. In 1870 Cecil Rhodes went to South Africa for his health. Within two years his genius for organizing and controlling joint stock companies and his ability to corner the market on diamonds had made him a millionaire. In later years, the British South Africa Company, which Rhodes headed, came to control South Africa completely. Although it was a private, profit-seeking company, it had all the power of a government, including the authority (given in its charter of 1889) to "make treaties, promulgate laws, preserve the peace, maintain a police force, and acquire new concessions."

The expansionist policies of the British South Africa Company led to the Boer War (1899–1902), which crushed the Dutch republics (the Orange Free State and the Transvaal republic) and gave Britain complete control over all South Africa. South Africa proved to be a rich mining region. But the legacy of British and Dutch imperialism is most vividly seen today in the suppression of the blacks, who constitute the vast majority of the population.

The other instances of imperialism in Africa are no less deserving of study. It must suffice in this short account, however, to mention that on the eve of World War I France held about 40 percent of Africa (much of it within the Sahara desert), England controlled 30 percent, and the remaining roughly 23 percent was divided among Germany, Belgium, Portugal, and Spain.

Imperialism in Asia

The results of the British takeover of India were evident by the turn of the twentieth century. In 1901 the per capita income was less than $10 per year; over two-thirds of the population were badly undernourished; most native Indian manufacturing had been either ruined or taken over by the British. Nearly 90 percent of the population struggled to subsist in villages where the average holding was only 5 acres and farming techniques were primitive. Much of the meager produce was paid out in taxes, rents, and profits that accrued to the British. Famine, disease, and misery were rife. In 1891 the average Indian lived less than 26 years and usually died in misery.

Much of the rest of Asia was also subjugated during this period. In 1878 the British overran Afghanistan and placed it under the Indian government, and in 1907 Persia was divided between Russia and Britain.

In 1858 the French had used the murder of a Spanish missionary as the rationalization for invading Annam, a tributary state of China. They soon established a French colony in what is now Vietnam. With this toehold the French succeeded, through war and intrigue, in bringing all the territory of Indochina under their domination by 1887.

The Malay Peninsula and the Malay Archipelago (which stretches for nearly 3000 miles) were also carved up. The British grabbed Singapore and the Malay States, the northern part of Borneo, and southern New Guinea. Another part of New Guinea was taken by the Germans, and most of the remaining islands (an area comprising about 735,000 square miles) went to the Dutch.

AMERICAN IMPERIALISM

Throughout much of the nineteenth century American imperialism channeled all its energies into conquering the continent and exterminating the native American Indian population. The Samoa Islands were America's first overseas imperialist acquisition. In 1878 the natives of Pago Pago granted the Americans the right to use their harbor. Eleven years later, the islands had been conquered and divided between the United States and Germany.

Similarly, Pearl Harbor became a U.S. naval station in 1887. In a very short time American capitalists controlled most of Hawaii's sugar production. The tiny minority of white Americans soon revolted against Queen Liliuokalani's rule and, with the help of U.S. Marines, subjugated the native population. In 1898 Hawaii was officially annexed by the United States.

It was also in 1898 that the United States used the convenient sinking of the battleship *Maine* as an excuse to declare war on Spain and "liberate" the Cubans from Spanish oppression. Recognizing that it was no match for the United States, the Spanish government accepted every American demand, but the United States declared war anyway as a "measure of atonement" for the *Maine*. The American victory gave it Puerto Rico, Guam, and the Philippine Islands outright, and the newly "independent" Cubans soon found American capitalists taking over most of their agriculture and commerce. Cuban independence had been restricted by a provision that the United States could intervene at its own discretion into Cuba's internal affairs "for the protection of life, property and individual liberty," a slogan that has been used to justify imperialism more than a few times. American troops invaded Cuba in 1906, 1911, and 1917 before secure control was finally established.

The Filipinos, who had been fighting for their independence from Spain, discovered the American brand no better than Spanish domination. President McKinley had decided that Americans were obligated "to educate the Filipinos and uplift and Christianize them;" but the Filipinos, who had been Roman Catholics for centuries, resisted American "Christianization." It took 60,000 American troops, as well as endless atrocities and concentration camps, before the Filipinos were finally "uplifted" and "educated."

In 1901, when the republic of Colombia refused to sell a strip of land (on which the Panama Canal was to be constructed) to the United States, President Roosevelt took action. A Panamanian insurrection was organized with American approval and help. United States warships were strategically placed to prevent Colombian troops from moving in to suppress the rebellion. The revolt started on November 3, 1903; on November 6, the United States extended diplomatic recognition to the "new nation"; on November 18, the United States had the Canal Zone on much more favorable terms than it had originally offered.

In 1904 President Roosevelt announced that the United States believed in the principle of self-determination for nations that acted "with reasonable efficiency and decency in social and political matters." He added, however, that "chronic wrongdoing, or any impotence which results in a general loosening of the ties of civilized society, may in America, as elsewhere, ultimately require intervention by some civilized nation. . . ."[7]

In 1909 U.S. Marines invaded Nicaragua to overthrow José Santos Zelaya, who threatened American economic concessions there. American troops were back in Nicaragua in 1912. In 1915 American Marines invaded Haiti, and in 1916 American troops overwhelmed the Dominican Republic and established a military government there.

By World War I the United States had seized or otherwise controlled Samoa, Midway Island, Hawaii, Puerto Rico, Guam, the Philippines, the island of Tutuila, Cuba, Santo Domingo, Haiti, Nicaragua, and the Panama Canal Zone.

IMPERIALISM AND EVOLUTIONARY SOCIALISM

The Boer War jolted British public opinion and resulted in strong conflicts among many radicals and socialists. On the one hand, it produced an abundance of jingoist sentiment and imperialist ideology that influenced some socialists; but on the other, J. A. Hobson's *Imperialism: A Study* caustically ridiculed this sentiment and ideology and advanced a theory of imperialism that was to have a profound influence on Marxists and many non-Marxist socialists.

Imperialism, according to Hobson, was a struggle for political and economic domination of areas of the world occupied by "lower races." Its "economic taproot" was the necessity for advanced capitalist countries to find markets for goods and capital produced domestically but for which there was inadequate domestic demand. Evoking traditions of nationalism and militarism, it could "appeal to the lust of quantitative acquisitiveness and of forceful domination surviving in a nation from early centuries of animal struggle for existence."[8]

The basic cause of the deficiency in domestic demand was, Hobson believed, a severely inequitable distribution of income that resulted in a distorted alloca-

---

[7] Quoted in G. C. Fite and J. E. Reese, *An Economic History of the United States*, 2d ed. (Boston: Houghton Mifflin, 1965), p. 472.

[8] Quotations in this paragraph are from J. A. Hobson, *Imperialism: A Study* (London: Allen & Unwin, 1938 [first published in 1902]), p. 368.

tion of resources, which led, in turn, to the quest for foreign markets. Hobson argued that the imperialist tendencies of the late nineteenth and early twentieth centuries could be reversed only by reform radical enough to effect a more equitable distribution of income. He summarized his position succinctly in the following passage:

> There is no necessity to open up new foreign markets; the home markets are capable of indefinite expansion. Whatever is produced in England can be consumed in England, provided that the "income," or power to demand commodities, is properly distributed. This only appears untrue because of the unnatural and unwholesome specialization to which this country has been subjected, based upon a bad distribution of economic resources, which has induced an overgrowth of certain manufacturing trades for the express purpose of effecting foreign sales. If the industrial revolution had taken place in an England founded upon equal access by all classes to land, education, and legislation, specialization in manufactures would have gone so far. . . .; foreign trade would have been less important though more steady; the standard of life for all portions of the population would have been high, and the present rate of national consumption would probably have given full, constant, remunerative employment to a far larger quantity of private and public capital than is now being employed.[9]

The issue of whether publicly to denounce English imperialism bitterly divided the Fabians. Sydney Olivier's insistence that the society's executive committee issue a pronouncement condemning the Boer War in particular and imperialism in general was rejected by one vote, but the committee agreed to the demand that the issue be put to a general vote.

Led by George Bernard Shaw, the pro-imperialist faction argued that small, backward nations could not manage their own affairs and should not be considered as nations at all, and that the advanced European nations thus had a duty to police and manage the internal affairs of these backward peoples for their own welfare. The debate was bitter. Finally, 45 percent of the membership voted to condemn English imperialism, and 55 percent opted to approve of or ignore imperialism. Immediately, 18 members of the society, including several of its most prominent personalities, handed in their resignations.

The sentiments of the German Revisionists were similar to those of the Fabians, the majority either approving of European imperialism or not considering it a proper issue on which to take a stand. Bernstein, for example, wrote: "Only a conditional right of savages to the land occupied by them can be recognized. The higher civilization ultimately can claim a higher right."[10] Orthodox Marxists, however, were virtually unanimous in condemning imperialism, which they analyzed as only the latest stage in the historical development of capitalism: Capitalists were forced by the mounting contradictions of the economic system to turn frantically to economic exploitation of more backward areas.

ROSA LUXEMBURG'S ANALYSIS OF IMPERIALISM

Rosa Luxemburg was one of the most important political leaders and exponents of orthodox Marxism. Her book *The Accumulation of Capital* contained a descrip-

[9] Ibid., pp. 88–89.
[10] Edward Bernstein, *Evolutionary Socialism* (New York: Schocken Books, 1961 [first published in 1899]), p. xii.

tion and analysis of imperialism that was to exert a strong influence on subsequent generations of socialists.

Luxemburg began her analysis by a review of Marx's analysis of the process of *capitalist commodity production*,[11] the process in which capitalists started with some given amount of money and purchased one commodity—labor power—and then sold a different commodity—that produced by labor in the production process. From the sales of the products of labor, they received a greater value than they laid out in expenses for raw materials, goods in process, and labor; that is, they received surplus value, or profits. The money they received in sales, however, had to be spent by purchasers of their commodities.

These purchasers of their commodities could be the laborers spending their wages for the means of subsistence, or other capitalists buying the raw materials and goods in process necessary for production. But we have already said that in order for surplus value to exist the proceeds from sales of commodities must exceed wages and expenditures on raw materials and goods in process. Part of the difference might be made up by capitalists' expenditures on consumption. Luxemburg observed, however, that capitalists' consumption expenditures typically make up only a small part of the surplus value they receive.

Another part of the deficiency in expenditures could be made up by capitalists purchasing capital goods that were not necessary to maintain the current level of production but were desired so that future production could be expanded. But the desire to expand production would have to be predicated on the expectation of greater demand for consumption goods, and it was the insufficiency of this demand for consumption goods that represented the crux of the problem. Capitalists would accumulate capital goods not for their own sake but only in the expectation that this accumulation would increase their profits. The inescapable conclusion, for Luxemburg, was that from within the internal sphere of a capitalist economy the expenditures of capitalists and workers could not for any lengthy period be sufficient to permit continuous realization of the surplus value generated from expanding commodity production.

But capitalism had been more or less continually expanding for well over a century, and Luxemburg sought to discover the source of the necessary additional expenditures that made this expansion possible. This source she found in the historical tendency of the capitalist mode of production to continually expand into noncapitalist areas, bring these areas under its control, and incorporate them within the domain of capitalist relations. The expenditures of these noncapitalist areas in the purchase of commodities produced in capitalist areas would represent the additional necessary demand:

> From the aspect both of realizing the surplus value and of procuring the material elements of constant capital, international trade is a prime necessity for the historical existence of capitalism—an international trade which under actual conditions is essentially an exchange between capitalistic and noncapitalistic modes.[12]

Luxemburg therefore believed that "imperialism is the political expression of the accumulation of capital in its competitive struggle for what remains still open of the non-capitalist environment."[13] The continuous diminution of the size of the

---

[11] See pp. 79–81.
[12] Rosa Luxemburg, *The Accumulation of Capital* (New York: Monthly Review Press, 1964) p. 359.
[13] Ibid., p. 446.

unexploited noncapitalist areas of the world had led to a situation in which "imperialism grows in lawlessness and violence, both in aggression against the noncapitalist world and in ever more serious conflicts among the competing capitalist countries."[14]

Within this theoretical framework Luxemburg wrote penetrating and insightful descriptions of the way in which the development of capitalism necessitated the growth of nationalism, militarism, and racism. In her analysis of military spending, for example, she understood the dual function such spending served in protecting capitalist empires around the world while providing the necessary stimulation of aggregate demand at home:

> . . . the multitude of individual and insignificant demands for a whole range of commodities . . . is now replaced by a comprehensive and homogeneous demand of the state. And the satisfaction of this demand presupposes a big industry of the highest order. It requires the most favorable conditions for the production of surplus value and for accumulation. In the form of government contracts for army supplies the scattered purchasing power of the consumers is concentrated in large quantities and, free of the vagaries and subjective fluctuations of personal consumption, it achieves an almost automatic regularity and rhythmic growth. Capital itself ultimately controls this automatic and rhythmic movement of militarist production through the legislature and a press whose function is to mould so-called "public opinion." That is why this particular province of capitalist accumulation at first seems capable of infinite expansion. All other attempts to expand markets and set up operational bases for capital largely depend on historical, social and political factors beyond the control of capital, whereas production for militarism represents a province whose regular and progressive expansion seems primarily determined by capital itself.
>
> In this way capital turns historical necessity into a virtue.[15]

This passage was written in 1913. This level of clear understanding of the role of military expenditures was not widely achieved among economists until about a half-century later, when the forces Luxemburg was describing had developed well beyond what they had been on the eve of World War I.[16]

Despite such brilliant insights, Luxemburg's analysis of imperialism rested on a faulty theoretical structure. Noncapitalist consumers are not automatically a source of increased demand. If products are to be sold to them, products must also be purchased from them—otherwise they would have no foreign currency with which to make the purchases. The net result on aggregate demand from this buying and selling cannot be determined in advance. Moreover, in less developed countries capitalist investments are soon yielding surplus value of their own. This tends to worsen rather than solve the problem of adequate demand.

Luxemburg's problem was that she focused on the wrong problem—underconsumption. The real driving force of imperialism was the search for profitable investment outlets to which the advanced capitalist countries could export capital. These deficiencies in the Marxist analysis of imperialism were corrected by Lenin.

---

[14] Ibid.

[15] Ibid., p. 466.

[16] For a further discussion of the importance of military expenditures in increasing domestic aggregate demand, see Chapter 11.

LENIN'S ANALYSIS OF IMPERIALISM

The most famous and influential socialist analysis was contained in Lenin's pamphlet *Imperialism: The Highest Stage of Capitalism,* published in 1916. Lenin attempted "to show, as briefly and as popularly as possible, the principal economic characteristics of imperialism."[17] The most important was that in the imperialistic phase of capitalist development the capitalist economies were thoroughly dominated by monopolies, a development Marx had correctly foreseen. By monopolies Lenin did not mean industries consisting of only one firm (the modern economic definition of monopoly); rather, he referred to industries dominated by trusts, cartels, combinations, or a few large firms.

Drawing heavily on the German experience, Lenin argued that the development of monopolies was closely related to important changes in the banking system. Banks had assumed a position of central importance in the drive toward cartelization and had come to exercise considerable control over many of the most important industrial cartels. This control was so extensive that Lenin spoke of the imperialistic phase of capitalism as the age of "finance capital."

Banks were able to mobilize huge sums of money for investment, but persistent downward pressures on domestic profit rates dictated that investment outlets be sought outside the home country. Lenin, unlike Hobson, did not believe the necessity to export commodities was the most important economic cause of imperialism. Rather, it was the necessity to export capital. Backward areas offered a large and inexpensive labor force and lucrative investment prospects.

In the imperialist phase of capitalism the various governments fought to gain access to privileged and protected markets for the combines and cartels within their own political boundaries. At the same time, these national combines and cartels sought to partition the world markets through international cartels. Deep-seated rivalry and competition, however, were more important than opportunistic short-run collaborations. Persistent national conflicts and wars were the inevitable result. In Lenin's words.

> The epoch of the newest capitalism shows us that certain relations are being
> established between capitalist combines, *based* on the economic division of the
> world; while parallel with this and in connection with it, certain relations are
> being established between political alliances, between states, on the basis of
> the territorial division of the world, of the struggle for colonies, of the "struggle
> for economic territory."[18]

Such a situation was, Lenin believed, inherently unstable. Imperialism would lead to wars among the advanced capitalist countries and to rebellions and revolutions in the exploited areas. As long as the capitalist system could support its imperialistic thrust, however, it would prolong its existence by providing outlets for excess investment funds. The extra profits that imperialism secured for the home country meant that the wages paid its workers could be raised. Thus, because it shared in the spoils, labor would be at least temporarily sapped of its revolutionary potential and controlled by right-wing labor leaders, "justly called social imperialists."[19]

---

[17] *Imperialism: The Highest Stage of Capitalism* (London: Lawrence & Wishart, 1939), p. 1.
[18] Ibid., p. 69.
[19] Ibid., p. 99.

If imperialism expanded the domain of capitalism and in doing so prolonged the system's existence, the tensions and conflicts it engendered were, Lenin believed, more severe than those of the competitive capitalism about which Marx wrote. Capitalism was still doomed, and socialism was still the wave of the future.

SUMMARY

The late nineteenth and early twentieth centuries witnessed the imperialistic carving up of most of the world's economically underdeveloped areas. The inhabitants of these areas were harshly and cruelly exploited for the profits of large corporations in the advanced capitalist countries.

The issue of imperialism split the evolutionary socialist movement. Many of the reform socialists, such as George Bernard Shaw and Eduard Bernstein, were strongly pro-imperialist. Others, among them J. S. Hobson, were strongly anti-imperialist. Hobson's analysis of imperialism stressed the maldistribution of wealth and income as the causes of this socioeconomic phenomenon. He advocated reforms to redistribute income and wealth within the capitalist framework.

Virtually all Marxist socialists opposed imperialism. Rosa Luxemburg saw the root problem as inadequate aggregate demand. Although her theoretical framework had some weaknesses, she had brilliant insights into the nature of imperialism, nationalism, racism, and militarism. Her weaknesses were corrected in Lenin's *Imperialism: The Highest Stage of Capitalism*. He stressed the importance of investment outlets and the capitalists' need to export capital. His analysis has remained the most influential Marxist critique of imperialism.

CHAPTER 11

KEYNESIAN ECONOMICS AND THE GREAT DEPRESSION

While the period from the Civil War to 1900 was one of rapid economic expansion in the United States, these accomplishments were dwarfed by the growth that occurred between 1900 and 1929. The following figures show the percentage increase in manufacturing production in several key industries between 1899 and 1927.[1]

Chemicals, etc.	239%
Leather and products	321
Textiles and products	449
Food products	551
Machinery	562
Paper and printing	614
Steel and products	780
Transportation and equipment	969

It has been estimated that U.S. wealth (the market values of all economic assets) reached $86 billion by 1900; in 1929, it stood at $361 billion.

This spectacular growth gave the United States a huge edge over all other countries in manufacturing output. The American prosperity of the 1920s was based on high and rising levels of output—though there were recessions in 1923 and 1927. The gross national product, the value of all goods and services produced, increased by 62 percent from 1914 to 1929. Only 3.2 percent of the labor force was unemployed in 1929, and labor productivity rose during that decade at least as fast as wages. Between 1921 and 1929, total automobile registrations increased from less than 11 million to more than 26 million; consumers spent tens of millions of dollars on radios, refrigerators, and other electric appliances that had not been available before. American manufacturing seemed to most people a permanent cornucopia destined to create affluence for all.

This leadership in manufacturing was associated with financial leadership in the world economy. The American economic empire began to rival that of England. By 1930 American businessmen owned large investments

[1] Figures taken from Leo Hubertman. *We the People* (New York: Monthly Review Press, 1964), p. 254.

around the world. The following figures give the values of these investments in 1930.[2]

Canada	$3,942,000,000
Europe	4,929,000,000
Mexico and Central America	1,000,000,000
South America	3,042,000,000
West Indies	1,233,000,000
Africa	118,000,000
Asia	1,023,000,000
Oceania	419,000,000

THE GREAT DEPRESSION

But this era of rapid growth and economic abundance came to a halt on October 24, 1929. On that "Black Thursday" the New York stock market saw security values begin a downward fall that eventually was to destroy all faith in business. Their confidence undermined, businessmen cut back production and investment. This decreased national income and employment, which, in turn, worsened business confidence even more. Before the process came to an end, thousands of corporations had gone bankrupt, millions were unemployed, and one of the worst national catastrophes in history was under way.

Between 1929 and 1932 there were over 85,000 business failures; more than 5,000 banks suspended operations; stock values on the New York Exchange fell from $87 billion to $19 billion; unemployment rose to 12 million, with nearly one-fourth of the population having no means of sustaining themselves; farm income fell by more than half; and manufacturing output decreased by almost 50 percent.[3]

America had plunged from the world's most prosperous country to one in which tens of millions lived in desperate, abject proverty. Particularly hard hit were the blacks and other minority groups. The proportion of blacks among the unemployed was from 60 to 400 percent higher than the proportion of blacks in the general population.[4] Certain geographic areas suffered more than others. Congressman George Huddleston of Alabama reported in January 1932:

> We have about 108,000 wage and salary workers in my district. Of that number, it is my belief that not exceeding 8,000 have their normal incomes. At least 25,000 men are altogether without work. Some of them have not had a stroke of work for more than 12 months, maybe 60,000 or 75,000 are working one to five days a week, and practically all have had serious cuts in their wages and many of them do not average over $1.50 a day.[5]

[2] Ibid., p. 251.

[3] Figures taken from Louis M. Hacker, *The Course of American Economic Gorwth and Development* (New York: Wiley, 1970), pp. 300–301.

[4] See Lester V. Chandler, *America's Greatest Depression* (New York: Harper & Row, 1970), pp. 40–41.

[5] U.S. Congress, Senate, Hearings before a subcommittee of the Committee on Manufactures, 72d Cong., 1st sess., p. 239.

Many cities reported that they could give relief payments for only a very short time, often one week, before people were forced to their own devices to subsist. The executive director of the Welfare Council of New York City described the plight of the unemployed:

> When the breadwinner is out of a job he usually exhausts his savings if he has any. Then, if he has an insurance policy, he probably borrows to the limit of its cash value. He borrows from his friends and from his relatives until they can stand the burden no longer. He gets credit from the corner grocery store and the butcher shop, and the landlord forgoes collecting the rent until interest and taxes have to be paid and something has to be done. All of these resources are finally exhausted over a period of time, and it becomes necessary for these people, who have never before been in want, to ask for assistance. The specter of starvation faces millions of people who have never before known what it was to be out of a job for any considerable period of time and who certainly have never known what it was to be absolutely up against it.[6]

The abject despair of these millions of people is at best suggested by a 1932 report describing the unloading of garbage in the Chicago city garbage dumps: "Around the truck which was unloading garbage and other refuse were about 35 men, women and children. As soon as the truck pulled away from the pile all of them started digging with sticks, some with their hands, grabbing bits of food and vegetables."[7]

What had happened to reduce the output of goods and services so drastically? Natural resources were still as plentiful as ever. The nation still had as many factories, tools, and machines. The people had the same skills and wanted to put them to work. And yet millions of workers and their families begged, borrowed, stole, and lined up for a pittance from charity, while thousands of factories stood idle or operated far below capacity. The explanation lay within the institutions of the capitalist market system. Factories could have been opened and people put to work, but they were not because it was not profitable for businessmen to do this. And in a capitalist economy production decisions are based primarily on the criteron of profits, not on people's needs.

THE ECONOMICS OF KEYNES

The socialist cause gained many enthusiasts in the 1930s. While the capitalist world was suffering what was perhaps its most severe depression, the Soviet economy was experiencing rapid growth. When the depression struck, it was a traumatic shock to many Americans, who had come to believe their country was destined to achieve unparalleled and unending increases in material prosperity.

The capitalist economic system seemed to be on the verge of total collapse. Drastic countermeasures were essential, but before the system could be saved the malady had to be better understood. And to that task came one of the most brilliant economists of this century: John Maynard Keynes (1883–1946). In this famous book *The General Theory of Employment, Interest and Money*, Keynes attempted to show what had happened to capitalism so that it could be preserved.

[6] Quoted in Chandler, op. cit., pp. 41–42.
[7] Quoted in Huberman, op. cit., p. 260.

Keynes began his analysis by looking at the process of production. In a given production period a firm produces a certain dollar volume of goods. From the proceeds of the sale of these goods, it pays its costs of production, which include wages, salaries, rent, supplies and raw materials, and interest on borrowed funds. What remains after these costs are paid is profit.

The important point to remember is this: What is a cost of production to the business firm represents income to an individual or another firm. The profit is also income—the income going to the owners of the firm. Because the value of production is exhausted by the costs of production and profits, and all these are income, it follows that the value of what has been produced must be equal to the incomes generated in producing it.

In terms of the entire economy the aggregate picture is the same as that for the individual firm: The value of everything produced in the economy during any period is equal to the total of all incomes received in that period. Therefore, in order for businesses to sell all that they have produced, people must spend in the aggregate all their incomes. If an amount equal to the total income in society is spent on goods and services, then the value of production is realized in sales. In that case profits remain high, and businessmen are willing to produce the same amount or more in the succeeding period.

Keynes called this a *circular flow:* Money flows from business to the public in the form of wages, salaries, rents, interests, and profits; this money then flows back to the businesses when the public buys goods and services from them. *As long as businesses sell all they have produced and make satisfactory profits,* the process continues.

But this does not happen automatically. When money flows from businesses to the public, some of it does not flow directly back to businesses. The circular flow has leakages. To begin with, all people do not spend all their incomes. A percentage is saved, usually in banks, and therefore withdrawn from the spending stream. This saving may be offset by other people, who borrow money from banks and spend more than their income. Keynes, however, pointed out that at the peak of prosperity saving is usually greater than consumer borrowing; thus there is usually net saving, or a net leakage, from circular income-expenditure flow.

Keynes also identified two other leakages: (1) People buy goods and services from foreign businesses, but the money spent on these imports cannot be spent on domestically produced goods. (2) The taxes people pay are also withdrawn from the income-expenditure flow.

These three leakages (savings, imports, and taxes) may be offset by three spending injections into the income-expenditure flow: (1) Imports can be offset by exports. They are exactly offset when foreigners buy goods produced in the United States in amounts equal to foreign imports purchased by Americans. (2) The government uses taxes to finance the purchase of goods and services. If it uses all taxes for this purpose and balances the budget, then government expenditures will exactly offset taxes in the spending stream. (3) If businessmen wish to expand their capital, they can finance investment in capital goods by borrowing the funds that were saved. Investment, then, may exactly offset the saving leakage.

If these three injections into the income-expenditure flow are just as large as the three leakages, then spending equals the value of production. Everything that has been produced can be sold, and prosperity reigns.

Keynes, however, believed it was unlikely that the process could continue uninterrupted for very long. Investment, which is necessary to absorb savings, enlarges the capital stock and hence increases the economy's productive capacity. In order to utilize the new productive capacity fully, production and income must increase in the next period. But with the higher income there will be more saving, which necessitates more investment; and this investment is by no means automatically forthcoming.

Keynes saw that individuals with higher incomes saved a higher percentage of their incomes than those with low incomes. He concluded that this pattern would hold for the whole society. As the aggregate income of society increases, total savings increases more than proportionately. In other words, at each new higher level of income a larger percentage of income is saved.

Thus investment would have to increase at a faster rate than income if it were to continually offset saving. Only this rapid increase would permit businesses to sell everything they produced; but the faster investment grows, the more rapid is the increase in productive capacity. Because of this, the economy must invest ever-greater amounts (both absolutely and relatively) in each successive period if the balance is to be maintained. However, according to Keynes, in any mature private enterprise economy the number of profitable investment outlets is limited. Hence, as the process of economic growth continues, the difficulty of finding sufficient investment outlets becomes more and more acute.

If it becomes impossible to find enough investment outlets, then investment falls short of saving and total expenditures for goods and services fall short of the value of those produced. Businesses, unable to sell all they have produced, find that their inventories of unsold goods are increasing. Each business sees only its own problem: that it has produced more than it can sell. It therefore reduces production in the next period. Most businesses, being in the same situation, do the same thing. The results are a large reduction of production, a decrease in employment, and a decline in income. With the decline in income, however, even less will be spent on goods and services in the next period. So businessmen find that even at the lower level of production they are unable to sell all they have produced. Again they cut back production, and the downward spiral continues.

Under these circumstances businesses have little or no incentive to expand their capital goods (because excess capacity already exists), and therefore investment falls drastically. Expenditures of all types plummet. As income declines, saving declines more than proportionately. This process continues until the declines in income have reduced saving to the point where it no longer exceeds the reduced level of investment. At this low level of income equilibrium is restored. Leakages from the income-expenditure flow are again equal to the injections into it. The economy is stabilized, but at a level where high unemployment and considerable unused productive capacity exists.

Keynes' analysis was not, in its essentials, drastically different from those offered by Marx (Chapter 6) and Hobson (Chapter 10). The principal cause of a depression was, in the opinion of all three thinkers, the inability of capitalists to find sufficient investment opportunities to offset the increasing levels of saving generated by economic growth. Keynes' unique contribution was to show how.

the relation of saving to income could lead to a stable but depressed level of income with widespread unemployment.

Marx (and Lenin) had believed the disease incurable under capitalism. Hobson had prescribed measures to equalize the distribution of income and thereby reduce saving as a cure. Could Hobson's prescription work? This probably is not a very meaningful question. In most industrial capitalist countries wealth and economic power determine political power, and those who wield power have never been willing to sacrifice it to save the economic system.

In the United States, for example, of the 300,000 nonfinancial corporations existing in 1925 the largest 200 made considerably more profit than the other 299,800 combined. The wealthiest 5 percent of the population owned virtually all the stocks and bonds and received over 30 percent of the income. Needless to say, this 5 percent dominated American politics. In these circumstances speculating about what would happen if the income and wealth were radically redistributed amounts to mere fanciful daydreaming.

Keynes' answer to the problem was more realistic. Government could step in when saving exceeded investment, borrow the excess saving, then spend the money on socially useful projects. These projects would be chosen in order not to increase the economy's productive capacity or decrease the investment opportunities of the future. This government spending would increase the injections into the spending stream and create a full-employment equilibrium. In doing so, it would not add to the capital stock. Therefore, unlike investment spending, it would not make a full-employment level of production more difficult to attain in the next period. Keynes summarized his position thus:

> Ancient Egypt was doubly fortunate, and doubtless owed to this its fabled wealth, in that it possessed *two* activities, namely, pyramid-building as well as the search for precious metals, the fruits of which, since they could not serve the needs of many by being consumed, did not stale with abundance. The Middle Ages built cathedrals and sang dirges. Two pyramids, two masses for the dead, are twice as good as one; but not so two railways from London to York.[8]

What types of expenditures ought the government to make? Keynes himself had a predilection toward useful public works such as the construction of schools, hospitals, parks, and other public conveniences. He realized, however, that this would probably benefit middle- and lower-income recipients much more than the wealthy. And because the wealthy have the political power, they would probably insist on policies that would not redistribute income away from them. He saw that it might be politically necessary to channel this spending into the hands of the large corporations, even though little that was beneficial to society would be accomplished directly. He wrote:

> If the Treasury were to fill old bottles with banknotes, bury them at suitable depths in disused coalmines which are then filled up to the surface with town rubbish, and leave it to private enterprise on well-tried principles of laissez faire to dig the notes up again . . . there need be no more unemployment. . . . It

---

[8] J.M. Keynes, *The General Theory of Employment, Interest and Money* (New York: Harcourt Brace Jovanovich, 1936), p. 131.

would indeed be more sensible to build houses and the like; but if there are political and practical difficulties in the way of this, the above would be better than nothing.[9]

The depression of the 1930s dragged on until the outbreak of World War II. From 1936 (the year Keynes' *General Theory* was published) to 1940, economists hotly debated the merits of his theory and policy prescriptions. When the various governments began to increase armament production rapidly, however, unemployment began to melt away. During the war years, under the stimulus of enormous government expenditures, conditions in most capitalist economies were rapidly transformed from a situation of severe unemployment to one of acute labor shortage.

The American armed forces mobilized 14 million people, who had to be armed, quartered, and fed. Between 1939 and 1944 the output of the manufacturing, mining, and construction industries doubled, and productive capacity increased by 50 percent. The American economy produced 296,000 planes, 5,400 cargo ships, 6,500 naval vessels, 64,500 landing craft, 86,000 tanks, and 2,500,-000 trucks.[10] During the war period the most pressing problem was a *shortage* of labor, as contrasted with the 19 percent unemployment that existed as late as the beginning of 1939.

KEYNESIAN ECONOMICS AND IDEOLOGY

Most economists believed this wartime experience had proved the basic correctness of Keynes' ideas. Capitalism could be saved, they proclaimed, by wise use of the government's powers to tax, borrow, and spend money. Capitalism was again a viable social and economic system.

But viability alone was insufficient as an ideology for capitalism. The USSR did not have unemployment in the 1930s, and its spectacular rate of growth during this period had proved the viability of the Soviet economic system. This challenge elicited a resurgence of the older neoclassical economic ideology. These older theories were cast in an esoteric and highly elaborate mathematical framework. Typical of the new economists was Paul A. Samuelson, whose book *The Foundations of Economic Analysis* is among the technically most formidable treatments of economics.[11] In 1947 The American Economic Association awarded him the first John Bates Clark Medal for the most outstanding contribution to economics made by an economist under 40 years of age. The book was also instrumental in securing the Nobel Prize in economics for Samuelson in 1970.

Samuelson has made an even more significant contribution in terms of his influence on the dominant economic ideology of capitalism in the past 25 years. His introductory text, *Economics,* has undergone ten editions, has been translated into almost every major language, and has sold millions of copies.[12] The

9 Ibid., p. 129.

10 All figures taken from Hacker, op. cit., p. 325.

11 Paul A. Samuelson, *The Foundations of Economic Analysis* (Cambridge, Mass.; Harvard University Press, 1947).

12 Paul A. Samuelson, *Economics* (New York: McGraw-Hill, 1948).

first edition set out mainly to explain and simplify Keynes' ideas. Each subsequent edition has tended to bring in more of the traditional neoclassical ideology of capitalism. In 1955 Samuelson offered his "grand neoclassical synthesis," an integration of Keynesian with neoclassical economics. The Keynesian theory would provide the knowledge necessary to maintain a full-employment economy, and the market system could operate within this Keynesian framework to allocate resources according to the time-honored principles of the neoclassical ideology. Almost every student of economics in the past 25 years has learned his elementary economics from Samuelson's textbook or from one of the many others that have attempted to copy his approach and content.

THE EFFICACY OF KEYNESIAN ECONOMIC POLICIES

After 1945, Keynesian economics became orthodoxy for both economists and the majority of politicians. Almost 3 million veterans were demobilized in that year. In 1946 another 11 million joined the civilian labor force. Congress and many economists feared a new depression and immediately took steps to apply the new Keynesian ideas. Passage of the Employment Act of 1946 legally obligated the government to use its taxing, borrowing, and spending powers to maintain full employment. The act declared that "it is the continuing policy and responsibility of the Federal government to use all practicable means . . . for the purpose of creating and maintaining . . . conditions under which there will be afforded useful employment opportunities, including self-employment, for those able, willing, and seeking to work, and to promote maximum employment, production and purchasing power." This was the first time the U.S. government ever acknowledged responsibility for employment, and it is still not really committed to full employment for all people.

Have Keynesian economic policies worked? The answer to this question is very complex. Since World War II there have been no major depressions in the United States, but there have been five recessions (the modern euphemism for a mild depression). In 1948–1949, a recession lasted for 11 months; in 1953–1954, for 13 months; in 1957–1958, for 9 months; and in 1960–1961, for 9 months. The 1969–1971 recession went on for over two years.

Because of these recessions, the economy's performance in the 1950s left much to be desired. The real rate of growth of GNP was 2.9 percent, which does not compare very favorably with the 4.7 percent for 1920–1929 or the 3.7 percent for 1879–1919. The brightest spot in the American economy's performance has been the growth rate in the 1960s, which averaged around 5 percent.

Unemployment for the 1950s and early 1960s averaged 4.5 percent, although it dipped to 3.5 percent in the mid-1960s. Moreover, inflation has been a persistent problem since World War II. From 1945 through 1968 the average annual increase in wholesale prices was 3.8 percent (most of which occurred in the late 1940s); the rate of increase from 1968 to 1970 was nearly 5 percent. The 1969–1971 inflation was accompanied by an economic recession in which unemployment soared to rates of over 6 percent. The simultaneous occurrence of both high unemployment and a high rate of inflation led to President Nixon's attempt to freeze wage and prices in late 1971, followed by government control over increases in wages and prices.

Economists like Samuelson argued that Keynesian policies, reflected in enormous government spending, resulted in the impressive growth performance of the 1960s; but they find the accompanying inflation quite mysterious. Before judging this performance, however, it is necessary to see what the American government substituted for the pyramids of Egypt and the cathedrals of the Middle Ages. In 1960 one observer wrote: "A central aspect of our growth experience of the past two decades is one which few spokesmen for the future candidly discuss. This is the fact that our great boom did not begin until the onset of World War II, and that its continuance since then has consistently been tied to a military rather than to a purely civilian economic demand."[13]

THE WARFARE ECONOMY

In 1940 military-related expeditures were $3.2 billion, or 3.2 percent of GNP. In 1943, at the height of World War II, military spending gobbled up almost 40 percent of GNP, while profits rose to unprecedented heights. The war provided capitalists with a clear example of how government military spending can end a depression and guarantee large returns to capital.

By 1947 military spending was back to only $9.1 billion, or 3.9 percent of GNP. During the rapid growth of the 1960s, military expenditures grew at approximately the same rate as GNP. If other expenses that are related to militarism but not included in the "defense" budget are taken into account, the total has been close to 15 percent in recent years.[14] The United States has spent and continues to spend more on militarism than any other country—more in absolute terms, relative terms, and per capita.

The result of these enormous expenditures has been the growth of the *military-industrial complex* as a necessary adjunct to economic prosperity. Its essential features have been described as follows:

> The warfare state we have constructed over the last two generations has a large clientele. At the top of the pyramid is the so-called military-industrial complex. It comprises, first, the Defense Department of the Federal Government, along with such satellites as the CIA and NASA. The admirals and generals, the space scientists and the intelligence men, like all government bureaucrats, are busily engaged in strengthening their influence. To this end they cultivate congressmen and senators, locate military establishments in politically strategic districts, and provide legislators with special favors. Former military men are drawn into the net of influence through the Army and Navy associations and through veterans' organizations. The military are supported by the industrial side of the complex. These are the large corporations on whom the military depend for the hardware of modern war. Some sell the bulk of their output to the military, like North American Aviation, Lockheed Aircraft, General Dynamics, McConnell-Douglas, and Thiokol Chemical. Others are important

[13] Robert Heilbroner, *The Future as History* (New York: Harper & Row, 1960), p. 133.
[14] See, for example, Daniel R. Fusfeld, "Fascist Democracy in the United States," *Conference Papers of the Union for Radical Economics*, December 1968, pp. 11, 34–35.

military suppliers but make the bulk of their sales in civilian markets, such as Western Electric, Sperry Rand, General Electric or IBM. Others, such as Dupont and General Motors, are only occasionally military contractors.[15]

The extent to which military production dominates the American economy is indicated by a recent survey showing that the five key military-related industries accounted for 7.9 percent of all employment in New York, 12.3 percent in New Jersey, 13 percent in Texas, 14.6 percent in Massachusetts, 15.7 percent in Maryland, 20.9 percent in Florida, 23.4 percent in Connecticut, 30 percent in Kansas, 31.4 percent in California, and 34.8 percent in Washington.[16]

Military expenditures operate in exactly the way Keynes believed pyramid building operated in the ancient Egyptian economy. For generals and most politicians, a tenfold overkill potential is twice as good as a fivefold overkill; two ABM (antiballistic missle) systems are twice as good as one but only half as good as four. And if the public cannot be easily convinced of this, the immense amount of research financed by the military-industrial complex comes to the fore. Weapons and delivery systems are rapidly superseded by new models. Horror stories convince the public that a further escalation of the arms race is necessary and that "obsolete" (and often unused) models must be scrapped.

Military spending keeps the capital goods industry operating near full capacity without raising the economy's productive capacity as rapidly as would be the case if they provided capital goods for industry. Demand does not tend to drop below supply as persistently as it formerly did; military spending increases demand without increasing productivity.

The neglect of these effects of the Keynesian military-induced prosperity is perhaps "the most important abdication of any by the economists."[17] This type of economic theory has led to "an ahistorcal, a technical or mechanical, a nonpolitical view of what the economy is and how it works."[18]

Very few Keynesian economists have been willing to come to grips with the implication of militarism as a tool of economic policy.

> The arms economy has been the major Keynesian instrument of our times. But its use has been cloaked as "national interest," its effects have been largely undermined, its international consequences largely deleterious and destabilizing, its importance making for uncritical acceptance and dependence by large segments of the society, its long-run effects hardly glanced at. The arms economy has done much more than distort the use of scarce creative scientific and engineering talent. . . . It has forced us to neglect a whole range of urgent social proprities, the consequences of which threaten the fabric of our society.[19]

SUMMARY

The severity of the Great Depression of the 1930s caused many economists to become dissatisfied with the orthodox neoclassical economists' view that unem-

---

[15] Ibid., p. 13.
[16] Ibid., p. 15.
[17] Sumner M. Rosen, "Keynes Without Gadflies," in T. Roszak, ed., The Dissenting Academy (New York: Random House, Vintage Books, 1968), p. 83.
[18] Ibid., p. 85.
[19] Ibid., pp. 86–87.

ployment was merely a short-run, ephemeral "adjustment" to a temporary disequilibrium situation. Keynes' new ideas were rapidly accepted by most important economists. World War II proved that massive government intervention in the market economy could create full employment; indeed, Hitler's Germany had already established this in the 1930s.

Since the war the United States has not had a major depression. Most economists agree that massive government spending is largely responsible for this improved performance of American capitalism. Critics have argued, however, that the social price of this prolonged prosperity has been the creation of a military-industrial complex that currently threatens the entire fabric of American society.

If this view is correct, then it is possible to conclude that Keynes' theories enabled the neoclassical ideology to come to grips with the most important economic problem of the 1930s but have obscured if not worsened other problems. Some of these problems and some contemporary ideologies of capitalism will be examined in Chapter 12.

CHAPTER 12

CONTEMPORARY AMERICAN CAPITALISM AND ITS DEFENDERS

Since World War II the American economy has experienced five mild recessions, albeit its growth has been fairly satisfactory by historical standards. Gross national product in constant (1958) dollars, grew from $355 billion in 1950 to $727 billion in 1969. Disposable personal income, again in constant (1958) dollars, grew from $250 billion to $512 billion over the same period.[1] Although the growth rate was slightly below the historical average in the 1950s, it was well above average in the 1960s.

The technological advances of American capitalism have been particularly impressive. For several decades before World War I, the increases in output per man-hour in American industry had been about 22 percent per decade. After World War II, output per man-hour increased by 35–40 percent per decade.[2] This growth was made possible by huge expenditures on research and development, which increased from $3.4 billion in 1950 to $12 billion in 1960; fully half of these funds came from the federal government.

With these improvements in technology and increases in production has come a greater concentration of economic power in the hands of a very small number of corporations. In 1929, the 100 largest manufacturing corporations had legal control (actual control being far greater) of 44 percent of the net capital assets of all manufacturing corporations. By 1962, this figure had increased to 58 percent.[3]

In 1962 there were 420,000 manufacturing enterprises. But a mere 5 of these enterprises owned 12.3 percent of all manufacturing assets; 20 owned 25 percent of the total. The total assets of the 20 largest firms were approximately as large as those of the 419,000 smallest companies combined. These 20 giants took a whopping 38 percent of all after-tax profits, leaving the smallest 419,980 to divide 62 percent. Furthermore, among the 180,000 *corporations* involved in manufacturing, the net profits of the 5 largest were nearly twice as large as those of the 178,000 smallest corporations.[4]

---

[1] Figures taken from *Federal Reserve Bulletin.* August 1970, pp. A68–A69.

[2] Louis M. Hacker, *The Course of American Economic Growth and Development* (New York: Wiley, 1970), p. 326. The increases in productivity in the 1920s had been even more impressive, however.

[3] Gardiner C. Means, "Economic Concentration," in *Hearings Before the Subcommittee on Antitrust and Monopoly of the Committee on the Judiciary, United States Senate* (Washington, D.C.: GPO, July 1964), pp. 9–19.

[4] Willard F. Mueller, "Economic Concentration," *Hearings,* op. cit., pp. 111–129.

Table 12.1 **Large Mergers and Acquisitions, 1966-1968**

	1966	1967	1968
Total number of acquisitions	1746	2384	4003
Number of acquired manufacturing and mining companies with more than $10 million in assets	101	169	192
Value of assets of acquired companies with more than $10 million in assets (in billions)	$4.1	$8.2	$12.6
Number of acquisitions made by 200 largest companies	33	67	74
Value of assets of companies acquired by 200 largest companies (in billions)	$2.4	$5.4	$6.9

The rate of concentration has quickened. In every year since 1959, there have been more than 60 mergers a year involving the acquisition of companies with over $10 million in assets. The number of mergers increased throughout the sixties. Table 12.1 illustrates this trend.[5] From 1968 to 1970 the evidence points to an ever-faster rate of acquisition. The process of increasing economic concentration, which began about 100 years ago, continues unabated today.

The post-World War II prosperity has not reduced the extremes of inequality in the United States. In the most complete study of the distribution of ownership of wealth ever undertaken,[6] it has been shown that the wealthiest 1.6 percent of the population owns over 80 percent of all corporate stock and virtually all state and local government bonds. Moreover, the concentration of ownership of these income-yielding assets has steadily increased since the early 1920s.

The distribution of income reflects the same extreme inequality. Despite the economy's impressive growth over the past three decades—and the much-publicized war on poverty of the early 1960s, which proved to be a half-hearted minor skirmish—poverty has remained an acute problem in the United States. In 1975, for example, 26 million Americans lived in families that had an annual income of less than $5500, the officially designated "poverty level."[7] The U.S. Bureau of Labor Statistics (BLS) reported that with the high prices that prevailed in 1975 it would require about $9198 for a family of four to live with "a sense of self-respect and social participation."[8] Thus most of these 26 million persons lived on less than half the amount necessary to generate "self-respect." Tens of millions more lived on less than $9198.

In stark contrast to this widespread poverty, the wealthiest 5 percent of the American population received over 20 percent of all income. At the top of this 5

---

[5] Table constructed from data of the Federal Trade Commission, derived by Paul Sweezy and Harry Magdoff, in "The Merger Movement: A Study in Power," *The Monthly Review*, June 1969, pp. 1–5.

[6] Robert J. Lampman, *The Share of Top Wealth-holders in National Wealth, 1922-1956* (Princeton, N.J.: Princeton University Press, 1962).

[7] Bureau of the Census, *Statistical Abstract of the United States for 1975* (Washington, D.C.: GPO, 1975), pp. 392, 401.

[8] Reported in *Los Angeles Times*, Sept. 26, 1976, p. 1.

percent was the elite 1.6 percent that owns most of the income-yielding stocks and bonds in the United States. The richest of the elite had incomes estimated between $50 million and $100 million per year (the latter amounts to about $275,000 per day).

Furthermore, taxes do little, if anything, to reduce the inequities in the distribution of income. It is commonly supposed that the U.S. tax system reduces inequality by taking a higher percentage of the income of the wealthy than is taken from the poor. The personal income tax does tend to reduce income inequalities, but the effect is much smaller than most people imagine. When economists analyze the total tax burden, however, they find that taxes actually increase inequality in the distribution of income because sales taxes, excise taxes, property taxes, and social security taxes all take a much larger percentage of the poor man's income than of the rich man's.

One economist, a recognized authority on taxes, has analyzed the total tax burden on incomes along the entire distribution spectrum. He found that families with incomes below $2,000 per year—certainly a level of abject poverty—paid out one-third of their income in taxes. As incomes got higher, people paid a lower percentage of their income in taxes. For example, families making between $10,000 and $15,000 paid out a proportion of their income that was nearly one-third lower than that paid by families with incomes below $2,000. Only among the wealthiest 5 percent of families did the total tax bite exceed that exacted from the poorest. The wealthy elite actually paid out, on the average, 36.3 percent of their income for taxes, a mere 3 percent higher than the poorest segment of society paid.[9]

Thus it appears that on the one hand American capitalism in the past three decades has proved fairly successful if judged solely by the criteria of economic growth and productivity (although there has been persistent unemployment and inflation). On the other hand, the extreme inequalities in the distribution of wealth and income have continued and even grown worse. It is not surprising, therefore, that these decades have seen numerous ideological defenses of American capitalism as well as socialist and radical critiques of the U.S. economy.

CONTEMPORARY CLASSICAL LIBERAL IDEOLOGY

Neoclassical economics was the principal purveyor of the classical liberal ideology of capitalism during the late nineteenth and early twentieth centuries. Since the 1930s, neoclassical economics has become more and more complex mathematically, which has enabled modern economists to gain many new theoretical and scientific insights. Its most important assumptions, however, those on which the entire theory rests, are still metaphysical in character. They have not been established on a scientific basis, either empirically or theoretically.

The finest summary of contemporary neoclassical economics is C. E. Ferguson's *The Neoclassical Theory of Production and Distribution*.[10] The mathemat-

[9] B. A. Musgrave, "Estimating the Distribution of the Tax Burden," in *Income and Wealth*, ser. 10 (Cambridge, England: Bowes & Bowes, 1964), p. 192.

[10] C. E. Ferguson, *The Neoclassical Theory of Production and Distribution* (London: Cambridge University Press, 1969).

ical reasoning in this book is so complex that very few people other than professional economists who are thoroughly competent in higher mathematics can understand it. Professor Ferguson is aware, however, of the tenuous nature of many of the assumptions of this ideology, which, like the medieval religious ideology of feudalism, ultimately must be accepted on faith alone. He admits this and asserts his personal faith: ". . . placing reliance upon neoclassical economic theory is a matter of faith. I personally have the faith; but at present the best I can do to convince others is to invoke the weight of Samuelson's authority. . . ."[11]

When the thrust toward esoterica removed classical liberal ideology from the level at which it could be widely understood, however, it also substantially reduced its effectiveness as a popular ideology of capitalism. To promote widespread popular acceptance of the ideology has been the task of numerous organizations. The best-known American organizations, which propagate a simplified, more popular version of the classical ideology, are the National Association of Manufacturers (NAM), the Foundation for Economic Education, the Committee for Constitutional Government, the U.S. Chamber of Commerce, and the American Enterprise Association.

A congressional committee found that out of $33.4 million spent "to influence legislation" $32.1 million was spent by large corporations. And of this $32.1 million about $27 million went to such organizations as those mentioned in the previous paragraph.[12] The NAM uses this money to publish a large amount of probusiness propaganda, including "an educational literature series, labor and industrial relations bulletins, news bulletins, a magazine of American affairs, and numerous studies on legislation, education, anti-trust laws, tariffs and unions."[13]

The Foundation for Economic Education reviews and distributes books that reflect the classical liberal ideology of capitalism and publishes and distributes, free of charge, a monthly journal, *The Freeman,* which propagates this ideology. The other organizations engage in numerous publishing and promotional activities designed to inculcate the same ideology as widely as possible.

The popularized statement of the classical ideology lays principal stress on the benefits of the free market. It is argued that the forces of supply and demand in a free market will always lead to results that are preferable to anything that could be achieved by the government or a central planning agency. The NAM, for example, asserts that the proper function of the government is to strengthen and "make more effective the regulation by competition."[14] Almost none of its literature, however, suggests much concern with the concentration of corporate power. Rather, the main economic problems are the powers of big labor unions and the "socialistic" welfare measures of the government.

In essence, most of this literature uses a drastically simplified version of some of the classical and neoclassical economists' analyses. It supports the view that

---

[11] Ibid., pp. xvii–xviii, Professor Ferguson's candid admission was prompted by a rather esoteric debate among academic economists. The debate proved conclusively that some of the most fundamental tenets of neoclassical orthodoxy were untenable. For a summary of the conclusions of the debate, see E. K. Hunt, "Religious Parable Versus Economic Logic: An Analysis of the Recent Controversy in Value, Capital and Distribution Theory," *Inter-Mountain Economic Review,* (Fall 1971; also see sec. III of E. K. Hunt and Jesse Schwartz, *Critique of Economic Theory* (London: Penguin, 1972).

[12] R. Joseph Monsen, Jr., *Modern American Capitalism* (Boston: Houghton Mifflin, 1963), p. 19.

[13] Ibid.

[14] National Association of Manufacturers, Economic Principles Commission, *The American Individual Enterprise System, Its Nature and Future* (New York: McGraw-Hill, 1946), p. 57.

any conceivable threat to the operation of the free market, whether real or potential, is an evil to be avoided at any cost. These organizations have had considerable success in propagating this point of view, particularly among small businessmen. (Big business, however, generally continues to look with favor on government intervention because it usually benefits from such actions.)

CONTEMPORARY VARIANTS OF THE CLASSICAL LIBERAL IDEOLOGY

Most critics of the classical liberal ideology emphasize its failure to come to grips with the realities of the concentration of immense power in the hands of considerably less than 1 percent of all corporations. Several attempts have been made to construct an ideology that retains the competitive, private enterprise flavor of classical liberalism while recognizing the existence of concentrated corporate power. Two of these will be discussed: the *contervailing power* ideology, associated primarily with the economist John Kenneth Galbraith, and the *people's capitalism* ideology, associated primarily with Professor Massimo Salvadori.

In his famous book *American Capitalism, the Concept of Countervailing Power,* Professor Galbraith recognized the existence of large, special interest power blocks in the American economy but argued then that they should not be of much concern because "private economic power begets the countervailing power of those who are subject to it."[15] The result of this newly created countervailing power is "the neutralization of one position of power by another."[16]

Thus strong unions neutralize strong business firms in the field of labor relations, and strong buyers' associations neutralize the monopolistic or oligopolistic powers of strong sellers. The result, then, is a kind of market equilibrium or invisible hand that harmonizes the interests of all. The harmonious whole is now simply made up of a few neutralized giants rather than numerous, atomistically competitive small firms.[17]

Another influential attempt to show the innocuous (or even beneficial) nature of corporate concentration was made by Professor Salvadori, who used the slogan "people's capitalism" to characterize what he believed to be the most essential feature of contemporary American capitalism: diffusion of ownership. The widespread diffusion of ownership of corporate stock, as well as other types of assets, means to Salvadori that capitalism is no longer a system where a tiny minority reaps most of the privileges but one in which the majority are rapidly becoming capitalists and getting a share of the privileges.[18] Salvadori has conveniently summarized his people's capitalism ideology:

[15] John Kenneth Galbraith, *American Capitalism, the Concepts of Countervailing Power* (Boston: Houghton Mifflin, 1956), p. 4.

[16] Ibid., p. 1.

[17] It should be mentioned that Professor Galbraith has published several books since *American Capitalism, the Concept of Countervailing Power* appeared. Even a cursory reading of these books shows that he has altered his opinions fundamentally. Nevertheless, because the ideology of countervailing power has been very influential, and because most of this influence flows from his book, we are justified in associating this ideology with his name.

[18] This is curiously similar to socialist Eduard Bernstein's idea, discussed in Chapter 9.

At present in the United States there are nearly half a million corporations; stockholders total about ten million (1959). Their numbers have increased rapidly in the post-war period. Standard Oil of New Jersey, for instance, had about 160,000 stockholders in 1946; twelve years later there were three times as many, close to half a million. As a rule, the larger the corporation the more widely spread the ownership. Large corporations in which a majority of shares are owned by an individual or by a family are fewer and fewer. It is already exceptional for a single individual to own more than four or five per cent of the stock of a given corporation. Unincorporated non-farm businesses number about four million; they belong to one or more individuals and this means millions of "capitalists." Nearly four million farmers (three-fourths of the total) are full owners or part owners of the farms they cultivate. Even considering that there is a good deal of overlapping among the three groups (shareholders, individual non-farm owners, farmers) one can say that at least one-fourth to one-third of all American families share the ownership of natural and artifical capital. There are also half a million independent professional people—lawyers, doctors, architects, engineers, accountants, etc.—whose other means of production are not only equipment of one kind or another but also skill and training, and whose income is related to the capital invested in acquiring professional efficiency; they are "capitalists" just as much as owners of natural and artifical capital. Most other families own durable consumer goods (houses, summer cottages, furniture, cars, electrical appliances, etc.), federal, state, and muncipal bonds, insurance policies and savings to the extent that they can consider themselves "capitalists."[19]

Thus bigness of corporations does not, for Salvadori, appear to be an issue. Ownership is becoming more equitably distributed because most people are becoming "capitalists," and hence, by implication, none is powerful enough to exploit another. Disciples point out that by 1970 there were approximately 30 million stockholders. In this view the United States is becoming a nation where the majority are capitalists.

Even many defenders of capitalism concede that Salvadori's analysis serves only to obscure the nature of the concentration of economic power in the United States and that it neither eliminates nor justifies this concentration. A. A. Berle, Jr., a distinguished scholar of American capitalism as well as a corporation executive, has written:

In terms of power, without regard to asset positions, not only do 500 corporations control two-thirds of the non-farm economy, but within each of that 500 a still smaller group has the ultimate decision-making power. That is, I think, the highest concentration of economic power in recorded history. . . . Since the United States carries on not quite half of the manufacturing production of the entire world today, these 500 groupings—each with its own little dominating pyramid within it—represents a concentration of power over economies which makes the medieval feudal system look like a Sunday school party.[20]

Contrary to the tone of this quotation, Berle is not a critic of American capitalism but one of the most important developers of a contemporary corporate, or collec-

---

[19] Massimo Salvadori, *The Economics of Freedom* (Garden City, N.Y.: Doubleday, 1959), pp. 70–71.

[20] A. A. Berle, Jr., "Economic Power and the Free Society," in Andrew Hacker, ed., *The Corporation Take-Over* (Garden City, N.Y.: Doubleday, 1965), p. 97.

tive, ideology of capitalism. Other conservatives have admitted that a very small percentage of all the millions of stockholders hold most corporate stock.

THE CONTEMPORARY CORPORATE ETHIC
AND CAPITALIST IDEOLOGY

The tactics of the late nineteenth-century robber barons led most people to reject the corporate ideology (discussed in Chapter 8). Their destructive competition and financial wheeling and dealing hardly supported the conclusion that they were becoming socialized stewards of the public welfare. And yet the classical liberal ideology had no real defense for the existing concentration of economic and political power. The Christian paternalist ethic, with its emphasis on the benevolence of the powerful, was still the only successful ideological defense of great inequalities of wealth and power.

It was simply not credible to cast the nineteenth-century capitalist in a kindly, paternalistic role. But some twentieth-century ideologists of capitalism have argued that capitalism has changed so drastically that capitalists have lost their importance in the system and have been replaced by a new class of professional managers. These theories envision this "new man," the professional manager, as the paternalistic steward of public welfare.

In 1932 A. A. Berle and G. C. Means published an important and influential book, *The Modern Corporation and Private Property.*[21] In it they argued that ownership of most of the colossal corporate giants had become so widely diffused that the owners of stock had lost or were rapidly losing control of these corporations. With no single owner holding more than 1 or 2 percent of the stock and with no effective ways of colluding, the owners were left with only the formal voting function when selecting the board of directors. Candidates for whom they could vote were selected by the existing board of directors. Thus the boards chose their own replacements and were essentially a self-perpetuating oligarchy. They wielded power but had no necessary connection with the owners of stock. They were not capitalists in the usual sense of the term.

In 1955 Berle wrote another book, *The Twentieth Century Capitalist Revolution,* in which he argued that corporations had developed a quasipolitical status. Managers were motivated primarily by the desire to promote the general public interest in their decision making, and any who were not so motivated would be forced by public opinion and the threat of government intervention so to act. This view has been widely accepted. Another economist, for example, wrote:

> No longer the agent of proprietorship seeking to maximize return on investment, management sees itself as responsible to stockholders, employees, customers, the general public, and, perhaps most important, the firm as an institution. . . . There is no display of greed or graspingness; there is no attempt to push off onto workers or the community at large part of the social costs of the enterprise. The modern corporation is a soulful corporation.[22]

[21] A. A. Berle and G. C. Means, *The Modern Corporation and Private Property* (New York: Macmillan, 1932).

[22] Carl Kaysen, "The Social Significance of the Modern Corporation," *American Economic Review,* May 1957, pp. 313–314.

The corporation was "soulful," of course, because in this economist's opinion its managers were conscientious, paternalistic stewards of society's welfare.

The managerial ideology was spelled out in some detail in a series of lectures delivered by prominent corporation managers at Columbia University in 1956. According to the chairman of General Electric, the lectures were intended "to coax us businessmen out of our offices and into the arena of public thought where our managerial philosophies can be put to the test of examination by men trained in other disciplines."[23]

One of the dominant themes in these lectures was that because American capitalism is "new," the complaints people may once have had against capitalism are no longer justified. Thus the chairman of Sears Roebuck asserted, "The historic complaint that big business, as the producing arm of capitalism, exploited the many for the profit of the few and deprived the workers of the products of their own labor had a valid basis in the facts of European capitalism, but lacks substance when applied to American capitalism today."[24]

Another theme was the justification of bigness on the grounds of better efficiency and higher quality. "The American public," asserted the chairman of U.S. Steel, "has gradually become accustomed to larger and larger groups and has become convinced that big production groups are outstanding in reliability and in the quality of their products and services and are necessary to perform America's larger production tasks in research, in production, and in the procurement of raw materials."[25]

Finally, the businessmen all saw managers as "professionals" who are as much concerned with "customers, share owners, employees, suppliers, educational institutions, charitable activities, government and the general public" as with sales and profits. They believed that managers "all know that special power imposes special responsibilities on those who hold it." Most managers, they asserted, fully accept "their responsibilities for the broader public welfare."[26]

Since 1942 this corporate managerial ideology has been assiduously disseminated by the Committee for Economic Development (CED). The CED readily accepted big business and also "the fact that government was big and was constantly growing bigger and that there was no returning to a simpler, happier past in this respect. It believed that the question was not *how much* government should do, but *what* it should do."[27] Government should not only accept all the duties assigned to it by the classical liberal ideology but also follow Keynesian policies to ensure stable full employment. Further, government should cooperate with corporate management in resolving conflicts and maintaining the tranquil, stable atmosphere within which management can effectively perform its public-spirited, paternalistic function of promoting the public welfare.[28]

Big business and big government are accepted by this ideology as not only inevitable but also necessary for maximum effiency. Big labor unions are also

---

[23] Quoted in Robert L. Heilbroner, *The Limits of American Capitalism* (New York: Harper & Row, 1966), p. 30.

[24] Ibid., pp. 31–32.

[25] Ibid., p. 32.

[26] Quotations in this paragraph are all from ibid., pp. 32–33.

[27] Karl Schriftgiesser, *Business Comes of Age* (New York: Harper & Row, 1960), p. 224.

[28] See Monsen, op. cit., pp. 25–29.

accepted as long as they recognize that most of their legitimate interests are in harmony with those of business and management.

Another important propagator of the managerial ideology has been the U.S. Information Agency (USIA), the offical government agency charged with the worldwide propagandizing of the "American point of view," The USIA operates on a grand scale. Its Voice of America broadcasts are heard around the world daily in scores of languages, and it publishes dozens of newspapers and magazines, maintains libraries, shows motion pictures, and engages in countless other propaganda operations.

Arthur Larson, who "was a semi-official ideologist to the Eisenhower Administration and a former head of the U.S. Information Agency,"[29] published a book, *What We Are For,*[30] in which he explained the philosophy of USIA propaganda. In the modern capitalist economy, Larson argued, the government should do only what "needs to be done" and cannot be done "as well" by private businesses.[31] Modern capitalism has a multitude of powerful interest groups, such as big business, big unions, big government, and so forth, that have no major or basic conflicts. Rather, their interests harmonize, and they mutually support each other. Larson assumed both that business managers are motivated primarily by the desire to promote social welfare to meet the "basic political and economic needs of all people"[32] and that businesses operate more efficiently than government. There is therefore a built-in preference for a minimal role for government in the economy.[33]

CRITICISMS OF CONTEMPORARY CAPITALIST IDEOLOGIES

Criticisms of capitalism have often gone hand-in-hand with criticisms of capitalist ideologies. In the remainder of this chapter criticisms of the ideologies of capitalism will be examined. Some of the principal criticisms of contemporary American capitalism will be discussed in Chapter 13.

Criticisms of Neoclassical Ideology

Neoclassical economics completely dominated orthodox academic economics in the late nineteenth and early twentieth centuries. From the 1930s on, however, it came increasingly under attack. In 1938 Oscar Lange and Fred M. Taylor published their significant book *On the Economic Theory of Socialism.*[34] Lange and Taylor accepted the neoclassical argument that a "purely" and "perfectly" competitive economy will lead to an "optimum allocation of resources," but they also showed that such an economy need not be a capitalist one. They demon-

---

[29] Ibid., p. 42.

[30] Arthur Larson, *What We Are For* (New York: Harper & Row, 1959).

[31] Ibid., pp. 16–17.

[32] Monsen, op. cit., p. 45.

[33] Larson, op. cit., p. 17.

[34] Oscar Lange and Fred M. Taylor, *On the Economic Theory of Socialism* (Minneapolis: University of Minnesota Press, 1938). Lange had published his essay two years earlier in *Review of Economic Studies,* October 1936, pp. 53–71, and February 1937, pp. 123–142.

strated that a socialist economy, in which the means of production were collectively owned, could also operate (through perfect planning or decentralized decision making) in a state of "optimal economic efficiency." Private ownership had absolutely no formal or theoretical importance in the neoclassical theory. Furthermore, under socialist ownership, they argued, the inequities of income distribution under a capitalist system would disappear.

The conclusion that many people drew from this book was that the neoclassical liberal ideology could be used equally as well (if not better) as an ideology of socialism. This was, indeed, a radical undermining of neoclassical economics as an ideology defending capitalism.

The classical liberal ideology was rejected by many, however, because it seemed to present a severely distorted picture of the realities of twentieth-century capitalism. Its basic assumption of pure competition—that no buyers or sellers were large enough to affect prices—was patently ridiculous. Moreover, it had little or nothing to say about the important problem of pollution of the environment. Economists also established that simple countercyclical policies of the Keynesian variety were insufficient to obviate the problems of capitalism's cyclical instability[35] and cannot cope with inflation.

The *coup de grâce* came in J. De V. Graaff's tightly reasoned *Theoretical Welfare Economics*.[36] Graaff showed that economists had not really appreciated the long and restrictive list of assumptions necessary for the optimally efficient allocation of resources envisioned in the model of a competitive, free-market capitalism to be realized. He cited 17 such assumptions,[37] many of which were so restrictive and unrealistic that Graaff concluded that "the measure of acceptance . . . [this theory] has won among professional economists would be astonishing were not its pedigree so long and respectable."[38]

A few of Graaff's 17 conditions will suffice to illustrate his point. Neoclassical ideology requires that any individual's welfare is identical with his preference ordering. In other words, children, dope addicts, fiends, criminals, and lunatics, as well as all other people, always prefer that which is best for them. Neoclassical theory also requires that neither risk nor uncertainty is ever present. In the opinion of many, this book completely destroyed the basis for the economic analysis on which the classical liberal ideology was constructed.

Criticisms of the Managerial Ideology

The managerial ideology has also come under extensive criticism. Many economists (including several in the neoclassical tradition) argue that bigness on the scale of American big business cannot be shown to be related to efficiency or better service. Giant corporations are much larger than maximum productive efficiency would dictate. These economists contend that a drastic reduction in

---

[35] On this last point see Milton Friedman, "The Effects of a Full Employment Policy of Economic Stability: A Formal Analysis," in *Essays in Positive Economics* (Chicago: University of Chicago Press, 1953, and William J. Baumol, "Pitfalls in Counter-Cyclical Policies: Some Tools and Results," *The Review of Economics and Satistics*, February 1961, pp. 21–26.

[36] J. De V. Graaff, *Theoretical Welfare Economics* (London: Cambridge University Press, 1967).

[37] Ibid., pp. 142–154.

[38] Ibid., p. 142.

the size of many corporate giants would greatly increase productive efficiency.[39] Examples like the electric power industry's competition with the Tennessee Valley Authority (TVA), the oligopolistic airlines' struggle with small, unscheduled competitors, and the challenge to the American steel industry from foreign competition are used to point out that private profits and monopoly power, not social welfare or social efficiency, are the prime motivations of big business.[40]

Critics also argue that managers have exactly the same motives as owner-capitalists. They cite an extensive study of the behavior of "management-controlled" giant corporations, which showed that managers were as profit-oriented as owner-capitalists. The author of the study concluded that "it would appear that the proponents of theories of managerial discretion have expended considerable time and effort in describing a phenomenon of relatively minor importance. The large management-controlled corporations seem to be just as profit-oriented as the large owner-controlled corporations."[41]

Many critics assert that modern managers have no more social conscience or "soul" than the nineteenth-century robber barons. The late Professor Edwin H. Sutherland, once known as the "dean of American criminologists" and former president of the American Sociological Association, conducted a thorough and scholarly investigation of the extent to which corporate executives were involved in criminal behavior. He took the 70 largest nonfinancial corporations, made only a few additions and deletions (due to special circumstances), and traced their criminal histories through official histories and official records.[42] There were 980 court decisions against these corporations. One corporation had 50 decisions against it, and the average per corporation was 14. Sixty of the corporations had been found guilty of restraining trade; 53, of infringements; 44, of unfair labor practices; 28, of misrepresentation in advertising; 26, of giving illegal rebates; and 43, of a variety of other offenses. There were a total of 307 individual cases of illegal restraint of trade, 97 of illegal misrepresentation, 222 of infringement, 158 of unfair labor practices, 66 of illegal rebates, and 130 of other offenses.[43] Not all of those cases were explicit criminal cases. But 60 percent of the corporations had been found guilty of criminal offenses an average of 4 times each.

From May 10, 1950, to May 1, 1951, a U.S. Senate Special Committee to Investigate Crime in Interstate Commerce, under the chairmanship of Senator Estes Kefauver, probed the connections of business and organized crime. Senator Kefauver, Democratic vice-presidential candidate in 1956, later wrote a book based on those hearings. Although he emphasized the fact that there was no evidence to link most big corporations with organized crime, he was nevertheless greatly alarmed at the extent of such connections:

> I cannot overemphasize the danger that can lie in the muscling into legitimate fields by hoodlums . . . there was too much evidence before us of unreformed hoodlums gaining control of a legitimate business; then utilizing all his old mob

---

[39] See, for example, Walter Adams, "Competition, Monopoly, and Planning," in M. Zeitlin, ed., *American Society, Inc.* (Chicago: Markham, 1970), pp. 240–248.
[40] Ibid.
[41] Robert J. Larner, "The Effect of Management-Control on the Profits of Larger Corporations," in Zeitlin, op. cit., p. 258.
[42] Edwin H. Sutherland, *White Collar Crime* (New York: Holt, Rinehart & Winston, 1961).
[43] These data are summarized by F. Lundberg in *The Rich and The Super Rich* (New York: Bantam, 1968), pp. 131–132.

tricks—strong-arm methods, bombs, even murder—to secure advantages over legitimate competition. All too often such competition either ruins legitimate businessmen or drives them into emulating or merging with the gangsters. The hoodlums are also clever at concealing ownership of their investments in legitimate fields—sometimes . . . through "trustees" and sometimes by bamboozling respectable businessmen into "fronting" for them.[44]

In 1960 Robert Kennedy, who later became Attorney General of the United States, published *The Enemy Within*. He gathered the material for this book while serving as chief counsel of the U.S. Senate Select Committee on Improper Activities in the Labor or Management Field. Kennedy, like Kefauver, stressed the fact that he was not condemning all or even most businessmen. He wrote that

we found that with the present-day emphasis on money and material goods many businessmen were willing to make corrupt "deals" with dishonest union officials in order to gain competitive advantage or to make a few extra dollars. . . . We came across more than fifty companies and corporations that had acted improperly—and in many cases illegally—in dealings with labor unions . . . in the companies and corporations to which I am referring the improprieties and illegalities were occasioned solely by a desire for monetary gain. Furthermore we found that we could expect very little assistance from management groups. Disturbing as it may sound, more often the business people with whom we came in contact—and this includes some representatives of our largest corporations—were uncooperative.[45]

Kennedy's list of the names of offending companies included many of the largest and most powerful corporations in the United States.

Ferdinand Lundberg has described the extent to which corporate leaders and management receive either very light punishment or no punishment at all when they become involved in improprieties or illegalities. Among the many cases he cites is that of

the bribe of $750,000 by four insurance companies that sent Boss Pendergast of Missouri to jail, later to be pardoned by President Truman. . . . It was almost ten years before the insurance companies were convicted. Then they were only fined; no insurance executives went to jail. There was, too, the case of Federal Judge Martin Manton who was convicted of accepting a bribe of $250,000 from agents of the defendant when he presided over a case charging exorbitant salaries were improperly paid to officers of the American Tobacco Company. While the attorney for the company was disbarred from federal courts, the assistant to the company president (who made the arrangements) was soon thereafter promoted to vice president: a good boy.[46]

Critics of the managerial ideology do not cite such studies and examples to show businessmen to be criminals. Obviously most of them are not. The point they wish to make is that the power of monetary incentives and the quest for profits are no less pronounced among managers than among owner-capitalists. In fact, the pressure to acquire ever-increasing profits is so strong on many businessmen and managers that some persistently resort to illegal or improper means. With such pressures, the critics argue, society can ill afford to turn to the

---

[44] Estes Kefauver, *Crime in America* (Garden City, N.Y.: Doubleday, 1951), pp. 139–140.
[45] Robert Kennedy, *The Enemy Within* (New York: Harper & Row, 1960), p. 216.
[46] Lundberg, op. cit., p. 135.

managerial class for paternalistic stewardship of the social and economic welfare.

SUMMARY

Since World War II the concentration of corporate power has become more extreme, and inequalities of income distribution have been reduced very little, if at all. Despite these facts, many contemporary ideologies continue to rely on the classical liberal defense of capitalism. Other ideologists continue to place the corporate ethic at the base of their defense of capitalism. The latter group stresses the "efficient, far-sighted policies" of the large corporations, and the "professionalism" as well as "broad, humanistic concerns" of corporate managers. Critics of this point of view argue that corporate managers are motivated by the same force that moved nineteenth-century capitalists: the quest for maximum profits.

CHAPTER 13

CONTEMPORARY AMERICAN CAPITALISM AND ITS RADICAL CRITICS

Radical criticism of American capitalism was widespread during the depression of the 1930s. During the late forties and early fifties, however, pervasive repression of dissent, combined with a relatively prosperous economy, effectively stifled most radical criticism.[1]

All this changed abruptly in the 1960s and early 1970s. The two most important galvanizers of this resurgence of radical criticism were the civil rights movement and the war in Vietnam.

THE CIVIL RIGHTS MOVEMENT

The struggle for equality for blacks in America really began in 1619, when the first black slaves were brought to the colonies. Since that time the struggle has been nearly continuous. In the 1950s, however, the blacks' quest for their basic human rights entered a new phase.

On May 17, 1954, in the case of *Brown* v. *Board of Education of Topeka,* the U.S. Supreme Court unanimously concluded "that in the field of public education the doctrine of 'separate but equal' has no place!" and declared that "separate educational facilities are inherently unequal."

In 1954 and 1955, the few black individuals who applied for admission to white schools were rebuffed and very often suffered severe reprisals. It began to appear that the Court decision would have little effect on the patterns of segregation that then existed. In December 1955, however, a black woman in Montgomery, Alabama, refused to give up her bus seat to a white man. She was immediately arrested. Within days the blacks of Montgomery had organized a boycott of the bus company.

After one year of intense and bitter conflict, the protest ended in victory. The 50,000 blacks of Montgomery succeeded in getting the local bus segregation law nullified. This victory had a symbolic significance that was far greater than the particular issue of bus segregation. Blacks everywhere vicariously shared a new

---

[1] For a thorough description of the repression of this period, see Fred J. Cook, *The Nightmare Decade: The Life and Times of Senator Joe McCarthy* (New York: Random House, 1971). Also see Cedric Belfrage, *The American Inquisition, 1945–1960.* (New York: Bobbs-Merrill, 1973).

sense of dignity, freedom, and power. They began to organize actively to fight white racism.

Their attempts met with fanatical resistance. In the fall of 1957 Arkansas Governor Orville Faubus used armed troops to bar the entrance of nine black students into Central High School in Little Rock. The federal government interpreted this as a blatant challenge to its authority and sent in paratroopers to enforce the federal court orders. Many southern communities chose to close their public schools rather than allowing them to be integrated.

In 1957 and 1960 Congress passed civil rights acts designed to extend voting rights to blacks. The Kennedy Administration urged young people, black and white, to concentrate on a massive registration drive to get southern blacks on the voting lists. Attracting both radical critics of capitalism and liberal young people who generally did not seriously question the basic social and economic system of capitalism, the civil rights movement was nationwide. In the early 1960s the liberals dominated the movement numerically. They believed that a massive protest against racism would open the public's eyes and that an aroused population would demand new laws that would improve, if not completely cure, the situation.

During this period civil rights activists organized sit-ins at segregated lunch counters and bus depots, pray-ins at segregated churches, and wade-ins at segregated beaches. Massive nonviolent demonstrations or nonviolent civil disobedience, they hoped, would reach the consciences of enough people to achieve integration.

Despite some successes in terms of new civil rights legislation, disillusionment began to affect large numbers of blacks as well as white civil rights workers. They began to realize that political franchisement had little effect on the vast economic inequalities blacks suffered. Of what use was the vote if a black man or woman could not secure a job, or if he or she was paid a salary that kept the family in a condition of poverty and degradation? Whereas in 1950 the average salary earned by a black was 61 percent of that earned by a white, by 1962 it had fallen to 55 percent. In the face of massive civil rights movement, the relative economic position of the blacks had actually deteriorated. Furthermore, whereas in 1950 the rate of unemployment among blacks had been slightly less than twice as high as that for whites, by 1964 it was significantly more than twice as high. In 1947 blacks constituted 18 percent of the poorest class in America; by 1962 they accounted for 22 percent of this class.

Many civil rights advocates became convinced that the most significant barriers to black equality were economic. They turned their attention to a critical analysis of American capitalism as a means of understanding the perpetuation, indeed the worsening, of the inequalities suffered by blacks.

THE WAR IN VIETNAM

The other major force that helped spark the resurgence of radical criticism was the war in Vietnam. Throughout the 1950s the U.S. government consistently fought against fundamental social and political change in less developed countries. In the guise of "protecting the world from communism," the United States had intervened in the internal affairs of at least a score of countries. In some, like Guatemala and Iran, U.S. agents actually engineered the overthrow of the legitimate governments and replaced them with regimes more to American liking.[2]

Most criticism was muted by the political repression of McCarthyism. The college students of the 1950s, the "silent generation," generally acquiesced in the national mood of anticommunism that provided the justification for political repression at home and extensive intervention in other nations' internal affairs. During the 1950s American intervention in Vietnam attracted little special attention. It was merely one of many countries that were being "saved from communism." In the 1960s, however, all this was to change drastically. The Vietnam War became a powerful force in regenerating radical criticism of American capitalism. For this reason, a brief examination of the origins of the Vietnam War is needed here.

During the World War II occupation of Vietnam, the French colonial regime collaborated with the Japanese. Toward the end of the war the Japanese locked up the colonial administrators and established a puppet regime under the Annamite Emperor Bao Dai. Throughout this period the Americans and the French had supported a resistance movement, the Vietminh, headed by Ho Chi Minh. When Japan surrendered, there was a peaceful transfer of political power to the Vietminh.

The French did not want to lose this part of their colonial empire but realized that they were too weak to inflict a quick military defeat on the new government. On March 6, 1946, they signed an agreement with the Ho Chi Minh government that read in part, "The government of France recognizes the Republic of Vietnam as a free state having its government and its parliament, its army and its finances, forming part of the Indo-Chinese federation and of the French Union."[3] This agreement clearly intended that the Ho Chi Minh government would enjoy a status similar to the governments of the members of the British Commonwealth. It legally established Ho Chi Minh's regime as the legitimate government of *all* Vietnam. Nothing that subsequently occurred changed this essential fact.

The French were confident, however, that they could make a subservient puppet of Ho Chi Minh. They failed completely in this task. Unable to reduce Ho Chi Minh to this role, they brought back Emperor Bao Dai, even though he had voluntarily abdicated his throne, changed his name, and retired to Hong Kong. They "installed" him as "chief of state" and declared the Vietminh to be outlaws. There followed six years of intense, bitter warfare. Finally, in 1954, the Vietminh decisively defeated the French. The Geneva Accords of July 1954, which arranged for the French surrender, called for a cease-fire and a *temporary* separation of opposing forces. Ho Chi Minh's followers were to move north of the seventeenth parallel, and Emperor Bao Dai's were to move to the south. This arrangement was to end within two years with a national election to choose the leader of all Vietnam. Shortly after these negotiations American-backed Ngo Dinh Diem ousted Bao Dai, proclaimed the existence of a "Republic of Vietnam," and appointed himself its first president.

There were no elections. The Americans and Diem simply asserted that there

[2] For a popular account of these interventions, see David Wise and Thomas B. Ross, *The Invisible Government* (New York: Random House, 1964).

[3] Quoted in Leo Huberman and Paul M. Sweezy, "The Road to Ruin," *Monthly Review*, April 1965, p. 787.

were now two Vietnams. The reason for refusing to have the election was candidly admitted by President Eisenhower in his book *Mandate for Change:*

> I am convinced that the French could not win the war because the internal political situation in Vietnam, weak and confused, badly weakened their military position. I have never talked or corresponded with a person knowledgeable in Indochinese affairs who did not agree that had elections been held as of the time of the fighting, possibly 80 percent of the population would have voted for Communist Ho Chi Minh as their leader rather than chief of state Bao Dai.[4]

Obviously the substitution of Diem for Bao Dai did not change the situation.

This American-imposed solution was rejected not only by Ho Chi Minh and his followers in the North but also by people in the South. So the war of national liberation, which had been fought against the Japanese and the French, was continued against the United States.

Americans were repeatedly told that their government was fighting a war to protect the South Vietnamese from the armed aggression of North Vietnam. The North Vietnamese were pictured as violators of the Geneva agreements, determined to enslave the South Vietnamese.

Critics of American policy challenged this official version of the nature of the war. Their assessment of what was happening in Vietnam received widespread support in academic circles, and college campuses became centers of antiwar sentiment. From the early 1960s through about 1966, most opposition of the war was largely confined to the campuses. During the last years of the decade, however, people from all segments of society actively opposed the war. The antiwar movement had become a mass movement.

Finally, in 1968, U.S. Secretary of Defense Robert S. McNamara, himself becoming disillusioned with the official rationale for the war, ordered the U.S. Department of Defense to prepare an in-depth account of how the United States became involved. In early 1971 the report was completed. The 7000-page document was obtained by the *New York Times*, which paid researchers to determine whether new facts had been brought to light. The Defense Department admitted that (1) the Eisenhower Administration had played a "direct role in the ultimate breakdown of the Geneva settlement";[5] (2) from 1954 onward, the United States had engaged in "acts of sabotage and terror warfare against North Vietnam";[6] (3) the United States "encouraged and abetted the overthrow of President Ngo Dinh Diem" when he was no longer considered to be of use; (4) for many years before 1965 the U.S. government undertook "the careful preparation of public opinion for the years of open warfare that were to follow."[7]

American involvement increased steadily until by 1968 the United States had an army of over 500,000 men on Vietnamese soil and were spending nearly $3 billion per month ($100 million per day!) in the attempt to impose a "suitable political solution" on the Vietnamese.

American battle casualties rose until hundreds of thousands of Americans were wounded and well over 50,000 Americans were killed. Young people every-

---

[4] Quoted in ibid., p. 789.

[5] Quoted in Neil Sheehan, "The Story Behind the Vietnam War, Based on a Pentagon Study," *New York Times News Service*, June 13, 1971.

[6] Ibid.

[7] Ibid.

where began to question the morality of the war. Beginning in 1964, teach-ins protesting the war were mounted on college campuses around the United States. Most organizers and participants were convinced that American involvement in the war was a tragic mistake that would be rectified if the public could be made aware of the facts of the situation.

The antiwar movement grew rapidly. President Johnson's landslide victory in 1964, as well as his decision not to seek another term in 1968, are often attributed, at least in part, to the powerful, widespread opposition to the war. After a few years of debate, however, antiwar critics were convinced that most Americans did not know the basic facts of Vietnam and wanted a hasty end to the war. Yet the American government, without giving any convincing reasons for its actions, continued to seek military victory.

Critics began to ask whether there was not some deeper motive than simple anticommunist sentiment propelling the American government. In particular, they began to search for an economic motive or rationale for the war. They began seriously to reexamine the older radical theories of capitalist imperialism.

THE WOMEN'S LIBERATION MOVEMENT

The women's movement, like the black movement, did not suddenly spring into being in the 1960s out of thin air. The earliest political activity of a significant number of U.S. women came in the 1820s and 1830s in the abolitionist movement to end slavery. Experience in the abolitionist movement made women aware of their own oppression and gave them the confidence to build a movement of their own, especially because they were ignored or dismissed by some of the abolitionists. The women's movement before the Civil War fought not only for the abolition of slavery, but also for ending the laws that made the man the sole controller of all property and all decisions in marriage (even giving men guardianship of the children in event of separation), as well as for the right to vote.

The aftermath of the Civil War gave the vote to blacks—or, rather, it gave the formal right to black *men,* but with no mechanism of enforcement in the South. Women, both black and white, were not given the vote. The women's movement fought a long, long battle until women were finally given the vote in 1920. The early movement had concerned itself with a broad range of issues, from poverty and divorce laws to working conditions, but the movement after about 1890 concentrated solely on the narrow issue of voting. By 1920 some 2,000,000 women were members of the leading woman suffrage organizations! Yet when the vote was given, most of these women thought the battle was won—so the women's movement collapsed and did not recover till the late 1960s.

A brief upsurge in the fight for women's rights occurred only in World War II, when millions of women were drawn into war work. The symbol of Rosie the Riveter replaced that of Jane the Housewife. Overnight it became fashionable for women to work in a war factory or a war office, and there was even discussion of child care to help working mothers. Moreover, the two political parties made considerable sympathetic noises in favor of the idea of an equal rights amendment for women in the federal consitution.

Unfortunately for women, the late 1940s and 1950s was a period of general repression on the American scene. People were happy to see the war's end and wanted nothing but smooth private lives of moneymaking, with no discussion or recognition of continuing social problems. All the radicals and liberals who advocated any social change were hounded by Senator McCarthy and a huge number of publicity-seeking inquisitors; one of those who made a successful career of red-witch-hunting was Richard Nixon. Women were told to leave their war jobs and get back to kitchen, children, and church (just as Hitler had told the German women). The media—and even conservative psychologists—painted a picture in which every woman was a happy housewife surrounded by hoards of gleaming children and gadgets.

Yet reality was quite different. Later studies have shown that most women who are nothing but housewives are dreadfully unfulfilled and unhappy. Moreover, even in the 1950s the number of women at work kept increasing, despite all the propaganda. By 1970 4 out of every 10 workers were women—and a majority of all women between 16 and 64 now work! Yet they work in the poorest jobs, such as domestic servant or secretary, and are paid less than men even for the same job. The average full-time woman worker only makes 59 percent of what a full-time male worker is paid. Furthermore, in every area women who are fully qualified are denied promotion. Only a few of the thousands of corporate executives are women; only 9 percent of full professors are women, only 16 of the 435 representatives in Congress are women; and no woman has ever been President, Vice-President, or a Supreme Court Justice.

In the 1960s women began to protest these conditions. The first result of protest was the Equal Pay Act of 1963. Then, in 1964, a provision for women was added to the Civil Rights Act, which prohibited discrimination in employment against minority groups. Yet the addition was made by a southern congressman who wanted to defeat the whole act by amending it to add the ban on sex discrimination—and its final passage was a political miracle. Even after it was passed, the agencies who were responsible for enforcing it treated the sex discrimination ban as a joke and made very little attempt to enforce it.

As a result, in 1966 the National Organization of Women was formed. It is a moderate organization that wishes to see the laws against sex discrimination fully enforced and has worked to get other laws—like the Equal Rights Amendment— passed so as to give women fully equal rights at last.

In the meantime radical women gained a great deal of experience in the civil rights movement and the antiwar movement. Once again, recognition of the oppression of blacks made women conscious of their own oppression. They therefore began to work to direct the Left movement toward the fight for equality for women as well as for minorities. In this, however, they were rebuffed by many male radicals who were unenlightened on the subject of women. Thus when the subject of women's rights was broached by black women in the civil rights organization called the Student Nonviolent Coordinating Committee, its leader Stokely Carmichael said: "The only position for women in SNCC is prone."[8]

By 1968 many radical women were fed up with most of the Left organizations, so they organized their own separate movement. The women's movement was never an intellectually or politically homogeneous movement, however. The National Organization of Women has always been its largest and best organized component. NOW advocates reforms which would not seriously alter the more

---

[8] Quoted in Judith Hole and Ellen Levine, *Rebirth of Feminism* (New York: Quadrangle, 1971), p. 110.

fundamental economic, social or political institutions of the United States. They seem to base their actions on the implicit acceptance of the view that sexism is primarily the result of ignorance. They believe that through education and political pressures applied to the Democratic and Republican parties most of the inequities suffered by women could be eliminated by legislative reform.

The most extreme segment of the women's movement is the separatists. They see all men as the enemy and believe that women's liberation cannot be achieved within a society of both men and women. They advocate a radically new society (or new enclaves in society) composed solely of women—they have a variety of plans or schemes by which to assure conception and biological propagation of the women. They see all oppression as merely so many aspects of "male institutions" and oppressive behavior as "male behavior" (whether the behavior is on the part of a man or a woman).

A third component of feminists are Marxist feminists. They see sexism as resulting from social institutions and systematically inculcated subjective attitudes about women, which in both cases serve to strengthen and perpetuate the capitalist system of power and privilege. All Marxist feminists agree that sexism is related to the class oppression that has existed for many centuries, and that sexism will never be eliminated until all class oppression is eliminated. There were and are, however, continuing disagreements among Marxists concerning the exact relationships between class struggles—in slavery, feudalism, capitalism, and other class-divided societies—and the psychological attitudes and prejudices relating to sexist discrimination.

Some Marxist feminists—probably a minority, but including several influential writers—stress that some form of sexual oppression may be a necessary prerequisite for the creation of the subjective attitudes necessary to create and maintain *any* form of class-divided society. They emphasize that any form of class domination requires authoritarian personalities in the dominant groups and repressed psychological attitudes for most people in the society. Therefore, they argue that sexism can be seen in some ways prior to, and more fundamental than, the class oppression that Marx showed to be one of the defining features of any class-divided mode of production, including capitalism.

The majority of Marxist feminists would agree that sexism has existed in many class-divided societies before capitalism, and would agree that the authoritarian and paternalistic psychology of sexism is a vital and important feature of all known class societies. Both groups of Marxist feminists would stress that the oppression of women does perform the function of helping to increase capitalist profits and to split men from women workers, so as to weaken the working class both politically and economically. According to the majority Marxist opinion, however, because sexism performs such a helpful function for capitalism, it will always be the prevailing ideology under capitalism, regardless of how many laws are passed against it. Therefore, these Marxist feminists consider that the struggle to abolish capitalism is the most important and fundamental way to fight sex oppression.

The minority group of Marxist feminists insist that if the fight to abolish both sexists institutions and attitudes is not made coequal with the fight to abolish the class division of society, then it is probable that the succeeding society that results from the socialist revolution may itself become a class-divided exploitative society. In the majority view, all class oppression must be abolished and social-

ism established as the *necessary prerequisite* for the liberation of women and all
human beings. The majority of Marxist feminists would agree with the minority (as
against some vulgar Marxists) that a socialist revolution is not a sufficient guarantee of women's liberation, that a continuing movement for women's liberation is
needed both *before* and *after* the socialist revolution.

CONTEMPORARY CRITIQUES OF AMERICAN CAPITALISM

The civil rights, antiwar, and women's liberation movements led to a burgeoning
literature critical of the basic institutions of American capitalism. Like earlier critiques, this literature censured the grossly unequal distribution of income,
wealth, and power in the United States. These critics, like the leftist Keynesians,
deplored the extent to which post-World War II economic stability had been
purchased at a cost of thoroughgoing militarism (discussed in Chapter 11).

On these points radical and liberal critics have been in agreement. Liberal
critics believe political reform and electoral politics are sufficient to correct these
perversions of the American economy. Radical critics, however, believe inequality and militarism are inherent in a capitalist economy and that it also necessarily
involves (1) imperialistic exploitation of underdeveloped countries as a means of
maintaining high output and large profits in the United States, (2) endemic discrimination against minority groups and women, (3) inability to control pollution
and resources exhaustion, and (4) a degrading commercialism and social alienation. In the remainder of this chapter some of the literature in these four general
areas will be described. Much of this literature has appeared in the *Review of
Radical Political Economics*, published by the Union for Radical Economics
(URPE). Its address is 41 Union Square West (Room 901), New York, New York,
10003. URPE is the main organization of U.S. radical economists.

AMERICAN IMPERIALISM

One of the first and most influential of these critics was Paul A. Baran. His book
The Political Economy of Growth,[9] first published in 1957, has undergone two
editions, has been translated into several languages, and has sold very well in
the United States and even better in most less developed countries. Baran argued that before a less developed country could industrialize it would have to
mobilize its *economic surplus*, or the difference between what is produced and
what has to be consumed in order to maintain the economy's productivity. It is
the source of investment capital with which the country can industrialize. Under
present institutional arrangements, most less developed countries either waste
their surpluses or lose them to imperialistic capitalist countries.

"Far from serving as an engine of economic expansion, of technological
progress and of social change, the capitalist order in . . . [underdeveloped] countries has represented a framework for economic stagnation, for archaic technology, and for social backwardness."[10] The peasant agriculture usually produces a

[9] Paul A. Baran, *The Political Economy of Growth* (New York: Monthly Review Press, 1962).
[10] Ibid., pp. 163–164.

sufficiently large surplus in these countries. In fact, Baran pointed out that the surplus is frequently as high as 50 percent of the total amount produced. "The subsistence peasant's obligations on account of rent, taxes, and interest in all underdeveloped countries are very high. They frequently absorb more than half of his meager net product."[11]

The problem is in the disposition of this surplus. Part goes to middlemen, speculators, moneylenders, and merchants—petty capitalists who have neither the interest nor the wherewithal to finance industrialization. A much larger part goes to the landowning ruling class, which uses its "share" to purchase luxury consumption goods, usually imported from capitalist countries, and the extensive military establishments needed to maintain their internal power.

Importing luxuries and military hardware necessitates sending exports to the industrialized countries. Exports usually consist of one or two primary agricultural products or mineral resources. The capitalist countries with which they trade have such monopsonistic buying power that the terms of trade are very unfavorable to the underdeveloped countries. The large, multinational corporations that purchase the raw materials are not interested in the industrialization of these countries. Thus foreign capitalist investment is limited to that necessary for the profitable extraction of resources.

An alliance between reactionary landowning class and foreign capitalists protects the interests of both by suppressing dissidence and keeping the masses at a subsistence standard of living. Thus landowners can maintain their position and capitalists are guaranteed cheap labor and large profits.

> Small wonder that under such circumstances Western big business heavily engaged in raw materials exploitation leaves no stone unturned to obstruct the evolution of social and political conditions in underdeveloped countries that might be conducive to their economic development. It uses its tremendous power to prop up the backward areas' comprador administrations, to disrupt and corrupt the social and political movements that oppose them, and to overthrow whatever progressive governments may rise to power and refuse to do the bidding of their imperialistic overlords.[12]

Baran believed the American government works hand in hand with American big business. Most U.S. economic and military aid provided to less developed countries is given, in his opinion, in order to prop up client governments. Often such governments are not strong enough to survive on their own, even with this aid. Under these circumstances the United States intervenes, either clandestinely (through CIA sabotage and intrigue) or directly (through the use of military force).

Baran and like-minded critics see the interventions in Guatemala, Iran, Korea, Cuba, the Dominican Republic, Vietnam, and Cambodia as examples of American endeavors to protect business interests, both current and potential, against threats from more progressive social and political movements. They point to 53 different "U.S. defense commitments and assurances" that commit the United States to the use of military force to maintain existing governments, very often against their own people.[13]

---

[11] Ibid., p. 165.
[12] Ibid., p. 198.
[13] See Harry Magdoff, *The Age of Imperialism, The Economics of U.S. Foreign Policy* (New York: Monthly Review Press, Modern Reader Paperbacks, 1969), pp. 203–206.

The dependence of less developed countries on a small number of export commodities is documented in a study based on International Monetary Fund data. Each of the 37 countries considered earns 58 to 99 percent of its export receipts from 1 to 6 commodities.[14] Furthermore, the United States depends on imports as the principal source for most of the 62 types of materials the Defense Department classifies as "strategic and critical." For 38 of these, 80 to 100 percent of the new supplies are imported; for 14 more, 40 to 79 percent are imported.[15]

A large and increasing percentage of U.S. corporate sales and profits results from exports and sales of foreign subsidiaries (many of which, of course, are in less developed countries).[16] Moreover, detailed examination reveals that the foreign trade of the less developed countries is very lopsided. Raw materials and metals in their first state of smelting constitute 85 percent of exports; manufactured goods (mostly textiles), only 10 percent. But about 60 percent of their imports are manufactured goods.[17] Because most manufactured imports are consumer goods, such a pattern of trade cannot lead to development but only to continued economic dependence.

Critics of this point of view (i.e., defenders of American economic foreign policy) argue that although foreign trade and foreign investments are important to American corporations, they also benefit the less developed countries. The orthodox argument is expressed in a widely used textbook:

> In general, a restrained optimism as to the future prospects for underdeveloped countries in their trading relations with the developed countries seems to be warranted. The most encouraging sign is the growing recognition on the part of developed countries that opening their markets to the export products of underdeveloped areas is an essential part of their accepted program to assist underdeveloped countries to grow.[18]

But this position does not deal directly with radical critiques of American economic foreign policy. It simply assumes that all the underdeveloped countries need is *more* trade. Another orthodox scholar who has studied the problem more thoroughly admits that "increasing the flow of private capital to underdeveloped countries will probably require a *recasting of economic policies* in both underdeveloped and advanced countries."[19] He does not go on to analyze what obstacles prevent this "recasting of economic policies."

Conservative defenders of American policies grant that developed capitalist countries have had immense economic, political, and military power, which they have used to influence and control peoples around the world. They deny, however, that this "imperialism" is basically economic in nature. Thus the widely respected economic historian Professor David S. Landes writes,

> It seems to me that one has to look at imperialism as a multifarious response to a common opportunity that consists simply in disparity of power. Whenever and wherever such disparity has existed, people and groups have been ready to

[14] Magdoff, op. cit., pp. 99–100.

[15] Percy W. Bidwell, *Raw Materials* (New York: Harper & Row, 1958), p. 12.

[16] Magdoff, op. cit., p. 57

[17] Pierre Jalee, *The Pillage of the Third World* (New York: Monthly Review Press, 1965), p. 8.

[18] Delbert A. Snider, *Introduction to International Economics* (Howmewood, Ill.: Irwin, 1963), p. 548.

[19] Benjamin Higgins, *Economic Development* (New York: Norton, 1959), p. 593; italics added.

take advantage of it. It is, one notes with regret, in the nature of the human beast to push other people around—or to save their souls or "civilize" them as the case may be.[20]

One radical critic has answered this assertion by noting that the modern capitalist drive to save people's souls from communism and to civilize them is perfectly compatible with economic motives. He cites the following quotation from an officer of General Electric Company: "Thus, our search for profits places us squarely in line with the national policy of stepping up international trade as a means of strengthening the free world in the Cold War confrontation with Communism." The critic, Harry Magdoff, summarizes his position: "Just as the fight against Communism helps the search for profits, so the search for profits helps the fight against Communism. What more perfect harmony of interests could be imagined?"[21]

Many books written in the 1960s attempted to explain contemporary American foreign policy—and in the cold war between the United States and the Soviet Union—in terms of American economic imperialism.[22]

RACISM AND SEXISM

Radical critics also point to the pervasive effects of discrimination based on race and sex that exists in capitalist countries, particularly in the United States. Virtually everyone agrees that racism and sexism create severe discrimination. Defenders of American capitalism explain this discrimination in one of two ways. The more reactionary is to argue that job discrimination merely reflects the innate inferiority of women and blacks. Few, if any, intellectuals embrace this position, but it apparently is accepted by a large minority in the United States. The other contention is that racism and sexism are products of a fairly universal human bigotry and are not related to capitalism or any other economic system.

Critics of capitalism point out that the wages of blacks and women make up a significant part of capitalists' wage costs. In 1970, for example, the wages of American women averaged only about 50 percent of the wages of men doing the same jobs. On that basis it would appear that approximately 23 percent of all manufacturing profits are attributable to the lower wages paid to women. Profits made as a result of racial discrimination would certainly be smaller, but they would still be significant.

In one of the most influential socialist critiques, Paul A. Baran and Paul M. Sweezy have argued that it is necessary to

consider first the private interests which benefit from the existence of a Negro subproletariat. (a) Employers benefit from divisions in the labor force which enable them to play one group off against another, thus weakening all. . . . (b)

[20] David S. Landes, "The Nature of Economic Imperialism," *The Journal of Economic History*, December 1961, p. 510.

[21] Magdoff, op. cit., pp. 200–201.

[22] See Magdoff, op. cit., D. F. Fleming, *The Cold War and Its Origins* (Garden City, N.Y.: Doubleday, 1961); Gar Alperowitz, *Atomic Diplomacy: Hiroshima and Potsdam* (New York: Simon & Schuster, 1965); David Horowitz, ed., *Corporations and the Cold War* (New York: Monthly Review Press, 1969); and David Horowitz, *Empire and Revolution* (New York: Random House, 1969).

Owners of ghetto real estate are able to overcrowd and overcharge. (c) Middle and upper income groups benefit from having at their disposal a large supply of cheap domestic labor. (d) Many small marginal businesses, especially in the service trades, can operate profitably only if cheap labor is available to them. (e) White workers benefit by being protected from Negro competition for the more desirable and higher paying jobs.[23]

They also assert that, in addition to increasing profits, discrimination increases social stability in a capitalist economy. The class structure of capitalism, they hold, leads to a situation in which

each status group has a deep-rooted psychological need to compensate for feelings of inferiority and envy toward those above by feelings of superiority and contempt for those below. It thus happens that a special pariah group at the bottom acts as a kind of lightning rod for the frustrations and hostilities of all the higher groups, the more so the nearer they are to the bottom. It may even be said that the very existence of the pariah group is a kind of harmonizer and stabilizer of the social structure.[24]

Although Baran and Sweezy's assertions pertain to racism, many critics argue that sexism performs much the same function in a capitalist society. These critics generally do not believe that capitalism is the original creator of racism and sexism but rather that capitalism perpetuates and intensifies racism and sexism because they serve valuable functions.

Today, transferring the locus of whites' perceptions of the source of many of their problems from capitalism and toward blacks, racism continues to serve the needs of the capitalist system. Although an individual employer might gain by refusing to discriminate and agreeing to hire blacks at above the going black wage rate, it is not true that the capitalist class as a whole would profit if racism were eliminated and labor were more efficiently allocated without regard to skin color. . . . The divisiveness of racism weakens workers' strength when bargaining with employers; the economic consequences of racism are not only lower incomes for blacks but also higher incomes for the capitalist class coupled with lower incomes for white workers. Although capitalists may not have conspired consciously to create racism, and although capitalists may not be its principal perpetuators, nevertheless racism does support the continued well-being of the American capitalist system.[25]

Similarly, the critics argue that sex prejudice helps divide the labor, civil rights, and radical movements to the benefit of American capitalists.

ALIENATION

Many contemporary radical critics have refined and elaborated on Marx's theory of the human alienation inherent in the capitalist economic system.[26] Baran and Sweezy, for example, maintain that total alienation pervades and dominates contemporary American capitalism:

[23] Paul A. Baran and Paul M. Sweezy, *Monopoly Capital* (New York: Monthly Review Press 1966), pp. 263–264.

[24] Ibid., pp. 265–266.

[25] Michael Reich, "The Economics of Racism," in David M. Gordon, ed., *Problems in Political Economy: An Urban Perspective* (Lexington, Mass.: Raytheon/ Heath, 1971), pp. 109–110.

[26] See Chapter 6.

Disorientation, apathy, and often despair, haunting Americans in all walks of life, have assumed in our time the dimensions of a prolonged crisis. This crisis affects every aspect of national life, and ravages both its social-political and its individual spheres—everyman's everyday existence. A heavy strangulating sense of the emptiness and futility of life permeates the country's moral and intellectual climate. High level committees are entrusted with the discovery and specification of "national goals" while gloom pervades the printed matter (fiction and non-fiction, alike) appearing daily in the literary market place. The malaise deprives work of meaning and purpose; turns leisure into joyless, debilitating laziness; fatally impairs the education system and the conditions of healthy growth in the young; transforms religion and church into commercialized vehicles of "togetherness"; and destroys the very foundation of burgeois society, the family.[27]

The fact of alienation, like the facts of racism and sexism, is explained by many defenders of capitalism as an unfortunate but inevitable by-product of industrial civilization. They point to all the boring and dangerous work that must be done, as well as to the narrow and fragmented personalities of the enormous number of bureaucrats. An industrialized socialist economy would, they assert, create the same type of alienation. Few people, regardless of political and economic views, would be willing to forgo the advantages of industrialization in order to combat alienation. And even if people did want to return to preindustrial society, there is simply no practical way of turning back time to some imagined golden age.

Socialist critics reply that although some amount of alienation will surely exist in any industrialized society, capitalism significantly intensifies alienation and makes it more pervasive. Erich Fromm, a famous psychoanalyst, social philosopher, and author, argues that the most important single cause of alienation is the fact that the individual feels no sense of participation in the forces that determine social policy. He sees these forces as anonymous and totally beyond the sphere of any individual's influence. "The anonymity of the social forces," writes Fromm, "is inherent in the structure of the capitalist mode of production."[28]

Fromm identifies several types of alienation created by the capitalist mode of production. Conditions of employment alienate workers. Their livelihoods depend on whether capitalists and managers are able to make a profit by hiring them, and thus they are viewed as means only, never as ends. The individual worker is "an economic atom that dances to the tune of atomistic management." Managers "strip the worker of his right to think and move freely. Life is being denied; need to control, creativeness, curiosity, and independent thought are being balked, and the result, the inevitable result, is flight or fight on the part of the worker, apathy or destructiveness, psychic regression."[29] The worker feels that the capitalist controls his or her whole life; both workers and consumers (and voters) feel weak and insignificant in view of the colossal power of the corporations over working conditions, prices, and even government policy.

And yet Fromm argues that the "role of the manager is also one of alienation," for the manager too is coerced by the ineluctable forces of capitalism and has very little freedom. He or she must deal "with impersonal giants; with the giant competitive enterprise; with giant impersonal markets; with giant unions, and the

[27] Baran and Sweezy, op. cit., p. 281.
[28] Erich Fromm, *The Sane Society* (New York: Fawcett World Library, Premier Books, 1965), p. 125.
[29] Quoted in ibid., p. 115.

giant government.''[30] His or her position, status, and income—in short, his or her very social existence—all depend on making ever-increasing amounts of profits. Yet the manager must do this in a world in which he or she has little personal influence on the giants surrounding the manager.

Fromm also maintains that the process of consumption in a capitalist society "is as alienated as the process of production." The truly human way of acquiring commodities, according to Fromm, would be through need and the desire to use: "The acquisition of bread and clothing [should] depend on no other premise than that of being alive; the acquisition of books and paintings on my effort to understand them and my ability to use them."[31] But in capitalist societies the income with which to purchase these commodities can come only through sales in the impersonal market.

As a consequence, those who have money are subjected to a constant barrage of propaganda designed to create consuming automata. Capitalist socialization processes make consumption-hungry, irrational, compulsive buying machines of us all. Acts of buying and consuming have become ends in themselves, with little or no relation to the uses or pleasures derived from the commodities.

> Man today is fascinated by the possibility of buying more, better, and especially, new things. He is consumption-hungry. The act of buying and consuming has become a compulsive, irrational aim, because it is an end in itself, with little relation to the use of or pleasure in the things bought and consumed. To buy the latest gadget, the latest model of anything that is on the market, is the dream of everybody in comparison to which the real pleasure in use is quite secondary. Modern man, if he dared to be articulate about his concept of heaven, would describe a vision which would look like the biggest department store in the world, showing new things and gadgets, and himself having plenty of money with which to buy them. He would wander around open-mouthed in his heaven of gadgets and commodities, provided only that there were ever more and newer things to buy, and perhaps that his neighbors were just a little less privileged than he.[32]

Finally, the most severe alienation is the alienation of a person from his or her "self." A person's "worth" in a capitalist market economy is determined in the same way as the "worth" of anything else: by sales in the marketplace. In this situation,

> man experiences himself as a thing to be employed successfully on the market. He does not experience himself as an active agent, as the bearer of human powers. He is alienated from these powers. His aim is to sell himself successfully on the market. His sense of self does not stem from his activity as a loving and thinking individual, but from his socio-economic role. . . . If you ask a man "Who are you?", he answers "I am a manufacturer," "I am a clerk," "I am a doctor." . . . That is the way he experiences himself, not as a man, with love, fear, convictions, doubts, but as that abstraction, alienated from his real nature, which fulfills a certain function in the social system. His sense of value depends on his success: on whether he can sell himself favorably, whether he can make more of himself than he started out with, whether he is a success. His body, his mind and his soul are his capital, and his task in life is to invest it favorably, to make a *profit* of himself. Human qualities like friendliness,

[30] Ibid., pp. 115–116.
[31] Ibid., p. 120.
[32] Ibid., p. 123.

courtesy, kindness, are transformed into commodities, into assets of the "personality package," conducive to a higher price on the personality market. If the individual fails in a profitable investment of himself, *he* feels that he is a failure; if he succeeds, he is a success. Clearly, his sense of his own value always depends on factors extraneous to himself, on the fickle judgment of the market, which decides about his value as it decides about the value of commodities. He, like all commodities that cannot be sold profitably on the market, is worthless as far as his exchange value is concerned, even though his use value may be considerable.[33]

Thus socialist critics argue that the impersonal nexus of the capitalist market mediates all human relationships. It makes profit and loss the ultimate and pervasive evaluative criteria of human worth. This means human alienation must inevitably be extremely severe in a capitalist market economy.

ENVIRONMENTAL DESTRUCTION

Capitalism must either experience economic growth or else suffer depression, unemployment, stagnation, and all the attendant social problems. But economic growth can also create situations in which the pursuit of profits comes into direct conflict with the public welfare. Critics of capitalism have argued that corporate profit seeking is generally accompanied by very little concern for conservation or for a clean, livable environment.

Pollution is of concern to defenders of capitalism as well as to critics. Defenders argue that it is a problem common to all industrialized economies. Critics assert that the problem is worse in a capitalist economy. Furthermore, they maintain that it would be virtually impossible to control pollution effectively in a capitalist system. This is so, they argue, because the basic economic cause of pollution in a capitalist economy is that business firms do not have to pay for *all* the costs incurred in the production process. They pay for labor, raw materials, and capital used up in production. But they use the land, air, and water for the disposal of waste products that are created in the process of production. Generally they pay little or nothing for the use of the environment as a garbage disposal.

It has been estimated[34] that each year businesses are responsible for over 25 billion tons of pollutants being spewed into the air and dumped into the water and on the land. This is about 125 tons of waste per year for every man, woman, and child in the United States. Included in this figure are about 150 million tons of smoke and fumes that blacken the skies and poison the air, 22 million tons of waste paper products, 3 million tons of mill tailings, and 50 trillion gallons of heated and polluted liquids that are dumped into streams, rivers, and lakes each year.

Critics argue that it is extemely difficult if not impossible for a capitalist economy to deal with these problems because those who receive the profits from production do not pay these social costs, and those who do pay the social costs have little or no voice in the operation of the businesses.

---

[33] Ibid., pp. 129-130.
[34] These estimates are taken from an important and impressive study on pollution: R. C. d'Arge, A. V. Kneese, and R. V. Ayres, *Economics of the Environment: A Materials Balance Approach* (Baltimore: Johns Hopkins Press, 1970).

In response to the widespread public demand for control of pollution and polluters, the government has given contracts to many corporations to devise new methods of combating pollution. In effect the government is asking private corporations to act as the controllers of other private corporations. Radical critics are convinced that this corporate integration of polluters and controllers will never lead to any substantial improvement. Most of the important pollution control companies have become subsidiaries of the giant corporations that do most of the polluting.

One radical critic has analyzed the effects of this corporate control.

> It is the chemical industry . . . that best illustrates the consequences of the incest between the pollution control business and the industrial polluters. First, the chemical industry is in the enviable position of reaping sizable profits by attempting to clean up rivers and lakes (at public expense) which they have profitably polluted in the first place. To facilitate this practically every major chemical company in the U.S. has established a pollution abatement division or is in the process of doing so. . . . A second consequence of placing the "control" of pollution in the hands of big business is that the official abatement levels will inevitably be set low enough to protect industry's power to pollute and therefore its ability to keep costs down and revenues high. According to a recent study by the FWPCA (Federal Water Pollution Control Administration) if the chemical industry were to reduce its pollution of water to zero, the costs involved would amount to almost $2.7 billion per year. This would cut profits almost by half. [35]

Under such circumstances the critics do not expect must progress in cleaning up the environment unless fundamental social, political, and economic changes occur first.

LIBERAL VERSUS RADICAL CRITIQUES OF CAPITALISM

The glaringly unequal distribution of wealth, income, and political power and the facts of militarism, imperialism, vicious discrimination, social alienation, and environmental destruction are all recognized and decried by both liberal and radical critics of capitalism. There is, however, an immensely important difference between the positions of liberals and radicals.

Liberals tend to see each of these social and economic problems as separate and distinct. The problems, they believe, are the results of past mistakes, inabilities, and ineptitudes or the results of random cases of individual perversity. Liberals also tend to consider the government as detached, disinterested, and motivated by a desire to maximize the welfare of all its citizens. Hence liberals generally favor government-sponsored reforms designed to mitigate the many evils of capitalism. These reforms never threaten the two most important features of capitalism: private ownership of the means of production, and the free market.

Radicals, however, see each of the social and economic problems we have discussed as the *direct consequence* of private ownership of capital and the process of social decision making within the impersonal cash nexus of the mar-

---

[35] Martin Gellen, "The Making of a Pollution-Industrial Complex," in Gordon, op. cit., pp. 469–470.

ket. The problems cannot be solved until their underlying causes are eliminated, but this means a fundamental, radical economic reorganization. If private ownership of capital is eliminated and if significant restrictions are placed on the areas in which the market determines social decisions, the resulting system would no longer be a capitalist economic system. It would of necessity be some type of socialist society.

RADICAL POLITICAL MOVEMENTS IN THE 1960s AND 1970s

In the 1930s and 1940s the "old left" political movements had gained substantially in both numbers and influence. The old left was almost entirely socialist, and their growth had been a consequence of the fact that the Great Depression of the 1930s had convinced many people that capitalism was an irrational, dying society. The principal organizations of the "old left" were the *Communist party,* the *Socialist Party,* and the *Socialist Workers party.* Although their membership constituted only a tiny percentage of the American population, they had an influence in labor organizations and in American social and political life that was far greater than their numbers would indicate.

The economic recovery of the late 1940s and 1950s combined with the harsh intellectual and political repression of McCarthyism had almost destroyed the leftist movement by the late 1950s and early 1960s. The civil rights and antiwar movements led to a widespread rebirth of the belief that many of the worst evils of American Society were the inevitable outcomes of the structure and organization of capitalism. Thus these movements led to a rebirth of the socialist movement.

But the radicals of the 1960s were generally very different from their counterparts in the 1930s. These differences—which resulted in their being called the "new left" in contrast to the "old left" of the 1930s and its surviving organizations—can be categorized under three headings. First, they initially believed that moral and emotional contempt were more important than intellectual understanding as potential sources for transforming American society. Often their own emotional intensity and moral fervor led them to believe a new American revolution was just around the corner. Second, they were so contemptuous of intellectual dogmatism and old left sloganeering that many members of the new left refused for several years to accept very many of the theoretical and empirical insights of the Marxist tradition. Third, their dislike of authority, authoritarian structures, and individual suppression was so great that they were unable to create any viable, effective organizations through which to further their aims.

The organization most typical of, and influential among, the new left was the Students for a Democratic Society (SDS). Organized in the early 1960s, it was most instrumental in disseminating the facts about the Viet Nam war and in mobilizing massive student resistence against the war. By 1968, however, two things had become obvious. First, their aversion to leftist dogmas was so great that it sometimes degenerated into anti-intellectualism. As a result, the organization was amazingly diverse in terms of its members' opinions about the nature of American society and the best tactics to use in attempting to restructure that society. Second, their aversion to authority (an aversion that they euphemistically extolled as "participatory democracy") had resulted in SDS being so loosely and ineffectively structured that they were hardly capable of any well-coordinated mass action at all.

It is not surprising that in 1969, shortly after then-President Nixon had been elected, SDS required relatively little effort on the part of government agents and provocateurs to precipitate its immediate and almost total disintegration.

But by this time the antiwar movement had a momentum of its own that was largely independent of the demise of SDS. Many moderate and liberal leaders had joined the bandwagon, and the Socialist Workers Party and the Communist Party had become active in the leadership of the radical wing of the anti-war movement.

By early 1973 several things became apparent. With the end of the Viet Nam war, hundreds of thousands of Americans who had opposed the war and had sometimes been thought to be a part of the Movement lapsed into a mood of relief and what appeared to be social and political indifference. People were weary of social conflict and hopeful that a peaceful, tranquil mood would come to prevail in the United States. The Watergate revelations and subsequent disclosures of the widespread, illegal operations of the American CIA and FBI showed Americans how far their government would go to crush political criticism at home and to maintain the world-wide American empire.

The result of these revelations was not, as leftists hoped, a widespread indignation and determination for radical social change. The more usual response was apathy and a naive hope and faith that these abuses and excesses had simply been the result of a few corrupt and unscrupulous politicians. Both the Republican and Democratic Parties chose presidential candidates, for the 1976 election, who could be portrayed as "simple, honest, just-plain-folks" politicians. Jimmy Carter was widely seen as a simple, honest, rural man who had not been corrupted by holding national office. And he was elected President.

The period from the early 1970s through 1977 (the date at which this was written) saw several important changes in the radical movement. Members of SDS and other like-minded radicals of the 1960s came to see that their hopes for radical social change in the near future were unrealistic. They saw that promoting such change would require a more adequate knowledge of the structure and functioning of capitalist socity. It would also require a much more effectively organized movement.

The first of these requirements led to a widespread tendency to study Marx and the ideas of Marxist theoreticians of the last hundred years. Radical students of the 1960s became radical professors in the 1970s. Organizations, such as the Union for Radical Political Economics (URPE), devoted themselves to the promotion and propagation of radical understanding of American capitalism. URPE currently has about 2000 members and publishes analyses of the current economic and political trends in the United States as well as studies aimed at increasing radicals' understanding of the nature and functioning of capitalism. These are published regularly in two journals—*The Review of Radical Political Economics* and *Dollars and Sense*—and a newsletter. Informal study groups have sprung up around the United States. Several universities have academic departments where radical professors now regularly teach Marxist views on history and the social sciences.

The widely felt need for better organization affected members of the new left in very diverse ways. A large part of them felt that no satisfactory nation-wide socialist organization existed, so they concentrated their efforts solely on local organizing. Another major segment joined the various "old left" organizations. During the 1970s several Maoist organizations (political organizations that base many of their ideas on the writings of Mao Tse Tung and the Chinese Communists), the Communist party, the Socialist Workers party, the Progressive Labor party, the International Socialists and other "old left" organizations have grown more rapidly than at any time since World War II.

A sizable part of the members of the SDS of the late 1960s and many other members of the "new left" retained their dissatisfaction with the "old left" organizations, however, while they still desired to organize on a nation-wide basis. The most important organization to come out of this group was the New American Movement (NAM), an organization formed in 1973 with approximately 50 chapters in various cities across the United States. The New American Movement aims to create a democratic socialist society in the United States, in which racism, sexism, imperialism, and all other forms of human oppression are eradicated. It believes that the old left socialist organizations are too thoroughly affected by past mistakes and outworn attitudes for them to be effective means for the economic, social, and political alterations that it believes ultimately will be necessary to create a humane, moral society in the United States.

By 1977 very little of the civil rights, or black, movement remained as a separate movement. Most of their more moderate demands for economic reform have been taken up by the liberal wing of the Democratic party. Their more radical demands for fundamental change in the social, political, and economic institutions as a means of achieving human equality have been taken up by most of the socialist organizations (which have always fought for racial equality). The black separatist movement of the 1960s, which wanted a separate all-black nation for themselves, appears virtually to have disappeared.

The women's movement has also changed in the 1970s. The women's separatist movement appears to be following in the footsteps of the black separatist movement. Its members, like the members of SDS in the 1960s, have an aversion to nearly all organizational forms and, consequently, have never been able to create a nationwide organization. Generally, their dislike of authority renders them ineffective as political organizations on the local level.

The National Organization of Women advocates few, if any, fundamental changes in social, political, or economic structures of capitalism. Consequently, while they do have a fairly effective nation-wide organization, they are definitely not socialist—though their rhetoric has recently become very radical on a number of important issues.

The Marxist feminist movement has had a considerable impact on several socialist organizations. This component of the women's movement has no effective national organization with an all-women membership, nor is it devoted solely to feminist issues. Marxist feminists, however, constitute a significant portion of the New American Movement (whose leadership bodies have always had more than 50 percent women), and feminist issues are very prominent in the program and activities of the New American Movement.

The socialist movement in the United States is much smaller and less effective than its counterparts in most advanced capitalist countries. In several Western European countries, coalitions of communists and socialists regularly receive somewhere near a majority of the votes in national elections. Socialist and communist parties in these countries have memberships in the millions. Because the United States is the most powerful of all capitalist countries, it is not surprising that its socialist movement is the weakest.

As we have seen in earlier chapters, socialist ideas and movements came into being with the industrial revolution, and socialists have always fought to eradicate the worst effects of capitalism. Socialists have also always fought and will continue to fight for the complete abolition of capitalism and its replacement by a democratic socialist society. As long as capitalism involves poverty, inequality, imperialism, unemployment and economic crises, environmental pollution, racism, sexism, and alienation, there will undoubtedly be socialists speaking, writing, organizing and acting in their efforts to create a better society.

SUMMARY

From the late 1950s to the early 1970s, the civil rights movement, the women's liberation movement, and the antiwar movement generated a resurgence of radical criticism of American capitalism. The radicals argue that inequality, discrimination, alienation, environmental destruction, militarism, and imperialism are integral parts of a capitalist economy. Unlike liberals, who believe that these evils are accidental and that the system can be reformed, radicals contend that these evils cannot be overcome unless the basic structure of capitalism is fundamentally changed.

The principal obstacle to the achievement of such reforms is the fact that political power is derived from economic power. Radicals see capitalist governments as plutocracies hidden behind phony façades of democracy. Both political parties, they point out, spend many millions of dollars on each election. As a consequence, both political parties are almost completely controlled by the wealthiest 2 percent of the population, which owns most of the income-producing capital.[36] In this situation one would not expect the wealthy elite to support any government that threatened to destroy the basis of their wealth, privileges, and power. Therefore fundamental reform seems unlikely unless a reform movement can establish a base of power independent of wealth. This explains the popularity at radical gatherings of the slogan "Power to the People!"

[36] For detailed evidence for this point of view, see G. William Domhoff, *Who Rules America* (Englewood Cliffs, N.J.: Prentice-Hall, 1967), and Domhoff, *The Higher Circles: The Governing Class in America* (New York: Random House, 1970).

PART TWO

PRICES AND POVERTY: An Introduction to Microeconomics

CHAPTER 14

MARKET ALLOCATION OF RESOURCES: Efficiency Versus Fairness

Part One of this book sketched some of the highlights in the history of economic thought and in the evolution of the private enterprise, or capitalist, system. In Parts Two and Three the actual working of the capitalist system is discussed. Part Two will concentrate on *microeconomics,* the economics of individual enterprises and individual workers and consumers; Part Three will deal with *macroeconomics,* the operation of the economy as a whole. Thus in Part Two we shall discuss, among other things, how enterprises set prices and make profits under competition and monopoly, how workers' wages are determined, how the government affects the distribution of income, and the economics of racial and sexual discrimination.

A private enterprise economy is one in which the factories, tools, and stocks of goods with which production is carried on are owned by private individuals. Individual ownership includes, of course, the corporate form of ownership. In the corporation, individuals own the whole capital, but each person's ownership is specified in the form of the stock or shares that he or she holds.

Most modern private enterprise economies are distinguished by socially and technologically complex methods of production and distribution. It is possible to imagine an economy of small farmers and artisan-producers in which each individual owns his or her own means of production and is a fairly independent producer. In the reality of the modern private enterprise economy, however, this type of individual independence is completely impossible. The factory system, which the Industrial Revolution ushered in, has made individual producers completely dependent. A worker in an automobile factory, for example, owns no tools of production. One worker cannot, alone, produce anything. He or she depends for continued existence on being able to sell his or her labor time to a company that employs hundreds of thousands of other workers. His or her work generally consists of one small, insignificant, and tedious operation (such as screwing a particular nut onto a particular bolt) that is repeated endlessly for eight hours.

In the American economy about 1.8 percent of the population owns 80 percent of all corporate stock. Most of the remaining 98.2 percent own little or no capital and depend on the *market* for their labor services to earn a living. When a worker succeeds in selling labor services, he or she is paid a wage that is then spent in the market for goods and services. By purchasing these goods and services, the worker is playing a small (usually *very* small) role in creating the demand that provides jobs for the other workers who produce these goods and services. In fact, in the U.S. economy the continued employment of any individual may depend on the actions and behavior of hundreds of thousands or even millions of other people. All these people are related to this individual through only one social institution: the market. It is therefore vitally important to understand how the market functions.

In a private enterprise economy the market determines what is to be produced. Capitalists, or their hired managers, are motivated primarily by their drive to maximize profits. They go to the market to hire labor and buy raw materials, which they combine with the factories, machinery, and tools they own in order to produce an output. (Many capitalists are strictly intermediaries and financiers and are not directly connected with productive output, but for our present purposes we shall ignore them.) They then sell their output in the market.

Their objective is to maximize the difference between their sales proceeds and their money expenses incurred in buying raw materials, hiring labor, and replacing used-up capital. This difference is, of course, profits. They constantly search for commodities that can be produced and sold profitably.

The capitalists' costs of production represent income to laborers and the owners of raw materials. Profit is the income that accrues to the capitalist. The recipients of these incomes spend them in the market for the goods produced by the capitalists' business firms. Thus money circulates from the business firms to the general public in the form of incomes generated in the production process. The money then returns to the business firms when the public purchases the goods and services these firms sell in the market.

There is thus an amazingly complex circulation of money from hundreds of thousands of business firms to hundreds of millions of people and back into the hands of the business firms. At all points the guiding force is the capitalists' constant search for profits. The decisions concerning what goods to produce (or even whether to produce), what inputs to buy, what wages to pay, and so forth are all determined by the criterion of profitability. All economic relations between people are mediated by the institution of the market. The market is obviously one of the most important social institutions in a private enterprise economy. In this and the several following chapters, we shall attempt to achieve a clearer understanding of what markets are and how they function.

It is important to begin by distinguishing a particular market and the market system (or, as it is often referred to, *the* market). Historically, a market was an area, usually near the center of a village or town, where producers and traders would meet and exchange goods. Later, any place where a merchant habitually sold commodities was a market. Today we sometimes refer to a grocery store as a market, but the word *market* is more generally used as an abstract concept. It refers, in general, to the negotiation of exchange transactions that generally involve money, and the determination of the prices at which these exchanges are transacted.

We speak of the stock market, the labor market, or the automobile market when we are referring to the buying and selling of stocks, labor services, or automobiles. We speak of the market or the *market system* when we wish to refer to monetary exchange and price determination in general. It is obvious that any market system that successfully facilitates price determination and exchange must contain complex systems of customs and traditions, laws, and agencies of law enforcement as well as the physical buildings in which business is transacted.

In this part of the book, physical settings of markets and many of the customs and laws that enable markets to function will be ignored. We shall concentrate on exchange (buying and selling) and the determination of price.

A market is basically a two-sided phenomenon with buyers facing sellers. Buyers have money they wish to exchange for goods, and sellers have goods they wish to exchange for money. The amount of a good that buyers would like to purchase at any given time is referred to as the *demand* for that good. Similarly, the amount of the good that sellers would like to sell is referred to as the *supply* of the good.

It should be stressed that demand is not necessarily related to need or desire. A penniless child longingly gazing through the window of a candy store adds nothing to the market demand for candy. Similarly, in the Great Depression of the 1930s millions of people went hungry while tons of wheat and thousands of cattle and sheep were destroyed and wasted because of the lack of any market demand for them. The problem, of course, was that, like the child at the candy store, the unemployed millions had no money to exchange for food.

DEMAND AND SUPPLY

Restated more formally, the definitions of demand and supply are as follows: *Demand for a good refers to the amount of that good buyers would like to purchase during a given period and at a given price.* Obviously demand must be expressed in terms of a given period if it is to have any meaning. The number of automobiles people wish to purchase is certainly very different over the course of a week as opposed to a year. Similarly, a given price must be specified. Clearly the number of Ford cars people would like to buy will be very different if the price is $500 than if it is $5000. An important point is that a demand for $100 worth of a good is simultaneously a willingness to supply $100 in money.

The definition of supply is very similar to that of demand. *Supply of a good refers to the quantity of that good sellers would like to sell during a given period and at a given price.* The supply of $100 worth of a good is simultaneously a demand for $100 in money.

If the reactions of buyers and sellers at different prices are considered, it becomes possible to define a demand schedule and a supply schedule. A *demand schedule* relates *various prices* of that good with the *amounts* of that good people would like to buy at each of the various prices. If the people of the United States were polled in order to determine the number of Ford Pintos they would like to buy at various prices, the results might be similar to those given in Table 14.1.

The information contained in this demand schedule can be shown on a graph as a demand curve. (See Figure 14.1.) A *demand curve,* like a demand schedule, relates prices to quantities demanded. The *DD* curve makes it possible to select any price and ascertain the quantity buyers would like to purchase at that price.

Why does the demand curve usually have a downward slope? At higher

Table 14.1 **Number of Ford Pintos Demanded at Various Prices**

Price	Quantity Demanded per Year (in 1,000,000s)
$1000	10
1500	8
2000	6
2500	4

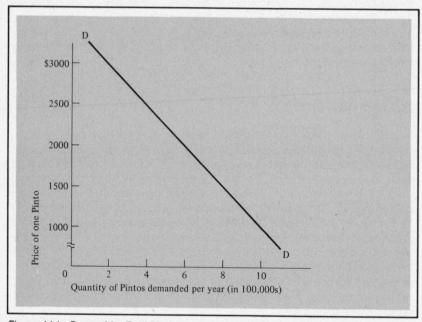

Figure 14.1 **Demand for Ford Pintos**

prices, people have a small demand—both because other goods appear more attractive and because they just don't have enough income to buy at those prices. As prices decline, people demand more—both because they can afford more and because these goods are now cheaper relative to other alternatives. We discuss these issues in more detail in later sections.

In a similar manner it is possible to find the number of Pintos the Ford Motor Company would desire to sell at various prices. Table 14.2 summarizes this hypothetical information. In Figure 14.2 the same information is expressed in the form of a supply curve, demonstrating the quantities sellers would like to sell at various prices.

Why does the supply curve usually slope upward? Ford is in business for profit. At higher prices it can make more profit, so it is willing to supply more Pintos at higher prices. This issue is also discussed more fully in later sections.

Market prices are determined by the forces of supply and demand. Sellers wish to exchange products for money, and buyers wish to exchange money for products. When a particular price is established, a specific quantity will be offered for sale and a specific quantity will be demanded. If these two quantities are equal, both sellers and buyers are able to conduct transactions in the desired quantities. For example, in Figure 14.3 the demand curve for Pintos (from Figure 14.1) is superimposed on the supply curve (from Figure 14.2). If a price of $2000 is established, the point at which the curves intersect indicates that buyers and sellers want to buy and sell 600,000 cars.

Table 14.2 **Number of Ford Pintos Supplied at Various Prices**

Price	Quantity Supplied per Year (in 1,000,000s)
$1000	2
1500	4
2000	6
2500	8

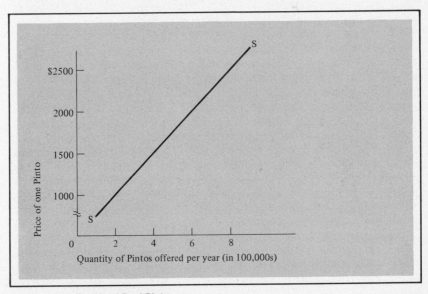

Figure 14.2 **Supply of Ford Pintos**

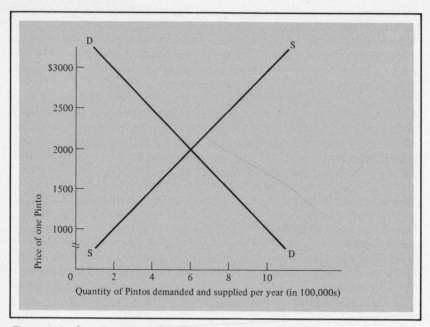

Figure 14.3 **Quantity of Pintos demanded and supplied per year (in 100,000s)**

When the desires of buyers and sellers are consistent and both are able to conduct their desired exchanges, the market is said to be in *equilibrium.* The notion of equilibrium is central to most economic theories. It generally means that supply and demand are equal and that the exchange desires of buyers and sellers are mutually consistent. At equilibrium prices everyone is able to buy or sell all that one chooses to buy or sell within one's budget.

If a price that is higher than the equilibrium price is established, then supply will exceed demand. This is called a situation of *excess supply.* In Figure 14.4, if the price of Pintos is set at $2500 an excess supply exists. Ford would like to sell 800,000 Pintos at that price, but buyers would like to buy only 400,000. There is an excess supply of 400,000.

In many markets there is a tendency for the forces of supply and demand to cause price changes that will eliminate excess supply and equilibrate the market. In the situation illustrated in Figure 14.4, thousands of Pinto dealers will find that at the established price of $2500 they are unable to sell the quantity of cars they had anticipated. As unwanted inventories of unsold cars accumulate, the dealers cut back or eliminate entirely their orders with the Ford Motor Company. With production geared for the 800,000 cars the manufacturer had hoped to sell, it is not long before large unwanted inventories pile up at the factory.

In order to reduce these inventories and stimulate sales, the manufacturer *may* reduce the price, which definitely would improve the imbalance between supply and demand. As long as the price remains above $2000, however, the excess supply will persist, and the motive to cut the price further will continue to exist. Only at the equilibrium price of $2000 will excess supply disappear and the market be cleared.

At a price below $2000 demand would exceed supply. (See Figure 14.5.) Dealers would find long lines waiting to buy the few available cars. Orders sent to Ford would go largely unfilled because these orders would far exceed the number of Pintos being produced. Figure 14.5 shows that at the low price of $1,000 Ford will offer to supply only 200,000 cars but consumers wish to buy 1,000,000 cars. There is therefore an excess demand of 800,000 cars.

Under these conditions it would be obvious to the dealers and the manufacturer that more cars could be sold at higher prices. The search for higher profits would dictate that the price be raised. As the price is raised, the amount of excess demand declines. But at any price below $2000 there will continue to be some excess demand. There will therefore continue to be an upward pressure on the price until it reaches the equilibrium level of $2000.

The rate at which price changes bring the market into equilibrium varies greatly from market to market. In some markets sellers are very sensitive to unwanted changes in inventories, so adjustments in price occur very quickly. The New York Stock Exchange is highly sensitive to hour-by-hour fluctuations in supply and demand. Frequent price changes serve to keep the market very near equilibrium at all times.

At the other extreme, what is for most people the most important of all markets—the labor market—may go for years in a situation of disequilibrium. With only a few exceptions (mostly in time of war), this market has had a persistent excess supply, which means, of course, involuntary unemployment for some people. This is a subject that will receive considerable attention in Part Three.

There are also many cases in which control of supply or demand gives an individual or group of individuals the power to *fix* prices. In this case excess

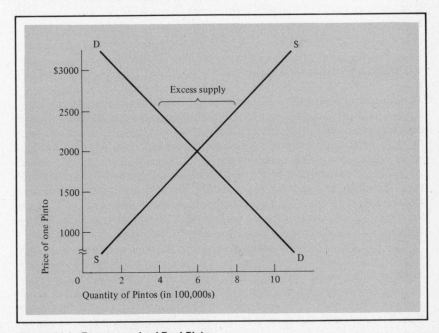

Figure 14.4 **Excess supply of Ford Pintos**

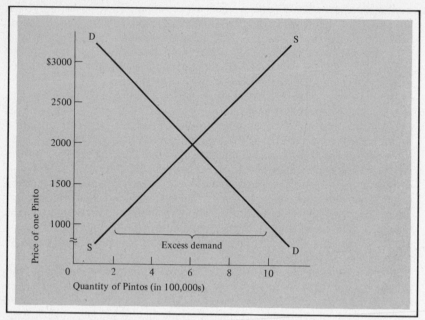

Figure 14.5 **Excess demand for Ford Pintos**

supply or demand may not lead to price changes if those changes are not in the best interests of the price fixer. We shall examine this fact and its implications in later chapters (18 and 19) on imperfect competition, *oligopoly* (when a few firms control supply), and *monopoly* (when one firm controls supply).

CHANGES IN DEMAND

There are three main factors that can change the demand for a particular commodity: (1) price changes, (2) changes in tastes or preferences, and (3) changes in income that consumers have to spend. We have already discussed price changes. With a given demand schedule, a lower price means more demand, while a higher one means less demand.

Suppose there is a change in preferences, with consumer preferences shifting from big, gaudy cars to small, economical ones like the Pinto. What happens to the demand schedule? At any given price, more will be demanded. This upward shift in demand is illustrated in Figure 14.6. The old demand curve, D_1D_1, is replaced by a new and higher demand curve, D_2D_2.

Now consider another influence on demand. Suppose that there was a general increase in the incomes of all people consuming Pintos. With the new, higher incomes individuals will probably buy *more* Pintos at *every* possible price. The higher incomes cause a *shift* in the demand curve. This produces a *new demand curve* (line D_2D_2). *At any price* the new demand curve shows that people wish to buy more at that price than they formerly did (when line D_1D_1 was the demand curve).

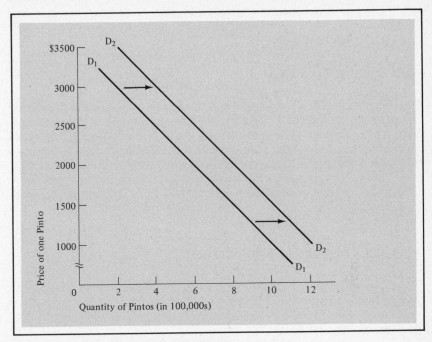

Figure 14.6 **Change in demand for Ford Pintos**

This increased demand is the result of the increase in income. In general, whenever there is a change in any of the factors (other than price) that affect demand, this change will be shown as a shift in the demand curve.

A bit of terminology here will make you sound like a sophisticated economist and may save you some confusion later on. Whenever an economist says flatly "demand has changed," he or she means *the whole demand curve has shifted.* An increase in demand means a shift of the curve outward (to the right, from D_1D_1 to D_2D_2); it means *more* Pintos are demanded at any given price. A decrease in demand means a shift of the curve inward (to the left, from D_2D_2 to D_1D_1); it means *fewer* Pintos are demanded at any given price.

When everything else stays the same (i.e., the curve does not shift) and only the price changes, the economist will *not* say "demand has changed." He or she will just say there has been "*movement along* the demand curve," or a change in quantity demanded. The economist will say, "at a higher price, less quantity was demanded" or "at a lower price, more quantity was demanded," but with no change or shift in the demand curve as a whole. In other words, with no shift in demand Ford could sell more Pintos only by lowering the price (and if Ford raises the prices it will sell fewer Pintos).

Of course, in reality both things often happen at once: (1) Prices of Pintos change, and (2) income and other factors affecting demand change. As a result of both (1) and (2), the quantity of Pintos demanded has changed. But it is impossible to be sure how much of the demand change was a result of the price change (movement along the demand curve) and how much was a result of changes in income and other factors (shift in demand curve). In other words, reality does not draw curves; only economists draw curves to try to analyze what is going on.

CHANGES IN SUPPLY

The explanation of shifts in demand and movements along demand curves may be repeated for changes in supply. The student should work this through in Figure 14.7. Consider, for example, the way higher or lower prices per car would cause Ford to move along the supply curve S_1S_1), offering more or fewer Pintos to the consumer market at different prices. But also consider the way lower costs per car (such as a lower price of steel per ton) might motivate Ford to offer more Pintos at each given price consumers would pay (i.e., a shift from supply curve S_1S_1 to S_2S_2).

CHANGES IN SUPPLY AND DEMAND

Finally, by putting the changes in supply and demand together it is possible to explain how prices are forced to change. The effect on the price of Pintos of an increase or decrease in demand (with supply conditions remaining unchanged) is shown in Figure 14.8.

An increase in demand for Pintos can be explained as a shift up from curve D_1D_1 to D_2D_2, or as a movement along the supply curve SS up and to the right.

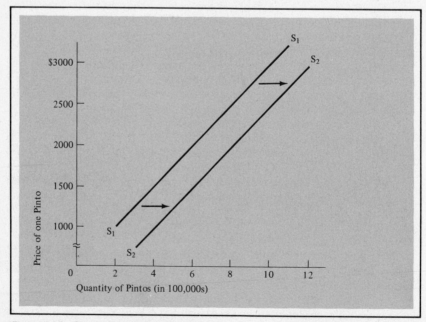

Figure 14.7 **Change in supply of Ford Pintos**

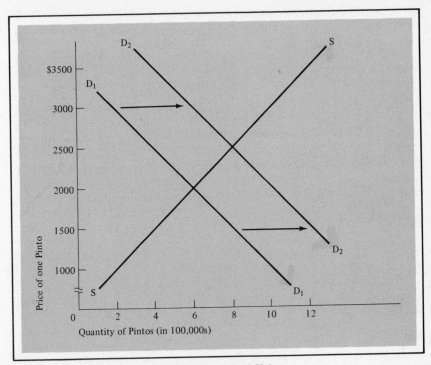

Figure 14.8 **Changes in demand and price of Ford Pintos**

Either description is correct. Either way, the fact is that Ford can sell *more* Pintos at a *higher price*. The quantity sold went from 600,000 to 800,000; the price went from $2,000 to $2,500. Of course there is nothing mysterious about that delightful result for Ford. It happened because it was assumed that demand shifted to Pintos (from Chevrolets or Volkswagens, perhaps). In the example in which Ford could sell more Pintos only at a lower price, it was assumed that there was *no* shift in demand to Pintos.

Similarly, in Figure 14.8 a decrease in demand for Pintos means a shift down from curve D_2D_2 back to D_1D_1. Suppose consumers shift demand from Pintos to Volkswagens. Then Ford will sell *fewer* Pintos at a *lower* price per car, assuming that the supply curve remains as drawn.

Now, on the other side, consider the changes in the supply of Pintos while the demand remains the same. (See Figure 14.9.)

An increase in supply means a shift over from curve S_1S_1 to S_2S_2. For some reason, perhaps lower costs per car or competition from Volkswagen, Ford is offering to supply more Pintos at every price at which consumers might demand them. There is an outward shift in the supply curve or a *movement* out *along* the demand curve. With demand unchanged, Ford is selling more Pintos by lowering their price. Whereas it previously sold 600,000 Pintos at $2,000 each, it now sells 800,000 at only $1,500 each.

A decrease in supply means shifting back from S_2S_2 to S_1S_1. Suppose, for example, that Ford's production costs rise for some reason. It may then charge higher prices *and* sell fewer cars. The supply curve has shifted, moving back along the demand curve, so that prices have gone up and fewer Pintos are being sold.

Of course in reality *both* curves may shift in the same period. Because of this possibility, it is usually impossible to tell which curve has shifted and which has remained stationary (or by how much each has moved) in the real world.

THE MARKET AS AN ALLOCATIVE DEVICE

One of the central problems with which economics deals is the allocation of scarce resources. Perhaps the most universal of social and economic problems faced by all societies is the fact that no society's capacity to produce or secure goods has yet been sufficient to satisfy all the wants, needs, and desires people have for these goods. Any good is considered by economists to be a *scarce good* when demand would exceed supply *if the good were to be given away freely in any desired quantity with no price charged for it.* It is obvious that most objects people need and desire are scarce goods.

Any society must devise a method of dividing up or allocating scarce goods among its citizens. In a slave economy, the slaves, like productive domesticated animals, were given enough to keep them fairly healthy so that they could work and reproduce themselves; the rest of the economy's output went to their masters. In the feudal economy (described in Chapters 1 and 2), conditions of land tenure largely determined the distribution and allocation of goods. The feudal

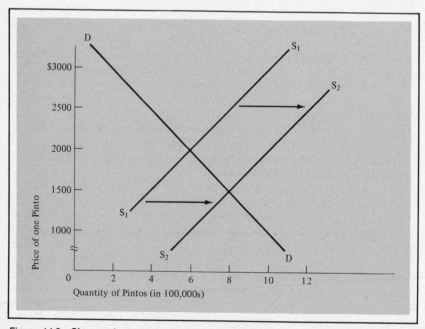

Figure 14.9 **Changes in supply and price of Ford Pintos**

serf, like the slave, got a minimal subsistence income, whereas the feudal lord, like the slave's master, received a much larger share in the fruits of production.

In a private enterprise economy, the market allocates scarce resources and goods. If the needs and desires for a particular good far exceed the available supply (as is the case with most goods), then the good goes to those who are willing and able to pay the highest price for it in the market.

It may be the case that many people desperately need a car like the Pinto but cannot afford its present price, although they could afford to pay a lower price. Now suppose the government fixed the price by law below the point at which supply and demand meet. There would still be two groups of people excluded from the consumption of Pintos: (1) Those who could not afford to pay even the lower price would again be excluded; (2) those who did not get their places in line before the supply of Pintos was exhausted would be excluded, in spite of the fact that they would have been willing and able to pay even the higher price. This kind of shortage may become a common situation in America if the wage-price controls begun in late 1971 are continued for a long period. In some socialist countries, such as the Soviet Union, price fixing of this type is fairly common. This explains the frequent reports of "shortages" and long queues in these countries.

Obviously, to the extent that markets tend to be self-equilibrating in a private enterprise economy and that there is no government price fixing, there will be a tendency for these shortages to be eliminated. It must be emphasized, though, that economists use the term *shortage* in a way that has no necessary relation to the abundance or lack of abundance of a good relative to people's need for it. The shortage is only relative to the demand *in money terms* by paying customers.

For example, imagine two economies, one in which an efficiently self-equilibrating market exists and another in which goods are all given away free on a first-come, first-served basis. In the first economy, there may be an extreme paucity of provision with only a tiny elite minority receiving most of the meager supply of available goods. If the markets are all in equilibrium, there are no shortages in the economist's sense, despite the fact that many may be dying of starvation. In the second economy, there may be an abundance of goods that are given away at no charge. Even though virtually everyone might be very well off relative to even the richest citizens in the first economy, if some people want more than is available to them there will be an economic shortage.

It is important to understand clearly the economist's meaning of the word *shortage* because the assertion that a market economy has fewer shortages than a nonmarket, or planned, economy is often misconstrued to imply that the material welfare of people in a market economy must be higher than that of people in a nonmarket economy. This welfare may or may not be higher, but it has nothing to do with the existence or nonexistence of economic shortages. In fact, in economies where the decision has been made *not* to use the market as the primary device to allocate scarce resources, the people have chosen to divide the produce of society by some nonmonetary means. They will no longer exclude those who cannot afford to pay the market price for a scarce good but must use some other principle of distribution.

How can market versus nonmarket means of allocating scarce goods be evaluated? Such an evaluation would require the weighing of many diverse considerations. The market tends to allocate scarce goods with a minimum of inconvenience and bureaucratic red tape. The whole process is generally quite efficient and impersonal. By contrast, look at two widely used nonmarket allocative mechanisms. First, there are rationing coupons like those used by the United States during World War II, which limit the amount of a scarce good any individual can purchase, regardless of the amount of money he or she has. Second, there is the first-come, first-served technique, in which those at the end of the queue are automatically eliminated when the supply of the good in question is exhausted.

The first of these nonmarket allocative mechanisms involves the high cost of extensive record keeping and some inevitable bureaucratic inefficiencies in the control and distribution of the coupons. The second method causes much wasted time as people wait in queues. It often leads to bitterness and resentment because people who can afford to buy the scarce commodity wait in line for a long time, only to find the supply exhausted when they finally work their way to the head of the line.

Thus it can be said that, in terms of convenience and efficiency, the market is probably superior to these two nonmarket allocative mechanisms (the superior efficiency relates only to the allocative process and implies nothing about technological efficiency in the production of goods and services in private enterprise versus nonmarket economies).

The market is frequently criticized, however, on the grounds that the resultant allocation of scarce goods is inequitable, unfair, and unjust. It is argued that in a private enterprise economy like the United States, where a few people receive the overwhelming bulk of all profits generated by the economy, an unjustly lopsided concentration of income and purchasing power is created. Many economists feel that as a consequence of this concentration of purchasing power the private enterprise economy emphasizes production primarily for the wealthy. In allocating scarce medical care, for example, the private enterprise system places more importance on psychiatric care for the neurotic pets of the wealthy than it does on the provision of minimal health services for the children of the poor.

To illustrate this last point, imagine a hypothetical island economy that is periodically struck with an epidemic of a disease that affects only children. From past experiences the islanders have found that when the disease strikes it randomly affects 80 percent of the children. They have also discovered a preventive antidote that reduces the chances of death if it is taken before the disease strikes. A child who has taken no doses of the antidote has a 90 percent chance of dying when he or she contracts the disease. With one dose of the antidote, the chance of death is reduced to 10 percent. Two doses reduce the chance to 8 percent; three doses reduce the chance to 6 percent; four doses reduce the chance to 5 percent. Beyond four doses the antidote has no further effect, and the chances of death remain at 5 percent.

Suppose that the island has 1000 children and that at the first sign of a new outbreak of the dreaded disease the people have produced and accumulated 1000 doses of the antidote. The antidote must be used immediately if the children's lives are to be saved. What system of allocation should the people use to distribute this extremely important scarce good? If the government on the island issues rationing coupons so that each child gets one dose of the antidote, then the following results could be expected: 800 children will get the disease, but since each has had one dose of the antidote, only 80 children will die; 920 children will survive the epidemic.

On the other hand, suppose the relative distribution of income and wealth that exists in the United States today. According to this income distribution, the islanders leave the allocation problem to the private-enterprise, free market system, with the following results: the 250 children who have the wealthiest parents will each take four doses of the antidote; of these 250, about 200 will get the disease and about 10 will die; of the remaining 750 children, 600 will get the disease and about 540 will die.

Using a nonmarket allocative mechanism, the islanders were able to save 920 children while 80 died. Given the unequal distribution of income and wealth that exists in the private enterprise market allocation, they saved 450 children while 550 died. This is admittedly a farfetched example with hypothetical percentages chosen to illustrate our point dramatically. But the point is there, and perhaps exaggeration is the most effective method of illustrating it. The student is urged to read *Don't Get Sick in America*,[1] a frightening but scholarly study that shows that this example is by no means as distorted as it might appear at first glance.

In ending this discussion on market allocation, it should be noted that one's view of the desirability of the market system depends on whether one is more impressed with the efficacy and impersonality of this allocation mechanism or with its lopsided results. Thus one defender of capitalism writes, "The case for capitalism is at its strongest on the simple thesis that the market knows best how to allocate and use the scarce resource of capital."[2] A critic of capitalism sees it differently: "The main reason that freedom of contract has never been as free as advertised—and it is a painfully obvious reason—is that sellers and buyers are not equal in bargaining power. So the terms of sale will simply reflect the power, or lack of it, that each party brings to the market place. So a market is also a financial slaughterhouse, where the strong chop up the weak."[3]

Even the "efficiency" of the capitalist market has been criticized as a very narrowly limited concept. As will be seen in Chapters 18 and 19, such efficient allocation of resources would operate only under pure competition; America, however, is characterized by a high degree of monopoly power. In Chapter 21 we explore the fact that if there is discrimination the market will reflect it and may reinforce it. In examining the aggregate economy in Part Three, we shall demonstrate that "efficient" use of resources applies only to employed resources but that the market system may leave many resources, both machines and human beings, unemployed. In Part Three we also note that private efficiency may ignore social costs such as pollution. This list of qualifications to market "efficiency" will be lengthened still further in Part Three, particularly when we consider the international market mechanism that includes the less developed two-thirds of the world.

SUMMARY

In a competitive market economy prices are determined by the conditions of supply and demand. Demand is based on consumers' desires and incomes. No

---

[1] Schorr, *Don't Get Sick in America* (Nashville, Tenn.: Aurora Publishers, 1970).

[2] Simon Webley, "The Utilization of Capital," in M. Ivens and R. Dunstan, eds., *The Case for Capitalism* (London: Michael Joseph, 1967), p. 41.

[3] D. T. Bazelon, *The Paper Economy* (New York: Random House, Vintage Books, 1963), p. 52.

cash, no sale. *If* there is pure competition, the market mechanism will allocate resources to each industry according to the cash demand for its product. Supply is based on the firm's costs of production. Thus, as costs go up, higher prices are required in order to induce the firm to supply more. As the price goes up, however, consumers will demand less. The equilibrium price will be the point at which supply and demand just balance. Its defenders claim that this system of production for private profit is efficient, even if it is not humane (but even its efficiency is very narrowly defined).

CHAPTER 15

PRICES AND INCOME:
The Neoclassical Theory

In Chapter 14 we examined the ways in which competition in the market allocates all resources under private enterprise capitalism. We explored the mechanics of price determination by supply and demand. All economists agree on the mechanics of supply and demand. Economists disagree, however, on the forces that determine supply and demand themselves, particularly the supply and demand for capital and labor. In this chapter we examine the neoclassical theory of how supply is determined by marginal cost and the cost of each "factor of production" is determined by its marginal product. In the next chapter we examine the Marxist or radical theory of these subjects.

UTILITY AND DEMAND

It has been demonstrated that the competitive market tends to allocate resources to produce things according to the pattern of consumer demand (with each customer's desires weighted according to how much money he or she has to spend). The heart of neoclassical economics, from early theorists like Stanley Jevons to most present-day textbook writers, is the notion that consumer demand, in turn, is determined by the utility of each commodity to the consumer. *Utility* is defined as *the pleasure or satisfaction one receives from consuming a good.* Most neoclassical textbooks state that utility alone determines how much people will be willing to pay for the good or how much of the good people will buy at various prices. However, several qualifications to this statement of the importance of utility must be made.

First, consumers often are persuaded by false and misleading advertising that they will receive a great deal more pleasure from a commodity than is attainable. On this basis they purchase the commodity, only to be disappointed and receive little or no satisfaction from it. Second, many actions are guided not by a search for pleasure, satisfaction, or utility but by habit, caprice, impulse, or any one of dozens of motives psychologists could list. Third, and most generally, a market society tends to inculcate a "buying mentality" in many consumers. The objective in making purchases sometimes becomes simply the spending of money per se rather than the satisfying of real needs or desires for the things purchased. This finding has been particularly emphasized in recent work in psychology concerning feelings of emptiness and alienation.[1]

[1] See the discussion by Erich Fromm in Chapter 13.

For these reasons, we believe the pattern of consumer demand is forced into a particular form by many things other than the actual pleasure or satisfaction derived directly from consumption of each commodity. But because the term *utility* is almost always used to explain demand, it will be retained but redefined for our purposes. We conceive of utility as synonymous with desire. If we say that a particular good possesses utility for a particular person, we simply mean that that person *desires to buy* the good in question. The desire may be the result of any number of motives. It may be a healthy desire that will, if satisfied, increase the person's well-being, or it may be a perverted or morbid desire that will, if satisfied, lead to pernicious or harmful results. In other words, the satisfaction of any particular desire cannot be said, a priori, to be either morally good or morally bad until there is sufficient information available to make an independent moral judgment.

DIMINISHING MARGINAL UTILITY

The neoclassical theory of demand begins with the principle of *diminishing marginal utility.* The marginal utility of a good is defined as the strength of the consumer's desire to purchase *one additional unit* of the good. The principle of diminishing marginal utility states that *as more and more of a good is acquired, the marginal utility of the good diminishes.*

On a hot summer day, for example, a person may desire a malted milk very intensely. But if he has one malted milk, the intensity of his desire for another diminishes. If he has two malted milks, the intensity of his desire for a third will be very low. He may have no desire at all for a third. Another way of stating this is to say that the marginal utility of malted milks diminishes as one more is bought.

HOW CONSUMERS MAXIMIZE UTILITY

When consumers spend their income, they strive to maximize their utility. Suppose their income permits them to purchase a large number of different groups, or *bundles,* of commodities. They will try to choose the bundle that satisfies their strongest or most urgent desires; that is, they will attempt to maximize their utility.

The consumer comes to the market with (1) a set of preferences or desires and (2) a certain amount of money income. Because the consumer's desires are constrained by his or her income, the consumer must pay attention to prices. It turns out that the consumer will maximize satisfaction or utility when income is spent so that *the marginal or additional utility derived from the last unit of each good purchased is exactly in proportion to the price paid for each good.* Another way to state this rule is to say that the consumer's satisfaction is maximized when an additional dollar spent for any one good yields exactly the same marginal utility as an additional dollar spent for any other good. This rule is explained further in a simple example whose calculations are shown in Appendix A to this chapter.

ELASTICITY OF DEMAND

Economists have developed concepts to describe demand curves in terms of how much the amount demanded reacts to a price change. If a small price change up or down causes a very big change in quantity demanded, the demand is said to be very *elastic.* But if a significant price change causes almost no change in quantity demanded, the demand is said to be very *inelastic.*

What kind of commodities have elastic demands (big reactions to price changes)? Mostly luxuries, such as movies or cake or Cadillacs. If the price is low enough, a consumer will be happy to buy a piece of cake or go to a movie or buy a new car. But if the price of one of these luxuries goes up while his or her income stays the same, the consumer will have to cut back on the luxury to buy more needed things. Demand for luxuries is very sensitive to prices; it is elastic.

The demand curve for cake might look like the one in Figure 15.1. The demand is elastic because when price declines, the rise in quantity is more than proportionate, so the total expenditure (or revenue to the seller) actually rises. Thus, at $3 only 100 cakes are sold and the total revenue is $300. But if the price goes down to $2, then 300 cakes are sold and the total revenue rises to $600.

What kind of commodities have inelastic demands (small reactions to price changes)? Mostly necessities, such as medicine or basic foods. If you are diabetic and need insulin to stay alive, then you will still buy almost the same amount even if its price doubles. If you live in China and your main food is rice, then if the price rises considerably you will reluctantly look for a substitute; but you may still demand quite a bit. If the price of rice falls, you may demand more; but if it was already 80 percent of your diet, you will not demand much more.

The demand curve for rice in China might look like the one in Figure 15.2. The demand is inelastic because when price declines, the rise in quantity is *less than proportionate,* so the total revenue declines. Thus, at $3 the quantity demanded and sold is 100 pounds and the total revenue is $300. But if the price goes down to $1, the quantity demanded only goes to 200 pounds and the total revenue *declines* to $200.

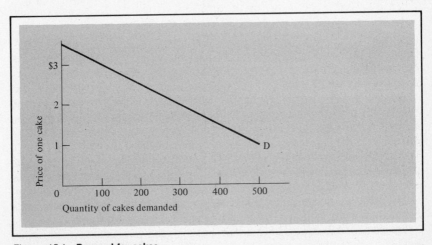

Figure 15.1 **Demand for cakes**

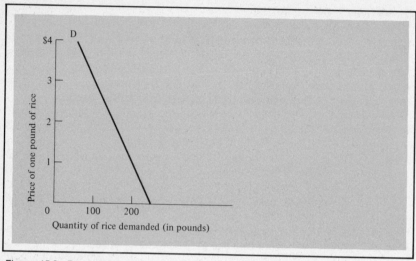

Figure 15.2 **Demand for rice**

These, then, are the concepts of elastic and inelastic demand. They can be expressed in a general formula to measure elasticity. Elasticity may be defined more precisely as

$$\text{Elasticity} = \frac{\text{percentage rise in quantity demanded}}{\text{percentage cut in price}}$$

Of course it is just as easy to talk about a decline in quantity demanded due to a price rise or, in general, the percentage *change* in quantity demanded due to a percentage *change* in price. Exactly how to calculate elasticity is shown in Appendix B to this chapter.

SUPPLY AND MARGINAL COST

Consumer behavior and demand have been examined in great detail. In order to complete the picture, it is necessary to examine the behavior of business enterprises in supplying goods, but only in enough detail to supply the information necessary for an understanding of price determination in the competitive market. The details of business price and output behavior are very different for pure competition and for various degrees of monopoly power; these details will be discussed in the chapters on competition and monopoly.

A firm's decision regarding the quantity of its product it wishes to supply at various prices depends on many things. The most important factor, though, is usually its costs of producing different quantities of its product. Just as neoclassical economics emphasizes marginal utility in determining consumer demand, it emphasizes marginal cost in determining business supply to the market.

Marginal cost is the additional cost of producing one more unit of output. Suppose a firm owns a single factory with 100 machines. It can increase its output only by adding more raw materials and more workers. Here, however, there is a law of increasing marginal cost for firms that is similar to the law of diminishing marginal utility for consumers.

Assume a given factory and machines (and no time to add more or improve technology). Then the lowest cost per unit is reached at some particular flow of raw materials and some *given number* of workers. To make it simple, assume that raw material flow is always adjusted to the number of workers. As the number of workers is increased, the cost changes. If there are too few workers, they will not be able to handle the whole factory efficiently. But as the number of workers increases beyond some point, they add less and less to the product; or, the marginal cost of one more unit of output rises. For example, if there are only 100 machines and each machine needs only one worker, what can more than 100 workers contribute? Certainly some are needed to bring in raw materials and to take them away, clean up, and repair. At some point, however, whether it is 125 or 150 or even 200, an additional worker could only add less than the previously hired worker.

Within these rigid assumptions it is hard to quarrel with this law. On this basis it is possible to picture marginal costs rising with output (after some minimal cost point is passed). Entrepreneurs will obviously not supply additional goods to the market at a price below their additional cost. Therefore, as the marginal cost of production rises for additional output, the prices at which additional supply will be offered must also rise.

In a perfectly competitive market the firm's supply curve is identical to its marginal-cost curve. The reason firms will supply goods at "cost" is that the traditional neoclassical definition of cost includes a "normal" profit. (The implications of this peculiar neoclassical definition will be examined in Chapter 19.) With imperfect competition or monopoly, the amount a firm will supply is not determined solely by its costs. (This will also be discussed in Chapter 19.) In the present context, however, it is sufficient to know that the firm's marginal cost is important in determining how much it will supply to the market.

THE PRICE AND OUTPUT OF AN INDUSTRY

Based on an understanding of the ways in which consumer desires (and income levels) determine demand and the ways in which enterprise costs determine supply to the market, it is possible to sum up the action of supply and demand for a whole industry. The mechanics of it were studied in Chapter 14. Here the main point is recapitulated in this new concept.

We shall illustrate the general way in which supply and demand determine price with the example of the mythical commodity called "Gadgets." It is assumed that the mythical industry of Gadget producers is composed of thousands and thousands of purely competitive firms. We are forced to use a fictitious commodity made by a fictitious industry because *few, if any, actual industries are purely competitive.* Later, in Chapter 19, we will explain the importance of the degree of competition in a given industry.

Figure 15.3 shows the usual supply and demand curve for Gadgets, a competitive industry. Supply *SS* is based on marginal cost; demand *DD* is based on marginal utility.

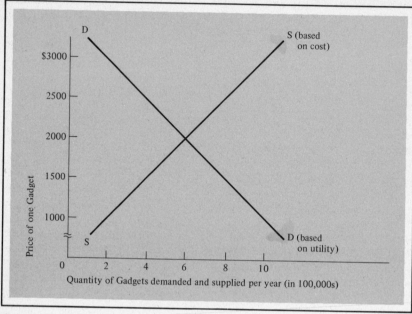

Figure 15.3 **Supply and demand for Gadgets**

The point at which supply and demand meet determines both the price of the Gadget and the number of Gadgets produced. At any lower price level, there is excess demand, and therefore the industry can produce more Gadgets *and* raise their price, hence making more profit. At any higher price level, there is excess supply, and therefore the industry is forced to produce fewer Gadgets and lower its prices.

The supply behavior is based on the marginal cost (always including a "normal" profit) of a Gadget to the Gadget Production Company.

This is a much oversimplified statement of the current view of price determination. Before it can be further refined and compared with earlier theories, one more tool is required: elasticity of supply.

ELASTICITY OF SUPPLY

It is not necessary to become involved in a detailed discussion of elasticity of supply because the concept is exactly analogous to that of elasticity of demand. Supply is elastic if it responds more than proportionately to a price change, and it is inelastic if it responds less than proportionately to a price change. More precisely,

$$\text{Elasticity of supply} = \frac{\text{percentage rise in quantity supplied}}{\text{percentage rise in price}}$$

Unlike demand, the quantity supplied moves in the same direction as price because a higher price means a higher profit (costs remaining the same), which induces a business to produce and sell more.

Inelastic supply reaction is found most often with perishable goods. Ripe tomatoes *must* be sold quickly, regardless of the price that can be obtained in the market. But durable goods such as furniture may show an elastic (sensitive) supply reaction to price changes. If the price of furniture falls, it can simply be stored and not offered for sale.

MOMENTARY SUPPLY AND PRICE EQUILIBRIUM

Even in the preceding examples, the length of time considered is clearly important. Besides tomatoes already in the market, what about the longer-run reaction of tomato growers? If the price falls for a long enough time, the number of tomatoes grown *will* decline considerably.

In the 1890s Alfred Marshall used this notion to clarify the concept of price determination. He distinguished the supply reaction to a price or demand change in three periods: momentary, short run, and long run. The momentary period is so short (an hour, a day, or a week, depending on the product) that the amount of supply in the market cannot be varied at all. The short-run period is long enough for a factory to produce more or less for the market within its capacity but too short for any new factories to be built or put into use. The long-run period is long enough for as many new factories to be built as are necessary to bring the supply up to the demand.

How does this time factor affect elasticity of supply (and thus, indirectly, prices)? Assume that at a given moment Gadget dealers have a certain supply of Gadgets on hand. No matter what sudden change there is in demand, they cannot sell more until they receive more: Momentary supply is perfectly inelastic.

Assume now that the one Gadget dealer in a town usually sells 10 Gadgets a week and that the factory delivers 10 Gadgets each Monday. One week the dealer sells 6 Gadgets up through Thursday. So on Friday there are 4 Gadgets to sell. But that Friday 8 customers want to buy Gadgets immediately (and are not willing to wait until Monday).

In this case the supply is fixed at 4, so the price will be raised to take advantage of the higher demand. Suppose the dealer has been selling at a price of $1800. Because 8 cannot be sold at $1800, the dealer may try to sell the 4 in stock at $2000. (See Figure 15.4.)

The Gadget dealer was ready for the usual Demand D_1D_1, but the demand shifted that day to D_2D_2. Still, the supply is perfectly inelastic for that day; the dealer simply cannot get more Gadgets to sell in that period. So the higher demand reaches equilibrium with the fixed supply at a higher price.

Most of the early utility theorists (from the crude J. B. Say to the very sophisticated Carl Menger) concentrated on market exchange and gave little consideration to changes in supply conditions. Consequently, it seems that this given momentary supply is the only case they considered. They stated (and it is true in this case) that marginal utility determines demand and that demand changes largely determine price changes. These theorists used this case to attack the older theory (of Marx and the classicals—Ricardo and Smith) that labor cost

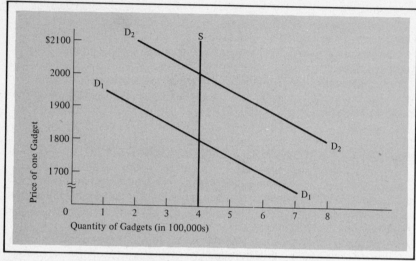

Figure 15.4 **Momentary equilibrium of Gadgets**

determines supply, which ultimately determines price. Certainly *in this case,* where supply is perfectly inelastic, supply cannot change and therefore cannot explain changes in price.

SHORT-RUN SUPPLY AND PRICE EQUILIBRIUM

What price will bring an equilibrium of supply and demand in the short run? Or how do supply and demand changes affect price in the short run? These are the questions emphasized by Alfred Marshall and in every neoclassical beginning text to the present day.

Briefly, in the short run marginal cost tends to rise when a firm tries to produce additional units of output beyond some point because the short run is, by definition, a period in which the firm has a *given* factory and machinery and no time to expand it. Technology requires some particular number of workers to run the plant at capacity (or at the cheapest cost per unit). When the firm tries to produce more than the capacity for which the factory is designed by adding more workers, the product per additional worker naturally declines; or, the marginal cost rises.

Because supply will never be below marginal cost, the supply curve naturally rises (up and to the right, as in Figure 15.5) as output expands. In other words, with rising costs the firm will supply more goods only at higher prices; or, the supply curve is more or less elastic, depending on the product, but is certainly no longer perfectly inelastic.

A shift upward in demand will raise prices, as in the previous case, but now the new equilibrium price is clearly also affected by the movement along the supply curve.

Figure 15.5 shows that an increase in demand for Gadgets raises *both* the price (from $2000 to $2500) and the quantity (from 600,000 to 800,000). The quan-

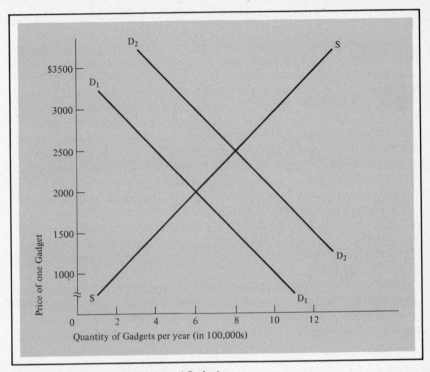

Figure 15.5 **Short-run equilibrium of Gadgets**

tity rises because the supply curve is somewhat elastic. This reflects the fact that existing Gadget plants have the capacity to turn out more Gadgets, *although at rising costs per Gadget.* It is clear in this case that both the quantity supplied and that demanded change and so together determine the new price equilibrium.

Alfred Marshall thus emphasized that supply and demand operate like the two blades of the scissors. Supply behavior is based on marginal costs. Demand behavior is based on marginal utility. It follows in the modern neoclassical view that both utility and cost together determine prices or values.

LONG-RUN SUPPLY AND PRICE EQUILIBRIUM

In the long run new factories can be built. Capital and labor can shift to industries where demand has risen. Therefore in the long run the quantity supplied can always rise as much as demand does.

Moreover, if Gadget Producers Company builds a new factory to produce more Gadgets, the new factory need have no higher cost per Gadget than the older factories. Hence the average cost (and the marginal, too) remain the same in the long run. Of course this is a rough approximation. In some cases better technology may allow the new factory to produce Gadgets at a lower cost per Gadget. In other cases expanded production with more use of a scarce raw material may drive the price of the raw material up, thus raising the cost per

Gadget. Here, for simplicity, the most common case—*constant cost* per Gadget in the long run—*is assumed.*

If, however, marginal costs are constant in the long run, then the supply curve will also be constant. It will be flat or a horizontal straight line on the graph. In short, supply will be perfectly elastic. Figure 15.6 illustrates this situation. In the long run what is the effect of an increased demand for Gadgets? More factories are built, and the supply adjusts completely to the demand. Moreover, the new factories have about the same cost per Gadget as the previous ones—assuming additional cost from greater use of resources is about canceled out by better technology.

In the long-run case, therefore, it can be asserted that the sole effect of an increase in demand is an equal increase in quantity produced. But the rise in demand has no effect on the price level. Of course at the initial moment of rise in demand, prices rose. However, that called forth more supply from existing factories in the short run, and therefore prices dropped a bit. In the long run the entire rise in demand was met by an equal increase in supply from new factories. Since the new factories have the same cost per Gadget as before, the price dropped back to its old level.

Therefore in the long run *demand determines the amount of production* (or the allocation of resources), *but supply alone determines the price level.* It can be said that the relative marginal utilities of different commodities determine the demand for them and the proportionate amounts of each produced. The long-

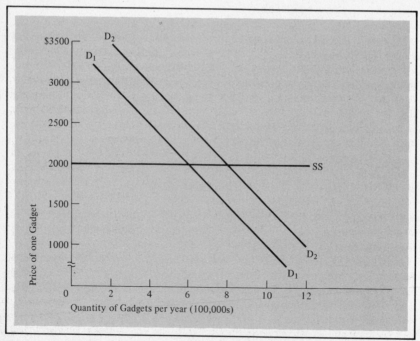

Figure 15.6 **Long-run equilibrium of Gadgets (SS line also represents price level)**

run price level, however, is determined solely by the level of costs per unit—that is, the supply conditions.

This is the case emphasized by the classicals and Marx. They were not so much interested in momentary or short-run market exchange and demand as in the long-run price or value of commodities. This they found to be determined solely by the cost of human effort or, as Marx put it, the total amount of human labor embodied in the product. He includes the labor involved in mining the raw materials and building the factories and machines used up in that production. This case, in which long-run labor cost determines price, is further explained in Chapter 16.

Marshall and the modern neoclassicals would agree that in this particular case of long-run supply, assuming constant costs, a change in marginal utility *does not* affect the price, but a change in the cost per unit *does* affect the price. The argument comes over the exact meaning of *cost*. The neoclassicals maintain that capitalists as well as workers put out an effort of some kind. The capitalist's "effort" may be a purely subjective "sacrifice" of immediate higher consumption for a later return on capital invested. Marx, however, insisted that it is only the workers' objective expenditure of labor that determines long-run price or value.

This dispute arises, of course, because there economists are concerned not only with the mechanics of price determination but also with the equitableness of income distribution. If the contributions to production by labor and capital are viewed differently, this obviously has much to do with how the distribution of income is viewed. Should Gadget workers or owners of Gadget stock receive the income from Gadget sales? This question of income distribution is discussed in the following sections.

THE DISTRIBUTION OF INCOME

The distribution of income is, perhaps, the most emotionally charged issue in economics. In a capitalist society differences in wealth and income distinguish and differentiate people in the most fundamental of ways. They determine who will live in slums and in mansions; who will be malnourished; who will have prestige, social power, and political power; who will be economically secure and emotionally self-confident; who will be economically insecure and lack confidence. And frequently these differences are the most important determinants of such diverse social issues as who commits what kind of crimes. For example, people who alter corporations' books in order to embezzle tens of thousands of dollars are generally relatively comfortable economically and if caught, generally receive comparatively light sentences. People who rob small amounts from liquor stores and gas stations, however, are more frequently economically destitute and always receive much harsher sentences. Thus, for these and many other reasons, the distribution of income is one of the most important aspects of any society.

Theories of what determines the distribution of income in a capitalist economy reflect the general ideological positions of the theorists vis-à-vis the evaluation of capitalism. Highly controversial issues are in question—for example, how capitalists make profits and whether workers are exploited.

THE MECHANICS OF INCOME DISTRIBUTION

Adam Smith talked about *rent* going to owners of land, *wages* going to labor, and *profits* going to the owners of capital. What determines the share of each of these types of income in the net national income? Economists' answers to this fundamental question differ greatly according to their basic world views. In fact, there are really two closely related questions: (1) What determines the share of each type of income? (2) Is the present distribution of income among different types good or bad?

To simplify the question, in this chapter we shall ignore the rent of land. In the modern United States and most industrialized economies, it is a very small category and thus not essential to the argument. That leaves two of Smith's categories: wages and profits. We define *wages* to mean all labor income, including time and piece wages, monthly salaries, commissions, bonuses, and managerial salaries. We define *profits* to mean all the return on capital. For the purposes of this argument, profits are included both as the return on the entrepreneur's own capital (*dividends*) and as the return on borrowed capital (*interest*). For other purposes in later chapters, it will be necessary to distinguish between these two forms of profits. *Capital* is the factories, machinery, raw materials, and money with which production and commerce are conducted.

The modern corporation owns its capital goods: factory, machinery, and raw materials. It pays wages and salaries to workers (including managerial salaries and bonuses). The workers use the capital goods to produce a product. The product is owned and sold by the corporation. What is the difference between a corporation and an unincorporated business? The most important difference is that the individual capitalist owners are not liable for the debts of the corporation.

The owners of the corporation are its stockholders. They each own a number of shares of *stock,* which represent their portion of the value of the corporation. To get the stock, of course, they paid money to the corporation. It uses that money to buy capital goods and to pay for labor. It may also borrow money; usually it issues bonds, which show how much the lender is owed (and how much interest he or she gets). The stockholders receive dividends, which are all the profits of the corporation from sales less all of the costs paid out (including wages, depreciation of capital, and interest to bondholders). If the corporation is unable to pay its debts, it is ruled bankrupt by the courts. Those who have lent money to it will divide all its remaining assets. If there are any assets left over, they go to the stockholders. But if there are insufficient assets to cover the debts, that's just too bad; no one can sue the stockholders.

THEORIES OF INCOME DISTRIBUTION

In discussing how income is distributed between wages and profits, economists have advanced two distinct and opposing views. The conservative view has generally dominated and is still taught as gospel in most American textbooks. It is a justification and apology for the status quo of U.S. capitalism. According to the conservative theory, (1) profits result from the sacrifices and productivity of capitalists (as wages result from the labor of workers), and (2) therefore the present distribution of income, in which many high incomes are made from profits, is just and equitable. The radical view has been advocated for at least 150 years, but it is just now gaining prominence in the United States. According to it, (1) capitalists are unproductive and extract their profits from the product of labor, and (2) therefore we need a new economic system in which private profit is eliminated. The radical theory is discussed in Chapter 16.

The Conservative Theory

The concept of profit as the reward to a capitalist for abstaining from immediate consumption was developed in the early nineteenth century by the economists W. Senior and J. B. Say. Each argued that provision of capital for production is a subjective cost, or disutility. The capitalist practices abstinence from consumption in order to invest capital and therefore is morally justified in making a profit from his investment. Similarly, wages result from subjective unpleasantness, or disutility, in providing labor.

In the 1870s Alfred Marshall[2] substituted *waiting* for *abstinence.* He argued that when the capitalist invests his capital in production he must *wait* to get the return from it until a future date. And the fact that he must wait to use all his wealth for consumption justifies his making a profit. Indeed, because he will not invest otherwise, a normal profit is simply a necessary cost of production.

The modern conservative theory of marginal productivity first appeared in full detail in John Bates Clark's *The Distribution of Wealth,* published in 1899.[3] It is dedicated to the propositions that workers and capitalists each receive in income exactly what they contribute as their marginal product and that this is an ethically just system. In other words, a worker's wage will just equal the additional (or marginal) product he or she adds to output. Likewise, the capitalist's profit just will equal the additional (or marginal) amount of product added by the piece of capital he adds to the productive process. This theory is gospel in all conservative textbooks, among them Paul Samuelson's famous work.[4]

The theory of marginal productivity is basically a very simple argument. Assume that there is a fixed amount of capital—that is, a particular factory and machinery. How many workers should be added by the rational capitalist to maximize his profits? Assume next that each additional worker adds something to the product, but that each additional worker adds less than the one before. This is the case because there is a fixed number of machines for them to use; therefore workers can add very little beyond the optimum capacity of the given factory. Suppose that there are five machines and ten workers and that most efficient functioning requires two workers per machine. Table 15.1 demonstrates the contribution to the marginal product of additional workers in this hypothetical factory.

The capitalist should continue to add workers until he finds that the last worker's product just equals his or her cost, or wage. If the wage rate is $70 a week, he should hire only 13 workers (or 12). Because the thirteenth worker makes no

[2] See Alfred Marshall, *Principles of Economics* (New York: Macmillan, 1953 [1st ed., 1890]).

[3] John Bates Clark, *The Distribution of Wealth* (Clifton, N.J.: Augustus M. Kelley, 1966 [first published in 1899]).

[4] Paul Samuelson, *Economics,* 10th ed. (New York: McGraw-Hill, 1977 [first published in 1948]).

Table 15.1

Number of Machines	Number of Workers	Total Product per Week	Marginal Product per Week
5	10	$1000	
5	11	1090	$90
5	12	1170	80
5	13	1240	70

additional profit for the capitalist, he should hire no more workers. The wage will just equal the additional (or marginal) product of the last workers.

Notice that what this theory has arrived at is a rule for capitalists to follow if they wish to maximize profits. If they do act this way (and they usually do), then the assertion that the wage is the same as the marginal product is at best a platitude: Workers are not hired if they produce a marginal product that is lower than the wage. This is simply because by hiring additional workers profits would be reduced. But some conservatives believe that they have thereby proved that this is a just and ethical distribution of income.

The conservative theory does exactly the same thing for profits. Assume that the capitalist employs a fixed number of workers. How much new machinery should he add? Suppose each machine adds less than the one before it. This is the case because there is a fixed number of workers; therefore additional machines cannot be used efficiently. Even if the capitalist could enforce a speedup, 100 workers could not handle 1000 machines. Stated with these rigid assumptions, the theory of diminishing marginal productivity is likewise a truism. But in the real world the capitalist adds both workers and machines, and new technology to boot, so there may be no diminishing productivity.

In this simple example, however, each additional machine adds less to the product than the previous one (because workers and perhaps factory space are limited). Thus the capitalist should add machines until the additional product of one more machine will just equal its cost. Beyond that point more machines give no more profit, so no more machines should be bought. Therefore the cost of providing an additional machine (whether out of the capitalist's own capital or from borrowed capital) will just equal the value of its additional (or marginal) product. Conservatives conclude that what is paid to capital is *its own* marginal product and that profits are a necessary cost of production and may be ethically justified.

Of course this argument applies only under pure competition; it does not apply in our present situation of pervasive monopoly power. Even Samuelson's conservative textbook agrees that *extra profits* (beyond the marginal product of capital) *are made under monopoly* to the degree that monopoly power controls the market. (This point is emphasized in Chapters 17, 18, and 19.)

RADICAL CRITIQUE OF MARGINAL-PRODUCTIVITY THEORY

It is important to note the grain of truth in Samuelson's conservative argument. It does show that marginal-productivity theory provides a general notion of how to make profits. It tells the capitalist to keep hiring workers (or adding machines) as long as they produce extra profit. When the additional profit approaches zero (because the additional product drops to the cost level), then the capitalist should stop adding workers (or machines).

Samuelson also shows that these are useful rules even for socialist planners to follow in allocating resources among investment projects. They must "introduce first those investment projects with the higher net productivity"[5] and use every additional worker and every additional machine in each project up to the point at which an additional unit would cost more than it adds to the product. In relation to the allocation of capital (factories and machines), this means that socialist planners must use something like a profit or interest rate to calculate which projects will bring the most return to society and which have returns too low to invest in. This argument, however, assumes that prices are useful measures of social benefits and social costs. Most radicals believe that prices, which are determined solely by the free play of supply and demand, are *not* useful indicators of social benefits and social costs.

Finally, Samuelson quietly adds a point about interest, or profits, under socialist planning that should be loudly and repeatedly stressed: "But, of course, no one necessarily receives interest income from them."[6] In other words, a planned socialist economy would have to calculate rates of return on different uses of capital to decide where to allocate it, *but it would not have to distribute any of these returns as income to any individual.*

We are concerned here, however, with the issue of how a capitalist system distributes income to individuals and groups. In relation to income distribution, radicals have attacked the marginal-productivity theory on several levels. They claim (1) that it is a tautology, (2) that the marginal product of capital cannot really be measured, and (3) that it confuses the productivity of capital and the productivity of the capitalist.

On the first level, it was indicated earlier that, given its assumptions, the analytic conclusions of marginal productivity follow practically by definition (but not its political-ethical conclusions). If it is assumed that the capitalist always acts to maximize profit, then he will never hire an additional worker who would cost more than he produces. He will only keep hiring workers who produce a surplus above their wages. If the product of the last worker hired is defined to be the marginal product, then it follows that his or her wage must be equal to that, neither more nor less. Similarly, a unit of capital will be utilized only if the additional product from its use equals the additional cost of its use. Given the assumption of profit maximization, these are tautologies in the sense that the conclusions are hidden in the definitions. It does tell the capitalist how to manipulate labor and other inputs to maximize profits, but it does not say whether this is good or bad for society.

---

[5] Samuelson, *op. cit.*, p. 580.
[6] *Ibid.*

It is possible that in some society it may be correct to allocate machines so that the return, or profit, from adding one more machine to production equals its cost. But this allocation rule certainly does not prove that it is necessary to have a society in which private capitalists provide the money to buy the machines. Nor does it prove that the capitalist's profit is justified even if it equals the marginal product of capital. This theory provides a particular description of the process of allocation of capital, but it represents no advance beyond older ethical justifications of profit income in terms of the capitalist's abstinence or waiting. (Incidentally, these older theories have long been ridiculed by radicals on the ground that the capitalist makes very little sacrifice in abstaining from consuming his whole income or waiting for his profit return. Should we sympathize with the sacrifice of a fellow who sits on his yacht and decides to invest 50 percent of his $1 million income rather than consuming it all?)

The second radical criticism is that the marginal-productivity theory is unrealistic because it does not refer to anything measurable. What is meant by a *unit of capital?* If it means a particular machine, of what relevance is theorizing about transferring it to a more productive use? Particular machines are designed to do particular jobs. If we find that a marginal product is less than its cost in an industry, how can the machine be moved to another industry? It is not designed for other work. Furthermore, the theory assumes that small units of capital can be added or subtracted at the margin. But most machines represent very considerable investments; they are not infinitely divisible.

Third, even admitting that the theory offers insights about how capitalists should invest and that it has some roughly definable meaning, still it pertains only to the production contributions of labor and physical capital. It says nothing about the capitalist's contribution. This is probably the most important point of criticism. Radicals admit that a machine may increase production, that workers need them, and that they increase the worker's productivity. In that sense Samuelson is right to say that "capital" has a "net productivity." But it is the physical capital that is productive (jointly with the worker), *not* the capitalist. The capitalist owns the capital, but he is not himself the machine. The machine does the work (with the worker); the capitalist gets the profit.

Radicals agree that machines are a necessary, or "productive," part of the physical productive process; they would even agree to the importance of managerial labor. Radicals argue, however, that this productivity of physical capital goods (created by another labor process in the past) is significantly different from the capitalist owners' ability to capture a certain portion of the product as interest or profit. "It is, of course, true that materials and machinery can be said to be physically productive in the sense that labor working with them can turn out a larger product than labor working without them, but physical productivity in this sense must under no circumstances be confused with value productivity."[7] In other words, "Under capitalism 'the productiveness of labor is made to ripen, as if in a hothouse.' Whether we choose to say that capital is productive, or that capital is necessary to make labor productive, is not a matter of much importance. . . . What is important is to say that owning capital is not a productive activity."[8] This is clear in the case of a mere coupon clipper (as most stockhold-

---

[7] Paul Sweezy, *The Theory of Capitalist Development* (New York: Monthly Review Press, 1958), p. 61.
[8] Joan Robinson, *An Essay on Marxian Economics* (New York: St. Martin, 1960), p. 18.

ers are today). The fact that some capitalists may otherwise perform productive labor through their own managerial work does not contradict the fact that they also make money through mere ownership of capital.

SUMMARY

According to neoclassical theory, demand for a good is based on its marginal utility, or the desires of the consumer plus the consumer's income. Supply is based on the marginal cost of production. At any given moment when supply is fixed, the changing demand sets the price. In a short run just long enough so that a factory may produce more or less, both supply and demand change and affect the price. In a long run long enough to build new factories, the demand will still determine how much is to be produced—that is, the allocation of resources to different industries. In the long run, however, any quantity that is demanded can be produced, so the price level will simply be determined by the cost (including an average profit). In other words, in the long run twice as much demand will mean twice as much production of the commodity; but *if cost per unit stays constant,* then the price will also stay constant. (Most neoclassical economists would say that cost usually does not remain constant even in the long run.)

According to neoclassical theory, workers receive the marginal product of labor and capitalists receive the marginal product of capital. This conservative theory tries to justify the present distribution of income. Critics admit that it says something about allocating labor and capital to different industries. But they claim that in relation to income distribution it explains nothing, is unrealistic and refers to nothing measurable, and confuses the product of capital with the product of the capitalist.

APPENDIX A

MARGINAL UTILITY AND DEMAND

Suppose that a consumer can spend income on only three commodities: apples, bread, and cake. It is then possible to determine the quantities of each to be bought in order to maximize utility. Utility will be maximized if the consumer buys the particular quantities of apples, bread, and cake that will leave the marginal utilities of each at a level at which the following condition holds:

$$\frac{\text{Marginal utility of apples}}{\text{price of apples}} = \frac{\text{marginal utility of bread}}{\text{price of bread}}$$

$$= \frac{\text{marginal utility of cake}}{\text{price of cake}}$$

The equality of these three ratios means that utility is maximized when the last dollar spent on apples yields the same utility as the last dollars spent on bread and cake. A numerical example will help explain this principle.

Table 15A.1 shows amounts of apples ranging from 1 pound to 6 pounds. The number of units of marginal utility for each pound of apples and the number of units of marginal utility per dollar for each pound of apples can be determined by reading across the table. The same kinds of assumptions are stated for bread and cake in Table 15A.2. Of course in reality it is not so clear that each consumer

Table 15A.1

Quantity (in pounds)	Marginal Utility of Apples (in Units of Utility)	Marginal Utility of Apples per Dollar (Price: $1)
1	12	12
2	11	11
3	10	10
4	9	9
5	8	8
6	7	7

Table 15A.2

Quantity (in pounds)	Marginal Utility of Bread (in Units of Utility)	Marginal Utility of Bread per Dollar (Price: $2)	Marginal Utility of Cake (in Units of Utility)	Marginal Utility of Cake per Dollar (Price: $3)
1	24	12	30	10
2	22	11	27	9
3	20	10	24	8
4	18	9	21	7
5	16	8	18	6
6	14	7	15	5

exactly measures or knows how many units of subjective utility is gotten from each additional commodity. (Could you measure *exactly* the relative desire or utility to you of one more apple versus one more loaf of bread?)

Still, the theory does help elucidate consumer behavior in a rough sort of way. Now imagine that a consumer with an income of $24 buys 6 pounds of cake for $18, 2 pounds of bread for $4, and 2 pounds of apples for $2. The consumer has spent the entire $24 income, but has not maximized utility. The ratios of marginal utility to price are not the same for the three commodities. The ratios are as follows:

$$\text{for apples} \quad \frac{11 \text{ units of utility}}{\$1} = 11 \text{ units of utility for last dollar}$$

$$\text{for bread} \quad \frac{22 \text{ units of utility}}{\$2} = 11 \text{ units of utility for last dollar}$$

$$\text{for cake} \quad \frac{15 \text{ units of utility}}{\$3} = 5 \text{ units of utility for last dollar}$$

The utility received from the last dollar spent on cake (5 units of utility) was considerably smaller than that of the last dollars spent on apples and bread (11 units each). Obviously this individual's utility could be increased if some purchases were shifted from cake to apples and bread.

If the consumer gives up 3 pounds of cake, 54 units of utility will be lost, but $9 will be gained to be spent on apples and bread. With this $9, the consumer purchases 3 more pounds of apples (thereby gaining 27 units of utility) and 3 more pounds of bread (thereby gaining 54 units of utility). Thus by shifting $9 worth of purchases the consumer gives up 54 units of utility and gains 81 units.

Obviously the second bundle of goods has more utility than the first. If the units of utility in the first bundle are added, they total 204 (6 units from cake = 135; 2 units from bread = 46; and 2 units from apples = 23). The total number of units of utility in the second bundle is 231 (3 units from cake = 81; 5 units from bread = 100; and 5 units from apples = 50). The ratios of marginal utility to price for the three goods in the second bundle are as follows:

$$\text{for apples } \frac{8 \text{ units of utility}}{\$1} = 8 \text{ units of utility for last dollar}$$

$$\text{for bread } \frac{16 \text{ units of utility}}{\$2} = 8 \text{ units of utility for last dollar}$$

$$\text{for cake } \frac{24 \text{ units of utility}}{\$3} = 8 \text{ units of utility for last dollar}$$

Thus the maximizing condition holds; that is,

$$\frac{8}{\$1} = \frac{16}{\$2} = \frac{24}{\$3}$$

Purchases cannot be shifted among the commodities any further without losing some utility. The reader should experiment with such shifts in order to be convinced that this is a maximum.

With this information it is now possible to demonstrate why demand curves slope downward and to the right—that is, why the quantity demanded *increases* as the price *decreases*. (See Chapter 14.) Imagine an initial position at which all consumers are maximizing their utility—that is, they have equated the ratios of their marginal utilities and prices for all the goods. It is then possible to trace the effects of a decrease in price.

If the price of one good, say apples, were to decrease, consumers would find that the utility received for the last dollar spent on apples would be higher than that received for the last dollar spent on other goods. Consumers would immediately shift some of their purchases from other goods to apples. Thus the initial result of a decline in the price of apples is an increased quantity of apples demanded.

But what determines exactly how much demand will shift to apples? Exactly how much will the demand for them increase when the price declines? That depends on their marginal utility (the desire for an additional apple) relative to the marginal utility of other goods (the desire for more bread and cake). As consumers buy more and more apples, their desire for an additional one declines. (This is just one illustration of the law of diminishing marginal utility.) At the same time consumers are buying less of all other goods (less bread and less cake). So the *marginal* utility of other goods rises; at the margin, their desire for an additional piece of bread or cake is now increased. The process of shifting demand from bread and cake to apples stops when an additional dollar spent for more applies (even at the new, lower price) yields just the same marginal utility as that spent for bread or cake (even at their old, unchanged prices).

APPENDIX B

ELASTICITY OF DEMAND

Elasticity of demand was defined in words as

$$\text{Elasticity} = \frac{\text{percentage change in quantity demanded}}{\text{percentage change in price}}$$

For those who prefer symbols to words, call elasticity E, quantity demanded Q, and price P, and let Δ mean "the change in." Then

$$E = \frac{\Delta Q/Q}{\Delta P/P}$$

The concept is important; the details of calculation are not. Nevertheless, the details may help you get the concept more firmly in mind.

Assume a move down the demand curve from some point 1 to point 2. The change in quantity demanded is $\Delta Q = Q_1 - Q_2$. The change in price is $\Delta P - P_2 - P_1$ because the price went down while quantity went up. The base for figuring the percentage could be either Q_1 or Q_2, with somewhat different results. As a convention economists always use the average, so $Q = (Q_1 + Q_2) \div 2$. Similarly, by convention $P = (P_1 + P_2) \div 2$.

The elasticity of demand for cake (shown in Figure 15.1) works out this way. Rise in quantity demanded is $300 - 100 = 200$. Average quantity, on which the percentage is based, is $(300 + 100) \div 2 = 200$. Fall in price is $\$3 - \$2 = \$1$. Average price is $(\$3 + \$2) \div 2 = \$2.5$. Therefore

$$E_{cake} = \frac{200/200}{1/2.5} = \frac{1}{0.4} = \frac{100\%}{40\%} = 2.5$$

The percentage change in demand (100 percent) is much greater than the percentage change in price (40 percent); therefore the demand is elastic. More precisely, demand is elastic if E is greater than 1, and here E is 2.5.

Similarly, the elasticity of demand for rice (shown in Figure 15.2) works out this way. Rise in quantity demanded is $200 - 100 = 100$. Average quantity is $(200 + 100) \div 2 = 150$. Fall in price is $\$3 - \$1 = \$2$. Average price is $(\$3 + \$1) \div 2 = \$2$. Therefore

$$E_{rice} = \frac{100/150}{2/2} = \frac{0.67}{1} = \frac{67\%}{100\%} = 0.67$$

Here the percentage change in demand (67 percent) is less than the percentage change in price (100 percent); therefore the demand is inelastic. Or, if you wish, it is inelastic because E is 0.67, which is less than 1.

To complete the concept, economists say that the demand curve is of *unitary elasticity* when E is 1. In this intermediate case the percentage change in demand is just the same as the percentage change in price.

At one extreme, a *perfectly inelastic* demand curve is shown by a vertical straight line. There is *no* change in demand when price changes. Thus E equals zero when demand is perfectly inelastic. However a *perfectly elastic* demand curve is shown by a horizontal straight line. When demand is perfectly elastic, E equals infinity. The firm can sell an infinite quantity of goods at the present price. Although these extreme cases are unrealistic, the concepts will be helpful later.

APPENDIX C

THE ETHICAL IMPLICATIONS OF UTILITY ANALYSIS

In Appendix A to this chapter we saw that when we assume (1) that individuals receive marginal utility from consuming commodities that is determined solely by the quantities of commodities they consume, and (2) that they arrange their purchases of commodities in such a way as to maximize their utility, then they end up by equating the marginal utility per dollar spent on each and every commodity.

More advanced textbooks on orthodox microeconomic theory show that on the basis of similar assumptions in the theory of production, that competitive capitalists maximize their profits when the cost of producing an additional, marginal unit of any two commodities is proportional to the prices of the two commodities. Furthermore, they show that competitive profit maximizing also leads to a situation in which the price of any factor of production, such as land, labor, or capital, is just equal to the value of the productive contribution of that factor in producing the last units of any commodities that require the use of that factor.

The entire analysis is based upon the assumptions of (1) diminishing marginal utility in the consumption of every commodity by each individual, (2) diminishing marginal productivity of any factor of production in the creation of all commodities, (3) utility and profit maximization, and (4) the uniform existence of competition in all markets. With these assumptions the conclusions of the previous paragraph follow from the logical principles of how constrained maxima are attained.

But traditional microeconomic theory does not stop there. It contains ethical or ideological elements as well. Neoclassical welfare economics accepts the above assumptions and conclusions and adds some important ethical assumptions. These assumptions are (1) an individual's utility is identical with his or her well-being or welfare; (2) the collective total of all individuals' utilities is identical with the social well-being or social welfare; and (3) the marginal utilities of different persons for all commodities in general (or the marginal utility of money) can not be compared between any two persons.

On the basis of these ethical assumptions, neoclassical welfare economics concludes that a competitive capitalist economy results in the following:

1. Each individual orders his or her purchases such that no change could take place without diminishing his or her welfare.
2. No alterations in the free market allocation of commodities among different individuals could take place without reducing at least one person's welfare.

3. No change in the allocation of productive factors, such as to change the proportions of the various commodities produced, could take place without reducing the total amount produced.
4. No change in the income payments to the owners of the various factors of production would be possible without either reducing the total amount produced or without some coercion that would leave some persons worse off than before.

The intricate arguments by which the conclusions are derived are too complex for this book. They are contained in intermediate and advanced microeconomic theory textbooks. All that we wish to do in this short appendix is to make two points. First, neoclassical welfare economics is the ultimate extension of the invisible hand argument of Adam Smith, which we discussed in Chapter 4. This theory attempts to show that a competitive capitalist economy maximizes social welfare and is therefore a perfect, ideal economy. Furthermore, since we cannot compare individuals' utilities, and since each factor of production is paid the value of its marginal contribution to production, the social distribution of income must be efficient and just.

The second point that we wish to make is that when microeconomic theory is used in this way (i.e., as an ideological justification for laissez-faire capitalism), it is subject to a large number of devastating criticisms. We will mention only a few of them.

First, the notion that a person's welfare is identical to his or her utility or desire for commodities ignores several important facts. Most desires are socially learned. Is it not possible to argue that some desires that are socially learned are really harmful to the true welfare of an individual? The ultimate consequences of using some electronic gadget or taking some variety of medicine may be so complex that no ordinary individual could possibly know their long-range influence on his or her welfare, but still want to consume them because others have said they will be beneficial. And since capitalists and their advertising campaigns are usually where we learn that we "want" something, we would have to assume that capitalists advertise in order to promote the social welfare rather than in order to make more profits. A most unlikely assumption. The absurdity of equating utility and welfare is most clearly seen when we look at small children or drug addicts. Everyone knows that these persons frequently want and feel that they need things that are harmful to their welfare. In short, to assume that each of us always wants that which best promotes our own welfare would require that we believe all individuals to be omniscient, perfectly adjusted saints.

Secondly, the assumption that we cannot compare the increase in the welfare of two different individuals when each receives an extra increment of income violates the most basic common sense of everyday life. Most of us feel certain that an extra dollar means much more to the welfare of a starving man than it does to the welfare of a millionaire. The assumption that we cannot make such comparisons is tantamount to arguing that the present extreme inequalities of wealth and income cannot be shown to be any worse than any alternative. The millionaire may believe this, but neither the starving man nor most of the rest of us believe this.

Thirdly, factors of production are not people. At least land and capital are not. Even if it could be shown that they received a reward equal to their marginal productivity (which the present writers believe to be impossible when sophisticated critiques of this theory are understood) it could never be concluded that the tremendously concentrated ownership of these factors in the hands of a tiny minority of the population is either fair or just.

There are many other ethical and theoretical arguments that show the weaknesses of neoclassical welfare economics, but we believe these three suffice to show the reader that economic theory never has been able to show, and cannot now show, that free-market capitalism is any sort of ethical ideal. Unfortunately, at the level of intermediate and advanced microeconomic theory (where these criticisms could and should be made with force and rigor) conservative economists dominate most universities. It is therefore important, even at the elementary level, to inform the reader about the tenuous nature of the welfare economics that are usually constructed upon the basis of orthodox utility theory.

CHAPTER 16

THE LABOR THEORY OF VALUE

The radical alternative to the utility theory discussed in the last chapter is the labor theory of value. The labor theory, however, has not always been used exclusively by radicals. Many of the rudiments of this theory were developed in Adam Smith's *The Wealth of Nations,* written in 1776, even though Smith is best known for his "invisible hand" argument for unregulated laissez-faire capitalism (see Chapter 4 above). The theory was refined and given a much more elaborate and logically consistent presentation in David Ricardo's *Principles of Political Economy and Taxation,* first published in 1817. Ricardo was a capitalist who made a fortune on the London Stock Exchange and was a consistent spokesman for the capitalists' point of view in nearly all practical, economic, and political issues of his era.

After Ricardo, however, most of the proponents of the labor theory were radical critics of capitalism. Karl Marx formulated the definitive version of the theory. He made substantial improvements in Ricardo's version of the theory. Most of the developments in the theory made over the last one hundred years have been refinements, elaborations, and extensions of Marx's version of the labor theory. One outstanding and important exception to the last statement was a book entitled *Production of Commodities by Means of Commodities* by Piero Sraffa, published in 1960. Although Sraffa for several decades had been a sympathizer of the Marxist tradition, in his book he developed Ricardo's version of the theory, rather than Marx's version. Sraffa's contribution contained insights and theoretical tools that could be reformulated in such a way as to refine and give added precision to the Marxist version of the labor theory. Our account will not be an attempt to reproduce the ideas of Marx, but to give a simplified version of the theory in its current state.

LABOR THEORY OF VALUE: FIRST APPROXIMATION

Capitalist society is a very complex mechanism in which we must explain the market value of products, the wage rate of workers, and the profits taken by capitalists. To make the learning process easier, we begin with the explanation of prices in a much simpler society, then slowly add all of the complexities until we achieve a fully realistic picture of modern capitalism. At the beginning we assume pure competition, perfect knowledge by all economic actors, very little government, full employment, and no international relations; each of these unrealistic assumptions will be dropped one at a time, some in this chapter and some in later chapters.

As a first approximation, let us imagine a simple society in which each individual producer performs all of the labor necessary to bring a particular commodity to market. This might be a society of independent farmers, hunters, and handicraft people. Each producer has free access to the natural environment. With his own labor, he fashions all of the tools and gathers all of the raw materials necessary to produce his commodity. He then performs the necessary labor to produce his commodity, using his own tools and raw materials, and sells his commodity on the market. (Usually a family produces as a unit in most such societies, so "he" may refer to male or female or a family.) With the proceeds of his sales he purchases, from other independent producers, those commodities which he needs and desires.

In such a society prices will perfectly reflect the amount of labor embodied in commodities. That is, prices will reflect the relationship between any given individual's productive effort and the productive efforts of all other individuals upon whom he is dependent. Let us suppose, for example, that the average amount of labor embodied in a pair of shoes is four days while that embodied in a loaf of bread is two days. In this society the forces of supply and demand will tend to adjust the prices of shoes and bread to that level at which two loaves of bread will exchange for, or cost as much as, one pair of shoes.

If money is used in the society, the same two to one ratio will tend to exist in the prices of the two commodities. Suppose a loaf of bread is $1.40 (an arbitrary sum of money). Then a pair of shoes will tend to be $2.80 as long as it requires twice as much labor. The resulting equilibrium level—*equilibrium* being defined as the point at which no further change is expected—is shown in Table 16-1.

If prices do not start at these equilibrium ratios, they will tend to get there by a series of adjustments based on the competition and self-interest of the individual producers. To illustrate this process of adjustment, let us assume that the price of bread is $1.00 per loaf and shoes are $3.00 per pair. At these prices one pair of shoes exchanges for three loaves of bread. Now in order for bread producers to obtain a pair of shoes they must work six days (needed to produce three loaves of bread). On the other hand, shoe producers need only spend four days to obtain a pair of shoes. Similarly, for the shoe producers four days of labor (needed to produce one pair of shoes) will exchange for three loaves of bread. Yet it takes the bread producers six days of labor to obtain three loaves of bread. In this circumstance, some bread producers are going to shift over to the production of shoes. This situation of disequilibrium is portrayed in Table 16-2.

Table 16.1 **Equilibrium Level of Exchange**

	Labor Time	Exchange for	An Equilibrium pair of prices
1 Pair of Shoes	4 days	2 loaves of bread	$2.80
1 Loaf of Bread	2 days	½ pair of shoes	$1.40

Table 16.2 **Disequilibrium in Exchange**

	Labor Time	Exchanges for	Prices
1 Pair of Shoes	4 days	3 loaves of bread	$3.00
1 Loaf of Bread	2 days	⅓ of a pair of shoes	$1.00

As the shift of producers from the bread industry to the shoe industry takes place, two things will happen. First, there will be a decline in the supply of bread available. With less bread available, the market mechanism will allocate the smaller supply by a competitive bidding up of the price by those most able to afford bread at a higher price. Those with less money, or a lesser desire to buy bread, will reduce their purchases at the new higher price. Secondly, there will be an increase in the supply of shoes available. In order to sell this increased supply, producers will bid down the price to induce consumers to buy more shoes.

These two price changes will continue until two loaves of bread exchange for one pair of shoes. For example, the price of shoes might decline to $2.80 a pair and the price of bread might increase to $1.40 a loaf. Only when the prices have adjusted to that point, at which they are proportional to the labor embodied, will there be no incentive for producers to leave one industry and enter another. Thus the market forces of supply and demand create equilibrium prices, the ratios of which are equal to the ratios of the labor embodied in the various commodities.

Effects of Changing Demand

One criticism of the labor theory often made is that it seems to rely only on the supply cost in labor units, but it ignores changes on the demand side. This is a misunderstanding of the labor theory. The labor theory says that equilibrium exchange ratios and prices will be set by proportionate amounts of labor, but it doesn't say that demand has no role to play. The demand will not set the price, but it will determine the *amount* produced.

Suppose an equilibrium price is achieved at $2.80 for a pair of shoes and $1.40 for a loaf of bread. Now suppose, by some quirk of consumer tastes, that the demand for bread doubles, while the demand for shoes declines. At first, the price of bread would increase. But then producers will shift to producing bread. Eventually, the amount of bread will reach the new higher ratio of demand to the amount of shoes produced.

The demand will have determined the *amounts* of each produced. The price of bread, however, will drop back to its old ratio to shoes. If not, we would again have a disequilibrium situation. So changes in demand cause temporary or short-run price changes, but their lasting effect is only on the amount produced. With a given long-run demand for goods equal to the amount produced, then the equilibrium *price* or exchange *value* is determined solely by the amounts of human labor embodied in each commodity.

The Value of Tools

Another often heard objection to the labor theory is that prices must be determined by value of the tools (and raw materials) used in addition to the human labor used. This is another misunderstanding of the labor theory. It was assumed in the above example that each producer made his own tools and obtained his own raw materials. The farmer grows wheat, makes his own plows and scythes, and bakes the bread. The shoemaker (say, for wooden shoes) makes his own axes and chisels, cuts down trees, and finally makes shoes.

All tools are produced by human labor. Any work in procuring raw materials is human labor. Therefore the labor theory includes *all* labor—for tools, processing raw materials, and production of the final product—in the exchange value or equilibrium price. Thus the $2.80 for a pair of shoes includes the labor that went into the tools and processing raw materials as well as the final manufacturing; the same is true of the $1.40 price of the loaf of bread.

Socially Necessary Labor

One naive objection to the labor theory stresses the fact that some labor produces nothing useful and, therefore, its product has a market value of zero. Marx always qualified the labor theory by referring only to "socially necessary" labor. For example, if a silly person labors for a year to produce a "What's-That," a commodity of no use to anyone, the commodity has zero exchange value even though it embodies a year's labor.

Slightly more complicated is the point that production is assumed to be at the present average level of technology. If a commodity is produced with less than the average level of technology, it requires more than the average labor necessary in the society, but its exchange value will only be the amount of socially necessary labor. For example, if a person were silly enough to produce a Ford auto in the backyard by hand, if it required twenty years of labor from 1956 to 1976, and if it were exactly identical to a 1976 Ford, then its price would also be identical.

Different Types of Labor

Another persistent objection to the labor theory of value is that various types of labor involve differing levels of skills, and that a commodity in which highly skilled labor is embodied would ordinarily seem to command a higher price than one in which unskilled labor is embodied. It is certainly true that commodities produced by an hour of skilled labor cost more than those produced by an hour of unskilled labor. But—apart from minor differences at birth—most work skills reflect the labor that went into producing that higher skill. For practical purposes, it is a sufficiently accurate representation of reality to assume that all differences in actual skills are a result of differences in training. When all of the labor time spent in teaching and acquiring skills is considered, all labor time can be reduced to a comparable equivalent of simple unskilled labor.

For example, in the above account of the production of shoes and bread, we can suppose that producing shoes requires much more skill than producing bread. Shoe producers must undergo a period of training to achieve their skills. We can then compute the additional time spent by the teachers and the trainees and then apportion this extra time over the average period during which shoe producers use these acquired skills. Perhaps it takes only three days of actual labor to produce a pair of shoes. But after apportioning the training time for the acquisition of skills, we find that the equivalent of four days unskilled labor time is spent producing each pair of shoes. Although this computation, which reduces skilled labor to an unskilled labor equivalent, becomes more complex when we introduce profits into the pricing scheme, it is always consistently solvable as long as skill differentials can be reduced to differences in the labor embodied in the acquisition of skills.

In the simple economy described in this first approximation, there are no wages or profits. All income results from the sale of commodities embodying the labor of the producers, and all income accrues to the immediate producers. Each producer specializes and then exchanges the material embodiment of his or her labor for the material embodiment of the labor of the other producers upon whom his or her continued existence depends. In this simple case it was easy to prove that the amounts produced were determined by consumer demands, but that the long-run exchange values or equilibrium prices were determined by the amount of labor expended by each producer (including the labor expended on tools and on training).

THE LABOR THEORY OF VALUE: SECOND APPROXIMATION

The second stage of our discussion of the labor theory of value provides a closer approximation to modern reality by introducing the central social relationship of capitalism, the class relationship between workers and capitalists. We now assume that different sets of workers extract raw materials, produce tools and machinery, and produce final commodities for consumption. The essence of capitalism is that capitalists own all of the raw materials, the tools and machinery, and all commodities up to that point in time at which the final consumer purchases a commodity. Capitalists also, at any given time, own most of the money in the economy. Laborers, in general, own nothing but their capacity to work—their labor power.

Production and the "Factors" of Production

Traditional economic theory sees production as a process in which three separate and distinct factors of production—land, labor, and capital—are combined to produce a variety of outputs. Each factor is said to make a definite measurable contribution to production. The rewards to the three factors are believed to be determined by the contributions that each factor makes to the production process. Thus the landlord receives rent for the use of his land, the worker receives wages for the use of his or her labor power, and the capitalist receives profits according to the productiveness of his capital (for more details of the traditional theory, see Chapter 15).

The labor theory of value begins with a completely different view of the production process. Production is seen as a *purely human activity,* in which humans expend labor on material objects. The labor theory starts with the fact that, unlike many species of animals, human beings rarely find a natural environment that is immediately adaptable for the satisfaction of their material needs. Subsistence requires the material necessities of food, shelter, and clothing. The enjoyment of pleasures beyond mere subsistence requires other material objects as prerequisites. Nature almost never provides in directly usable form the material prerequisites for human subsistence and pleasure.

To sustain life, people must transform the natural environment from its unusable state to a state that is serviceable for human needs. This transformation is solely and purely a human activity. The outer crust of the earth existed for untold thousands of years before the appearance of the first human beings. No person is responsible for its existence, nor is anyone responsible for the particular properties of the natural environment, by virtue of which it can be adapted to fulfill people's needs.

People could not live in a vacuum, nor could they live in the void of outer space. This seemingly obvious statement must be stressed, because distortions and misrepresentations of the labor theory have asserted that the theory ignores the "contributions" of the natural environment. The labor theory begins by taking the earth or natural environment as given independently of any human being or human endeavor. Production consists *solely* of human exertion applied to raw materials in order to transform them into products of human labor that are capable of sustaining life. The raw materials are certainly necessary—people, like all life forms, must have an environment in which to exist—but their existence has never involved a social or human cost. In the traditional view, production is seen as a process in which people and resources are coequal contributors, and in which some people ought to be paid for "nature's contribution." In the labor theory of value, production is seen as a strictly human endeavor of *laboring* to transform the preexisting natural environment into products, which are usable for people.

The earliest and most primitive forms of production were probably very simple and direct. Shelters were made from caves or with trees and branches; fruits and nuts were picked and gathered; small animals were killed for food and clothing. From this simple state of affairs, in which life must have been very difficult and precarious, all human progress was based on finding new, more complex methods of producing that would increase human productivity. This usually meant producing tools that would render people more effective in transforming their environment. All human beings of which we have any direct or indirect knowledge have used tools. Increases in human productivity have been the results of increased knowledge of ways in which the natural environment could be transformed, and increasingly sophisticated and complex tools with which to effect the transformation.

Thus if tools are considered to be "capital," then always and everywhere capital has been integral to human production. Traditional economic theory does define tools as part of capital. Therefore traditional economic theory says that not only human labor, but also capital is a factor of production. The owners of capital are said to receive profits because capital is "productive." The profits are thought to be determined by the productivity of capital. *Capital,* in the traditional theory, is defined as those material objects that have been previously produced and are necessary for future production; for example, factories, machines, tools, and partially processed raw materials are said to be capital. Traditional economists conclude that capital is and always will be part of production; therefore capitalists deserve a profitable return on capital. This assertion confuses material things with human relations.

In the labor theory, on the contrary, factories, tools, machinery, and partly finished raw materials are defined to be the *means of production.* (In previous societies land was the most important means of production, but now it plays a minor role.) The means of production are the physical aspect of capital. But capital in our economy also has a monetary aspect. When a banker loans a billion dollars to a corporation, and the corporation uses it to buy means of production (or physical capital), that billion dollars is not just money, it is financial capital.

Both the physical and monetary aspects of capital are important, but they do not sufficiently define capital. For example, if a worker has $10 in money, and if that is not enough to go into business, the money is not "capital." Or if a worker has a tool, such as a lawn mower, that the worker uses for his or her own private purposes, the tool is not "capital."

The answer to the problem, therefore, is that what we mean by "capital" in a capitalist society is determined by a set of human relationships. One class, called capitalists, "owns" the physical and monetary capital. Another class, called workers, uses the physical capital to produce things. Workers produce both consumer goods and more physical capital. *The human relations*—codified into laws—between workers and capitalists *determine what we call capital.* For example, if a capitalist hires many workers to cut lawns as a paid service to consumers, then the lawn mowers he owns are capital—and if he spends $10 to repair one of those lawn mowers, that $10 is capital.

Of course, the reason that economists study such human relations—and argue about definitions of capital or theories of value—is ultimately to justify or attack the system of private profit. This is why conservatives insist that it is the only way to do things, while radicals point out that capital may be owned by a collective group or all of society and profit may be collective or social rather than private.

The argument about profits becomes confused because human relations of production under capitalism have a superficial appearance that deceives us into thinking they are relations between things, not people. These personal and social relationships appear, in a capitalist, commodity-producing society, as the ratios of prices among commodities, including the price of physical capital and the price of labor (wages). Exchange values reflect the social division of labor and are determined by the relationships between the labor expended on one product and the general total of all social labor. Thus human, social relationships appear to be merely impersonal, nonhuman relationships among commodities.

This identification of human relationships as commodity relationships is not, however, simply an illusion based on erroneous perception or imagination. One of the defining features of capitalism is that in this social system, and this system alone, the human element of the production process is reduced to a commodity—labor power—to be bought and sold on the market in the same manner as any other commodity. Labor power can never be made into a commodity unless and until the people who produce are effectively denied any means of independently producing. This, in effect, denies them any way of remaining alive except to sell their power to produce—their labor power—to those who have the control over whether or not production can take place. In capitalism, private ownership of the means of production insures that workers must sell their labor power or starve—so labor becomes a commodity and human relations are seen as commodity relations.

Origins of the Worker-Capitalist Relationship

In Chapters 2, 3, and 4 of this book, we described in some detail the evolution of capitalism from the earlier feudal economy. The feudal economy produced on isolated agricultural estates and also had some independent handicraftsmen in the guilds in the few urban areas. Rather than review that complex evolution here, we have chosen to highlight one feature—the origins of the worker-capitalist relation—by means of an unrealistic, but dramatically clear, parable.

Imagine a tropical island on which neither clothing nor shelter need be produced. The only necessary production on this island is the catching of fish. In order to catch enough fish to feed everyone, each of the 100 inhabitants of the island must spend six hours a day fishing. When the fish are caught, they are divided equally among the 100 citizens of the island. The fish are caught by hand.

One day after the fishing is completed, several people are discussing the process of fishing, and it occurs to them that the hemp, which grows wild on the island, could be dried and woven into ropes; the ropes could be tied together in a fashion such as to produce a fishing net; the net would enable them to catch substantially more fish per hour spent fishing. So they decide that for a period of time 50 people will work full-time producing nets, while the other 50 will fish twelve hours a day to produce enough fish to feed everyone.

The people who are producing nets are laboring only in order that more fish can be caught, so the net producers are, in reality, working to catch fish in the future. When the nets are completed, they represent partially caught fish; they are the material embodiment of a part of the labor that will go into the catching of fish. The islanders discover that, using the nets, each fisherman can catch twice the average number of fish in each hour of fishing than before the nets. It appears as though the 100 islanders can spend only three hours per day fishing and three hours producing various luxury goods to enhance the enjoyment of life for themselves.

But the most cunning and unscrupulous of the islanders has an idea. He gathers nine of the strongest and most brutal islanders, and in a secret conference explains his plan. The next day they announce to the other islanders that a new principle called private property ownership is being instituted. The ten of them are the owners of all of the hemp, all of the rope, and all of the nets, and have ownership of the waters surrounding the island. "We will have," they proclaim, "a private enterprise economy." They explain that this means that each of the other 90 people will be perfectly free to choose to work for them or not. Those who work for them will be paid a wage equal to one-half of the nets they make or one-half the fish they catch. Those who do not work for them will get nothing. Anyone using the hemp, the rope, the nets or the water without their permission will be punished for violating the laws of private property.

Two or three of the most daring of the islanders refuse and begin fishing for themselves. They are immediately beaten up and tied to trees and forced to go without food or water for two days. The other islanders are told that this is the punishment for violating the laws of private property. In fear of receiving the same punishment and not wanting to starve, the other islanders "freely" apply for jobs. Fifty of them are put to work catching the same number of fish as were previously caught by all 100 of the islanders. Ten are put to work repairing nets and producing new nets as replacement for nets that wear out, and 30 are put to work producing luxuries for, or being servants of, the ten capitalists.

Only this new relationship between the 10 capitalists and the 90 workers transforms the water, the hemp, the rope, and the nets into privately owned capital. If all of the islanders had continued using the nets and dividing the produce among themselves, there would be no capital and no profit. Profit now consists of the fish eaten by the capitalists and the luxuries or personal services provided for the capitalists. Considered another way, only the labor of the net producers and fishermen is actually necessary as a minimum if the islanders are to continue producing and survive. The 30 luxury producers and servants provide *surplus labor,* and surplus labor is the source of the capitalists' profits.

Thus private ownership of the means of production is essentially a *social relationship* between the owners and the nonowners. In the parable, as in reality, it is a coercively established and coercively maintained system of privileges for the owners and sanctions for the nonowners. (Of course, capitalism was *not* the result of a consious conspiracy by a few people; moreover, workers today are persuaded more by propaganda than by force.) Only when such a social relationship exists do the nets, tools, and other means of producing things become privately owned and are used as a means to get workers to produce private profit.

To complete our parable, we find the capitalists announcing that there are inheritance laws, so that when they die their children will own the means of production. When the second generation of capitalists takes over, productivity has increased sufficiently to reduce the amount of labor necessary to provide food at the given level of technology in the society. The new capitalists, accustomed to a life of ease and luxury, now appoint some of the islanders as policemen to enforce the laws of private property. The capitalists now have no function but to enjoy their leisure, their luxuries, and the services provided for them.

They fear, however, that since the workers greatly outnumber the policemen, there may be a revolt that would put an end to their privileges. They decree that each worker needs to be schooled in "social science." They hire "social scientists" who devise a theory that the production of fish requires both labor and capital. The workers, these social scientists proclaim, receive a wage, which is determined by their productivity, and the capitalists receive profits that are determined by the productivity of their capital. Each worker is free to work or starve as he or she chooses, and each person, whether capitalist or worker, receives a reward determined by the productivity of the factor of production (either labor or capital) which they own. Therefore the system is fair and just. (This theory was examined at some length in the previous chapter.)

To the extent that the workers believe the social scientists, all is peaceful and tranquil. If they do not accept this "theory" and attempt to withhold some or all of their surplus produce from the capitalists, the police punish them for violating the laws of private property. Such is the parable that illustrates the essential social feature that transforms a society of free and independent producers into a society of a few capitalists (who receive all profit) and many, many workers (who receive only wages).

Commodity Exchange Under Capitalism

A *commodity* is defined as any product sold in the market. Some societies do not produce commodities for the market. In the parable above, when the 100 fishermen fished collectively and then divided the product equally, there was no market exchange. They produced products only for their use value. *Use value* is defined as all of the concrete, particular characteristics of a product, by virtue of which individual consumers can derive utility from the product.

Capitalists, on the contrary, do *not* invest money in a business to produce use values, but to obtain exchange value. *Exchange value* is defined as the quantity of other commodities—or the quantity of money—for which a commodity will exchange in the market. For example, General Motors does not produce autos as use value for its workers. G.M. produces autos strictly for sale in the market, to obtain exchange values.

The capitalist has no personal concern about the use values he produces; that is, he has no concern, whether his commodity be guns or medicine, or what use is made of it, as long as he receives his exchange value. He has only the indirect concern that if no person buys his commodity, then the exchange value cannot be realized in money. Money is the medium of exchange, and, as such, it is the universal expression of exchange value. The exchange value of a commodity is only realized when it is exchanged for money. Persons having money can, through exchange, give up possession of generalized exchange value (money) for possession of the use value of a commodity. So a capitalist's only concern is that someone have both the money and the desire to possess the use value of his commodity. This permits him to realize the exchange value of the commodity.

The society of independent producers in our first approximation was, like capitalism, a society that produced commodities for exchange in the market. The *form* of the process of exchange, however, is strikingly different in a simple economy of independent producers (our first approximation) and in a capitalist economy. In the simple economy of independent producers, each producer expended his or her own labor to produce a commodity. This commodity was then exchanged for money. The money, in turn, was exchanged for other commodities that the producer wished to consume. The circulation of commodities and money could thus be depicted as follows:

commodities → money → commodities

In this simple economy exchange is an exchange of use values, with money merely mediating the exchange. Thus in our earlier example the shoemaker exchanged a pair of shoes for $2.80 in money, then used the money to buy two loaves of bread. The shoemaker bought the bread for direct consumption as a use value.

The situation looks quite different to a capitalist in a capitalist economy. Eventually, of course, the capitalist—like the independent producers—exchanges his commodities in the market for money and uses the money to buy other commodities, both for personal consumption and expanding production. But, unlike the independent producer, the capitalist does not begin by expending his own labor to produce a commodity.

On the contrary, the capitalist begins by investing money. With his money the capitalist buys raw materials, plant, and equipment (which are commodities), and he buys labor power (which is now also a commodity). He then sells the commodities that the laborers, using his tools and materials, produce. Thus the new circulation of commodities and money can be depicted as follows:

$$\text{money} \rightarrow \text{commodities} \rightarrow \text{money}$$

In this process the capitalist begins with money and ends up with money. The acquisition of commodities now merely mediate in the exchange of money for money.

But why should anyone wish to exchange money for money? The answer is obvious: The capitalist expects to end up with more money than that with which he started. And in the usual operation of a capitalist economy, he does just that. Thus a more accurate depiction of circulation in capitalism would be

$$\text{money} \rightarrow \text{commodities} \rightarrow \text{more money}$$

where the money the capitalist ends up with is greater than the money he started out with.

Profits and Prices

We must now explain how a capitalist can begin with a fund of exchange value (money), make a series of exchanges, and then end up with another fund of exchange value (more money), which is greater than that with which he started. This "more" or "extra" exchange value is called *surplus value,* and at the present stage of the argument, surplus value is the equivalent of profits. The question to be answered, then, is: How do all capitalists, as a class, make profits by buying and selling?

To begin, we must reject the notion that profits are made because a capitalist buys commodities from other capitalists at prices below their equilibrium exchange values, or sells commodities to other capitalists at prices above their equilibrium exchange values. This may be the source of profits for some particular capitalists, but it can never be the source of profits for all capitalists as a class. This is so because any time a profit is made by buying below the exchange value, the seller incurs an identical loss. Similarly, when a profit is made by selling above the exchange value, the buyer incurs an identical loss. It is obvious that, in the aggregate, such gains and losses exactly cancel out. But capitalists, as a class, make profits. We must therefore seek the source of aggregate profits elsewhere.

Another possible source of profits might be the monopoly power of certain capitalists. By securing a monopoly, they can charge as high a price as the "traffic will bear" and secure high profits. While monopoly power is certainly a source of extra high profits for certain capitalists, it is not the source of profits for all capitalists. Capitalists operating in industries that are highly competitive also receive profits. Therefore to get at the basic and ultimate source of profits, we shall, at this stage in the argument, assume that there is pure competition and *there are no monopolies.*

Does this system of competitive capitalism have the same results for prices as the system of independent competitive producers described in our first approximation? Remember, there we found that the equilibrium price or exchange value was solely determined by the labor embodied in each commodity. When capitalists employ workers for a private profit, does this result change? In our example bakers sold bread for $1.40 a loaf, while shoemakers sold shoes for $2.80 a pair. Now suppose there is the same technology under capitalism. A loaf of bread still requires two days labor, while a pair of shoes still takes four days labor. What will be the exchange rates and prices under capitalism?

Suppose we begin with some other, arbitrary prices, such as only $1.00 for bread but $3.00 for shoes. In this case, the shoe-producing capitalists make a higher than average rate of profit (an extra 20¢ a pair), since they are selling above the value of the product, measured in labor days. The bread-making capitalists, however, are making below the average rate of profit because they are selling (a lower 40¢ a loaf) below the value of the product, measured in labor days.

With competition among capitalists prevailing in every industry, however, the principal result would be that an equal rate of profit would tend to be established in each and every industry. The *rate of profit* measures the increase of money (profit) to the money invested. With pure competition capitalists can enter or leave any industry with relative ease. This means that if different profit rates exist in different industries, then capitalists (seeking to maximize their profits) will leave those industries having low profit rates and enter those industries having high profit rates. In our example this would reduce the supply of bread, and hence raise the price of bread in this low profit industry. But these price changes would increase profits in bread (the low profit industry) and reduce profits in shoes (the high profit industry). As long as any difference in profit rates remains, the process will continue. It is obvious that where competition prevails, the forces of supply and demand will tend to equalize all rates of profit. Therefore eventually the prices of shoes and bread will reach their *equilibrium* two to one ratio at $2 to $1, or at $2.80 to $1.40, or some other combination, just so the ratio of prices is the same as the two to one ratio of labor expended on the products. Therefore we conclude that, in the long-run in equilibrium under capitalism, competitive profit making insures that prices will be in the same ratios as exchange values determined by the labor expended.

How Capitalists Make Profit

We seem to be further than ever from explaining profit. If capitalists must sell at equilibrium prices equal to the labor value of the product, how do they ever make a profit? The answer to the mystery lies, not in selling prices and exchange, but in the capitalist process of production.

The capitalist begins with money. He purchases material commodities, such as plant, equipment, and raw materials. He also purchases some units of the commodity, *labor power,*—that is, the right to direct workers' expenditure of labor power for some hours or days. We assume that he buys both the material commodities and the labor power at their equilibrium prices. The labor power works with the material commodities. The use value of the labor power—the actual exertion of muscular and intellectual energy in producing—is used up. New commodities are produced. They are sold at their equilibrium value. Somehow, the process ends with the capitalist having more money than that with which he started. The whole process may be depicted this way:

Money → Commodities → Production → More Commodities → More Money

Since the capitalist both bought commodities and sold commodities at equilibrium prices, he must have made the extra money in the production process. In other words, the commodities he bought to be used as productive inputs must have created more value in production than their own value. The secret answer to the origins of surplus value (or profit) is just this: *The capitalist buys the worker's labor power as a commodity in the market at its market value, then sells the product of the worker at a higher value.*

To show how this happens, consider an example of the process for one capitalist. He begins by using his money to buy two kinds of commodities, which Marx called constant capital and variable capital. *Constant capital* is defined as all the money spent for raw materials, machinery, factory construction, and any other products of previous labor purchased by the capitalist. The term constant capital is usually used to refer to the money spent and also to the commodities bought, since they are two forms of the same thing.

Since these products are all the result of previous labor, they may also be considered as simply so many units of labor. A *unit of labor* is defined as the product of the work of one laborer for one production period. In our example we assume that the capitalist buys constant capital embodying four units of labor. Why did Marx call these commodities (such as machinery) by the term constant capital? Because he wished to stress that this type of commodity enters the production process with a certain value (such as four units of labor), which value remains constant during the production process.

Variable capital, on the other hand, is defined by Marx to be the amount of money expended on the wages of labor during the production period. The term variable capital may be used both to refer to the money expended on wages and also the commodity that is bought for that money, namely labor power, the worker's ability to expend muscle and energy. This type of "capital" is variable in that a worker may expend more or less energy in a single day, depending on how many hours he or she works and on the intensity of labor demanded by the capitalist. When workers are forced to work faster than the previous average, this is called *speed-up.* In our example we assume the capitalist buys the labor time of ten workers, that is, ten units of labor power.

We assume that the capitalist hires ten workers. He pays them the market value of the only commodity they sell, namely ten units of labor power. What is the value of a unit of labor power? We do *not* mean the ethical value of an honest day's work—nor do we mean the product of a day's work, since that is called a unit of labor. We mean, How much must the capitalist pay in the market-place to hire one worker's labor power for a day?

In Marx's terms, what is the labor value of the commodity labor power? The reader will recall that one of the distinguishing features of capitalism is that human productive endeavor becomes a commodity—labor power. The exchange value of labor power is determined in the same way as that of any other commodity. There is some amount of labor that must be expended in order to create and maintain an adequate supply of labor power. In order for laborers to be able to continue offering their labor power for sale to capitalists, they must consume a certain amount of those commodities necessary to sustain life. In order to maintain the labor force over a longer period it is necessary for laborers to receive a sufficient amount of these necessities for them to rear a family and, in effect, grow their own replacements.

Those commodities that a laborer must have to sustain himself or herself are socially necessary costs of production, just as the food and shelter for farm animals is a necessary cost of producing agricultural products. Thus *the labor embodied in the production of the commodities that a worker and his (or her) family must consume to sustain themselves is the labor value of the commodity labor power.* As in the case of any other commodity, this is an average long-run result, which is the effect of all the factors affecting competition for jobs and wages in the labor market. These include the size of the unemployed army of workers kept in reserve, the strength of individual capitalists and their associations, the opposing strength of the trade unions, and the role of the capitalist state in labor struggles. Of course, in some short-run situations, such as a depression, a worker may be paid less than the value of his or her labor power.

How many hours a day must a worker work in order to produce the (long-run) value of his or her labor power? The answer is many hours less than he or she actually does work in a day, since the extra labor (beyond the value of his or her labor power) is the source of surplus value for the capitalist.

For simplicity, in our example we assume it takes exactly one-half of the worker's day to produce the market value of his or her labor power, say, four hours out of an eight-hour day. This means that one-half of labor exerted creates the market value of labor power, and one-half of the labor exerted creates surplus value. Looked at in another way, each worker labors one-half of the day for his or her own subsistence (wages) and one-half a day for the capitalists' surplus value (profit). We can call the first half of the worker's day *necessary labor,* because it is a socially necessary cost of production. The second half of the day can be called *surplus labor,* because it is not a socially necessary cost of production. Surplus labor creates commodities, which constitute the surplus value or profits. In other words, surplus labor represents labor extended beyond the period during which a worker produces the value equivalent of his or her wages, and it can therefore be called unpaid labor. Unpaid labor is the only ultimate real source of profits.

Our example of capitalist production is illustrated in Figure 16.1. The picture shows that the capitalist buys 4 labor units worth of constant capital, that is, raw materials, plant, and equipment. The capitalist also buys 10 units of labor power, that is, he hires ten workers for a day. In the production process, the 4 units of labor embodied in the raw materials, machinery, and other material inputs are used up to produce 4 units of labor embodied in new commodities (say, a commodity called "widgets"). The 10 units of labor power are used up in the production process to produce commodities (widgets) embodying 10 units of labor. By

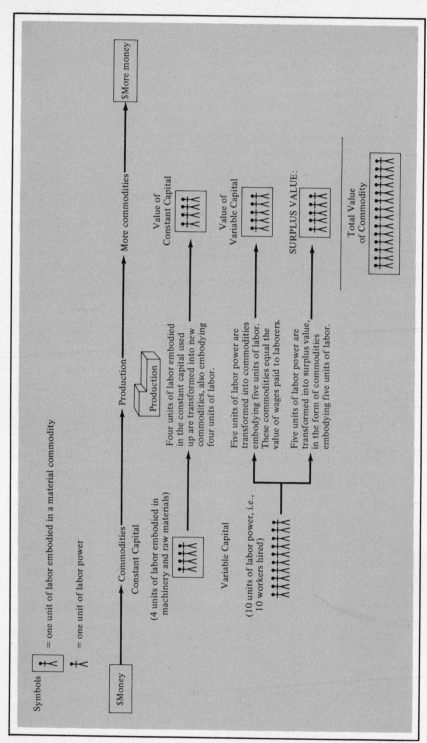

Figure 16.1 **The origin of surplus value**

our assumption of the wage level, however, the workers are paid an amount of money sufficient only to buy 5 units of labor embodied in commodities (widgets). This leaves the capitalist with commodities embodying 5 units of labor; this is the surplus value or profit.

If we add together the value of the constant capital used up (4 labor units of commodities), plus the value of the variable capital used up (wages in the form of commodities embodying 5 units of labor), plus surplus value (profit in the form of commodities embodying 5 units of labor), then the total value of the commodities produced is 14 units of labor. Thus:

Total value = constant capital + variable capital + surplus value
Or
14 units of labor = 4 units + 5 units + 5 units

In modern accounting terms, which blur and disguise some important concepts, the same equation may be expressed as

Price = Material costs (including depreciation) + wages + profit

What is disguised here is that the commodities represented by each of these terms actually embody a certain number of units of labor. Money often disguises labor values. With this warning—and given certain unrealistic assumptions to be modified in stage three of our argument—the terms in the equation may be transformed from labor units into money terms. If we arbitrarily assume that 1 unit of labor is valued at $10 in the market, then the equation becomes

Price of $140 = $40 material costs + $50 wages + $50 profit

Exploitation, or surplus value, is defined here as the difference between the value produced by the worker (value of units of labor produced) and the worker's wage (value of labor power). It is a strictly scientific concept, though the word also has ethical connotations (like every concept in economics). The *rate of exploitation* is defined as

$$\text{rate of exploitation} = \frac{\text{surplus value}}{\text{variable capital}} = \frac{\text{profit}}{\text{wages}}$$

or, in this example,

$$\frac{5 \text{ units of labor}}{5 \text{ units of labor}} = \frac{\$50}{\$50} = 100\%$$

The rate of exploitation is defined from the worker's point of view.

On the other hand, the *rate of profit* is a capitalist concept, designed to measure the profitability of various capital investments. The rate of profit is defined to be

$$\text{rate of profit} = \frac{\text{surplus value}}{\text{variable capital} + \text{constant capital}}$$
$$= \frac{\text{profit}}{\text{wages} + \text{material costs}}$$

In this example,

$$\text{rate of profit} = \frac{5 \text{ units of labor}}{9 \text{ units of labor}} = \frac{\$50}{\$90} = 56\%$$

Obviously, the rate of profit depends not only on the ratio of profits to wages but also the ratio of material costs (constant capital) to wages (variable capital). This latter ratio is defined as

$$\text{organic composition of capital} = \frac{\text{constant capital}}{\text{variable capital}} = \frac{\text{material costs}}{\text{wages}}$$

In other words, the *organic composition of capital* is the ratio of material costs (past labor) to present labor costs in production. In our example, it is

$$\text{organic composition} = \frac{4 \text{ units of labor}}{5 \text{ units of labor}} = \frac{\$40}{\$50} = 80\%$$

Our second stage, or second approximation to reality, could also be extended to the circulation of *all* capital. This task is mainly accomplished in Part III of this book. Here, we may briefly note that capitalists as a whole will produce the constant capital directly in the form of new machinery and raw materials to replace those used up. So 4 million labor units of constant capital will be used by workers to produce 4 million labor units of new constant capital. Capitalists as a whole will produce the value of variable capital in the form of consumption goods for workers. So to pay wages to 10 million workers (units of labor power), they will order the workers to produce 5 million units of labor in the form of consumable commodities. Finally, this leaves 5 million units of labor power for production of surplus value or profits. The capitalists take their profits in two forms. Some, perhaps 2 million labor power units, will go to produce commodities for luxury consumption. The rest, perhaps 3 million labor power units, will be used to produce new capital goods for expansion of business, thus leading to larger production and larger profits in the next period.

THE LABOR THEORY OF VALUE: THIRD APPROXIMATION

So far we have swept under the rug one complication in the labor theory. We showed how competition among capitalists forces an equal rate of profit in all industries. But competition of workers for jobs—and the struggle between workers and capitalists in each industry—also tends to produce an equal rate of exploitation in all industries (assuming, for the moment, there are *no* unions or business monopoly power). If there are equal rates of profit and equal rates of exploitation in all industries, that doesn't seem to pose any problem.

It sounds logical, and is logical, that equally exploited workers should produce equal rates of profit. The problem is, however, that the rate of profit is measured against not only living labor but also the previous labor embodied in constant capital (costs of raw materials and depreciation of machinery). Remember that the rate of profit is equal to profit divided by wages *and* the constant capital. But this *implies that the rate of profit is determined not only by the rate of exploitation of labor but also by the ratio of labor costs to material costs* (the organic composition). Yet this implication forces us to say that, where labor is equally exploited, lower material costs mean higher rates of profit. We would have to conclude that rates of profit are different in different industries according to the ratio of labor to material costs.

Yet we know that competition leads to equal rates of profit. In earlier sections we solved this problem by just assuming (implicitly) that technology or the organic composition was the same in all industries. Realistically, that is not true. So how can there be the same rate of profit in all industries if there are differing ratios of labor to machinery and material costs?

The answer is that, in this more realistic approximation, when the organic composition differs from industry to industry, money prices will diverge from labor values in such a way as to systematically redistribute the surplus value from one industry to another. In this stage of our presentation, money prices will no longer be identical to labor values, and profits will no longer be identical to surplus value when surplus value is stated in terms of labor values. Two points must emphatically be made, however. Both points stress the fact that the modifications introduced in this section do not in any way alter the conclusions we arrived at in the first two stages of the argument. First, prices still reflect the social division of labor and the production by separate capitalist firms, in which all coordination of production is affected by the market. Second, living labor power remains the sole source of surplus value, and surplus value is the sole source of profit. In particular, the source of profit remains the difference between the price of labor power and the prices of the commodities, which embody the labor into which that labor power was transformed in the production process.

A significant part of the reasoning at the third stage of our presentation is analytically more difficult than the main body of this chapter (or our entire book, generally). We must therefore refer the interested reader some literature which is somewhat more technical.[1] The reader who works through this literature will see that even though prices may deviate from labor values, and the profit of any capitalist may deviate from the surplus value generated by the labor power which he purchases, the ratio of the money value of all commodities produced to the money value of all labor power is equal to the ratio of the labor value of all commodities produced to the labor value of all labor power. Thus the nature and source of profits remain the same as in the second stage of our analysis, even though they are redistributed among capitalists.

If competition equates the rates of profit in all industries, and if differing organic compositions of capital exist, then the *surplus value must be redistributed through price changes* that equate the rates of profit. Some surplus value must be taken from those industries with a low organic composition and given to those

[1] See for example Ronald L. Meek, "Some Notes on the 'Transformation Problem'," in *Economics and Ideology and Other Essays* (London: Chapman and Hall, 1967), pp. 143–157, and Alfredo Medio, "Profits and Surplus Value," in E. K. Hunt and Jesse Schwartz, eds. *A Critique of Economic Theory* (Baltimore: Penguin, 1972), pp. 312–346.

industries with a high organic composition. The latter industries have more constant capital and it therefore requires more surplus value for them to achieve the socially average rate of profit. The former industries have less constant capital and it therefore requires less surplus value for them to achieve the socially average rate of profit. To effect this redistribution of surplus value, it is necessary for competition to raise the prices in industries with a high organic composition and lower the prices in industries with a low organic composition. A commodity produced with the socially average organic composition will have a ratio of money price to labor value that is equal to the ratio of the total monetary value of all goods to the total of all labor embodied in those goods. That is, a commodity with an average organic composition will have a price that is proportional to the labor embodied in it.

Thus, in its third approximation to reality, the labor theory of value does not assert that all money prices will be proportional to labor values. It does assert that *deviations from this proportionality will be systematically predictable.* In any science it is not expected that a valid theory is one that permits of no exceptions or deviations. The most that is ever expected of a scientific theory is that in its most complex and complete form, it be capable of systematic prediction of when and how observed phenomena will deviate from the general outcome, which the theory predicts in its most simplified and qualified form. The labor theory of value, when judged by this standard, is seen to be scientifically sound.

LABOR THEORY OF VALUE: FURTHER APPROXIMATIONS

Our exposition of value, wages, and prices is still at a very high level of abstraction. Several further approximations are needed to be more realistic, and many chapters of this book will deal with those more realistic situations. First, there is *not* pure competition but a high level of industrial concentration, as described in fact and theory in Chapters 18 and 19. Second, all workers are not treated equally; there is discrimination, by race and sex and other prejudices, as shown in Chapter 21. Third, there is not equilibrium at all times but rather frequent periods of unemployment and price inflation, as explained in Chapters 22 through 28 and 30 and 31. Fourth, there is not a purely private economy but extensive government intervention through regulations, laws and police, military spending, business subsidies, taxation, and other ways, all discussed in Chapters 20 and 29. Fifth, goods and services are not all measured just in the market but have noneconomic benefits and losses, such as polluting products, discussed in Chapters 32 and 33. Finally, the U.S. economy does not form its prices in isolation from all others but has vital international relationships, as described and explained in Chapters 34 and 35.

SUMMARY

The labor theory of value is based on an intellectual perspective that sees production as a transformation of unusable resources into usable products of human labor. The only ingredient in this transformation is human labor. The natural resources represent the material that is transformed—and production could certainly not take place in a vacuum with nothing to transform—but the natural resources contribute nothing toward their own transformation. They simply exist and their existence and potential for being transformed is a prerequisite for human life and human production. Tools and machines are used in production, but they are merely natural resources that have been previously transformed by human labor.

Produced means of production have been used in every human society of which we have any knowledge. By themselves, however, these means of production are not capital. They become capital only in a market-oriented, commodity-producing society in which they are owned and controlled exclusively by a small social class—the capitalists. The existence of a capitalist class, which owns and controls the means of production, necessarily involves the coexistence of a working class with no means of sustaining itself except through the sale of the commodity labor power. Thus, the widespread sale of labor power as a commodity is one of the most important distinguishing features of capitalism.

In the first stage of our presentation of the labor theory of value, we showed that in a commodity-producing society in which each producer owned his or her own means of production, commodity prices would be proportional to the labor embodied in the production of the commodities. Prices would reflect the social division of labor and the mutual interdependence of all producers—an interdependence that is expressed in millions of market exchanges.

In the second stage, or second approximation, of our argument we showed that the basis of profits is the fact that only a portion of a laborer's productive effort goes toward producing the value equivalent of his or her means of subsistence (that is, toward producing the value of his or her own labor-power). The remainder of this productive effort is surplus labor, and surplus labor creates profits.

The third approximation, increasing the realism of the argument, showed that differing organic compositions of capital cause prices to deviate from strict proportionality to quantities of labor embodied in commodities. These deviations, however, follow a predictable pattern and do not alter any of the important conclusions arrived at in the first two approximations of the argument.

Further approximations to reality show how production, prices, and wages are affected by monopoly power, trade union struggles, discrimination, unemployment, government activity, and international relationships.

CHAPTER 17

INCOME DISTRIBUTION AND THE LABOR MOVEMENT

In this chapter, we first present the facts of income distribution today. Then we examine the history of the U.S. labor movement to see how it has affected the distribution of income.

Poverty and Inequality

In 1974 the United States government stated that an urban family of four lived in poverty if it received less than $5038 per year. In that year twenty-four million, three hundred thousand persons received lower incomes than this officially defined poverty level.[1] That income figure, however, was absurdly low. Given the rampant inflation of the late 1960s and 1970s, the government's figure would more aptly describe a family in a state of desperate destitution. Inflation so eroded the purchasing power of the dollar in the early 1970s that an average American working family could just get by. In fact, the median family income for 1974 was $12,836. Yet 20 percent of the people, or about 42 million people, lived in families that received about half or less than half of that income, that is, less than $6500 dollars that year. In our opinion it would be a conservative estimate to say that these 42 million persons lived in poverty.

In fact, the government's definition of poverty is based on computations made by scientists working for the Agriculture Department. They computed that a person, who knew all about nutrition and was a skilled calculator of budgets, could just get by if he or she carefully and skillfully used every penny of his or her food budget for food that would just suffice for "emergency or temporary use when funds are low." Even the government did not believe that anyone could get along on that amount for very long! But most of the poor remain poor year after year.

In 1969 even Agriculture Department spokespersons conceded that the food plan used in computing the poverty level "is not a reasonable measure of basic money needs for a good diet." Furthermore, the yearly upward adjustment in the food budget to reflect cost of living increases is defective. It is based on the average change in a broad cross-section of prices. But poor people spend the largest single part of their income on food, and food prices increased faster than

---

[1] All data in this section, unless otherwise footnoted, are from U.S. Department of Commerce, Bureau of the Census, *Statistical Abstract of the United States*, 1975 (Washington, D. C.: GPO, 1975), pp. 392 and 401.

other prices during the 1970s. Thus the government's poverty budget would buy considerably less food for a family in 1975 than it would in 1970.

In fact, one branch of the United States government has recognized the total inadequacy of this definition of poverty. The Labor Department's Bureau of Labor Statistics calculates what they call a "lower budget" for an urban family. This budget is intended to reflect how much a family can just barely get by with if it has adequate food, shelter, clothing, medical care, and education. It would require, in their opinion, an average family to have $9198 to just get by in 1975. There are 60.3 million people living in families that did not receive family incomes sufficient for even this minimum.

Furthermore, the percentage of total income received by the poorest 20 percent and the second poorest 20 percent has not changed much since World War II. Table 17-1 shows the percent of total income received by each fifth of the population, from lowest to highest, since 1974. Also included is the percentage received by the highest 5 percent.

Two conclusions are obvious from table 17-1. First, the distribution of income remains amazingly stable over the years. There is no observable trend toward a decrease in the degree of inequality. Second, on the average for the entire period the highest 5 percent of income receivers receive as much income as the lowest 40 percent all combined.

The data for 1975 show a worsening of inequality.[2] The number of persons living below the official poverty level (which inflation pushed up to $5500) increased substantially to nearly 26 million people. At the same time, the share of income going to the richest 5 percent of the population increased. In that year, income inequalities based on racial and sexual differences were also typical. For males working full-time year round, the average income of blacks was only 73 percent that of whites. The average income of a woman working full-time year round was only 59 percent that of men. These differences did not reflect the true magnitudes of the inequalities based upon race and sex, however, because

Table 17.1 **Income Inequality from 1947 to 1974**

Income Group of Family	Percentage of Income Received						
	1947	1950	1955	1960	1965	1970	1974
Lowest fifth	5.1	4.5	4.8	4.8	5.2	5.4	5.4
Second fifth	11.8	11.9	12.2	12.2	12.2	12.2	12.0
Middle fifth	16.7	17.4	17.7	17.8	17.8	17.6	17.6
Fourth fifth	23.1	23.5	23.5	23.9	23.9	23.9	24.0
Highest fifth	43.3	42.7	41.8	41.3	40.9	40.9	41.0
Highest 5 percent	17.5	17.3	16.8	15.9	15.5	15.6	15.3

Source: U.S. Department of Commerce, *Statistical Abstract of the United States*, 1975 (Washington, D.C.: GPO, 1975), p. 392.

[2] Data in this paragraph are from a U.S. Census Bureau Study, reported in the *Los Angeles Times*, Sept. 26, 1976, p. 1.

blacks and women are much more likely to be able to find only part-time jobs or to be unemployed.

Moreover, even leaving aside race and sex, these data do not really show the extent of inequality of incomes because they are taken from tax reports that use biased data. The higher one's income is, the more tax loopholes permit one to not report as income a great deal of money that comes into one's possession. If true incomes were reported, the higher incomes would be much larger than is shown on the table (see Chapter 20 for details).

INCOME BY SOURCE

The most important factor differentiating incomes is their source. Capitalists receive income from owning while nearly everyone else gets their income from working. The very wealthy who receive extraordinarily high incomes are capitalists. Our table gave the figures for the highest 5 percent of income recipients. Included among these were many doctors, lawyers, corporate executives, and so on. But the truly wealthy are the capitalists who constitute approximately 2 percent of the population.

Of this 2 percent about one-half, or one percent of the population, are the elite, powerful capitalists. Two different scholarly studies have attempted to ascertain what percentage of the ownership of corporate stocks was in the hands of the wealthiest one percent of Americans. For 1958 Robert Lampman estimated that this wealthy one percent owned 75.4 percent of all corporate stock. A study for the year 1972, by James D. Smith and Stephen D. Franklin, produced the somewhat more conservative estimate that this one percent owned 56.5 percent of all corporate stocks.[3] Whichever method of estimating one believes to be more accurate (and the authors believe that Lampman's study was more accurate), it is obvious that this one percent of the population is truly a wealthy power elite that receives the bulk of the income from ownership. Incomes in this elite one percent range up to highs of over $100 million per year (or more than $270,000 per day, 365 days per year).

Those who receive property income, such as the profits from corporate stocks mentioned above, may be called the "capitalist" class. Property income includes corporate profits, the profits of unincorporated businesses, income from rents, and income from interest. Among the very wealthy, defined as those individuals with incomes over $1,000,000, over 95 percent of their income (in 1971) came from such ownership of property, so these were truly capitalists.[4] At the other end of the spectrum, for all those individuals under $10,000 income in 1971, wage and salary income from labor came to over 90 percent of total income, so these were truly "working" class people.

We can also make some estimate of the total shares of labor income and property income in the United States. Government data, however, do not exactly fit the categories of any economic theory, so conservative, liberal, and radical economists always fight over how to define these amounts, even when we all use

---

[3] These results are reported in U.S. Department of Commerce, *Statistical Abstract of the United States* (Washington, D.C.: GPO, 1975), p. 110.

[4] See Sam Bowles and Herb Gintis, *Schooling in Capitalist America* (New York: Basic Books, 1975), p. 90.

the same government data. In 1975 the total amount of property income[5] was as follows (in billions of dollars):

Business Proprietors' Income	$95
Rental Income	37
Corporate Profits before tax	115
Net Interest Income	75
TOTAL PROPERTY IMCOME	$322

This data on property income (showing $322 billion) is still badly understated because it is reported for tax purposes, but many tax loopholes allow much property income not to be reported at all.

The total amount of wages and salaries in national income in 1975 was $807 billion.[6] This amount is drastically overstated for two reasons. First, there are *no* tax loopholes available for wage and salary income, so it is relatively overstated compared to property income. Second, it includes vast amounts of "managers' and executives' salaries," which are often property income in disguise (so they can be deductions from corporate taxes). The most interesting comparison is what Marx called the rate of exploitation or the rate of surplus value, which is *roughly* translatable into the ratio of property income to labor income:

$$\text{Rate of Exploitation} = \frac{\text{Property income}}{\text{Labor income}} = \frac{\$322}{\$807} = 40\%$$

Finally, how many people are in which class according to the source of their income? Again, the government does not use exactly our categories, but some of the main trends can be obtained from the government data. Table 17-2 shows the results.

From this table we see that wage and salary workers are now the overwhelming majority (or 84 percent) of Americans. Yet their income share is far, far below 84 percent, especially since the income data above include managers' salaries as labor income. Managers and officials are now a not insignificant 7 percent of the labor force. The self-employed 80 percent in 1780 were mostly farmers. The self-employed have now shrunk to only 9 percent, including 2 percent farm owners, 4 percent independent professionals and artisans, and 3 percent self-employed businesspersons. So this 9 percent is all that is left of the old middle class; even adding managers and officials we get only 16 percent "middle class."

But where is the capitalist class? The government data hides the capitalist class. The top corporate executives are hidden among the managers and officials. The biggest millionaire coupon-clippers are hidden among the self-employed businesspersons. Nevertheless, from the estimates of wealth stated earlier, especially holdings of corporate stock, we find that the entire capitalist class is only about one percent of the population.

[5] Data from U.S. Department of Commerce, *Survey of Current Business*, Dec. 1976, p. 6. Because they contain a lot of tax loopholes, we have *not* included the "inventory valuation adjustments" nor the "capital consumption adjustments."

[6] Data from *ibid*. We do not include so-called "supplements to wages and salaries" because these are mainly employer social security contributions *paid to government* and expenses of business executives for trips and entertainment.

Table 17.2 **Evolution of the U.S. Labor Force**

Year	Wage & Salary Workers	Self-employed	Managers and Officials
1780	20%	80%	0%
1880	62	37	1
1969	84	9	7

Note: The data from 1780 exclude slave workers.
Source: All data presented here from government sources, as discussed in the excellent article by Michael Reich, "The Evolution of the U.S. Labor Force," in R. Edwards, M. Reich, and T. Weisskopf, eds. *The Capitalist System* (Englewood Cliffs, N.J.: Prentice-Hall, 1972), pp. 174–183.

THE LABOR MOVEMENT BEFORE THE CIVIL WAR

The labor movement was very weak in the United States before the Civil War (the War Against Slavery). There had been a few strikes and a few unions, but most unions were very temporary and soon disappeared. One reason was that the industrial working class was such a small part of the population. In the North most of the population in the early nineteenth century was composed of small farmers, where the whole family ran the farm. In the South the main laboring population were the slaves, though there were also many poor white farmers. In 1860 there were still only 1.3 million factory workers.[7] The Civil War greatly stimulated industry, however, so that by 1870 there were 2 million factory workers and 3.6 million other wage workers.

Another factor that made the organization and maintenance of unions so difficult was that workers were split by all kinds of prejudices, in part stimulated by the employers. Throughout American history, there have been large numbers of new foreign-born workers who could be pitted against the native-born. There was also a slow influx of women into industry, who were paid very low wages but who were prohibited by men from entering most unions until after the Civil War (and who are still not allowed into most union leadership).

The most important prejudice weakening American labor, however, was the racial prejudice of whites against blacks as well as the objective fact of slavery in a large section of the nation. In the South it was often said, by *The Charleston Mercury* newspaper, for example, "Slavery is the natural and normal condition of the laboring man . . . and the Northern states will yet have to introduce it. The theory of a free society is a delusion."[8] Moreover, before the Civil War these slaveowners often elected the President, dominated the Supreme Court, man-

[7] This fact, and any other facts in this section not otherwise footnoted, comes from the beautiful book by Richard O. Boyer and Herbert M. Morais, *Labor's Untold Story* (published by the United Electrical, Radio, and Machine Workers of America, 11 East 51st Street, New York, N.Y., 10022, first ed. 1955, third ed. 1970). A more complete, scholarly history is Philip S. Foner, *History of the Labor Movement in the United States* (New York: International Publishers, several volumes, first volume in 1947).
[8] Quoted in Boyer and Morais, op. cit., p. 13.

aged Congress, had a strong control over both political parties, and pushed racism as God's will through organized religion in the South and to some extent even in the North. The slaveowners used their power to buy up much of the press, to control some of the few existing universities (and all the southern schools), to dominate the officers' corps in the U.S. Army, and to get the nation into war with Mexico in order to expand into the West. In 1857, in the Dred Scott case, the U.S. Supreme Court held that slavery was legal *everywhere* in the United States, regardless of state laws. In pure economic terms, this meant that white workers in the North could not get high wages or maintain strong unions because the South was always willing to produce the same product more cheaply with slave labor.

After the Civil War, the northern industrialists took over control of the country, pushed capitalism into the West and the South, and made immense fortunes (some of which were begun by selling poor quality goods to the Union armies). This was the era of the robber barrons, who made fortunes by ripping oil, timber, gold, and coal from the earth, often leaving ruined land and dust bowls behind them. Yet millions of people lived in abject poverty in unsanitary slum conditions.

THE NATIONAL LABOR UNION

The Civil War laid the basis for trade unions by the abolition of slavery and by the stimulation of industry, which resulted in a growing class of poorly paid factory workers. William H. Silvis was the man who helped organize and lead the first nationwide labor federation. He was born in 1828 in Pennsylvania in a family of ten children (which was typical in those days) with little money in the family and little food to eat. He worked as an iron molder, and in 1863 helped to organize a national union of iron molders. He was appalled by the poverty of the working class—for example, the fact that in New York City little girls worked from 6 in the morning till midnight for three dollars a week! As a union organizer he started out on a national organizing tour with only $100 in his pocket.

Not only did he see the poverty of the workers, he also noted that employers were beginning to organize on a national scale (for example, the Iron Founders Association was organized in 1866). Silvis pointed out these facts, not only to thousands of individual workers but also to many other trade union leaders. As a result, in August 1866 in Baltimore, the National Labor Union was formed and Silvis became its president. But labor was still divided. Many delegates were opposed to admitting women, but Silvis fought for and won the inclusion of women in the National Labor Union (NLU), though many of its constituent unions would not admit women for many years.

Silvis also fought for the inclusion of blacks, 4 million of whom were now free workers, in the NLU. On this point, however, he was defeated. Not only were many of the delegates prejudiced against blacks, but they were single-mindedly interested in a campaign for the eight-hour day and did not want to hear about any other issue. The only major resolution passed declared

> The first and great necessity of the present to free the labor of this country
> from capitalistic slavery is the passing of the law by which eight hours shall be
> the normal working day in all the states of the American Union.[9]

[9] Quoted in ibid., p. 32.

The campaign for the eight-hour day did spread like wild fire, and Eight-hour Leagues were formed all over the United States, with 50 in California alone. By 1868 the U.S. government was forced to pass an eight-hour day for all of its own employees. Yet private industry resisted, state laws were declared unconstitutional by the Supreme Court, and a federal law was passed only in 1938 by the New Deal. Before that time, many Congressional investigations found amazingly long working hours even for women and children in most parts of the United States. Still, the agitation of the NLU did reduce the average working day from 11 hours in 1865 to 10.5 hours in 1870.

Silvis worked so hard as an organizer that he died in 1869 at the age of 41. As a memorial, the NLU finally admitted blacks to membership at its 1869 convention. But it was too late for this gesture to succeed. The National Labor Union was already becoming a largely middle-class reformers' organization, with neither white nor black workers in it. By 1868 two-thirds of its membership was composed of doctors, lawyers, farmers, preachers, and other nonworking-class people. As a result, after the 1869 convention the NLU leadership declared that trade unions were *not* the best road to reform. So their union affiliates began to fall away, and by the 1871 convention only two union delegates showed up. The NLU, like many other organizations of this period, turned to the crank ideas of a currency reform that would make easy money available to everyone. In 1872 the NLU supported a National Labor Reform Party, running on the single plank of currency reform, which left workers so uninterested that it got only 30,000 votes. Thus, the NLU killed itself by not acting like a labor federation but like a middle-class reform group with crankish ideas. This pattern repeated itself in many "labor" organizations in the last half of the nineteenth century.

THE KNIGHTS OF LABOR

After some years of rapid industrial expansion after the Civil War, a major depression began in 1873 and lasted for six lean and hungry years. By 1877 there were about 3 million unemployed, a huge percentage of the labor force. In 1873 there had been thirty national trade unions, but unemployment, lockouts, and blacklists destroyed most of them, so only eight or nine national unions remained by 1877. Yet workers and the unemployed were becoming more militant under the intolerable conditions. There was a large demonstration in New York City, where signs proclaimed, "The Unemployed Demand Work, Not Charity." The noble police, bought and paid for by big business, attacked the demonstration with clubs and sent many women and children to hospitals. *The New York Times* said that all the demonstrators were foreigners and communists, a theme that has been repeated ever since.

In Pennsylvania in the 1870s the police fought pitched battles with the miner's union. Because many of them were Irish immigrants who belonged to the Ancient Order of Hibernians, most of the union leadership was charged with being Irish revolutionary terrorists. The police and the newspapers invented the name "Molly McGuires" for them, though this organization never existed in the United States. Ten of the miners were charged with killing a policeman, were rapidly convicted in a witch-hunting atmosphere, and were hanged on June 21, 1877.

In another action, in July of 1877, a strike against the Baltimore and Ohio erupted in violence when strike-breakers tried to move the trains. The Philadelphia militia came to Pittsburgh, were met by a large hostile crowd, and fired into it. They killed 20 men, women, and children! That night they were surrounded in their barracks by thousands of miners and steel workers. The militia ran away at midnight to escape the wrath of these many thousands of people. The newspapers again reported that the strikers and all their supporters were communists and anarchists, so the newspapers praised the police and militia for their violence. The *New York Tribune* said, "These brutal creatures can understand no other reasoning than that of force and enough of it to be remembered among them for generations."[10]

At the same time, a new national union federation was growing from a small and strange beginning. In 1869 a small union called the Garment Cutters Association was disbanded and immediately reconstituted itself as the Knights of Labor. Its national officers were called the Master Workman, the Veritable Sage, the Worthy Foreman, the Unknown Knight, and the Treasurer. People wishing to become members paid $1, went through a large number of ritual initiation ceremonies, and were sworn to secrecy. There had been so much violence against the labor movement that the Knights felt that only secrecy would allow them to survive. No women were admitted until 1882. For a long time the Knights of Labor was a very small organization; it was known only for its secrecy, so the newspapers charged that it was a subsidiary of the Irish Molly McGuires, trying to overthrow the government of the United States.

By 1877, however, the National Labor Union had disappeared, and the great strikes, as well as the violence with which they were met, convinced many workers that some new national organization was needed. By the end of 1877, the Knights had expanded to 14 district assemblies from Massachusetts and New York to Indiana and Illinois, with much strength in Pennsylvania. The Knights had a program opposed to monopoly corporations, which they thought should be publicly owned; specifically, they argued for public ownership of the railroads, telephones, and telegraph companies. In 1881 the Knights finally decided to give up their secrecy and go public, though they retained secret initiation rights. In 1878 the Knights had only 9,287 members, but they grew to 52,000 by 1883 and to over 600,000 members by 1886.

Part of the secret of their swift growth was that their local assemblies would accept anyone from any trade or occupation, male or female, black or white. Their slogan was, "An injury to one is the concern of all." Yet their admission of anyone, without limitation by trade, was also a weakness. Many of their assemblies had a middle-class composition and were more interested in grand reforms than immediate issues of labor versus capital.

The Grand Master of the Knights of Labor in the years 1880 to 1886 was Terrence V. Powderly. He was a rather conventional believer in reform policies. He stressed the popular panacea of currency reform. On the other hand, he absolutely opposed strikes and actually acted as a strike-breaker in some circumstances. He felt that strikes could never cause reforms, never change unjust laws, and never solve labor's problems. He even attempted in 1886 to stop the tide of workers organizing in favor of the eight-hour day, which he also felt to be

---

[10] Quoted in ibid., p. 69.

a side issue. When millions of workers organized to strike for the eight-hour day on May 1, 1886, Powderly did all he could to oppose this movement. That was the last straw for many members of the Knights, so the Knights declined as fast as they had previously risen.

THE AMERICAN FEDERATION OF LABOR

A third national federation of labor unions also grew out of the depression of 1873 and the violent strikes of the late 1870s. In 1881 a number of unions met together to form the Federation of Organized Trades and Labor Unions of the United States and Canada, which changed its name in 1886 to the American Federation of Labor (AFL). The AFL was formed by a number of labor leaders who considered themselves socialists, its leader Samuel Gompers among them. In 1886 the AFL adopted a preface to its Constitution that said,

> A struggle is going on in the nations of the world between the oppressors and oppressed of all countries, a struggle between capital and labor which must grow in intensity from year to year and work disastrous results to the toiling millions of all nations if not combined for mutual protection and benefit.[11]

Moreover, the first main action of the AFL was a very militant one. The AFL became the main force behind the eight-hour day movement. The AFL called on all labor to strike for the eight-hour day on May 1, 1886. It is ironic that many years later the AFL declared it was subversive and communistic to demonstrate on May 1st. The May 1st demonstrations were supported by many hundreds of thousands of workers, were peaceful, and were very successful in their publicity. On May 2nd, however, at a protest meeting against police brutality in Haymarket Square in Chicago, some unknown person tossed a bomb that killed one policeman. Using this as an excuse, the police rounded up several trade union leaders and some anarchists, a long framed-up trial took place, and four of the men— who had been nowhere near Haymarket—were executed.

The AFL gradually took an entirely different, very peaceful and less and less militant path as time went by. Its leaders declared that they had *no* ultimate ends of social change, that they were interested only in immediate monetary gains for the workers. Moreover, the AFL came to rely more and more heavily on organization of the highly skilled workers in very narrowly defined craft unions. At no time until the 1930s did the main leaders of the AFL willingly organize masses of unskilled workers in industrial unions. On the contrary, they often had a large number of small craft unions all competing for members among the skilled workers and totally neglecting the unskilled, especially black and women workers. They practiced what came to be known as "business unionism," meaning a dollars-and-cents orientation toward higher wages as their first and last priority, the amassing of huge treasuries to support their power, the use of large staffs of highly paid professional organizers, and big salaries for their top union executives.

There were many attempts to reform the AFL, to bring it closer to the needs of the millions of unorganized workers. This was particularly true in the period of 1900 to 1920, when the Socialist party flourished in the United States. By 1912 the

[11] AFL, quoted in ibid., p. 90.

Socialists had elected over 1000 local and state officials and two congressmen, had newspapers that sold to millions of people, and had hundreds of thousands of dues-paying members. In 1912 Eugene Debs, who was born and raised in Terre Haute, Indiana, ran for President of the United States as a Socialist and received over a million votes. Even later, in 1920, when he was in prison for opposing the First World War, Debs still took almost a million votes again, though he could do no personal campaigning from his prison cell. Throughout this whole period, the Socialists opposed the business unionism and narrow craft organization of Samuel Gompers and other AFL leaders. The Socialist candidate for President of the AFL frequently took about one-third of the votes.

Although the Socialist party produced many leaders, Gene Debs was by far the most remarkable. He grew up in the Midwest, was very tall, a powerful speaker, and reminded people of Abe Lincoln. Debs worked on the railroads for many years. He wrote,

> As a locomotive fireman, I learned of the hardships of the rail in snow, sleet
> and hail, of the ceaseless danger that lurks along the iron highway, the
> uncertainty of employment, scant wages and altogether trying lot of the
> workingman, so that from my very boyhood I was made to feel the wrongs of
> labor . . .[12]

In 1893 Gene Debs organized a single railway union to replace the 22 squabbling craft unions of the AFL on the railways. At that time Debs was still quite conservative in much of his thinking, was not a Socialist, and supported the Democratic party. In 1894, however, Debs's fledgling union was manipulated into a premature strike when it was still growing and not yet mature. Even then the union (the American Railway Union) would have won against the bosses; but U.S. Army troops were called into the center of the strike, in Chicago, and broke the strike with violence. At the same time Debs and all the union leadership were put in jail for six months for violating the Sherman Antitrust Act on the theory that they had restricted trade and competition! (Yet up to that time, no monopoly corporation executive had ever been tried under the Act, much less sent to prison!) During his time in prison, Debs studied Marxist political economy and became a socialist.

Soon after 1920 Debs died, the Socialist party split into many warring sects of socialists and communists, and government repression was very severe. The President of the National Association of Manufacturers said, numerous times, that the American trade union movement was an un-American, illegal, and infamous conspiracy of communists and anarchists. After the Bolshevik revolution in Russia, "Innumerable . . . gentlemen now discovered they could defeat whatever they wanted to defeat by tarring it conspicuously with the Bolshevist brush."[13] On January 2, 1920, *The New York Times* screamed in a banner headline, "200 Reds Taken in Chicago. Wholesale Plot Hatched to Overthrow U.S. Government." Attorney General Palmer, who was very pro-business and anti-labor, on the night of January 2, 1920, did indeed arrest *ten thousand* American workers, mostly union members and union leaders, who were taken out of their beds and thrown into prison. They were all charged with being illegal or undesirable aliens and indicted for deportation. As it turned out, about 6500 were released with no

[12] Debs, quoted in ibid., p. 115.
[13] Frederick Lewis Allen, quoted in ibid., p. 204.

charges at all—they were not aliens but American citizens, just a mistake, sorry. The other 3500 were held for deportation, but the great majority of these also won their cases and were acquitted.

In all of this period, the AFL continued placidly to organize small numbers of skilled, almost all white, mostly male, workers. The more militant unions were independent of the AFL—unions such as the Western Federation of Miners, which in the period 1896 to 1914, fought to organize the miners of the West. Particularly in Colorado, the government of which was owned lock, stock, and barrel by the mining and banking interests of the Rockefellers, the miners fought pitched battles against scabs supported by local, state, and even federal troops. There were a number of massacres in which wives and even children of the miners were killed. For a time the Western Federation of Miners was the most important founder and supporter of the International Workers of the World (IWW). The IWW, organized as a rival federation to the AFL, was highly militant, explicitly socialist, and did win some important strikes, such as the strike by the (mostly women and children) textile workers in Lawrence, Massachusetts, in 1912. Yet the IWW did not pay enough heed to the immediate needs of the workers, nor did they heed the necessity for routine organizing in an efficient manner in periods other than the most red-hot strike situations. So the IWW faded away after a short, but glorious, history.

THE GRAPES OF WRATH AND THE RISE OF THE CIO

The 1920s were a time of little trade union activity and very little radical political activity, partly because of government repression, partly because of splits in the socialist movement, and partly because of a long business upswing with only mild recessions. In 1929, however, began the Great Depression, which went on and on through 1930 and 1931 and 1932 and 1933, with only a slight recovery after that, reaching the level of production of 1929 only in 1937. World capitalist production fell by 42 percent and U.S. capitalist production by 50 percent between 1929 and 1932. At least 50 million people were unemployed throughout the world, with over one-fourth of the U.S. labor force unemployed by official statistics. The capitalist system planted the grapes of wrath in workers and reaped a major expansion of the trade union movement in the United States.

Yet the AFL did very little in the first years of the depression, even coming out *against* unemployment compensation. For a while the most important organized activity of workers was in the National Unemployed Council, which had branches all over the United States. Its main activity was the prevention of evictions. Where families could not pay the rent, the police showed up to evict them, but the members of the Unemployed Councils showed up as thousands of people determined not to allow such evictions. For example, in the eight months ending June 30, 1932, in New York City 185,794 families got eviction notices, but about 77,000 of these were moved back into their homes by people from the Unemployed Councils.

Although there were big increases in the votes for the Socialist and Communist parties, the main political event of the 1930s was the election of Franklin Roosevelt and the New Deal. The New Deal, supported by the labor unions, promoted the Civilian Conservation Corps to give employment to the unemployed. In 1935, it passed the Wagner Act or National Labor Relations Act, which guaranteed the right to strike and collective bargaining, and made illegal some anti-union activities of corporations. In 1938 the New Deal passed the Fair Labor Standards Act, which legislated maximum hours of work and minimum wages.

With some support from the New Deal legislation, workers at first tried to organize in the AFL. But the AFL unions were not interested in nor designed to accommodate millions of unskilled workers. Moreover, the employers counterattacked by huge expenditures on propaganda claiming that the trade unions as well as Roosevelt and the New Deal were all a communist plot. In addition to propaganda, General Motors alone from January 1934 to July 1936 spent $994,855.68 to hire private spies and private police to sabotage and attack the labor unions.

One memorable strike that did occur was that of the longshoremen on the West Coast in 1934. When they first tried to bargain with the employers, the employers simply fired all the union leaders. When the leaders were reinstated by order of the regional labor board, the employers still refused to recognize or bargain with the union. Eventually, about 35,000 maritime workers were out on strike, the center of the strike being the Embarcadero at the port of San Francisco. The strikers wanted pay of $1 an hour and a union hiring hall to replace the usual "shape-up" system whereby employers hired on whim from those who showed up at the docks. On July 3, 1934, the police decided to break the mass picket lines to allow scabs to work. One reporter wrote,

> The police opened fire with revolvers and riot guns. Clouds of tear gas swept the picket lines and sent the men choking in defeat. . . . Squads of police who looked like Martian monsters in their special helmets and gas masks led the way, flinging gas bombs ahead of them.[14]

But this was only the preliminary. The pickets returned on July 5th, a Thursday (known as Bloody Thursday), and they were joined by many young people from the high schools and colleges as well as hundreds of other union members. The police charged, using vomiting gas, revolvers with live ammunition, and riot guns. Hundreds were badly wounded and two workers were killed.

The pickets finally were driven away and the employers thought they had won. But many union locals as well as the Alameda Labor Council called for a general strike. In spite of a telegram from the President of the AFL forbidding any strike, the workers of San Francisco launched a general strike to support the longshoremen and in protest against the killings by the police. The general strike was amazingly successful:

> The paralysis was effective beyond all expectation. To all intents and purposes industry was at a complete standstill. The great factories were empty and deserted. No streetcars were running. Virtually all stores were closed. The giant apparatus of commerce was a lifeless, helpless hulk.[15]

During the general strike, labor efficiently allowed into the city emergency food and medical supplies, but nothing else. Thousands of troops moved into the city, but there was no violence; labor simply refused to go to work. The general strike lasted until July 19th, when the local AFL officials, refusing to call a roll-call

14 Mike Quinn, quoted in ibid., p. 285.
15 Mike Quinn, quoted in ibid., p. 287.

vote of the central labor council, announced that a majority of the council had called off the strike.

Yet after that, the longshoremen's pickets were not disturbed, lest the general strike should break out again. The longshoremen had their wages raised to 95 cents an hour and won the union hiring hall. Later, the U.S. Immigration Department tried five times to deport the union leader, Harry Bridges, who had come from Australia, on charges that he lied when he said he was not a communist—but after five long cases, the Supreme Court finally ruled that all the cases were frame-ups and that there was not sufficient evidence that he was a communist.

By 1935 the U.S. government had recognized the right of collective bargaining for most workers, wages were still very low, unemployment was still very high, and millions of workers were in a very militant mood. Many of the unorganized workers tried to organize new locals of the AFL, but the AFL was not much interested in them, and the very narrow jurisdictional rules of the AFL craft unions made organizing very difficult in the mass industries. Thus, when John L. Lewis pulled out of the AFL and organized a new federation, it was welcomed with open arms. Besides Lewis and the United Mine Workers, the AFL was left behind by the Typographical Union, the Amalgamated Clothing Workers, the Textile Workers, the Mine, Mill and Smelter Workers, the International Ladies' Garment Workers, and a few more unions. Altogether, some 1 million workers left the AFL to form the Congress of Industrial Organizations (the CIO).

There were immediately a number of mass organizing campaigns and strikes, many of them in the new form of the "sit-down." In this form, workers simply sat down in a plant and took it over till their demands were met. The advantage was that scabs could not be brought in unless the workers were forcefully pushed out, but that was difficult without injuring the company's equipment, which most companies were loath to do. On January 29, 1936, at 2 a.m. the rubber workers in Firestone Tire Plant No. 1 in Akron, Ohio, simply pulled the switch and stopped the assembly line, and sat down. In three days they won their strike, including union recognition. The wave of sit-down strikes spread rapidly across the nation, partly as a fad, but mostly as a serious new offensive by workers for their rights. Most of the new unions formed by workers went into the CIO. New unions were formed of Rubber Workers, Electrical Workers, Steel Workers, and the United Automobile Workers, each of which became massive unions. In one year from its formation, the CIO grew from 1 million to 2 million members. The AFL—and numerous newspapers—denounced the CIO as a communist conspiracy, but nobody paid much attention.

One of the hardest fought strikes was in Michigan against the automobile companies, where working conditions pushed the men to desperate organization. In the summer of 1936,

> During July, a torrid heat wave sent the thermometer boiling to over 100 degrees for a week straight. But the assembly lines pounded away mercilessly while many workers fell at their stations like flies. Deaths in the state's auto center ran into the hundreds within three or four days . . .[16]

The auto companies would not even recognize the unions. The new United Auto Workers struck the main plant of General Motors in Flint, Michigan. On Decem-

[16] Henry Krause, quoted in ibid., p. 299.

ber 30, 1936, the Flint workers sat-down in the plant—as did GM workers in many other plants around the country. But GM had always owned the town of Flint completely, being the only major employer in town. Some GM officials organized vigilante squads, the police cooperated closely with GM, and the courts willingly issued injunctions against the strikers. But the workers held firm in the plant for day after day, their beards growing longer and longer. The hardest fight was by the wives of the strikers, who had to bring in food to them in a running battle against the local and state police. One woman wrote later,

> Motorists had been warned to drive elsewhere. The police stationed themselves around the plant with tear gas and guns. They had gas masks on when the women came with the evening meal. . . . The women began passing the food through the windows. . . . Then came the tear gas.[17]

On the worst day of the fight, 14 women fell from gunshot wounds, but the food continued to come into the plant.

All of the nation's newspapers said this was a prelude to revolution; they quoted Alfred Sloan, head of GM, who said it was all a communist attempt to Sovietize the auto industry and then the whole country. Enormous pressure was brought to bear on the young liberal governor of Michigan to bring in the National Guard to clear the plant of strikers. At last, he capitulated and went to tell John L. Lewis of his decision, but John L. reminded him of the governor's own grandfather, who had been an Irish revolutionary, and John L. said he himself would go to the plant and be the first to fall from the National Guard's bullets. The governor retreated and finally decided not to use the National Guard. Then, on the 44th day, General Motors surrendered to the strikers' demands (because their competitors were taking the market away from them). The union was recognized, speed-up reduced, and wages started to rise from their level of 30 cents an hour.

Soon after this, there was an enormous effort to organize the steel industry. After seeing the GM strike, United States Steel gave in and recognized the Steel Workers union. But Republic Steel held out, using their own police to massacre ten peaceful pickets on Memorial Day in 1937. Nevertheless, soon all the steel companies recognized the union. By 1938 the CIO grew to nearly 4 million members. Even the AFL woke up enough to begin to get new members.

Then came the Second World War in which the corporations made record profits, while thousands of soldiers were dying. Nevertheless, the war did bring full employment and another vast growth in union membership. Women particularly flooded into the war industries, and female union membership grew from 800,000 in 1938 to 3,500,000 by the end of 1944.

The overall data on the growth of unions is shown in Table 17.3 and Figure 17.1. The data show that, excluding agriculture, in which unions have had few members, the percentage of unionized workers was only about 11 percent in 1930. The militant organizing drive of the CIO brought in many millions of unorganized and unskilled workers, raising union membership to about 30 percent in the late 1930s. Then the full employment of the Second World War brought union membership to a high of 35.5 percent in 1945.

[17] Mary Heaton Vorse, quoted in ibid., p. 305.

Table 17.3 **UNION MEMBERSHIP, 1945–1972 (Union Members as percent of all Employees in Nonagricultural Employment)**

Year	Percent Unionized	Year	Percent Unionized	Year	Percent Unionized
1930	11.3	1954	34.7	1963	29.1
1945	35.5	1955	33.2	1964	28.9
1946	34.5	1956	33.4	1965	28.4
1947	33.7	1957	32.8	1966	28.1
1948	31.9	1958	33.2	1967	27.9
1949	32.6	1959	32.1	1968	27.8
1950	31.5	1960	31.4	1969	27.0
1951	33.3	1961	30.2	1970	27.3
1952	32.5	1962	29.8	1971	27.0
1953	33.7			1972	26.4

Source: U.S. Department of Labor, Bureau of Labor Statistics, *Handbook of Labor Statistics 1976* (Washington, D.C.: GPO, 1976), p. 297.

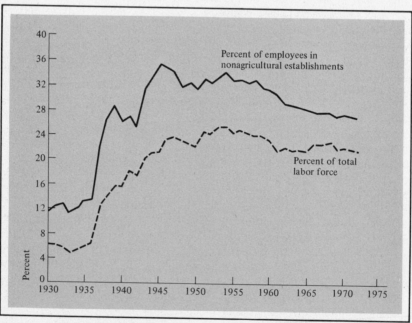

Figure 17.1 **Union membership shown as a percentage of total labor force and of employees in nonagricultural establishments, 1930–1972 (excludes Canadian membership).** (Source: U.S. Bureau of Labor Statistics, *Handbook of Labor Statistics, 1974,* Washington, D.C.: GPO, 1974.)

THE COLD WAR AND THE DECLINE AND FALL OF THE CIO

At the end of the Second World War, the prospects for American labor looked very bright. Allied with the Soviet Union, we had won a war against fascism. Our country was filled with democratic, pro-union propaganda; and the government was run by a Democratic party, supposedly allied with labor. There had been a great deal of discussion of civil rights in the U.S. government, and black soldiers came home expecting to find equal opportunities. Women had been widely recognized as equal workers, and both parties accepted the Equal Rights Amendment into their platforms. Then a counterattack was launched by all the most antiblack, antiwomen, antilabor, and pro-big-business forces in the United States.

The main weapon of this attack was the Cold War, in which it was said that the one and only threat to Americans came from the Soviet Union and the communist "conspiracy." The first success of this attack was the election of an overwhelmingly conservative Republican Congress in 1946, which immediately passed the very antilabor Taft-Hartley Act, cancelled all rent and price controls, attacked child care centers as a communist device, and totally ignored the need for civil rights for minorities. One of the main instruments of the antilabor attack was the House Un-American Activities Committee, which helped the Republican campaign, as early as the 1944 anti-Roosevelt campaign, by stating that, "The political views of the Communist Party and the CIO Political Action Committee coincide in every detail."[18]

Although the Un-Americans had been attacking labor unions as a communist conspiracy through this Congressional Committee ever since 1938, they stepped up the level of their slanders in the period 1946-1948 (and to some extent throughout the 1950s). Every union that showed the slightest militancy immediately had its leaders subpoenaed before the House Un-American Committee— and later before Senator Joe McCarthy's committee.

The Taft-Hartley Act of 1946 must be seen in the context of this Cold War against "Russians and communists." It restored to courts the power to issue anti-union injunctions. It gave the Labor Board the right to order a 60-day cooling off period during which a strike would be illegal. It outlawed mass picketing, the closed shop, and the right of labor to contribute to political campaigns—but gave employers the right to sue unions for "unfair labor practices." And it forced all union leaders to take an anti-communist oath, which meant that they could be sentenced to prison if a jury could be convinced that they were communists. In those days of hysteria, it was easy to get juries to convict alleged communists. For example, Clinton Jencks of the Mine, Mill, and Smelter Union was accused by a stool-pigeon of being a communist, tried in a farcical trial, and sentenced to five years in prison. It required many years of legal fighting, during which Jencks suffered both personally and as a union organizer who could no longer help the union, for the U.S. Supreme Court to hold many aspects of the trial and "evidence" to be insufficient *and* unconstitutional. This was the experience of many thousands of Americans who lost their jobs or careers because they were too strongly prolabor and had been labelled "communist" by some committee or

[18] House Un-American Activities Committee, quoted in ibid., p. 338.

prosecutor (the FBI even went around asking employers, "Did you know that Mr. X is a Communist?").

Under this kind of red-baiting pressure, the CIO finally caved in and split. In 1948 the CIO leadership issued an order that all of their unions must vote for Harry Truman and the Democratic party or risk expulsion, though many of the CIO unions had already declared for the new Progressive party. As a result, by 1949 the CIO expelled all of the unions suspected of leaning to the left: the United Electrical Workers; the International Longshoremen's Union; the Mine, Mill and Smelter Workers; and seven other unions. Altogether, about 1 million workers were expelled from the CIO. Moreover, all remaining union activists realized that they had better be silent or they would be expelled by the CIO or smeared by Senator McCarthy or by the House Un-American Committee.

In this situation not only the independent unions, but also the AFL and the CIO, all lost members. Most union leaders became very timid and/or corrupt and/or collaborated with the boss. The AFL and CIO merged in 1955, but even this merger did not restore their strength or vigor; it merely marked the end of the militant CIO. Therefore, total union membership fell from 35.5 percent of the nonagricultural labor force in 1945 to only 26.7 percent in 1972.

Of course, unions are stronger in the manufacturing sector than in the rest of the economy. The manufacturing sector, however, has declined in importance relative to other sectors, especially service industries. Moreover, union power has been declining even in the manufacturing sector. The changes in percent of unionization in manufacturing are shown in Table 17.4.

Table 17.4 shows that union strength declined by 5.3 percentage points in all manufacturing from 1958 to 1972. When manufacturing is divided into eight industrial groups, the percentage of workers in unions rises slightly in only one group, while it falls in seven groups. The loss of bargaining strength, with a lower

Table 17.4 UNIONIZATION IN MANUFACTURING BY INDUSTRY (union members as percent of employees on payrolls)			
	1958	1972	Change in Percentage Points from 1958 to 1972
All Manufacturing	52.4	47.1	−5.3
Food, beverages and tobacco	55.1	53.4	−1.7
Clothing, textiles and leather	50.1	41.6	−8.5
Furniture, lumber, wood, and paper	50.3	50.1	−0.2
Printing and publishing	39.7	32.7	−7.0
Petroleum, chemicals, and rubber	39.6	34.7	−4.9
Stone, clay, and glass	44.6	48.0	+3.4
Metals and machinery	52.3	47.1	−5.2
Transportation equipment	78.7	59.1	−19.6

Source: U.S. Department of Labor, Bureau of Labor Statistics, Handbook of Labor Statistics, 1974 (Washington, D.C.: GPO, 1975), p. 367.

percentage of the labor force enrolled in unions, helps explain the weakening position of labor versus capital.

SUMMARY

Income distribution in the United States is very unequal. A large percentage of Americans still live below the official poverty level. Yet a small percentage, around one percent, are very wealthy, living mostly on income from profits, rent, and interest. Over 80 percent of Americans earn mostly wages and salaries, and just barely make ends meet.

Income distribution is not just a matter of the impersonal forces of supply and demand but the very direct personal confrontation of workers and bosses as part of those forces. The history of labor unions in the United States has been very violent. There were few unions till the Civil War and the industrialization following that war. The most important labor federation for many decades was the American Federation of Labor, which mainly organized highly skilled, white, male workers and left most of the labor force unorganized. During the New Deal of the 1930s, the situation changed enough that the Congress of Industrial Organizations was able to organize millions of new workers. All unions grew during the Second World War. Then in the following period of repression against so-called "communists," the labor movement split and declined. So the percentage of union members has been declining ever since, though some signs of renewed militancy have appeared in unions in the 1970s.

CHAPTER 18

MONOPOLY POWER

The world of numerous, small competitive capitalist enterprises, which Adam Smith thought would produce the best result for all concerned, is gone forever (if it ever existed). Since the period of the 1890s and early 1900s, western Europe and the United States have been characterized by the domination of a relatively few giant firms. This new stage of monopoly has not ended capitalism, but it has intensified many old qualities and added some entirely new and unpleasant features.

In the monopoly stage of capitalism the setting of prices and outputs is quite different than under competition, and the profit result is equally different. The amount of waste, manipulation of the consumer, limitation of the worker's wages, and conflict between profit seeking and social needs (such as the need for a decent environment) exist on entirely new scales. If Adam Smith's harmony-of-interests theory ever had a grain of truth, it is surely not applicable to the monopoly stage of capitalism.

THE TREND OF CONCENTRATION

In a purely competitive economy each competing business unit would be so small that its actions taken alone could not appreciably influence the quantity of goods or the price in the market. Such, more or less, was the U.S. economy during the early nineteenth century. Small farms and small businesses produced most of the output, and there were no giant corporations dominating an entire industry (though there were many local monopolies). As late as 1860, there were still no incorporated business firms in many of the major urban industrial centers. Since that time, the picture has changed drastically.

The size of corporations rose rapidly in the post-Civil War period. By 1900 the share of manufacturing output produced by corporations had grown to two-thirds. Some of the big corporations developed by virtue of rapid internal growth; others arose through mergers of formerly independent firms.

Mergers have come in waves. The first massive movement, which lasted from the early 1890s to the outbreak of World War I, was characterized by *horizontal* mergers, in which a big corporation absorbed other corporations that were its direct competitors. The result of such mergers was, of course, industries dominated by fewer and much larger corporations. The second wave came in the 1920s. It was characterized by *vertical* mergers, which occurred between firms producing goods in sequence, as when a giant corporation absorbs its suppliers or absorbs the firms to which it sells its output. The 1960s witnessed a third and unique wave. Most of these mergers were of the *conglomerate* variety, in which a giant corporation absorbs other corporations that have no relation to it. The aim is simply to establish a colossal corporate empire that will give its controllers immense economic and political power.

From 1950 through 1959 there were an average of 540 corporate mergers a year. From 1960 through 1967 the average was 1100 a year. In 1968 there were 2655 mergers. More and more of these were conglomerate mergers between two giants in different industries. From 1948 through 1953 conglomerate mergers accounted for 59 percent of the total. From 1960 through 1965 they comprised 72 percent of the total. In 1968 conglomerate mergers accounted for 84 percent of all mergers.[1]

The enormous size and power of the 100 largest conglomerates may be seen in the data on how many large firms in each separate industry are under their control. "In more than half of the 1014 product classes in manufacturing as a whole, at least one of the 100 largest was among the 4 largest producers, and in 31 percent at least 2 came from the 100 largest. It is thus obvious that the 100 largest companies are not limited in their operations to only a few large-scale industries but rather are broadly represented among the largest producers of manufacturing products throughout most of the wide spectrum of U.S. industry."[2]

Today there still are millions of very small industrial enterprises, but a few hundred corporate giants hold most of the wealth and do most of the producing. Table 18.1 reveals the extremely high concentration of corporate assets in a comparatively few firms. At the bottom, a large number of small corporations held a minuscule portion of total corporate assets. At the top, a few giant corporations held 60 percent of all assets. That some 1300 U.S. corporations would hold almost $2 trillion in assets is incredible; that amount is more than the total value of

Table 18.1   **Distribution of Corporate Assets (all U.S. corporations, 1971)**

Size (in assets)	Corporations (number in group)	Corporations (percent in size group)	Assets (percent owned by group)	Assets (amount owned by group)
$0–100,000	958,089	57%	1%	$33 billion
100,000–500,000	515,813	31	4	116 billion
500,000–5,000,000	177,121	10	8	226 billion
5,000,000–250,000,000	30,226	2	27	784 billion
250,000,000 and over	1,349	0.08	60	1.729 trillion
Total	1,682,616	100.00%[1]	100%	2.889 trillion

Source: U.S. Internal Revenue Service, *Statistics of Income, Corporation Income Tax Returns for 1971* (Washington, D.C.: G.P.O. 1975).
[1] Data add to more than 100% because of rounding.

[1] All data in this paragraph are from the Federal Trade Commission and were cited in Federal Reserve Bank of Cleveland, *Economic Commentary*, May 12, 1969, p. 3.
[2] John Blair, *Economic Concentration* (New York: Harcourt Brace Jovanovich, 1972), pp. 53–54.

all western European assets. Among those 1300 corporations, there is still a great concentration within just the top 200 or 300 corporations.

The figures for all corporations average out differences in various sectors. In the important sector of banking alone, for example, there are approximately 13,775 commercial banks, but a mere 14 of them hold 25 percent of all deposits, and the 100 largest banks hold 46 percent of all deposits.[3]

Another function of banks is to hold assets in *trust* for individuals and corporations. Banks exercise the voting power for these stocks, which gives them immense power without having legal ownership. Forty-nine of the largest banks hold over 5 percent of the common stock in 147 of the 500 largest industrial corporations in the United States. They also hold at least 5 percent of the common stock in 17 of the largest companies in the fields of merchandising and transportation. These banks are represented in the boards of directors of the majority of the largest corporations in the fields of manufacturing, merchandising, utilities, transportation, and insurance.

Finally, let us turn to the decisive sector of manufacturing taken alone. In the general category of manufacturing enterprises, there were 180,000 corporations and 240,000 unincorporated businesses in 1962.[4] Ninety-eight percent of all manufacturing assets were owned by the corporations. Of the 420,000 manufacturing firms, the 20 largest (not 20,000, but 20!) owned 25 percent of total assets of manufacturing firms. The largest 50 firms owned 36 percent, and the largest 200 owned 56 percent. If adjustment is made for giant firms that are owned by even larger giants (i.e., if their ownership is added together), we arrive at a much higher percentage of control. The fact is that, after adjustment for ownership of subsidiaries, a mere 100 firms owned 58 percent of the net capital assets of all the hundreds of thousands of manufacturing corporations. Another index of the imbalance of economic power is the fact that the largest 20 manufacturing firms owned a larger share of the assets than the smallest 419,000 firms combined.

When profits earned are examined, the contrast is even more striking. The net profits of the 5 largest corporations were about twice as large as those of the 178,000 smallest corporations combined. In order to appreciate the size of these giants, consider just one of them, General Motors. "General Motor's yearly operating revenues exceed those of all but a dozen or so countries. Its sales receipts are greater than the combined general revenues of New York, New Jersey, Pennsylvania, Ohio, Delaware, and the six New England states. . . . G.M. employees number well over 700,000 and work in 127 plants in the United States and 45 countries spanning Europe, South Africa, North America, and Australia. The total cash wages are more than twice the personal income of Ireland."[5]

If the individual industries which are the arenas of most direct competition are examined, the picture of economic concentration may be even more sharply

---

[3] The figures on concentration in banking are taken from the Patman Committee Staff Report for the Domestic Finance Subcommittee of the House Committee on Banking and Currency, *Commercial Banks and Their Trust Activities: Emerging Influence on the American Economy* (Washington, D.C.: GPO, July 1968), p. 5.

[4] The data that follow are taken from Willard F. Mueller, "Economic Concentration," in hearings before the Subcommittee on Antitrust and Monopoly of the Committee on the Judiciary, United States Senate, 88th Cong., 2d Sess., *Part 1: Overall and Conglomerate Aspects* (Washington, D.C.: GPO, July 1964), pp. 111–129.

[5] Richard Barber, *The American Corporation* (New York: Dutton, 1970), p. 20.

drawn than in the aggregate data. Let an *industry* be defined so that there is easy substitution among the products of all firms within it, and very little possible substitution with products of outside firms. In most industries, just three or four giant monopolistic firms control most of the production, and most of these top firms, as shown above, are part of the 100 largest super-giant conglomerates. Many small firms also exist in most industries, but altogether they produce a small percentage of the total output. U.S. government data for 1963, adjusted slightly for more precise market definition, showed that 39.6 percent of all industries were highly concentrated, that is, had 50 percent or more of their product sold by four companies.[6] Another 32.1 percent of all U.S. industries were moderately concentrated, that is, had 25 percent to 49 percent of their product sold by four companies. Only 28.3 percent of all industries were somewhat competitive, that is, less than 25 percent of their product was sold by four companies.

Moreover, among the top companies are many interlocking directorates. In 1965, the 250 largest corporations had a total of 4007 directorships, but these were held by just 3165 directors.[7] Among these, 562 men held 2 or more directorships, and 5 men held 6 each! Other studies have traced control to eight main groups: three that each held large blocs of stock in several corporations were Rockefeller, Mellon, and DuPont; two that used financial control over several corporations were Morgan-First National and Kuhn-Loeb; three were groups known for their local control in the cities of Boston, Chicago, and Cleveland. In addition, as seen earlier, there is now formal control by large conglomerates (themselves usually part of one of the major interest groups) of top corporations in each of several industries.

INCREASING BUSINESS CONCENTRATION

The size and power of the largest firms keep increasing, even as a percentage of the immense and increasing U.S. total capital. Table 18.2 shows that the percentage of all U.S. manufacturing assets owned by the 200 largest rose by 3 percent points in the Great Depression. It fell a little in World War II as small and medium-sized firms expanded even more rapidly than the giants to meet the unlimited government demand. The share of assets of the 200 largest rose again by 13 whole percentage points from 1949 to 1968. The share of value added in manufacturing (another measure of concentration) produced by the 200 largest corporations also rose 12 percentage points from 1947 to 1967 and rose another percentage point from 1967 to 1972.[8]

Since 1950, 1 out of every 5 of the 1000 largest manufacturing companies has been swallowed by an even larger giant. Since 1959 big business has been absorbing other business firms with $10 million or more in assets at a rate exceeding 60 a year. In 1966 101 companies, each with assets of more than $10 million, were absorbed by other companies; in 1967 the number was 169; in 1968 it was 192. Obviously oligopolistic business giants are far from satisfied with the im-

---

[6] All data from Census Bureau, *1963 Census of Manufacturers* adjusted by Blair, op. cit., p. 14.

[7] All data in this paragraph from Blair, op. cit., p. 76.

[8] U.S. Department of Commerce, "Concentration Ratios in Manufacturing," *1972 Census of Manufacturing* (Washington, D.C.: GPO, 1975), SR 2-4, Table 1.

Table 18.2 **Share of 200 Largest Manufacturing Corporations**

Year	Percentage of Total Manufacturing Assets
1929	45.8%
1939	48.7
1949	47.1
1959	54.8
1969	60.2
1973	60.3

Source: Federal Trade Commission, reported and discussed in John Blair, *Economic Concentration* (New York: Harcourt Brace Jovanovich, 1972), p. 64. Data for 1973 from David Penn, "Aggregate Concentration," *Anti-Trust Bulletin* (Spring 1976).

mense size and power they already have. There is nothing to lead us to believe that these mushrooming industrial empires are about to discontinue merging. Furthermore, the few large firms control most research and thus will continue to grow more rapidly. A 1960 survey showed that just 4 firms accounted for 22 percent and 384 firms accounted for 85 percent of all industrial research and development.[9] Finally, it is worth noting that much of the increase in concentration comes during depressions. In every depression millions of small businesses are driven to the wall and go bankrupt. Then the big fish eat the little fish, buying up most assets for a song. The result is that each recession or depression further increases monopoly power.

The economy of the United States has thus changed from a predominantly competitive to a predominantly monopolistic production situation. The monopolies are still growing through conglomerate mergers of giants in different industries. The apparent degree of concentration may not change in each industry, but the same conglomerate may now control a large firm in each of many industries. Thus the data on particular industries, which indicate that the shares of the 3 or 4 largest have not increased much for several years, severely understate the trend toward concentration of power in the 100 largest manufacturing firms.

THE REASONS FOR MONOPOLY

One fundamental cause of the emergence of the giant corporation is the economy of scale that can be derived from large production units that turn out cheaper goods by using more specialized machinery, more specialized workers, and mass production assembly lines. Small firms are driven out of business by the cheap goods produced through large-scale applications of technology. The large firm gains a monopoly by selling at a lower price while making more profit.

In addition to improved technology based on the economies of scale, there is another reason for the greater profitability of huge firms like General Motors.

[9] See John K. Galbraith, *The New Industrial State* (Boston: Houghton Mifflin, 1967), p. 23.

These firms grow internally or via merger far beyond the technologically neces-sary minimum because they wish to exercise monopoly power over the market. With small competitors eliminated or dominated, the few remaining giant firms can restrict output and set higher prices to make higher profit rates.

The huge firms try to gain monopoly control of a whole industry to escape what they call the "rigors of competition" or "cut-throat competition"—meaning that they want the freedom to set their prices wherever they please without fear of competition. Their behavior and excuses are ironic because they tell everyone else how great the free, competitive market is.

The giant monopolistic firms attempt to eliminate risk and uncertainty, not only controlling their own industry's output, but also (1) buying out raw material suppliers, (2) buying out dealers and outlets for the finished product, (3) using vast nationwide advertising, and (4) linking up with banks and other financial sources. With these motivations there is no clear upper limit to desirable size. The motto seems to be "the bigger the better."

PRICES AND PROFIT MAXIMIZATION

What is the effect of monopoly on the price structure? The essence of the mo-nopolist's position is the ability to keep competitors out of the market by means of greater efficiency, control of natural or financial resources, control of patents, or any other legal or illegal methods. Thus prices can be as high as the market will bear, and there is no competitive mechanism to bring the higher profit back down to the average rate of profit in industry as a whole.

Although the monopolist can make a higher than average rate of profit, profit cannot be made out of thin air. Total profits still remain within the limits of total revenue minus costs. To some extent monopoly does not affect aggregate prices or aggregate profits but only redistributes aggregate profits. From a given amount of aggregate profits, monopolists may take away part of the profits of small businessmen and farmers by competing for the consumer's dollar. They may also increase their share of profits through their power to buy raw materials and food at low prices and sell finished goods at high prices to these small entrepreneurs. However, monopolists may also increase total profits by using their power to raise prices or to restrict money wages in order to lower the workers' real wages.

Monopoly price and quantity of production are set by monopolists as they see fit. In order to maximize profits, however, they can only set the quantity at the point of greatest difference between total revenue (determined by demand) and total cost (determined by the cost of labor plus material costs). Once the quantity is set, even a monopoly can sell only at a price determined by the demand at that point. The difference between this and the competitive situation is that under monopoly the quantity supplied is set lower so that the price is higher. Therefore the short-run rate of profit is higher than the average under competition. The long-run rate of profit remains higher because capital cannot freely enter the industry.

Contrary to this view, many economists claim that modern businessmen do not always attempt to maximize profits. The capitalist today, however, is not the individual businessman but the corporation. Whether the businessman is rational and calculating in private life is essentially irrelevant to the functioning of the system. In corporate decisions there can be no doubt that the making and accumulating of profit hold as dominant a position today as they ever did. Like the individual enterprise of an earlier period, the giant corporation is an engine for maximizing profits, but it is not used merely as an enlarged version of the personal capitalist. There are two differences: (1) The corporation has a much longer time horizon, and (2) it is a much more rational calculator.[10]

Having said that much, it is important to avoid a dogmatic notion that every corporate decision is made in terms of immediate dollars and cents returns. Certainly corporate management may sacrifice short-run profits to ensure the security of their market control, to spur company growth, and even to act as dictated by the somewhat vague concept of prestige. Thus prices are not always set as high as the market will bear. It could be said that management maximizes a multiple set of objectives. Equally well (because the difference is only semantic), it could be emphasized that each of the other objectives is merely a rational way to achieve maximum long-run profits, which are the real sole objective.

WHO CONTROLS THE CORPORATION?

Liberals agree that monopoly is an evil aspect of capitalism, but they believe a remedy short of doing away with capitalism is possible. Some rely on stricter enforcement of antitrust laws. Others admit that these laws have clearly proved inadequate and advocate stricter laws. Still others claim that a process of internal change in giant corporations is automatically eliminating most of its negative qualities. John Kenneth Galbraith is the leading spokesman of the latter view.

Galbraith maintains that there is a great contradiction between the notion that the modern corporation is controlled by the management and the fact that it nevertheless ruthlessly tries to maximize profits for its stockholders. Furthermore, he argues that the most important factor of production is no longer capital but the specialized talent of scientists and technologists, and that real power passes from stockholders and top management to the members of the *technostructure* (i.e., the technical personnel, including scientists and technicians). According to Galbraith, the members of the technostructure do not get the profits they are supposed to maximize. Because the technostructure supplies talent, not capital, why should they worry about the return of capital? He says that the modern corporation has the capacity to shape society, but its resources are used to serve the deeper interests or goals of the technostructure, which possesses the real power.[11]

Galbraith agrees that a few hundred giant corporations control the market, regulate output and prices, and exercise enormous political control. Yet with a wave of his hand he eliminates the corporate executive and puts the control of the corporation in the hands of scientists and technically skilled workers. He then finds that the technostructure really manages the corporation and that, for their own reasons, they manage it in the best interests of all society. In other words,

---

[10] In this respect, see James Earley, "The Impact of Some New Developments in Economic Theory: Discussion," *American Economic Review*, May 1957, pp. 333–335.

[11] Galbraith, op. cit., Chapters 5, 6, 7, 8.

Galbraith is very critical of capitalism, especially of the tremendous centralization of the means of production, but nevertheless is apologetic in the sense that he concludes that the industrial system has actually solved (or is solving) its problem.

The radical view is that Galbraith ignores the real position of modern corporate management. In the first place, the fact that so many top executives hold stock means their motivations cannot possibly be inconsistent with profit seeking. For example, in early 1957, 25 managers of General Motors owned an average of 11,500 shares each.[12] They might not be able to affect policy even with that amount of stock in General Motors, yet each owned roughly $500,000 in the company, so it is improbable that any manager was indifferent to profits. Further, among stockholders there are more managers than representatives of any other group, and a larger proportion of managers own stock than in any other group.

Galbraith, of course, argues that it is not the motivation of the managers but the motivation of the technostructure that is decisive. Radicals counter that the goals of the technostructure would be the same as those of the managers: survival of the firm, growth, independence from outside control. All these demand profit-making activity. More important, it flies in the face of reality to believe that the technicians control the corporations. The managers hire and fire the technicians, not vice versa. In the end it is the boss rather than the hired hand who makes the decisions (and will use expert advice only to make more profitable decisions).

MONOPOLY PROFIT RATES

The monopoly structure of American capitalism has been examined and the price-setting behavior of its management investigated. How do monopolistic structure and behavior affect the performance of American capitalism? In this section the effect on profit rates is reviewed. First the sources, in theory, of monopoly profit are briefly recapitulated; then the facts of monopoly profit are presented.

The whole point of monopoly control of markets is, of course, to restrict output and charge higher prices. All consumers are hurt by higher monopoly prices. Workers may have a constant wage in dollars, but as prices rise their buying power falls. If we reduce the figure for money wages by the percentage of price increases, the result is called the *real wage*. For example, if money wages stay at $100 while prices rise by 7 percent, the real wage declines. Therefore, if money wages stay constant, we may say that price increases by monopolies lower real wages and thereby increase their profits.

Purchasers of producer goods also suffer from monopoly prices, so the profits of small businesses and farmers are lowered. Some large firms also have extra market power as large buyers of commodities from small business, forcing down the prices of these small suppliers.

The giant firm also has extra power in the labor market, so it may add to its profits by buying labor at a rate lower than the average wage. This factor may, of course, be somewhat offset by trade union action. In the modern world of mo-

[12] Gabriel Kolko, *Wealth and Power in America* (New York: Praeger, 1962), p. 13.

nopoly, wages are not determined simply by automatic market supply and demand. They are determined by the bargaining strength of capital and labor, with monopoly capital usually in the stronger position. Workers are thus squeezed from both sides by monopoly. On the one hand, the monopolies can pay lower money wages by exerting their power in the labor market. On the other hand, monopolies can charge workers higher prices as consumers.

Additional monopoly profits come from lucrative government military contracts, which are financed from the workers' tax money, thus again increasing total profits (see Chapter 29). Extra-high returns from foreign investments abroad also add to monopoly profits; that is, profits are extracted from workers in foreign countries (see Chapter 35). In summary, monopolies, or oligopolies if there are more than one large firm controlling the industry, make profit far above the average rate in several ways: (1) selling at higher prices to consumers, thereby lowering the real wage, (2) selling at higher prices to small business and farmers, (3) buying at lower prices from small business and farmers, (4) buying labor power at lower wages from workers, (5) selling to the government at higher prices, and (6) buying labor power and materials at lower prices in foreign countries. Through these relatively high prices and low costs (always relative to a competitive firm in the same situation), the monopoly or oligopoly firms extract more profits from worker-consumer-taxpayers here and abroad; they also transfer some profits from small business and farmers to themselves.

Turning to the facts, we may investigate first how the profit rates of an enterprise are affected by its absolute size. The size of a business is indicated by the total amount of its assets, and the profit rate is the total profit divided by the capital investment of all the stockholders. Profit rates by asset size for all corporations since 1931 are given in Table 18.3.

In an economy of pure and perfect competition, all profit rates should be equalized in the long run. As Table 18.3 demonstrates in the U.S. economy the long-run profit rate is not the same for all corporations. On the contrary, the

Table 18.3 **Long-Run Profit Rate by Corporate Size (All U.S. Manufacturing Corporations, 1956–1975)**

Size (by assets)	Profit Rate (profit before taxes divided by sales)
$0 – 1,000,000	3.7%
1,000,000 – 5,000,000	5.3
5,000,000 – 10,000,000	6.7
10,000,000 – 50,000,000	7.4
50,000,000 – 100,000,000	8.1
100,000,000 – 250,000,000	8.5
250,000,000 – 1,000,000,000	8.8
$1,000,000,000 – and over	11.7

Source: U.S. Federal Trade Commission, *Quarterly Reports of U.S. Manufacturing Corporations* (Washington, D.C.: G.P.O., 1956–1975).

smallest corporations have much lower profit rates than the corporations in the largest-size groups. This is a proof of the existence of monopoly power and imperfect competition.

Economic concentration, however, has another important aspect. The indicator of market power is a firm's relative size and importance in its own industry. A *concentration ratio* in each industry may be defined as the percentage of sales controlled by the eight largest corporations in the industry. Several studies have found a definite relationship between an industry's concentration ratio and its profit rates. Some evidence is presented in Table 18.4

Table 18.4 Monopoly Power and Profit Rates (all U.S. manufacturing corporations)

Industry Group	Concentration Ratio 1972	Profit Margin 1972	Average Profit Margin of Sector in			
			1972	1967	1958	1954
Monopoly Sector (over 50% concentration)						
Motor Vehicles	88%	8.7%				
Tobacco (except cigarettes)	87	11.3				
Instruments	65	13.9				
Primary Nonferrous Metals	64	5.6	8.9	10.7	9.6	11.0
Electrical Machinery	62	7.1				
Primary Iron & Steel	56	5.0				
Chemicals	55	11.3				
Petroleum & Coal Products	55	8.3				
More Competitive Sector (under 50% concentration)						
Food	49%	4.7%				
Paper	47	6.8				
Textiles	46	4.7				
Leather	41	5.1				
Fabricated Metals	39	6.5	6.2	6.1	5.0	5.8
Apparel	33	4.3				
Lumber	31	8.0				
Furniture	29	6.7				
Printing & Publishing	29	8.7				

Source: U.S. Federal Trade Commission data on profits and U.S. Census Bureau data on concentration, compiled by Kathleen Pulling, *Cyclical Behavior of Prices and Profits, U.S., 1949–1975* (unpublished Ph.D. dissertation, University of California, Riverside, 1977).

Notes: A *concentration ratio* is the percentage of industry sales controlled by the eight largest sellers. The ratio for each industry group is a weighted average of the ratios in each of its component industries. Three groups (nonelectrical machinery; stone, clay, glass; and rubber and plastics) are excluded because their concentration ratios were sometimes over and sometimes under 50 percent in this period. A *profit margin* is the percentage of profit to sales in each industry group. The four years shown are the years in which censuses of manufacturing were taken.

The very high concentration of production that exists in many industry groups reflects the fact that in the majority of U.S. industries the bulk of production is concentrated in a few giant corporations, with hundreds of smaller companies producing very little. Moreover, inspection of the table reveals a considerable rise in profit rates as the degree of concentration rises. Thus the average profit margin in the monopoly sector (over 50 percent concentration ratio) is much higher than is the average profit margin in the competitive sector (under 50 percent concentration ratio) in all four years for which data is available. The conclusion is that the giant corporations, with larger size and greater market power, have higher rates of profit than the small competitive firms.

This analysis may be extended to the trend of aggregate profits under capitalism. It appears that the giant corporations have steadily reduced production costs per unit and that there have been powerful impulses toward innovation. Yet monopoly cannot be considered a rational and progressive system because although it reduces costs, it continues to set extremely high prices. Moreover, its increased productivity does not benefit everyone but only a few. Profit rates increase, and the share of profit in national income rises. Contrary to the nineteenth-century economist's version of falling rates of profit, under monopoly the rate tends to rise.

MONOPOLY AND WASTE

To some extent, large firms are more efficient because of economies of scale. Production cannot reach optimum efficiency below a certain point, or quantity of output. Thus the fact that large firms account for most U.S. output means that most of the economy has the ability to produce at lower costs than ever before. Studies of cost data reveal the possibility of high efficiency at a fairly constant level beyond the necessary minimum scale of production.[13] Of course, because the very large firms also have disproportionately larger research facilities and control a very large percentage of all unexpired patents, they have the greatest potential for increasing efficiency. Moreover, many investment projects require resources beyond the means of small firms.

But the large, entrenched firm stands to lose most from the obsolescence of present machinery and from product improvements that reduce the number of units the customer need buy—for example, a longer-lasting light bulb. Therefore if the large firm has an oligopoly position and faces no serious competitive pressure for improvement, it may develop, patent, and not use important inventions. Monopoly power has paradoxical effects on innovation. Giant firms have a rapid rate of technological progress, but they retain a large amount of technologically obsolete equipment.

Monopoly power may also be used to restrict supply in order to raise prices. Thus, as will be seen in Chapter 31, monopoly power is one of the principal causes of inflation. Monopolies will expand production as rapidly as possible only in extraordinary periods of unlimited demand. This usually occurs only when government demand skyrockets, as in World War II. In wartime, monopolies can

[13] See J. S. Bain, "Price and Production Policies," in Howard S. Ellis, ed., *A Survey of Contemporary Economics* (New York: McGraw-Hill, 1948), p. 140.

cease restricting output but still charge prices as high as the government will allow.

Moreover, as is also shown in chapter 31, the existence of economic concentration may have increased the severity and possibly the number of depressions because of (1) its destabilizing effects on remaining small businesses and (2) its lowering of workers' ability to consume. It would seem that this is another reason why the net effect of monopoly may be to lower the rate of economic growth.

On the other hand, breaking up large firms into smaller units would probably not increase economic growth. Reducing the American economy to small firms would certainly cause a major decrease in economic efficiency because of the loss of economies of scale—and most likely would have negative effects on investment. It is impossible to go backward to a competitive small business economy; the only answer seems to be to go forward to public and workers' control of the giant corporations.

The rate of growth (and waste) under monopoly is also affected by the fact that the sales effort has greatly expanded. Once a relatively unimportant feature of the system, sales effort has become one of its decisive nerve centers. The impact of advertising and related expenditures on the economy is outranked only by that of militarism. In all other aspects of social existence, the influence of advertising is second to none. In an economic system in which competition is fierce and relentless but in which the small number of rivals rules out price cutting, advertising becomes to an ever increasing extent the principal weapon of the competitive struggle. There is little room under atomistic competition for advertising; in monopoly it is the most important factor in the firm's survival.

Relatively large firms are in a position to exercise a powerful influence on the market for their output by establishing and maintaining a pronounced difference between their products and those of their competitors. This differentiation is sought chiefly by means of advertising, trademarks, brand names, distinctive packaging, and product variation. If successful, it leads to a condition in which consumers believe the differential products can no longer serve as close substitutes for each other.

Advertising involves a massive waste of resources, a continual drain on the consumer's income, and a systematic destruction of the consumer's freedom of choice between genuine alternatives. Furthermore, advertising in all its aspects cannot be meaningfully dealt with as some undesirable excrescence on the economic system that could be removed if we would only make up our minds to get rid of it. Advertising is the very offspring of the monopoly form of capitalism, the inevitable by-product of the decline of price competition; it constitutes as integral a part of the system as the giant corporation itself. The economic importance of advertising lies partly in its causing a reallocation of consumers' expenditures among different commodities. Even more important, however, is its effect on the magnitude of aggregate effective demand and thus on the level of income and employment. In other words, it generates useless expenditures by consumers, which soak up part of its overproduction by getting consumers to spend money beyond their direct needs.

Advertising affects profits in two ways. The first effect is the fact that part of advertising and other selling expenses are paid for through an increase in the prices of consumer goods bought by productive workers. Their real wages are reduced by this amount, whereas total profit is maintained by the higher prices.

The other, more complicated, effect is that the profits and wages some capitalists and workers make from the business of advertising constitute an expense for other capitalists. This component of the outlays on advertising and sales effort does not constitute an increase in total profit but does cause its redistribution. Some individuals living off profit are deprived of a fraction of their incomes in order to support other individuals living off profit, namely those who derive their incomes from advertising itself.

Furthermore, in making it possible to create the demand for a product, advertising encourages investment in plant and equipment that otherwise would not take place. The effect of advertising on the division of total income between consumption and saving is not measurable but is clear in direction and probably very large. The function of advertising, perhaps its dominant function today, is to wage a relentless war on behalf of the producers and sellers of consumer goods against saving and in favor of consumption.

Actually much of the newness with which the consumer is systematically bombarded is either fraudulent or related trivially, and in many cases even negatively, to the function and serviceability of the product. Moreover, other products are introduced that are indeed new in design and appearance but that serve essentially the same purposes as old products they are intended to replace. The extent of the difference can vary all the way from a simple modification in packaging to the far-reaching and enormously expensive annual changes in automobile models.

In addition, most research and development programs, which constitute a multibillion-dollar effort in the United States, are more closely related to the production of salable goods than to their much touted mission of advancing science and technology. For example, if monopoly profit and dealers' markups were excluded, then the real cost of production of the 1945 automobile, built with the technology of 1975, would have been far less than it was in 1945. The big three in auto making have always spent enormous sums on changes in automobile styles each year, which are of no use to consumers, but help sell more cars. Thus the total amount of waste from all the time and effort devoted directly and indirectly to selling products under monopoly must considerably lower the rate of economic growth.

Not only does monopoly greatly increase the waste of capitalism but it also raises pollution and environmental destruction to a new level. In the competitive model, apologists could claim that consumer preference dictated what was produced and therefore that pollution was merely an unfortunate by-product of the demands of the public. The apologists argued that these unfortunate by-products of public preference could be handled by some minor public action in beautifying the environment. Under monopoly, such apologetics are no longer possible; it is clear that consumer preference is manipulated and directed toward whatever products are most profitable to produce, and therefore "environmental damage becomes a normal consequence of the conflict between the goals of the producing firm and those of the public."[14]

So far, only the civilian wastes and peacetime pollution caused by monopoly have been considered. The full effect of monopoly power, however, depends on its political influence (see Chapter 20), its close relationship with the military (see Chapter 29), and its vast international spread (see Chapters 34 and 35).

[14] John K. Galbraith, "Economics as a System of Belief," *American Economic Review*, May 1970, p. 477.

SUMMARY

In several waves of mergers since the late 1890s, the American economy has been converted from one of numerous small competitive industrial enterprises to one dominated by giant corporations. In each industry three or four corporations together make the decisive output, investment, and pricing decisions. All small businesses together produce a small percentage of total output and receive an even smaller percentage of profits. The high degree of concentration increases instability and unemployment in at least two ways: First, driven to the wall, small businesses reduce employment and sometimes set off depressions; many go bankrupt, thus worsening the depression. Second, the giant corporations keep their own prices and output high by restricting the supply of output and further reducing employment.

Giant firms increase their prices rapidly during prosperity, causing inflation by pushing profits up through the use of monopoly power over the market. Since the 1950s they have even had the power to continue raising prices during recessions (though more slowly than during expansions). The giant firms also mount giant advertising campaigns, wasting vast resources on the false claim that their products are better than others. Finally, the giant firms contribute giant pollution to the air, land, and sea; it is just not profitable to spend their money on purifying devices for their industrial processes or for their consumer products, such as cars.

CHAPTER 19

PROFIT MAXIMIZATION IN ALTERNATIVE MARKET STRUCTURES

In this chapter we wish to explore in detail how a firm maximizes its profit.[1] *Profit* is the difference between revenue (or sales proceeds) and costs. The revenue a firm gets in a given supply-and-demand situation depends on how much competition it faces in its industry.

An *industry* is the total of all firms selling a particular product. Thus, when we speak of the steel industry or the automobile industry, we are referring to all the individual business firms producing steel or automobiles. Industries are said to fall within one of four categories: pure competition, monopolistic competition, oligopoly, or monopoly. Actually, this is an oversimplification because no real industry falls *exactly* into one of these four categories, but they are convenient tools of analysis.

MARKET STRUCTURES AND THE DEGREE OF COMPETITION

A *purely competitive industry* is one in which four essential conditions are present: (1) The industry is made up of a very large number of firms, and there are also a large number of buyers of the product they sell. (2) Each seller supplies so small a percentage of the market that its actions have virtually no effect on the price at which the industry sells the product, and each buyer demands so small a percentage of output that his purchases alone also have virtually no effect on the price at which the industry sells the product. (3) It is very easy for new firms to get into the industry or for old firms to leave it. (4) Each firm produces a product that is so nearly identical to the product of the other firms that consumers are largely indifferent about which firm within the industry produced the product they buy.

A *monopoly* exists when there is only one seller of a product that has no close substitutes. In a monopolistic industry one firm *is* the industry. If the monopolist's position is to be maintained, he must erect barriers that prevent competitors from entering the industry. If he is successful in doing this, the payoff is generally very large. Because he has complete control over the price of his product (within the

---

[1] Those readers who are merely looking for a general overview of economics may wish to skip the technical details—sections with symbols and graphs—that are explored in this chapter.

limits set by the demand schedule), he can set the price at the level that will maximize profits.

Between the extremes of pure competition and monopoly, economists make two further classifications. Closer to pure competition is *monopolistic competition*. A monopolistically competitive industry has a large number of small sellers who engage in some slight amount of *product differentiation*. A product may be differentiated in many different ways; for example, one seller packages his product more attractively or gives friendlier service. In any event, some consumers prefer one or another particular seller's product. For this reason, firms have a small degree of control over price, and a firm cannot enter the industry as easily as it can enter a purely competitive industry.

Closer to a monopoly (and often tantamount to it) is an *oligopoly*. An oligopolistic industry has a few giant sellers, each of which controls a significant share of the market. Entry into an oligopolistic industry is very difficult, often as difficult as into a monopolistic industry. There is generally, but not always, some product differentiation. The most significant feature of an oligopoly is the fact that, because of the interdependence of its members, no firm can make significant changes in price without reckoning with the reactions of its competitors.

DEMAND AND PRICE FOR A PURELY COMPETITIVE FIRM

For a whole industry, a larger amount can be sold *only* at a lower price (or lower average revenue). This is not the case for a single competitive firm. In purely competitive industry, each firm is so small that whatever quantity it chooses to sell will have a negligible effect on the supply for the entire industry. Therefore it can sell all that it wishes at the going price.

The situation for both a purely competitive industry and one firm within that industry is demonstrated graphically in Figure 19.1. Figure 19.1(A) shows the supply and demand for coats which is assumed to be a purely competitive industry. Figure 19.1(B) shows the price (or demand curve, since they are the same in this case) for the individual coat-making firm.

The price of a coat ($100) is determined in the industrywide market for coats by the intersection of the industry supply and demand curves. The graph shows that *at this price the individual firm can sell any quantity it wishes*. Because it has been assumed that the individual firm cannot affect supply for the entire industry, and because the market demand is equal to the supply at the prevailing price ($100), the firm never experiences any problem in selling all it wishes to sell at this price.

Therefore the demand curve for the individual firm's output is a horizontal line at the industry-determined price. The firm sells any quantity it chooses at this price. Assume that it decides to raise its price in order to increase its revenue. Because the firms in a purely competitive industry all produce an identical product, no consumer will pay more than $100 for one firm's product when he can buy an identical product from a competitor for $100. Similarly, the firm will never sell any quantity at a price below $100. Because it can sell any quantity it chooses at $100, there would be no incentive for it to lower the price. Thus the firm in a purely competitive industry faces a given price; it cannot vary it upward,

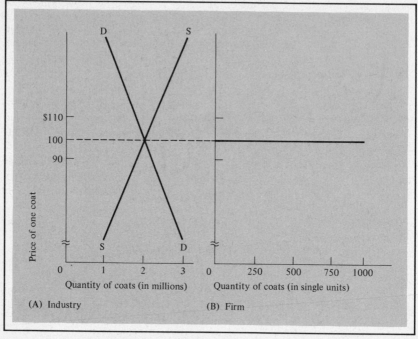

Figure 19.1 **Supply and demand for coats**

and it does not wish to vary it downward. (The situation is very different for a monopoly.)

SUPPLY AND THE COSTS OF PRODUCTION

A firm's decision regarding the quantity of its product that it wishes to supply at various prices will depend, to a large extent, on the costs of producing different quantities. In this section we shall analyze the firm's cost during the short run, when its output is limited to the productive capacity of current plant and equipment. Over a longer period the firm could construct a larger plant and install new equipment, thus expanding its scale of operations; but for the shorter period considered here, these capital goods are fixed in size and number.

Because the amount of a firm's plant and equipment is fixed in the short run, some of its costs must be considered fixed whether it produces nothing or operates at capacity. *Fixed costs* include the costs of maintaining plant and equipment, rent, and costs of watchmen, guards, and others. Obviously, if the firm produces more goods, then the *average* fixed cost will decline because the same cost is spread over, or divided by, more units.

Even during the short run, however, some costs—notably those of labor and material—are variable. The firm can produce more or less of its product by hiring more or fewer workers and using more or less raw materials.

The *average* variable cost for a unit of output is obtained by taking the total cost of labor and raw materials and dividing it by the quantity produced. If one laborer combined with a given amount of raw materials produced ten coats, and if each additional laborer combined with the same amount of raw materials continued to produce ten coats, then the average variable cost per unit produced would remain the same regardless of the amount the firm produced. The average-variable-cost curve would be a straight horizontal line, showing that the quantity of coats produced had no effect on its magnitude.

This situation does not obtain in most types of productive processes. Generally the firm's plant and equipment have been designed and constructed to operate most effectively at a particular level of output. The production of a single commodity usually involves numerous productive processes, which occur at different rates and are difficult to coordinate. For maximum efficiency no single process should be halted or stopped because it is outstripping the other processes; nor should other processes be stopped because this process cannot keep pace.

After engineers have calculated the various rates at which different productive processes will take place, the plant is constructed and equipped in such a way that there is some *optimal* level of production at which all productive processes can be effectively coordinated. Average variable costs are lowest at the optimum level of production but higher both below and above that level.

Because average fixed costs fall continuously, the total result is that average cost per unit may fall rapidly at first and continue to fall until the optimal point is achieved; then average cost may slowly rise. This usual short-run behavior of average costs (a U-shaped curve) is illustrated in Figure 19.2.

According to Figure 19.2, the quantity of 1000 coats is the production level at which all production processes are most effectively coordinated and plant and equipment are most efficiently utilized (the cost is only $75 per coat). At smaller quantities, bottlenecks occur and some equipment is *underutilized;* consequently, average costs are higher. At larger quantities, plant and equipment are being *overutilized* and various bottlenecks and inefficiencies are encountered; consequently, average costs are higher. The further a firm gets from the opti-

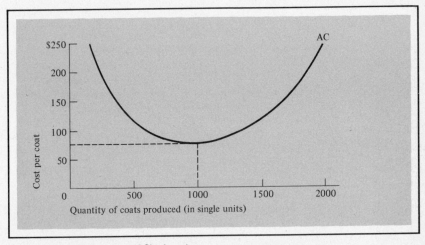

Figure 19.2 **Average cost (AC) of coats**

mally efficient quantity (1000 coats in this case), the higher its average costs are. This is true whether the firm produces smaller or larger quantities than the optimal amount.

Because it is the basis of the supply curve, marginal cost is even more important than the average cost. *Marginal cost* is defined as follows:

$$\text{Marginal cost} = \frac{\text{increase in total cost}}{\text{increase in quantity}}$$

Because we may speak of decrease as well as increase, we may substitute the word *change* for *increase* in the definition to make it more general.

In Figure 19.3 marginal cost represents the increase in total costs of production attributable to an increase in output of one additional coat. If the change in cost attributable to producing one more coat is lower than the average cost of producing the product, then it may be said that the lower marginal cost is pulling the average cost downward. This is similar to the case of a person taking several tests. The last test score pulls the average score up or down, depending on whether it is higher or lower than the average. Thus it is possible to conclude that as long as the average cost is declining, the marginal cost must be below it. When the average cost is rising, the marginal cost must be above it, pulling it upward. These relations between the average and marginal cost are illustrated in Figure 19.3.

Notice that at low production levels, those at which each additional coat is produced at less cost, marginal cost is very low (only $25 at 500 coats) and is well below the average. But at production beyond the optimal capacity, when the average cost of producing coats is rising, marginal cost rises rapidly to a high level ($150 at 1500 coats), and goes further and further above the average.

These mechanical relations may be summarized as follows: (1) average cost is at its minimum when it is equal to marginal cost; (2) when marginal cost is below average cost, it is pulling average cost downward; (3) when marginal cost is above average cost, it is pulling average cost up.

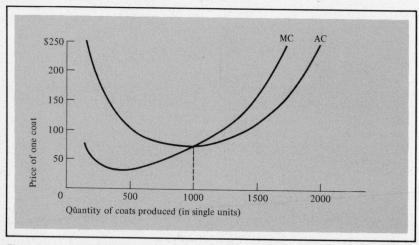

Figure 19.3 **Average cost and marginal cost (MC) of coats**

CLARIFYING THE MEANING OF COSTS

Two more points relating to the traditional (neoclassical) economist's treatment of costs must be clarified. The economist's concept of costs differs from the accountant's definition of the term. For the accountant a cost must involve a monetary outlay. In other words, he records costs only when money changes hands. Economists include two types of costs in their analyses: explicit costs and implicit, or imputed, costs. *Explicit costs* are the accountant's costs; *implicit costs* include those that the company's owner would have to pay if, for example, he did none of the managerial work himself. Thus a normal wage for the managerial and other labor he performs is counted among implicit costs.

Assume, for example, that a man saves $20,000 and opens a service station. During the first year his accountant calculates that his total revenue was $32,000 and his costs $22,000. The accountant informs him that he has made a profit of $10,000. A traditional economist would assess his costs differently. Suppose that the owner worked 60 hours every week and that it would have cost him $3 per hour to hire a man to do this work. The economist would subtract the imputed wage of $9,360 and inform the owner that he had registered a profit of only $640 rather than $10,000. All economists agree that everyone deserves pay for his or her own labor, including managerial labor.

The traditional economist, however, would consider another, more dubious, implicit or imputed "cost." The man invested his own $20,000 in the station. He gave up the opportunity to invest it elsewhere—say, in 6 percent government bonds. Therefore the neoclassical economist says that he also had an implicit cost of $1,200 in interest forgone, so he "really" made a loss.

For neoclassical economists *profits* means only *excess* profits—that is, they are excess over all explicit and implicit costs, including a "normal" or average profit (or interest). Although this definition is useful in one way, it has a very conservative bias in another sense. It is useful in that the capitalist *does* require the bribe of an average rate of profit to get him to use his capital in production. He usually considers normal and necessary the rate that has been the average for the last few years. Thus only if an average profit is included with costs can it be said that supply behavior is determined completely by costs. This definition is employed here because it is convenient to be able to say, in agreement with all current economics books, that in pure competition the supply curve is identical with the marginal-cost curve—this point is examined later.

The neoclassical definition of costs sneaks in the idea that the capitalist *deserves* to receive an average profit as a cost of providing capital for production. It is true that physical capital goods are necessary for production, that in any society limited capital goods must be allocated to maximize returns, and that allocation is a social cost because it means other areas cannot use those capital goods. It is also true, given a private enterprise system, the capitalist entrepreneur must be bribed with the average profit to get him to furnish his capital. It was shown in Chapter 15, however, that the productivity of capital goods implies neither that the capitalist is productive nor that he deserves his profit. In other words, a socialist society would provide capital to itself out of public funds; it would consider provision of capital a cost of production; and it might even calculate rates of profit in each industry to decide where to allocate capital. (See

Chapter 38.) But a socialist society would not pay the profits to any private individual.

There is only one other essential point to be made in this discussion of costs. Total cost can be shown quite easily on a graph of per-unit costs. Because the average cost is the total cost divided by the quantity produced, it follows that total cost is given by the product of average cost multiplied by the quantity produced. In Figure 19.4 total cost is shown as a shaded rectangle. Taking any quantity (for example, 700 coats in Figure 19.4), we go up the average-cost curve and then over to the cost axis of the graph. Here the average cost per unit required to produce 700 coats is found: $80. We know that the total cost will equal 700 × $80. But because line 0-to-700 and line $0-to-$80 are adjacent sides of a rectangle, their product is equal to the area of the rectangle. Therefore the shaded rectangle in Figure 19.4 represents the total cost of producing 700 coats: 700 × $80 = $56,000.

MAXIMUM PROFIT UNDER COMPETITION

In an earlier section it was shown that once the price of the industry's product is determined, then the individual competitive firm faces a demand curve (or a given price) that is a straight horizontal line. It is further assumed that each firm has the U-shaped short run average-cost curve described earlier. In Figure 19.5 the demand curve has been superimposed on the cost curves in order to present the whole picture for the competitive firm.

In order to understand the firm's reaction to the market price ($100), it is necessary to ascertain what motivates the firm's owners (or managers). The answer provided by the vast majority of economists, from Adam Smith to the present, is that the one overriding objective of all capitalists, or their managers, is to maximize their profits. We accept this answer provisionally and treat each firm as a profit maximizer.

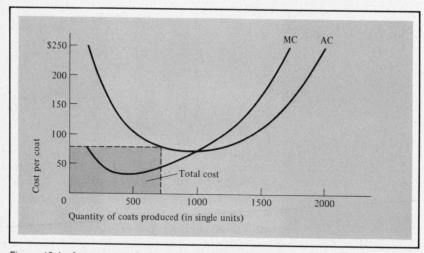

Figure 19.4 **Average, marginal, and total cost of coats**

The manager whose cost and revenue curves are pictured in Figure 19.5 will maximize his profits by producing and selling 1200 coats. At this quantity the firm's marginal cost is equal to its price. The rule for maximizing profit under competition is to produce the quantity *that equates marginal cost and price.* There are two shaded rectangles in Figure 19.5. The combined area of the rectangles is equal to the firm's total income from sales or revenue (because it represents the price times the quantity the firm sells). The area of the lower rectangle is equal to the firm's total cost (because it is the product of the firm's average cost times the quantity it produces). The area of the upper rectangle is equal to the firm's profit (because it represents total revenue minus total costs, which is, by definition, profit.)

In order to understand why 1200 coats is the quantity that maximizes the firm's profit, imagine that the firm produces and sells a smaller quantity of the product. For any quantity below 1200, the firm's price per unit is higher than its marginal cost. Consequently, if the firm produces and sells an additional coat, this last coat will add more to the firm's total revenue than it adds to the total cost. The last coat therefore adds to the firm's profit. As long as the firm is producing fewer than 1200 coats, it can add to its profit by producing and selling more coats.

However, imagine that the firm is producing more than 1200 coats. For any quantity above 1200 the firm's marginal cost exceeds its price per unit. If the firm were to produce and sell one less coat, the reduction in its costs would exceed the reduction in its revenue. Its profit would therefore increase. As long as the firm continues to sell more than 1200 coats, it can add to its profit by producing and selling less. It is now easy to see why the competitive firm maximizes its profit by equating its marginal cost and its price.

For any price that prevails in the market, the marginal-cost curve will indicate what quantity the firm would like to sell. But a line showing the quantities a firm would like to sell at various prices is exactly what we defined a supply curve to be. Therefore *in pure competition a firm's marginal-cost curve is its supply curve.*

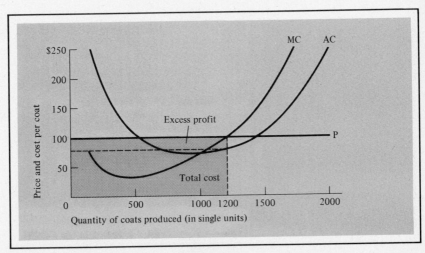

Figure 19.5   **Price (or demand) and cost of coats**

Because the industry is simply the total of the firms within it, the industry's supply curve is the summation of the marginal-cost curves of all these firms.

EQUILIBRIUM FOR THE FIRM AND THE INDUSTRY IN PURE COMPETITION

In the purely competitive industry price is determined by the intersection of the industry supply and demand curves. The individual firm adjusts its quantity in order to maximize profit. Figure 19.6 (A) shows an individual firm's cost and revenue curves.

In Figure 19.6 the firm and industry are in short-run, but not long-run, equilibrium. The industry is in short-run equilibrium because it is producing at the point where its price and marginal cost are equal. But neither the industry nor the firm is making excess profit.

Two points should be made about the firm's excess profit: (1) It is assumed that all firms have access both to the same technology that this firm is using and to inputs of comparable quality. It can be concluded, therefore, that the cost curves of virtually all firms in the industry are nearly identical to those of the firm pictured in Fig. 19.6(B). (2) It must be remembered that the firm's cost curves include an imputed cost covering an average return on the owner's capital; thus normal, or average, profit is included in the cost.

It must be concluded, therefore, that the firms in this industry are making excess profits above an average return on capital. Because it is easy to enter a purely competitve industry, capitalists who are making only an average profit in other industries will be attracted to this industry by the lure of excess profits.

An industry is said to be in long-run equilibrium when there is no tendency for firms either to enter or to leave it. The industry pictured in Figure 19.6 is not in long-run equilibrium because it is earning excess profits and therefore new firms will be entering it.

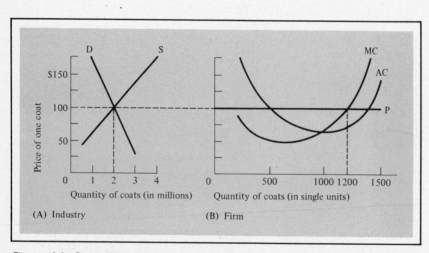

Figure 19.6 **Competitive equilibrium in the coat market**

As new firms enter, their additional outputs must be added in order to derive the industry's new supply curve. This means that the supply curve will shift to the right. Figure 19.7 illustrates the original situation depicted in Figure 19.6 but also shows what happens as the supply curve shifts to the right (from the original position, S_1). When the supply curve shifts, it must ultimately shift to S_2. If it stops short of S_2, excess profits will continue and more firms will be attracted, shifting the curve farther to the right until it reaches S_2.

With the greater supply provided by the new firms entering the industry, all excess profits have been eliminated. At the new, lower price of $75, the firm reduces its output from 1200 to 1000 coats in order to equate its marginal cost with the new price. This lower output maximizes the firm's profits in the new conditions. At that point, however, it is also true that the firms' average cost is just equal to its price per unit. The decline in price from $100 to $75 has eliminated the firm's excess profits (because its average cost is also $75).

With no excess profits there is no longer any incentive for new firms to enter the industry. The firms within the industry are receiving a normal, or average, rate of return on their capital and labor. Therefore there is no tendency for firms to leave the industry. It can now be said that when the new supply curve results in the establishment of a new price equal to the long-run average cost of each firm, then the industry is in long-run equilibrium because the number of firms within the industry has been stabilized.

Thus, when both the individual firms and the purely competitive industry are in long-run equilibrium, the following equality holds for each firm:

$$\text{Price} = \text{marginal cost} = \text{average cost}$$

The fact that price equals marginal cost indicates that the firm is satisfied that its current level of output is the most profitable one for it. The fact that price equals average cost indicates that there will be no tendency for firms either to enter or to leave the industry (because the average cost includes just an average rate of profit).

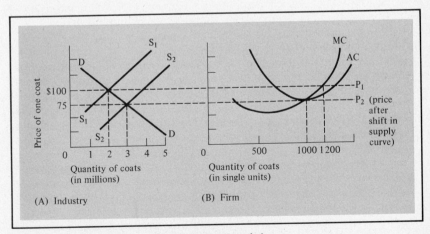

Figure 19.7 **Change in equilibrium in the coat market**

Our account of long-run equilibrium in a purely competitive market differs somewhat from the accounts that are found in many conservative textbooks. When the firm was making excess profits by producing and selling that quantity of output at which the industry price equaled its marginal cost, the conservative economists depict two different series of changes that lead to long-run equilibrium for both the firm and the industry. First, they say that new firms will enter the industry for the same reasons that we have already given. Second, they say that the existing firms may expand their productive capacity and generate entirely new and different *long-run cost curves.* The expansion of each individual firm's productive capacity was ignored in our account and we must explain why we omitted this consideration.

In the standard conservative textbook it is argued that in the long run the firm has no fixed costs because all factors of production, including the size or productive capacity of the factory, can be varied and therefore all costs become variable costs in the long run. If all costs are variable then there is no immediate or obvious reason why the long-run average-cost curve should be U shaped. In the short run, the U-shaped cost curve is derived from the fact that a particular factory was designed to operate most efficiently when a certain number of workers are employed in the factory. If either fewer or more workers than this optimum number of workers are employed, the production process will be less efficient. A short-run U-shaped average-cost curve reflects the fact that a given factory operates most efficiently when producing that level of output for which it was technically designed, and that if either more or less than that amount of output is produced, then production will be less efficient and costs will be higher.

In the long run the firm can expand its factory size or the number of factories it owns. It is our belief that if a firm multiplies the number of factories it owns while each factory incorporates the same technology as all of the other factories, then the firm's long-run average costs will be relatively constant. That is, the average cost per unit of output for a second factory, utilizing exactly the same technology as the first factory, ought to be identical, at a given level of output, as the average cost per unit of output in the first factory. If this is true, and we believe that in general it is, then in the long run the firm could produce larger quantities without increasing its average costs per unit of output simply by constructing more factories. Therefore, the long-run average-cost curve would be a horizontal line showing constant returns to scale as the firm multiplies the number of factories that it owns.

If we drop the assumption of a fixed technology and allow for technological change, then the effects of such changes in technology as have generally occurred in the history of capitalism are to make production more efficient and hence to make average costs decline in the long run. Therefore, we conclude that in the long run a firm's average-cost curve will probably be constant (or horizontal) or else declining—depending upon whether technology remains constant or changes.

This poses a problem for conservative economists. They like to argue that in the long run something approximating pure competition can reasonably be expected to obtain in a capitalist economy. But if a single firm can, in the long run, produce ever larger quantities of output at a constant or a declining average cost, then what is there to prevent a single firm from growing so large that it takes over the entire industry and creates a monopoly? Or what prevents a few firms from growing so large that they create an oligopolistic industry? In our opinion, this is exactly what has happened in many of the most economically significant industries in most capitalist economies. But this is precisely what most conservative economists want to deny.

One way in which they can deny this tendency to oligopoly or monopoly in capitalism is to argue that long-run average-cost curves are U shaped and that the point of optimum efficiency or the point of minimum average cost per unit of output occurs when the firm is producing only a small, insignificant part of the total output of the entire industry. If the firm then attempted to expand its output it would incur higher costs and would therefore be unable to profitably compete at that higher level of output. Therefore the U-shaped average-cost curve "saves" the "realism" of the theory of pure competition.

But the reasons which the conservative economists put forward to support the idea of a long-run U-shaped average-cost curve seem to us to be quite unconvincing when applied to the actual existing conditions in most industries. Therefore, we generally reject the notion that such cost curves characterize most actual industries. And because we reject this notion, in our demonstration of long-run equlibrium we had to show the change in the industry supply curve as being entirely the result of new firms entering the industry.

In our view, it is only when the increase in the industry's supply curve is the consequence solely of new firms entering the industry that the notion of a purely competitive industrial equilibrium for a long-run period can be defended. Therefore, without asking why existing firms do not expand their capacity, we simply showed that if they do not do so then it is theoretically possible for a long-run purely competitive equilibrium to obtain. The important question, of course, is why we should ever expect this type of solution to actually occur in reality. This raises the issue of the relevance of the competitive model.

RELEVANCE OF THE COMPETITIVE MODEL

The reader has probably wondered which industries in the contemporary American economy are purely competitive. Only one or two industries (out of many thousands) in the entire American economy present a factual resemblance to the model just worked through.

The most obvious choice of a purely competitive market might be from agriculture. Traditionally, in the wheat industry, for example, each farmer produced a homogeneous product, and no farmer produced enough to affect the price significantly. Each would take as given the price determined in the market. Whether he sold all or none of his crop at this price was virtually irrelevant to the determination of price.

Over the past several decades, however, two important changes have occurred in agricultural markets: (1) The government has intervened extensively in the market through various schemes of subsidies and production controls. (2) The agricultural industry has been increasingly coming under the control of giant corporations that in no way resemble the small, relatively powerless firms pictured in the theory. These two developments have so fundamentally altered the agricultural market that the model of pure competition definitely does not explain or describe it.

If only one or two industries even resemble the model, then a question must be asked: What is the relevance of this analysis to the American economy of the 1970s? The answer is that such analysis reveals more about the thinking of many economists than it does about the functioning of the economy.

The model of pure competition is the basis of the neoclassical economists' claim that the unencumbered private enterprise market system results in a situation of optimum production and distributional efficiency. In Chapter 7 we saw that neoclassical economics arose as an apology for the status quo in capitalism. From the analysis just presented it can be seen that in pure competition each firm, in equilibrium, produces the quantity at which its costs are minimized and its production is most efficient. The firm receives only the socially defined normal rate of profit. No excess profits exist. The consumer gets the product at the lowest possible price. The theory also claims that every factor of production gets the value of what it contributes to production (although the theory says nothing about the inequitable ownership of factors of production that prevails).

Such is the economic ideal for the neoclassical, laissez faire economists: a beautiful, well-ordered, just world. But examination of the contemporary American economy reveals that theirs is a totally illusory world.

A tiny minority of the neoclassical economists have honestly admitted the degree to which reality differs from their ideal.[2] But most persist in arguing that what extists bears a reasonably close resemblance to their model. Thus the neoclassical analysis is generally used to show that the free enterprise market economy is the best and most just of all possible worlds. Therefore the theory of pure competition is studied here primarily to understand the basis of a very important conservative ideology supporting capitalism. (The model of pure competition, in its simplest form, also provides analytic tools that can be used to study more realistic cases.)

DEMAND AND REVENUE FOR A MONOPOLY

A *monopoly* exists when a single firm constitutes the entire industry. The firm sells a product for which there are no close substitutes, and potential competitors are prevented in one way or another from entering the industry.

Under competition, the demand curve for a whole industry slopes down and to the right (because the quantity sold increases only when the price falls). The demand curve for a competitive firm, however, is a horizontal straight line (because the firm's output is so small, it can sell as much more as it wishes at the same price). A monopoly firm, by definition, is the only seller of a commodity; it *is* the industry. Therefore *the demand curve for a monopoly firm is exactly like the demand curve for a whole competitive industry:* it slopes down and to the right. The monopoly demand curve shows that, unlike the owner of a competitive firm, who faces a given price, the monopolist can *choose* to sell more goods at a lower price or fewer goods at a higher price (he is not a price taker but a price fixer).

[2] See, for example, the chapter on Henry C. Simons in William Breit and Roger L. Ransom, *The Academic Scribblers* (New York: Holt, Rinehart & Winston, 1971), pp. 205–222.

Thus a market demand curve shows the maximum revenue per unit of the commodity that a monopolist will receive at any particular level of sales he may choose. When they view it from this seller's standpoint, economists call the demand curve an *average-revenue curve.* It shows the average revenue per unit of the commodity sold for any level of sales.

Figure 19.8 shows a demand curve for a monopolized commodity—say, aluminum (for many years the Aluminum Company of America [ALCOA] had a pure monopoly of aluminum). It can be labeled a demand curve *or* an average-revenue curve. The curve in Figure 18.8 is labeled "demand = average revenue" to underscore this equivalence. At $1000 per ton, consumers wish to purchase 10 million tons. Alternatively, if the monopolist wishes to sell 10 million tons, then $1000 is the maximum price he can charge.

When ALCOA (assumed here to be a pure monopoly) decreases the price of aluminum and, hence, increases its sales of aluminum, two separate effects result in change in its total revenue: (1) the *quantity effect* and (2) the *price effect.* More aluminum can be sold only by lowering the price of aluminum. The decline in the price of aluminum multiplied by the quantity of aluminum sold at the old price is an amount of revenue that the firm loses in order to expand sales. Thus, when the quantity sold is increased by a lower price, the quantity effect always increases total revenue, while the price effect decreases total revenue. The net change in total revenue may be positive or negative, depending on whether the quantity effect or the price effect is larger.

Assume that ALCOA (or any monopoly) wishes to know how much total revenue will be increased if sales are increased by one ton. The information ALCOA is looking for is what economists call the *marginal revenue,* which may be defined as the change in the total revenue the firm will receive as a result of sale of one additional unit, in this case one more ton of aluminum. Marginal revenue is defined as follows.

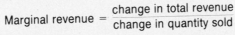

$$\text{Marginal revenue} = \frac{\text{change in total revenue}}{\text{change in quantity sold}}$$

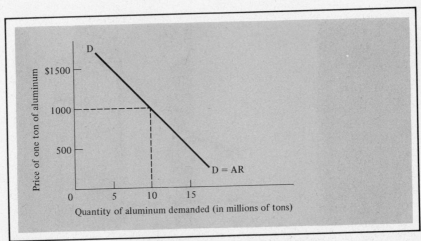

Figure 19.8 **Demand and average revenue (AR) from aluminum**

The average and marginal revenue curves of a monopoly are illustrated in Figure 19.9

Notice that at any quantity of aluminum the marginal revenue is lower than the average revenue. Whenever the average revenue is decreasing, the marginal revenue must be lower than the average revenue. Again, this is similar to the case of a person taking a series of tests. If the average score declines as more tests are taken, it must mean that the marginal score (or the score on the last test taken) is below the average. In fact, it is the lower marginal score that pulls the average score down. Similarly, if the average revenue is decreasing, the marginal revenue must be below it and pulling it down.

When 10 million tons of aluminum are sold, marginal revenue is zero, or total revenue can be increased no further with the given demand: the quantity effect just offsets the price effect.

At quantitites below (to the left of) 10 million, the quantity effect is more significant than the price effect, and therefore the marginal revenue is positive. As the quantity of aluminum sold increases, the price effect becomes more important and the quantity effect less important, until at 10 million they are equal: At higher quantities of aluminum (to the right of 10 million), the price effect is more important, and therefore the marginal revenue is negative. It is possible to conclude from this that a monopolist would always sell a smaller quantity than 10 million tons because if he expands sales to 10 million, the increase in revenue as a result of the last unit sold is zero. If he sold a greater quantity, he would actually lose revenue because marginal revenue is negative at quantitities above 10 million.

EQUILIBRIUM FOR THE MONOPOLY

In order to see the equilibrium price a monpolist will charge and the quantity he will sell, the monopolist's revenue curves must be superimposed on his cost

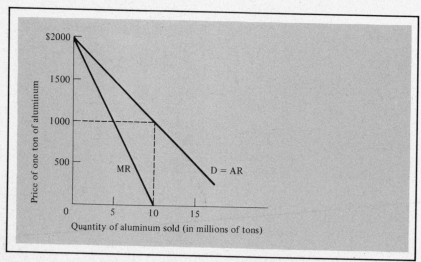

Figure 19.9 **Average revenue and marginal revenue (MR) from aluminum**

curves. From the discussion in the previous section, it is known the average-revenue curve will slope downward and to the right and that the marginal-revenue curve will be below it and have a steeper slope. These curves are pictured in Figure 19.10. The profit-maximizing position is reached when the monopolist produces and sells the quantity (6 million tons) at which *marginal revenue equals marginal cost.* The reason for this is easy to comprehend. Below this level, one additional ton of aluminum brings in more revenue than its additional (or marginal) cost. Above this point, one additional ton of aluminum costs more than the average it brings in to ALCOA. Notice how the monopoly rule differs from the competitive rule that price should equal marginal cost. Because the monopolist has the entire market, his demand curve slopes downward, and therefore his marginal revenue is below the average revenue. In the competitve case, the firm is so small that the demand curve appears purely elastic in relation to it. Therefore the competitve price or average revenue *equals* its marginal revenue. Because the monopolist's marginal revenue is lower (and the more general rule is that marginal cost equals marginal revenue), the monopolist chooses to supply less output to the market than would be the case in a competitive industry with similar cost and demand curves.

The average-revenue curve in Figure 19.10 indicates that $1500 is the maximum price at which 6 million tons can be sold. The shaded area shows the excess profits received at that price. For a monopoly, unlike a purely competitive firm, the making of excess profits is the usual and expected case. Nothing in the short or the long run tends to reduce these excess profits (except for changes in general business conditions as the economy undergoes cyclic fluctuations, a topic that will be examined in Part Three).

In addition to the high price the monopolist charges and the excess profits he makes, he almost never produces at the most efficient level of production. As shown in Figure 19.10 the monopolist stops producing before reaching the point

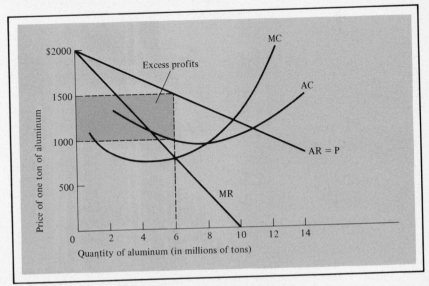

Figure 19.10 **Equilibrium for a monopolist selling aluminum**

at which his average costs are minimized. He does this, of course, because he is interested in maximum profits, not maximum efficiency. If he had produced the quantity that minimized his costs, he would have been forced to sell his product at a much lower price, and this would have reduced his excess profits. The reader can now easily see what is meant by the age-old charge that monopolies restrict output and sales in order to increase their excess profits. The reader can also see why, from the very beginning of the capitalist, private enterprise economic system, most businessmen have tenaciously fought to acquire monopoly power.

MODIFICATION OF MONOPOLY ANALYSES

In the discussion of the market equilibrium for a monopolist, it was assumed both that the monopolist took his revenue and cost curves as given and that he maximized his profits by equating marginal cost and marginal revenue within the fixed constraints of externally determined revenue and cost curves. These assumptions enabled us to examine only one aspect of the monopolist's ceaseless drive for more excess profits. The monopolist can also increase excess profits by shifting his cost curves downward and his revenue curves upward.

Shifts in revenue curves can be effected in several ways. The first and most obvious method is through advertising. If the monopolist can persuade more consumers that they want or need his product, then he will be able to sell more of it at all prices along the demand curve—that is, the demand curve will shift upward and to the right. Thus we are literally bombarded with advertising. In a thousand and one ways at least, businessmen endlessly attempt to convince us to consume ever-increasing amounts of their products.

Another way monopolists can increase the demand for their products is by convincing the government that it should erect and maintain protective tariffs to eliminate foreign competition. Although a firm or a group of firms often manages to achieve a monopoly within national boundaries, only very infrequently can a worldwide monopoly be achieved (however, many American-based multinational firms are working feverishly in that direction). To the extent that consumers buy a close foreign-made substitute for a monopolist's product, the demand for his product is reduced. Protective tariffs can eliminate foreign competition and thereby increase demand for the monopolist's product. Over the past several centuries businessmen have—generally with considerable success—sought the aid of governments in creating and protecting their firms' domestic monopolies by enacting protective tariffs. Such tariffs increase monopoly revenues at the expense of the consumer, who is forced to pay a higher price for "protected products." They are much like a tax levied by the government against all consumers, part of the proceeds of which is turned over to the monopolist to augment his excess profits.

Many large business firms are also able to increase the demand for their products through massive sales to the government. The bulk of these sales are connected with military procurement. For many of the largest U.S. corporations, these sales represent from 5 to 100 percent of their total sales. This topic is pursued in greater depth in Part Three.

There also are many ways business firms can shift their cost curves downward. They can press for government legislation that weakens labor unions; the Taft-Hartley Act of 1947 is an example of very restrictive legislation. They can also work to elevate "cooperative" and "reasonable" men to positions of leadership in unions, men who will not press very hard for wage increases that would disturb the status quo in the wage and profit distribution. They can also get the President to appoint business-leaning "public" men to positions in regulatory agencies. These measures enable large firms to keep their wage costs to a minimum.

Monopolies also seek to achieve a monopsonistic position. A *monopsony* exists when a firm is the *only buyer* of a particular resource or intermediate product. A monopsonist can offer a very low price for the resource he is purchasing, and the seller must accept the offer or not sell his resource. Thus resource costs can be decreased if the firm can achieve monopsonistic buying power, which is no less actively sought than monopolistic selling power.

The immense political power that stems from their economic power permits giant corporations to reduce costs in other ways. The government is often persuaded to allow them to use government-owned facilities for production connected with the armaments they are selling to the government. These facilities are generally used *free of charge*. And when the government has charged rent, it has reimbursed the corporations and given them extra profits on this rent; this is the so-called cost-plus contract. In other words, the government has actually paid the giant corporations to use government-owned facilities free of charge. Such a case was described by a U.S. Senate Committee report on pyramiding missile profits:

> Much of Western Electric's Nike production was done at two government surplus plants, which under the ordinary method of doing business with the government would have been supplied to Western Electric without cost. However, Western Electric instead of having the plants supplied free, rented them from the Government. Western Electric included the rentals as part of its overall costs and then charged the government a profit on these costs. The total rentals paid to the government by Western Electric for these plants amounted to over $3,000,000. When added to Western Electric's costs, the rentals generated additional profits to the company of $209,000. In such a situation, there could be little resistance on the part of Western Electric to having the government raise the rent, because as the rent went up, so did Western Electric's profit, since the complete amount of the rent was repaid by the landlord back to the tenant together with a profit.[3]

These are only a few of the ways large monopolistic corporations are constantly striving to use their economic and political power to maximize profits.

WHO ARE THE MONOPOLISTS?

Most introductory economics textbooks identify pure competition and monopoly as the extreme cases along the spectrum of industrial organization. They argue (and we agree) that there are almost no purely competitive industries. Most mo-

[3] U.S. Congress, Senate, Government Operations Subcommittee, *Pyramiding of Profits and Costs in the Missile Procurement,* Senate Report No. 970 (Washington, D.C.: GPO, 1964).

nopolies, they assert, are either local or regional in scope, ranging from the single grocery store in a small village to the single giant real estate developer in a large city. They maintain that national monopolies are as rare as purely competitive industries. According to these textbooks, monopoly theory is of intellectual interest primarily as an extreme case with little actual or practical applicability at a national level in the American economy.

This view, we believe, is in error because it adheres strictly to the definition of monopoly as existing when there is only one seller. It interprets one seller to mean one firm. Admittedly, there are very few national markets where a single business firm is the only seller. Most important nationwide markets are dominated by a few giant corporations; they are oligopolies. In a later section of this chapter, however, we shall see that despite some distinct differences between oligopolies (a few firms) and monopolies (a single firm), most oligopolies act *as if* they were monopolies. We shall argue that our analysis of monopolies applies generally to oligopolies on questions of pricing, output, and the shifting revenue and cost curves. If our analysis is correct, so that we can redefine monopolies to include industries that behave as if they were a single seller, then monopolies dominate almost all the important national markets in the United States.

NATURAL MONOPOLIES AND GOVERNMENT REGULATION

There are some industries that economists call *natural monopolies*. The technology used in these industries creates a cost curve on which the minimum average cost is not reached until a firm is producing a very large quantity. Generally, before the minimum average cost is reached a single firm can supply the entire market with the commodity in question. If two firms divided the sales between them, each would produce such a small quantity that its average cost would be much higher than that of a single firm supplying the entire market. In this circumstance a free market will always lead to one firm's acquiring a monopoly position.

The most common examples of natural monopolies are public utilities such as electric and telephone companies. Because each of these companies supplies a commodity that is a vital necessity for most individuals and most other business firms, they are almost always regulated by the government. This regulation generally takes the form of an imposed price ceiling (although the regulating agencies are often controlled by the monopolies, so the price ceiling is usually high enough to allow considerable excess profits).

The governing agency can reduce the monopolist's excess profits by lowering the price he will charge the public and/or increasing the quantity of the product he will sell. If the government wishes to increase the public welfare and still allow the monopolist to choose a profit-maximizing quantity to sell, it will generally attempt to set the price at the level at which the monopolist's marginal cost is equal to his average revenue. This type of price ceiling is illustrated in Figure 19.11.

For quantities at which the price ceiling is below the firm's average-revenue curve, that ceiling becomes, in effect, an average revenue and a marginal revenue for the firm. The reasoning is analogous to that for a firm in pure competi-

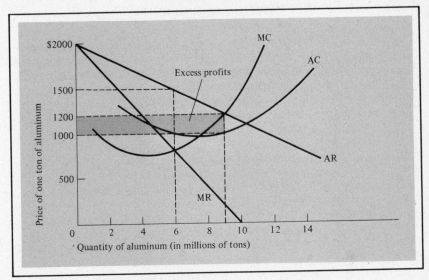

Figure 19.11 **Ceiling on price of aluminum**

tion, whose price is determined independently of its actions. The monopolist, unlike the purely competitive firm, however, cannot sell any quantity he wishes at that price. For quantities at which his original average-revenue curve falls below the price ceiling, the maximum price he can charge is determined by his average-revenue curve. In Figure 19.11, for quantities up to 7 million tons the price ceiling serves as an average-revenue and marginal-revenue curve. At quantities larger than 7 million tons, the firm reverts back to its original revenue curves. If the firm is not regulated, it will charge $1500 and sell 6 million tons. The price ceiling is imposed at the price ($1200) that will equate the firm's average revenue and its marginal cost (as under competition). The firm then treats the price ceiling as a marginal-revenue curve for quantities up to 9 million tons (where the price ceiling equals the average revenue and the marginal cost). He is then selling more at a lower price and receiving less profit.

Although the general public and other business firms are obviously better off after the price ceiling has been imposed, it is obvious that the monopolist is still making large excess profits (i.e., his average-cost curve is still below his average-revenue curve). But as long as the monopolist is left free to choose the quantity he wishes to sell, there is no price that will both clear the market (i.e., equate supply and demand) *and* in any way result in better service for the public. For example, if the price ceiling were set at a lower level, the quantity the firm wished to sell would fall short of the quantity the public wished to buy, so a market disequilibrium would result. If the price ceiling were set at a higher level, the government would merely be returning the monopolist nearer to his original profit-maximizing position at the expense of the general public's and other business firms' welfare. This happens frequently because of the monopolists' control of the regulatory agencies.

MONOPOLISTIC COMPETITION AND OLIGOPOLY

In the United States today there are about 12 million business firms (of which nearly 14 percent are corporations). If agriculture is excluded as a special case not clearly fitting into any market structure, well over 99 percent of the remaining firms fit into the category we call monopolistic competition. Judged in terms of number of firms, it is by far the most important category of industrial organization.

The overwhelming majority of business firms are, however, minute firms in the fields of retailing, wholesaling, and the service industries (e.g., small drugstores, hot dog stands, barber shops, and so forth). In a very important sense the more basic industries (e.g., mining, agriculture, banking, transportation, manufacturing, and communications) are the foundation on which the prosperity of the nation depends. Those who control these industries dominate the entire economy. Almost all the basic or fundamental industries are completely controlled by giant oligopolistic corporations. Therefore, judged in terms of economic power, oligopoly is by far the most important category of industrial organization. Of the approximately 180,000 U.S. manufacturing corporations, for example, a mere 100 (0.004 percent) own 58 percent of total net capital assets.

If we were to describe America's industrial landscape, we would begin with a vast plain of millions of tiny pebbles, representing all the economically powerless, monopolistically competitive business firms. At the center of this enormous plain would rise a few hundred colossal towers, representing the important oligopolistic corporations. These few hundred towers would be so large that they would dwarf into insignificance the entire plain below them.

EQUILIBRIUM FOR A MONOPOLISTICALLY COMPETITIVE FIRM

Monopolistic competition exists in an industry made up of many small firms, each producing a slightly differentiated product. An example of a monopolistic competitor is the neighborhood gas station, which differs slightly, but only slightly, from its competitors. The differentiation may be merely in the packaging, the location of a retail store, or the service offered; but in any case it creates a certain amount of consumer loyalty, which creates demand curves that slope downward and to the right. If a firm raises its price, it will lose only a portion of its customers to competitors. Many will continue to buy the product at higher prices. But if a firm lowers its price, it will attract a few of its competitors' customers.

The monopolistically competitive firm maximizes its profits when it equates marginal cost and marginal revenue. In many cases, if the firm has recently substantially differentiated its product, it may make large, monopolistic, excess profits. Such a situation is shown in Figure 19.12.

A monopolistically competitive market, however, has no significant barriers preventing the entry of new firms. New firms, seeing the excess profits, will begin producing and selling highly similar products and will drain the demand away from the firm pictured in Figure 19.12(A). As a consequence, the original firm's average-revenue curve will shift downward and to the left. As long as excess profits remain, new firms will continue to enter and the average-revenue curve

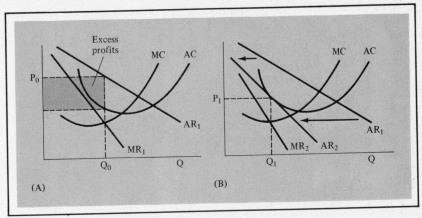

Figure 19.12   **Average revenue (A) before and (B) after new firms enter**

will continue to shift downward and to the left. Therefore the downward shift will come to a halt only after the average revenue curve just touches, but does not cross, the average-cost curve.

This situation is pictured in Figure 19.12(B). The average-revenue curve just touches, but does not cross, the average-cost curve. At that quantity the firm's marginal cost is equal to its marginal revenue; to maximize its profits, it produces at this point. It is also the quantity at which the firm's average revenue is equal to its average cost.[4] All the excess profits have been squeezed out by the entry of new competitors.

Notice, however, that the new equilibrium is always above the minimum point of the firm's average-cost curve. In Figure 19.12(B) the new demand curve, because it is still not flat as in pure competition, meets the average-cost above the minimum point. The price is above the minimum cost level, but there are no excess profits because at the actual production level costs are also higher than the minimum. In other words, the firm in monopolistic competition produces less output at a higher price and at a higher cost than the purely competitive firm in long-run equilibrium. We can therefore say that, in equilibrium, monopolistically competitive firms incur waste by never producing at their most efficient level. (In fact, only a purely competitive firm can be shown to produce efficiently in a private enterprise economy.)

The only way in which the firm can hope to regain some of its lost excess profits is to convince the public, usually through advertising, that its product has been more substantially differentiated from those of its competitors. But when one firm advertises and attracts new customers, its competitors generally retaliate by competitively advertising their own products. The net result often is that things are brought back to the point at which they were before the first firm began to advertise. Now, however, no firm is willing to curtail its advertising for fear of losing its customers to competitors who continue advertising.

[4] It might seem to the reader that this result is attributable to the way in which we arbitrarily drew the curves in Figure 19.12. This is not so, but to prove it involves some knowledge of calculus, so we leave the proof to more advanced books.

Advertising becomes almost a pure waste that is locked into the system. We say "almost" a pure waste because we grant that advertising may occasionally impart useful information. Most advertising, however, is so notorious for its use of half-truths, emotional appeals, brainwashing, and psychological appeals to people's most basic frustrations that few people can tell when any genuinely useful information is being offered. Most of us consciously dismiss advertising as a totally unreliable source of information, even though we may unconsciously be affected by the constant barrage of advertising aggressively hurled at each of our senses.

Another waste of monopolistic competition is the tendency to duplicate needlessly the same service. For example, how many times have you seen four gas stations on the same street crossing on all four corners? This is totally inefficient from a social point of view.

Thus we have sketched the picture of monopolistic competition, a picture that fairly adequately describes the overwhelming majority of small businesses in a private enterprise economy. Millions of tiny, nearly powerless businessmen work feverishly to create or protect some amount of monopolistic excess profits. Millions of competitors try equally hard to take away those excess profits. No competitor is able to sustain the acquisition of excess profits for a very long period, but each perpetually struggles, worries, competes, connives, and battles in a never-ending war in which there are no victors. Millions of firms almost never produce at the most efficient, lowest-cost level of production; billions of dollars are wasted on the aggressive propagation of inane, mind-dulling, and obnoxious advertising.

OLIGOPOLY

An *oligopoly* exists when a few business firms dominate an industry. Unlike any of the industrial categories discussed up to this point, an oligopolistic firm does not face a definite, unambiguous demand curve for its product. The amount the oligopolist can sell at any price can be substantially affected by his rivals' actions. Furthermore, because his actions similarly affected his rivals, any time he changes his price he must assume that other competitors will react in some way to this change. His rivals' reactions will, in turn, affect the customers' response to his initial price change. He must be prepared to respond to any unexpected moves by his competitors. Thus the fact of *interconnectedness* and *mutual dependence* of oligopolistic firms is the outstanding feature of an oligopolistic industry.

How can the effects of competitors' reactions be analyzed? First, their reactions to a price increase and to a price decrease can be differentiated. If a firm raises its price it will automatically lose many of its customers to its rivals, who sell a highly similar product. Consequently, its action is not likely to provoke a reaction from its rivals. They are happy to acquire new customers.

However, if the firm lowers its price it will attract its rivals' customers if they do nothing to retaliate. Rather than losing their customers, they are likely to lower their prices by the same amount. It might seem that these price changes would cancel each other out, leaving each firm selling the same quantity at a lower price. This is not the case, however. When all the firms lower their prices, they attract new customers. Furthermore, old customers may buy more of the product sold by the industry.

Figure 19.13 provides two demand curves for an oligopolistic firm in an oligopolistic industry: Ford Motor Company (and our old friend the Pinto). Demand curve D_1D_1 is constructed on the assumption that rivals ignore price changes made by Ford. Demand curve D_2D_2 is constructed on the assumption that rivals follow suit and change their prices by the same amount. For demand curve D_1D_1, marginal-revenue curve MR_1 is constructed. For demand curve D_2D_2, marginal-revenue curve MR_2 is constructed. Demand curves D_1D_1 and D_2D_2 intersect at the price and quantity that prevailed before the price change.

From the discussion of oligopoly behavior it is assumed here that, begining at $2,000, Ford's rivals will not react if it raises its price. Therefore for all prices above $2,000 (and quantities below 600,000 Pintos), the curves D_1D_1 and MR_1 are Ford's actual demand and marginal revenue curves. If Ford lowers its price below $2,000, the rivals will lower their prices accordingly. Therefore for prices below $2,000 (and quantities greater than 600,000 Pintos), the curves D_2D_2 and MR_2 are the firm's actual demand and marginal-revenue curves.

By eliminating the irrelevant sections of the two demand curves, it is possible to construct the firm's actual demand and marginal-revenue curves. In Figure 19.14 these curves are constructed and the firm's cost curves superimposed upon them. Two things should be carefully noted: The average-revenue or demand curve is kinked (where the demand curve abruptly turns down), and the marginal revenue (at 600,000 cars) suddenly falls off into the negative quadrant of the graph.

It is clear from the graph that Ford will lose profits if it changes its price either upward or downward from the initial price of $2,000. It is also clear that it would be highly unlikely that the revenue curves could ever shift so far downward and

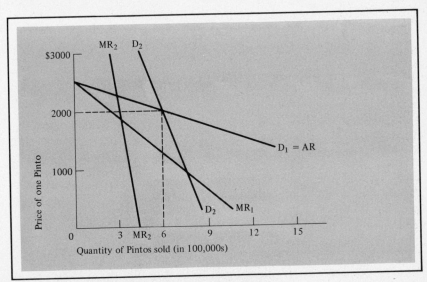

Figure 19.13 **Oligopoly demand curves for Ford Pintos**

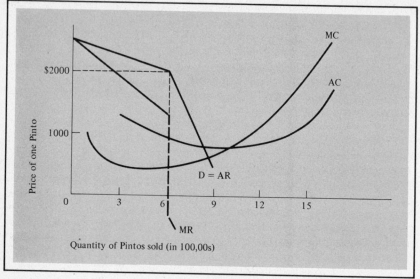

Figure 19.14 **The kinked demand curve for Ford Pintos**

to the left that Ford would lower the price it charged. An increase in costs or an increase in the revenue curves would have to be fairly substantial for the firm to raise its price, unless business conditions led rival firms to raise their prices as well.

This analysis helps explain the historically observed fact that prices in oligopolistic industries are very stable in the face of short-run small variations in demand. It also helps explain why, over the longer run, oligopolistic prices almost never fall. Rather, they show a persistent tendency to rise during periods of inflation and remain stable during periods of recession or deflation.

Oligopoly Prices

The analysis does not show, however, how the price charged by oligopolists is arrived at. Whatever price is established, a kink will develop at that price. But how is the price established in the first place?

Most textbooks develop elaborate models of oligopolistic behavior based on the assumption that regardless of how many times the actions of rivals upset their expectations, the rivals never learn that they are mutually dependent.[5] The German economist H. von Stackelberg developed a sophisticated analytic model of oligopolistic behavior that proved that oligopolistic rivalry will never result in the establishment of a stable price unless all the firms accept a single firm as a leader and all other firms accept positions as followers.[6] In other words, stability requires that a single firm (or any other single decision-making body) make the

[5] For a good, brief discussion of three such models, see Richard A. Bilas, *Microeconomic Theory* (New York: McGraw-Hill, 1967). pp. 213-219.

[6] H. von Stackelberg, *The Theory of the Market Economy,* trans. A. T. Peacock (New York: Oxford University Press, 1952), pp. 194-204.

decisions in the oligopoly and that the remaining firms accept the decisions made by the leader.

What type of decisions will be made by the oligopolistic leader in a private enterprise economy? The answer to this question is simple once the absurd assumption that oligopolistic firms do not recognize their mutual dependence is rejected. "If we assume that they recognize it [their mutual dependence], then they will set industry price at the monopoly price. The number of firms in the industry does not matter so long as they realize their interdependence."[7]

In other words, the large corporations prevent price competition, although they do compete through alleged quality differences and advertising. With no price competition the sellers of a given commodity have an interest in seeing that price or prices established are such as to maximize the profits of the group as a whole, so each product is priced *as if* it were sold by a single monopoly corporation. This is the decisive fact in determining the price policies and strategies of the typical large corporation. And it means that the appropriate price theory of an economy dominated by such corporations is not competitive price theory but monopoly price theory. What nineteenth-century economists treated as a special case is now the general situation.

It is true that there is little open collusion in the United States because of the antitrust laws. Yet some kind of tacit collusion probably exists to a large degree in most industries, reaching its most developed form in what is known as *price leadership.* It is a mutual security pact in which no formal communication is necessary.

In this situation, when one firm raises or lowers the price, all the others will follow. When collusion is forbidden, the price leader calculates the share of the total market demand that his rivals will supply at various prices. He then chooses the price where the remaining demand (after the rivals have chosen their appropriate supply quantities) will maximize his profits. For the industry as a whole this solution approximates the pure monopoly solution. So long as all firms accept his solution, which is really nothing else but a corollary of the ban on price competition, it becomes easy for the group as a whole to feel its way toward the price that maximizes the industry's profit. In the appendix to this chapter we examine the exact mechanism of price leadership and other mechanisms by which oligopolies set a monopoly-like price.

There is the qualification that oligopoly prices do not in fact move upward or downward with equal ease, as they would in a pure monopoly. If one seller raises his price, this cannot possibly be interpreted as an aggressive move. The worst that can happen to him is that the others will stand pat and he will have to rescind (or accept a smaller share of the market). In the case of a price cut, however, there is always the possibility that aggression is intended—that the cutter is trying to increase his share of the market by violating the taboo on price competition. If rivals interpret the initial move in this way, the result may be a price war with losses to all. Hence everyone is more likely to be careful about lowering prices than about raising them. Under the present situation of oligopoly, in other words, prices tend to be stickier on the downward side than on the upward side, and this fact introduces a significant upward bias into the general price level in a capitalistic economy dominated by oligopolies.

[7] Bilas, op. cit., p. 219.

OLIGOPOLY OR MONOPOLY?

In the first section of this chapter, four general classifications of market structures (pure competition, monopolistic competition, oligopoly, and monopoly) were described. We found that there were almost no purely competitive industries. In the previous section, it has been argued that, in their decisions regarding pricing, output, and sales, there is very little difference between oligopolies and monopolies.

Are there other differences of sufficient importance to make the oligopoly category a useful analytical tool? Or would it be better to drop oligopoly and simply refer to all industries that are dominated by a few giant corporations as monopolies?

The principal difference between oligopolistic and monopolistic firms is the rivalry that exists among the former. Although they have found by experience that this rivalry is mutually disastrous when it is extended to competitive pricing, they remain rivals. Their competition is generally confined to advertising, sales promotion, and cost reduction campaigns, and their actions do not differ substantially from the monopolist's behavior, particularly in attempts to shift revenue curves upward and cost curves downward.

It seems, therefore, that only when the passage of time results in a substantial shift of relative power within an oligopolistic industry are there important differences between a monopoly and oligopoly. During such a situation a struggle for the industry's price leadership might develop. Such a struggle might result, temporarily, in destructive price competition (or worse). But once a new leader emerged, the industry would generally return to the types of policies that make it hardly distinguishable from a monopoly.

Thus, the oligopoly category is useful for analyzing temporary situations during which destructive competition takes place. It might also be useful to differentiate between monopolies and oligopolies in analyzing differences between advertising and sales promotion techniques for firms that sell commodities for which there are close substitute (oligopolistic firms) and for those that sell products for which there are no close substitutes (monopolistic firms).

In almost any other situation or context, the differences between monopolistic and oligopolistic firms are insignificant. In most discussions it is quite appropriate to refer to all giant corporations as monopolistic firms, as is generally done in ordinary conversation. The economist's narrower definition of monopoly, while sometimes helpful, is so restrictive that it eliminates almost all existing business firms. Yet the formal analysis of a monopolist's pricing and output decisions forms the basis for understanding the behavior of most giant corporations.

SUMMARY

In this chapter we defined four types of market structures: pure competition, monopolistic competition, oligopoly, and monopoly. Pure competition and monopoly were analyzed in depth. Purely competitive industries are almost nonexistent. They are studied because the analysis of pure competition is the foundation of the classical liberal, laissez faire policy prescription. Because a purely competitive firm will tend to produce at its most efficient, low-cost level of output, the level at which the firm earns no excess profits, pure competition is also some-times used as a theoretical norm against which to evaluate and compare existing industries.

Monopolistic firms, however, almost never produce at the most efficient, low-cost level of output. Furthermore, they generally receive large excess profits because of their control over the price they charge consumers. Even if the gov-ernment were to attempt to control a monopolist in order to mitigate the exploita-tion of the general public, the monopolist would probably continue to make ex-cess profits.

Most American business firms fit into the market structure of monopolistic competition. Our analyses have shown that although these firms do not generally receive excess profits, they incur waste by never producing at their most efficient level and by wasting enormous amounts of resources on competitive advertising.

A comparatively few powerful oligopolistic giants dominate the industrial land-scape of American business. Oligopolies generally set prices as if they were monopolies (this point is developed further in the appendix that follows). Large excess profits and inefficiency characterize their operations.

APPENDIX

PRICE DETERMINATION IN AN OLIGOPOLY

The simplest and most direct method of oligopoly pricing occurs when the oligopolistic firms form a formal cartel. A *cartel* is an association that acts as a monopoly. Within a cartel each firm is treated as if it were merely a separate plant owned by the monopoly.

Figure 19A.1 shows that a cartel's price determination is identical to that of a monopoly. The monopolist has a single marginal-cost curve; the cartel's marginal-cost curve is determined by adding together the various individual oligopolists' marginal-cost curves. The industry price is set at $2,000, and 3 million compact cars is the quantity sold by the industry. Each firm produces the quantity at which its own marginal cost is equal to the industry's marginal cost (and marginal revenue).

Cartels, as such, are illegal in the United States. But many oligopolistic industries have found several ways of engaging in covert collusion that enables them to cooperate in such a manner that their pricing and output decisions become almost tantamount to a formal cartel.

When this type of collusion is not possible, many oligopolistic industries rely on the price leadership of the dominant firm within the industry. The dominant firm may be either the largest or the most efficient; sometimes it is both. In this situation the dominant firm sets the price. The other firms take that price as given

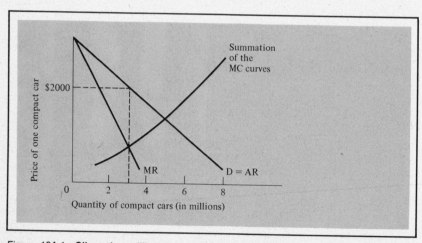

Figure 19A.1 **Oligopoly equilibrium in compact car industry**

the same way a purely competitive firm accepts the industry price as given. They produce up to the point at which their marginal cost is equal to that price (which they take as their marginal revenue).

In order for the dominant firm to maximize its profits, it must know approximately what the marginal costs are for the other firms. For some time U.S. Steel was the price leader in its industry. Figure 19A.2 illustrates how price is determined in such an industry. DD is the industry demand curve; the demand curve for U.S. Steel is labeled $D_{uss}D_{uss}$. The summation of the marginal-cost curves for all firms other than the price leader is also shown.

The demand curve for the price leader (D_{uss}) is computed in the following manner: Whatever price the leader (U.S. Steel) selects, it knows the other firms will produce up to the point at which their marginal cost equals that price. U.S. Steel knows, therefore, that the other firms, taken collectively, will produce the quantity (in Figure 19A.2, 70 million tons) at which the summation of their marginal-cost curves equals the price it establishes. The demand for the leader's output will be the total market demand at that price minus the quantity the other firms sell. In other words, the leader's demand curve at any price will be equal to the difference between the market demand curve and the summation of the other firm's marginal-cost curves.

For example, if the leader establishes a price of $2000 the other firms will produce all that can be sold at that price (because at that point market demand equals the summation of the marginal-cost curves). At prices below $2000 the summation of the marginal-cost curves falls successively farther to the left of the demand curve. Therefore as price declines, the demand remaining for the leader increases.

The marginal revenue (MR_{uss}) is derived from U.S. Steel's demand curve. The leader will maximize its profit by producing the quantity (30 million tons) and establishing the price ($1500) for the industry. The remainder of the firms will produce, among them, 70 million tons, and the entire industry will produce 100 million tons (equal to U.S. Steel's 30 million plus the others' 70 million).

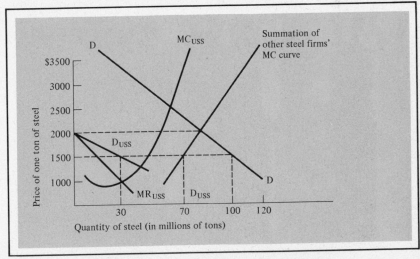

Figure 19A.2 **Price leadership by U.S. Steel (USS) in oligopoly industry**

It should be stressed that the follower firms only very superficially resemble firms in a purely competitive market. Although they take the price that has been established and adjust their output so that their marginal cost is equal to that price, their long-run normal position is one in which they also make monopolistic, excess profits. Because the oligopoly, like the monopoly, manages to keep new firms out of the industry, there are no market forces that would tend to erode profits.

A third method of establishing a monopoly price is through the creation of a government regulatory agency to supervise the industry. Although these agencies ostensibly exist to protect the general public's interests, very often they function as means of coordinating the industry and establishing a monopoly price (this was discussed in Chapter 8).

CHAPTER 20

GOVERNMENT AND INEQUALITY

In Chapter 17, we examined the distribution of income in the United States and found a small number of very rich people, who are mostly recipients of profit income from capital. We also found a very large number of poor and low-income people, who are mostly wage workers or unemployed workers. In Chapter 18, we found that even in the corporate world there are a few very big fish and millions of small ones. Clearly, economic power lies in the hands of a few thousand owners and executives of the major corporations.

In this chapter the relationship of economic power to political power will be examined. First we shall explore the degree to which their vast economic power gives disproportionate political power to that same relatively small number of top corporate owners and executives. Then we shall see how the resulting government affects economic inequality via taxation, welfare, farm subsidies, antitrust laws, and education. In Chapter 29, government policies, particularly military spending, will be considered in relation to unemployment and inflation.

HOW ECONOMIC INEQUALITY PRODUCES POLITICAL INEQUALITY

In spite of our formal political democracy, money talks in politics as elsewhere. Thus it is no surprise that many writers, not all radical, have alleged that those with economic power are dominant in U.S. politics. While he was President of the United States, Woodrow Wilson wrote, "Suppose you go to Washington and try to get at your Government. You will always find that while you are politely listened to, the men really consulted are the men who have the biggest stake—the big bankers, the big manufacturers, the big masters of commerce, the heads of railroad corporations and of steamship corporations. . . . The masters of the Government of the United States are the combined capitalists and manufacturers of the United States."[1]

How far can Wilson's hypothesis be substantiated by the facts? Do the large number of low-income workers or the few high-income, upper-class capitalists dominate U.S. politics? The economics of class structure has been examined; now we must ask about consciousness of class background because this will affect political behavior. A careful study conducted in 1964 found, contrary to the

---

[1] Woodrow Wilson, *The New Freedom* (Garden City, N.Y.: Doubleday, 1914), pp. 57–58.

myth of an all-middle-class America, that 56 percent of all Americans said they thought of themselves as "working class." Some 39 percent considered themselves "middle class." (It is true, though, that 35 percent of all those questioned said they had never thought of their class identification before that moment.) One percent said they were "upper class," and only 2 percent rejected the whole idea of class.[2]

An individual's political behavior is strongly influenced by class background. But that leads to a puzzle. If a majority identify with the working class, and everyone has one vote, why do parties favorable to the working class not win every election? Why do government policies usually support not working-class interests but (as Woodrow Wilson asserted) those of the wealthy capitalist class? More precisely, given formal democracy and capitalism, exactly how does our extreme economic inequality tend to be translated into inequality of political power?

In the first place, there is the simple fact that the degree of political participation tends to vary with class background. "The average citizen has little interest in public affairs, and he expends his energy on the daily round of life—eating, working, family talk, looking at the comics [today, TV], sex, sleeping."[3] More exactly, 86 percent of those identified in another 1964 study as middle class voted, but only 72 percent of the working class voted. Similarly, 40 percent of the middle class had talked to others about voting for a party or candidate, but only 24 percent in the working class had talked about it. Among the middle-class people interviewed, 16 percent gave money to a political cause, 14 percent attended political meetings, and 8 percent worked for a party or candidate; in the working class, figures on the same activities were only 4 percent, 5 percent, and 3 percent, respectively.[4]

Thus political participation of all kinds increases with income. Some of the reasons are obvious. Lower-income workers have less leisure, less money above minimum needs, more exhausting jobs. Furthermore, detailed studies show that because workers have less education and less access to information, they have less knowledge of the importance of various issues, which accounts, in part, for their lower participation. The same studies show more cross-pressures on workers—for example, the racial antagonisms that conveniently divide and weaken their working-class outlook.[5]

Unequal political power is also achieved through control of the news media. Even if the average worker "had an interest in politics, he would have great difficulty getting accurate information; since the events of politics unfold at a great distance, he cannot observe them directly, and the press offers a partial and distorted picture."[6] Even the quantity of news is limited. Although 80 percent of Americans read newspapers and 88 percent have television sets, only 2.8 percent of total newspaper space and even less television time is devoted to political news.

[2] This study is reported in Marian Irish and James Prothro, *The Politics of American Democracy* (Englewood Cliffs, N.J.: Prentice-Hall, 1965), p. 38. To avoid the imputation of a radical bias, we have taken all of the data in this section from their widely used traditional textbook. In turn, all of their footnotes refer to well-known conventional political scientists.

[3] Ibid., p. 165.

[4] Ibid., p. 38.

[5] Ibid., p. 193.

[6] Ibid., p. 165.

If the quantity of political news is deplorable, its quality is abysmal or worse. The first problem is that only one view is available to most people because of increasing concentration of newspaper ownership. In 1910 some 57 percent of American cities had competing daily papers, but in 1960, only 4 percent had competing dailies. Furthermore, news media tend to have a conservative bias because (1) they do not want to offend any powerful interests; (2) they especially do not want to offend major advertisers, all of which are big businesses; and (3) most important, "Since the media of communication are big businesses, too, the men who control them quite naturally share the convictions of other businessmen."[7]

Economic power also worsens the substantial inequality of political power available to different pressure groups. Thus a standard political science textbook points to *status* as the most important factor in determining the influence of a pressure group. After listing other sources of status, it concludes, "Finally, since status is so closely tied to money in the United States, the group with greater status will almost automatically be able to command greater financial resources. And it costs money to engage in pressure politics. . . ."[8]

The fact of economic power weighs all the more heavily because advertising is now a vital component of politics. ". . . Pressure groups . . . are now spending millions of dollars every year on *mass propaganda*. Not only broad groups like the National Association of Manufacturers, but even individual companies maintain elaborate bureaucracies to sell 'correct' ideas on general policy questions along with favorable attitudes to the company."[9]

The vast amount of business advertising reinforces the general ethos of capitalism. What is its message? Ours is a lovely country; material luxuries represent the ultimate goal; everyone can have these material luxuries. A certain percentage of business advertising is devoted to specifically political issues. Yet the government permits *all* business advertising to be counted as a cost, which can be deducted from income when taxes are computed. Of course labor unions are not allowed this tax deduction for political advertising.

ECONOMIC POWER AND THE PRESIDENT

There is no great mystery about how economic power gains dominance over the President. Money, big money, is required for presidential campaigns. For example, just in the few months of primary campaigns in 1972, Edmund Muskie spent about $2 million. It is estimated that President Nixon spent $29 million in the 1968 campaign and about $55 million in the 1972 campaign. Two traditional political scientists admit that "because campaigns are exceedingly costly, the wealthier a person is, the more strategic his position for bringing pressure to bear on politicians."[10]

In return for the money showered on him, Nixon appointed conservative businessmen to most cabinet and subcabinet positions; to almost all committees and

[7] Ibid., p. 184.
[8] Ibid., p. 245.
[9] Ibid., p. 249.
[10] Robert Dahl and Charles Lindblom, *Politics, Economics, and Welfare* (New York: Harper & Row, 1953), p. 313.

agencies; to most high posts in the Republican party; and to many ambassador-ships (including 16 of the 19 in Western Europe). Obviously these positions are desired and used in furthering the interests of these individual businessmen and of all business; an example is the business favors done by Nixon's friend, John Mitchell, who became Attorney General. This process, by which the President is elected by economic power and then appoints economically powerful people to positions from which they can further extend and defend economic power, may be called a feedback mechanism. In later sections, we shall look at how the political feedback mechanism causes Presidential bias in favor of big business on farm subsidies, tax loopholes, military spending, and so forth. More direct feedback mechanisms to influence the political process itself include police to stop demonstrations, the use of the CIA and FBI to attack "radicals" (meaning anyone opposed to the administration), and the use of the President's prestige in TV and press announcements to promote big-business policies.

The scandals of the Nixon era revealed—more dramatically than ever be-fore—a truth that has long been known to serious economists. When conserva-tives talk about "law and order" they mean primarily the protection of private property here and abroad—by any means available. Thus, letting the police shoot Chicano farm workers because they are striking is "law and order." Break-ing into and bugging the Watergate Democratic headquarters (or breaking into and robbing a psychiatrist's office in the Pentagon Papers case) is "law and order" because it protects the administration that protects private property. Bombing Cambodia—even though it is unconstitutional because Congress did not authorize it—is "law and order" because it protects the friends of capitalism abroad. Thus the conservative view of "law and order" is always to protect prop-erty (or "national security," which is the same thing) but not people. *This func-tion of "law and order" (or protection of private property) is the main function of the U.S. government.*

CONGRESS AND ECONOMIC POWER

Nor is Congress immune to the lure of economic power. Members of Congress need money to get elected and reelected; they need it for advertising, to pay for TV, to pay air fares, and for many other basic necessities of political life. Lincoln is said to have spent only 26 cents on his campaign, but in the 1950s members of congress spent about $15,000 to $25,000, and in the 1970s many members of congress were spending over $100,000 on each campaign. In the 1976 race for Governor of West Virginia, Jay Rockefeller spent $1.6 million in the primary con-test alone, or $8.85 per vote.[11]

The Republican and Democratic parties together spent about $140 million in 1952, $155 million in 1956, $175 million in 1960, $200 million in 1964, $300 million in 1968, and $425 million in 1972.[12] One investigation found that the Democratic

---

[11] Reported in editorial in *The Nation* (November 6, 1976).
[12] See M. Cummings and D. Wise, *Democracy Under Pressure* (New York: Harcourt Brace Jovanovich, 1971), pp. 304–305. Also see Associated Press, "New Study Sets 1972's Political Campaign Cost at $425 million," *Sunday Press-Enterprise*, April 25, 1976, p. 1.

party's money comes about 55 percent from corporations, 20 percent from big labor, 15 percent from racketeers and gangsters, and 15 percent from middle-class Americans in small contributions. The Republicans usually collect about twice as much in total, most of which comes from big business. Conservative Senator Russell Long guesses that "about 95 percent of congressional funds are derived from businessmen."

Members of congress are also indirectly affected by economic power through the strong influence of the President. Furthermore, big business can threaten to open or close plants in a particular congressional district. Business can give a member of congress free time on radio or TV or a free plane ride. In addition, there are about 5000 fulltime lobbyists in Washington, about 10 for each representative (and many are ex-members of congress or good personal or business friends of members of congress). Except in emergencies, lobbyists do not directly buy votes. They merely serve as the main channel for the largest campaign contributions, buy lunches and dinners, and supply petty cash, credit cards, profitable investment opportunities, legal retainers to members of congress (most of whom are lawyers), lecture fees, poker winnings (members of congress *always* win), vacations, and fringe benefits ranging from theater tickets to French perfume. The two largest lobbies are the oil interests (which make billions in special tax loopholes) and the military armaments industry. All of this power is so strong—and so necessary for election—that even liberals will be found voting consistently for the direct needs of business interests in their districts, no matter how they may vote on broader issues. Thus one friendly senator, Boies Penrose, said to a meeting of businessmen (back in 1900, when such things were said more frankly), "I believe in a division of labor. You send us to Congress; we pass laws under . . . which you make money; . . . and out of your profits you further contribute to our campaign funds to send us back again to pass more laws to enable you to make more money."[13]

ECONOMIC BACKGROUND OF POLITICAL LEADERS

Upper-income members of the capitalist class (mostly white, male, Anglo-Saxon, Protestants) hold a disproportionate percentage of the top political positions. From 1789 to 1932, the fathers of U.S. presidents and vice presidents were 38 percent farm owners and only 4 percent wage earners or salaried workers. Similarly, from 1947 to 1951, the fathers of U.S. senators were 22 percent professionals, 33 percent proprietors and officials, 40 percent farm owners, and only 4 percent wage earners or salaried workers. Finally, from 1941 to 1943, the fathers of U.S. representatives were 31 percent professionals, 31 percent proprietors and officials, 29 percent farm owners, and only 9 percent wage earners or salaried workers.[14]

Data for 1970 show that 266 of the 435 members of the House of Representatives (about three-fifths) had outside financial interests providing over $5000 in

13 Quoted in Mark Green, James Fallows, and David Zwick, *Who Runs Congress?* (New York: Bantam, 1972, The Ralph Nader Congress Project), pp. 7–8.
14 Cummings and Wise, op. cit., p. 39.

income per year beyond their congressional salaries.[15] This figure may be an underestimation because income of wives and children was not listed (nor was income under $5000 listed). To make $5000 a year from stocks and bonds requires at least $70,000 or $80,000 in holdings. Very wealthy men, with fortunes ranging from many tens of thousands of dollars up to the figure of slightly under $3 million listed for Representative Pierre Du Pont, sit in Congress.

What are the sources of their wealth? A total of 102 members of congress held stock or well-paying executive positions in banks or other financial institutions; 81 received regular income from law firms that generally represented big businesses. Sixty-three got their income from stock in the top defense contractors; 45, in the giant (federally regulated) oil and gas industries; 22, in radio and television companies; 11, in commercial airlines; and 9, in railroads. Ninety-eight members of congress were involved in numerous capital gains transactions; each of them netted a profit of over $5,000 (and some as high as $35,000).

In the executive branch, upper-income, business-oriented individuals have had a majority of all the important positions throughout U.S. history. This includes the members of the cabinet, their assistants and department heads, and heads of most regulatory agencies. They quite naturally, with no conspiracy, tend to consult big businessmen and business groups as experts (such as the Committee for Economic Development or the Council on Foreign Relations). Wealthy families have also contributed a majority of federal judges, top military men, and top leaders of intelligence agencies. Finally, it should be noted that there is much crossing over at the top: Ex-generals often become corporate executives, and corporate executives often get to be cabinet members.

The results of the importance of wealth in getting elected, as well as the effects of wealth on ideological outlook, can be seen clearly in the U.S. Senate in Table 20.1.

The table shows at least 21 millionaires in the Senate but only 5 below $50,000 in wealth (though this lowest category includes 99 percent of Americans). The table

Table 20.1 **Wealth and Ideology in the U.S. Senate, 1975**

Wealth Group	Senators in Group	Average Liberal Rating by ADA, 1975
under $50,000	5	92%
$50,000 - $250.000	30	59
$250,000 - $500,000	18	53
$500,000 - $1 million	4	53
$1 million or more	21	29

Source: Ralph Nader study, reported in Jim Chapin, "The Rich Are Different . . ." *Newsletter of the Democratic Left,* November 1976, p. 3. The results are for 88 Senators for whom questionnaire or other data were available; no data on 22.

[15] All of these data were taken from statements filed with the House Committee on Standards of Official Conduct in April 1971; they were discussed in an article in the *Los Angeles Times,* May 24, 1971, pt. I, p. 12.

also shows that senators are consistently less liberal as they have more wealth. The poorest (not very poor) were given a liberal voting rate of 92 percent by the Americans for Democratic Action (ADA), but the ADA gave only a 29 percent liberal voting record to the 21 millionaires. These results fit almost too well with a vulgar Marxist economic determinism. There are certainly many exceptions; for example, the very liberal Senator Ted Kennedy is a millionaire.

Of course no serious radical would state the thesis of big-business control of government as if it were total. There are many qualifications. For example, although most members of Congress are rich, white males, the influence of wealth in Congress is much less than it is in the cabinet and in other executive offices. Similarly, in state and local governments the influence of the wealthy is very strong, but certainly they do not have exclusive control. Moreover, even among the members of the capitalist class in high positions there are many differences of opinion, mistakes in perceiving their own interests, and conflicts of interest between different business groups. Thus the rule of the capitalist class is by no means monolithic; it rules through the forms of shifting coalitions and liberal or conservative styles, as reflected in the Democratic and Republican parties. Finally, the working class (including farmers, industrial workers, intellectual and professional workers, the poor and unemployed, and workers from minority groups) can sometimes organize sufficiently to overcome the power of money by pure weight of numbers, may exert pressure, elect a few representatives, and sometimes even prevail on particular issues.

EFFECTS OF GOVERNMENT ON ECONOMIC INEQUALITY

Although everyone knows that there is extreme inequality in the United States, liberals argue that the inequality is much reduced by higher tax rates on the rich, welfare payments to the poor worker, subsidies to the poor farmer, public education for the poor, and antitrust laws, which decrease the concentration of income and power. Thus Paul Samuelson asserts that the U.S. government has reduced income inequality, though he admits that it has not been much of a change: "The welfare state, through redistributive taxation and through educational opportunity . . . has moved the system a bit toward greater equality."[16] Radicals object to this conclusion on several grounds.

First, radicals present the facts on the history of income distribution, which were given in Chapter 17. These facts show that (1) there was very, very little overall change in income distribution between 1910 and 1970; (2) the share of the poorest 20 percent of the population has actually declined; (3) the share of the richest 20 percent has fluctuated, going down very, very slightly by 1970. Therefore, in spite of many promises by liberal U.S. government administrations, there has been no reduction of inequality since 1910.

Second, the main function of the system is the preservation of "law and order," which means that police and armies and courts and prisons all protect the private ownership of vast fortunes for the rich. Government thus preserves capitalist control of land and factories. With the help of government in breaking

[16] Paul Samuelson, *Economics*, 9th ed. (New York: McGraw-Hill, 1973), p. 804.

strikes, the rich can continue to pay low enough wages to farm and industrial workers to continue to make the high profits by which they grow richer.

Third, radicals have shown that the administration of every program from taxation to welfare has been such that the rich have benefited more and the poor less than the law would seem to indicate at first glance. We look in detail at each program in the following sections.

Taxation

It is certainly true that income tax rates rise as income rises, so that in theory individuals in the higher income brackets not only must pay more taxes but also must pay a higher percentage of their income in taxes. Indeed the theoretical tax rate today seems to take most of an individual's income, once that income exceeds $1 million.

In practice rich taxpayers find many loopholes that allow them to pay much lower tax rates. Thus in 1957 the highest tax rate had risen to an apparently confiscatory 91 percent, yet that category of taxpayers paid only 52 percent to the government.[17] In 1969, the tax rate paid by all taxpayers with incomes reported over $1 million was only 34 percent, and since they don't have to report all of it the rate was actually only 20 percent.[18]

One kind of loophole for the rich is *capital gains*. This is the income derived from sale of a piece of property (including corporate stock) at a higher price than that at which it was bought. The increase in value of the property (held more than six months), or capital gain, is taxed at only one-half the rate for ordinary income. In 1957 20 percent of incomes above $100,000 a year was in the form of capital gains. But it should be noted that this loophole does not save money for the poor. For taxpayers in the $3500-$4000 income bracket, capital gains accounted for only 0.3 percent of income.

Another large loophole is the tax-free bonds. The interest on federal bonds cannot be taxed by states, and the interest on municipal bonds cannot be taxed by states or by the federal government. Of course to make a significant amount of money from bonds a very large investment is necessary, and bonds are typically sold in large lots that only the rich can afford. Other loopholes include homeowners' preferences, dividend exclusion, depreciation allowances, and depletion allowances (especially gas and oil).

As a result of these loopholes, some startling statistics have appeared. In 1965 a certain taxpayer had an income of $20 million but paid no taxes. In 1974 some 3,302 people earning more than $50,000 paid *no* federal taxes—and that included 5 people with incomes over $1 million in that single year. *It has been estimated that the total loss of government revenue from all loopholes in the income-tax laws is about $77 billion a year.*[19]

---

[17] For this and much of the following information, see Gabriel Kolko, *Wealth and Power in America* (New York: Praeger, 1962), chap. 2.

[18] John Gurley, "Federal Tax Policy," *National Tax Journal*, September 1967.

[19] J. Lechman and B. Okner, "Individual Income Tax Erosion by Income Classes," in U.S. Congress, Joint Economic Committee, *Economics of Federal Subsidy Programs*, pt. I (Washington, D.C.: GPO, 1972), pp. 13–40. The 1974 data is from Internal Revenue Service, reported by Associated Press, "Vote Would Close Loopholes for Rich," *Riverside Daily Enterprise*, May 13, 1976, p. A3.

Whereas the rich, with their income from property, can find many tax loopholes, there are none for the average worker with wage income. Consequently, there is in fact only the slightest redistribution of income as a result of the federal income tax. The data for 1962 indicate that the richest fifth (or top 20 percent) of the population had 45.5 percent of all income before taxes. After taxes, their percentage of national income had decreased by only 1.8 percent. The poorest 20 percent had increased their share by only 0.3 percent; the second fifth, by only 0.6 percent; and the third fifth, by only 0.5 percent. Thus *after* taxes the richest 20 percent still had far more income than the poorest 60 percent.

Even more important is the fact that the federal income tax amounts to only 40 percent of all taxes and is the only one that is progressive to even a slight extent (*progressive* means that the tax falls more heavily on the upper-income groups). The other 60 percent of taxes are mainly *regressive,* according to most observers, in that they fall more heavily on the lower income groups. "We might tentatively conclude that taxes other than individual income taxes do not reduce, and probably increase, income inequality."[20]

Most of the regressive taxes are state and local, such as the sales tax and the property tax. In terms of percentages these fall much more heavily on lower- and middle-income groups than on the rich. For example, a tax on gasoline or telephone service is spread quite equally among the population; therefore these taxes take a much higher percentage of a poor person's income. In 1958 people in the lowest income class ($9000-2000) paid 11.3 percent of their income in state and local taxes. But each higher income group paid a smaller and smaller percentage: 9.4 percent ($2000-4000 group), 8.5 percent ($4000-6000), 7.7 percent ($6000-8000 group), 7.2 percent ($8000-10,000 group), 6.5 percent ($10,000-15,000 group), and 5.9 percent (over $15,000 group).[21] Thus the higher the income group, the lower its state and local tax rates.

In addition, a large amount of taxes are paid in the form of compulsory contributions by workers to the social security system. These taxes are highly regressive because even the poorest workers pay a large part of the tax.

When all kinds of taxes—federal, state, and local—are added together, the proportionate burden on the poor seems to be actually larger than on the rich. Although the rich pay a larger total of taxes, the percentage of their income going to taxes is actually less than the percentage of poor families' income going to taxes. In 1967 the poorest families, those with less than $3000 income, paid 34 percent of their income in taxes. In the same year, the richest families, those with incomes over $25,000, paid only 28 percent of their income in taxes. In fact, in 1967 the richest 5 percent of taxpayers had 15 percent of all income before taxes; but they had 17 percent of all income after all federal, state, and local taxes were paid.[22]

In the last 30 years, the tax burden has actually been shifting further away from rich capitalists and toward all workers and the poor. In 1944 corporate

[20] F. Ackerman et al., "Income Distribution in the United States," *Review of Radical Political Economy,* Summer 1971, p. 24.

[21] All data from Kolko, loc. cit. For further shocking data, see Arnold Cantor, "State Local Taxes: A Study of Inequity," *AFL-CIO American Federationist,* February 1974, revised and reprinted by AFL-CIO May 1976.

[22] See Joseph Pechman, "The Rich, the Poor, and the Taxes They Pay," *The Public Interest,* Number 17, Fall 1969, pp. 113-137.

income taxes were 34 percent of all federal income taxes, but corporate taxes fell to only 14 percent of federal taxes by 1974.[23] At the same time, social security taxes (paid mostly by workers) rose from 4 percent of federal taxes in 1944 to 29 percent in 1974. Similarly, among the federal individual income taxpayers, the share paid by the lowest 20 percent of income recipients rose from 4 percent in 1950 to 11 percent in 1970—while the share of taxes paid by the top 4 percent of income recipients fell from 43 percent to just 27 percent.[24]

In conclusion, the whole tax system redistributes very little, if any, income from rich to poor. It certainly does virtually nothing to mitigate poverty or reduce inequality.

Welfare

Liberals assert that absolute poverty is the only income problem left, ignoring the fact that extreme inequality of income creates a relative, or social, poverty as well. They argue that because a growing number of people are getting larger welfare payments, the poverty problem will be solved. But poverty is not defined simply as an absolute income level of less than $3000; it is *relative* to the society in which a person lives. The people in India live on a median income of $100. There, a person earning $3000 per year might be considered wealthy. But there can be no doubt that an American family living on that income could afford neither the cultural nor the physical necessities of life. So even if one earns $3000, in a society as affluent as the United States he or she still lives in relative poverty. Therefore "brutalizing and degrading poverty will exist as long as extreme income inequality exists."[25]

Because taxation does not redistribute income, the question is whether welfare programs have a significant effect in that direction. In the first place, expenditures for welfare have been fairly small. In 1968 welfare spending under all federal, state, and local programs was only $26.9 billion. This included public aid, unemployment payments, workmen's compensation, health and medical programs, public housing, and educational aid to low-income students. These payments do help the poor somewhat, but the effect is small; it has virtually no effect in altering the relative positions of the poorest or the richest segments of society.

This $26.9 billion was only 3.82 percent of all personal income in 1968. Therefore, although it could make a few people better off, it could not change things very much.

What has been the historical trend of welfare payments? In 1938, welfare payments were 6.7 percent of personal income; in 1950, welfare was down to 3.86 percent; in 1960 it was down a little more, to 3.31 percent. Thus the 3.82 percent level in 1968 was back to the 1950 level and still just about half the 1938 level. Not only is welfare a small percentage of personal income, but it also has actually decreased as a percentage in 30 years of much-touted new programs. Furthermore, there are qualifications. Some of that 3.82 percent does not go to the poorest groups. Welfare money spent on school lunches or university scholarships benefits middle-class children as well.

[23] *Economic Report of the President,* 1976 (Washington, D.C.: GPO, 1976).
[24] U.S. Department of Commerce, *Statistical Abstract of the United States* (1960 and 1974), discussed in *Economic Notes,* newsletter published by Labor Research Association, April 1975, p. 4.
[25] Richard Edwards, "Who Fares Well in the Welfare State," in R. Edwards, M. Reich, and T. Weisskopf, eds. *The Capitalist System* (Englewood Cliffs, N.J.: Prentice-Hall, 1972), p. 244.

Moreover, the poor help pay for welfare, so the net amount received is even less. It is estimated that in 1968 the poorest 40 percent of the population (those with incomes below $7500) paid in taxes about $6 billion of the money budgeted for welfare. This estimate assumes that taxes fell equally on the entire population and were not regressive, as the total tax burden may well be. Thus net welfare to the poor (assuming that all the welfare payments went to the poorest 40 percent) was not $26.9 billion but $26.9 minus $6 billion, or $20.9 billion. The percentage of income paid in net welfare is even smaller than it looks at first. It is no wonder, then, that our tax and welfare systems have not resulted in any significant redistribution of income.

Interestingly, this pattern of small effects and no significant reduction in income inequality over many decades also holds true for the capitalist countries of western Europe. Even in Denmark and Sweden, where taxation and welfare programs are supposed to be very, very progressive, recent studies have shown little change in income distribution (after taxes and welfare) for several decades. A UN report reveals that for all western Europe "the general pattern of income distribution, by size of income, for the great majority of households, is only slightly affected by government action."[26]

The problem is that the social and economic conditions of a private enterprise economy lead to a psychology in which one works only if one has to work. Thus only by offering extremely unequal incomes for differing amounts of work done can work incentives be maintained under this system. It would take very different institutions with very different education and propaganda to change this psychology. Thus U.S. welfare programs are very carefully designed to go to those who do not work: children, the old, the blind. No welfare income goes to those who work hard but are paid low wages (who constitute about half of the poverty group) because that might lower their "incentive." A few programs give the low-paid worker minimum health and education so that he or she is able to work but very carefully do not provide any food, clothing, or shelter. This philosophy of welfare leads to extreme degradation of welfare recipients. In order to galvanize the working poor to ever greater effort, welfare recipients are kept in such a pitiful, dehumanized condition that anyone would rather work, even at the most disagreeable jobs and at the lowest pay.

The dole a welfare recipient receives is grossly insufficient for even the barest subsistence livelihood. Moreover, in return for this paltry sum the individual loses many basic civil rights supposedly guaranteed to everyone. The single woman supporting a family on welfare, for example, must permit welfare workers to search her house and subject her to a demeaning interrogation to ascertain if her personal sexual conduct is proper and fitting. This is only one of many ways welfare recipients are degraded and dehumanized. It is quite absurd to argue that programs like these will ever eliminate poverty.

Farm Subsidies

The rural poor have suffered the most pathetic poverty. For most of the twentieth century the incomes of small-farm owners and farm workers have lagged far behind other U.S. incomes. For that reason, liberals have persuaded Congress to

26 U.N. Economic Commission of Europe, *Incomes in Postwar Europe: A Study of Policies, Growth, and Distribution* (Geneva: United Nations, 1957), pp. 1–15.

pass various bills aiding farmers with subsidies. What has been the practical effect of these subsidies?

First, the high economic concentration among the business firms engaged in farming should be noted. At present the richest 10 percent of all farms produce over 50 percent of total agricultural output. The poorest 50 percent of all farms produce only 5 percent of farm output. Concentration in agriculture has greatly increased in the period since subsidies were initiated.

Second, the farm support programs benefit mainly the richest farmers and give very little support to the poorest farmers. In 1963–1965, the poorest 20 percent of all farms received only 1 percent of the farm subsidies given in sugar cane, rice, and feed grains, 2 percent of those in cotton, 3 percent of those in wheat, 4 percent of those in peanuts and tobacco, and 5 percent of those in sugar beets. At the same time, the richest 20 percent of all farms (with the highest incomes before subsidies) received 83 percent of the farm subsidies given in sugar cane, 69 percent of those in cotton, 65 percent of those in rice, 62 percent of those in wheat, 56 percent of those in feed grains, 57 percent of those in peanuts, 53 percent of those in tobacco, and 51 percent of those in sugar beets.[27]

Third, it appears in fact that the net result of the farm program is to increase the percentage of total farm income going to the richest farmers and to decrease that going to the poorest farmers. Roughly, this can be seen from the fact that in 1963 the poorest 20 percent of all farmers and farm managers received 3.2 percent of farm income, whereas the richest 20 percent received 50.5 percent of farm income. Yet the data cited on subsidies showed that many of the farm programs gave less than 3.2 percent of the benefits to the poorest farmers and more than 50.5 percent to the richest farmers. Thus not only do most of the benefits go to the richest farmers but their share of the subsidies is *higher* than their share of the presubsidy income, so the disproportionate subsidies make farm income more extremely unequal than it would be without them. Clearly income inequality in farming is actually increased by the farm programs. In other words, it appears to be a regressive program, although we cannot say just how regressive: "the net effect of these programs may be less regressive than the data suggest—or possibly more regressive—but the pattern is clear."[28]

The discussion up to this point shows the effects of the farm programs on farmers who own their own farms. There is a fourth factor: what are the effects on farm workers, who own nothing but their power to labor? The answer is very simple. The main farm programs provide farm owners—mainly on the largest, richest farms—price supports to maintain prices at a certain level above costs, and payments to keep some land out of production in order to reduce the supply of farm goods. No money from these programs goes to farm workers. In fact the programs may hurt farm workers to the extent that the programs pay to keep land out of production, thereby increasing unemployment. "The State pays the *owners* of farm property not to produce, but pays virtually nothing to *farm workers* who become unemployed as a result of this dole to property owners."[29]

---

[27] All data from James Bonnen, "The Effect of Taxes and Government Spending on Inequality," in *The Capitalist System*, pp. 235–243.

[28] Ibid., p. 242.

[29] Howard Wachtel, "Looking at Poverty from a Radical Perspective," *Review of Radical Political Economics*, Summer 1971, p. 12.

Finally, the net result of this program—to help farm workers not at all, to help poor farmers slightly, and to help rich farmers very much—is not at all surprising. Indeed it represents the continuation of a consistent pattern in U.S. history. Large corporations have always been the ones helped by government subsidies. In the nineteenth century, for example, three-fourths of all railroad construction was paid for by the government, and huge amounts of land were given to the railroads. Merchant shippping today gets large subsidies. Largest of all is the amount the government gives business for "research and development" ($17 billion in 1969 alone) both directly and indirectly through academic institutions.

Education and Inequality

Government-subsidized education is often thought to decrease the inequality of incomes. "The government gives free education to all," goes the argument, "so anyone can improve his station in life by going to school for a longer period."

Clearly there is a significant positive correlation between amount of education and level of income. Thus in 1968 those with only eight years of schooling had a median income of only $6600.[30] The median income for high school graduates was $8,300, and that for college graduates was $11,800. In part, more schooling is the *cause* of better jobs and better pay for the individual. In part, however, better schooling is the *effect* of having a high income (and to some extent individuals from high-income families may get high-income jobs merely because their fathers own the businesses in which they work).

It is a fact that individuals from high-income families are able to get more schooling in the United States than individuals from low-income families. This may be seen in the following data from a survey that classified students graduating from high school in 1966 according to their family's income in 1965.[31] Of those in the under-$3000 income group, only 20 percent started college by February 1967. Other figures for the same period are 32 percent in the $3,000-4,000 group, 37 percent in the $4,000-6,000 group, 41 percent in the $6,000-7,000 group, 51 percent in the $7,000-10,000 group, and 61 percent in the $10,000-15,000 group. Fully 87 percent of those with family incomes over $15,000 started college. Thus the higher one's family's income, the greater one's chance of going to college.

Children of richer parents get more schooling mainly because they can afford to keep their children in school longer than poor parents can. They can pay high tuitions in private schools that admit students even with low grade averages. Even in the public universities, where the tuition may be much lower or nonexistent, there are still living expenses. Many students must drop out of college or not enroll simply because they have no money on which to live while in school.

Furthermore, children of richer families have a better chance to do well in school and learn more. Opportunities and encouragement provided in the home and community are much more likely to produce highly motivated children who know how to study. Cultural background is very important in performance on IQ tests and college entrance record examinations. These examinations, which purport to test general ability, in reality are designed to conform to middle-class,

[30] All data in this paragraph are from Ackerman et al., "Income Distribution in the United States," op. cit.
[31] Ibid.

white, urban experience. A student from a poor or black or rural background will lack the necessary cultural references to understand the questions or have any intuition of the answers. This has been proved over and over again, but the tests are still used. They determine which "track" (discussed below) an elementary student is put into, and they determine who enters college. Thus it is no surprise that only 7 percent of all college students come from the poorest 25 percent of all families.

Another condition that hurts students from poor families and helps those from richer families is the fact that schools in different areas get very different amounts of money. Central-city slum schools often receive less money per student and almost always attract less competent teachers. Suburban township schools are apt to receive more money per student and attract better teachers.

Students in elementary and high schools are put into different *tracks*.[32] One track is vocational training, which prepares the poor for manual labor. Another track, college preparation, equips students from upper-middle-class and richer families for college, in order to get high-income jobs (so that their children can go to college, and so forth). In elementary schools it is often called *ability grouping* of the bright and the stupid. But the degree of ability is determined by IQ tests that do not assess innate intelligence but, as noted previously, discriminate on the basis of class background.

The tracking system exists both within and between high schools. Within some high schools, counselors push the poor and the minority groups into vocational training and the rich into college preparation. Within others, such pushing is hardly necessary because of the vast differences among schools. Schools in the black slums provide only basic, or vocational, training. Schools in the richest areas give only college preparation. These different tracks are enforced both formally by the tests given and informally by counselors and teachers. One investigation in New York showed that middle-class white children were usually offered voluntary classes in how to pass college examinations, but that in Harlem even seeing the old tests was "against the rules."[33]

We may conclude with certainty that our educational system does not reduce inequality from generation to generation. On the contrary, the richer students have more opportunities to get a good elementary and high-school education, to get into college, to remain in college, and therefore to get a high-income job after college—and then to send their children to college. Thus the educational system seems to transmit inequality from one generation to the next.

Government and Business

In the United States the Industrial Revolution commenced after the Civil War. In more than a century of American industrial capitalism, the relationship between government and big business is seen by some observers as having been desultory and often contradictory. This is because many government programs and legislative acts were designed to promote big business, whereas some laws, particularly antitrust legislation, were ostensibly designed to curb the size and power of big business.

---

[32] The best description of "tracking" is in Florence Howe and Pual Lautner, "How the School System Is Rigged," in *The Capitalist System*, (Englewood Cliffs, N.J.: Prentiss-Hall, 1972), pp. 229–235.

[33] Ibid., p. 234.

Thurman Arnold, former "trust-busting" head of the federal government's antitrust division, believes that these contradictory policies and laws have stemmed from "a continuous conflict between opposing ideals in American economic thinking."[34] The power of "economic thinking," taken alone, explains very little, however. A more realistic explanation of these seeming contradictions would be based on the two broadest objectives of government in its dealings with big business.

First, the government has been committed to the maintenance of the capitalist system and the promotion of the interests of big business. This commitment has generally dominated the relationship between government and business. The interests of various capitalists and business firms, however, are not always mutually compatible. Many conflicts are so intense that, if left unresolved, they could eventually threaten the very existence of the capitalist system. Government's second objective, therefore, is to act as the arbiter in these rivalries and to resolve the difficulties before they become so extremely serious.

The antitrust laws have given the federal government a measure of power to enforce its function as arbiter. Interpreted in this way, the government's policy toward business has not been contradictory. Nor has this policy been designed, as many liberals believe, to curb the immense power of giant corporations. Rather, it has always attempted to promote the general interests of all capitalists and all businesses. Sometimes the individual interests of capitalists have coincided, as, for example, in the late-nineteenth-century attempt to crush labor unions. But in instances of industrial or commercial rivalry between two giant corporate empires, the interests have been in conflict. In such cases the general interests of all capitalists would depend on at least partial restriction of one or both of the rivals.

American industrialization was aided significantly by the intimate association of government and business. Big business was supported by protective tariffs, which began with the Morrill Tariff of 1861 and were expanded significantly in 1890, 1894, and 1897. Thus large corporations were protected from foreign competition and could use fully their domestic monopoly powers to charge high prices.

The due process clause of the Fourteenth Amendment had been intended to give equal rights to blacks. In the late nineteenth century, however, it was not used to help blacks at all. Rather, it was interpreted to prohibit state regulation of corporations (who were considered legal "persons"). The courts denied state governments the right to interfere in any way with even the most abusive, malicious, and socially deleterious corporate behavior.

The railroad magnates were among the most important entrepreneurs in the American Industrial Revolution. Through bribery, chicanery, and fraud, they amassed great personal fortunes. Building railroads was never more than the vehicle from which they launched their financial schemes. The federal government responded by generously giving federal lands to the railroads. Between 1850 and 1871 the railroads were handed 130 million acres of land, an area as large as all the New England states plus Pennsylvania and New York. During the same period, state governments gave the railroads another 49 million acres. All

---

[34] Thurman Arnold, "Economic Reform and the Sherman Anti-trust Act," in J. A. Garraty, ed., *Historical Viewpoints: Volume Two, Since 1865* (New York: Harper & Row, 1969), p. 151.

this, and yet some economic historians still refer to the second half of the nineteenth century as an age in which government stayed out of business affairs!

Toward the end of the nineteenth century, the relationship between the federal government and big business became a symbiosis in which the government governed in ways big business wanted it to govern and big business furnished the money, organization, and power structure through which politicians could come to power in the federal government. When progressive elements of the Democratic party saw that Democratic President Cleveland's relationship with big business was hardly distinguishable from the Republican–big-business relationship, they captured control of the party and nominated William Jennings Bryan, a champion of the workers and farmers. William McKinley, the big-business Republican candidate, raised campaign funds estimated to total as much as $15 million, 50 times more than Bryan's $300,000. From that time on, the Democratic party has been more careful about picking a candidate of whom at least a large segment of big business approves.

Regulatory Agencies

Since the late nineteenth century the U.S. government has established many regulatory agencies, such as the Interstate Commerce Commission, supposedly designed to protect consumer and environmental interests. Thus telephone and electric companies are given monopolies, but public agencies are placed above them to regulate their profits. These commissions are commonly thought to be the watchdogs of the public interests, but they often turn out to be merely a legal way to give monopoly powers to an oligopoly. The commissions are generally dominated by those they are supposed to regulate, and neglect the public interest. For example, when the public does not give them careful attention, the public utilities commissions normally grant most price increases desired by the regulated companies. Similarly, when California passed a new law by voters' initiative (against strong pressure from the construction industry) to regulate building on the California shoreline in the interest of environmental protection, Governor Reagan appointed to the agencies responsible for enforcement mostly representatives *opposed* to the protection of the shoreline.

While public agencies have always been dominated by business interests, some of the most obvious cases occurred during the Nixon administration. The Federal Power Commission is an important agency supposed to protect consumer and environmental interest concerning gas and electricity. All five of the members appointed by Nixon were either businessmen in the gas or electric businesses or lawyers for these firms. As is usual, the Senate went along with the appointments in the first four cases. In the fifth case, however, Robert Morris was rejected when, on June 13, 1973, the Senate finally asserted its power to turn down such openly biased appointments. Senator Magnuson said that in the case of Morris the Senate was "again asked to accept . . . one more nominee whose professional career has been dedicated to the furtherance of the private interests of that industry." He pointed out that Morris had represented Standard Oil of California for 15 years. In fact, from 1964 to 1971 he had spent most of his time lobbying for Standard Oil against public interests on natural gas matters before the Federal Power Commission!

Antitrust Laws

There have been four major laws designed ostensibly to decrease the monopoly power of big business. The first was the Sherman Antitrust Act of 1890, which forbade any contract, combination, or conspiracy to restrain trade.[35] In fact, it forbade any agreement not to compete, regardless of how the agreement was achieved. It also forbade monopolies or attempts to monopolize.

The Clayton Act of 1914 forbade corporations to engage in price discrimination—that is, to force some customers to pay more than others. It also prohibited *interlocking directorates* where this would lead to a substantial reduction of competition.

The Federal Trade Commission Act of 1914 outlawed *unfair* methods of competition and established the FTC to investigate the methods of competition used by business firms. Finally, The Celler-Kefauver Act of 1950 forbade the purchase of either the stock of a competing corporation (which had already been illegal) or the assets of competing corporations (hitherto a big loophole in the laws).

The antitrust laws were supposed to limit the concentration of economic power among corporations. Yet, as one observer has written, "the fact that after the passage of the Sherman Act the country witnessed a spectacular merger movement, another wave after the passage of the Clayton Act (1914), and again after the Celler-Kefauver Act, indicates that the laws have been ineffective in 'limiting the concentration of control.' "[36]

For the first two decades after the passage of the Sherman Act, the antitrust laws were used almost exclusively to break the power of labor unions to strike against employers. Although there have been periodic convictions of business firms throughout the twentieth century, most observers agree that virtually all the important oligopolistic corporations are constantly violating most of the antitrust law sanctions. There is almost no price competition among the giants. There are many, many instances of interlocking directorates, and almost no one doubts the pervasive existence of illegal collusion among giant corporations.

Why, then, are a few corporations occasionally singled out for conviction for violations of which virtually all corporations are guilty? We believe that in these cases the government uses the antitrust laws to act as arbiter in the irreconcilable conflicts between various corporations. Antitrust convictions are generally mildly punitive government actions, taken when the government decides which group of corporations should be supported in a particular conflict of interest. This was most apparent recently when the U.S. government acted against certain conglomerate mergers in which "young newcomers" tried to take over old, established corporations.

The government does not really attempt to eliminate the pervasive illegal policies of corporations. Throughout American history the government has done everything it could to create and promote the interests of monopolistic businesses. For the good of all, a few must occasionally be slapped on the wrists. Antitrust laws make this possible. They therefore operate to blunt some of the traditional antimonopoly sentiment and to resolve some conflicts between different corporate interests.

---

[35] For a more detailed historical account of the Sherman Act and its early enforcement, see Chapter 8.
[36] Douglas F. Dowd, *Modern Economic Problems in Historical Perspective* (Boston: Raytheon/Heath 1965), p. 49.

Government Purchasing Policy

Federal, state, and local governments buy one-quarter to one-third of our national product. Profit rates of corporations selling to government are much higher than the average profit rate. The largest single government purchase is of military supplies, where the most spectacular profits are made. Through this mechanism, government purchasing policies tend to shift income to the corporations and to their rich stockholders. All government spending will be analyzed in detail in Chapter 29.

SUMMARY

The economic power of a comparatively few corporations and individuals, examined in previous chapters, was shown here to result in a disproportionate degree of political power for this group. This is not an accident but a perfectly natural result of their control over the press, television and radio, advertising, financing for political campaigns and for lobbying, foundations, and many other avenues of control open to those with wealth.

Because of this natural influence (not a conspiracy), government policies do not decrease inequality in the American economy. In fact, after considering only the policies that are supposed to reduce inequality (such as taxation, farm subsidies, and education), we can conclude that many of them actually increase the degree of inequality. If we had considered all government policies, the net effect would undoubtedly have been to substantially increase inequality. Given the present sources of political power, it appears very doubtful whether the government will ever take actions that would substantially reduce poverty and inequality.

CHAPTER 21

ECONOMICS OF DISCRIMINATION

Most elementary economics books ignore racial and sexual discrimination as social phenomena outside of economics. These phenomena, however, have political-economic roots and, in turn, affect the economy in important ways.

TYPES OF DISCRIMINATION

In the United States racism involves prejudice and discrimination against many minorities. The most common form is use of an ideology claiming that another race is inferior in order to justify profit-making activity and discrimination against the members of the other race. For example, the white colonists in America declared that the Indians were inferior and then stole their land and almost eliminated them.

Ironically, each succeeding wave of white settlers was met by a form of discrimination called *nationalist* prejudice, which was directed at them by those who were already here. Thus all Eastern Europeans were held to be backward in culture; Italians were all lazy; Irish were all loud and uncouth. Against Chinese and Japanese immigrants there was a combination of nationalist and racist prejudice. During World War II all Americans of Japanese ancestry on the West Coast were confined to concentration camps. (German Americans never were.) Finally, nationalist and racist prejudice also combines to support discrimination against Americans of Mexican and Puerto Rican origin. (Both were incorporated into the United States through imperialist expansion, one group in the war against Mexico and the other in the war against Spain.)

Religious bigotry is another form of discrimination closely related to national chauvinism and racial prejudice; indeed, all are similar both in cause and in effect. In Europe, Protestants and Catholics killed each other for centuries; and in America, the Catholic minority is still subjected to a certain amount of prejudice and discrimination. Much worse, of course, was the many-centuries-long oppression of the Jews, forcibly converted, limited to certain occupations, often taxed to bankruptcy, and periodically massacred. Yet in the late nineteenth and early twentieth centuries, it appeared that anti-Jewish sentiment was dying away; and it has never been as severe in America as in some other countries, although it certainly exists. But just as the Jews began to feel secure, Hitler's fascism unleashed the worst racist atrocity in the history of the world. More than 6 million Jewish men, women, and children were tortured, gassed, and burned to death.

Another racist atrocity was the enslavement of black Africans throughout three centuries and their shipment under horrifying, inhuman conditions to various places of prison and work, especially the American South. This enslavement was not done in the name of Aryan domination, as was Hitler's killing of the Jews and other "inferior" peoples, but in the gentle name of Christianity, it being the white man's burden to bring civilization and the true faith to the black man. One result of this enslavement is that blacks today constitute the largest single minority in the United States, and one of the most oppressed.

When blacks were slaves doing simple agricultural work in the South, racism played its usual function of explaining that blacks were inferior to whites, that slavery was their natural condition, that such simple labor was all they could do, and that they were very happy in this condition. Now that blacks are a large part or a majority in many American cities and do all the complex tasks required to run American industry and urban life, the prejudices have changed somewhat, but the discrimination is as fierce as ever.

Last but not least, there is sexist discrimination against women in America. It will be shown that both the attitudes and the actual discrimination against the female 51 percent of Americans is very similar in nature to the discrimination against racial, national, and religious minorities.

THE IDEOLOGY OF RACISM

The main point of racism is that minority groups are held to be biologically inferior. Racism is called an "ideology" because it is a systematic set of beliefs claiming the superiority of one group to others; it is a "prejudice" in that no amount of evidence can shake these beliefs—and even inconsistent beliefs do not bother the true believers.

Adolf Hitler and his Fascists carried racism to its ultimate in the 1930s, when he proclaimed that white, male, non-Jewish Germans (called "Aryans") were a master race, superior to all other groups. He created a stereotype, or ideal picture, of all Aryans as big, strong, blond, and superintelligent—even though Hitler himself was none of these. His stereotype of the Jew was small, dark, greedy, and cowardly. His stereotype of all other peoples were likewise physically weak and mentally inferior. His stereotype of women had them all stupid and good for nothing but sex and childbearing; Aryan women were also dumb sex-objects, but were beautiful as well. Such stereotypes were not mere harmless nonsense; on this basis Hitler killed millions of Jews and Russians, enslaved hundreds of millions of people, and particularly enslaved all women.

Similarly, slave owners in the U.S. South before the Civil War claimed that all blacks were biologically inferior. The stereotyped blacks were stupid and lazy, shuffled their feet when they walked, but liked to sing and dance (to celebrate their happy life as slaves). The stereotype also said that blacks were oversexed. This stereotype has long provided an excuse for white men to rape black women, while lynching black men for imaginary rapes of white women.

There are still racists who claim that all blacks are mentally inferior. For example, Dr. William Shockley, a white male physicist, claimed in 1973 that in data "from Negro populations with average IQ's of 80 in Georgia and 90 in California that each 1 percent of Caucasian ancestry raises average IQ by one point for these low IQ populations."[1] So the blood of the "master race" raises intelligence! Yet over and over again anthropologists and psychologists have demonstrated that so-called IQ scores are related to socioeconomic status and cultural background (because of the way the tests are designed), but are *not* related to race, religion, national origin, or sex.

Such unscientific stereotypes are common in everyday thinking and strongly affect and harm blacks in occupational and professional roles. The following incident illustrates the awful power of prejudiced stereotypes:

> A young Negro lawyer recently recalled his first case, in which he was called upon to defend a burglar. The thief, white, appeared before the judge dressed as he had been when apprehended by the police, in dirty work clothes, his hair mussed, an unshaven face. The lawyer . . . was neatly dressed in a business suit, was well-shaven, and was carrying a briefcase. The judged looked at both men and asked, unjokingly, "Which man is the lawyer?"[2]

Can you imagine how much attention the judge paid to the black lawyer's arguments?

FACTS OF RACIST DISCRIMINATION

Black families have much lower income than white families. Because of the victories of the militant civil rights movement of the 1960s, the median family income of blacks moved up from 54 percent of white income in 1964 to 61 percent in 1969.[3] Because of white backlash in the early 1970s—under the leadership of Nixon and Ford—median black income fell back to 58 percent in 1975. In fact, black family income in 1975 in terms of real purchasing power was slightly below the 1969 level.

In absolute terms the median black family in 1975 earned $8779, but the Federal government estimates a lower middle-class "intermediate budget for a family of four" at $15,318. So most black families are far below the lowest middle-class income level. In fact, 31 percent of all black families in 1975 were below the official (understated) poverty level of $5500 for an urban family of four. The percentage living in poverty increased from 1974 to 1975 because of the increase in unemployment. (During the good years of the 1960s, the percentage of blacks living in poverty declined from 48 to *only* 28 percent, so the rise back to 31 percent in 1975 represented considerable backsliding).

Even by August 1976, when unemployment had lessened a little, white unemployment was still 7 percent, but black unemployment was almost 14 percent. In the same month white teen-age unemployment was 17 percent, but black teen-age unemployment was still an almost unbelievable 40.2 percent! All of these unemployment figures are official U.S. Labor Department data, but we shall show in Chapter 22 that these official data are drastically understated. The National Urban League calculates that, when discouraged workers and part-time workers who want full-time jobs are counted, the actual unemployment rate in the second quarter of 1976 was 25 percent of all black workers and 64 percent for black

[1] United Press story in *Press-Enterprise*, October 23, 1973, p. A–2.
[2] Quoted in Cynthia Epstein, *Woman's Place* (Berkeley: University of California Press, 1971), p. 190 n.
[3] All data in this section from U.S. government sources, reported in *Newsweek*, October 4, 1976, pp. 73–79.

teen-age workers! The problem is that blacks were fired twice as fast as whites in the 1975 depression but were hired back more slowly than whites.

Even worse off than black males are black females, because they suffer from both racist and sexist discrimination. Whereas the median black family in 1975 earned $8779, the median black female-headed family earned only $4898, or 40 percent less. This median family income was far below the official poverty level of $5500. While some of this was due to unemployment, most black female family heads were very hard working, full-time workers being paid below-poverty wages.

In the political sphere, although blacks comprise 11 percent of the U.S. population, blacks in 1975 were only 3 percent of the U.S. House of Representatives and only 1 percent of the U.S. Senate. In the same year, blacks were only 4 percent of state legislatures, and less than 1 percent of elected city and county officials.[4]

Another basic area of continuing discrimination is in education. By 1974, in the appropriate age groups, only 72 percent of blacks had completed high school, only 18 percent of blacks enrolled in college, and only 8 percent finished 4 years or more of college.[5] By 1974 whites in the same age groups still had much higher educational rates: 85 percent finished high school, 25 percent enrolled in college, and 21 percent finished 4 years or more of college. Most blacks who dropped out of school did so because of economic pressures.

Finally there is continued job segregation against blacks. Black men and women are overrepresented among lowly paid factory workers and domestic servants. Yet in 1970 blacks were still only 5 percent of highly paid professionals, 7 percent of clerical workers, and only 2.6 percent of highly paid managers and administrators.[6]

WHAT CAUSES RACISM?

The most conservative view is now, as always, that there are inherited biological differences, making the blacks (and Mexicans, Indians, Jews, Catholics, ad infinitum) intellectually and physically inferior. The inferiority is the cause of lower income, less educational achievement, and so forth. Moreover, they are lazy and like to live in squalor. Because these arguments are not backed by any scientific evidence and because refutations do not lessen the prejudice one bit, we may leave this view without further comment. Races are, of course, defined by their superficial physical differences, but there are no important biological differences among the races of humankind, much less any inherited intellectual differences.

Most sociologists are liberal enough to admit that blacks are not inherently inferior. They still insist that the problem lies in the minds of blacks and whites. Many assume that all whites have racist attitudes. Many assume that all blacks have attitudes making it more difficult for them to get good jobs, such as "low

[4] See "Voters and Elected Officials," *Economic Notes,* February 1976, pp. 5–6.
[5] See Barbara Becnel, "Profiling the Black Worker, 1976," *AFL-CIO American Federationist* (July 1976), p. 6.
[6] See U.S. Census Report P-60, discussed in "Black Labor Since Reconstruction," *Dollars and Sense,* Summer 1976, p. 15.

aspiration patterns that set limited achievement goals."[7] The traditional sociologists' solution would seem to be that we have to employ an unprejudiced psychoanalyst (from Mars?) to change the attitudes of all whites and blacks through therapy.

Radicals agree that it is a fact that most whites have racist prejudices. It is also a fact that some blacks still have attitudes of inferiority that impede their progress, though most of the reports on black attitudes are myths used to excuse discrimination. It must be emphasized that the discrimination caused by white racism is a thousand times more of a barrier to blacks at present than any remaining black attitudes of inferiority.

But the most important question is, Why do these white racist attitudes persist? Hundreds of comparative studies of other societies show that whites are not born with attitudes of racial superiority and blacks are not born with attitudes of racial inferiority. These attitudes are inculcated by society. They are given to children by the older generation in the family; by the educational system (e.g., in stereotypes in textbooks); by the media (e.g., in stereotypes on TV, in newspapers, books, and magazines); and by political leaders (like George Wallace).

This leads to the next question: Why does the establishment permit and encourage racist stereotypes? Of course, the degree of open stereotyping has been reduced in recent years but only under the pressure of the civil rights movement. It is the contention of radicals that racism plays an important function in supporting the status quo and that the capitalist establishment benefits from it directly and indirectly.

WHO BENEFITS FROM RACISM?

Conservative economists agree with the conservative sociologists that no one benefits from discrimination, that it is merely a matter of irrational and inexplicable tastes or preferences. Conservatives emphasize that discrimination by business is irrational because (so they claim) profits are lost as a result. They argue that if there is discrimination in other areas of the economy, then each capitalist is presented with a supply of qualified blacks willing to work for wages below the going wages. Since the capitalist can purchase these workers at lower wages, more profits could be made by doing so. Therefore, capitalists who are willing to hire blacks (below the going wage) will make more profits, while those who refuse to hire blacks at any wage will lose profits. Thus the conservative Milton Friedman claims,

> a businessman or an entrepreneur who expresses preferences in his business
> activities that are not related to productive efficiency is in effect imposing
> higher costs on himself than are other individuals who do not have such
> preferences. Hence, in a free market they will tend to drive him out.[8]

The conservative economists conclude that the capitalists who discriminate do so for irrational reasons and lose money because of the discrimination. They

---

[7] Louis Ferman, Joyce Kornbluh, and J. Miller, eds. *Negroes and Jobs* (Ann Arbor: University of Michigan Press, 1968).

[8] Milton Friedman, *Capitalism and Freedom* (Chicago: University of Chicago Press, 1962), p. 108.

further argue that under pure competition capitalists who discriminate will eventually be put out of business because of their higher costs per unit. Thus competition will tend to end discrimination and push black wages ever closer to white wage levels.

Most liberal economists seem to agree with most of these premises, which flow from good neoclassical economics. They argue, however, that the U.S. economy is characterized by a high degree of monopoly rather than pure competition. By the exercise of their monopoly power in the labor market and in the commodity market, firms can hold down all wages and pass on to consumers some of the cost of discrimination. In other words, the liberals agree with the conservatives that racism is an inexplicable attitude, but they contend that it costs the capitalist only a little to indulge his strange preference. Therefore, they believe it might be a long time, if ever, before capitalism automatically ended discrimination, so the government should pass reform laws to end discrimination.

Radicals, on the other hand, do not believe that capitalists lose money from discrimination or that their attitudes are inexplicable. How could discrimination continue for such a long time if capitalists lose from it? Capitalists *gain* in many ways from racist discrimination and hence have an interest in continuing it. They gain because (1) racist prejudice divides workers, making unions weaker and resulting in lower wages for all workers; (2) the same division makes capitalist politicians safer from attacks by labor; (3) racist discrimination makes it easy to keep blacks as an unemployed reservoir of cheap labor for boom times; (4) racism provides white politicians with a scapegoat for many social problems; and (5) racism helps inspire soldiers when they are supposed to kill Asians in Vietnam. As a result white capitalists as a whole benefit from racism, though white workers as a whole lose from racism.[9]

Radicals maintain that in the pre-Civil War South racism was a useful apologia for slavery. It meant that the slave owners would have no guilty consciences, the slaves might accept their lot more easily, and the Northerners would not interfere. Racism declared that slavery was divinely ordained by God as a benefit to the inferior black. Thus its first function was to justify economic exploitation.

This function of racism continues today, when apologists contend that black and Chicano workers are poorly paid only because they are inferior workers. More important, to the extent that white workers believe the racist ideology, unions are weakened by excluding black workers—or accepting them reluctantly and keeping them from equal power in unions. White and black workers have frequently broken each others' strikes in the past, though they are now learning to work together. In the areas of strongest racism and weakest unions, such as the South, black workers' wages are very low, but white workers' wages are almost as low. For this reason, one honest liberal economist has concluded, "Far from being indifferent to the existence of discriminatory attitudes on the part of workers, the capitalist gains from them and may find it profitable to invest in their creation."[10]

Another reason that racism is profitable to capitalists is the provision of a handy, but disposable, labor force. If an employer has 10 black and 10 white

[9] This point is fully discussed and proven statistically in Michael Reich, "The Economics of Racism," in David M. Gordon, ed., *Problems in Political Economy* (Lexington, Mass.: Raytheon/Health, 1971).
[10] Morris Silver, quoted in Ray Franklin and Solomon Resnick, *The Political Economy of Racism* (New York: Holt, Rinehart & Winston, 1973), p. 23.

workers, and must fire half for a couple of months, which will he fire? If "he is rational and seeks to minimize his labor turnover costs, he will lay off his ten black workers on the assumption that they will be unlikely to get permanent or better jobs elsewhere because of the discriminatory practices of other employers."[11] Thus the capitalist can (and does) fire black workers in each recession and easily hires them back in times of expansion. He also gains by not paying the fringe benefits due workers who stay on the job for a longer time.

Radicals assert that blacks are exploited within the United States, both as an internal colony and as workers. Blacks today constitute about one-third of the entire industrial labor force and an even larger percentage of unskilled manual laborers. Racial discrimination keeps them "in their place" as a large pool of unskilled and often unemployed workers to be used to hold down wages in times of high demand for labor; racial prejudice justifies that place. Thus racism is in this respect only one more added apologia for considerable extra profits extracted at the expense of the lowest-paid part of the American working class.

Because that exploitation is at the heart of the system, legal reforms cannot give much help to most blacks. Radicals claim that

> the system has two poles: wealth, privilege, power at one; poverty, deprivation, powerlessness at the other. It has always been that way, but in earlier times whole groups could rise because expansion made room above, and there were others ready to take their place at the bottom. Today, Negroes are at the bottom, and there is neither room above nor anyone ready to take their place. Thus only individuals can move up, not the group as such: reforms help the few, not the many. For the many, nothing short of a complete change in the system—the abolition of both poles and the substitution of a society in which wealth and power are shared by all—can transform their condition.[12]

Radicals maintain the political function of racism is to find a scapegoat for all problems. For example, the white is told that the dirt and violence of the modern city is all due to the black. Similarly, Hitler told German workers that unemployment was all due to Jewish bankers, while the middle class was told that all the agitation was due to Jewish communists.

The second political function of racism, according to radicals, is to divide the oppressed so the elite can rule. For example, no one is more oppressed or poverty-stricken than white southern sharecroppers. But they have always fought against their natural allies, the blacks. Instead, the poor white has given political support to the wealthy white southerners who not only monopolize southern state and local politics but also wield disproportionate influence in Congress because they succeed to and hold key committee chairmanships and leadership positions by virtue of seniority. The same kind of divide-and-rule tactic is used in northern cities.

Radicals also claim that racism is a particularly handy tool of imperialism. England especially has long used the strategy of divide and rule: Hindu against Moslem, Jew against Arab, Protestant against Catholic, Biafran against Nigerian, black against Hindu in Guyana. And America is quite willing to use the same tactic: Vietnamese against Cambodian, Thai against Laotian. Moreover, "inferiority" (inherited or acquired) is still being given as a reason for lack of develop-

---

[11] Franklin and Resnick, op. cit., p. 20.
[12] Paul Sweezy and Paul Baran, *Monopoly Capital* (New York: Monthly Review Press, 1966), p. 27.

ment—where imperialism is the real reason. Finally, national chauvinism, or patriotism, always asserts that aggression comes from the other, evil people and that "our" pure motives should not be questioned.

SEXIST IDEOLOGY: STEREOTYPES OF WOMEN

Just as the ideology of racism relies on stereotypes of blacks, the ideology of sexism relies on stereotypes of women. One stereotype of women is that they are all sentimental and impulsive, emotional and foolish; not hard-headed, hard driving, and logical, as in the stereotype of men. For example, former Vice-President Agnew, who was forced to resign because of his criminal activity, says, "Three things have been difficult to tame—the ocean, fools, and women. We may soon be able to tame the ocean; fools and women will take a little longer."[13]

Yet the opposite stereotype of women also exists. She is narrow in vision; interested in little, material things; grasping and evil. For example, the men who wrote the Bible claim: "And the Lord God said unto the woman, What is this that thou has done? And the woman said, The serpent beguiled me, and I did eat." On this basis medieval men stereotyped all women as sly, sharp, aggressive witches.

Of course these two stereotypes are contradictory. How can all women be greedy, sharp, and aggressive and at the same time sentimental and foolish? Such inconsistencies never seem to bother prejudiced people. Neither are racists and sexists bothered by conflicting evidence; they always see things the way they wish to see them: "Thus, an anti-Semite watching a Jew may see devious or sneaky behavior. But in a Christian he would regard such behavior only as quiet, reserved, or perhaps even shy."[14] Since prejudice distorts "evidence," no amount of evidence can change it.

As an example of how prejudiced stereotyping is much too stubborn for evidence, imagine an employer interviewing a series of people for an executive job. Suppose he believes in the usual stereotype of women. Suppose the first woman is sophisticated and careful before speaking. He thinks: She is too passive and "feminine" for the job. Suppose the second woman objects to something he says. He thinks: She is an aggressive bitch. Suppose the third person is a man: he gets the job. In many real cases like this imaginary one, prejudiced stereotypes are not harmless; they lead directly to discrimination.

Above all, sexist stereotypes are intended to justify the domination of women by men. This is very apparent in a statement by Napoleon Bonaparte:

> Nature intended women to be our slaves . . . they are our property, we are not theirs. They belong to us, just as a tree that bears fruit belongs to a gardener. What a mad idea to demand equality for women! . . . Women are nothing but machines for producing children.[15]

Sexism, or the theory of male supremacy, is an ideology that serves to justify discrimination against the majority of Americans. Although sexism is similar in the pattern of discrimination and in ideology to racism, it is more pervasive, more

[13] Quoted in Kirsten Amundsen, *The Silenced Majority* (Englewood Cliffs, N.J.: Prentice-Hall, 1971), p. 114.

[14] Philip Goldberg. in Athena Theodore, ed., *The Professional Woman* (New York: Schenkman Publishers, 1971), p. 168.

[15] Quoted in "Know Your Enemy," in Robin Morgan, ed., *Sisterhood Is Powerful* (New York: Vintage, 1970).

deeply ingrained, and harder to combat. Clearly the black woman is held to be doubly "inferior" and suffers the most discrimination.

SEXIST DISCRIMINATION

Back in 1890 women constituted only 17 percent of the labor force, though many more were unpaid workers on farms owned by their husbands.[16] From this period comes the myth that all women are housewives and play no role in the paid labor force. The myth no longer has even a semblance of truth. By 1940 women were 25 percent of the labor force. In World War II women suddenly became 36 percent of the labor force, then dropped to 28 percent in 1947 as they were pushed out of jobs by returning veterans. Since then, there has been a steady rise till in 1975 women were 40 percent of the labor force.

A majority of all women (54 percent) in the working ages (18 to 64) were in the labor force in 1974. Moreover, 58 percent of all working women were married at that time. So most women work at a paid job. And most women workers really have two jobs, a paid job plus the unpaid job of housewife. Even women with small children now work outside the home; in 1974 54 percent of women with children under 17 were in the labor force.

Working women mostly work for the same reason as men—economic necessity. About 42 percent of women workers were single, divorced, separated, or widowed, so they had no choice but to work. Women head 12 percent of U.S. families, but about half of families living in poverty.

But why are more and more married women working in paid jobs? Because, with inflation, their wages are more and more necessary to attain a minimum decent standard of living. Women work more if they have more years of education and fewer small children. If we look at women with the same education (e.g., 4 years of high school) and the same age level of children (e.g., ages 6 to 17), then we find that the percentage of women working declines as the husband's income level is higher (e.g., from 67 percent working with husband's income level of $3,000 to $5,000—down to 49 percent working with husband's income level at $10,000 and over). In summary 71 percent of all working women are single, divorced, separated, widowed, or have husbands below the $10,000 income level, so they work out of dire need.

Although most women are forced to work outside the home, these jobs pay them less than men workers receive because of discrimination. Figure 21.1 shows that the wage gap is large and has been widening in both absolute and percentage terms for many years. The median full-time, year-round woman worker earned only 65 percent of men's median wages in 1955, but this percentage *dropped* by 1974 to only 57 percent![17] Of course, the discrimination is compounded by racism as well as sexism, so a full-time, year-round black woman worker earned only 54 percent as much as a white male worker in 1974. This wage discrimination is true even in specific professions where everyone has high educational qualifications; for example, in 1970 male economists earned 23 per-

16 All data in this section, unless otherwise stated, comes from an excellent study by U.S. Department of Labor, Women's Bureau, *1975 Handbook on Women Workers* (Washington, D.C.: U.S. GPO, 1975).
17 Data in this paragraph from U.S. Women's Bureau, *The Earnings Gap Between Men and Women* (Washington, D.C.: U.S. GPO, 1976), pp. 6–12.

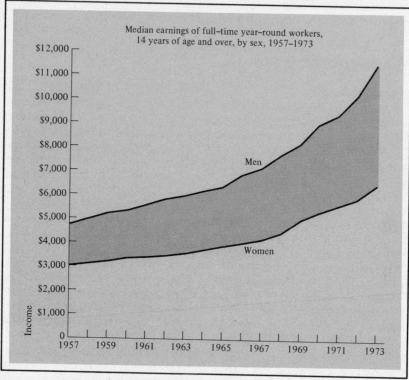

Figure 21.1 **The wage gap between men and women, 1955–1975.** (Source: U.S. Department of Labor, Women's Bureau, *1975 Handbook of Women Workers*, Washington, D.C.: U.S. GPO, 1976, p. 129.)

cent more than female economists; and male mathematicians earned 50 percent more than female mathematicians.

Some of the wage gap is thus caused by direct discrimination within an occupation. Another factor causing the wage gap is discrimination in promotion. For example, in 1973–1974 in all college and university faculties women were 45 percent of the low-paid category of instructors but were only 24 percent of the higher category of assistant professors, only 15 percent of the still higher category of associate professors, and only 9 percent of the highest paid category of professor. The same pattern is true of all occupations. For example, women were 90 percent of all bank tellers, but only 19 percent of bank officers.

The largest single cause of the wage gap, however, is segregation that keeps women out of many high-paying occupations and pushes them into a few low-paying occupations. These low-paying occupations are then relatively overcrowded with the large supply of women workers forced into them, so the employers can continue to pay low wages. Thus in 1973 over 40 percent of all women workers were crowded into just ten narrowly defined occupational groups: secretary (women were 99 percent of the total workers in the occupation), retail trade salesworker (69 percent), bookkeeper (88 percent), private household worker (98 percent), elementary school teacher (85 percent), waitress (83 percent), typist (97 percent), cashier (87 percent), sewer and sticher (96 percent), and registered nurse (84 percent). Men, on the hand, were spread out over a wide range of occupations.

At the other end of the spectrum, women are present in very small numbers in the high-paying occupations and professions. The percentage of women in high-paying jobs did increase in the late 1960s and early 1970s as a result of the women's movement. Pressure from the women's movement achieved the passage of anti-discrimination laws. Propaganda from the women's movement changed the consciousness of men and women and opened up new vistas on possible careers for women. Even with this movement, which caused large increases in the percentages, women in 1973 were only 18 percent of all managers and administrators, and were only 10 percent of all engineering and science technicians (even though the number of women in engineering went from 7,000 to 20,000).

Because of the women's movement—and because of economic necessity—women penetrated the skilled trades, though still in small numbers. Women increased their percentage, from 1960 to 1970, as carpenters (from 0.4 to 1.3 percent), electricians (0.7 to 1.8 percent), plumbers (0.3 to 1.1 percent), and machinists (1.3 to 3.1 percent). For similar reasons, women overcame prejudice in the professions. So from 1960 to 1970 women increased their percentage of all lawyers (from 2 to 5 percent), doctors (7 to 9 percent), and dentists (2 to 3 percent). Moreover, from 1969 to 1973, women increased from 7 to 16 percent of all law students, and women increased from 9 to 15 percent of all medical students.

Yet these are still small numbers of women in the higher-paying professions. The earnings gap between men and women has continued to increase because (1) most new women workers have gone into the poorest-paying occupations, (2) some discrimination in wages for the same jobs continues, (3) and women are still not promoted as often as men.

In addition the total income going to women is reduced because women workers are unemployed in a higher proportion than male workers. In 1975 the unemployment rate for white male workers was 7.2 percent, but it was 8.6 percent for white women workers. Also in 1975, as a result of racism, the unemployment rate for black male workers was 13.7 percent, but it was 14.0 percent for black women workers.[18]

WHAT CAUSES SEXISM?

The ideologies of racism and sexism are similar in many ways. Both are based on the supported inferiority of some groups of human beings to others: "All discrimination is eventually the same thing—Anti-Humanism."[19] Even in the present "enlightened" age, the ideology of sexism continues in unabated fury. Thus the conservative view still justifies lower pay for women: "If a woman were more like

[18] See U.S. Department of Labor and Department of H.E.W., *Employment and Training Report of the President* (Washington, D.C.: U.S. GPO, 1976).
[19] Congressman Shirley Chisholm, "Racism and Anti-Feminism," *The Black Scholar*, January–February 1970, p. 45.

a man, she'd be treated as such."[20] This view ignores the main point: that millions of women get less pay for doing the same work as men.

A more "liberal" statement of sexism comes from Dr. Edgar Benson, member of the Democratic party's Committee of National Priorities (and a close friend of former Vice President Hubert Humphrey), who says "that physical factors, particularly the menstrual cycle and menopause, disqualify women for key executive jobs."[21] Is it not fortunate that instead of nervous females, who might get us into wars and crises like Vietnam and Watergate, we have had our destiny in the hands of a series of calm, masculine politicians?

All tests show that men and women are equal in intelligence, although they usually progress at different rates in childhood learning, with women leading in the early years.

Radicals certainly admit that there are physical differences between men and women. With respect to working ability, however, the evidence indicates that male and female workers are equal on the average. In fact, in some primitive societies women normally carry heavier loads then men. The question is one of training and expectations. Listen to the lot of a slave woman of the American South as stated by the great black abolitionist Sojourner Truth: "Look at my arm! I have ploughed and planted and gathered into barns, and no man could head me—and ain't I a woman? I have borne thirteen children, and seen most of 'em sold into slavery, and when I cried out with my mother's grief, none but Jesus heard me—and ain't I a woman?"[22]

Even in social and sexual matters, in the radical view, it is not a given, eternal fact that man must always dominate. In some primitive societies men and women appear to have about equal social and sexual roles. This is especially true in societies in which the economic roles of the two are roughly equal in importance, as when women gather wild food and men hunt. In other primitive societies, in which women conduct agriculture and hunting is unimportant, women appear to play the dominant role. If nothing else can be said without controversy, at least modern anthropology makes clear that there are many types of family organization (including various kinds of group marriages), not just one eternal type.

Only with the coming of civilization—meaning economic stratification and the possession of property in land, cattle, slaves, or serfs—does the woman also become a piece of property. In fact, for purposes of clear inheritance of property the woman of the upper class in ancient civilizations was very well guarded; only the male could freely violate the theoretical monogamy system. This was the beginning of the double standard.

The particular attitudes of American men and women are carefully inculcated, not inherited. "Women are taught from the time they are children to play a serving role, to be docile and submissive. . . ."[23] These attitudes are taught by the family, the schools, the media, the church, corporations, and the government—in which white males are usually dominant.

[20] Angus Black, *A Radical's Guide to Economic Reality* (New York: Holt, Rinehart and Winston, 1970), p. 37.

[21] Quoted in the *San Francisco Chronicle*, July 27, 1970, p. 9.

[22] Quoted in Bird, op. cit., p. 25.

[23] Marilyn Goldberg, "The Economic Exploitation of Women," *The Review of Radical Political Economics,* Spring 1970, p. 35.

It has often been said that the position of women in a society mirrors the general condition of human rights in a society. Even in the nineteenth century, the connection was pointed out to those radicals who wished to ignore it: "Every socialist recognized the dependence of the workmen on the capitalist . . . but the same socialist often does not recognize the dependence of women on men because the question touches his own dear self more or less clearly."[24] In the twentieth century, the ideology of women's inferiority reached its high point in Nazi Germany. The Nazi directive to women was to be with "children, kitchen, and church."

WHO BENEFITS FROM SEXISM?

As in the case of racism, conservative economists argue that capitalists actually lose by discriminating against qualified women. Such discrimination, they say, means paying men for a job that women could do equally well for less pay.

The Establishment economist Barbara Bergmann repeats this argument:

> We come . . . to the allegation, usually made by radicals out to discredit capitalism, that women's subjection is all a capitalist plot. Who benefits financially from maintenance of the *status quo?* The most obvious beneficiaries of prejudice against women are male workers in those occupations in which women are not allowed to compete. . . . It is not the male workers or their wives who do the discriminating, however. The employers of the male workers (almost entirely males themselves) are the ones who do the actual discriminating, although of course they are cheered on in their discriminatory ways by their male employees. The employers actually tend to lose financially since profits are lowered when cheap female help is spurned in favor of high-priced male help.[25]

So in her view it is not the capitalists but only the male workers who gain from discrimination. The poor capitalists, who actually do the discriminating, lose by it. But why do capitalists in business for profits systematically choose to lose money? She says they lose financially but gain psychologically: "It feels so good to have women in their place." Neither she nor any one else with this view answers the obvious question: If it causes financial losses (even small ones), why hasn't such discrimination tended to decline and disappear under capitalism?

The truth is, according to radicals, that capitalists do not merely gain psychologically while incurring losses from sex discrimination. On the contrary, capitalists gain from sexism both in power and in *profits.* Moreover, all workers, male as well as female, lose from sexist attitudes.

How do capitalists make profit from sexism? Obviously they use it as an excuse to pay women lower wages. More important, sexist prejudice divides male and female workers, making it more difficult to organize strong unions. In the United States one of every four men workers are unionized, but only one of every seven women workers. The prejudice of union men is apparent in the fact that women constitute 20 percent of all union members but less than 1 percent of all union executive board members. Even in unions like the International Ladies Garment Workers Union, which is over 75 percent female, only a few tokens are

[24] Statement by August Bebel, *Women and Socialism* (New York: Schocken, 1971, originally 1892).
[25] Barbara Bergmann, "Economics of Women's Liberation," *Challenge* 16 (May/June 1973): 14.

on the executive board. Furthermore, in the past unions have done little, if anything, for women's specific grievances and have even joined employers in agreements for lower wages and worse job categories for women.

Union men often pay for their prejudices in broken unions and lower wages. For example, "Standard Oil workers in San Francisco recently paid the price of male supremacy. Women at Standard Oil have the least chance for advancement and decent pay, and the union has done little to fight this. Not surprisingly, women formed the core of the back to work move that eventually broke the strike."[26] Because it reduces union bargaining strength, sexism causes lower wages for *both* men and women. The evidence shows that in areas where most of the labor force is female the pay for both men and women is lower than average, even though the workers in many of those areas have higher qualifications (shown in more education) than the average worker. An excellent piece of research has shown this for all the clerical occupations in which women predominate. (See Table 21.1)

Table 21.1 **Education and Income of Clerical Workers, 1960**
(all data for full-time, year-round workers;
all occupations listed have at least 51 percent women)

Clerical Occupation	Percent that median education in occupation is above median education of all U.S. male workers		Percent that median wage in occupation is below (or above) median of all U.S. male workers	
	Men	Women	Women	Men
Library Attendants and Assistants	+23%	+18%	-46%	-45%
Doctors, Dentists, Office Attendants	+12	+12	-47	-32
Bank Tellers	+14	+12	-37	-16
Bookkeepers	+14	+12	-36	-11
File Clerks	+12	+10	-41	-25
Office Machine Operators	+13	+12	-32	-4
Payroll clerks	+13	+12	-27	0
Receptionists	+13	+13	-29	-23
Secretaries	+15	+14	-29	+5
Stenographers	+14	+14	-30	+2
Typists	+13	+13	-36	-20
Telephone Operators	+11	+10	-33	+7
Cashiers	+8	+8	-47	-22
Other Clerical Workers	+12	+12	-34	-1

Source: Derived from Valerie Oppenheimer, *The Female Labor Force,* Population Monograph Series no. 5 (Berkeley: University of California, 1970)

[26] Kathy McAfee and Myrna Wood, "Bread and Roses," in Roberta Salper, ed., *Female Liberation* (New York: Knopf, 1972), p. 156.

The table shows that in these occupations women's education is far above the median of U.S. workers, but their wages are far below. Moreover, the same is true of the men in these predominantly female occupations; their education is much above, while their wages are much below the U.S. median. Therefore, *sexist discrimination not only hurts female workers but also hurts male workers*—and the lower wages produce higher profits.

In addition to weak unions, another reason for low wages in the predominantly female occupations is that women are systematically excluded from other occupations and pushed into these. Such segregation causes overcrowding or oversupply in the areas where women are allowed to work, thereby lowering wages in these jobs. Some economists admit that males in these occupations will be hurt, but they argue that males in other occupations will have higher wages because the exclusion of women lowers labor supply. Thus they claim that some male workers may gain from sexism. This is partially true, but it ignores the weakening of unions in all areas and the other unfavorable sociopolitical effects for all workers mentioned below. It might also be noted that the sectors employing mostly white males are sectors with strong monopoly power, where higher wages are passed along in higher prices to all consumers.

Again, like blacks, women have a much higher unemployment rate. This is partly because the boss knows they can't easily get other jobs because of discrimination. So the boss can keep a core of skilled white males but hire (cheaply) blacks and women from the army of unemployed when they are needed most at peak seasons. Thus the capitalist also avoids paying women fringe benefits, which accrue only to workers employed for a long time.

The glorification of housework can also be profitable. In the words of one male advertiser, "property manipulated . . . American housewives can be given the sense of identity, purpose, creativity, the self-realization, even the sexual joy they lack—by the buying of things."[27] Thus advertisers use the sexist ideology to instill "consumerism" in women. The sexist image of the good woman shows her in her kitchen surrounded by the very latest gadgets, with the best cake mix, made up with miracle cosmetics. Commercials imply that she is a failure if her floors are not the shiniest and her laundry the whitest in the neighborhood. This image helps business sell billions of dollars of useless (or even harmful) goods.

Sexism is also profitable because women's unpaid work in the home is crucial to provision of the needed supply of labor. Housework is equivalent to about one-fourth of the GNP, though it is not counted in the GNP. If business had to pay women in full to raise and clean and cook for the labor force, it would seriously reduce profits. The labor of women as housewives is vital to industry; there would be no labor force without it, yet it goes unpaid. Furthermore, women in the family are not only profitable to capitalism through their unpaid material labor but perhaps even more in the psychological jobs that women (under sexist conditioning) do in the family. The woman in the sexist family helps provide "good" workers: "A woman is judged as a wife and mother—the only role she is allowed—according to her ability to maintain stability in her family and to help her family 'adjust' to harsh realities. She therefore transmits the values of hard work and conformity to each generation of workers. It is she who forces her children to stay in school and 'behave' or who urges her husband not to risk his job by

27 Quoted in Betty Friedan, *The Feminine Mystique* (New York: Dell, 1963), p. 199.

standing up to the boss or going on strike."[28] Moreover, as a result of their dependent role in the sexist family, women themselves are socialized to be passive, submissive, and docile as workers.

The last, but not the least, important profit to capitalism from sexism comes in its increased support for political stability. On the one hand, the woman's psychological role in the sexist family has the same effects politically as economically: (1) It tends to make her more fearful and conservative, and (2) she tends to influence her husband in this direction and (3) to pass it on to her son and, especially, to her daughter. Sexism is also used as a political divide-and-rule tactic much like racism. White politicans blame all urban problems on blacks. Secretary of the Treasury Schultz during the Nixon administration blamed unemployment (and accompanying pressure for low wages) on the competition of women workers. Thus conservative politicians try to make women a scapegoat for men's problems instead of an ally against the system.

LIBERATION MOVEMENTS

Discrimination means terrible socioeconomic conditions for many minority groups. These poor conditions have led to strong protest and liberation movements by many minority groups, such as blacks, Chicanos, and Indians. There are reform groups, such as the National Association for the Advancement of Colored People, who believe laws against discrimination can achieve equality under capitalism. There are also radical groups, such as the Black Panthers, who do not believe full equality is possible under capitalism but want to see an entirely new, restructured system to achieve full equality in a democratic socialist society.

The same reformer-versus-radical split exists among groups favoring women's liberation. There are many reforms on which all of those fighting against sexism can agree. For example, we need free child care centers, equal pay for equal work, equal access to all education, equal access to equal kinds of jobs, free birth control information and devices so that women can determine when they wish to have children, and as a last resort, free and legal abortions when necessary.

The problem is that it is unlikely that these reforms will change basic attitudes, nor is it clear that all these reforms can actually be achieved under capitalism. It is a fact that the lower wages of women are a source of additional profit. Perhaps even more important, it is a fact that the submissive attitude of women, encouraged by church and television alike, serves as an important prop to the status quo. There are thus strong and vested interests in favor of maintaining the ideology of male supremacy and the practice of sexual discrimination so long as capitalism exists.

SUMMARY

National, religious, and racial discrimination exist in America against blacks, Mexican and Puerto Rican Americans and other "ethnic groups," American Indi-

[28] McAfee and Wood, op. cit., p. 156.

ans, Japanese and Chinese Americans, Catholics, and Jews. The well-documented oppression against blacks is very severe in housing, education, jobs, health, and every other area of life (and even in death; there are segregated cemeteries). The racist ideology against blacks originated as an apology for slavery, but it continues as an apology for low wages, high ghetto rents, exclusion of blacks from the political process in the South and elsewhere, and many other profitable reasons for maintaining racist myths.

Prejudice and discrimination against women are much older, having been present in many previous societies. American women continue to suffer from fewer educational opportunities, fewer job opportunities, lower pay for the same jobs, and a sexist ideology that says they are inferior. The ideology and discriminatory patterns continue to be supported, in part, because some important interests find them very profitable.

Women as well as blacks, Chicanos, and other minorities have organized liberation movements. They are achieving some limited reforms under capitalism. Their more radical groups are also playing a major role in the fight for a better—equalitarian and socialist—society.

PART THREE

UNEMPLOYMENT AND INFLATION:

An Introduction to Macroeconomics

CHAPTER 22

AGGREGATE PROBLEMS:
Unemployment and Inflation

Inflation means rising average prices. Unemployment means willing and able workers with no jobs. Never before in U.S. history have Americans suffered from both unemployment and inflation at the same time. It was first noted on a small scale in the 1950s and 1960s but became most dramatic in the depressions of 1970 and 1975.

A depression is a large downturn in output and employment. A recession is a small downturn in output and employment. Since no one agrees on what is "small" or "large" in this context, the terms are best defined by means of an ancient, but accurate, old joke: A "recession" is when the other guy is out of work; a "depression" is when you are out of work. Some apologists for the present government prefer to call a depression by a more euphemistic term like "rolling readjustment." Whatever the term, it hides a lot of human misery.

HISTORY OF UNEMPLOYMENT IN THE U.S. ECONOMY

Alternating periods of expansion and decline of output and employment—called business cycles—have occurred regularly in the United States for over 150 years. The very earliest cycles were clearly tied to events abroad. In its infancy, from 1776 to 1840, the American economy depended heavily on the export trade to Europe. The country prospered with every quickening in the flow of ships and goods from Atlantic ports. When this flow was interrupted, distress in the coastal towns persisted until some new stimulus brought a return of strong demand for American shipping. Most profits came from commerce, and large foreign commerce at that. It was in commerce and shipping that the most important capital investment was occurring. Therefore, between 1800 and 1815, a remarkably close correlation existed between the demand for American exports and the health of the American economy as a whole.[1] In 1836, when European economic

[1] See W. B. Smith and A. H. Cole, *Fluctuations in American Business, 1790-1860* (Cambridge, Mass.: Harvard University Press, 1935).

activity declined and the American expansion faltered, Europeans sold many of their holdings and withdrew their funds, intensifying the major depression that followed.

After 1840 foreign influence persisted, but the course of the economy was increasingly shaped by the domestic environment. By midcentury American business cycles were more clearly internally generated; a pattern of fluctuation characteristic of modern capitalist economies had set in. In the nineteenth century, depressions or recessions began in 1857, 1860, 1865, 1869, 1873, 1882, 1887, 1893, 1895, and 1899. The twentieth century witnessed depressions or recessions beginning in 1902, 1907, 1910, 1913, 1918, 1920, 1923, 1926, 1929, 1937, 1945, 1948, 1953, 1957, 1960, 1969, and 1973. There has been a somewhat regular pattern of expansion and contraction in business activity. The average business cycle of peacetime expansion and contraction lasts about 45 months. The economy always expands in wartime, so cycles with a war are much longer. In the majority of cycles, the expansion lasted much longer than the following contraction, but there have been several lengthy contractions.

During the period of American industrialization (1870s through 1920s) ". . . millions lived in abject poverty in densely packed slums . . . They struggled merely to maintain their families above the level of brutal hunger and want for such little pay that their status was a tragic anomaly in light of the prosperity enjoyed by business and industry."[2] Prosperity was enjoyed by business and industry in most years. Output, productivity, and profits all climbed impressively. Yet the last decades of the nineteenth century saw frequent periods of distress and depression. From 1873 to 1879, thousands of small businesses failed, farms were lost to foreclosure, and the accumulated savings of thousands of families, caught by bank failure, disappeared. Estimates of unemployment during the long depression that began in 1873 range from 1 to 3 million. When recovery came in the 1880s, output expanded more rapidly than at any other time in U.S. history, and yet the decade was interrupted by three years of depression. Vigorous expansion did not return to the economy until late in the 1890s; the depression of the early 1890s is generally regarded as the most severe on record prior to the Great Depression. Over 4.5 million workers, or almost 20 percent of the labor force, were unemployed in 1894 and unemployment remained high until 1899.[3]

The inadequacies and deficiencies of the banking community and of the monetary system operated to aggravate the mild as well as the severe cyclic disturbances, not only in the nineteenth century, but also well into the twentieth century. As the economy matured, the frequency of banking crises accelerated. Precipitous monetary failures occurred in 1873, 1874, 1890, 1893, and again in 1907.

World War I brought economic expansion. It was followed, however, by the severe depression of 1920–1921. Production fell by 20 percent and employment dropped 11 percent within a year (Figure 22.1).

The rebound out of the 1921 trough was a strong one, and notwithstanding the downturns of 1923–1924 and 1926–1927, the 1920s were growth years. Major

[2] Foster R. Dulles, quoted in Richard O. Boyer and Herbert Morais, *Labor's Untold Story* (New York: Marzani & Munsell, 1955), p. 34.

[3] See Stanley Lebergott, *Manpower in Economic Growth: The American Record Since 1800* (New York: McGraw-Hill, 1964).

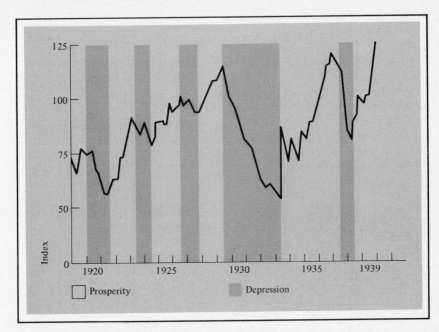

Figure 22.1   **Index of industrial production, 1919–1939 (seasonally adjusted; base: 1935–1939 = 100).** (Source: Federal Reserve Board, reprinted in U.S. Department of Commerce, Bureau of the Census, *Historical Statistics of the United States, 1789–1945*, Washington, D.C.: GPO, 1949, p. 330. Depression dates from the National Bureau of Economic Research.)

advances in productivity took place, employment was high, and prices were steady or gently falling. Major new industries led the expansion. Automobile production tripled during the decade, making up one-eighth of the value of manufacturing by 1929. The automobile's stimulus to the construction, steel, glass, rubber, oil, retail trade, and service industries led to widespread increases in production. These were boom years for new housing and business construction as well. Radio was a growth industry, while production of other consumer durables reached record levels.

In October 1929 the stock market collapsed. It would be difficult to support a view that the stock market break was the basic cause of the depression of the 1930s. Manufacturing had begun to falter at least three months earlier, and the construction industry had been depressed for almost two years. But the collapse of the stock market was spectacular. Buyers for securities vanished as everyone rushed to sell. Debts that could not be paid encompassed the lenders in the downward spiral of asset values. Moreover, the loss of wealth was being matched by the loss of income as prices, sales, and production continued to fall. There were signs that the debacle had ended in early 1931, but instead of beginning to recover, the downward momentum suddenly quickened. By 1933 at least 25 percent of the labor force was unemployed. The homeless, the hungry, and the desperate were never fully counted. The economy improved slightly until 1938, when it took another plunge downward. Full employment was restored only by the all-out war spending of World War II.

Table 22.1 **Timing of Business Cycles in the United States since 1949**

Standard Reference Dates			
Monthly		Quarterly	
Trough	Peak	Trough	Peak
Oct. 1949	July 1953	4-1949	3-1953
Aug. 1954	July 1957	3-1954	3-1957
Apr. 1958	May 1960	2-1958	2-1960
Feb. 1961	Nov. 1969	1-1961	4-1969
Nov. 1970	Nov. 1973	4-1970	4-1973
March 1975	—	1-1975	—

Sources: U.S. Department of Commerce, *Business Conditions Digest* (monthly). Method of dating first proposed by Wesley Mitchell and Arthur Burns, *Measuring Business Cycles* (New York: National Bureau of Economic Research, 1946)

Since World War II the American economy has been plagued by instability, although depressions approaching the seriousness of the Great Depression have been avoided. Several small recessions of the 1950s were followed by prolonged prosperity in the 1960s, but in 1969 another recession hit the economy. In 1974–1975 the economy suffered from the worst and longest depression since the 1930s, with unemployment officially recorded over 9 percent.

Table 22.1 records the dates of business cycle peaks and troughs since World War II. A *trough* is the low point of business activity and employment. A *peak* is the highest point of business activity and employment. A *business cycle* is defined as the expansion of business activity from initial trough to peak *plus* the following contraction of business activity from peak to final trough.

THE MISERY OF UNEMPLOYMENT

Even in minor depressions, millions of people are unemployed and suffer extreme deprivation; for example, cases of malnutrition were found in 1975 among families of those long unemployed. For the society as a whole, recessions and depressions mean periods of unused resources, lower output and employment, and a much slower long-run rate of growth. Many attempts have been made to calculate the amount of loss to society for unemployment. One careful estimate put the total loss for the years 1953 to 1972 at 45 million labor-years, valued at $1.8 trillion in 1970 dollars.[4] A *labor-year* is the amount of work one person can produce in a year. If these calculations were extended back to cover all the depressions in U.S. economic history, the total loss would be astronomical.

[4] Leon Keyserling, "What's Wrong with American Economics," *Challenge* vol. 16 (May/June 1973), pp. 18–25.

Depressions and economic instability have other effects, however, that cannot be calculated in economic terms. There are sociological effects, as reflected in population growth, higher divorce rates, crime, physical and mental ill health, and even suicide rates.[5] If few resort to suicide, the total effect is nonetheless incalculably great on all who lose jobs, small businesses, or farms; who wander about on an enforced "vacation" with meager subsistence provided by private or public charities; who find all of their previous plans destroyed.

Even in the Great Depression, most unemployed workers tortured themselves with the idea that each of them, individually, was at fault:

> The suddenly-idle hands blamed themselves, rather than society. True, there were hunger marches and protestations to City Hall and Washington; but the millions experienced a private kind of shame when the pink slip came. No matter that others suffered the same fate, the inner voice whispered, "I'm a failure."[6]

Unemployment thus caused millions of individual tragedies as well as vast social wastefulness.

Conservatives do a lot of shouting about "law and order," yet they ignore the causes of crime—unemployment being one of the most prominent. Tom Wicker noted,

> In 1974, as a declining economy progressively forced people out of work, the rate of crime rose by 17 percent nationally, compared to a rise of only 0.75 percent in 1973. The rate of violent crime doubled, the rate of property crime tripled, and . . . [a] link to rising unemployment was suggested.[7]

What suggested the link between crime and unemployment to Wicker were three facts. Those cities that had the largest increases in unemployment also had the largest increases in crime. Those months that had the largest increases in unemployment also had the largest increases in crime. Finally, the type of crime that increased most was the type most likely to be committed by a poor, unemployed person, that is, street crimes of muggings and robberies for small sums of money. Nor is the relation between unemployment and crime purely economic; the unemployed are angry and frustrated and live in a society where affluence is flaunted at them every day.

When a newspaper casually mentions that 7 million Americans want to work but cannot find jobs, these are not just 7 million statistics but 7 million afflicted individuals. If a large firm closes down or moves to a new location, it leaves behind engineers and executives suddenly reduced from a useful job at $400 a week to enforced idleness on unemployment compensation, as well as a large number of unskilled workers with no future prospects. At times whole mining towns seem to lose animation, and hundreds of miners' wives line up at soup kitchens and welfare departments for food allotments. In the "prosperous" year of 1959, a 38-year-old unemployed auto worker represented millions of others when he said, "I've been looking for work all over but I can't get a job. I hate

---

[5] For the Great Depression of the 1930s, there is an immense literature on each area; for an overall study of the effects of earlier business cycles, see D. C. Thomas, *Social Aspects of the Business Cycle* (New York: Knopf, 1927).

[6] Studs Terkel, *Hard Times: An Oral History of the Great Depression* (New York: Pantheon Books, 1970), p. 5.

[7] Tom Wicker, "Unemployment and Crime," *New York Times*, April 25, 1975, p. 33.

being on welfare. It's enough to make a man jump into the river."[8] When the majority of the people are working for good wages, very few really want to subsist as a useless stick of wood on a few dollars a week.

In the depressed years 1974 and 1975, there were hundreds of published reports of individual hardship cases. To cite two at random:

> In Athens, Ohio, Jonathan Patrick, an unemployed musician, tried to earn a living by selling flowers on the street, but he found that few people had the money to buy them. He said, "When people can't enjoy a flower, something is wrong, deep down. People say they don't have the money, or they pretend not to see, or they hurry by and look away."[9]

Skilled, well-paid workers are also caught by the depression.

> Robert Cleland, age 26, was a draftsman at Chrysler in Detroit. He has a wife, two children, a new house, a car, and many payments to make. In February 1975, he was unemployed and said: "Once upon a time, I believed in the American Dream. Everything I have, I earned by long hard work, and now it seems a total hassle to hang onto it. The good things of the dream are slipping away. You're damn right there's a depression."[10]

The depression of 1974–1975 put many white middle-class suburban families on food stamps for the first time. Many, many small businesses went bankrupt. Many small farmers were forced off the land.[11]

THE TRUE EXTENT OF UNEMPLOYMENT

Table 22.2 lists the official U.S. government estimates of maximum unemployment in various depressions.

The official data are horrifying enough, since every unemployed individual is a tragedy, but these data drastically understate the real amount of unemployment. Let us examine the unemployment data in detail for the trough of the 1974–1975 depression.

The officially recorded unemployment rate for the second quarter of 1975 was 8.8 percent. For the entire second quarter of 1975, there were 92,575,000 persons in the labor force including 84,384,000 employed and, officially, 8,191,000 unemployed (or 8.8 percent).[12] There were also 58,358,000 persons *not* in the labor force. Any reader of these statistics must be curious as to why over 58 million of the 151 million adult population are not in the labor force. According to the Labor Department survey most of that 58 million do not want a job now; however, some do want a job but are simply too discouraged to look for a job (at least, they had not looked in the last four weeks of the survey). It breaks down this way: 58,358,000 not in the labor force = 53,353,000 who do not want a job

[8] Reported in an excellent survey by A. H. Raskin, "People Behind Statistics: A Study of the Unemployed," *New York Times,* March 16, 1959, p. 1.

[9] This case is taken from among many in the excellent article by Associated Press writer Victoria Graham, printed in *Riverside Press-Enterprise,* February 9, 1975, p. C1.

[10] Ibid., p. C2.

[11] Ibid., p. C2.

[12] All data from U.S. Department of Labor, Bureau of Labor Statistics, *Employment and Earnings,* July 1975. Data for all persons 16 years and over, seasonally adjusted.

now + 5,156,000 who want a job but are too discouraged to look. When asked why they do not want a job now, the 53 million said,

attending school	6,291,000
ill, disabled	4,780,000
keeping house	31,438,000
retired	7,607,000
other	3,237,000
Total	53,353,000

Some of these reasons, such as "keeping house," are clearly the result of social conditioning, but let us accept all of these people as voluntarily not working.

That leaves the suspicious category of over 5 million "discouraged" workers not counted in the labor force. This category is particularly suspicious because it always rises in recessions and depressions, so it automatically lowers the unemployment rate. For example, in the fourth quarter of 1973 at the peak of the expansion, there were 4,349,000 discouraged workers, but as the depression continued, the number of discouraged grew by 837,000. For this reason, strange things can happen in the official statistics. For example, from January to February 1975, the number of people employed at jobs declined by one-half million, yet there was no change in the unemployment rate. The reason is that the official labor force shrank by the same amount. *The New York Times* explained this apparent lack of increase in the official unemployment rate by saying that

... There was a decline in the number of people at work in February, but the unemployment rate remained static because about 580,000 already jobless persons stopped looking for work last month, in many cases because they felt

Table 22.2 **History of Unemployment**

Depression Years	Officially Reported Maximum Unemployment
1926—1927	4%
1929—1933	25
1937—1938	20
1945—1946	4
1948—1949	8
1953—1954	6
1957—1958	8
1960—1961	7
1969—1970	6
1974—1975	9%

Source: U.S. Department of Labor, all except last reported in Geoffrey Moore, "Recession?" *Economic Outlook USA*, Vol. 1 (Summer 1974), p. 4. Annual rate in worst month of each depression.

there were no jobs to be found. . . . the government did not count them statistically as unemployed.[13]

If unemployment can be solved no other way, it can always be solved by redefining the statistics.

The Labor Department also asked the over 5 million discouraged workers why they had given up looking for a job. Reasons for not looking were

school attendance	1,394,000
ill health, disability	631,000
home responsibilities	1,135,000
think cannot get a job	1,153,000
other	873,000
Total	5,186,000

Remember that all of these 5-million-plus discouraged workers *want* a job now! Clearly, the 1,153,000 who did not look (mostly after many months of looking) because they "thought they cannot get a job" should be counted as unemployed. If they are included in the labor force as unemployed, then the quarterly rate rises from the official 8.8 percent to 10 percent. This is a very minimal adjustment.

The government, however, only recorded this answer of complete discouragement if no other answer was given. Since all these workers want a job now, "school attendance" meant answers like "I couldn't find a job so I went back to school." The euphemism of "home responsibilities" meant "there aren't any jobs for secretaries, so I'm keeping house now." Therefore, it would seem more accurate to say that *all* these discouraged workers were involuntarily unemployed. If they are all classified as in the labor force and unemployed, then the unemployment rate goes from the official 8.8 percent to 13.7 percent (or 13,777,000 people). This figure represents the maximum adjustment for discouraged workers but still leaves out other causes for the official understatement of unemployment.

The second largest cause for the official understatement is the peculiar handling of part-time workers. In the second quarter of 1975, the Labor Department found 79 million full-time and 13.5 million part-time employed, but the department states: "persons on part-time schedules for economic reasons are included in the full-time employed."[14] What does the term *economic reasons* mean? By economic reasons the department means that people wanting full-time jobs could only get part-time jobs because the economy was in such a bad condition. So the department's statement really says "persons on part-time schedules who wanted, but were unable to get, full-time jobs are included in the full-time employed." Peculiar indeed!

According to the Labor Department's own data, in the second quarter of 1975 an average of 3,878,000 persons could find only part-time work "for economic reasons," though they desired full-time work.[15] The average hours worked by

[13] "The Labor Force Is Shrinking Drastically," *The New York Times*, March 9, 1975.
[14] U.S. Department of Labor, op. cit., p. 51.
[15] This was the average for April, May, and June. See U.S. Department of Labor, op. cit., May, June, and July 1975.

these people were only 21 a week, or about half the full-time work week. Therefore, they should be counted as half-employed, an average of 1,939,000 additional unemployed. With this correction alone, the unemployment rate rises from
an official 8.8 percent to 10.9 percent.

From these two adjustments, then, we can examine a minimum and maximum
statement of unemployment for the second quarter of 1975.

Table 22.3 reveals that the official unemployment rate of 8.8 percent for the
second quarter of 1975 should be raised to 12 percent on a very conservative
adjustment, an increase of almost half. A more realistic adjustment reveals an
unemployment rate of 15.7 percent, or almost double the official figure.

Unfortunately, even the maximum correction does not necessarily correct all
the downward biases in the Labor Department unemployment data. The department treats as fully employed many *unpaid* family workers. In the peak expansion
year of 1973, there were still 1.6 million unpaid family workers, including 700,000
in agriculture.[16] This phenomenon of work without pay in the family unit—because no other job is available—is called *disguised unemployment.* The person
usually adds little or nothing to the family income (for example, on a very small
farm) but shares in that small income. During a depression, disguised unemployment always increases as more people are forced to share the limited family
resources, and final figures for 1975 will show a large increase in this category.

The averages at a given time also hide the extent of the spread of insecurity
among workers. In the peak business year of 1973, the official unemployment
rate was 4.9 percent, but some 14.2 percent of all workers were unemployed for

Table 22.3 **Corrected Unemployment Rate**
(2nd Quarter of 1975, seasonally adjusted)

Minimum Correction	
1. Official unemployment	8,191,000 (or 8.8%)
2. Involuntary part-time unemployment	1,939,000
3. Minimum adjustment for discouraged	1,153,000
Minimum corrected unemployed	11,283,000
12.0% unemployed = 11,283,000/93,728,000 (in labor force)	

Maximum Correction	
1. Official unemployment	8,191,000
2. Involuntary part-time unemployment	1,939,000
3. Maximum adjustment for discouraged	5,186,000
Maximum corrected unemployed	15,315,000
15.7% unemployed = 15,315,000/97,761,000 (in labor force)	

Source: U.S. Department of Labor, *Employment and Earnings,* July 1975.
Note: Another extremely useful set of estimates of unemployment and underemployment are
presented in David Gordon, "Counting the Underemployed," in David Gordon, ed., *Problems
in Political Economy* (Lexington, Mass: D.C. Heath, 1977, 2nd ed.), pp. 70-75.

[16] U.S. Department of Labor, *Manpower Report of the President,* April 1975, p. 274.

some period during the year.[17] If the same ratio holds true in 1975, we may expect 25 to 30 percent of all workers to suffer a period of unemployment at some time during the year.

UNDEREMPLOYMENT

There is also what some economists call subemployment or underemployment. Because of general wide-spread unemployment, a skilled person may accept an unskilled job at low pay if that is all that is available. The threat of unemployment holds millions of workers to very low pay at jobs below their qualifications. Final data on 1972, a year of expansion and relatively low unemployment, reveal that there were 6 million full-time employed workers who earned less than the government's own official poverty standard.[18] In the depression years of 1974 and 1975 (with the added burden of inflation) the position of the working poor became considerably worse.

Underemployment means that millions of unskilled workers work full-time but are paid below the poverty level. Underemployment means that millions of skilled workers must work in unskilled jobs far below their capacity. Finally, underemployment means that hundreds of thousands of college graduates work at jobs requiring almost no education. For example,

> In one case in 1975 Jim Stephens (a fictitious name, but a real case) earned his bachelor's degree in biology. He was unable to gain immediate acceptance to the limited number of spots in medical schools, so he tried to get work as a lab technician. Since it was the middle of the depression, he was unable to get even a lab technician job. Therefore, he became a cab driver.[19]

A survey of placement services found that among the college graduates of 1975, many architecture B.A.s became construction assistants, many English B.A.s have been reduced to clerical work, some people with education degrees have been forced to work in factories (because cities and states are too cheap to employ more teachers), and a few Ph.D.s have been discovered working as bartenders. A year after the 1974 graduation 27 percent of the graduates "said they had more education than their jobs required and 24 percent said their work didn't make use of their skills."[20] This high rate of underemployment of college graduates continued into 1977.[21]

UNEMPLOYMENT OF MINORITIES AND WOMEN

All women and both sexes in many minority groups—including blacks, Chicanos, Puerto Ricans, Jews, Italians, Irish, and many others—suffer discrimination in the

---

[17] Ibid., p. 274.

[18] See Thomas Vietorisz, R. Mier, and B. Harrison, "Full Employment at Living Wages," *The American Annals of Political and Social Science* (March, 1975). Also see the very clear analysis of unemployment and subemployment in Paul Sweezy and Harry Magdoff, "Capitalism and Unemployment," *Monthly Review*, vol. 27, June 1975, pp. 1-130.

[19] G. G. LaBelle, Associated Press release, *Riverside Press-Enterprise*, August 27, 1975, p. 11.

[20] Ibid.

[21] See Paul Steiger, "The 'Underemployed': A Growing Class," *Los Angeles Times* (February 20, 1977), p. 1.

United States. The discrimination is justified by various kinds of prejudices, which falsely claim the groups are "inferior."[22] The discrimination includes discrimination in housing, education, loans, types of jobs, and employment. Here we consider only that facet of discrimination that results in higher unemployment rates. In the case of young people, some unemployment results from prejudice against youth, but some also results from lack of qualifications, to the extent that training and experience are qualifications. In the case of women and minorities, since anthropologists find that all groups are created with equal qualifications, *all* higher rates of unemployment must be due to discrimination, including some present employment discrimination and some previous discrimination in education, training, or previous jobs.

Even the official U.S. data show these extremely high unemployment figures. In June 1975 average unemployment for all workers was 9.1 percent.[23] Table 22.4 shows that women suffered more unemployment than men, blacks suffered more than whites (almost double), and youths suffered more than adults (far more than double). Thus white males 20 years and over were best off, while black women workers ages 16–19 suffered the most unemployment. A rate of 7.6 percent for all white males is bad enough, but an unemployment rate of 43 percent for all young black workers reveals a condition of unbelievable depression for this group. Figure 22.2 shows that blacks have had almost double the unemployment rate of whites for many years.

Yet these official data of unemployment do not tell the full story. The *underestimates* of unemployment are even greater for women, minorities, and youth than

Table 22.4 **Unemployment by Race, Sex, and Age (June 1975 rates, in percentages)**

Category	All Workers, 16 and Over	Young Workers, 16–19 Years
All	9.4%	23.6%
All whites	8.4	—
All blacks	15.4	—
All men	8.4	—
All women	10.2	—
White men	7.6	20.8
White women	9.4	21.4
Black men	15.4	42.8
Black women	15.5%	43.0%

Source: U.S. Department of Labor, *Employment and Earnings* (July 1975).

[22] The best discussion of prejudice and discrimination against women in employment is in Barbara Deckard, *The Women's Movement* (New York: Harper & Row, 1975), chapters 5 and 6. An excellent discussion of prejudice and discrimination against blacks in employment is in Ray Franklin and Solomon Resnick, *The Political Economy of Racism* (New York: Holt, Rinehart and Winston, 1973).

[23] Data from U.S. Department of Labor, Bureau of Labor Statistics, *Employment and Earnings* (July 1975). *All workers* refers to everyone counted in the labor force age 16 and over. These data are not seasonally adjusted because they are not available in that form.

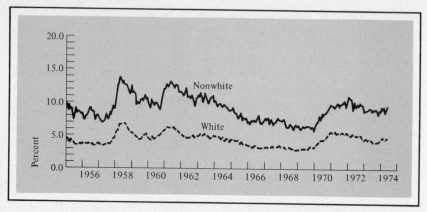

Figure 22.2 **Unemployment rates by race (seasonally adjusted).** (Source: U.S. Department of Labor, Employment and Earnings, Washington, D.C.: GPO, monthly.)

for white male adults. The two most important reasons are the same factors discussed above as major reasons for underestimating all unemployment. First, even more women that men and, proportionately, even more blacks than whites, fall into that strange category: "not in the labor force, but want a job now." In the second quarter of 1975, only 1,592,000 men, but some 3,583,000 women were counted as not in the labor force because they were discouraged from looking, even though they wanted a job now. At the same time, the discouraged workers included 3,699,000 whites and 1,196,000 blacks. As a proportion of the population or the labor force, this was much higher for blacks than whites. Even as a proportion of those counted as not in the labor force, the discouraged were 7.2 percent of the whites but 16.6 percent of the blacks.

Second, both blacks and women (and youth) are proportionately much larger percentages than adult white males of those who are employed part-time but desire full-time jobs and cannot find them. Corrected unemployment figures in Table 22.5, adjusting for only these two factors, give a more realistic picture of the burdens of unemployment by race, sex, and age of workers.

On any calculation (1) a higher percentage of blacks than whites are unemployed, (2) a higher percentage of women than men are unemployed, and (3) a higher percentage of young than old workers are unemployed. Moreover, the differences become greater—both absolutely and relatively—when these corrections remove the various underestimations. For example, black women have only a slightly higher rate of unemployment than black men in the official data (15.5 to 15.4 percent), but the difference is much greater in the adjusted data (31.3 to 23.9 percent).

The group of black women, ages 16 to 19, reflects all three kinds of discrimi-. nation in an official unemployment rate of 43 percent. With a correction merely to include those part-time workers who want, but can't find, full-time work, the rate for this group for June 1975 rises to 49.2 percent unemployed. If data were available on how many are too discouraged to look for work from this group, but are not counted in the labor force, the minimum and maximum corrected rates of unemployment would be well over 50 percent.

Table 22.5   **Corrected Unemployment by Race, Sex, and Age
(June 1975 rates, in percentages)**

Category	Official Unemployment	Minimum Corrected Unemployment[a]	Maximum Corrected Unemployment[b]
White men	7.6	9.9	12.0
White women	9.4	13.3	18.8
Black men	15.4	20.1	23.9
Black women	15.5	22.9	31.3
All youth, 16–19	23.6	30.9	40.5
All workers	9.1	12.4	16.3

Source: U.S. Department of Labor, *Employment and Earnings*, July 1975, pp. 26 and 59. Not seasonally adjusted.

[a] *Minimum corrected unemployment* means that unemployment is adjusted to include one-half of those part-time workers who desire full-time jobs but are unable to get them; and both unemployment and labor force are adjusted to include those workers officially not in the labor force but who want work now, but are discouraged from looking because they think they cannot get a job. Discouraged are from quarterly survey.

[b] *Maximum corrected unemployment* means that unemployment is adjusted to include one-half of those part-time workers who want full-time jobs but are unable to get them, and both unemployment and labor force are adjusted to include those workers officially not in the labor force but who want jobs now, but are discouraged from looking for any reasons.

There are also other reasons to believe the official rates underestimate unemployment of youth, minorities, and women. It was shown earlier that large numbers of unpaid family workers are counted as employed. Yet a disproportionate number of these are young and/or female and/or blacks in the South.[24]

Furthermore, the category *white* includes Chicanos and Puerto Ricans, whose unemployment rates are far higher than average.[25] On the other side, the category *black* includes several other small racial minorities, particularly Chinese and Japanese, whose unemployment rates are much lower than blacks' rates. Thus the unemployment gap between whites and blacks is somewhat larger than it appears in the official data.

Finally, subemployment or underemployment is far more prevalent among young workers, women, and minorities that it is among white male adults. For example, in 1970 the median wage of full-time employed workers was $7,870 for white men, $5,314 for black men, $4,584 for white women, and only $3,487 for black women.[26] As a result, in 1970 only 5 percent of U.S. families headed by white males were below the official poverty line, but 33 percent of all black families were below the poverty line; 37 percent of all families headed by white women were below the poverty line, and 62 percent of all families headed by

[24] The data (from the Census Bureau) and a more complete argument are in the excellent book by Victor Perlo, *Economics of Racism, USA* (New York: International Publishers, 1975).
[25] Ibid.
[26] All data here from U.S. Department of Labor, discussed in Chapter 21.

black women were below the poverty line. The official poverty line was $4,275 per family. Since the average wage of full-time employed black women was only $3,487, it is easy to see how most families headed by black women were in poverty even though most of these women worked full-time. Of course, in the depression of 1974–1975 when unemployment was especially bad among blacks and women, their poverty situation worsened.

In addition to underemployment causing their low wages, underemployment is also reflected in the poor jobs given some highly qualified groups. For example, in 1972 women with college degrees had only a slightly higher median wage than men with eighth-grade education. Among women with four years of college, 17 percent take jobs as unskilled or semiskilled workers. Even among women with five years or more of college, 6 percent take unskilled or semiskilled jobs. [27]

Why is unemployment so high among women and minorities? The reason lies both in prejudice and in the fact that this unemployment pattern is also profitable to employers. If an employer has ten black and ten white workers, and must fire half for a couple of months, which will be fired? If "he is rational and seeks to minimize his labor turnover costs, he will lay off his ten black workers on the assumption that they will be unlikely to get permanent or better jobs elsewhere because of the discriminatory practices of other employers." [28] Thus the capitalist fires black workers and women in each recession and hires them back in times of expansion. The employer also gains by not paying the fringe benefits due workers who stay on the job for a longer time.

SEASONAL UNEMPLOYMENT

In addition to general or cyclical unemployment, workers are also unemployed in a seasonal pattern. For example, agricultural workers are very fully employed at harvest time but are often unemployed many months in the year.

To eliminate the seasonal pattern from consideration and analysis, the Labor Department publishes seasonally adjusted unemployment rates. Although the techniques now used are quite complex, the basic idea of the adjustment is quite simple: raise the unemployment rate in months that normally have high seasonal employment and lower it in months with normally low seasonal employment. Accordingly, the Labor Department reported in the first six months of 1975 the data in Table 22.6.

The seasonally adjusted results, which are the ones given publicity, were more pleasant for the Ford administration since they put the unemployment rate over 9 percent only in one month, whereas the unadjusted rates were 9 percent or more in four months. One should always take the seasonal adjustment with a grain of salt because it may, in a sense, understate or overstate the impact of a depression depending on the time of the year. Nevertheless, all data used in this book from here on are seasonally adjusted.

The whole concept of seasonal unemployment is dubious if it means that this sort of unemployment is an act of nature and nothing can be done about it. It is

[27] See Deckard, op. cit., Chapter 5.
[28] See Franklin and Resnick, op. cit., p. 20.

Table 22.6 **Unemployment Rates, Seasonally adjusted and not seasonally adjusted, 1975**

Month	Not Seasonally Adjusted	Seasonally Adjusted
January	9.0%	8.2%
February	9.1	8.2
March	9.1	8.7
April	8.6	8.9
May	8.3	9.2
June	9.4%	8.6%

Source: U.S. Department of Labor, *Employment and Earnings* (July 1975), p. 19.

true that nothing can be done about it in a pure unplanned capitalist economy. But in a planned economy, like Cuba, which under capitalism had large numbers of unemployed sugar workers in the winter, these workers can easily be given other work, such as constructing rural housing, roads, or dams.

FRICTIONAL UNEMPLOYMENT

Frictional unemployment is supposed to mean those workers who are temporarily unemployed only because they are moving from one job to another, usually in the wake of technological progress. For example, workers building stage coaches may be unemployed for a short time until they move into the automotive industry. This concept has a small grain of truth but has been used in deceptive ways.

It is said that frictional unemployment is natural because it results from technological progress, so nothing can be done about it. Yet in a planned economy all such workers could be retrained by the government. The main problem, however, is that conservatives overestimate frictional unemployment in order to deny that there is much (or any) general unemployment caused by capitalist business cycles.

In World War II, when there was unlimited government demand, unemployment fell to 1 percent. Since frictional unemployment results from technological progress, and since such progress was very rapid in World War II, frictional unemployment should never be higher than the 1 percent recorded in World War II. Yet in the Truman period Democratic economists started saying frictional unemployment was 1.5 to 2 percent. In the Eisenhower administration Republican economists said frictional unemployment was 2.5 to 3 percent. In the Kennedy-Johnson administrations Democratic economists spoke of 3.5 to 4 percent frictional unemployment. Nixon's economists talked about 4.5 to 5 percent, and Ford's economists talked about 6 to 8 percent frictional unemployment.

THE PROBLEM OF INFLATION

Inflation is defined as a rise in the average price level of all goods. A rise in one price offset by a fall in another is not inflation; this is constantly occurring as a result of shifting demand, such as a shift from butter to margarine. Furthermore, we must distinguish the effects of a slow and gradual inflation from those of a very rapid, or galloping, inflation. If inflation results in the rise of prices by a few percent per year, then it is only a social irritant. It does work a great injustice on those who possess savings, who have made loans, who must live on a fixed income, or whose wages lag behind prices, because these groups find the purchasing power of their incomes steadily declining. In particular, the aged face an economic disaster when they retire. This decline of real wages and real savings exacerbates many economic and political conflicts. For a country as a whole, gradual inflation of domestic prices may reduce the volume of goods sold abroad; and for goods that still face competition, entire overseas markets may be lost.

The situation is much more serious, however, when the rate of price inflation reaches several hundred percent per year, as happened in Germany in the early 1920s. Rampant inflation brings such a rapid decline in the value of money that ultimately there can be complete dislocation and collapse of the economy, with correspondingly violent political reactions. At such times money and the market system fail completely. Productive effort is paralyzed, and exchange retrogresses to barter. In recent years there have been several underdeveloped countries, such as Brazil and South Vietnam, in which galloping inflation threatened to disrupt all normal economic processes.

Even in the United States, the magnitude of inflation is indicated by the fact that the consumer price level quadrupled between 1900 and 1958, and doubled between 1938 and 1958.[29] During the six years from 1945 to 1950, wholesale prices rose 52.6 and consumer prices 33.7 percent. Nevertheless inflation in the United States was in the very gradual category of 1 or 2 percent a year in most years from 1951 to 1965. After the escalation of the war in Vietnam in 1965, however, inflation became progressively worse. It was one of the major economic issues in the 1968 and 1972 presidential elections. By 1974 the Gallup poll reported that 62 percent of Americans felt it was the worst single national problem.

In U.S. history mild inflations have occurred in almost every business cycle expansion. Major inflations also occurred in every war, including the Revolutionary War, the War of 1812, the Civil War, World Wars I and II, the Korean War, and the Vietnam War. On the other hand, deflations, or declining prices, occurred in almost every depression or recession up through the recession of 1948. Although it seems hard to believe, there have been long periods of declining prices in U.S. history.

Until 1950 there was never any inflation during a recession or depression. In the recessions of 1954 and 1958, however, there were price rises in several industries in the midst of unemployment, though the overall price level didn't change much. In the recessions of 1969–1970 and 1974–1975 there were *both* high unemployment and inflation. Inflation in 1974 and 1975 reached rates of 12

[29] See Willard Thorp and Richard Quandt, *The New Inflation* (New York: McGraw-Hill, 1959), p. 1.

percent to 14 percent in several months in spite of unemployment rates of 8 and 9 percent and over. This is a new phenomenon in U.S. history.

THE HUMAN IMPACT OF INFLATION

Inflation hurts everyone whose income does not rise faster than the rate of inflation. When it comes in a time of high unemployment, it means a crushing burden on those whose money income is actually falling. Economists use the term *real* income to refer to an income after adjustment for price changes. If your income in money terms rises by 10 percent, but the consumer price level rises by 15 percent, then your real income has declined. Obviously, those on fixed money incomes will suffer the greatest declines in real income. So the elderly and retired are hurt the worst. Any unemployed worker has a miserable fixed income on the government dole.

The combined impact of depression in keeping wages down—and of inflation in raising prices—has brought lower real wages to most American workers in the decade from 1965 to 1975. Thus the weekly take-home pay, after federal taxes, of a worker with three dependents rose rapidly from 1965 to 1975 in money terms. Without adjusting for inflation, weekly take-home pay rose from $86.30 in 1965 to $151.99 in 1975.[30] It rose every single year. It is not money, however, but what it will buy, its real purchasing power, that is important to workers. This amount rose a little in the expansions of 1965–1968 and 1970–1972 but fell even more in the recession and depression years. As a result, when the weekly money wage is adjusted for inflation, there is an actual decline in the decade. The *real* weekly take-home pay (in constant 1967 dollars) declined from $91.32 in 1965 to $87.46 in April 1975. Besides showing how labor has suffered from inflation, these data cast doubt on the theory that inflation has been caused by high wages.

As a result of the mixture of severe unemployment and rapid inflation, the total number of Americans living in poverty increased by 5.6 percent in 1974 and increased by another 10.7 percent in 1975.[31] Altogether, in 1975 the official U.S. government figures show that 25.9 million Americans were living below the government-defined poverty level! Yet the poverty level was probably understated at the official figure of $5,500, since this includes only a "temporary" and inadequate diet, with very little for clothing or shelter. The official estimate was that 42 percent of the increase in poverty was due to unemployment; most of the rest was caused by inflation.

Of course, U.S. inflation is not as bad as German inflation was right after World War I. The price level often doubled in a day or even an hour. By 1923 one U.S. dollar was worth 4.2 billion German marks. According to the novelist Thomas Mann,

> Peasants filled their houses with sewing machines, pianos, and Persian rugs, and refused to part with their eggs and milk except in exchange for articles of permanent value. . . .

[30] U.S. Department of Labor, Bureau of Labor Statistics, *Employment and Earnings,* August 1975 and earlier issues.
[31] U.S. Census Bureau, *Money, Income and Poverty Status of Families and Persons in the U.S., 1975* (Washington, D.C.: U.S. GPO, 1976).

> *You took your money as fast as your legs would carry you to some innocent grocer. . . . If you were lucky, he had the mark quotation for 9 A.M., but not for noon. . . . You might drop in at the tobacconist's for a cigar. Alarmed at the price, you'd rush to a competitor, find that his price was still higher, and race back to the first shop, which may have doubled or tripled its price in the meantime. . . . On Friday evenings, you could see workers coming out of the factories with baskets, sacks, and suitcases full of money. . . . It became necessary to pay wages daily. . . .*[32]

That inflationary experience was the breeding ground of Hitler's fascism.

The current U.S. inflation (and depression) is bad enough for many individuals. For example, many retired workers find their retirement income is below poverty levels, so they must sell many of their small stock of possessions just to stay alive.[33] Many people still working have to give up all quality foods and change to cheaper kinds of food.[34] It must be stressed that inflation usually hurts the poor worse than the rich. Inflation redistributes income to the rich by raising the value of the property they hold, including property in land, buildings, and corporate stock.

BLAMING THE VICTIM

Conservative economists have always tended to blame the unemployed for unemployment. Some conservative politicians still claim that anyone who *really* wants a job can get one. In the next chapter we shall see that, using the strange proposition called Say's Law, conservative economists for many decades proved to their satisfaction that a general depression is impossible, so involuntary unemployment on a large scale is impossible. They admitted only *frictional* unemployment—that is, a temporary depression in a few industries until workers can move to other industries that are booming.

On the basis of these arguments, conservative economists concluded that all unemployed (beyond the frictional unemployed) must be lazy loafers unwilling to work at the prevailing wage. The unemployed must, according to these economists, voluntarily leave their jobs to look for easier for better-paying jobs elsewhere. Imagine arguing this notion during the 1930s when official unemployment was over 25 percent. Do all workers periodically get fits of laziness or greed? Are millions only pretending to be unhappy when out of a job and living on a thin handout from the government?

As we shall see in the next chapter, this argument always leads conservative economists to the conclusion that all workers would be fully employed if only they would accept lower wages. These views have been revived in more sophisticated technical form by modern conservatives. For example, Armen Alchian argues that when demand declines, workers are faced with a choice.[35] They can agree to continue working at a lower wage or voluntarily quit their present jobs

[32] Lecture by Mann in 1942, quoted by George F. Will in "The German Inflation of the 1920s." *Riverside Press-Enterprise*, February 7, 1975, p. D9.

[33] Victoria Graham, "Great Recession," *Riverside Press-Enterprise*, February 9, 1975, p. C1.

[34] Ibid.

[35] Armen Alchian, "Information Costs, Pricing, and Resource Unemployment," *Western Economic Journal*, vol. 7, June 1969, pp. 107–129.

and go hunting around for a better one. Since many workers are ignorant of the true facts of the job market, they spend many months hopping around looking for nonexistent jobs at their old wages. Meanwhile, these millions of ill-informed workers may be considered voluntarily unemployed or frictionally unemployed or "employed" in acquiring information.

One of the problems with this argument is that its description is contrary to fact. Bosses (such as General Motors) seldom call their workers together for a cozy chat to say "you accept a lower wage or be fired"; they usually just fire thousands of workers without warning. (Moreover, we shall see in the next chapter that accepting lower wages would *not* lower the unemployment rate.) Alchian has tried to answer this criticism. He claims that capitalists have learned from experience that, when given the choice of lower wages or quitting, most workers will quit. Instead of going to the bother of offering this choice, employers just anticipate the workers' choice and fire them "to the mutual satisfaction of both employee and employer."[36] Since in reality most unemployed would accept lower wages, and since there is no evidence that employers think in this contorted fashion, it is hard to see why so many economists have treated his theory so seriously.

Alchian's argument about voluntary, frictional unemployment while looking for better jobs has been particularly applied to women workers and young workers. Three authors of a recent textbook say

> The size of frictional unemployment is rising. Voluntary quits and job hopping represent a large and growing phenomenon in the United States labor market. Unusually large numbers of younger (and inexperienced) workers and middle-aged women have been entering the labor force recently. These workers are typically more selective about the types of jobs they will accept.
>
> Unemployment during job search to improve wages or working conditions is considered to be voluntary and not a proper concern of government policy.[37]

So women and young workers, "voluntarily quit" and "job hop" and they "are typically more selective about the type of jobs they will accept." The mildest comment one can make about this argument is that it is both illogical and a travesty of the facts. Logically, one would expect that women and young workers would be far more anxious to hold on to any job, no matter how bad and lowly paid, than an older male because they know that they will face discrimination in getting a better job. They are certainly not more selective because they cannot afford to be. The fact is—according to numerous Labor Department surveys—that women voluntarily quit any given job much *less* than men at that job.[38] The argument, therefore, seems compounded less of evidence and more of prejudiced notions about women and unemployed young workers (of whom a high proportion are black, though this is not always mentioned).

The conservative economists extend the argument to blame the victims not only for unemployment but also for inflation. Alchian's view is that voluntary unemployment lowers the supply of willing workers, so raises wages and thus raises prices. In Alchian's view workers must suffer several months of futile job

[36] William Hosek, *Macroeconomic Theory* (Homewood, Ill.: Irwin, 1975), p. 293. Hosek has a summary and discussion of Alchian.

[37] William Mitchell, John Hand, and Ingo Walter, eds., *Readings in Macroeconomics* (New York: McGraw-Hill, 1975), p. 152.

[38] The official data are fully presented and discussed in Barbara Deckard, op. cit., pp. 85–86.

hunting before they learn to accept lower real wages—and only these lower real wages will stabilize the price level. In later chapters we shall see that conservatives now view some level of unemployment as natural. The *natural* level of unemployment is that level necessary to stop inflation; and they argue that any steps to lower that natural level will only result in more inflation. We shall also find in later chapters that the conservative view, that workers are themselves responsible for unemployment and inflation, is incorrect.

SUMMARY

The U.S. economy is subject to alternating periods of expansion and contraction. In each contraction period, the amount of unemployment rises to extremely high levels, causing many kinds of individual and social misery. Even in the present (1977) period of expansion, there continues to be very high levels of unemployment, underemployment, and inflation.

CHAPTER 23

THE INSTITUTIONAL SETTING

Why are millions and millions of people unemployed in the U.S. economy? It seems strange—like a scene from *Alice in Wonderland*—that millions of people lack jobs when there is so much to do. After all, by official government count, millions of people are in poverty; they lack the necessary food, clothing, and shelter for a decent life. Couldn't millions of unemployed be employed to produce these urgently needed amounts of food, clothing, and shelter? It seems barbaric and inexplicable to have even one person languishing in unemployment while there is so much to be done.

Our economy experiences periods of prosperity and depression, or boom and bust. These are caused by the imbalance of *aggregate supply* and *aggregate demand*. Aggregate supply is defined as the total output that business produces and plans to sell. Aggregate demand is defined as the total dollar amount of goods that consumers, investors, and governments plan to buy. Sometimes the aggregate supply of produced goods is either too small or too great in terms of the aggregate demand for goods. Certainly if aggregate supply and demand were always equal, there could be no such periodic phenomena as overproduction and underproduction. Depressions occur when the aggregate demand is insufficient (in money terms) to purchase the whole supply.

The first question to be asked is simple but basic. In what kind of economy must total supply and demand always be equal? Under what economic institutions is it possible for demand to be greater or less than supply? We shall find that in all pre-capitalist systems, there was never a problem caused by lack of demand, though other kinds of catastrophes often hurt the economy. Under capitalism, however, there is periodically a lack of effective demand for goods and services. The *effective demand* for products under capitalism is a demand backed by money. The poor may desire more food. That is not an effective demand unless they have the money to buy the food. Only if there is a demand in money terms is it effective in getting a capitalist to produce and to hire more workers.

THE CAPITALIST SYSTEM

What exactly is meant by capitalism? *Capitalism* may be defined as a system in which one class of individuals, the capitalists, own the means of production. These means of production are called *capital goods*, such as factories and equipment. The capitalists hire another class of individuals, called *workers*, who own nothing productive but their power to labor. The product of the workers' labor is owned by the capitalists. The capitalists sell the product in the market place for a certain amount of money. The capitalists will produce only so long as they expect to make a profit in the market above and beyond all their expenses.

It is this system that creates the possibility of an alternating cycle of boom and bust, with episodes of massive unemployment, sometimes accompanied by high rates of inflation. Previous economic systems, such as slavery or feudalism, did have unemployment or inflation at times, but they were rare and usually caused by a natural catastrophe, such as a flood or an epidemic. Only modern capitalism shows a systematic business cycle with periodic mass unemployment caused by a lack of effective demand. Only modern capitalism shows the unique phenomenon of high unemployment and high inflation at the same time, not as a function of natural catastrophe but as a result of the normal functioning of the system. It is worth noting these differences from previous systems in some detail to understand the nature of the business cycle.

PRODUCTION FOR THE MARKET

It is characteristic of the private enterprise economy, which was fully developed in England by the end of the eighteenth century, that most production was directed solely toward its sale on the market. This was hardly ever true of earlier societies. In the most primitive societies, almost all productive activity is directed at production of food by gathering or hunting. These activities are necessarily carried out by the collective unit of all the males and/or females of the tribe. Generally, almost all of the produce is distributed according to some fixed scheme among the tribe's membership.

Even at a somewhat higher economic stage, production is still for use, and not for sale. None of the Indian tribes of the Americas, not even the Aztecs, bought or sold land or produced crops to sell for a profit to others. In fact, "for the red man soil existed only in order to meet the necessities of life, and production, not profit, was the basis of his economy. . . . Unemployment was certainly never a problem in the Indian communities of early America."[1] Because there was little division of labor within the tribe, there was little if any trade among its members. Furthermore, very little commerce was transacted between the most primitive tribes, and that "was virtually restricted to materials small in bulk and precious for their decorative or magical qualities."[2] We find that all over the world for thousands of years almost all economic systems, whether tribal or feudal, were based on relatively self-sufficient agricultural units.

In the Roman Empire, there was a great deal of trade, but most of it was in luxury goods.[3] This trade therefore did not affect the self-sufficiency of the basic agricultural unit, the slave-run plantation, although a lack of surplus food could bring starvation to large numbers of city dwellers. As one authors says, ". . .Notwithstanding the phenomenal expansion of trade and industry, the vast masses inside the Empire still continued to win their livelihood from the soil. Agriculture

[1] John A. Crow, *The Epic of Latin America* (Garden City, N.Y.: Doubleday, 1948), p. 54.
[2] Grahame Clark, *From Savagery to Civilization* (London: Cobbett Press, 1946), p. 96.
[3] See, for example, the brief account in F.W. Walbank, *The Decline of the Roman Empire in the West* (London: Cobbett Press, 1956), pp. 11–13.

remained throughout antiquity the most usual and most typical economic activity, and land the most important form of wealth."[4]

The same was true of feudal England, where the primitive level of technology made impossible the supply of large urban populations and even greatly restricted trade between the villages. As a result, in the England of that day "towns developed slowly; each group of burgesses solved their local problems on their own initiative and in their own time. Even in 1377 not much more than eight percent of the population were townsmen, and only a minority of these had independent dealings with continental markets."[5]

Of course in the later medieval period there were areas of more highly developed industrial production, such as Flanders and northern Italy; and even relatively backward England carried on a systematic wool trade with Flanders. Yet these were exceptions to the general rule of the feudal economy and may be considered early signs pointing to the end of that economy.

If there happened to be a surplus from the slave or feudal estate, then it might be marketed in return for foreign luxury items to be used by the lord of the estate. Finding a market, however, was not a matter of life and death for the economic unit. If the surplus found no market, the manor was still supplied with its necessities for that year, and it could and would continue the process of production for the next year's needs. What could disturb such economically self-sufficient societies were only the catastrophes that were more or less external to the economy—natural disasters such as droughts, plagues, or floods, or political troubles such as government interference, war, or revolution. These phenomena could and did depress production in various randomly spaced intervals, as well as seasonally because of the special seasonal sensitivity of agriculture.

This type of economy could not, however, conceivably face the problem of lack of effective demand for all commodities because the economic unit directly consumed most of the products of its own land and could do without trade altogether. Thus in discussing the business cycle of depression and prosperity, Mitchell observes that ". . . the total number of past business cycles may well be less than a thousand. For business cycles are phenomena peculiar to a certain form of economic organization which has been dominant even in Western Europe for less than two centuries, and for briefer periods in other regions."[6]

In the period of transition from feudalism to capitalism in the England of the sixteenth, seventeenth, and eighteenth centuries, the majority of the people still lived on the land and consumed their own products. As time went on, however, more and more products, both agricultural and industrial, were delivered to the market place. By the end of the eighteenth century, the private enterprise system of production for the market embraced most economic activity. By the nineteenth century, one business entrepreneur might own a factory producing millions of shoes, though his whole family could consume only a few pairs. The shoes had to be sold in order to buy other consumer goods for his family, pay wages to his employees, and replace and expand the plant and equipment of his business.

In the United States, the transformation to a market economy took place in the nineteenth century. In 1800 two-thirds of the U.S. population labored in agricul-

---

[4] Ibid., p. 18.
[5] Marion Gibbs, *Feudal Order* (London: Cobbett Press, 1949), pp. 7–8.
[6] W. C. Mitchell, *Business Annals* (New York: National Bureau of Economic Research, 1926), p. 47.

ture, and most of the remainder were employed in commerce and shipping. Except for the foreign trade sector, markets were small and local. Many families and communities were almost self-sufficient. Native industry, which had a foothold in 1800, spurted during the War of 1812, when imports from England were cut off. By 1815 New England mills and factories were capable of supplying textiles and simple manufactures to the nation. Transportation networks were built to link communities and regions. This permitted farmers to specialize in commercial crops for cash income with which they purchased in the market the necessities of life. By 1840 a large national market for manufacturers had been created. Families turned away from self-sufficiency and purchased cloth, flour, farm implements, and household items. Rapid industrialization followed. In 1860, the United States was producing more than one-fifth of world manufacturing output, and by 1913 American production had risen to one-third of the world total.

The process of industrialization, starting first in England and spreading to the rest of western Europe and the United States, had changed the character of production and employment. Production required a greater number of stages, or steps, as materials and products became less simple. Labor grew more specialized, and labor's employment came to be linked with the expanded use of capital.

In the modern market economy, every person's productive effort is related to sales in the market, and every person's income depends on the income of others. A man working in an automobile factory, for example, depends for his continued employment on millions of people buying cars each year. In turn, most of these car buyers depend on millions buying the products they produce. If consumers are unable to buy their cars, the automobile worker immediately loses his job. The car manufacturer needs less steel, less rubber, less paint, and so on. Each of these industries, in turn, lays off workers. The process goes on and on because of the interconnectedness of the market economy. Each time more workers lose their jobs, their income ceases. They can no longer buy the hundreds of goods and services they normally purchase, and the crisis widens and becomes more severe.

The sale in the market of privately produced goods and services generates all income. Decisions to purchase are made by thousands of small- and large-income receivers, and the total of these purchasing decisons makes up the total, or aggregate, demand. In previous economic systems, the self-sufficient economic unit—the craftsman producing a trickle of handmade items for known customers—could not possibly be troubled by lack of demand for his or her product. When almost all that was produced by the economic unit was consumed by it, Say's law had to be true. In the industrialized private enterprise system, however, *the businessperson produces for the market and cannot continue production if there is no market demand for his or her products*. This, then, is the first major institutional feature of the private enterprise economy. Appearing in the eighteenth century and continuing to the present day, it is one of the factors that make business cycles possible.

REGULAR USE OF MONEY

Another institutional condition that opens up the possibility of a lack of aggregate demand is the regular use of money in exchange. The monetary system takes the place of the barter system of exchanging good for good. It was seen that production for the market makes cyclical unemployment possible. Use of money in the market exchange will be shown to be a second necessary condition for the emergence of business cycles.

The Uses of Money

Money replaced the barter system because it is much more convenient to use. What precisely are its functions in the modern economy? Traditionally, money is said to have four functions:

1. Money is the *unit of accounting,* or the standard of value—that is, it is a measuring stick for everything else. All contracts are drawn up in money terms, with so much money to be paid for a certain product at a certain time. We think of a coat or a table as being worth so many dollars.
2. Money is the *medium of exchange,* or actual intermediary between commodities (including services). Under barter, one commodity is exchanged for another commodity. In the monetary economy, a commodity is exchanged for money; then the money may be exchanged for another commodity.
3. Money is a *store of value,* or a device for hoarding. When money is received as an income, it need not be spent immediately. Instead, if it is in a nonperishable form such as gold, it may be buried or stored away and hoarded until the possessor chooses to use it. In the modern world money is deposited in a bank account, which is completely nonperishable; the money may even grow by earning interest while it is on deposit.
4. Money is a *standard of deferred payment,* or a unit of accounting for future payments on debts. In other words, I may buy something from you now but promise to pay for it later. My promise is always in terms of so many units of money, not, for example, in so many pairs of shoes. In the United States paper money is a legal tender (or legally acceptable unit) for the payment of any debt.

Our "money" today is (1) coin and paper currency in circulation plus (2) all demand deposits (checking accounts) in commercial banks. (In Chapter 30 the evolution of money, from commodities such as gold to its present complex forms in the U.S. economy, will be explored in detail.)

These are the four traditional concepts of the use of money, but they are grossly oversimplified and misleading. For one thing, a piece of paper cannot produce an automobile; only human beings can produce things. The piece of paper has power to command labor only because it faithfully reflects the human relationships on which our society is built. It is not really money but people who command and manipulate other people.

Moreover, the monetary system is often inadequate to fulfill these functions, which traditional views assume it will smoothly achieve. In Chapter 31, and briefly here, we shall see that it fails in all its functions during an inflation. In Chapter 28, and again briefly here, we shall see that the monetary system helps make depressions possible *and* tends to intensify them.

The Abuses of Money

Money does not serve its four functions equally well under all conditions. Imagine that there is catastrophic inflation, with prices doubling every hour, which means that the value of money falls by half each hour. Money then functions badly as a unit of accounting because the same product sells at such rapidly changing prices that neither consumers nor sellers can keep track of them. With rapid inflation money is also a poor medium of exchange: People may refuse to accept it at all because its buying power is so uncertain and may diminish further before it can be spent.

With rapid inflation money is also a very bad store of value because money hoarded away now will buy so very much less in the future. Instead of keeping money, everyone rushes to buy goods or real property that will be worth more and more units of money as the inflation continues. Anyone with cash savings in paper money or bank accounts or government bonds is badly hurt, so it may happen that no one will put money in banks or buy government bonds at almost any interest rate. Finally, with rapid inflation money cannot function as a standard of deferred payment because the standard itself keeps changing. If someone lends $100 today and it is worth only $1 when it is paid back tomorrow, then the lender is very badly hurt. When people refuse to accept the medium of exchange because they have lost confidence in it, economic activity falls to the level that can be maintained by barter.

The use of money, even in ancient times, brought many new complications onto the economic scene. In the Roman Empire, for example, vast amounts of money were needed by the government to support wars of expansion, large standing armies, police and bureaucracy, and an unfavorable balance of trade (due to import of luxuries from the East). The emperors were eventually forced to the expedient of debasing their coins by "clipping" (decreasing the metallic content of coins) or mixture with less valuable metals. As the government debased the coins and as production of goods declined in the later days of the empire, the amount that could be bought with the coins declined rapidly; in other words, a catastrophic inflation occurred.[7]

Despite their difficulties with it, the regular use of money did not lead to the modern type of depression because most of the Roman economy was still contained in self-sufficient agricultural units.[8] The luxury trade did suffer from the extreme inflation but only as one more affliction in addition to colonial wars and slave revolts, the extreme inefficiency of employing slave labor, and the Roman citizens' attitude that any participation in the work process was degrading (because only slaves should work).

With the breakup of the Roman Empire, trade suffered a considerable decline. In early feudalism the pattern was overwhelmingly that of the isolated, self-sufficient manor. Barter therefore grew in importance, and the use of money declined. On each manor, in return for the lord's protection, the serf provided all the services and consumer goods needed and required by the lord, his family, and his retinue. However, when technology began to improve, industry and commerce slowly began to revive in western Europe. The widespread trade of the later medieval period eventually led to the replacement of barter by a money economy; at the same time, following the pattern discussed in the previous section, production was increasingly designed for sale in the market rather than use at home.

[7] See, for example, Walbank, op. cit., pp. 42–43, 51–52.
[8] See ibid., p. 18.

The modern private enterprise economy demands continuous use of money as the go-between in market exchange by the entire population. In a barter economy it is possible for one commodity to be brought to market in larger supply than there is demand for it; but it is impossible for "total supply" to exceed "total demand" because the two are identical; both are the same aggregate bunch of products brought to the market. The important point, however, is not the definitional identity of total supply and demand in a barter economy. It is that there may be a mismatch of particular supplies and demands but no lack of *aggregate* demand. For example, those who bring cows to market may find more shoes and fewer coats produced than they desire; that is, they would rather "spend" their cows for fewer shoes and more coats than are available. The excess supply of shoes is balanced by the excess demand for coats. The result is only a temporary, or frictional, unemployment of shoe producers, which could be cured by a shift to coat production. It is true that in the actual medieval economy rigid feudal restrictions did not allow many such shifts in production or occupation, but it was just these restrictions that the classical economists wished to abolish.

The mistake made by the classical adherents of Say's law (that total demand equals supply) was to apply rules of a barter economy to a money economy. They extended the argument by means of the general observation that money is merely the means of exchanging two commodities, so that the operation of the money economy is "essentially" the same as that of the barter economy. Thus we find Ricardo contending that "productions are always bought by productions, or by services; money is only the medium by which the exchange is effected."[9] One function of money is to facilitate the exchange of commodities, but it has other uses as well. In the modern economy, the seller obtains only money for commodities, money that may or may not be used immediately or later to buy other commodities. Thus money functions as the means for the storage of value for future use. The wants of humankind may be infinite, but it is not always the case that all buyers have money to buy what they want. There is therefore *no inherent necessity in a money economy that sellers should find buyers for all commodities brought to market.*

The problem is not an aggregate lack of money in the economy. While those who wish to buy have no money, those who have money may be taking it out of circulation and not using it in any way, or *hoarding* it. The chain of circulation may then be broken at any point at which the flow of money is stopped or withdrawn from the system. In that case the reduction of the flow of circulation, like the reduction of the volume of water flowing in a stream, causes a slowdown in the movement of products being circulated by this means. While it is basically true that products exchange for products even after the introduction of money, the mere necessity of the money bridge makes all the difference in the world. If the bridge is absent, finished commodities may pile up in warehouses, while potential consumers are unable to buy them. Only money can make a possible consumer into an actual buyer in the private enterprise system.

An excess of supply in this economic system does not mean everyone is fully satisfied. People's wants are elastic; we may have as much of a particular commodity as we want at one time, but there is always an infinity of other things that we desire, things that still have use value or utility for us. Therefore the problem

---

[9] Ricardo, op. cit., p. 275.

is not overproduction of the total commodities relative to what people want or desire. The problem is rather that there may be too many commodities on the market relative to the *effective demand,* which is limited by definition to desires that are backed by money in the marketplace.

CREDIT MONEY

In the United States at present, the largest part of the money supply, about four-fifths of the whole, is pure credit money. *Credit money* consists of demand, or checking, deposits at banks, which are dollar amounts owed by the banks to the holders of the accounts. Credit money is created whenever a bank makes a loan to a customer and "credits" his or her checking account with the amount of the loan. Except for the legal constraints on the lending of money, banks could go on creating money without limit as long as people had confidence in the acceptability of the money. Only the smallest portion of the money supply consists of coins and paper money issued by the U.S. Treasury. A somewhat larger portion is paper money issued by the Federal Reserve System (Fed). Technically, even these parts of the money supply are credits to the private sector because they are debts of government agencies that are payable on demand. Dollar bills, however, are no longer payable in gold, so a $10 bill presented to the Treasury or the Fed could be paid by any legal tender—say, two $5 bills. Thus the Treasury or the Fed may create money simply by using the printing press. Although Congress does impose a legal limit, it often raises that limit.

The use of credit intensifies all money problems; not only may a person sell something and not immediately purchase something else, but also it is possible to sell something and not receive the proceeds of the sale for some time. If Brown owes Smith, and Smith owes Johnson, and Johnson owes Martin, a break anywhere along this chain of credit circulation will be disastrous for all of the later parties in the chain. Moreover, the credit chain in the modern private enterprise economy is usually circular in nature, so that the reverberations reach the starting point and may begin to go around again. This does not, of course, explain why the chain should ever break in the first place.

It has been amply demonstrated that when money and credit institutions become the usual way of doing business, the business cycle of boom and bust becomes a possibility. Does this mean that these institutions are sufficient to explain the business cycle? We know that money and credit existed in ancient Rome and in the sixteenth to eighteenth centuries in western Europe, yet the financial disturbances of those times do not seem to have been the same phenomena as the modern type of business cycle. It is true that after the development of money and credit every catastrophic natural happening or violent political event might be reflected in a financial panic. For example, when the English fleet was burnt by the Dutch in 1667, and in 1672 when Charles II stopped payments from the Exchequer, there were sudden runs on the London banks. In the eighteenth century, financial crises resulted from the Jacobin conspiracy in 1708, the bursting of the South Sea stock speculation bubble in 1720, the fighting with the Pretender in 1745, the aftermath of the Seven Years' War in 1763, and the disturbances caused by the American Revolution.[10] These panics were un-

---

[10] See discussion of all these events in W. C. Mitchell, *Business Cycles* (Berkeley: University of California Press, 1913), pp. 583–584.

like the modern business cycle, both in cause and effect, because they originated in external causes and resulted in only limited depressions in a few trades for brief and random periods. The first truly general industrial depression of the modern type appeared as late as 1793 in England.[11]

In summary, there is evidence of a long period of extensive use of money and credit with only temporary and externally caused financial panics. Conversely, in the nineteenth and twentieth centuries there have been depressions, as well as many minor recessions, that did not produce financial panics. There is no reason, all other things being equal, why money and credit should not flow steadily through the process of circulation, so long as business expectations remain optimistic. It may be tentatively concluded that the regular use of money and credit is a necessary prerequisite, but not a sufficient explanation, of business cycles. (The analysis and problems of money and credit are explored in much more detail in Chapters 30 and 31.)

PRODUCTION FOR PRIVATE PROFIT

We have examined two conditions—production for the market and regular use of money—that must be present if business cycles are to occur. These are cycles in which demand fluctuates below the full-employment level of supply. But at least one more institutional condition is necessary before we can contend that total demand may not equal supply in this economy (or that Say's law does not hold true). It is the existence of private ownership of production facilities and production for private profit. Even in an economy characterized by exchange in the market through the medium of money, supply and demand can be kept in balance, or quickly brought back into balance, if both supply and demand are consciously planned by the same national agency.

A centrally planned socialist economy is one in which the government owns and plans the use of all means of production. Most business cycle economists admit that industrialized socialist economies do not experience the business cycle phenomena characteristic of industrialized private enterprise economies. This is the case because a socialist economy can make one unified plan for growth without concern for private profit. Thus all of the data on Soviet economic development indicate continuous full employment (except for retraining time or movement between jobs).

In a private enterprise economy, each individual enterprise makes its own plans on the basis of its own estimate of whether it will obtain a private profit by undertaking production. In the national plan of a socialist economy, *the same agency decides both the aggregate supply and the aggregate demand.* It sets the aggregate consumer demand by setting wages, and it controls the aggregate investment demand directly through the government budget.

Of course socialist planners may make mistakes in allocation of resources and new investment, especially because there are changes in technology and other new conditions each year. They may allocate resources to uses that are not as productive as others, or even order the production of one thing (say, automobiles) but not order enough production of other things going into it (say, rubber tires). In such cases there may be supply bottlenecks holding back pro-

[11] Ibid.

duction in some industries and temporary oversupply and unused capacity in others. Such mistakes may lower the rate of growth or even cause output to fall in one year (as happened in Czechoslovakia in 1963).

Moreover, much recent data on eastern Europe and the Soviet Union show a cyclical recurrence of slow-growth periods. Each time the economy starts growing rapidly, the bureaucrats get overoptimistic. They push production more rapidly than is physically possible, leading to supply bottlenecks. If they order too many new factories to be built at once, the result is half-built factories and little or no increase in current output. Nevertheless, there remain very important distinctions from a private enterprise economy. There need be no secondary effects, no cumulative collapse of production, because socialist investment is not based on private profit (and the economy does remain at full employment). Naturally, the fact that a socialist economy is not subject to cyclical unemployment does not prove by itself that it is better or worse than a private enterprise economy. For that overall judgment, we would have to consider all the criteria for comparing economies, including full employment, efficiency, growth, distribution of income, and political and social effects.

In an economy based on private ownership of individual competing units, the sum of decisions to produce may not equal the sum of decisions by other individuals and businesses to spend—that is, to consume and invest. If the sum of the outputs produced at present prices is greater than the sum of the monetary demand, then there is not enough revenue to cover the costs of production and also yield a profit for the private entrepreneur. This criterion is decisive because *if the private entrepreneur can make no profit, he or she will not continue production,* machinery will stand idle, and all of the workers will be unemployed.

SUMMARY

Some classical economists believed aggregate demand always automatically adjusts to aggregate supply (Say's law). This was true of earlier societies in which production was for self-sufficient isolated units, and the little exchange that existed was by barter. It is also roughly true in socialist economies, where production and investment are planned for social use. Say's law is *not* true for modern private enterprise, capitalist economies, in which (1) production is for the market, (2) exchange operates by means of money and credit, and (3) the aim of production is private profit. Thus, despite its impressive long-run growth, the American economy has been plagued by instability. The growth of large-scale, oligopolistic, corporate capitalism in the late nineteenth century only increased this instability. As a result, ever since the Industrial Revolution and the establishment of full-blown capitalist systems, western Europe and the United States have been subject to periodic depressions of "overproduction" in which output falls, factories are idle, and millions of workers are unemployed and on relief. This periodic unemployment means that every worker and small-business owner lives with uncertainty and great tension every single day. While society loses much product, millions of individuals lose jobs, are plunged into poverty, have a feeling of total helplessness and uselessness, and suffer greatly increased physical disease (including malnutrition) and mental disease (including rises in every indicator of ill health from insomnia to suicide).

CHAPTER 24

NATIONAL INCOME ACCOUNTING:

How to Map the Circulation of Money and Goods

The Department of Commerce publishes detailed national income accounts (which are discussed in a lengthy appendix to this chapter). These accounts report the total flow of money and goods in the nation for a given period the same way private accounting reports the flow of money and goods through a single private enterprise. Many economists have labored to map this circulation of money and goods in the nation—just as biologists map the circulation of blood through the body. The two most famous economists who have labored at this task are Marx and Keynes.

J. M. Keynes (1883–1946) made his major contribution in the midst of the Great Depression of the 1930s. He wanted to trace these flows in order to find out how it was possible for a nation to have a lack of demand for goods while millions of people were hungry, poorly clothed, and ill-housed. He found the answers by tracing how money may leak out of the system, how those who have money may hoard it and not spend it, while those who badly need goods have no money. He concentrated on the total or aggregate demand for goods coming from consumer spending on consumer goods and the demand from investors' spending on goods necessary for production.

Karl Marx (1818–1883) wrote in the middle of the nineteenth century, when he had already witnessed a major depression each decade for several decades. In the midst of the misery of early British industrialization, he was especially sensitive to the effects of depression on unemployment among the workers. He also analyzed demand for goods from a class point of view, noting that workers account for most of consumer demand but that their demand is very much restricted by the limits of wage income.

The aggregate concepts of Keynes, which are stated in this chapter and the next, constituted a radical new way of thinking for orthodox, mainstream economists. Before Keynes, most orthodox academic economists denied the possibility of aggregate disequilibrium. Since there was no possibility of aggregate disequilibrium (depression or inflation), they had seen no need for aggregate concepts.

Keynes changed all that and made the aggregate concepts the basis for a whole new aggregate or macroeconomic analysis.

The unorthodox Marx had made such an analysis long before, but it was ignored. We shall see in the following chapters how Marx also went further to analyze not total flows but flows by class—thus, not just total income but workers' income and capitalists' income. Some followers of Keynes also look at these facts, but it is not their usual emphasis.

THE CIRCULAR FLOW OF GROSS NATIONAL PRODUCT

Gross National Product (GNP) is defined as the total value of all the finished goods and services produced by a nation in a year's time. Each good or service is valued at its market selling price. The market pricing system thus provides a yardstick by means of which totally different and otherwise unrelated items can be compared and aggregated.

The national flow of production and income may be thought of as a circular flow of supply and demand between households and businesses. In this simplified picture of the economy, there is no foreign trade because if it were included, the circle of supply and demand would be broken at that point. The government sector also is not included for the sake of simplicity. Understanding the circular flow in this uncomplicated economy is essential to understanding the concepts of aggregate supply and aggregate demand. The same concepts underlie the construction of the national income and product accounts.

In a capitalist economy some households own property while others own only their power to work. The workers' households supply certain amounts of labor. The capitalist owners of property buy this labor and add to it the appropriate amounts of factories, machinery, and raw materials. At each given level of technology this will enable business to supply households with a certain amount of consumer goods and to supply other businesses with new *capital goods*. Capital goods are defined to include new factories and new machinery as well as raw materials supplied to business.

Consumer goods keep the households alive and ready for labor, and the new capital goods are available for further business expansion. Of course the services supplied by households to business as well as the products supplied by businesses to households are furnished for payment, not free of charge. In a primitive economy, services can be bartered directly for products, but a complex economy cannot be based on such a system of exchange. Payment must be made by means of money, which is the only type of effective demand in the U.S. economy.

In our simplified version of an economy (with no foreign trade and no government) the demand that calls forth the supply of business goods and services may be divided into two spending flows: private consumption and private investment. Thus *aggregate demand for the national product is equal to private spending for consumption and investment.* This concept of demand, based on consumer and investor spending, was Keynes' main analytic tool.

The payment for the supply of services from households may be similarly divided into various income streams: wages, rent, interest, and profits. Wage income includes hourly wages, piecework wages, salaries, and commissions.

Profit income includes profits of both corporate and unincorporated business. Rental income includes the rent from land as well as buildings. Interest income includes all returns on borrowed money. It is assumed at this point that all of these business incomes are actually paid out to households.

The circular flow of supply and demand is depicted in Figure 24.1, which indicates how (1) money spending flows from households to business in return for (2) the flow of products from business to households. At the same time (3) the services and property of households flow to business in return for (4) the flow of money income from business to households. Notice that money moves in one direction around the circuit, whereas goods and services meet it in their equal and opposite movement. If there is no hitch, the supply and demand will flow smoothly and just balance each other in both sets of transactions.

Gross national product may be calculated in two different ways, corresponding to the money flow from households to business or the equal money flow from business to households. In the first, the aggregate money demand for all products, or the *flow of money spending* on consumer goods and investment goods, is examined.

$$\$ \text{ GNP} = \$ \text{ spending} = \$ \text{ consumption} + \$ \text{ investment}$$

This flow of money spent for products must correspond to the equal and opposite flow of products to their final buyers. In the marketplace the money flow

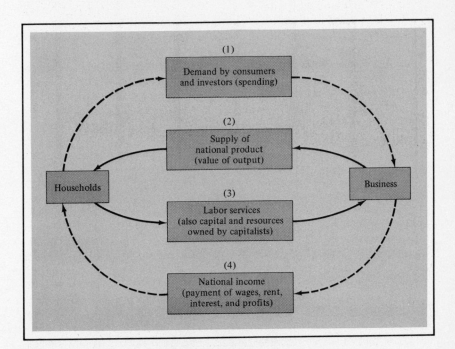

Figure 24.1 **Circular flow of supply and demand**

from purchasers is precisely the measure of the value of the GNP sold by business. Thus in Figure 24.1 the two upper loops, labeled (1) and (2), show the movement of money in one direction and the equal movement of goods and services in the other direction. *The two are equal by definition* because the exchange price has been agreed to by both buyers and sellers. In the next chapter we will see how Marx and Keynes analyzed the problems that result when consumers and investors *intend* to spend *less* than the value of goods supplied at present prices.

The second way of calculating GNP is to add up the money paid out by businesses for all of their costs of production. Most of these costs of production constitute *flows of money income* to households. These incomes include wages paid for the services of labor, rent for the use of land, interest for the use of borrowed capital, and profit for capital ownership. Thus the two lower loops of Figure 24.1, labeled (3) and (4), depict the movement of goods and services to business in one direction and the equal movement of money as income to households in the other.

Actually businesses have other costs that have not yet been discussed. These costs make the second way of calculating GNP a little more complicated than suggested by the simple diagram in Figure 24.1. One of these costs is *depreciation,* or the funds set aside to replace the machinery and factory buildings that are used up or eventually worn out in the process of production. These funds are paid out not to any individual but to other businesses when it is time to replace the worn-out instruments of production. So when depreciation is added to the flows of money incomes, we get

$$\$ \text{ GNP} = \$ \text{ wages} + \$ \text{ rent} + \$ \text{ interest} + \$ \text{ profits} + \$ \text{ depreciation}$$

Marx emphasized this second way of looking at the flow of GNP. He agreed that the business pays out wages to workers. He also noted that business paid other businesses to replace the depreciated machinery. He stressed, in addition, the property incomes—rent, interest, and profit—that capitalists exploited from workers. Thus, he emphasized,

$$\$ \text{ GNP} = \$ \text{ wages} + \$ \text{ property incomes} + \$ \text{ depreciation}$$

We can calculate GNP, as Keynes did, in terms of all spending to purchase output; or we can calculate GNP, as Marx did, in terms of all the money flow through business to workers and capitalists (and for depreciation to other businesses). By definition the GNP calculated by either method must be equal to the same money value. Indeed, the U.S. Department of Commerce, which makes these calculations, always does arrive at the same amount by either method (after allowing for statistical mistakes).

GROSS NATIONAL PRODUCT IN REAL TERMS

To know whether a change in GNP reflects a change in national welfare, we must determine whether the change was due to a change in the economic measuring rod (prices) or a change in the *real* quantity of goods and services produced. If the national product doubles in money value but the price level has also doubled, then the real product—the goods and services available to the nation—has remained the same. Or, if GNP in current prices has risen 5 percent but the overall price level has risen 3 percent, physical output has increased by only 2 percent.

In calculating GNP the government must use current prices. But to make comparisons between years when price changes have occurred, the money value of GNP can be deflated by dividing the current value by an index showing how much prices have changed:

$$\frac{\text{Prices} \times \text{quantity produced} = \$\,\text{GNP}}{\text{Price index}} = \text{real (or deflated) } \$\,\text{GNP}$$

The Department of Commerce compiles price indexes for the many components of GNP. It also deflates each component by its index. Each index is constructed from the price changes that have occurred in the items that make up that component. By choosing a base year, such as 1929 (1929 = 100), against which all price changes are measured, deflated GNP data can be made comparable over the years.

POTENTIAL GROSS NATIONAL PRODUCT

Many times, part of the nation's productive capacity goes unused. Factories may stand idle or only partially used while millions of unemployed workers search for jobs. During such periods economists can calculate the approximate *potential* GNP that would obtain *if* the unemployed laborers could be put to work and *if* the factories not being utilized could be used to full capacity. The difference between potential and actual GNP is a widely used measure of the economic costs of recessions and depressions.

PER CAPITA GNP

We have noted that the actual GNP in real terms is used as a reflection of national welfare. But suppose we want to know the welfare not for the nation but for each individual. If China has the same national product as England, then the average Chinese is much worse off than the average Englishman because of the tremendous difference in population. Therefore to measure the individual welfare the GNP of a nation must be divided by the number of its population. This result is the per capita GNP. Notice, however, that per capita GNP is only an average; it does not say anything about how the GNP is distributed among individuals.

NET ECONOMIC WELFARE

Finally, suppose we have deflated GNP by price rises and by population increases. Is the resulting real per capita GNP a good measure of individual human welfare? More and more economists are coming to the conclusion that it is not a good welfare measure.

On the one side, there are some goods and services not included in the GNP because they are not given a value in the market. For example, the work of housewives is not counted in the GNP. Yet women work long, hard hours in the home, and their labor equals about one-fourth of the official GNP value. This exclusion is very inconsistent because a maid's labor is counted in the GNP to the amount of her salary, yet if she marries the house owner her labor is no longer counted and GNP is reduced. The reason for this exclusion is the sexist idea that women don't really work very hard, plus the capitalist notion that services are valuable only if they are sold in the market.

On the other side, many costs to the public are not subtracted from GNP, even though they are caused by the private capitalist production of GNP. For example, production and use of cars and trucks causes air pollution. This pollution costs the public in terms of health, such as eye and respiratory diseases, and even property damage, such as harm to trees and plants. Thus GNP should be reduced by the amount of this damage.

Moreover, some large portion of GNP is composed of wasteful or harmful goods that reduce or do not increase human welfare; this portion should not be included in GNP. For example, cigarettes are part of GNP, but they are harmful. Advertising "service" is part of GNP, but over 90 percent of it is pure propaganda or misinformation. The largest single waste is military spending, yet all of those billions of dollars spent to stockpile bombs and tanks are included in GNP.

It might also be noted that some projects benefit the public beyond the cost shown in GNP. For example, a dam built by the government for water and power (and counted in GNP at cost) may also produce recreation and beauty.

Therefore a new measure is needed, and some economists have argued for *net economic welfare* (NEW) to replace official GNP. NEW would equal GNP but in addition would (1) *add* housewives' labor, (2) *add* unpriced benefits (e.g., recreation from dams), (3) *subtract* unpriced costs (e.g., pollution from industry and cars), and (4) *subtract* all harmful and wasteful products.

SUMMARY

Goods flow from business to households, while labor services flow from households to business; money travels in the opposite direction around the circle. The gross national product is the money value of all the goods produced in a year. It should be corrected for inflation of prices or increase of population if it is to begin to measure welfare. But it should also be corrected to add housewives' labor and other benefits not priced in the market, and we should subtract from it all the harmful and wasteful products (including the military) plus all the costs of pollution and other environmental destruction. Only with these major corrections would a new measure of GNP reflect human welfare.

APPENDIX

THE NATIONAL INCOME ACCOUNTS IN DETAIL

We saw in Chapter 24 that if government and foreign trade are omitted, then GNP may be calculated as spending for consumption plus spending for investment.

We are now ready to bring government into the calculation of GNP and to admit that goods are sold and brought abroad. Government could be viewed as a giant household or business; but because government output of services is not sold in the marketplace, there is no obvious way to value the services it provides. The U.S. government is not to any appreciable extent an owner of any instruments of production; it receives its income by taxing the incomes of labor and of privately owned instruments of production. Yet government spending in the private sector is a very significant part of overall demand, and government employs about 18 percent of the labor force.

For our purposes the role of government in the economy will be simplified by assuming that it merely siphons money from the circular flow by taxing and injects it back into the spending stream by buying goods and services from businesses. The types of goods and services government buys and the uses to which it puts them will be considered in later chapters. Gross national product, with government spending in the economy and with foreign trade, when calculated from the expenditure side, becomes

$$\$ \text{ GNP} = \$ \text{ spending} = \$ \text{ consumption} + \$ \text{ investment}$$
$$+ \$ \text{ government} + \$ \text{ net exports} \tag{1}$$

Net *exports* are the difference between what is sold and what is bought abroad. Exports bring a flow of dollars into the country in exchange for goods produced at home but sold abroad. Imports result in a flow of dollars out of the country for the purchase of goods produced abroad. If more is exported than imported, the net figure is an addition to the total amount of spending taking place for domestically produced goods and services. Foreign trade is also discussed in greater detail in a later chapter.

With governments in the picture another cost of doing business must enter the calculation of production costs: sales or excise taxes. These taxes include general sales taxes on all or most commodities, such as a 5 percent state tax on all sales. They also include special taxes, such as the tax on cigarettes, that effect only the purchasers of one commodity. In either case the government extracts the money at the point of purchase before it can be considered as income by business. These are sometimes called indirect taxes because they are not a direct tax on the income of any individual or business. From the income or cost side GNP includes the sales taxes as a cost of doing business. Thus

$$\$ \text{ GNP } = \$ \text{ cost of production } = \$ \text{ wages } + \$ \text{ interest } + \$ \text{ profit} + \$ \text{ rent } + \$ \text{ sales taxes } + \$ \text{ depreciation} \tag{2}$$

Net National Product

Net national product (NNP) differs from GNP in only one respect: NNP does *not* include the amount of depreciation that has occurred during the year. *Depreciation* is defined as the amount of capital used up in the production process. The NNP is very useful as a measure of what part of the economy's total production is actually available for use. Certainly production that merely replaces machinery that has worn out and is no longer usable should not be considered as adding to the amount of capital available to the economy. Thus to compare useful production in two countries we would compare NNP, not GNP, because when we compare product actually available for use, we are not interested in the amount of depreciation or capital used up in producing the available product. To arrive at the figure for NNP, simply subtract depreciation from GNP.

$$\$ \text{ NNP } = \$ \text{ GNP } - \$ \text{ depreciation} \tag{3}$$

In the national accounts depreciation is called *capital consumption allowance*. Unfortunately, the capital consumption allowance does not alwyas reflect physical depreciation accurately because it involves many problems of estimation that are affected by the practices of accountants. These accountants must view not only the expected life of capital equipment but also the implications for tax liability. From the cost or income side NNP can be calculated by eliminating depreciation (or the capital consumption allowance).

$$\$ \text{ NNP } = \text{ wages } + \$ \text{ rent } + \$ \text{ interest } + \$ \text{ profits } + \$ \text{ sales taxes} \tag{4}$$

If we were still excluding government, NNP and national income would be identical. *National income* is defined as the income of the nation in a year's time that is wholly derived from the production of final, usable goods and services. It is the income going to *all* the economic classes: wages to workers, rent to landlords, interest to lenders, and profit to capitalists. Sales taxes and all other indirect business taxes go to the government and do not become income to any class of citizens. When they are subtracted from NNP, the national income is simply

$$\$ \text{ National income } = \$ \text{ wages } + \$ \text{ rent } + \$ \text{ interest } + \text{ profits} \tag{5}$$

or

$$\$ \text{ National income } = \$ \text{ NNP } - \text{ sales tax} \tag{6}$$

PERSONAL AND DISPOSABLE INCOME

The government imposes various taxes on the national income but also adds to the income stream many kinds of welfare payments. Therefore the total of payments to all classes in production (i.e., the national income) is not the amount of income that households actually have at their disposal. Households' income comes from production *plus* various welfare payments *minus* various taxes.

In order to proceed from national income to the income that actually goes to people (i.e., *personal income*), various additions and subtractions must be made. First, corporate profits do not go directly to any individual; corporate profits must be subtracted from national income in the process of determining the personal income actually going to individuals. Second, individuals pay out of their wage income certain compulsory contributions for social insurance to the government (these are payments for what is usually called *social security*); these also must be subtracted from the national income. Third, individuals make various payments of interest on loans to financial institutions and to government; these also must be subtracted to find personal income.

On the positive side, the government makes many *transfer* payments that transfer income to individuals, thus adding to personal income. These transfers include unemployment compensation, farm subsidies, business subsidies, and social security benefits. Second, corporations pay dividends out of profits. Third, business makes a few transfer payments, such as retirement benefits. Fourth, a great many wealthy individuals receive interest payments from the government or from corporations. All such payments must be added to national income if we wish to calculate personal income. Totaling all the additions and subtractions from national income, the result is personal income. The procedure is indicated by the following unwieldly equation:

$$
\begin{aligned}
\$ \text{ Personal income} =\ & \$ \text{ national income} \\
& -\ \$ \text{ corporate profits} \\
& -\ \$ \text{ interest paid by individuals} \\
& -\ \$ \text{ social security taxes} \\
& +\ \$ \text{ government transfer payments} \\
& +\ \$ \text{ dividends} \\
& +\ \$ \text{ business transfer payments} \\
& +\ \$ \text{ personal interest income} \qquad (7)
\end{aligned}
$$

Finally, there is *disposable personal income,* which is the amount of money actually at the disposal of individuals and households for spending on consumption or for personal saving. In order to find this quantity, *personal income taxes,* which are the taxes an individual or household must pay in proportion to its yearly income, must be deducted. The result is expressed as

$$
\begin{aligned}
\text{Disposable personal income} =\ & \text{personal income} \\
& -\ \text{personal income taxes} \qquad (8)
\end{aligned}
$$

Consumers may now spend and save out of disposable personal income. If consumption expenditures are subtracted, we arrive at personal saving. A simplified listing of the accounts discussed here (with actual figures for 1975) is shown in Table 24A.1.

Saving and Investment

It is necessary to distinguish between the concepts of wealth, capital, and investment. *Wealth,* the broader concept, is the total holding by everyone of all durable consumer goods plus the ownership of natural resources *plus* the total holding of the entire stock of capital. Wealth is not measured in the national income and product accounts. A high level of production certainly means that a large stock of wealth exists in the form of productive capital. The national accounts, however, measure only the value of the flow of production, and hence income. They are not designed to measure the holding of wealth either as capital or, for that matter, in the form of claims measured in money, which would be called *financial wealth.* Capital is defined as the total value of all existing buildings and factories, machines and equipment for production, and inventories. *Inventories* are defined as the existing stocks of raw materials, goods in process, and finished goods stockpiled.

Investment may then be defined simply as the *change* in capital, its increase or decrease within a year or some other period. This means that any individual investment that does not increase the amount of capital, such as the purchase of old shares of stock by one individual from another, does not count as net invest-

Table 24A.1 **National Income Accounts for 1975 (in billions of dollars)**

Gross National Product	$1,516	
− Depreciation (or Capital consumption)		−$161
= Net National Product	=1,355	
− Indirect Business Taxes (mostly sales taxes)		− 147
= National Income	=1,208	
− Corporate Profits		− 92
− Interest Paid by Individuals		− 74
− Social Security Taxes		− 110
+ Government Transfer Payments		+ 169
+ Dividends		+ 32
+ Business Transfer Payments		+ 6
+ Personal Interest Income		+ 111
= Personal Income	=1,250	
− Personal Income Tax		− 169
= Disposable Personal Income	=1,081	
− Consumption Expenditures		− 997
= Personal Saving	= 84	

Source: Federal Reserve Bulletin (October 1976), p. A55.

ment for the nation. Even if a corporation sells new stock, the proceeds do not become net investment in the economy until the corporation actually uses the money to purchase new factories, equipment, or inventories. In other words, the investment discussed here is not mere financial dealing or individual investment of money, but the *real*, or physical, expansion of the nation's economic capacity. More specifically, this year's investment consists of new construction, new producer's durable equipment, and the change in business inventories.

Only one more distinction in this area of analysis need be made. The total investment in the economy is called *gross investment.* It includes both *net investment,* or investment to expand productive capacity, and *replacement investment,* or investment needed to replace the depreciation of present productive capacities.

There is, of course, a close connection between net and gross investment and net and gross national product. The connection can be easily stated through the spending approach to national product. Leaving aside government spending and net export spending, we find that

$$\text{\$ Gross national product} = \text{\$ consumption} + \text{\$ gross investment} \qquad (9)$$

In this equation gross investment includes replacement investment, which is equal to depreciation. Similarly, without government or net export, we find that

$$\text{\$ Net national product} = \text{\$ consumption} + \text{\$ net investment} \qquad (10)$$

Having defined investment, we must now define saving. Most of our national product goes for consumption—that is, the aggregate purchase of consumer goods and services by all U.S. households. *Whatever part of national income or product is not used for consumption is defined as saving.* Thus the following definition may be written (aside from government and foreign trade):

$$\text{\$ Net national product} = \text{\$ consumption} + \text{\$ saving} \qquad (11)$$

Aside from the government, there are only two sources of saving in the economy. These are (1) the personal saving of individuals and households and (2) the retained profits of businesses. Notice that the depreciation funds put aside by business, a form of gross savings, come of the gross national product. Therefore net saving is what remains from net national product after consumer spending, while gross saving is what remains from gross national product after consumer spending out of it.

Notice that both saving and investment are each by definition equal to national product (net or gross) less consumption. Therefore they must by definition equal each other. Leaving out government and foreign trade, we may write

$$\text{\$ Consumption} + \text{\$ net investment} = \text{\$ consumption} + \text{\$ saving} \qquad (12)$$

The equality between saving and investment is an accounting identity. Both are equal to national income minus consumption, by definition. Had we started from GNP, depreciation funds would have been included on both sides, making gross investment equal to gross saving of business and individuals. (The following equations will hold for net or gross amounts, so we do not distinguish between them.)

With government included, the identity becomes

$$\begin{aligned} \$ \text{ Consumption} + \$ \text{ investment} + \$ \text{ government} = \\ \$ \text{ consumption} + \$ \text{ savings} \\ + \$ \text{ taxes} \end{aligned} \tag{13}$$

This is so because national product is now the sum both of the three spending flows and of the three allocations between consumption, saving, and tax payments. The sum of investment spending and government spending is identical with the sum of private saving and taxation. If government spending and taxation are equal, the government budget in the national accounting framework is in balance. In practice, the difference between government spending and government taxation is called *government saving,* which may be positive if taxes exceed government spending or negative if there is a budget deficit.

When foreign trade is added, the identity becomes

$$\begin{aligned} \$ \text{ Consumption} + \$ \text{ investment} + \$ \text{ government} \\ + \$ \text{ exports} = \$ \text{ consumption} \\ + \$ \text{ saving} + \$ \text{ Taxes} + \$ \text{ imports} \end{aligned} \tag{14}$$

This identity can be understood as representing, on the left side, the expenditures for goods and services by the four spending sectors and, on the right side, the uses of national income. The difference between exports and imports is often called *net exports.*

If it is positive, it indicates that foreigners cannot pay for all U.S. exports with the money spent on imports from them. Hence they are increasing the total demand for U.S. goods. Since they are putting money into the U.S. economy, net exports is also called *net foreign investment.*

By rearranging accounting terms and subtracting consumption from both sides, the overall identity between saving and investment can be written as follows:

$$\begin{aligned} \$ \text{ Investment} + (\$ \text{ exports} - \$ \text{ imports}) = \$ \text{ saving} \\ + (\$ \text{ taxes} \\ - \$ \text{ government}) \end{aligned} \tag{15}$$

The sum of net domestic private investment and net foreign investment is identical to the sum of net private saving and governmental saving. Or, in brief, saving equals investment in the national accounts.

The Value Added Concept

The GNP of the United States includes only final products. It avoids counting the value of the same product more than once when this product appears at various intermediate stages of the production process. Suppose *both* the value of all the steel produced and the value of all the automobiles produced were counted in GNP. Since a great deal of steel is used in automobile production, we would be counting the value of that steel twice, once by itself and once as a principal ingredient in automobiles.

The correct procedure is to include only the *value added* by capital and labor (and land) in each industry—that is, the increase in the worth of the product in the production process of that industry beyond the worth of the raw materials bought from other industries. Therefore the value added by capital and labor (and land) to the raw material in the steel industry would be counted. Then the value added by capital and labor (and land) in making automobiles out of the steel would also be counted. But the value of the steel, or any other product from another industry, used by the auto industry would not be counted again. The whole calculation of gross product (using the cost of production, or income, approach) may be illustrated as follows:

$$\begin{aligned}
&\text{Gross product in steel and auto industry} \\
&= \text{steel (wages + profits + rent + interest + depreciation)} \\
&+ \text{auto (wages + profits + rent + interest + depreciation)} \quad (16)
\end{aligned}$$

Notice that neither the cost of the iron or coal used in the steel industry nor that of the steel or rubber tires used in the auto industry is included; both are values produced by other industries and not values added by this industry. The value added is thus less than the price in each industry by exactly the amount of goods and materials bought from other industries.

SUMMARY

For the purposes of analysis economists try to keep accounts measuring all of national output. Everything put together is called the *gross national product,* the demand for which comes from consumers, investors, government, and foreign buyers. Although it is an important measure, we should not be mesmerized by the size of GNP because it includes many wasteful or even harmful goods and services (advertising, cigarettes, military). A second concept is the *net national product,* which equals GNP minus depreciation. Third, *national income* equals NNP minus sales taxes (and a few similar taxes). Fourth, *personal income* is what actually winds up in the hands of individuals; so it equals national income earned in the usual ways plus welfare and subsidies and interest payments from the government minus profits kept by corporations and corporate taxes and employees' social security taxes paid to the government. Fifth, *disposable income* is equal to personal income minus personal income taxes. Finally, *savings* equals disposable income minus consumption. Because investment is also defined as all income or output minus consumption, saving and investment are equal by definition in the national income accounts (but, as will be seen in the next chapter, what some people plan to save and others plan to invest may not be equal).

CHAPTER 25

INCOME DETERMINATION

In this chapter we discuss three very different analyses of how national income is determined, why unemployment and inflation occur, and what are the correct political policies to cure these problems. The first is the conservative position, presented by J. B. Say and almost all the classical and neoclassical economists. The second is the liberal position presented by J. M. Keynes and his followers. The third is the radical position, presented by Karl Marx and many other radicals.

THE CONSERVATIVE VIEW OF J. B. SAY

The conservative view, first presented by J. B. Say (1767–1832), is that unemployment and inflation are accidents caused by factors external to the economy. They are always minor and temporary; and the capitalist economy, if left to itself, will always automatically come back to full employment and stable prices in a short time. *Say's Law* states that any supply of goods calls forth its own demand, so there can *never* be overproduction relative to demand for any length of time. Every supply of output leads to income, which leads to an equal amount of demand.

In its most rigid form Say's law states that aggregate demand must always equal aggregate supply at any level of supply, including the full-employment level. This denies the possibility of either a deficiency or an excess of aggregate demand and therefore denies the possibility of depressions or inflations in general business activity. Say's law does *not* state that aggregate supply and aggregate demand are "identical" or are equal by definition: ". . . Though Say's law is not an identity, his blundering exposition has led a long series of writers to believe that it is one—and this in no less than four different senses."[1] Rather, *Say's law says that an increase of supply, through various automatic processes, calls forth an equal amount of demand.*

Aside from a few dissenters, whole generations of economists refused to accept the possibility that there could be involuntary unemployment or an excessive supply of goods. Furthermore, they never challenged the assumption that all commodities could always be sold at prices equal to their full, long-run costs. They admitted only the possibility of temporary, accidental maladjustments in one or a few industries. Such maladjustments were sure to be corrected as soon

[1] Joseph A. Schumpeter, *History of Economic Analysis* (New York: Oxford University Press, 1954), p. 618.

as competition could force capital to switch from one industry to another. In a typical statement Ricardo argued, "Too much of a particular commodity may be produced, of which there may be said to be such a glut in the market as not to repay the capital expended on it; but this cannot be the case with all commodities."[2]

The kernel of truth in Say's law is the platitude that every purchase constitutes a sale, and every sale means some money income to someone, which again may, and ordinarily will, be used for more purchases. Ricardo phrased the case for Say's law in this way: "No man produces but with a view to consume or sell, and he never sells but with an intention to purchase some other commodity which may be useful to him or which may contribute to future production. By purchasing them, he necessarily becomes either the consumer of his own goods, or the purchaser and consumer of the goods of some other person."[3]

This argument implies that there can be no depressions in modern private enterprise economies. Yet observation reveals that such economies have never been without periodic depressions within the last century or more. Say's law is, indeed, true for certain earlier types of economies; these could not have less aggregate demand than supply because production was for the use of self-contained communities with little external trade and little use of money. Under capitalism, however, the economy has changed; as we saw in Chapter 23, (1) production is for private profit, (2) output must be sold in the market for a profit, and (3) money is used as a medium of exchange and may be hoarded rather than respent.

By ignoring these historical changes, the classical economists, such as Say or Ricardo, built an analytic model that fit a primitive economy or a Robinson Crusoe island but is inadequate for modern capitalism. Leaving aside government and foreign trade for the moment, the essentials of J. B. Say's view of the economy can be portrayed in a very simple picture (Figure 25.1).

There is an important grain of truth in what J. B. Say claimed. It is true that output, which is supplied to the market and sold there, generates income. The capitalist pays out wages, rent, and interest. The residual from sales, whether positive or negative, may be called profits. These incomes all go to households (if we assume that corporations pay out all profits to stockholders). The households normally use all the money for consumption and investment. Since saving is defined as all nonconsumption, it is automatically equal to investment in this case.

Say and the other classical economists claimed that all income not spent for consumption would always be invested because if more money is saved than invested, competition among lenders will cause the rate of interest to fall. A lower rate of interest stimulates investment, which rises until it equals the amount of saving. Thus the total spending for consumer and investment goods would always rise to equal the total amount of goods produced.

A second classical argument claimed that, even if supply of goods were temporarily greater than demand (because of an irrational lack of investment), this

---

[2] David Ricardo, *The Principles of Political Economy and Taxation* (London: Gonner, Bell, & Sons, 1891 [reprinted from 1821 edition]), p. 276.

[3] Ibid., p. 273.

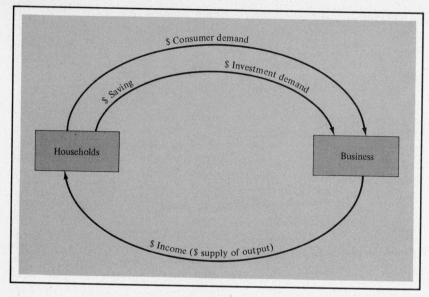

Figure 25.1 **Conservative (J. B. Say) view of income flow**

imbalance would quickly be cured by competition. Under competitive conditions the excess supply of output would quickly cause prices to drop. At the new, lower prices, demand would automatically rise to equal the supply.

The third and final classical argument asserted that, even if prices don't drop and the supply of goods is temporarily excessive, this causes very temporary unemployment. The unemployment causes competition among workers, which leads to lower wages. The lower wages stimulate capitalists to demand more labor (since it's cheaper now), which brings back full employment. Therefore the classical economists concluded that the capitalist system will automatically restore full employment with stable prices after any temporary dislocation. So the government should do nothing.

THE LIBERAL VIEW OF J. M. KEYNES

Keynes (1883–1946) is perhaps the most important economist of the first half of the twentieth century. His background does not appear to be that of a radical or an earth shaker. Born into a respected English family and educated in the best British schools, Keynes worked for His Majesty's Civil Service and the Bank of England, edited the *Economic Journal,* and wrote careful treatises on Indian finances and formal logic as well as the general problems of money. Keynes was always considered one of the Establishment in cultural, governmental, and financial circles, yet he rocked the Establishment both in England and the United States by demolishing the myth of Say's law and automatic full employment.

Say's law had been attacked by such unorthodox economists as Malthus and Marx. Keynes, however, attacked it in detail, using the respectable academic tools of the classical and neoclassical economists. In his most famous book, written at the depths of the Great Depression, he destroyed Say's law and proved that the equilibrium level of the economy might be either at a point of heavy unemployment or at overly full employment and inflation.[4]

EQUILIBRIUM OF AGGREGATE SUPPLY AND DEMAND

Keynesian economists use the idea of an equilibrium of the forces of aggregate supply and demand as their important analytical tool for understanding the level of output and employment. *Aggregate supply* is defined as the total output that business produces and plans to sell.

Aggregate demand is defined as the total dollar amount of final goods and services that consumers, businessmen, government, and foreigners *plan* to buy from the business sector. *Equilibrium* exists when planned aggregate demand equals planned aggregate supply at present prices.

It was noted in Chapter 24 that statisticians make supply and demand equal in the national income accounts, but that is only by including unwanted and unplanned accumulation of inventories as "demand" by definition. The situation is quite different if the demand that arises from planned (or intended) spending is examined. Planned spending is defined as all spending except the spending on unwanted increases in inventories. Planned supply and planned demand will be equal only when the economy is at *equilibrium*. Equilibrium means that buyers' and sellers' desires exactly agree at present prices. If however, 1000 bushels of ripe tomatoes go unsold, then the supply at present prices is greater than the planned demand.

The problem may be explained another way by saying there is equilibrium only if consumption plus planned investment are equal to consumption plus saving. *Saving* is defined to be the difference between income and planned consumption spending. Keynes argued that equilibrium is maintained only if saving out of income is just equal to planned investment spending.

The problem of economic equilibrium is illustrated in its simplest form in Figure 25.2. Business pays the national income to households. Then, if there is equilibrium, all of that income is spent by households to buy goods from business. This implies that all income that is not spent for consumption is saved in the form of investment spending. If some savings are not invested, but are diverted into hoards of money, then there will not be equilibrium of supply and demand.

The picture in Figure 25.2 assumes that

$ Saving = $ investment demand + $ hoarding or $ dishoarding

---

[4] John Maynard Keynes, *The General Theory of Employment, Interest and Money* (New York: Harcourt Brace Jovanovich, 1936).

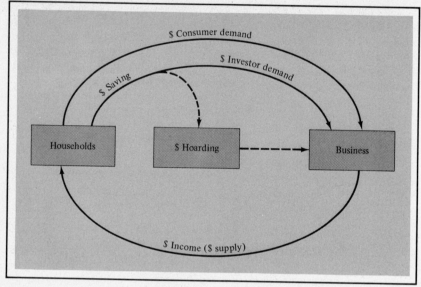

Figure 25.2 **Liberal (J. M. Keynes) view of income flow**

DISEQUILIBRIUM, UNEMPLOYMENT, AND INFLATION

Say assumed that all output supplied to the market meant income and that all income is invariably spent, either for consumption or investment. Keynes, on the contrary, points out that some income may not be spent for either consumption or investment in a given period. "Hoarding" means *not* spending income. If all income is not spent, then some income drops out of the circular flow of money into inactive hoards. For example, money deposited in banks, if the banks do not lend it to anybody, is not spent.

Keynes pointed out that if all the money income—wages, profit, interest, and rent—from supplying goods to the market is not spent, then there may be disequilibrium. *Disequilibrium* here means simply that the total money demand for all goods is less than the value of all goods at present prices. When demand is less than supply, inventories accumulate and capitalists lose money, so they cut back on production and fire workers. The economy may reach equilibrium again only at a much lower level of supply, where a vast number of workers are unemployed.

Keynes described this new situation of an unemployment level of equilibrium as one in which some savings are not invested but are hoarded, thus reducing demand. He pointed out that Say was wrong to think lower rates of interest would automatically stimulate investment. Investors invest only for profit, but suppose the outlook is for very little profit or even losses. No capitalist will be willing to borrow money even at very low interest rates because of the risk involved based on the poor profit expectations in the future—so saving may remain permanently higher than investment.

Moreover, Keynes argued that Say was wrong to think lower prices would automatically increase demand. He pointed out that lower prices will decrease wage and profit incomes, but the lower incomes mean less spending and even less demand.

Finally, Keynes argued that Say was also wrong to think lower wages would mean more demand for labor. Wages are the largest single component of consumer demand. If wages are lowered, demand for goods falls. Yet a falling demand for goods means capitalists' demand for labor may fall even further.

The opposite situation may result in inflation. Remember that inflation means rising prices (whereas deflation means falling prices). Suppose that planned demand is greater than supply, or that planned investment is greater than saving. As a result, at present prices, excess demand drives prices and outputs upward. At first, the only effect might be prosperity or rising output and employment. But when the barrier of full employment is reached, output can rise no higher, so a still-higher demand can result only in higher prices or inflation. In the case of inflation, according to Keynes, spending may be greater than national income because additional money moves out of hoards into investment, as shown in Figure 25.2. This movement of money out of hoards is called *dishoarding.* Spending can also exceed income if the spenders are borrowing from banks and the banking system as a whole is creating new money.

KEYNES AND CONSUMER BEHAVIOR

Having decided that inflation and depression are determined by the movements of aggregate demand relative to supply, Keynes' main enterprise is the explanation of those movements. He gives particular attention to deducing the psychological bases for the decision of households to save or consume at different economic levels.

Keynes begins by classifying the elements of aggregate demand for net product into two categories: consumer spending and net investment. Consumer demand is determined for the most part by the level of national income. His reasoning as to consumer behavior is based on certain broad psychological presumptions: (1) At a very low income level, the average individual still needs some minimum consumption and therefore will spend all his or her income on consumption and may even dip into savings or go into debt to spend more than his or her whole current income on consumption. (2) As the individual's income rises, a smaller percentage of it is needed to cover minimum needs, so at some break-even point he or she reaches an equality of income received and consumption spending. (3) As income rises to a very high level, consumption needs and desires may be filled through the use of a smaller portion of income, so an increasing percentage may be saved.

This usual behavior of consumers is illustrated in Figure 25.3. The line labeled "Income (consumption + saving)" shows the total income at each point; it is equal by definition to the income spent for consumption plus the income saved. *If* income exactly equaled consumption at every income level, then that line (at 45°) would also show consumer spending. In reality they are different. The line labeled "Consumption" shows how much consumer spending there actually is at each level of income. The space between these two lines obviously reflects the

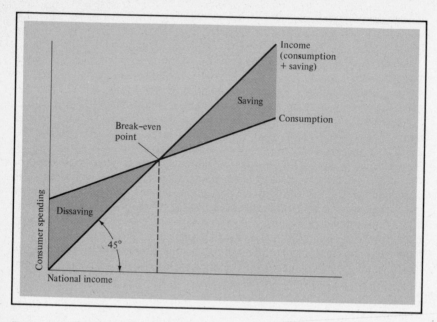

Figure 25.3 **Consumption and income**

amount by which consumption differs from income. At low levels of income, consumer spending by the poor is greater than their income, so there is *dissaving* (using up of reserves or going into debt) by these consumers. At high levels of income, consumer spending by the rich is much less than their income, so there is saving by this group.

This Keynesian schedule of aggregate consumer spending at different income levels is called the *consumption function*. It tells us that in the short run consumption is not some constant proportion of income. Rather, as income rises, consumption rises, but consumption rises more slowly than income. Therefore *as income rises, the proportion of income spent on consumption declines.* The relationship between income and consumption is explored more thoroughly in Chapter 26.

KEYNES AND AGGREGATE DEMAND

Consumption spending is the largest component of aggregate demand. In a simple economy, with no government and foreign transactions, consumption and investment together constitute aggregate demand. As has been seen, the demand may be greater or less than the aggregate supply of output that could be produced if everyone were fully employed. Consumption spending is generally considered the most stable component of aggregate demand. If consumption really behaves in a stable fashion, then, given any level of investment, our knowledge of consumer behavior enables us to derive the level of equilibrium income associated with that level of investment.

Take any arbitrary level of investment. Assume that this level of investment is constant, that is, does not change when income changes. (The actual behavior of investment is quite complex and will be investigated in detail in Chapter 27.) This investment is combined with consumer demand, according to Keynes' view of consumer behavior, in Figure 25.4. The aggregate-demand, or spending, line is derived by adding the constant amount of investment to the consumption schedule at every level of income. *If* demand equaled supply at every level of output, then the economy would always be on the 45 degrees break-even or equilibrium line, but that is not necessarily so.

Figure 25.4 illustrates the economic results at three levels of supply or output. If there is a relatively small labor force available, then full employment can produce only Output 1, a relatively low level of output. If there is a larger labor force, then full employment can produce Output 2. With a relatively large labor force, full employment can produce Output 3, a relatively high level of output.

It is clear that there is only one level of Output at which aggregate demand (equal to consumption plus investment) is equal to aggregate supply (output, or consumption plus saving): Output 2. This is called the *equilibrium level of income and output*. If full employment happens to produce this level, there is no problem.

Assume, on the contrary, that there is a large labor force, which at full employment produces Output 3. At this level it is obvious that the total of planned spending (aggregate demand) is less than the level of output (aggregate supply). The difference, labeled "Unemployment Gap," represents goods and services produced that neither business nor consumers want to buy. These goods and services become unwanted inventories. In the next production period businessper-

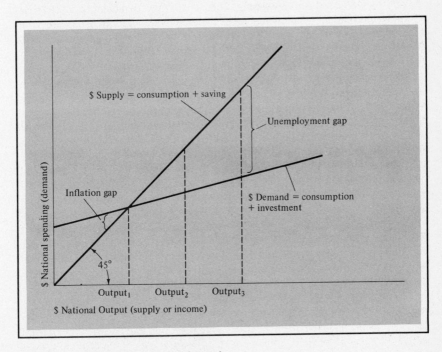

Figure 25.4 **Aggregate supply and demand**

sons will cut back on production to avoid the continued buildup of unwanted inventories. This decrease in production (and in the number of workers employed) must continue until Output 2 is reached. At this point output is just equal to what will be voluntarily purchased. The expectations of both businesspersons and consumers are consistent at Output 2. There are no longer forces at work that will lead to changes in output and income. This is why Output 2 is called the *equilibrium* level of output. But remember that all of the workers fully employed *could* produce Output 3, so at level 2 there is unemployment. It is an *equilibrium below full employment.* Only if all the unemployed workers died of a plague or were killed in a war would this be an equilibrium with full employment.

Now assume the opposite case. If we begin with a much smaller labor force that can produce only Output 1, aggregate demand will be higher than aggregate supply. (See Figure 25.4.) Businesspersons will be able to sell more than they have produced. This can be accomplished only with an unplanned and unwanted reduction of inventories—*disinvestment* to the national income accountant. If inventories are reduced to zero and no more can be produced (because full employment has already been attained), then how will the businessperson react to the excess of demand over the supply of goods? Obviously, because no more goods can be produced, he or she will raise prices. This is the inflation situation.

If, in this case, full employment of workers can produce only output and national income at Output 1, the aggregate supply available at that level is less than the aggregate demand. In other words, in that instance saving (plus consumption) is less than investment (plus consumption). This implies that there is an excess of investment funds, which comes from dishoarding of previous savings or from an increased money supply. Then there may be attempts to increase output beyond the full-employment level. Because output cannot rise beyond the full-employment level, prices must then begin to rise. Therefore the result of the gap between the demand for output and the smaller supply of it is price inflation. The inflationary tendency will continue until the money value of national output and national income approaches the Output 2 equilibrium level. Although *physical* output cannot go above the given full-employment level of Output 1, the money level of national output can rise further because output in money terms equals output in physical terms times the (rising) price level.

The Keynesian analysis, in its simplest form, demonstrates how the nation's income is determined by the equilibrium between aggregate demand and aggregate supply. It shows that this level of income may be well below the level that could be generated by producing with the labor force fully employed, so the equilibrium level of a capitalist economy may be such as to cause large-scale unemployment. On the other side, the Keynesian analysis shows that the level of income and spending may be above the production possible with the labor force fully employed, in which case the equilibrium level of a capitalist economy may be such as to cause considerable price inflation. Notice that this simplest Keynesian analysis does not explain how there could be both inflation and unemployment at the same time; it seems to exclude that possibility.

Keynes' solutions to unemployment and inflation are those of the liberal reformer. He proves that unregulated capitalism may produce long periods of unemployment or inflation. Nevertheless, he believes that capitalism can be saved by government intervention. If there is unemployment, aggregate demand can be raised by more government spending or lower taxes. If there is inflation, aggregate demand can be lowered by less government spending or by higher taxes.

THE RADICAL VIEW OF KARL MARX

Long before Keynes was born, Karl Marx (1818–1883) made the same critical attack on Say's law; he also proved that capitalism is subject to periodic attacks of mass unemployment. Unlike Keynes, however, he argues that the capitalist diseases of unemployment and inflation cannot be cured by reforms but only by replacing capitalism completely with the new economic system of socialism. These policy differences are discussed in later chapters.

Marx's distinctive contribution to income determination analysis is to point out the very different demand behavior resulting from workers' wage income and from capitalists' property income. This distinction is shown in Figure 25.5.

Marx divides income into two flows:

$$\text{\$ Wage income} + \text{\$ property income} = \text{\$ national income}$$

Wage income here includes all income earned from labor, such as piecework wages, hourly wages, and salaries. Property income includes all unearned income deriving from ownership of property, such as profits from ownership of capital, rent from ownership of land, and interest from ownership of money. As we saw in Chapter 16, Marx argued that all property income is derived directly or indirectly from the labor done by workers.

The important point here is that workers' wages and capitalists' property income reveal very different spending patterns. On the one hand, most workers' income is in the lower income categories. Thus most of workers' income is spent for consumption, while very little, if any, is saved. For simplicity, Marx considers that the low wages of debt-ridden poor workers are balanced by the higher wages of better paid workers. Therefore, Marx assumes that aggregate wages just equal the consumer spending of workers:

$$\text{\$ Wage income} = \text{\$ workers' consumption}$$

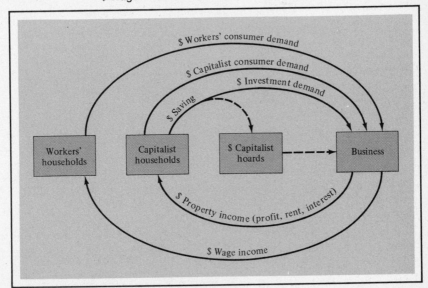

Figure 25.5 **Radical (K. Marx) view of income flow**

The data in later chapters will indeed indicate that the *average* worker—the average of poorly paid and better paid, in good times and bad times—saves almost nothing.

Capitalists, on the other hand, receive very high incomes from profits, rent, and interest. Therefore, as will be shown in later chapters, capitalists do save large parts of their income. As a result, the pattern of spending from capitalist income shows two flows. Capitalists not only spend on consumer goods, including luxuries, but also save some of their income:

$$\text{\$ Capitalist consumption} + \text{\$ capitalist saving} = \text{\$ property income}$$

What happens to capitalists' savings? In what forms do they save? A large part of it will be invested for profit. The capitalist buys stocks and bonds in corporations, and the corporations invest the money in factories, equipment, and inventories of goods on hand. Some of the money is invested indirectly through deposits in banks and insurance companies, who lend it to corporations, who use it to buy capital goods. If often happens, however, that there are no more profitable ways to invest the remaining amounts of capitalist saving. In that case, some of capitalist savings are not profitably invested but are held idle in banks or other hoards. As a general proposition,

$$\text{\$ Capitalist investment} + \text{\$ capitalist hoarding} = \text{\$ capitalist saving}$$

Of course, in a year with very high profit expectations, capitalists may invest beyond their current income by lowering their saving hoards or dishoarding.

Marx thus agress with Keynes that saving may be greater than planned investment (causing unemployment) or saving may be less than planned investment (causing inflation). Marx, however, stresses that these problems arise because of (1) the distribution of income under capitalism and (2) the behavior of capitalists seeking profits.

SUMMARY

This chapter shows three views of income determination. The conservative, J. B. Say, sees an automatic adjustment mechanism keeping the circular flow of the economy uninterrupted at full employment. The liberal, J. M. Keynes, sees the flow interrupted by hoarding, with no automatic return to full employment, but believes the capitalist government can correct the imbalance. The radical, Karl Marx, agrees that capitalism often operates with unemployment; he separates the flows into workers' and capitalists' income and spending, and finds the problem to be caused by the basic relations of capitalism and to be unsolvable within capitalism.

CHAPTER 26

CONSUMPTION

The largest single element of spending for U.S. products comes from the consumer demand for goods and services. What determines consumer demand? Obviously, the total amount of income available is an important factor. Rich and poor, however, have very different spending patterns. Therefore, another factor determining consumer demand is the degree of inequality in the distribution of income between rich and poor.

INEQUALITY IN INCOME DISTRIBUTION

The facts of inequality in U.S. income distribution were presented in full in Chapter 17 of this book, so we need only summarize that data here. First, a large percentage of U.S. families live below the officially defined poverty level. Second, distribution of income is very unequal, with the richest 10 percent of families getting more income than the poorest 50 percent of families put together. Third, there has been little, if any, change in inequality in this century. Fourth, the richest one-tenth of 1 percent of families control most property, particularly corporate stock, so 90 percent of their income is from profit, rent or interest. Fifth, the poorest 70 percent of the population own almost no property producing income, so almost 100 percent of their income is wage or salary income from labor.

CONSUMER PSYCHOLOGY AND SOCIAL STRUCTURE

Keynesian economists use certain shorthand terms to describe the relationship between consumption and income. The *average propensity to consume* is the portion of income spent for consumption, or the ratio of consumption to income at any particular level of income. If consumption is $600 billion while national income is $800 billion, then the average propensity to consume is $600/$800 or 75 percent. Similarly, the *average propensity to save* is the ratio of saving to income at this particular level of income. (Remember that saving is defined as all income not consumed.) If saving is $200 billion and income is $800 billion, then the average propensity to save is $200/$800 or 25 percent.

Keynesian economists also speak of the *marginal propensity to consume,* which can be thought of as the portion that will be spent out of any additional increment to income. It is defined as the ratio of the change in consumption to the change in income. If consumption increases by $0.8 billion, while income increases by $1.0 billion, then the marginal propensity to consume is $0.8/$1.0 or

80 percent. Similarly, the *marginal propensity* to save is the ratio of the change in saving to the change in income. If saving increases by $0.2 billion, while income increases by $1.0 billion, then the marginal propensity to save is $0.2/$1.0 or 20 percent.

The Keynesian use of the word *propensity* to describe consumer behavior seems to imply that consumers follow some purely innate psychological laws. On the contrary, according to radical economists, consumer behavior is determined not by any natural drives but by social conditioning. We are not born with a desire for television sets. Nor is there any innate compulsion to consume exactly 90 percent of our income and save 10 percent. Our desires for television sets, as well as our decisions on the ratio of consumption and saving to income, are determined by society's attitudes, ideologies, and institutions. Certainly family background has a significant influence on consumption habits, as do secular and religious educational systems. And last but not least, the vast volume of advertising in the U.S. economy affects the pattern and even the aggregate amount of consumption.

Thus consumer psychology is largely socially determined. Even more important than consumer psychology or desires, however, are the objective social facts of how income is distributed. Even if they have the very same psychological attitudes, an unemployed worker with a tiny income will not be able to save anything (and may dissave, or go into debt), whereas a businessperson with a million-dollar income may consume only 10 percent of his or her income (and still have a very high consumption standard). Thus the data show that groups with very low incomes spend all (or more than all) their incomes on consumption. In the terminology of Keynesian economics, low income groups have a high propensity to consume. On the contrary, the data show that groups with very high incomes spend only a small proportion on consumption. The high-income groups spend a large number of dollars on consumption, but this leaves them with a high proportion of unused income, which they save in various forms. In the terminology of Keynesian economics, the high-income groups have a low propensity to consume and a high propensity to save.

Obviously, a change in the distribution of income will affect the proportion of income spent on consumption. Hence if society taxes the rich and gives to the poor, the proportion of income spent on consumption (the propensity to consume) will usually rise. But if society taxes the poor and gives to the rich, the proportion of income spent on consumption will usually fall.

Propensity to consume for the whole nation therefore depends mainly on just two factors (although it is influenced by many others): (1) consumer psychology as determined by social conditioning and (2) how society distributes income. In this context the term *propensity to consume* is perhaps misleading. A more neutral term, perhaps *consumption ratio*, might more easily include behavior based on both psychological desires and income distribution. Because most economic literature does use *propensity to consume*, it is used here; but the reader must remember that it refers, not to innate drives, but to socially conditioned psychology and the objective facts of income distribution.

Using the usual terminology, we can say that an income shift from the rich to the poor will tend to raise the national propensity to consume because the poor have to consume all their income. An income shift from the poor to the rich will tend to lower the national propensity to consume because the rich consume a much lower proportion of their income.

Further, most of the income of the rich comes from ownership of property (profits, rent, interest, and dividends). But most of those whose income comes almost solely from wages and salaries fall into the lower-income groups. Thus we expect to find workers forced to spend almost all of their low incomes; while capitalists are able to save a good-sized proportion of their high incomes. This theoretical expectation is confirmed by some data given by the conservative Milton Friedman; his data show the reality of this difference in class behavior. In the period 1948–1950, Friedman found that business owners saved 23 percent of their income, farmers saved only 12 percent, and nonfarm wage workers saved a mere 4 percent.[1] Friedman's data thus reveal that the average worker spends 96 percent of his or her income for consumption. Although a few better-paid workers save some money (especially in expansions), large numbers of poorly paid workers go into debt (especially in depressions). Other studies have found capitalists saving as high as 30 to 40 percent of their incomes, so the difference is truly striking.

Thus the effects of shifts between property income and wage income are similar to those of shifts between rich and poor. If less goes to capitalist property owners and more to wage workers, the result is a higher propensity to consume because wage workers consume almost all their income. If less goes to wage workers and more to property owners, the result is a *lower* propensity to consume because property owners consume a small percentage and save a very large percentage of their income.

CONSUMER BEHAVIOR OVER THE BUSINESS CYCLE

The changes in consumption and saving at different levels of income, as postulated in consumption theory, may be illustrated by actual data. In 1929, at the peak of prosperity, the level of consumer expenditure reached its highest point of the decade, as did national income. Personal saving was also at a record level of $4.168 billion.[2] By 1933, in the depth of the depression, aggregate income had fallen by half. Consumption had also fallen, but not as swiftly, because people were spending on consumption more than their aggregate income by dipping into their savings accumulated in previous years and by going into debt. As a result, personal saving was actually negative in 1933, at −$648 million (dissaving).

From these data, the conclusion is: Total consumer spending rises when national income rises, and falls when national income falls. Consumption, however, rises more slowly than income and also falls more slowly than income. In an expansion a sizable portion of high incomes is usually saved; whereas in a depression, when income suddenly falls, all or more than all income is often spent on consumption. In other words, when national income rises in prosperity, the

[1] Milton Friedman, *A Theory of the Consumption Function* (Princeton, N.J.; Princeton University Press, 1957), pp. 69–79.

[2] Data from U.S. Department of Commerce, *Statistical Abstract of the United States, 1964* (Washington, D.C.: GPO, 1964).

average propensity to consume (the ratio of consumption to income) generally falls; but when national income declines in a depression, the average propensity to consume generally rises.

There is, in fact, a great deal of evidence from other cycles that indicates "that as income falls in the business cycle, consumption will fall proportionately *less* than income; and again when income rises cyclically, consumption will rise proportionately less than income."[3] Furthermore, this relationship is consistent with the fact that the ratio of additional consumption spending to additional income (the marginal propensity to consume) is far less than 1. Using the statistics for 1947 to 1958, it has been calculated that only 88 percent of additional disposable income is usually spent on consumption (and only 58 percent of additional GNP is spent on consumption).[4] The important fact, however, is that the average propensity to consume, or the proportion of consumer demand to income, has declined in every expansion and risen in every depression.

These cyclical patterns can be seen most clearly if each cycle is divided into nine stages. Stage 1 is the initial trough at the bottom of the last depression; stages 2, 3, and 4 divide up the expansion; stage 5 is at the cycle peak; stages 6, 7, and 8 divide up the contraction; and stage 9 is the final trough in the new depression. The cycle average for each series is set at 100, so the figure for each stage is a percentage of that cycle's average. The patterns in the 1970–1975 cycle for national income, national or aggregate consumption, and the ratio of consumption to income are shown in Table 26.1 and Figure 26.1.

Table 26.1 Cyclical Patterns of National Income and Consumption (United States, quarterly data, 4th quarter 1970 to 1st quarter 1975)

	Trough (4Q, 1970)	Expansion			Peak (4Q, 1973)	Contraction			Trough (1Q, 1975)
Stages	1	2	3	4	5	6	7	8	9
National income	89	93	98	105	107	105	103	100	100
Aggregate consumption	91	94	99	105	104	102	103	100	101
Average propensity to consume	114	107	101	94	90	94	98	102	105

Source: U.S. Department of Commerce, *Survey of Current Business,* (July 1972, July 1973, July 1974, August 1975). Dates of peaks and troughs of cycle from Table 22.1
Note: Average value from 4th quarter 1970 through 1st quarter 1975 set equal to 100. Average value of national income was $652 billion. Average value of aggregate consumption was $527 billion. Average value of the ratio of consumption to income, that is, average propensity to consume, was 0.81. The values of national income and consumption are in real terms, that is, in constant 1958 dollars, deflated for price changes.

[3] Alvin Hansen, *Guide to Keynes* (New York: McGraw-Hill, 1953), p. 76.
[4] See Bert Hickman, *Growth and Stability of the Postwar Economy* (Washington, D.C.: Brookings Institution, 1960), p. 224.

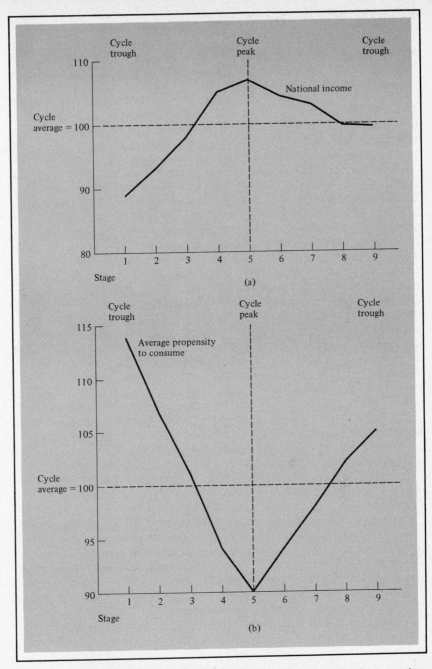

Figure 26.1 **(A) National income and (B) average propensity to consume. Average value of variable from 4th quarter 1970 through 1st quarter 1975 set equal to 100. The data is quarterly from 4th quarter 1970 to 1st quarter 1975 for the United States. The movements of national income are shown in real terms, that is, in constant 1958 dollars, deflated for price changes.** (Source: U.S. Department of Commerce, *Survey of Current Business,* July 1972, July 1973, July 1974, and August 1975.)

National income rises from the initial trough at stage 1 (in the fourth quarter of 1970) to the cycle peak at stage 5 (in the fourth quarter of 1973) by 18 points. The term *points* is used throughout this book to refer to the amount of rise or decline in one of these cycle patterns, in which the average over the whole cycle is always set at 100 points. Since this base remains the same for all comparisons in this cycle, the comparisons are clearer than statements of *percentage point* rises or falls from various bases. Reduction of data to a base of 100 for each cycle also allows comparisons between different cycles and different economic variables.

While national income rose 18 points in the expansion, consumption rose only 13 points in the expansion. Similarly, in the contraction from the peak (at stage 5, in the fourth quarter of 1973) down to the final trough (at stage 9, in the first quarter of 1975), national income fell 7 points, while consumption only fell by 4 points. These data illustrate the fact that consumption rises and falls more slowly than income. The result of these different movements of income and consumption is that the ratio of consumption to income, the average propensity to consume, is highest at the trough of the contraction. As shown in Figure 26.1b., the ratio of consumption to income then falls to its lowest point at the cycle peak, rising to another high point at the end of the following contraction.

In the four previous cycles, from 1949 through 1970, the result is the same. Since the index for each cycle is based on setting its own average equal to 100, the patterns can be averaged without distortion. For those four cycles, in the average expansion national income rose 25 points, while consumption rose only 18 points. For those four cycles, in the average cyclical contraction national income fell by 3 points, while consumption actually rose by 0.6 points.[5] In these very mild contractions, income fell little and consumption stayed almost constant. (All these data are in terms of real purchasing power; everything rose more in money terms.)

Why does the average propensity to consume tend to fall in each business expansion? Many Keynesians argue that, as income rises, the average psychological propensity of consumers is fixed at the norm set by their previous spending level. There is a long lag before they consider a higher level to be normal and necessary. In the meantime the percentage saved must increase.

Many other economists, particularly radicals, have considered more specifically the differing consumer behaviors of affluent capitalists and lower income workers. As capitalist income rises in an expansion, capitalists do consume a smaller and smaller proportion of it. Partly, this is because they still consider their earlier consumption level normal and satisfactory. Partly, it is because the profit outlook has become more optimistic, so they wish to save a larger part of their income in order to invest it in profitable enterprises.

Workers, on the other hand, continue to spend almost their whole income on consumption. Since their standard of living was below normal at the bottom of the depression, they use most of their increased income to pay off debts and buy necessities. At any rate, their propensity to consume remains over 95 percent even at the peak of the cycle.

Since the capitalists have a much lower propensity to consume than the work-

---

[5] Data from U.S. Department of Commerce, *Business Conditions Digest*, October 1974; and U.S. Department of Commerce, *National Income and Product Accounts of the United States, 1920–1965* (Washington, D.C.: GPO, 1966).

ers, the distribution of income between worker and capitalist is very important in determining the national average propensity to consume. Even if there were no changes in psychological propensities to consume in either class, a shift in income distribution could explain a change in the average propensity to consume. The declining average propensity in an expansion may be explained by a shift of income from workers (with high propensities to consume) to capitalists (with low—and falling—propensities to consume). The rising propensity to consume in a depression could be explained by an income shift back from capitalists to workers.

CYCLICAL SHIFTS IN INCOME DISTRIBUTION

Wages do rise and fall proportionately less than aggregate income, while profits fluctuate more than the total national income. "Thus in a time of great activity, wages and salaries constitute a smaller fraction of increased national income than in a time of depression."[6] The aggregate data demonstrate that the ratio of wages to national income falls in economic expansion but rises in depression. In the 1970–1975 cycle, wages (employee compensation in terms of real purchasing power) rose 15 points in the expansion, and fell 7 points in the contraction.[7] On the other hand, profits (corporate profit and inventory valuation adjustment in terms of real purchasing power) rose 33 points in its expansion and fell 27 points in its contraction. While wages peaked in stage 5, profits peaked in stage 4. We find that profits rose much faster than wages in the expansion and declined faster in the contraction.

As a result of the more rapid rise and fall of profits, the ratio of profits to wages changes systematically over the business cycle. In the 1970–1975 cycle, the *ratio* of profits to wages rose 29 points to its peak and fell 23 points to its trough (Figure 26.2). Thus there was an income shift toward high-income capitalist profits in the expansion and back toward lower-income workers' wages in the contraction. This was a major reason for the declining propensity to consume in the expansion and the rising propensity to consume in the contraction.

To avoid confusion, it must be stressed that real wages, profits, consumption and income all rose in the expansion and all fell in the contraction. But the *ratio* of consumption to income and the *ratio* of wages to profits both declined in the expansion and both rose in the contraction. In the expansion workers have more real income, but a smaller proportion of all income—and vice versa in contraction.

In the four business cycles from 1949 to 1970, the patterns of profit and wage behavior were similar, except that the downturns in profit and profit ratios occurred much earlier in the expansion. This led some observers to make it an absolute rule that profits and profit ratios decline in early expansion, although this was true only for these particular expansions. In these four expansions, total corporate profits in real terms reached a peak each time in mid-expansion (in

[6] John M. Clark, *Strategic Factors in Business Cycles* (New York: National Bureau of Economic Research, 1951), p. 155.
[7] All data in this entire section from U.S. Department of Commerce, *Survey of Current Business*, August 1975; and from U.S. Department of Commerce, *Business Conditions Digest*, October 1974.

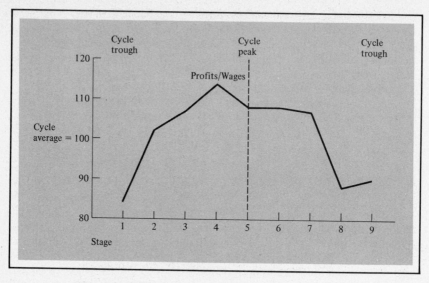

Figure 26.2 **Ratio of profits to wages, 1970–1975**

stage 3). In all four expansions total real wages rose to its peak at the end of expansion (in stage 5). As a consequence, in these four cycles the *ratio* of profit to wages rose to its peak in mid-expansion (in stages 2 or 3). Most recently, in the 1970–1975 cycle, this important ratio of profits to wages peaked toward the end of expansion (in stage 4).

Why do wages rise so slowly in expansions, particularly in the early half of expansion? In the recovery phase of the cycle, there are still large numbers of unemployed willing to take new jobs at low pay. The bargaining power of unions in the early phases of business expansion is also relatively weak, partly because of the existence of the reserve of unemployed workers, but also because of the general attitudes toward wage changes. The public is sympathetic to workers resisting wage cuts but less sympathetic to fights for wage increases. Even workers are more easily aroused by anger and militancy to resistance to wage cuts than they are enthusiastic to strike for wage increases. In early expansion, however, the big profit increases come primarily from increased productivity. Expansion, particularly the initial recovery, is a period of investment in new machinery, which increases productivity of workers and lessens the need to hire more workers. Finally, increased demand for goods causes prices to rise during expansion. It takes workers a while, however, to realize that these price increases are holding down their real wages (this is called the money illusion).

Why do wages usually keep rising to the peak of expansion? By the peak of expansion, there is much less unemployment. This gives unions greater bargaining power. Worker militancy also increases as workers become fully aware that productivity increases are raising profits, while price increases are slowing the increase of real wages. For these reasons, real wages as well as money wages usually continue to rise to the peak of expansion.

Why do real wages fall relatively slowly in contraction? During the recession, workers strongly resist wage cuts, while productivity and prices usually rise much more slowly than in expansion (because of declining demand). Thus the recession usually witnesses a shift to a lower ratio of profit to wage as profits fall faster than wages. In the next chapter we will examine why profits usually rise so rapidly in early expansion, level off (or even decline) in late expansion, decline rapidly in early contraction, and usually bottom out (or even rise) in late contraction.

CYCLICAL INTERACTION OF INCOME DISTRIBUTION AND CONSUMPTION

Earlier sections have implied how cyclical changes in income distribution affect the cyclical behavior of consumer demand, but it is useful to make this explicit as a conclusion of this chapter. Early in cyclical expansions, the ratio of profits to wages rises drastically. This income shift lowers the ratio of consumer demand to income and output. In the later stages of expansions, the ratio of profit to wages levels off or declines a little, though it is still above the cycle average until the business peak is reached. This slight easing of inequality is not enough to get consumer demand to rise rapidly (and is too late to stop the process of contraction), but it does keep consumption steady or slowly rising until the contraction begins.

In the early part of most contractions wages fall, but profits fall even more rapidly. The improved equality of income distribution raises the ratio of consumption to income. Therefore, consumption does not fall as rapidly as income, so consumer demand sets some floor to the contraction.

A numerical example may clarify how a shift in income distribution affects consumer demand. Suppose at the beginning of an expansion that all workers receive $50 billion in wages and all capitalists receive $50 billion in profits. Suppose also that workers spend for consumption 100 percent of their income, while capitalists spend for consumption only 50 percent of their income. Then consumer demand equals $50 billion out of wages plus $25 billion out of profits, or a total of $75 billion. This would be an average propensity to consume of 0.75.

Now assume workers still have an income of $50 billion and still consume $50 billion. Profits, however, expand in an upturn to $100 billion. If capitalists still consume only 50 percent, then they will consume $50 billion. The new expanded level of consumption is now $50 billion of wages plus $50 billion of profits. This is a total of $100 billion of consumer spending out of a total income of $150 billion, so the average propensity to consume has declined to 0.67. (Actually, the decline will be greater because the average propensity to consume of capitalists also declines in the expansion.) This decline means a widening gap between consumption demand and output as the expansion continues. The gap is closed in the contraction because income shifts back to workers, so consumer demand drops more slowly than income.

SUMMARY

Consumer behavior is determined by both social conditioning and income distribution. Income is distributed very unequally, a few rich families having very high incomes, a large number of poor having a very low income. The poor (mostly wage earners) consume a very high percentage of their income. The rich (mostly profit and interest receivers) consume a small percentage of their income.

In expansion periods the average propensity to consume falls, partly because of the psychological behavior of capitalist profit makers, but partly because there is a shift of income from low-income wage earners to high-income profit makers. In depression periods the average propensity to consume rises, partly because of the psychological behavior of capitalist profit makers, but partly because there is a shift in the percentage of income going to low-income wage workers (though their absolute income levels are falling).

APPENDIX A

ASPECTS OF THE CONSUMPTION FUNCTION

The APC was defined as the ratio of consumption to income at any particular level of income. Similarly, MPC was defined as the ratio of change in consumption to change in income. Figure 26A.1 illustrates the consumption function. The

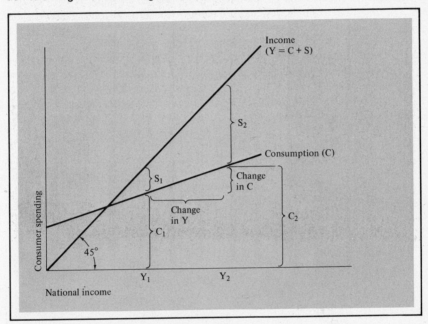

Figure 26A.1 **Propensities to consume and save**

DEFINITIONS
Average propensity to consume (APC) = C/Y
Average propensity to save (APS) = S/Y
Marginal propensity to consume (MPC) = (Change in C)/(Change in Y) = $(C_2 - C_1)/(Y_2 - Y_1)$
Marginal propensity to save (MPS) = (Change in S)/(Change in Y) = $(S_2 - S_1)/(Y_2 - Y_1)$

IDENTITIES
1. $Y = C + S$
2. $Y_2 - Y_1 = (C_2 - C_1) + (S_2 - S_1)$ or change in Y = change in C + change in S
3. $C_1/Y_1 + S_1/Y_1 = 1$ or APC + APS = 1
4. $(C_2 - C_1)/(Y_2 - Y_1) + (S_2 - S_1)/(Y_2 - Y_1) = 1$ or MPC + MPS = 1

accompanying definitions and identities should be reviewed thoroughly to understand the pertinent terms used by Keynesian economists.

As the level of income rises, APC falls; that is, the ratio of C_2 to Y_2 is less than the ratio of C_1 to Y_1. Notice that the MPC is simply the slope of the consumption function. It is assumed for simplicity that MPC is constant, which means that additions to income will result in equal additions to consumption. In reality, though, MPC probably declines somewhat as income rises.

As the level of income rises, APS rises; that is, the ratio of S_2 to Y_2 is greater than the ratio of S_1 to Y_1. Because MPC is assumed to be constant, MPS stays constant; that is, additions to income produce equal additions to saving.

Four simple identities result from these definitions. First, consumption plus saving (or dissaving) must always equal income. Second, the change in consumption plus the change in saving (or dissaving) must always equal the change in income. Third, because consumption plus saving equal income, APC plus APS must always equal 1. Fourth, MPC plus MPS must always equal 1.

A numerical example may more clearly fix these definitions. Assuming that consumption for each level of income is known, then all the other quantities may be calculated according to their definitions.

In Table 26A.1 the simplest possible assumption is used: Consumption rises by $1000 with each $2000 rise in income. This is a constant MPC (and a constant MPS). Nevertheless, because it was assumed that consumption began above income (because some minimum consumption is necessary even at very low income levels), the table also reveals a falling APC with a rising APS.

Table 26A.1 **Income and Consumption Relationships**

	Assumptions			Calculations	
Income (Y)	Consumption	Periods	Saving (S) = Y–C	Average Propensity to Consume = C/Y	Average Propensity to Save = S/Y
$ 0	$2,000	1	– $2,000	2/0 (or + infinity)	2/0 (or – infinity)
$ 2,000	$3,000	2	– $1,000	3/2 (or 1.50)	1/2 (or – 0.50)
$ 4,000	$4,000	3	$ 0	4/4 (or 1.00)	0/4 (or 0.00)
$ 6,000	$5,000	4	$1,000	5/6 (or 0.83)	1/6 (or 0.17)
$ 8,000	$6,000	5	$2,000	6/8 (or 0.75)	2/8 (or 0.25)
$10,000	$7,000	6	$3,000	7/10 (or 0.70)	3/10 (or 0.30)

APPENDIX B

THE MULTIPLIER

Some economists believe that Keynes' most important conceptual contribution to macroeconomics is the consumption function and that the most important analytic tool to come out of the Keynesian dissection of consumption is the multiplier. The *multiplier* expresses the relation between an initial increase (or decrease) in one of the components of aggregate demand and the total increase (or decrease) in national income caused by it. The initial spending change may come from any one of the components of aggregate demand, but investment spending is the most volatile. Investment spending characteristically rises sharply or falls drastically during cyclical fluctuations. Its fluctuations are usually of much greater amplitude than those of consumption.

Obviously it is vital that government policy makers know how any change in spending, whether in direct government spending or in private investment encouraged by government spending, will affect national income. This question first received considerable attention during the 1930s, when New Deal politicians debated ways of combating the depression.

We leave government spending for a later chapter and concentrate here, as Keynes did, on the effects of changes in investment spending. In precise terms the *investment multiplier* may be defined as the ratio of change in national income to change in investment. This is more than a definition; there is a casual relationship running from change in investment spending to change in income. Change in investment usually causes a larger change in income and output because some of the money spent on investment will be *respent* by its recipients for additional consumption.

Assume that during a period with some unemployment a firm decides to construct a large new factory. This sudden increase in investment spending will increase the incomes of the contractors who supply the necessary machinery and materials and provide jobs for previously unemployed workers. Now assume that the initial increase in spending and income is $1000. The recipients of this income will immediately respend most of it for consumer goods, which will result in new income for businesspersons and workers in the consumer goods industries. These income recipients will, in turn, spend much of their new income on more consumer goods. Exactly how much additional spending occurs in each round will depend on the marginal propensity to consume of the income recipients. But it is already clear that any additional consumer spending must mean that the total income generated will be more than the original $1000 of investment spending.

The easiest way to see how the multiplier is supposed to work is to study a numerical example. In the example in Table 26B.1, only some initial change in investment and a certain marginal propensity to consume need be assumed. One

Table 26B.1 **How the Multiplier Works**

1. Suppose an increase in investment of $1000.
2. Also suppose a marginal propensity to consume of 4/5, or 80 percent.

Number of Rounds of Spending	Increase in Investment	Increase in Consumption	Increase in National Income	Increase in Saving
0	$1000 —		→$1000 —	→$ 200
1	0	$ 800 ←	→ 800 —	→ 160
2	0	640 ←	→ 640 —	→ 128
3	0	512 ←	→ 512 —	→ 102
4	0	410 ←	→ 410 —	→ 82
5	0	328 ←	→ 328 —	→ 66
6	0	262 ←	—	
—	0	—	—	—
—	—	—	—	—
—	—	—	—	—
—	—	—	—	—
—	—	—	—	—
—	—	—	—	—
Infinite Number of Rounds of Spending	Total Increase in Investment $1000	Total Increase In Consumption $4000	Total Increase in National Income $5000	Total Increase in Saving $1000

thousand dollars of investment becomes $1000 of income when it is spent. It is assumed that 80 percent, or $800, of that income is respent on consumption, which means another $800 of national income going to other individuals. They will then spend 80 percent, or $640, of *that* income, and so it goes. In the first round, 20 percent, or $200, leaks out into saving; and in the second round, 20 percent of the remaining income, or $160, leaks out into saving. The process ends only when the last $1 of the increased income is saved. At that point the whole $1000 of investment has been saved, but there already have been many rounds of consumption spending in between. In this example the total of all the rounds of consumption spending (or respending) will eventually approach $4000, and national income will approach a level that is $5000 higher than before.

If investment returns to its old level after completion of the factory, the entire process will then work in reverse. Therefore, when the multiplier is used as an analytical tool, it is necessary to distinguish between a one-time injection of new investment spending and a rise in the level of new investment spending that is sustained over a long period of time.

If the $1000 increase in investment is considered as a one-time injection of new spending, then the totals at the bottom of Table 26B.1 represent only temporary additions to consumption, saving, and national income. After these one-time increases are realized, however, total spending will eventually return to its original level. But if the $1000 increase is a new, stepped-up rate of investment spending that continues through several subsequent periods, the totals represent the rise from the old, lower levels to the new, higher levels of spending flows, which will persist in each future period.

From this description of how the multiplier works, it should be clear that if less is saved out of each increment to income, then each increment to consumption spending will be larger. In other words, if the marginal propensity to save declines, the subsequent increases in consumption and income will be larger.

The multiplier formula is just a shortcut for finding where the process of Table 26B.1 ends without repeating the calculation a great many times. Because the formula works equally well for an initial increase *or* decrease in investment, we shall speak generally of changes rather than increases or decreases. By definition:

$$\text{Multiplier} = \frac{\text{change in income}}{\text{change in investment}} \tag{1}$$

However, movement from one to another equilibrium position is assumed; therefore, at the end the change in saving must equal the change in investment. Substituting saving for investment, we get

$$\text{Multiplier} = \frac{\text{change in income}}{\text{change in saving}} \tag{2}$$

or, by simple mathematical manipulation,

$$\text{Multiplier} = \frac{1}{\dfrac{\text{change in saving}}{\text{change in income}}} \tag{3}$$

Lo and behold! The denominator of this fraction is nothing but the marginal propensity to save. So the formula to remember is just

$$\text{Multiplier} = \frac{1}{\text{MPS}} \text{ or } \frac{1}{1 - \text{MPC}}, \tag{4}$$

because the marginal propensities to save and consume always add up to exactly 1.0.

Look again at the example in Table 26B.1. It has been established that *total increase in income = increase in investment × the multiplier.* In this example the increase in investment is $1000. What is the multiplier? The MPC is ⅘, so the MPS is ⅕. The multiplier must equal 1 divided by ⅕, which is 5. So we may write

Total increase in income = $1000 × 5 = $5000

This demonstrates how the multiplier is used to find the end result of investment spending.

Notice that if the multiplier is reduced, then the investment spending has less effect. At one extreme, if the multiplier is just 1, the change in income is just equal to the change in investment. At the other extreme, if the multiplier approaches infinity, any small change in investment will cause an infinite change in income.

Of course the value of the multiplier is controlled by the MPC or MPS. If MPC falls, so does the multiplier (because less is respent out of each increase in income). A multiplier of only 2 means an MPC of only ½. A multiplier of only 1 means everything is saved and the MPC is zero. But a multiplier of infinity means all income is immediately respent for consumption, the MPC is 1, and the MPS is zero.

There are some obvious weaknesses or, at least, qualifications that must be kept in mind when the multiplier theory is used. First, so far the time element has been ignored; it takes a certain amount of time before income received is respent for consumption, and still more time before the second and third and later rounds of responding may occur. If the time lag happens to be very long or varies widely, a much more complicated multiplier will be needed to get a realistic answer to the change in income for one year.

Second, it has been assumed that MPC remains constant until the process is completed. In reality MPC often changes and is effected by many psychological and institutional factors. For example, the accumulated savings of World War II greatly increased the propensity to consume in the immediate postwar years.

Moreover, saving is not the only leakage from the income stream. Higher or lower taxes will also change MPC out of national income. Furthermore, if purchase of imports (e.g., Volkswagens) increase, there will be a leakage from domestic consumer spending. Thus the domestic MPC may change too often to permit accurate prediction of the multiplier for more than a few months in the future.

Third, the multiplier formula assumes that investment will remain the same while consumption and national income are expanding rapidly. Obviously the simple multiplier theory cannot be used if further changes in investment are to be considered.

For all of these reasons, we conclude that while the multiplier is a helpful explanatory device, it cannot be relied on for an exact estimate.

SUMMARY OF MULTIPLIER

The investment multiplier measures the change in national income that results from a change in investment. The formula for estimating this multiplier is roughly 1 divided by the MPS. This formula is far from exact because it neglects (1) time lags; (2) leakages from increased saving, taxes, and foreign imports; and (3) further changes in investment.

APPENDIX C

DATA ON CYCLICAL CHANGES IN INCOME DISTRIBUTION

Table 26C.1 **Ratio of Profit to Wages, 1970 to 1975**
(United States, quarterly data, 4th quarter 1970 to 1st quarter 1975)

	Trough (4Q, 1970)	Expansion			Peak (4Q, 1973)	Contraction			Trough (1Q, 1975)
Stages	1	2	3	4	5	6	7	8	9
Wages	91	94	99	104	106	104	103	102	99
Profits	78	90	100	111	109	107	101	94	84
Ratio of profits to wages	84	102	107	113	108	108	103	88	90

Source: U.S. Department of Commerce, *Survey of Current Business, (January 1973, July 1974, August 1975).*
Note: The average value from 4th quarter 1970 through 1st quarter 1975 is set equal to 100. The average value of wages (all employee compensation in real terms) was $485 billion. The average value of corporate profits (with inventory valuation adjustment, all in real terms) was $62 billion. The average value of the ratio of profit to wages was 0.19. The value of this ratio is consistently understated in the official data for a number of reasons, including drastic overstatement of "wages" and drastic understatement of "profits." All property income is 25 percent of national income in the same official data, also badly understated.

Table 26C.2 **History of Ratio of Profits to Wages**

| | Level of Profit/Wage Ratio at Each Cycle State | | | | | | | | |
| Stage of Cycle | Trough | Expansion | | | Peak | Contraction | | | Trough |
	1	2	3	4	5	6	7	8	9
1949–1954	96	114	108	95	90	75	81	82	87
1954–1958	98	110	105	99	94	89	82	77	80
1958–1961	96	98	108	104	101	96	93	90	88
1961–1970	91	103	112	96	75	70	70	70	65
1970–1975	84	102	107	113	108	108	103	88	90

Sources: U.S. Department of Commerce, *Business Conditions Digest*, (October 1974). U.S. Department of Commerce, *Survey of Current Business* (August 1975).

Note: Quarterly data. "Wages" include all compensation of employees. "Profits" include all corporate profit and inventory valuation adjustment. Ratio for each quarter is profits divided by wages. Average value of ratio over each entire cycle is set equal to 100. Actual averages in the five cycles were 0.21, 0.19, 0.17, 0.17, and 0.19, respectively, all badly understated in the official data as shown earlier.

CHAPTER 27

INVESTMENT

Attempts to explain investment behavior constitute the heart of many business cycle theories. Economists have long realized that, from the standpoint of understanding business cycles, investment spending is the most crucial and violently fluctuating component of aggregate demand. Yet it is also the most difficult to explain and accurately predict.

GROSS AND NET INVESTMENT

Gross investment is defined as the total value of all capital goods produced in a year. *Net investment* is simply the change in the stock of capital within a given period. The stock of capital grows as new capital goods are produced and purchased. On the other hand, the stock of capital is steadily diminished through use, wear and tear, and obsolescence. To determine net investment, the amount by which the old capital stock has diministed in the period is subtracted from the amount of gross investment.

For example, in the crucial year 1929, $8.7 billion was invested in new construction and $5.8 billion in new producers' durable equipment, and there was a $1.7 billion increase in business inventories, or a total of $16.2 billion gross investment.[1] Because allowances for depreciation (or decline of the old capital stock) amounted to $8.6 billion in that year, it can be assumed that $8.6 billion of the gross investment was for replacement. By definition the net investment must have been at the level of $7.6 billion (because $16.2 gross minus $8.6 depreciation = $7.6).

Although it was assumed that the amount of replacement investment can be measured by the estimated depreciation, the decision to replace depreciated capital goods is not automatic. In 1933 gross investment was only $1.4 billion, but depreciation was still $7.2 billion. Therefore net investment was actually at the negative level of −$5.8 billion. The capital stock, and hence the economy's productive capacity, was rapidly diminishing. (Notice that gross investment could never be negative, for at worst no new capital goods would be produced. In that event, net investment would be negative and equal to depreciation.)

In an investigation of aggregate demand, it is gross investment that is important. Any investment spending is a part of the demand for currently produced capital goods. If growth of productive capacity is being considered, however, then net investment indicates by how much the capital stock has increased and

---

[1] All data in this paragraph and the next paragraph are from Wesley C. Mitchell, *What Happens in Business Cycles?* (New York: National Bureau of Economic Research, 1951), pp. 154–157.

thereby permits an estimation of the increase in the economy's capacity to produce.

INVESTMENT FLUCTUATES VIOLENTLY

In the last chapter it was shown that consumption fluctuates much less than national income. This is because in an expansion, when income is increasing and shifting from wages to capitalist profits, capitalists do not increase their consumption proportionately. Capitalists already have more than adequate consumption and they are tempted in the boom to invest more of their income. In expectation of high profits and expanding demand, investment rises rapidly.

Conversely, in a depression, demand is falling and the profit outlook is miserable, so capitalists rapidly reduce their investment. Capitalists then spend for consumption a higher proportion of their declining income. Moreover, income shifts back toward workers who spend an even higher proportion of their own declining income for consumption.

It is, therefore, no surprise that investment fluctuates far more violently than consumption. During the 1970–1975 cycle consumption rose 14 points in the

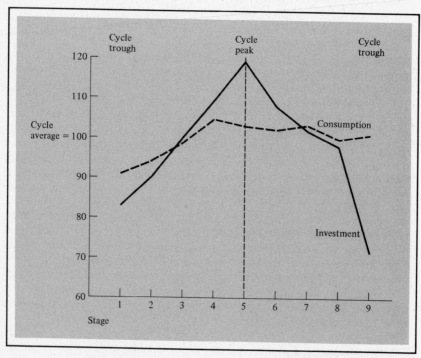

Figure 27.1 **Investment and consumption, 1970–1975. The average value for each variable over the whole period, 4th quarter 1970 to 1st quarter 1975, is set at 100. Average value of real gross private domestic investment was $124 billion. All data are in real terms, quarterly, for the United States.** (Source: U.S. Department of Commerce, *Survey of Current Business*, Washington, D.C.: GPO, August of 1971, 1972, 1973, 1974, and 1975.)

expansion and fell 4 points in the depression. Gross investment, on the other hand, rose by 35 points to the cycle peak and fell by an enormous 46 points to the cycle trough.[2] Incidentally, net investment fluctuated, as usual, even more violently. Figure 27.1 compares the cyclical behavior of consumption and gross investment in this cycle.

The same relationship has held true in most previous cycles. In the four mild cycles from 1949 to 1970, consumption rose in the expansions an average of 18 points and actually rose slightly in the contractions an average of 0.6 points. In the same four mild cycles, investment expanded an average of 30 points and contracted an average of 13 points.[3]

DECISION TO INVEST

The businessperson who contemplates the purchase of new plant or equipment will not decide to make the purchase unless the profit he or she expects to receive from this investment is greater than, or at least equal to, the purchase price of the capital goods. Obviously, profits are exceedingly important in determining the level of investment—and hence output, income, and employment—in the U.S. economy. Indeed the prime motivation for investment in a private enterprise economy is the expectation of future profit on the new investment. But because future profits cannot be known with certainty, it is mainly on the basis of the present level of profits and changes in profits that businesspeople form their expectations. Accordingly, high or rising profits will lead to optimistic expectations and new investment, whereas low or falling profits will lead to pessimistic expectations and a decline in new investment.

The other and quite distinct reason for the importance of profits is the fact that more profits provide the funds for more investment. If there are no profits, the firm may lack funds to invest even if it wishes to do so. Although the capital funds can sometimes be borrowed, more profits make it easier for the firm or its stockholders to obtain credit. Moreover, most firms are quicker to invest from internal sources, and in practice most expansion is financed with retained profits.

A great many empirical studies have found a close relationship between investment decisions and total profits or profit rates.[4] One study of data from 1947 to 1960 in fifteen industries found a significant correlation between total profits and investment decisions (evidenced by new capital appropriations) in every one of the industries.[5]

Various other studies have found a positive correlation of investment with profits after taxes as well as profits before taxes, total profits, the rate of profit (on sales or on investment), the level of profits, the change in profits, present profits, and previous profits lagged by one quarter or two. One reason that all these variables have been correlated with investment in various studies is that they are

[2] U.S. Department of Commerce, *Survey of Current Business*, August 1971, August 1972, August 1973, August 1974, August 1975, p. D5.

[3] Ibid.

[4] See the summaries of several earlier studies plus their own results in the definitive book by John Meyer and Edwin Kuh, *The Investment Decision* (Cambridge, Mass.: Harvard University Press, 1959), pp. 27–29, 134–135.

[5] Howard Sherman and Thomas Stanback, Jr., "Cyclical Behavior of Profits, Appropriations, and Expenditures: Some Aspects of the Investment Process," *Proceedings of the American Statistical Association*, September 1962, pp. 274–286.

all correlated with each other; in other words, most of the different measures of profits move in the same direction in each period. Nor can we say that only one of these measures is appropriate to all problems; different ones are needed to answer different questions. For example, a long-run investment decision between different industries is probably most influenced by the rate of profit on investment in each industry. On the other hand, in making a decision on whether to invest at all in a particular phase of the business cycle, or whether to postpone or increase the investment, businesspeople seem most heavily influenced by the movements of the profit rate on sales in the past few quarters. At any rate, there is no reason to doubt that investment behavior is most influenced by recent profit performance of corporations.

THE ACCELERATOR

We have seen that the basis for investment decision making is the expected profit from the investment. But it is difficult to estimate expected profits, so economists and businesspeople use crude substitutes to make rough guesses. The most widely used index on which to base guesses of the profitability of investments is changes in demand for output.

This approach then investigates the ratio between increased demand for output and increased capital investments. If this ratio is known and stable, we could predict the change in capital (that is, investment) from a change in output demanded. The *accelerator* is defined as the ratio between investment decisions and changes in output demanded. In other words, the accelerator is the coefficient by which we multiply a change in output demanded to predict the level of investment.

Notice that the businessperson invests in (net) new machinery only to *increase* his or her output. So the accelerator coefficient relates investment decisions, not to the level of demand for output, but to the change (increase or decrease) in demand for output. Since the rate of change of demand fluctuates more than the level of demand, this helps explain why investment fluctuates more violently than the level of output. Appendix A to this chapter discusses the accelerator concept in detail, but it also discusses all of the weaknesses of this concept.

PSYCHOLOGICAL ATTITUDES

Because investment decisions are based on projections of sales, revenues, and profits into the future, it would be easy to say that fluctuations in aggregate investment are caused by changes in investor confidence about economic conditions. Although it points to a vital aspect of economic behavior, such a formula actually explains nothing. There can be no denying the sensational effects of changes in expectations on real economic conditions in the private enterprise system. Between 1929 and 1932 children did not have enough to eat, men jumped from tall buildings, rich women pawned their fur coats. What caused the trouble? Pessimism?

Certainly there was pessimism in the Great Depression of the 1930s. But what caused the pessimism? In 1929 most indexes of production, new investment, and profits turned down in the summer, but the stock market crash and the collapse of expectations did not occur until autumn. For example, the industrial peak was reached in June 1929, but stock prices did not peak until October 1929. In a competitive, private enterprise economy, especially as it increases in complexity and interrelatedness, a single enterprise cannot accurately predict its future costs and receipts; therefore it tends to keep an optimistic outlook until it encounters obstacles. In fact, the usual order of events in depressions appears to be that production and financial indexes decline first, despite the most extreme optimism. It is only then, because of the change in objective economic conditions, that the optimism changes to pessimism, which reinforces the depression and may postpone the recovery. The reverse process seems to occur in economic expansions, when rises in production and profits are followed by a shift from pessimism to optimism.

Of course, after an expansion begins, it is true that the optimism of businesspeople goes beyond a rational response to profit increases, so it carries the expansion far beyond the point that cold calculation would carry it. Such frenzied speculation helps make the peak conditions into a bubble easily burst. Similarly, after a depression begins, pessimistic business expectations (usually overreacting in an irrational manner) cause a much greater decline in business activity than the objective condition warrants. But the ultimate cause of pessimism in businesspeople's attitudes is the previous objectively recorded decline in profits or profit rates.

INVESTMENT DETERMINED BY PROFITS

In the expansion phase of the cycle, particularly in the early expansion, profits and profit rates rise rapidly. This causes a powerful spurt of investment. At the peak of expansion, profits and profit rates are squeezed by various forces. This profit squeeze causes—via still more pessimistic expectations of future profits— a decline in investment. The decline of investment continues throughout the contraction as profits continue to decline. Toward the end of the recession, profits and profit rates bottom out and expectations become more optimistic. This ending of the profit squeeze (and expected upturn of profits) leads to the beginning of a new investment boom.

Let us see the degree to which the messy facts of the real world bear out that scenario. Figure 27.2 shows the behavior of investment and profits in the 1970–1975 cycle. It is apparent that they are very closely correlated. Profits rise to stage 4, then decline. Investment continues rising to stage 5, then declines. So investment follows profits neatly, with a one-stage time lag.

To be more comprehensive, let us examine the timing and expansion amplitude (increase) of gross investment and corporate profits in the last five cyclical expansions. The data shows the close relationship of investment and profits in each expansion.[6] In the first three cycles, profits peaked in mid-expansion (stage 3), while investment peaked in mid to late expansion (stages 3 or 4). In the last two cycle expansions, profits peaked in middle to late expansion (stage 4), while investment—reacting with a time lag—did not peak until the cycle peak (stage 5.) This delayed reaction of investment to changes in profits and profit rates is nor-

[6] See U.S. Department of Commerce, *Business Conditions Digest,* October 1974; also U.S. Department of Commerce, *Survey of Current Business,* August 1975. The Five expansions began in 1949, 1954, 1958, 1961, and 1970.

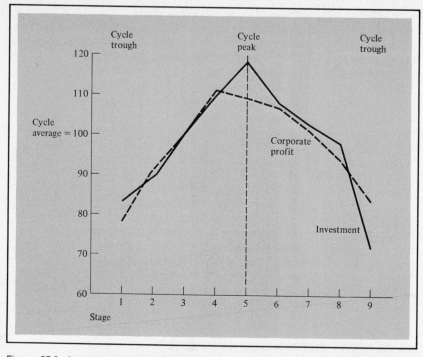

Figure 27.2 **Investment and profits, 1970–1974. Average value for each variable over whole period, 4th quarter 1970 to 2nd quarter 1975, is set at 100. Average value of gross private domestic investment was $124 billion. Average value of corporate profit was $62 billion. All data are in real terms, quarterly, for the United States.** (Source: U.S. Department of Commerce, *Survey of Current Business*, August of 1971, 1972, 1973, 1974, and 1975.)

mal because it takes businesspeople some time to make new plans, and some time to carry out new plans.

Moreover, the amplitude of expansion of investment is highest in those three cycles (beginning 1949, 1961, and 1970) in which profits also expanded the most. Investment expanded the least in the other two cycles, when profits also expanded the least. It is reasonable to conclude that investment expansion is stimulated and determined by the rise of profits. Investment declines, usually with some time lag, after businesspersons have observed that profits are being squeezed to lower levels.

The same close relationship of investment to profits appears in the contractions. The evidence reveals that investment declines during the whole period of profit squeeze in the contraction. At the end of a contraction, when profits bottom out (or at least fall more slowly), then investors regain their confidence and begin to increase investment in the early stages of the next cycle.

PRODUCTION AND REALIZATION OF PROFIT

Investment is a function of profits (and profit rates). What, then, determines how much profit is made in the U.S. economy? In making profits the capitalists face two problems. The first problem is to create or produce a profitable commodity—that is, a commodity that embodies a profit margin above costs at going prices. The second problem is to sell the commodity on the market at the going price—that is, to realize the profit embodied in the commodity.

In formal terms,

$$\$ \text{ sales revenue} - \$ \text{ costs of production} = \$ \text{ profit}$$

The sales revenue depends on the effective or money demand for all commodities, including the demand for consumer goods and services and the demand for investment goods and services. In the last chapter we examined the limitations of consumer demand. If a capitalist has produced a consumer commodity embodying a profit above costs, but there is no consumer demand for it, then the capitalist cannot realize a profit and therefore sustains a loss.

The capitalist may also produce a commodity (such as a machine) designed to meet the demand of investors. If the capitalist sells a machine to other capitalists, just as much profit may be realized from that sale as from the sale of a refrigerator to a consumer. Investment demand, however, is a much smaller part of total demand than consumer demand. It is also partly derived from consumer demand. Therefore, when consumer demand is limited (by income and the distribution of income), investment is also limited. In the last chapter we saw that consumer demand rises more slowly than national income or output; this drastically limits the realization of profits as the expansion progresses.

Before profit can be realized, it must be produced. In the process of production the capitalist buys labor from workers and raw materials and equipment from other capitalists. These human and material inputs must be used to produce a product that will sell (assuming demand does not change) above the cost of these inputs. How does the capitalist usually achieve this magical production of profits above all costs? In Chapter 16 we saw that the value of a commodity is determined by the total labor that goes into it. This price will include present labor in production *plus* the previous labor embodied in plant, equipment, and raw materials used up in the production process. The value of the product includes the entire value of the product of the previous labor (expressed mostly in depreciation costs). But the market value of present labor is far below its contribution to the value of the product, so capitalists make a surplus value or profit from the labor of the present workers. The *production* of profit then depends on keeping down costs, but the *realization* of profit depends on keeping up prices by sufficient consumer and investor demand.

WAGE COSTS OVER THE CYCLE

Profits may be expanded by high prices and low costs, or may be squeezed by high costs and low prices. Let us begin by examining one kind of costs—wage costs. If wages rise relatively to prices in some part of the cycle, then profit rates are reduced (all other things remaining constant). If, on the contrary, wage costs fall relative to prices, then profit rates rise if nothing else changes. Finally the rise and fall of profit rates influences the rise and fall of investment.

Several theories of the business cycle, to be examined in the next chapter, do allege that high wages in expansion cut into profits, and therefore cause the downturn. Thus, in this theory, labor is itself responsible for unemployment—again, blaming the victim. But this should mean that there is a shortage of labor causing high wages in each boom. Actually, there is a chronic long-run continuing unemployment in the United States. As we shall see, even at the peak of the boom considerable unemployment continues. Except in wartime, the only authenticated nationwide shortages of labor occurred in one or two railway booms in the nineteenth century. Otherwise, unemployment is the rule in peacetime expansion, so even unions can raise wages only very slowly.

Let us examine the data on cyclical behavior of wages. We saw in Chapter 26 that total profits rose faster than total wages in every expansion, though wages catch up a little near the peak; and that total profits fall faster than total wages during most of the contraction. The individual capitalist firm, however, is not concerned with the relative share of wages and profits in national income. The firm is concerned with its cost in the production process, so we must examine labor costs per unit. It is the labor cost (plus other costs) per unit that, in relation to prices, determines what the margin of profit will be.

Obviously, labor costs per unit depend in the first place on the hourly wage rate. Figure 27.3 shows the behavior of the hourly wage rate over the 1970–1975

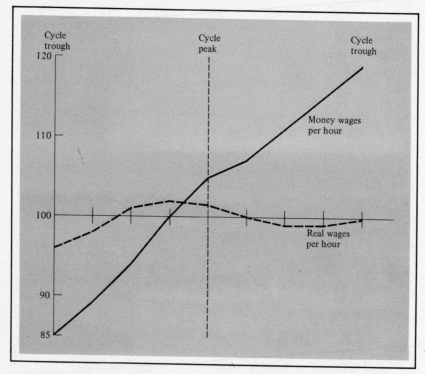

Figure 27.3 **Wages per hour, U.S., 1970–1975. Real wages equal money wages divided by the price index.** (Source: Bureau of Labor Statistics, Employment and Earnings, January 1973, July 1974, September 1975, Table C–10.)

business cycle. It reveals continuous and enormous rises in the amount of money paid in wages per hour. But it also reveals a very different behavior for *real wages,* that is, the money wage deflated by the price level. Workers are obviously interested in real wages because that is the purchasing power of their wages. Yet capitalist profit also reflects real wages because this ratio of money wages to prices is a major determinant of the profit margin. In other words, *if* prices stay constant and money wages rise, the capitalist may make less profits—but if prices rise more than wages, the capitalist may increase his profit margin.

Figure 27.3 reveals that real wages per hour, the ratio of money wages rates to prices, rose very slowly in most of the expansion from 1970 to 1973 (by only 4 points from trough to peak). This is usual, and it marked some increase in hourly labor costs to capitalists. In the contraction of 1973 to 1975, real wages fell slowly (about 3 points from peak to trough). This fall in hourly wages was some relief to capitalists, again a normal part of every recession or depression. We discussed in the last chapter why hourly wage rates behave this way, rising slowly in expansion and falling slowly in contraction.

Capitalists, however, are not as much concerned with hourly labor costs as with the labor cost per unit of output. The labor cost per unit is determined both by the hourly wage rate *and* by the productivity of labor, that is, the product per worker in each hour. As technology improves, each worker produces more in an hour. If the capitalist can grab most of the productivity increase, then his or her labor costs per unit may even decline. In other words, the capitalist tries to increase productivity, the product per worker, faster than real wages increase. Unions try to keep real wage increases at least up to increases in productivity, so as to maintain the worker's share in the product. Unions usually lose in every expansion.

In the expansion of 1970–1973, output per labor hour—or productivity of workers—did rise considerably (by 11 points from trough to peak). Since this rise in productivity per hour was much greater than the rise in real wages per hour, the *real labor costs* of capitalists per unit of output *actually declined* in most of the expansion period![7]

TOTAL COSTS OVER THE CYCLE

Costs may be divided in two categories. One category is labor costs, discussed in the last section. A second category includes the costs of material goods bought from other capitalists. This category includes the costs of plant and equipment, which appear as production expenses in the form of depreciation allowances. The other large category of production cost is the price paid for raw materials and intermediate goods used up in production.

In a careful study of costs and prices, Frederick Mills collected data for many cycles—from the 1890s to the 1930s—on prices of consumer goods, producer goods (i.e., plant and equipment), and raw materials.[8] Mills found that in the average expansion period consumer goods prices rose slowly. He found, how-

[7] Data from U.S. Department of Labor, see Appendix B to this chapter from complete citation and data.
[8] Frederick Mills, *Price-Quantity Interactions in Business Cycles* (New York: National Bureau of Economic Research, 1946), pp. 132–133.

ever, that producer goods prices rose sharply and raw materials prices rose even faster. Similarly, in the average depression consumer goods prices fell, but producer goods prices fell much more—and raw materials prices fell even further. Because of rapid shifts in demand and slow changes in supply, prices of all capital goods (and especially raw materials) rose more rapidly in expansions and fell more rapidly in contractions than did prices of consumer goods.

In recent business cycles, some changes have occurred since costs seldom decline in recessions. Still it appears that nonwage costs, mainly materials, do still rise more rapidly than other prices in expansion, and fall more (or rise less) in recessions. As Figure 27.4 shows, in the expansion from November 1970 to November 1973, the price of finished goods rose considerably (by 13 points), but the price of raw materials rose an extraordinary amount (by 50 points) in the same period. Thus, *the rising costs of raw materials did contribute to the profit squeeze in the expansion in 1973.*

In the contraction from November 1973 to March 1975, the price of finished goods actually *rose* (by 18 points). The price of raw materials, however, reached a peak in the stage just after the cycle peak, then *declined* for the rest of the contraction. (See Figure 27.4) Thus the movements of raw material prices actually helped U.S. profit margins in most of the contraction because they fell in most of the period.

PROFITS DETERMINED BY DEMAND AND COSTS

Profits cannot be squeezed from one side alone. The profit squeeze in expansion must be explained by both the limited demand for goods and services (the prob-

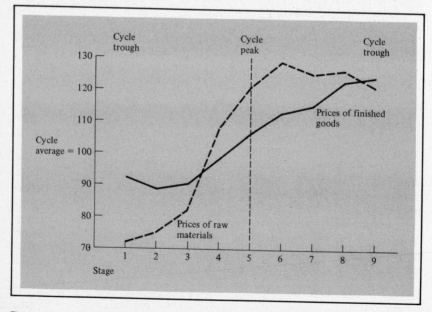

Figure 27.4 **Prices of finished goods and prices of raw materials.** (Source: U.S. Bureau of Labor Statistics, *Monthly Labor Review,* January 1971 to August 1975.)

lem of realizing profit) and the rising costs of equipment and raw materials (the problem of producing profit). In the last chapter we saw that consumer demand is limited in the expansion by a falling propensity to consume among capitalists and a shift in income from workers' wages to capitalist profits. In this chapter we have seen that prices of raw material, equipment, and other intermediate goods all tend to rise faster than the prices of finished goods, especially consumer goods.

The results of the squeeze by limited demand and rising costs were shown in this chapter as reflected in the declines in total profits and profit rates in the mid and late expansion. The same squeeze shows up in profits per unit, which rose enormously in most of the expansion (by 29 points), then fell in the very last segment of expansion (by 2 points).[9] The profit squeeze came because total costs rose even faster than prices at the cycle peak.

As shown in earlier sections, these changes in profits and profit rates explain why businesspeople change their levels of investment. In the early expansion period, rapidly rising profits led to high levels of investment. The profit squeeze at the peak of expansion reduced investment. Falling profits in the depression reduced investment rapidly. Finally, a slight recovery in profits led to recovery in investment.

The capitalist system was once again temporarily "cured" of its illness by the drastic means of a depression. Although high rates of inflation and unemployment lingered on (keeping millions of people in poverty), the rising profit margins would lead to new investment and new prosperity for business. This completes the description of each of the variables in the business cycle; the next chapter will attempt to tie them together in a full theory of the business cycle.

SUMMARY

Investment shows violent fluctuations over the business cycle. In percentage terms consumption fluctuates much less. Investment depends on profit expectations. Profit expectations depend on expected revenues from sales and expected costs of production. Actual profits rise rapidly in early expansions as costs are low and demand rises rapidly. Then profit is squeezed by limited demand and high costs. In contractions, profit falls rapidly, reflecting falling demand. Finally, profit recovers as demand levels off and costs per unit fall. Business investments rise and fall even more than the objective increases and declines in profit rates would indicate because or irrational and exaggerated psychological reactions ("confidence" or "lack of confidence").

[9] Data from U.S. Labor Department, see full data and citation in Appendix B to this chapter.

APPENDIX A

THE ACCELERATOR

What is the systematic reasoning that links investment to a change in output? With a given technology, a factory needs a certain amount of capital equipment to produce a certain output. Assume that there is an increase in demand for a factory owner's products, so that the owner wishes to increase the factory's output beyond the present capacity. If the technology stays the same, capital equipment must be increased in proportion to the increase in output demanded. Therefore the factory owner's demand for new capital (net investment) bears a precise relation to the increase in output.

This reasoning may be extended to the determination of net investment in the whole economy. At a given level of technology aggregate output can be increased only with a certain aggregate increase in capital (net investment). Therefore the demand for an increase in capital is in some ratio to the decision to increase output. That ratio is by definition the accelerator. Thus, in general, we may say that

$$\text{Change in capital} = \text{accelerator} \times \text{change in output}$$

By definition *capital* means the value of productive facilities. But the expenditure to increase productive facilities is by definition *net investment*. Because net investment is precisely the change in capital, we may write

$$\text{Investment} = \text{accelerator} \times \text{change in output}$$

We may simply note the definition that

$$\text{Accelerator} = \frac{\text{investment}}{\text{change in output}}$$

and remember that this theory claims that the accelerator ratio is some precise and roughly constant number.

In the United States yearly output runs at about one-third of the value of all capital. Therefore it may be assumed that roughly three units of new capital are required to add one unit to national product. The accelerator coefficient thus may be thought of as relating about three units of net investment to each added unit of output.

As an example, the output of shoes may be related to the investment in new shoe machinery. More demand for shoes means more investment in equipment. But if demand for shoes stays the same, there should be no further investment in shoe machinery. Finally, if demand for shoes declines, then the accelerator causes disinvestment. *Disinvestment* here means that some shoe machinery is allowed to wear out and is not replaced.

If the value of the accelerator is known, then what will happen to net investment for any movements of output can be predicted exactly. Table 27A.1 picks some arbitrary changes in the output of shoes to see what will happen to investment in shoe machinery (given an accelerator set at 3).

The movements of shoe production are given arbitrarily; the rest of the table follows by assumption and definition. Thus from period 1 to period 2, output rises by $10, but because $3 of capital is required to produce $1 of output, capital must rise by $30. In other words, under this assumption a change in output of $10 causes net investment of $30. Similarly, in the next interval, a $20 rise in output causes $60 of investment. A *smaller* ($5) rise in output from period 3 to period 4 causes a *decline* in investment to only $15, and in the next interval, output does not change, so net investment, or the change in capital, must be zero.

From period 5 to period 6, output declines slightly, but investment must decline by three times as much. Next, a larger decline in output means a much larger decline in investment, and then a smaller decline in output causes a rise in investment to a less negative level. When output stops declining for a period, investment rises to zero. Finally, a small ($10) rise in output again leads to $30 of investment. Throughout, the level of net investment, or the change in capital, is related to the *change* in output. The desired new investment will always be the excess of desired capital over actual capital.

Table 27A.1   **The Accelerator in Shoe Production**

Time Period	Shoe Production Output	Change in Output	Shoe Machinery (Capital)	Change in Capital (Net Investment)
1	$100	$10	$300	$30
2	110	20	330	60
3	130	5	390	15
4	135	0	405	0
5	135	−5	405	−15
6	130	−20	390	−60
7	110	−10	330	−30
8	100	0	300	0
9	100	10	300	30
10	110		330	

Note: This table assumes that $3 more of capital is required to produce $1 more of output. The figures for output of shoe machinery are chosen arbitrarily. The figures for shoe machinery (capital) must then be three times the output of shoes. The change in output is the difference between output one period and the next. The change in capital (net investment) is the difference between capital one period and the next, but is also always three times the change in output.

To illustrate the most important features of this process, the movements of output (shoe production) and net investment (increase or decrease in shoe machinery) may be graphed. The data in Table 27A.1 are used as the basis for the graph in Figure 27A.1.

Notice that in Figure 27A.1 the movements of net investment in shoe machinery do not resemble the movements in the output of shoes; investment moves earlier and more sharply. However, the movements of investment in shoe machinery are exactly similar to the movements of the *change* in the output of shoes (multiplied by 3).

Several studies have indicated that in the long run, when productive capacity must grow if output is to grow, there is a roughly stable relationship between net investment and the change in output. In any short-run period, however, concern is focused on investment as an immediate psychological reaction to prospective changes in the amount of output demanded. It is easy to see that in the short run the rigid relationship between investment and change in output posited by the accelerator theory must be qualified in many ways.

First, even if the accelerator holds true for a ten-year period, does investment react exactly in that ratio to a change in demand in a one-month period or even in a whole year? In reality the time lag between changed demand and net investment varies from industry to industry and even from phase to phase of the business cycle. A long and complicated process takes place before investment spending actually results. If demand improves, the corporate directors must

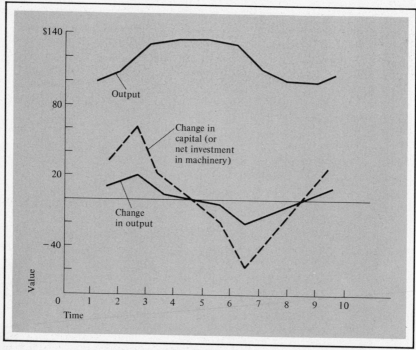

Figure 27A.1 **Output and investment in shoe production**

come to *expect* increased future demand. But entrepreneurial expectations may also be affected by noneconomic psychological or political factors. Then the directors must appropriate funds for investment purposes and perhaps arrange outside financing. Next engineers must design new factories or new machines. Even after the construction actually begins, it is some time before all the investment funds are fully spent.[10]

Second, the accelerator assumes that each industry faced with higher demands is already running at full capacity. That is not true, however, in a depression or in the early stages of recovery from a depression. During a depression there is much idle machinery and many empty, unused factories. Therefore in such periods any new demand can be met easily *without net investment.* Thus the accelerator is notably weaker whenever there is much unused capacity to produce.

Third, the accelerator ignores the physical limitations on the amount of investment or disinvestment in any given period. No matter how much the demand increases at the peak of prosperity, the investment goods industries can produce only so much in a given time. Therefore it must be assumed that these industries have just enough excess capacity to produce the investment goods called forth. Similarly, falling demand in a depression may indicate much disinvestment. But the whole economy can disinvest (or reduce its capital stock) in one year only to the extent of the depreciation of capital in that year. In other words, capital can be reduced in the economy as a whole only as fast as it wears out or becomes obsolete.

Fourth, the simple accelerator ignores the effects of changes in the relative levels of prices and costs. At the peak of prosperity, the great demand on the capacity of the capital goods industries may raise the cost of capital goods and thus weaken investment incentives. The level of wage costs also changes systematically over the cycle. Moreover, a firm needs financial capital for investment, which depends mostly on reinvestment of profits; if there is not enough profit, then the firm must borrow in the capital market and must face higher interest costs. On the other side, prices show long-run as well as cyclical fluctuations, which affect expected revenues.

These costs and price changes, which are summarized by profit changes, affect investment as much as or more than the simple amount of output demanded. Therefore, the profits—or the rate of profit—are a better predictor of investment than amount demanded. For both profits and output demanded, the *change* in the indicator may impress investors more than a continuing high or low *level* of that indicator (but the *level* of profits does control how much capital is actually available for investment).

Finally, the accelerator only tries to explain net investment. Since replacement is not automatic, it is gross investment that must be explained. Replacement investment—in addition to net investment—is sometimes speeded up and sometimes postponed. To explain these changes in replacement policy we must again turn to changes in expectations of profit and available funds from profits.

---

[10] The timing of investment spending is discussed in detail in Howard Sherman and Thomas Stanback, "Cyclical Behavior of Profits, Appropriations, and Expenditures," *Proceedings of the American Statistical Association,* September 1962, pp. 274–285. Also see Bert Hickman, "Diffusion, Acceleration, and Business Cycles," *American Economic Review,* September 1959.

SUMMARY OF ACCELERATOR

The accelerator principle says net investment is related in a definite ratio to the change in output during the business cycle. Although this is roughly true, several factors indicate that there is no reliable single fixed figure for the accelerator ratio. First, there is a long and varying time lag from the first indication of increased demand for output to the actual investment expenditure. Second, in a recession, the accelerator is greatly weakened. Third, investment cannot make as extreme swings as predicted because there is an upper limit, given by the capacity of the capital goods industries, and a lower limit, given by the amount of depreciation. Fourth, the simple accelerator is modified by changes in the relationship of prices and costs because these changes affect profits and, consequently, investments. There is no space here for a discussion of other modifications, such as the fact that the accelerator may work only in the aggregate and not at all in many individual industries. For all that, the accelerator does embody a large grain of truth and emphasizes the basic fact that new capital goods are built to meet new demand. It also explains, in part, why investment fluctuates so much more violently than consumer demand; it is related not to the level but to the *change* in demand. In Chapter 28 we shall combine the consumption function with the accelerator to explain a simple business cycle theory.

APPENDIX B

DATA ON INVESTMENT, PRICES, COSTS, AND PROFITS

Table 27B.1 **Investment, Price, Cost, and Profits, 1970–1975**

	Initial Trough Nov. 1970	Expansion			Peak Nov. 1973	Contraction			Final Trough March 1975
Stages	1	2	3	4	5	6	7	8	9
Real gross investment	83	90	100	109	118	108	102	98	72
Real corporate profit (total)	78	90	100	111	109	107	101	94	84
Profit per unit	77	93	99	106	104	101	105	103	101
Real consumption	91	94	99	105	104	102	103	100	101
Implicit price deflator	90	92	95	99	104	107	111	116	118
Real wages per hour	96	98	100	102	101	100	100	99	99
Money wages per hour	86	90	95	101	105	107	111	115	117
Real labor costs per hour	101	100	99	98	100	100	102	103	103
Money labor costs per unit	91	92	94	97	104	107	113	119	122
Output per labor hour	92	97	101	103	103	101	101	100	100
Prices of finished goods	93	89	91	98	106	113	115	123	124
Raw materials	71	75	82	108	121	129	125	126	121

Sources: Prices of finished goods and raw materials from U.S. Bureau of Labor Statistics, *Monthly Labor Review*, January 1971 to August 1975. Unit profits, implicit price deflator, wager per hour, labor cost per unit, and output per labor hour are all from U.S. Bureau of Labor Statistics, *Employment and Earnings*, January 1973, July 1974, September 1975, Table C-10. Gross investment and total corporate profits from U.S. Department of Commerce, Survey of Current Business, August of 1971, 1972, 1973, 1974, and 1975.

Notes: Data are monthly or quarterly; quarterly data use the quarterly trough and peak dates. The average for each series is set equal to 100 over the whole cycle.

The data in Table 27B.1 are provided in order to picture the cycle more concretely. To understand them one should graph each series separately or with another related series.

CHAPTER 28

UNEMPLOYMENT AND BUSINESS CYCLES

This chapter begins with the conservative and liberal theories of cyclical unemployment, then presents a modern radical theory.

CONSERVATIVE NEOCLASSICAL THEORIES

Until the 1930s the main body of neoclassical economic theory did not try to explain, but rather tried to explain away, the business cycle. It was argued that the amount of general unemployment was exaggerated and that there were only partial and frictional fluctuations of production. Moreover, each depression was said to be the last. Indeed, in the 1920s they were said to be gone forever after more than 100 years of business phenomena. In the 1960s conservatives repeated their opinion that "the business cycle has disappeared."

These attitudes are traceable, in the main, to the general social outlook of economists, who supported the status quo. In part, however, they may have resulted from the lack of much theoretical interest in the movements of aggregate demand. Neoclassical economists dealt mainly with demand for particular products based on the subjective utility to individual consumers. Individual desire, however, must obviously be limited and must begin to decline after some given quantity is consumed. Thus a typical neoclassical economist asserts, "It is natural . . . that after the brisk demand of the . . . American public for motor cars in 1922–1923, the intensity of the desire for these articles should fall away."[1] This neoclassical approach leads naturally to thinking of unemployment as a problem of absolute overproduction, of too much production. When, however, the entire economy is examined, and not just each individual product, it becomes clear that the problem in a major depression is not that more is produced than people subjectively desire to consume. On the contrary, there is not nearly enough produced to fulfill the desires or even the minimum health needs of the population; there is too much output only relative to effective purchasing power.

As long as most economists accepted Say's law, which insists that there cannot be a general deficiency of effective demand relative to supply, there were only a few logically possible explanations for the fluctuations of aggregate output. One such explanation was that external or noneconomic shocks to the economy may limit supply or bring sudden demands. For example, sunspots may cause bad weather, and bad weather leads to bad harvests; unions may go on

[1] D. H. Robertson, *Banking Policy and the Price Level* (Clifton. N.J.: Augustus M. Kelley, 1949), p. 10.

strike; governments may foolishly interfere with production activities; wars may stop the flow of raw materials or bring sudden demands for military production; and so forth. Thus one famous economist declares, "Major depressions have been produced by a variety of different types of 'shocks,' not by a regular cycle-producing mechanism."[2]

Certainly such shocks as wars and bad weather do affect the economy; but such occurrences do not always coincide with the major swings in the economy, some of which occur in the absence of any apparent outside shock. Furthermore, noncapitalist economies have reacted quite differently to outside shocks. Therefore we may at least ask what mechanisms in the American economy give rise to cyclical movements as a result of these random shocks. We shall also try to understand how the internal operation of the capitalist economy might produce a business cycle even with no external shocks.

Since conservatives refuse to believe that the private capitalist economy could possibly generate its own depressions, they examine every other accidental or shock explanation with great care. The modern conservative school known as monetarists believes the whole problem is due to government mistakes in handling the monetary system. They argue that fluctuations are not caused by the capitalist system but by the government issuing too much money or too little money.[3] Granted that the U.S. capitalist government makes mistakes in its monetary policies, is it conceivable that the government has made the same mistake every few years for the last 150 years? Such theories of "mistakes" do not explain the systematic behavior of the capitalist economy, in its expansions and contractions, which follow regularly one after the other.

Another conservative notion is that depressions are due to inexplicable waves of psychological pessimism. Such pessimism may cause temporary panics during which money is hoarded and credit is withheld. Typical of these explanations is the statement that "the chief cause of the evil is a want of confidence."[4] The defect of such theories lies in the fact that no one has ever demonstrated cycles of optimism and pessimism in businesspeople independent of the economic cycle. In fact, the height of optimism is always reached, as in 1929, at the peak of the business cycle. Only *after* economic conditions have objectively worsened are there irrationally large reactions by businesspersons, which intensify the economic downturn. Similarly, irrational optimism may intensify an economic expansion after conditions have objectively improved.

LIBERAL KENESIAN THEORIES

The economist whose name is connected with the theoretical revolution of the 1930s in Keynes. As has been seen, Keynes' contribution was the demolition of Say's law. He recognized the possibility that the economy as a whole may be in equilibrium at other than full employment—that is, that more or less may be demanded than is supplied at full employment at the present price level. Yet, one of his most prominent followers comments that "Keynesian economics, in spite

---

[2] James S. Duesenberry, *Business Cycles and Economic Growth* (New York: McGraw-Hill, 1958), p. 11.
[3] See William Mitchell, John Hand, and Ingo Walter, *Readings in Macroeconomics* (New York: McGraw-Hill, 1975), pp. 271–272.
[4] Alfred and M. P. Marshall, *The Economics of Industry* (New York: Macmillan, 1881).

of all that it has done for our understanding of business fluctuations, has beyond doubt left at least one major thing unexplained; and that thing is nothing less than the business cycle itself."[5] Keynes' popularity perhaps is attributable to his having said, in a striking manner, the right thing at the right time, for he not only explained the possibility of depressions and inflations but also laid down possible solutions for these problems within the bounds of the private enterprise economic system.

The simplest Keynesian theory of the business cycle was stated by Alvin Hansen and Paul Samuelson.[6] It provides only a bare sketch of reality. The theory consists of just three relationships. First, aggregate demand is composed of planned consumption spending plus planned investment spending. Of course this demand may be greater or less than the full-employment supply of output.

How much income is spent for consumption depends on the second relationship: Consumption is determined by some given propensity to spend out of last year's income, and the average propensity to consume declines as income rises. How much income is spent for investment depends on the third relationship: Investment is determined by the change in income or demand during the previous year (by the so-called accelerator coefficient). If these three statements are accepted as reasonable approximations of reality, what kind of cyclical behavior results?

Assume that national income is expanding in the early expansion phase of the business cycle. The increase in income causes an even greater demand for new capital goods, or net investment. But an initial increase in investment spending causes a further increase in consumer spending and in national income. Then the process continues because the increase in income leads to more investment, which leads to more consumption and income, causing still more investment, and so forth. The consumption and investment relations together thus spell out a cumulative process: An initial expansion in the economy leads to continuing expansion.

Assume now that national income is contracting in the depression phase of the business cycle. The decrease in income causes a large disinvestment of capital. The vast decrease in investment spending means much less income and less consumption. The further decrease in income leads to further disinvestment, which causes a further lowering of consumption, and so forth. Thus the combination of consumption and investment relationships also explains the cumulative process of contraction in the depression. An initial decline leads to continuing decline.

What is more difficult to understand is why the economy ever passes from the process of continuous expansion to the continuous contraction of depression, or, for that matter, how we move from depression back to expansion. The same theory can also explain these turning points, although not as persuasively as it explains cumulative expansion or contraction.

At the peak of expansion it is true that income, consumption, and investment are all increasing. Yet the careful observer can begin to discern strains and even cracks in the impressive facade of prosperity. Consumption increases, but the

[5] J. R. Hicks, *The Trade Cycle* (New York: Oxford University Press [Clarendon Press], 1950), p. 1.
[6] See Paul Samuelson, "Interactions Between the Multiplier Analysis and the Principle of Acceleration," *Review of Economic Statistics*, May 1939, pp. 75–78.

propensity to consume begins to decline as the proportion of income saved increases. As a result, the aggregate demand out of national income rises more and more slowly. But a smaller increase in national income means, according to the investment relationship, an absolute decline in net investment. A decline in net investment, however, causes a decline in national income, which causes a fall in consumer spending. Thus begins the process of contraction into depression.

Similarly, at the lowest point in a depression (the trough) it is true that income, consumption, and investment are all contracting. Yet as total consumption declines, the propensity to consume rises. As a result, the aggregate demand out of national incomes falls more and more slowly. But a *smaller* decline in national income means, according to the accelerator, an absolute rise in the level of investment (or at least less disinvestment). This causes a rise, no matter how small, in aggregate spending. Then the rise in spending means more income and a rise in consumption. Thus begins the process of recovery and expansion.

Some readers may gain understanding from an arithmetic example of the whole process of expansion, downturn, depression, upturn, and again prosperity. Such an example can be constructed from the simple assumptions about consumption and investment behavior. Assume that net investment always equals the preceding change in income (that is, the accelerator is exactly 1). Also assume that the marginal propensity to consume is 0.90, or 90 percent of the previous period's income, to which we must always add some arbitrary minimum consumption (say, $96 billion). The resulting cyclical process of expansion and contraction is shown in Figure 28.1.

The time periods here may be taken as 2 or 3 months. Notice that after the initial rise the national income falls for 10 periods (from $1 trillion to $920 billion), then rises for 10 periods (from $920 billion to $1 trillion), and then begins to fall again. This same fluctuation will continue forever, or as long as we keep the same assumptions. Consumption is always determined by the preceding national income, and net investment is always determined by the difference between the two preceding national incomes. National income itself is always the sum of the consumption plus the net investment of the same period. Thus does the simplest (or multiplier-accelerator) theory give a consistent picture of how the economy produces depression out of expansion and expansion out of depression in a continuing business cycle.

THE UNDERCONSUMPTIONIST VERSION OF LIBERAL THEORY

All economists agree that the simplest liberal Keynesian multiplier-accelerator theory is too simple to explain many of the facts. The liberal economist John Hobson[7] argued that consumer demand is too restricted because wages are too low. He believed unemployment cycles could be cured under capitalism if workers were given higher wages—a theory that appeals to many trade unionists.

Hobson did *not* say that workers' wages—or even their share of income—are always declining. That could explain how capitalism gets into a depression but

---

[7] For an exhaustive description of the many varieties of under consumption theory, see Gottfried Haberler, *Prosperity and Depression* (Cambridge, Mass.: Harvard University Press, 1960).

Arithmetic Example of Simplest Business Cycle Theory [a, b]

(Assumes the consumption is always $96 billion plus 90 percent of the previous period's income, and that net investment is always equal to the change in income to one period ago from two periods ago. Also assumes that national income is expanding from $996 billion in first period to $1000 billion in second period. All figures in billions of dollars.)

Time period	Consumption	National income	Net investment
1		$ 996	
2		1000	
3	$996	1000	$ 4
4	996	996	0
5	992	988	−4
6	985	977	−8
7	975	965	−11
8	964	952	−12
9	953	940	−13
10	942	930	−12
11	933	923	−10
12	927	920	−7
13	928	925	−3
14	928	933	5
15	936	944	8
16	945	956	11
17	957	969	12
18	969	982	13
19	978	991	13
20	987	996	9
21	995	1000	5

[a] Some of the numbers are not exact because of rounding.

[b] The arrows show lines of influence. Only the first few arrows are shown. The student should fill in the rest of the arrows. The result will show the pattern is repeated in every period.

Figure 28.1

not how it gets out of it. What Hobson argued is that while total wages rise in the expansion period, the *share* of wages in national income falls. We saw in Chapter 26 that it is true that the wage share declines—while the profit share rises—in every expansion on record (and that the opposite happens in most contractions).

Hobson asked, What is the effect on consumer demand of this shift from wages to profits? He argued that profit makers have much higher incomes than wage workers. Therefore they save more and have a lower propensity to consume. Since they now have a larger share of national income, the national propensity to consume will decline. Again, we saw in Chapter 26 that this is a true statement.

Hobson concluded that in every expansion period the propensity to consume tends to fall, mainly because of the shift from wages to profits. Hobson thought this was sufficient to explain how inadequate consumer demand at the cycle peak causes a depression, while the opposite process would initiate a recovery.

Critics noted that this argument is not sufficient. Though there may not be enough consumer demand to buy all new production, investor demand may fill the gap. As one conservative economist says, "It will not do to explain insufficiency of investment by the insufficiency of effective demand because effective demand would be sufficient if aggregate investment were."[8] Of course if consumption were not rising at all, more investment could only mean the production of factories to produce more factories to produce more factories, and so on.

The underconsumptionist argument may be buttressed in a modern Keynesian framework by explaining investment with the help of the accelerator principle. As we saw in Chapter 27, the accelerator principle says that investment is determined by the increase in aggregate demand. But consumer demand is the largest component of aggregate demand. When consumer demand rises more slowly at the peak, it means aggregate demand also increases more slowly. When the increase in aggregate demand is less and less, the accelerator principle says investment will actually fall. This sets off a depression. This process is depicted in Figure 28.2.

The opposite process at the bottom of the depression initiates a recovery and expansion. Wages do not fall as rapidly as profits in the contraction. For this reason (and other reasons) consumer demand falls more slowly than income or production. Therefore, aggregate demand reaches a floor and stops falling (or falls very slowly) at the trough of the contraction. When aggregate demand is constant, the accelerator principle says that net investment will stop falling and will actually rise from its negative level to at least become zero. Continued production at this stabilized level sets the stage for a renewed expansion.

Since the problem of a depression, as they see it, is lack of demand, the underconsumptionists argue for higher wages as a solution. Presumably, higher wages would increase consumer demand, allow capitalists to realize more profits, and keep the expansion going forever. They ignore the fact that wages are not only the largest component of consumer demand, wages are also the largest component of costs. If costs rise, the capitalist makes less profit, so the solution of higher wages leads to other problems.

THE CONSERVATIVE OVERINVESTMENT THEORY

Overinvestment theorists, such as Frederick von Hayek, argue that a crisis arises from high costs.[9] The high level of investment and production leads to a demand for more labor and materials than are available, causing the price of labor and raw materials to rise. Some of Hayek's work also stresses the cost of rising interest rates at the cycle peak.

The heaviest emphasis by overinvestment theorists is usually on the threat to

---

[8] William Fellner, "The Capital-Output Ratio," *Money, Trade, and Economic Growth: Essays in Honor of John Henry Williams* (New York: Macmillan, 1951), p. 121.

[9] For an exhaustive description of the many varieties of overinvestment theory, see Haberler, op. cit.

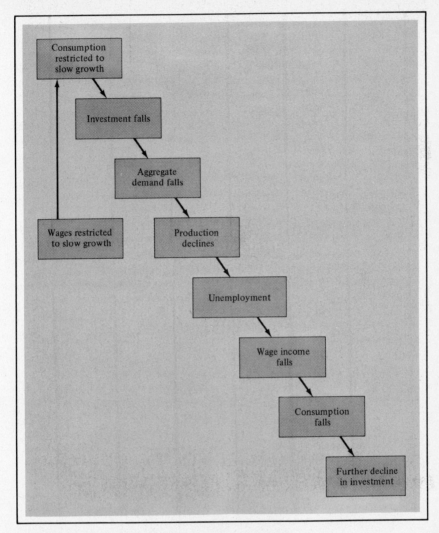

Figure 28.2 **Underconsumption view of crisis at cycle peak**

profits from rising wage costs as the economy nears full employment. In wage negotiations employers use this argument to prove that higher wages will lead to less investment and production, and so to unemployment. Therefore, they tell unions to hold down wage requests.

In reality, the argument that high wages in expansion lead to low profits, which leads to a crisis, ignores some crucial facts. As we saw in Chapter 27, labor costs per unit usually fall in most of the expansion because of rising productivity. Moreover, when labor costs rise somewhat near the end of expansion, they rise less than other more rapidly expanding costs.

Some overinvestment theorists also emphasize that the expansion leads to rising costs of new capital equipment, rising costs of raw materials, and rising interest rates making borrowing more expensive. Assuming that these costs increase faster than the prices of the commodities produced, capitalist profits per unit must decline. When profit rates decline, there is a decline in investment and production, so depression begins. Paradoxically, in this view too high a level of investment leads to high costs, which eventually leads to a crisis characterized by declining investment. This view of the crisis is pictured in Figure 28.3.

To summarize the overinvestment theory: In expansion, rapidly rising demand for labor and investment goods (overinvestment) causes a rapid rise in the cost of these goods to investors. The prices of consumer goods rise more slowly, squeezing profit margins in that sector, and as a result, the increase of total profits proceeds more slowly. Because investment is determined by the increase in profits, less increase in profits causes less investment. Less investment causes less income, which causes less consumption, and so forth until the depression is well under way.

The opposite process takes place in the contraction period and eventually leads to recovery. In the contraction there is a rapidly falling demand for labor and investment goods, so there is a fall in the cost of these goods to investors. Since the prices of finished goods fall more slowly (or rise more rapidly if there is an inflation in the midst of recession), the profit margin eventually improves. This

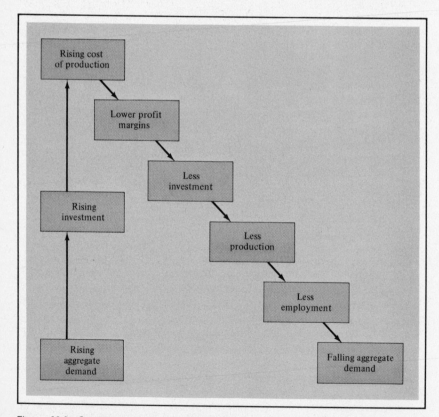

Figure 28.3 **Overinvestment view of crisis at cycle peak**

improvement of the profit margin then leads to more investment and a new expansion.

Since the problem causing the depression is a profit reduction owing to higher costs, these theorists argue the position that the government could cure the problem by taking appropriate steps. The steps they urge, however, are the exact opposite of the underconsumptionist suggestions. Their solution—which is pleasing to business—is to hold down costs, particularly wage costs. Those who emphasize the rising costs of labor claim that more employment can only come by cutting wages. A recent textbook says, "The general solution to involuntary unemployment is a reduction in real wages until the amount of labor demanded equals the amount supplied."[10] The Nixon administration followed this advice by putting very strict controls on wages, while keeping very loose controls on prices.

The notion of solving unemployment by cutting wages conveniently ignores the fact that lower wages mean less demand for consumer goods, which makes it harder for capitalists to realize their profits. Both Marx and Keynes emphasized this fact.

Nevertheless, some radicals join conservatives in blaming the depression crisis on low profits caused by high wages. Thus two radicals, citing the *Wall Street Journal* as their source, say, "Knowledgeable observers of the labor scene have pointed directly to an increasingly obstreperous labor force as an influence on the decline in productivity during the expansion."[11] Like the conservatives, they argue that high employment levels lead to a militant or "obstreperous" labor force that forces higher wages and lower productivity, thus causing a crisis by squeezing profits. They do not seem to recognize that, on the one hand, capitalists must produce profits by forcing workers to create a surplus value above costs; on the other hand, however, capitalists must also realize their profits by sales in the market, which require high consumer demand and high wages. In simpler terms, the criticism is that profits cannot be squeezed from only one side at a time; they are squeezed from both sides. The capitalists' dilemma is that they would like both lower wage costs *and* higher consumer demand.

Other overinvestment theorists, who emphasize rising costs of capital and capital goods, advocate other policies to cut costs. Most would lower costs of capital to investors through government influence on interest rates. Specifically, they would have the Federal Reserve System manipulate money and credit supplies so as to lower interest costs (for details of this procedure, see Chapter 30). Even though the costs of buying physical capital goods would be unaffected, investors could borrow money capital more cheaply. Therefore, their own profits would be higher; investment would be stimulated, and the economy would recover.

The theme that higher costs, particularly wage costs, cause lower production and lower investment, is repeated over and over again by conservative economists and the business press. In October 1974 an economist wrote in the *Wall Street Journal*,

---

[10] Richard Leftwich and Ansel Sharp, *Economics of Social Issues* (Homewood, Ill.: Irwin, 1974), p. 249.

[11] Raford Boddy and James Crotty, "Class Conflict and Macro-Policy," *Review of Radical Political Economics*, vol. 7, Spring 1975, p. 8. A similar view is given in Andrew Glyn and Bob Sutcliffe, *British Capitalism, Workers, and the Profit Squeeze* (Baltimore: Penguin Books, 1972).

The cost of labor is soaring. . . . One reason many analysts view the trend as "ominous" is that it could soon begin to erode company profits sharply and trigger increasing layoffs. So far, corporations generally have managed to boost their prices even more rapidly than labor costs have risen. . . .[12]

This article admits that prices had actually risen faster than labor costs in the year from September 1973 to September 1974. In fact, we saw in the last chapter that real wages were falling while corporate profit rates were still rising in that period. This article is merely worrying that *maybe* corporate profits could soon begin to fall, not that they had already.

Propaganda from Wall Street has even convinced a few radical economists that "The overall profit rate of U.S. corporations has been falling since at least 1965."[13] A look at the data in Table 28.1, taken from equally conservative sources, indicates that that claim is totally false. Profit rates—both before and after taxes—of all manufacturing corporations did fall in the recession of 1969–1970. Then, however, profit rates rose steadily during the next expansion and continued to rise in the inflation-in-recession year of 1974. Petroleum profit rates behaved the same, except that their after-tax profit rate rose unbelievably to almost 20 percent in 1974!

It is somewhat more scientific to test the proposition that profit rates are falling by examining the average for entire cycles of boom and bust periods. Table 28.2 shows that profit rates have fluctuated enormously but have shown no trend. Profit rates were very, very low in the 1930s during most of the Great Depression. Profit rates rose greatly in World War II but were held down somewhat by wartime controls. When controls came off, profit rates rose again. They reached their

Table 28.1 **Profit Rates on Stockholders Equity, U.S. 1965–1974**

Year	Petroleum (after taxes)	All Manufacturing (after taxes)	All Manufacturing (before taxes)
1965	11.9%	13.9%	21.9%
1969	11.9	12.4	20.1
1970	11.0	10.1	15.7
1971	11.2	10.8	16.5
1972	10.8	12.1	18.4
1973	15.6	14.8	21.6
1974	19.9%	15.4%	23.4%

Sources: Profit rates after taxes from First National City Bank, cited in Labor Research Association, *Research in Economic Trends*, vol. 1, September 1975, Number 3, p. 6. Profit rates before taxes from Federal Trade Commission and Securities and Exchange Commission, *Quarterly Financial Reports of All Manufacturing Corporations* (Washington, D.C.: GPO, 1st quarter 1965 to 4th quarter 1974).

[12] Alfred Malabre, Jr., "Real Cost of Labor Outpaces Pay Gains As Productivity Lags," *Wall Street Journal*, October 31, 1974.

[13] Andrew Zimbalist, "Limits of Work Humanization," *Review of Radical Political Economics*, vol. 7, Summer 1975, p. 55. He cites as his source an editorial of the *Wall Street Journal*, February 20, 1975.

height in the Korean War, when only minimal controls existed. Profit rates then fell for two cycles. They were revived again by the Vietnam War and thus rose in the last two cycles.

The old overinvestment theorists argued that at the peak of the cycle rising costs squeeze profits, which lowers investment and causes a depression. The newer conservatives stress a longer-run view that rising costs are pushing profit rates lower continuously, so the lower rates reduce incentives to invest, while the lower amounts of profit reduce the capital available for investment for long-run growth. For example, "the total amount of new investment capital that will be needed for continued economic growth between 1974 and 1985 has been set at $4.7 *trillion* by a recent New York Stock Exchange study."[14] A very similar estimate by the Ford administration's Commerce Department is cited by the U.S. Treasury Department as a basis for arguing that present levels of corporate profits after taxes are insufficient to fill these immense capital needs.[15] Treasury Secretary William Simon then drew the conclusion (which all this was leading toward) that the corporate tax rate should be lowered, perhaps to zero![16] He also favored lower tax rates on capital gains based on the same argument.

The conservative arguments about lack of profits leading to lack of capital for investment, both in depressions and over the long run, have several things wrong with them. First, it was shown above that profit rates in the United States have not fallen in the long run. Similarly, a careful British study found that the same conservative propaganda about a profit crisis in their economy is mythical,

Table 28.2 **Profit Rates on Stockholders' Equity, 1933-1975 (all U.S. manufacturing corporations)**

Cycle	Average Profit Rate	Events
1933–1938	3.8%	Great Depression
1938–1945	16.2	World War II
1945–1949	17.8	Recovery from war
1949–1954	24.3	Korean War
1954–1958	21.0	Continuing cold war
1958–1961	17.3	Lessening cold war
1961–1970	19.3	Vietnam War
1970–1975	19.5%	Vietnam War, wage-price controls

Sources: 1933 to 1949, annual data from U.S. Internal Revenue Service, *Statistics of Income, Corporate Income Tax Returns* (Washington, D.C.: GPO, 1935-1951), 1949 to 1975, quarterly data from U.S. Federal Trade Commission and Securities and Exchange Commission, *Quarterly Financial Report of Manufacturing Corporations* (Washington, D.C.: GPO, 1st quarter 1949 to 4th quarter 1975).

[14] Bill Wycko, "The Work Shortage," *Review of Radical Political Economics,* vol. 7, Summer 1975, p. 16.
[15] See "A Shortage of Capital," *Riverside Press-Enterprise,* Riverside, Calif., June 20, 1975, p. A-3.
[16] See *Riverside Press-Enterprise* "Lower Corporate Taxes," June 20, 1975, p. A-3, and July 9, 1975, p. A-3.

that in fact the share of profits after taxes in the United Kingdom has been stable from 1950 to 1973.[17]

Second, profits do drop in each recession or depression, but that does not mean that there is a lack of capital. In a depression, there is a surplus of capitalist saving with no profitable place to invest it. For example, Treasury Secretary Simon made his statement that cried about lack of capital for investment in June 1975. But according to the government's own figures, in May 1975 fully 25 percent of all U.S. plant and equipment was standing idle.[18] How can the problem be lack of capital when 25 percent of existing physical capital is not utilized?

Finally, it is clear that all this mythology is designed to justify either controls on wages or lighter taxes on corporations. Moreover, a congressional investigation shows that corporations are already paying very little in taxes because of the loopholes in the law.[19] Although the corporate rate is supposed to be 48 percent, in 1974 the actual rate paid by 142 major corporations was only 23 percent. Eighteen of these corporations (including Chase Manhattan, Mobil Oil, and Bank of America) paid 10 percent or less; and eight of the corporations (including Ford Motor Company, with $351.9 million adjusted net income) paid no taxes at all. Representative Charles Vanik, chairman of the congressional investigation, concluded: "If U.S. corporations are already paying little or nothing in federal income taxes, it makes no sense to give them tax relief in an effort to stimulate investment capital."[20]

A GENERAL (RADICAL) THEORY OF THE BUSINESS CYCLE

Although the liberal underconsumption and conservative overinvestment theories appear superficially opposed, the radical view treats them as two different aspects of a more general process.[21] At the peak of prosperity, the limited consumer demand and the rising cost per unit act together to squeeze profits and choke off economic circulation. At the trough of the depression, the end of decline in consumer demand and the falling costs per unit increase profits and stimulate economic activity.

The theory that depression is caused by both limited demand (underconsumption) and high costs (overinvestment) is a radical one because it shows that cycles of expansion and depression are inevitable under capitalism. Some liberals believe they could prevent depressions by giving higher wages to increase demand, but that ignores the cost problem. Some conservatives would prevent

[17] M. A. King, "The United Kingdom Profits Crisis: Myth or Reality?" *The Economic Journal*, vol. 85, March 1975, pp. 33–54.

[18] U.S. Department of Commerce, *Survey of Current Business*, July 1975. Their data is an understatement because it does not include plants that are 100 percent idle.

[19] All data in this paragraph from an investigation by a taxation subcommittee of the House Ways and Means Committee chaired by Representative Charles Vanik, reported in "Corporations Evade Taxes," *Riverside Press-Enterprise*, October 8, 1975, p. 1.

[20] Representative Charles Vanik quoted in *ibid.*

[21] The radical view was first developed by Karl Marx in various works. Its history since Marx is given in Paul Sweezy, *Theory of Capitalist Development* (New York: Monthly Review Press, 1958). It is further developed in Michal Kalecki, *Theory of Economic Dynamics* (New York: Monthly Review Press, 1968). Also see John Strachey, *Theory of Capitalist Crisis* (New York: Covici-Friede, 1935). Obviously, some contemporary radicals violently disagree with our interpretation of Marx.

depressions by lowering wages and interest rates, but that ignores the demand problem. Actually, most traditional economists now agree with radicals that cycles of boom and bust are inherent in unregulated capitalism. They have fallen back to the second line of defense: that depressions can be prevented by the monetary and fiscal policies of the U.S. government (an issue discussed in Chapter 29).

The general radical theory may be stated here, very briefly, within the same framework we used earlier. Demand for output consists of consumption plus investment. Cost of output consists of wages plus plant, equipment, and materials used up. Total profit is the difference between the value of output demanded and the cost of output produced.

Almost all economists agree that the crisis leading to a recession or depression is caused by a profit squeeze. Anyone doubting this should reexamine the data in Chapter 27 on profits and profit rates. In the cycles of the 1950s and early 1960s, both profits and profit rates rise to mid-expansion (stage 3), then begin to fall. In the cycles of the late 1960s and early 1970s, profits peak in late expansion (stage 4) and then begin to fall. The question is only: What causes the profit squeeze? Limited revenue or rising costs or both?

Conversely, both total profits and rates of profit fall enormously in the early stages of the contraction. Then in the trough of the contraction, profits and profit rates are almost constant at a low level. These trends set a floor to the recession and prepare for a recovery. The question is only: What ends the profit squeeze? Rising revenue or lower costs or both?

In the early expansion, prices rise very slowly (actually declining in the first stages of some cycles). The reason goes back to the fact that aggregate wages, and therefore consumer demand are rising very slowly (and the propensity to consume is falling). Fortunately for the capitalists, cost per unit is rapidly declining in this period. The reason is that rapidly rising productivity creates falling labor costs per unit. In other words, the product is getting larger and capitalists are keeping a higher percentage of it. Since costs are falling while prices are slowly increasing, the result is a great increase in the profit rate.

At some point in the expansion (whether mid-expansion or late expansion), the situation becomes quite different. This new situation does not occur suddenly: It is the result of a slow but inexorable process. On the one side, costs per unit decline more slowly or begin to rise in mid-expansion, finally rising considerably in late expansion. Prices, after declining or rising slowly in early expansion, pick up speed in mid-expansion, then rise more slowly at the peak (as demand weakens). As a result, profits already show very little increase in mid-expansion and usually decline toward the end of the business cycle expansion.

Why does demand weaken in late expansion? Total wages rise considerably, but the share of labor is below its cycle average (though the share did rise a little in the late expansions of some cycles in the 1950s and 1960s). Therefore, aggregate consumer demand rises, but the propensity to consume is still below its long-run average. Thus the price increase is limited by the limits of effective demand under capitalism.

Why do costs rise more rapidly than prices in late expansion? This is due partly to the fact that labor costs per unit rise because of falling productivity. The main reason for the cost rise, however, is that nonlabor costs, especially raw materials, rise much faster.

Since costs are rising more rapidly than prices (because of limited demand), profit is squeezed. If profit is squeezed in mid-expansion, then investment declines soon after. If profit declines in late expansion, then investment declines soon after (at the peak). Whether investment declines in mid or late expansion, its decline is decisive. Falling investment leads to an eventual decline in income, which causes a further decline in demand, leading to falling production and unemployment.

From the viewpoint of the capitalist system, are wages and salaries too high or are they too low? On the one hand, since in most expansions labor costs per unit are slowly rising (though Hultgren actually found them declining a little at the peak), wages are cutting into the production of capitalist profits, so they are too high. On the other hand, since consumer demand is not rising rapidly enough to raise prices faster than costs, aggregate wages—the main support of consumer demand—are too low. Remember that the *ratio* of aggregate wages to profits is lowest in early expansion; and, although it rises a bit in late expansion, it is still below the cycle average (so the propensity to consume is still below its cycle average). In this sense, wages are both too high and too low. The system cannot be saved from crisis by lowering wages because this weakens demand and prevents realization of profits. The system cannot be saved from crisis by raising wages because this reduces the rate of profit created in production.

Schematically, the profit squeeze at the cycle peak may be depicted as in Figure 28.4, which shows only the essentials. The profit squeeze at the peak is caused by both rising costs and restricted demand. This profit squeeze leads to less investment, which leads to a contraction. During the ensuing contraction, the profit squeeze first worsens, then begins to ease. In the recent cycles, with

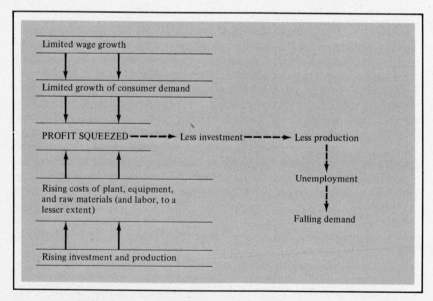

Figure 28.4 **Radical view of profit squeeze at cycle peak**

continuing inflation, prices are still rising in the early stages of contraction. Yet total costs rise more rapidly. Therefore, the profit squeeze continues and deepens. In this period the share of labor does rise but only because profits are falling. The statistical fact that their percentage share of income is rising cannot comfort workers much when their own real income is dropping.

In later contraction, the situation begins to ease somewhat for the capitalist. Prices decline a little, or at least rise a little less rapidly. Costs per unit, however, rise very little in the mid-contraction and actually decline at the depression trough. Since the profit rate finally stops declining (and may even rise at the trough), capitalists see a ray of hope on the horizon. Therefore, they start some investment, increase current production, and the recovery begins.

FACTORS INTENSIFYING CYCLICAL UNEMPLOYMENT

We have now stated the basic theory of business cycles, but it is still quite abstract. To get closer to reality we must examine many other factors that do not cause, but do seem to intensify, cyclical upswings and depressions. Among these factors are (1) monopoly rigidities in the economy, (2) irrational optimism and pessimism, (3) foreign trade and investment, (4) postponement or hurrying of major inventions and innovations, (5) depreciation and replacement cycles, (6) panics and expansions in money and credit, (7) some kinds of government intervention, and (8) inventory cycles. The effects of business optimism and pessimism were discussed earlier in this chapter. Monopoly power, government intervention, money and credit, and international relationships are discussed in later chapters.

Inventions

One factor intensifying the business cycle is the postponement of major inventions and innovations in depressions and their hurried introduction in periods of expansion. An invention is a new discovery; an innovation is the industrial use of that invention.

There is no apparent reason to assume that the whole mass of investors should have ideas in bunches.[22] Of course one major invention is likely to lead to many others in that field or in closely related fields, but unusual inventive activity in one area may be canceled on the average by unusual lack of activity in some other area. There would still be some random variation in the rate of invention, but it would be within moderate limits around the given rate, certainly not enough by itself to set off a major depression or recovery.

The rate of invention, however, may be influenced by the state of the economy. In a period of prosperity, increased demand for output means increased desire for better technology with which to expand output rapidly. And more funds

---

[22] For the opposite view, that inventions inevitably tend to appear in waves and that business cycles "are due to the intermittent action of the 'force' of innovation," see Joseph A. Schumpeter, *Business Cycles* (New York: McGraw-Hill, 1939), p. 175.

may be available for research. By contrast, research expenditures dropped in the severe depression of 1929–1933.

The rate of innovation (putting inventions to an economic use) does have its random movements. But the only movements great enough to cause significant intensification of the business cycle are the declines in innovation registered after depressions have begun and the rise in innovations registered after expansions have begun. It thus appears that changes in the rate of innovation are determined mostly by changes in business conditions; so innovations are not shocks from outside that initiate business cycles. Since, however, most innovations are made in expansions and are postponed in depressions, they are a factor intensifying the business cycle.

Replacement

Another intensifying factor is the postponement or hurrying of investment to replace depreciated capital equipment, which is normally more than 50 percent of all investment.[23] If replacement spending is greater or less than current allowances for depreciation, then total demand is greater or less than it would have been. Furthermore, most changes in the difference between replacement and depreciation are not random with respect to the business cycle. During a depression, when there is no desire to maintain a high level of output, many necessary replacements may be postponed. Yet depreciation allowances continue, and thus this source of saving may be far greater than the replacement investment during such a period. In fact, because depreciation is related to aggregate capital accumulated in many previous years, it declines only very slightly except in very long depressions.[24]

Replacement expenditures are often postponed because they are not needed during depressions, so the continued saving of funds for eventual replacement of depreciated machinery means a net loss of demand. This reduction of demand intensifies the depression. On the other hand, when a long period of prosperity begins, firms spend replacement funds sooner than necessary; the latest innovations are made as replacements long before the old machinery has finished its useful life. This extra investment demand then adds fuel to the expansion under way.

Inventories

Still another intensifying factor is the rise and fall of inventories. Inventories are stocks of goods held by producers, wholesalers, or retailers. Cycles are caused partly by fluctuations in investment in producers' equipment and factories but also by fluctuations in investment in inventories. Changes in inventory investment play a very important role in most business cycles. For example, in the five business cycles from 1919 through 1938, the average change in inven-

---

[23] See Simon S. Kuznets' data, discussed in R. A. Gordon, "Investment Opportunities in the United States," in *Business Cycles in the Post-War World* (New York: Oxford University Press, 1952), p. 293.
[24] See Wesley Mitchell, *What Happens During Business Cycles* (New York: National Bureau of Economic Research, 1946), p. 142.

tory investment accounted for 23.3 percent of the average rise in GNP in expansions and 47.5 percent of the decline in GNP in contractions. In the same period, changes in construction and producers' durable equipment together accounted for an average of only 20.5 percent of the rises and 37 percent of the declines in GNP.[25] This finding was confirmed for the 1945–1960 period when changes in inventories again constituted very large percentages of the cyclical changes in GNP.[26] If the longer and more severe major depressions or expansions are examined, it appears that much of the decline or rise occurs in investment in plant and equipment. Examination of the shorter, less severe, minor recessions or expansions reveals, however, that most of the decline or rise of investment is in inventory investment.

In the upswing of the cycle, when sales are rising and businesspersons are optimistic, there is a high level of inventory investment. Businesspeople try to keep their inventories in some desired ratio to sales but are never able to keep enough on hand during rapid expansions. Moreover, their optimism leads them to overexpand inventories. The high and rising level of investment in inventories is one more factor pushing demand upward during the expansion.

Only after the peak of the cycle is passed and a depression begins do business inventories finally catch up with sales expectations. Then, as sales are falling and businesspersons become pessimistic, they soon start to lower the level of inventory investment. Businesspeople lower their inventory investment just to keep the same ratio of inventories to sales, but then they lower it even further because of pessimistic expectations. By the trough of the cycle, businesspeople believe they have far too many goods on hand to sell in a reasonable time, so they frantically try to reduce their inventories by not buying new goods. Then inventory investment becomes quite negative—that is, it is less than what is sold. Thus inventory investment reacts to the same factors as plant and equipment investment (falling consumer demand, relatively high costs), and the precipitous decline in inventory investment makes the depression that much worse by further lowering the demand for goods.

SUMMARY

Our basic business cycle theory has been modified to a considerable degree. The rigid consumption function and investment accelerator mechanisms, basic to all the theories of the cycle examined in this chapter, are not by any means the full explanations of the history of economic expansions and contractions. We saw in the underconsumptionist theory that it is not enough to consider how consumption is determined by the level of income. Income must be separated into wages and profits; and the shift from wages to profits in prosperity, with a return to a lower profit ratio in depression, must be considered. There is a higher prospensity to consume out of wages, so a shift to profits means a lower national propensity to consume.

---

[25] See Moses Abramowitz, *Inventories and Business Cycles* (New York: National Bureau of Economic Research, 1950), p. 5.

[26] See Thomas Stanback, Jr., *Post-War Cycles in Manufacturers' Inventories* (New York: National Bureau of Economic Research, 1962), p. 6.

We also examined overinvestment theories, which stress changes in costs of capital goods and raw materials and their effects on profit margins. We found that in each expansion, wage costs per unit usually rise slower than prices, but that raw material costs do rise more than prices of finished goods. Finally, we found that both booms and busts are intensified by many other secondary factors, including irrational psychological reactions, money and credit panics and speculation, monopoly power, postponements (or speedups) of innovations, postponements (or speedups) of replacements for depreciated capital, inventory investment or disinvestment, government intervention, and international relationships.

APPENDIX A

MARX ON CYCLES

Some economists swear by Marx; others swear at him. There have been many interpretations of the views of Karl Marx on the cyclical economic crises of capitalism, but the various interpretations disagree violently.[1] Here, a few quotes are given from Marx just to get the flavor of his views for those who are interested. Remember that Marx defined "surplus value" as that value of the product extracted from the workers by the capitalist beyond all wage costs and other costs. It is the source of all profit, rent, and interest.

Marx points out that making profits requires not one step, but two. First, the capitalist must extract surplus value from the workers by holding down wages; but, second, the capitalist must sell the goods that embody the surplus value.

> The creation of . . . surplus value is the object of the direct process of production. . . . But this production of surplus value is but the first act of the capitalist process of production. . . . Now comes the second act of the process. The entire mass of commodities . . . must be sold. If this is not done, or only partly accomplished . . . the laborer has been none the less exploited, but his exploitation does not realise as much for the capitalist. . . . The realization of surplus value . . . is not determined . . . by the absolute consuming power, but by the consuming power based on antagonistic conditions of distribution, which reduces the consumption of the great mass of the population to a variable minimum within more or less narrow limits.[2]

Profits, therefore, may be and are squeezed from two directions at the peak of expansion: (1) by rising costs of production, which may prevent creation of surplus value, and (2) by limited demand, which may prevent realization of surplus value.

Sometimes Marx emphasized the limited demand resulting from the exploitation of workers. "The ultimate cause of all real crises always remains the poverty and restricted consumption of the masses."[3] Expansions are brought to an end by the limits imposed by class structure:

> The epochs in which capitalist production exerts all its forces are always periods of overproduction, because the forces of production can never be utilized beyond the point at which surplus value can be not only produced but also realized; but the sale of commodities, the realization of the commodity capital and hence also of surplus value, is limited not only by the consumption requirements of society in general, but by the consumption requirements of a society in which the great majority are poor and must always remain poor.[4]

[1] See Howard Sherman, "Marxist Models of Cyclical Growth," *History of Political Economy* vol. 3, Spring 1971, pp. 28–55. Also see Howard Sherman, "Marx and the Business Cycle," *Science and Society,* vol. 31, Fall 1967, pp. 488–504.

[2] Karl Marx, *Capital* (Chicago: Charles Kerr, 1907), vol. 3, p. 286.

[3] Ibid., p. 568

[4] Ibid., vol. 2, p. 363, footnote.

On the other hand, Marx criticized and ridiculed the naive underconsumptionists of his day. He insisted that wages do not remain constant; wages rise in total and in hourly rates in the typical expansion.

Marx also acknowledged that, in some extraordinary cases, capitalist investment could be so rapid as to cause a shortage of labor. This shortage leads to high wages, cutting into the rate of profit, and causing a crisis. "If the quantity of unpaid labor supplied by the working class, and accumulated by the capitalist class, increases so rapidly that its conversion into capital requires an *extraordinary* addition to paid labor, then wages rise, and all other circumstances remaining equal, the unpaid labor diminishes in proportion."[5] (Italics added.) He goes on to say that this fall in the rate of profit leads to a depression, which causes wages to fall again.

Note, however, that Marx calls this an extraordinary rise in wages. He also says that such cases have only occurred in exceptional periods, such as the U.S. railway boom of the nineteenth century. Marx emphasized that in most periods of normal capitalist expansion, there is a rising rate of exploitation, that is, profits are rising faster than wages. Marx makes the point very clear:

> The falling tendency of the rate of profit is accompanied by a rising tendency of the rate of surplus value, that is, the rate of exploitation. Nothing is more absurd, for this reason, than to explain a fall in the rate of profit by a rise in the rate of wages, although there may be exceptional cases when this may apply.[6]

If rising wages were not the cause of the profit squeeze, what was? One side of the squeeze was the rising cost of capital goods, including plant, equipment, and raw materials. Marx points out that the rising cost of capital goods is a normal occurrence as capitalists accelerate their demand in an expansion:

> The same phenomenon (and this as a rule precedes crises) can occur if the production of surplus capital takes place at a very rapid rate, and its retransformation into productive capital so increases the demand for all the elements of the latter that real production cannot keep pace, and consequently there is a rise in the prices of all the commodities which enter into the formation of capital.[7]

SUMMARY OF MARX'S THEORY

In every capitalist expansion, the rate of profit first rises rapidly. At the peak of expansion, however, the rate of profit falls because it is assaulted from two sides. On one side, costs per unit of raw materials and machinery used up in production (all of what Marx called constant capital) rise rapidly, thus limiting the production of surplus value or profit. On the other side, it is harder to realize surplus value or profit by selling the output produced because demand is limited. Demand is limited because wages are limited (a rising rate of exploitation in Marx's terms). The squeeze on profits causes a business downturn or depression. In the depression, the process finally reverses itself, producing a new boom.

[5] Karl Marx, *Capital* (New York: International Publishers, 1967), vol. 1, p. 620.
[6] Karl Marx, *Capital* (Chicago: Charles Kerr, 1907), vol. 3, p. 281.
[7] Karl Marx, *Theories of Surplus Value* (New York: International Publishers, 1952), p. 371.

CHAPTER 29

GOVERNMENT:

Welfare or Warfare

In American society the economy is powerfully influenced by the government, though the government is dominated to a large extent by economic power. The U.S. government has always affected the economy in many ways, from the inflationary spending of the Revolutionary War period through the deficit financing of the 1930s. An essentially new relationship has emerged, however, in recent years. Since 1941 the government has become, by far, the largest single source of demand. The newly emerged economic structure is dominated not only by large private firms but also by pervasive governmental activity, mostly centered around military production. It follows that the actions of the U.S. government now form an integral part of the American economy. The following sections present a brief introduction to the taxing and spending policies by which the governmental activity has affected economic growth and stability. (Earlier, in Chapter 20 we discussed the role of government in relation to the distribution of income. In Chapter 30 government monetary policy will be discussed. In Chapter 31 direct wage and price controls will be considered.)

GOVERNMENT AND THE EARLY ECONOMY

The history of U.S. governmental activity is a record of the conflicts between the interests of sectors, regions, and groups, and most often these interests have been economic. As Madison said,

> But the most common and the most durable source of faction has been the various and unequal distribution of property. Those who hold and those who are without property have ever formed distinct interests in society. Those who are creditors, and those who are debtors, fall under a like discrimination. A landed interest, a manufacturing interest, a mercantile interest, a moneyed interest, with many lesser interests, grow up of necessity in civilized nations, and divide them into different classes, actuated by different sentiments and views. The regulation of these various and interfering interests forms the task of modern legislation. . . .[1]

From the Revolutionary War through the nineteenth century, the government was concerned primarily with the protection of property, the promotion of busi-

[1] James Madison, *The Federalist*, no. 10.

ness, and the establishment of the necessary institutional framework for a commercial, industrial economy.

One of the earliest demands on the national government was for tariff protection. American shipping and young, inefficient manufacturing industries wanted protection from European competition. From the very first, U.S. tariff policy was generally designed to serve American business interests and to ensure high profits by reducing foreign competition. Even when businessmen held the doctrine of laissez-faire in the very highest esteem, they continued as a group to advocate tariffs. Allowing for a few brief, exceptional periods, the government gave them their tariffs and protected their internal monopolistic powers.

Just as important to the economy was a sound currency. The government actively pursued a policy of providing a stable and adequate money supply, and eventually central control over the monetary system, called for in the Constitution, was realized. The *proper amount* of money was a matter of considerable dispute throughout the nineteenth century. Many interests argued for more abundant, or easy, money; others argued for restricted, or tight, money.

Many sophisticated arguments were given in defense of easy and tight money. These arguments, however, often only thinly veiled the pleading of special interests. The advocates of easy money were the farmers and small businessmen, particularly along the frontier, who needed credit to buy and develop land. The eastern capitalists, who were generally creditors, did not enjoy the prospect of lower interest rates or plentiful dollars. Usually the federal government was accused of aligning with the eastern money interests. This widespread view helped Jackson kill the second United States Bank, which would have established a uniform banking and monetary system.

The conflict became particularly intense in the last third of the nineteenth century, when the average price level fell continuously. This was very damaging to debtors who borrowed money when it was worth less and paid it back when it was worth more. Farmers in particular became a disgruntled class. With the advent of mechanized agriculture, they had gone deeply into debt. Agricultural prices fell precipitously, but freight rates failed to decline substantially. As money became worth more and more, they were continuously and ruthlessly squeezed. During this period agricultural and labor interests united to demand currency reform and the abolition of the gold standard. This cry for easy money was one of the unifying forces in the Populist political movement.

Table 29.1 **State Governments' Uses of Borrowed Money in 1838**

Banking	$ 52,640,000
Canals	60,201,551
Railroads	42,871,084
Turnpikes	6,618,868
Miscellaneous	8,474,684
Total	$170,806,187

Source: Tenth Census of the United States, vol. VII (Washington, D.C.: GPO), p. 526.

Another important function of the government in the eighteenth and nineteenth centuries was the creation of efficient transportation networks, a primary prerequisite for the growth of a commercial, private enterprise system. The importance of a stable currency and efficient transportation can be seen by examining the projects state governments financed through borrowing. Table 29.1 gives a breakdown of the nearly $171 million of state government debts in 1838.

Although the market was potentially national in size, a huge investment in transportation was necessary before regional markets could be united. Between 1815 and 1860, federal and state governments made 73 percent of the total investment in canal development, and governments were large suppliers of capital funds for railway construction before the Civil War.

After the Civil War, the railroad boom became even more important to the American economy. Between 1865 and 1914, railroad mileage increased from about 37,000 to almost 253,000 miles. During this period, the federal government became a major source of railroad financing. Earlier, between 1850 and 1871, the U.S. Congress had given away 175,350,000 acres of choice public lands to the railroads—a gift to private enterprise of taxpayers' property worth about $489,000,000.[2] In addition, in the same period, the government had granted the railroads $65,000,000 in special low-cost credit.

Thus throughout the period during which American capitalism was developing into an industrial giant, the government was instrumental in providing the institutional and economic framework in which profitable business could be conducted. Private enterprise profited handsomely as taxpayers subsidized many of the business and industrial ventures that helped provide these necessities.

FISCAL POLICY

The economic role of government that most directly influences the level of output, income, and employment is its taxing and spending of money, or *fiscal policy*. During most of American history the federal government has based its taxing and spending decisions on the political value of the project on which the money was to be spent. The effects of fiscal policy on output, income, and employment were ignored until the depression of the 1930s.

The prevailing economic philosophy was that taxes should be used only to finance necessary government expenditures. It was thought to be an unsound financial practice for governments to borrow money. If a balanced budget, in which expenditures equaled taxes, could not be achieved, it was thought to be preferable to have taxes exceed expenditures so that any debts incurred in the past could be retired. Only the Great Depression and the World War II experiences forced a change in this policy. The trend since that time has been for government spending to rise much more rapidly than taxes.

Federal government spending in the United States in 1921–1929 was only 1 percent of GNP. In 1930–1940, as the New Deal responded to the Depression, it had increased to 4 percent of GNP. With World War II government spending rose to the incredible height of 41 percent of GNP in 1943 and 1944. After the war it

[2] G. C. Fite and J. E. Reese, *An Economic History of the United States,* 2d ed. (Boston: Houghton Mifflin, 1965), p. 330.

fell somewhat, but it bounced up again in the Korean war, so federal spending averaged 11 percent of GNP in 1945-1959. In 1960-1970, partly owing to the Vietnam War, federal spending averaged 13 percent of GNP—about two-thirds or more being military.[3] Total government spending—including state and local as well as federal—rose to 31 percent of GNP in 1970.

GOVERNMENT EXPENDITURES AND AGGREGATE DEMAND

In the income determination model discussed in Chapter 25, we assumed an economy in which there was no government economic activity. We now move a step closer to reality by considering government spending and taxes.

Taxes, like saving, are a leakage from the income stream. Government expenditures, like investment, are an injection into the spending stream. Aggregate supply is now the total of consumption, saving, and *taxes*. Aggregate demand is the total of consumption, investment spending, and *government spending*. The equilibrium of aggregate supply and demand is depicted in Figure 29.1.

Figure 29.1 is exactly like earlier pictures of supply and demand except that government expenditures and taxes have been added. In this picture Income 2 is the equilibrium level of income, where aggregate supply and demand just hap-

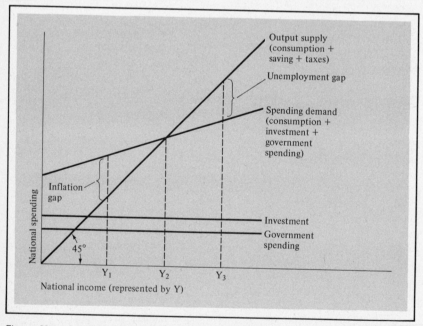

Figure 29.1 **Aggregate supply and aggregate demand. All amounts represent planned decisions, not mere accounting statistics.**

---

[3] James Cypher, *Military Expenditures* (Ph.D. dissertation, University of California, Riverside, 1973), chap. 6.

pen to balance. Suppose that full employment will produce some much higher level of output and income, such as Income 3; then there is a lack of aggregate demand at that higher level, only Income 2 is actually produced, and there is vast unemployment. On the other hand, suppose that we have many fewer workers or less technology so that only a much lower level of output and income can be produced, such as Income 1. At that low level of output, there is a great excess of money demand for goods, but no more can actually be produced, so prices must rise and there is inflation until Income 2 is reached in money terms.

All of this duplicates what was said in Chapter 25 on income determination (which the student should review). What is new is that with government in the picture something can be done about either the unemployment or the inflation, assuming we don't have both at the same time. If there is unemployment—because full employment is at Income level 3, which is far above equilibrium—then the government can add to demand in one of two ways. It can directly increase government spending, which is a component of demand, and/or it can lower taxes, which increases the income available to be spent for consumer or investor demand.

On the other hand, if there is inflation because demand is at too high a level (perhaps because of vast government military spending), then the government can reduce demand in one of two ways. First, it may lower the level of government spending. Second, it may raise taxes, which reduce the amount people have left over for consumer or investor spending. These are the simple mechanics of fiscal policy; we will now proceed to its problems.

AUTOMATIC STABILIZERS

Excessive or deficient demand can be combated in two ways: with *automatic* fiscal devices and with *discretionary* fiscal policies. Automatic fiscal policy is built into the present structure of governmental taxing and spending to react automatically to inflation or depression. Discretionary fiscal policies are changes in the fiscal structure made by current and conscious government decisions. Since World War II the government has placed more reliance on automatic than on discretionary fiscal measures. The fiscal structure is supposed automatically to expand net government demand in depressions and to decrease net government demand in inflations.

To understand the working of the automatic stabilizers, we must glance back at the circular flow of income and spending. The circular flow, with the addition of government income and spending, is illustrated in Figure 29.2. Note that some government money flows *to* business (demand for goods and services) and households (welfare payments). The government receipts flow *from* business (sales taxes, corporate profit taxes, and social security taxes) and households (personal income taxes). An automatic stabilizer is a government device built into the fiscal system that automatically increases or decreases government flows to or from the rest of the economy in response to changes in economic conditions.

In a depression, when GNP tends to drop, the stabilizers should automatically increase government money flows to businesses and households and/or decrease money flows from businesses and households to the government. This

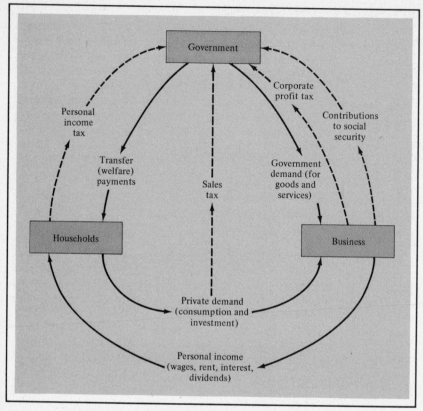

Figure 29.2 **Circular flow of income. International transactions are excluded, otherwise net exports would be an additional demand for products.**

will prevent disposable personal income from dropping as rapidly as otherwise, and thus investment and consumption expenditures can be maintained at a higher level. Similarly, in an inflation, the automatic stabilizers are supposed to decrease the amount given and increase the amount taken away from business and households, thus decreasing the total amount of consumer and investor spending. In either case the net changes in government flows should have a multiple effect.

Now what are the magic devices by which the government is supposed to keep the economy automatically stable? On the spending side of the ledger, the government makes many types of welfare payments that automatically increase in depression and automatically decrease in expansions. For example, as full employment is approached, there will be very little unemployment compensation; but in a depression, with growing unemployment, this may become a significant source of buying power.

On the taxation side, the total amounts of federal income tax collected had declined in most recessions faster than personal income, so it usually left people with more to spend. The federal income tax acted this way because individuals automatically pay a lower tax rate if their incomes decline. Therefore, the federal tax system was an important automatic stabilizer.

Unfortunately, the depression of 1973–1975 was in the midst of a continued price inflation. Therefore, personal incomes rose in the depression in money terms, though they fell in terms of purchasing power. Thus the percentage of taxes rose in the 1973–1975 depression. For middle-income taxpayers, with an intermediate income by government standards, in 1974 personal income taxes went up 27 percent and Social Security taxes went up 22 percent over 1973. As a result of the inflation, this was the first depression in American history in which the burden of personal income taxes actually increased. Instead of being the most important automatic stabilizer, the federal income tax operated as a major automatic destabilizer!

DISCRETIONARY FISCAL POLICIES AND SOCIAL PRIORITIES

Because the automatic devices have failed to stabilize the economy, liberal Keynesian economists maintain that discretionary fiscal measures are necessary to eliminate depression and inflation. They contend that the legislature merely needs to increase spending and lower taxes in depression, and lower spending and increase taxes in inflation. But these measures also are subject to political and economic complications.

There are three different policy views of what government discretionary fiscal policy ought to be. The most conservative economists, such as Adam Smith or the contemporary American Milton Friedman, argue that no discretionary fiscal measures are needed. The government should stay out of the economy. Friedman agrees with Adam Smith that the less government the better. He attributes many of our economic problems to too much government interference with private enterprise, which would otherwise automatically adjust to all situations in a near-perfect manner. To the extent that conservatives admit any need for government policy, they say that only monetary measures are necessary. Conservatives favor measures affecting the money supply (via interest rates, for example) rather than any fiscal measures of spending or taxation because they feel that monetary measures do not directly interfere with business. They view an adequate money supply merely as one of the prerequisites for a private enterprise economy. Other prerequisites which they believe government should provide, include police and armies to maintain "law and order," primarily to protect private property from its domestic and foreign enemies.

The second, the liberal, view is that of such economists as John M. Keynes or the contemporary American Paul Samuelson. Liberals admit that capitalism has real problems, such as general unemployment and inflation. Liberal Keynesians argue that adequate government measures of increased or decreased spending and increased or decreased taxation are necessary to correct these problems. Finally, they used to maintain that such measures can *always successfully bring about full employment* with stable prices. Some of them now, however, define full employment as "only" 4 or 5 percent unemployment and stable prices as "only" 2 or 3 percent inflation per year.[4] Others, including Samuelson, simply admit that

---

[4] See, for example, James Tobin and Leonard Ross, "Living with Inflation," *New York Review of Books,* May 6, 1971.

ending inflation *and* getting full employment at the same time is one little thing not yet solved by establishment economists: "Experts do not yet know . . . an incomes policy that will permit us to have *simultaneously* . . . full employment and price stability."[5]

The radical view is expressed by Karl Marx or the contemporary American Paul Sweezy. Radicals argue that problems like periodic unemployment are deeply rooted in the capitalist system and cannot be cured by any amount of monetary or fiscal measures. They contend that the *U.S. economy has reached full employment only during major wars.* In normal peacetime years, they believe unemployment and/or inflation is the usual state of capitalism. They argue that the necessary drastic fiscal measures cannot be taken by capitalist governments because powerful vested interests oppose each such step, aside from military spending.

Suppose we accept the liberal Keynesian argument that government intervention can prevent large-scale unemployment or runaway inflation. The basic fiscal formula, to which may be added certain monetary measures, is to raise taxes and lower spending during inflations, while lowering taxes and raising spending during depressions. Moreover, corporate executives and members of congress alike are by now well aware of and receptive to these techniques. But that by no means settles the issue (even aside from the problem of simultaneous unemployment and inflation discussed in Chapter 31).

The problem remains: Which spending? Whose taxes? Suppose we agree to spend the large amounts of money necessary to maintain full employment. Many outlets that would be socially beneficial conflict with the vested interests of large corporations or wealthy individuals. Larger welfare payments tend to raise the wage level; government investment in industrial ventures or in public utilities tends to erode monopolistic privileges. The issue is the political constraints to economic policies.

In the years immediately after World War II, the problem was to spend $15–20 billion annually. This might have been a very agonizing social and political issue except for the advent of the Cold War.

Dollars for Cold War armaments did not violate any vested interests. Military spending is considered an ideal antidepression policy by big business for three reasons. First, such expenditures have the same short-run effect on employment and profits as would expenditures on more socially useful projects. Second, military spending means big and stable profits, whereas welfare spending may shift income from rich taxpayers to poor recipients. Third, the long-run effect is even more favorable because no new productive equipment is created to compete with existing facilities. During the part 25 years, the main change has been that the necessary addition to the income stream has risen to at least $70–80 billion a year. *If it were politically possible, the whole amount could be spend on useful public commodities,* such as housing or health or education, rather than on military waste. These useful types of public spending are *not* politically feasible in such large amounts, however, as long as the U.S. government is dominated by big business.

One popular cure for depression is reduction of taxes to allow more money to flow into private spending. Given the composition of the U.S. government, how-

[5] Paul Samuelson, *Economics*, 9th ed. (New York: McGraw-Hill, 1973), p. 823.

ever, tax cuts always end up benefiting mainly the rich and the corporations. Even in the liberal Kennedy administration, the taxes of the poor were reduced very little and of the rich very much, resulting in a redistribution of income to the deserving members of the wealthy class. Especially in a depression, however, the wealthy will not spend their increased income. The consumption of the wealthy remains at adequate levels even in a depression, and they have no desire to invest in the face of probable losses. Hence the political restriction as to *who* gets the tax cuts makes this policy economically ineffective.

Similarly, all economists (and even most businesspeople) may see a need for more and more vast government spending under capitalism. The prime political question, however, is spending on what, for it is here that vested interests come into play. Thus even small vital expenditures on medical care have sometimes been defeated by the American Medical Association. Powerful vested interests oppose almost every item in the civilian budget as soon as expansion proceeds beyond the necessary minimum. What kind of interests must be defeated to have the necessary spending to fill a $70–80 billion deficiency in demand? Constructive projects such as the Missouri Valley Authority could develop dams, irrigation, and cheap power, but these have been fought tooth and nail by the private power interests (and, indeed, might lower private investment by direct competition). There could be large-scale public housing, but private contractors have long kept such programs to a minimum.

There might be other welfare spending—for example, on hospitals and schools. The rich, however, see these as subsidies to the poor for things that the rich can buy for themselves out of their own pockets. Proposals to increase unemployment compensation or lower taxes paid by the poor encounter even greater resistance because they would transfer income from the rich to the poor. Likewise, billions could usefully be spent in aid and loans to the less developed world, where poverty and human suffering are so widespread. That, however, could be passed on a massive scale only over the bodies of hundreds of members of congress, who represent well the wishes of their self-interested constituents and have no concept of the long-run gain to world trade and world peace. If any of these measures are to some extent allowed, it is only after a long political fight, certainly not promptly enough to head off a developing depression.

We could list, one by one, all the areas in which powerful vested interests stand in opposition to the satisfaction of some of the nation's most basic social needs. These interests will not tolerate government competition with private enterprise, measures that undermine the privileges of the wealthy, or policies that significantly alter the relative distribution of income. They therefore tend to oppose all government nonmilitary spending—except direct business subsidies. The only major exception to this generalization is government spending on highways, which is actively promoted by the largest and most lucrative single industry after defense: the automobile producers.

MILITARY SPENDING VERSUS WELFARE SPENDING

From all of the facts just given, we conclude that welfare or constructive spending on a large scale is opposed by too many special interests to be politically feasible. Our hypothesis is that *only large-scale military spending brought the United States out of the great depression of the 1930s, and only large-scale military spending has kept the United States out of a major depression.* The liberals like Samuelson are much more complacent; speaking about mass unemployment and galloping inflations, he says they are things of the past. He asserts that these are ancient problems that are solvable and have been solved: "For example, however true it might have been in the turn-of-the-century era of Lenin . . . , it is definitely no longer the case in the age after Keynes that prosperity of a mixed economy (i.e., capitalism plus government) depends on cold-war expenditures and imperialistic ventures."[6]

It is a fact, however, that our economy has boomed by spending immense sums of money to kill the people of Vietnam. How would Samuelson replace that crutch to the economy? He says: "Does building missiles and warheads create jobs . . . ? Then so too will building new factories, better roads and schools, cleaning up our rivers, and providing minimum income-supplements for our aged and handicapped."[7] Certainly it is true that jobs could be created in all these constructive ways rather than the destructive ways of warfare. *But*—and it is a big *but*—we are talking about *government spending,* so we must remember that vested interests will obstruct programs that might harm them. Yet for the government to build new factories means direct competition with private industry. For the government to build schools means to take money from rich taxpayers and transfer it to the education of poorer citizens. To clean up the rivers means both more use of tax money and forcing private industry to spend money on purifying its wastes. Giving to the aged and handicapped means again adding taxes and shifting income to the poor.

The political reality is that vested interests oppose each of these programs with violent rhetoric and successful political pressure. Thus Congress does not even talk about building government factories for peaceful use—in fact, government atomic energy plants have been given away free to private capitalists. Presidents Nixon and Ford, both of whom were supported primarily by big business, vetoed a large number of liberal Keynesian bills to stimulate employment by more public jobs or by more spending for health, education, or welfare. President Carter is committed to some Keynesian-type spending to stimulate the economy. Yet he also has many ties to business, has many conservative economic advisors, and says he is a "fiscal conservative." Therefore, we predict that he will *not* launch constructive projects on the massive magnitude needed to approach full employment but will continue to allow a relatively high level of unemployment. We also predict that, in spite of his explicit promise to cut military spending, he will *raise* military spending during his term in office.

Paul Samuelson says that radicals have asked, "Politically, will there be as much urgency to spend what is needed for useful, peacetime full-employment programs as there is urgency and willingness to spend for hot- and cold-war purposes?" And he answers, "It was proper to ask this question back in the 1950s. But . . . experience since then has shown that modern electorates have become very sensitive to levels of unemployment that would have been considered moderate back in the good old days. And they do put effective pressure at

[6] Ibid., p. 823.
[7] Ibid., p. 824.

the polls on their government."[8]   But in the first place, the pressure is only to get jobs—not necessarily to get welfare rather than warfare jobs; so both Republican and Democratic administrations continue military spending to avoid unemployment—and do not do large amounts of constructive spending.

In the second place, Samuelson just assumes that "the people" make our governmental decisions, but we saw in Chapter 20 that the dominant power in governmental decision making in the United States is big business. It would have been nice to test what the liberal McGovern would have done in power. Perhaps he would have been able (with much popular support to overcome business pressure) to substitute a little more welfare for a little less warfare. But that was not the record of previous liberal administrations: the Kennedy administration vastly increased military spending, invaded Cuba, and expanded the Vietnam War; and the Johnson administration further expanded the Vietnam War on a vast scale.

We have seen that Keynesian liberals fail to see the political constraints that make military spending the only allowable solution to unemployment. The political nature of the problem has become even more apparent in the inflationary situation of the past 20 years. The Korean and Vietnam wars caused so much government demand for military supplies that inflation resulted, prices rising especially in 1950–1953 and 1967–1974. To cure inflation the simple Keynesian prescription is to increase taxes and reduce spending.

But whose taxes, which spending? Major increases in taxes on the wealthy are not easily passed by our government. And there is not that much room for further taxes on the poor and the middle class without provoking rising discontent. So it is easier to reduce government spending. But not military spending; politicians and spokespersons for industry and the military continue to convince the nation that these are absolutely necessary. Thus welfare spending is cut. Already a tiny percentage of the American government budget, welfare has nevertheless been cut further as a tool to fight inflation. Hence the burden of inflation has fallen on the common man and woman in the forms of rising prices, rising taxes, and falling welfare spending all at the same time.

The question of social and political priorities often boils down to a conflict between the genuine needs of the majority versus the desires of the tiny minority that possesses immense economic and political power. The majority of Americans need more education, health, and welfare; but a powerful minority favors military spending.

THE MILITARY ECONOMY

To measure the full extent of the military impact on the economy, we must recall that the U.S. Department of Defense is the largest planned economy in the world today outside the USSR. It spends more than the net income of all U.S. corporations. By 1969 it had 470 major and 6,000 lesser installations, owned 39 million acres of land, spent over $80 billion a year, used 22,000 primary contractors and 100,000 subcontractors—thus directly employing in the armed forces and mili-

[8] Ibid., pp. 824–825.

tary production about 10 percent of the U.S. labor force.[9] Some key areas of the economy are especially affected. As early as 1963, before U.S. entry into the Vietnam War, studies show that 36 percent of the output of producers' durable goods were purchased directly or indirectly by the federal government, mostly for military use.

How did the U.S. economy come to have such an enormous military sector?[10] Of course in World War II the United States had an enormous military production. It was assumed by every policy maker, including economists and businesspersons and political leaders, that the United States would mostly disarm after the war. It was also assumed that this would lead to a depression: therefore every possible solution was considered, with most analyses leading to the sole suggestion of renewed military spending. It was in this atmosphere that the Cold War was born; it provided every possible increase in military spending. In fact, since the United States had a monopoly of atomic bombs, the USSR was very unlikely to be aggressive. Moreover, Soviet foreign policy was mostly very cautious and conservative (so much so that revolutionaries in other countries accused them of betrayal for *not* supplying arms). In reality, the USSR had its sphere of influence—Eastern Europe—which the United States has not invaded, while the United States has spheres of influence and imperial power in much of Latin America, Africa, and Asia, which the USSR has never invaded. Thus, despite the Cold War rhetoric, the two major powers have never clashed militarily (except by indirectly supporting others).

Therefore the armaments spending justified by the Cold War rhetoric was not militarily necessary. It was utilized, as in Southeast Asia, to protect U.S. investments abroad but also in large part to support the U.S. economy at home. Thus we find in both world wars that the industrialists dictated to the government exactly how the procurement process should be run, completely dominated the Department of Defense, and made enormous rates of profit. This condition has continued ever since.

How big is U.S. military spending? It certainly includes all Department of Defense spending, but it goes considerably beyond that. How far is controversial, but the most careful study to date (by James Cypher) includes half of all "international affairs" spending, veterans benefits, atomic energy and space appropriations (all military-related), and 75 percent of the interest on the public debt (since at least 75 percent of the debt was used to pay for wars). Other things that are too hard to get exact data on are major parts of the budget for research and development, the CIA, and other intelligence agencies—and of course the deaths, wounds, and alienation of young Americans. For the five quantifiable items in military spending, Cypher adds up the grand total of $1.7 *trillion* from 1947 through 1971—enough to buy our entire gross national product for 1969 *and* 1970.

Yet this amount of direct military spending (even if it included the things we can't quantify) still underestimates the impact of military spending on the U.S.

---

[9] These data come from U.S. Defense Department documents that are reported in Seymour Melman, *Pentagon Capitalism* (New York: McGraw-Hill, 1970).

[10] Most of the analysis and all of the facts in the rest of this chapter come from James Cypher, *Military Expenditures and the Performance of the Post-war Economy, 1947–71* (Ph.D. dissertation, University of California, Riverside). This dissertation is a gold mine of information and the best discussion now available of military spending.

economy. There is a very large indirect or secondary effect on (1) additional consumer goods from the spending of those who receive military dollars and (2) additional investment in plant, equipment, and business inventories by military industries. Economists measure the secondary effects of military spending by the government multiplier (discussed in detail in the appendix to this chapter), which measures the ratio of the total increase in all spending to every dollar of increase in government spending. Estimates of the multiplier from military spending range from about $1.85 to $3.50 of total spending for every dollar of military spending.

The most important measure of military spending is as a percentage of our whole gross national product (GNP). From 1947 to 1971 it ranged from a low of 10.1 percent of GNP in 1948 to a high of 21.9 percent in the Korean War year of 1952. It was at 13.5 percent and 13.2 percent in 1967 and 1968, during the Vietnam War peak, and slowly fell to 12.6 percent in 1969, 11.6 percent in 1970, and 11.1 percent in 1971 (with another major rise in 1972). For the whole 1947–1971 period, direct military spending averaged 13.2 percent of GNP. Now if we are quite conservative and assume a multiplier of only 2, it is apparent that direct and indirect military spending accounted for the demand for 26.4 percent of GNP. This means that if military spending and its indirect effects had not been present in this whole period and all other things had been the same (which is very unlikely), we would have had a depression greater than that in the 1930s—when unemployment was 24.3 percent. Of course if the military multiplier is actually 3, then total demand for GNP would fall by 39.6 percent if we ended all military spending—always assuming we did nothing else. Actually we have seen that the U.S. government might increase welfare spending a little, but it is not politically feasible on the scale required.

It is worth noting just how military spending has affected the U.S. economy at various times. As late as 1939 it had very little effect, being only 2.6 percent of GNP. In World War II it rose to about 40 percent of GNP, which brought full employment (and even a shortage of labor). After World War II there were several times when the drop in military spending seems to have been the main catalyst setting off a recession. Thus in 1948 it fell by 11 percent, followed by a recession in 1949. In 1953 it fell by 17 percent and in 1954 by 30 percent; and there was a recession in 1954. In 1957 military spending grew only 2.6 percent, followed by a recession in 1958. In 1960 it fell 3 percent, followed by recession in 1961. In 1969 it grew by only 3 percent, and it fell by 2 percent in 1970, followed by the recession of 1971. All this suggests that military spending must keep rising at a considerable rate to prevent recessions and that when it falters it sets off a recession.

Obviously this is no simple case of cause and effect. In the first place, it holds true only when the economy does not have other sources of major new demands (but that has not occurred ever since the first rush of consumer spending after World War II). And there is still an underlying private cyclical mechanism that makes the economy react as it does. Moreover, it can be offset by other policies on the required scale. Thus in addition to the years mentioned, there is one other time when military spending faltered but did not set off a recession. In 1965 military spending did not change at all, but this lack was offset by the massive tax cut of 1964–1965, which did stimulate some private spending.

On the other side, it should also be noted that military spending seems to have increased each time the U.S. economy needed to get out of recessions. Thus in the recession of 1949, military spending was immediately increased by 7.6 percent; in the recession of 1958, it was increased by 8.1 percent; and in the recession of 1961, it was increased by 6.6 percent. It was also increased by 7.6 percent in 1955, which may have helped us out of the 1954 recession. In 1971 wage-price controls were used in the new unemployment-inflation situation, but it appears that military spending did take another jump upward in 1972 to help with the continuing unemployment.

Thus our automatic and inherent pattern of business cycles has now been overlaid with a more politically motivated business cycle. When there is an all-out boom, business influence gets government to reduce military spending. This reduction is desired (1) to avoid inflation and (2) to avoid full employment, which means "uppity" workers and higher wages. Since, however, it is hard to time the military spending reductions exactly when desired and very hard to estimate exactly how much is needed, this always seems to do more than just limit the boom; it almost always seems to turn into a full-scale recession. Indeed, in Chapter 28 we saw why the capitalist economy never stands still but always has cumulative forces pushing it rapidly up or down once it gets going. Thus when vested interests reduce military spending a bit—in order to limit the boom—this action may set off a recession. As the recession gets worse and profits decline, the same political-economic power is used to start increasing military spending again, which may set off another boom. This, of course, is much too sketchy and rigid a schema to encompass all the many factors effecting current economic history, but it is an important framework for understanding.

Finally, we must note why big business is so happy with a normally high level of military spending. On the aggregate level, we saw that it is used to protect U.S. investments abroad, to get the economy out of recessions, and to prevent a major depression; but there is an additional incentive for the individual defense contractor. This incentive is based on the fact that the rate of profit is very high in military production and that most of these profits go to a few very large firms. Almost all military contracts go to some 205 of the top 500 corporations, and just 100 of them get 85 percent of all military contracts.

There are some studies of military profits, but all of them understate the profit rates. In reporting to the government the military firms overstate their costs—and since they do not operate under competition but in a cosy relation with the Pentagon, they probably overstate costs more than most firms. Thus they allocate costs of other parts of their business to military contracts and add in all sorts of other unrelated costs—some have even tossed in the costs of call girls to influence government inspectors (called "entertainment" in their accounts). They also make many hidden profits through the use of complex subcontracting procedures to subsidiaries, unauthorized use of government-owned property, and getting patents on research done for the government.

Still, a study by the General Accounting Office (GAO) of the U.S. government has definitely spelled out their high profit rates.[11] First the GAO asked 81 large military contractors by questionnaire what their profit rates were for 1966 through 1969. The replies, which were limited by self-interest, still admitted an average profit rate of 24.8 percent—much higher than nonmilitary profits in the same industries. But spot checks showed that these profit rates were still very much underreported. So the GAO did its own audit of the books of 146 main military

[11] Fully discussed in Cypher, chap. 5.

contractors. The study found that the profit rate of these merchants of death was a fantastic 56.1 percent rate of return on invested capital!

SUMMARY

In the nineteenth century, federal and state governments subsidized canals and railroads. Since the 1930s, the U.S. government has tried to modify the business cycle by increased government spending and lower taxes in depressions—while at the peak of each expansion the government reduces spending and increases taxes to prevent full employment (supposedly to fight inflation). Government spending in depressions has never gone into constructive projects—schools, hospitals, housing—on the massive scale required because of the political power of the capitalist class, who oppose these projects and desire military spending for greater profits.

Military spending took the United States out of the Great Depression and has prevented a major depression ever since. It directly employs about 13 percent of the labor force and indirectly another 13 percent or more in most years. A decline of military spending has set off several recessions, while increases in military spending have encouraged recoveries from several recessions. Any constructive government spending tends to compete with private enterprise and to redistribute income from rich to poor. Military spending alone does not compete with private enterprise; it indirectly stimulates private consumption and investment and redistributes income from the poor to the rich (because of the very high profit rates paid to military producers). Therefore very powerful economic interests are against constructive or welfare spending but favor military spending. While enough military spending can produce full employment, it seems a highly irrational economic system that can guarantee full employment only in this way—since it also implies high taxes, inflation, and death.

APPENDIX

THE GOVERNMENT MULTIPLIER

The obvious objectives of government fiscal policy are to increase the net flow of demand during depressions by increasing spending and lowering taxes, and to reduce the net flow of demand during inflation by reducing spending and raising taxes. Not only the direct effects but also the secondary effects of these policies are important. For example, in a depression it is hoped that increases in government spending will mean more income to businesses or individuals and that this, in turn, will lead to further increases in private consumption and investment.

The secondary effects of a government expenditure may be quantified in terms of the government multiplier. The *government multiplier* is the ratio of increase in national income to an increase in government spending. The reader will recall that the investment multiplier was defined as the ratio of an increase in national income to an increase in private investment.

Take the very simple assumption that consumption reacts in a given ratio to an increase in income (while investment remains constant). This means every increase in income automatically leads to a certain increase in consumption spending. This spending means a further, though smaller, increase in income, some of which will be spent for a second round of consumption, and so forth.

The formal apparatus for studying the government multiplier is exactly the same as that for the investment multiplier. It may help to review a numerical example in which we assume (1) a certain increase in government spending with a given marginal propensity to consume and (2) that the increase in government spending takes place without any change in tax receipts. Under these simple assumptions, the formula for the government multiplier is

$$\text{Government multiplier} = \frac{1}{\text{MPS}}$$

or

$$\text{Government multiplier} = \frac{1}{1 - \text{MPC}}$$

Remember that MPS stands for marginal propensity to save and MPC stands for marginal propensity to consume. Also remember that MPS is just 1—MPC. And MPC is defined as the ratio of an increase in consumption to an increase in income. Thus in Table 29A.1 the government multiplier is 5 and the national income increases by $5000.

Table 29A.1 **How the Government Multiplier Works**

1. Suppose government increases its spending by $1000 (while private investment does not change).
2. Also suppose a marginal propensity to consume of 4/5, or 80 percent.

Increase in Government Spending	Increase in Consumption	Increase in National Income	Increase in Saving
$1000		$1000	
0	$ 800	$ 800	$ 200
0	$ 640	$ 640	$ 160
0	$ 512	$ 512	$ 128
0	$ 410	$ 410	$ 102
0	$ 328	$ 328	$ 82
—	—	—	—
—	—	—	—
—	—	—	—
—	—	—	—
Total Increase in Government Spending	Total Increase in Consumption	Total Increase in National Income	Total Increase in Saving
$1000	$4000	$5000	$1000

Suppose, in different economic conditions, that only half of additional income is always consumed and fully half is saved. Then only half of new government spending will be respent for consumption. But half of that amount, as it becomes income, will be spent in a second round of consumption. Then half of the second round of consumption will be spent for a third round of consumption, and so forth. The end result is that if MPC is just ½, the multiplier approaches 2. That is, the total additional consumption will just equal the additional government spending, so the total increase in income is just twice the initial increase in income received from the government. Thus if the government spends an extra $1 billion, a multiplier of 2 says that a total increase of $2 billion in national income will be generated, of which $1 billion will be the secondary consumer spending.

For similar reasons, if MPC rises to ⅔, the government multiplier rises to 3. If, however, the marginal propensity to consume is zero, then the multiplier is 1. In this case there are *no* secondary effects because *all* of the first round of spending is saved. In the other extreme case, if MPC moves toward 1, the multiplier moves toward infinity—that is, the secondary effects are infinite because all income is immediately respent for consumption.

Of course, the government multiplier ratio is an artificial concept because it does not take into account all the changing factors and complications involved.

The first qualification is the fact that the second, third, and fourth rounds of spending do not occur instantaneously; it takes time before income is respent for consumption. Long or varying time lags make it much more difficult to speak of an exact multiplier. Second, the multiplier explained here assumes that investment is a given constant and is not affected by changes in income. As has been seen in earlier chapters, however, there is probably a close connection between investment and the change in income. If this is so, changes in government spending, as well as the secondary changes in consumer spending, may directly affect investment. However, government spending may have negative psychological effects on investment if it is thought to take away funds by taxation or to compete by means of cheaper products. At any rate government spending is likely to have some direct or indirect effect on investment, and as a result investment may not legitimately be considered a constant in this regard.

The third major set of qualifications to the government multiplier arises from the fact that MPC does not remain constant, yet it is the very rock on which the multiplier theory is founded. It does not remain constant because, for one thing, consumption is actually influenced by many factors other than income. The marginal consumption ratio also varies because there are different leakages from the process at different times. For example, the effect of an increase in government spending on national income may be partly siphoned off by the levy of higher taxes or merely by automatic movements into higher tax brackets. Furthermore, it may happen that increased spending for imports removes some portion of income from the domestic multiplier process. For all of these reasons, MPC may change too often for any accurate prediction of the multiplier beyond a short period of only one or two rounds of the process.

The fourth and last qualification has to do with how the government spending is financed. If the government takes back through taxation the same amount that it spends, then there is no net addition to consumer spending, only the initial government spending is added to the economy, and the multiplier will be only 1. The national income will increase by the amount of the increase in government spending.

If increased government spending is financed by sale of government bonds, or *deficit spending,* the effect on the private economy depends on how the bondholders would have used the money had they not lent it to the government. If they would have spent it all for consumption or investment anyway, then there would be no net stimulation to the private economy. If they would have spent only a small percentage of it (which is often the case), then the government spending would have a very powerful net effect on the private economy.

Finally, the most inflationary method of financing government spending is to print new money because this withdraws nothing from the private sector either by taxation or borrowing. In a deep depression, a government may finance expenditures by printing money; at full employment, it will attempt to use only taxation; and with a small degree of unemployment, it may use borrowing.

Summary

Government spending has both direct and indirect effects. The indirect effects occur through the additional consumer and investment spending the government stimulates. These indirect effects are called multiplier effects. The multiplier measures the total change in demand resulting from a change in direct government spending. Economists estimate it with the formula, multiplier = 1/ MPS, but this formula is very rough and inaccurate because it leaves out many factors.

CHAPTER 30

MONEY, BANKING, AND MONETARY POLICY

Aggregate demand is the total planned spending of money in exchange for the economy's current output of goods and services. In order to isolate what determines the level of this demand, we assumed that the money supply remained constant when we examined changes in investment or consumption spending. Using this approach, any fall in total demand implies a rising flow of money into hoards; while any rise in total demand, as would occur when planned investment exceeds the flow of saving, implies that dishoarding is occurring. Therefore in equilibrium there is neither hoarding nor dishoarding, planned investment equals planned saving, and the total money supply is being used recurringly in exchange for goods and services. In this case a constant sum is being held in money balances. More realistically, when total demand is rising, the money supply may also be rising because new money may be created by the commercial banking system. Conversely, when total demand falls, the money supply may shrink because new credit money is not created and loans are repaid to banks. Our purpose in this chapter is to examine the money supply and to investigate the money creation powers of commercial banks.

The present money supply consists of coins and paper currency outside of commercial banks and checking accounts (demand deposits) in commercial banks. In August 1976 the total U.S. money supply was $306 billion, including $79 billion in currency and $228 billion in demand deposits. The recent growth of the money supply and its component parts is shown in Figure 30.1.

Demand deposits, which account for a fairly constant percentage of the money supply (76.4 percent in 1947 and 77.2 percent in 1973), are the debts of commercial banks. When we say banks create money, we refer to the fact that banks have the ability to create demand deposits. After considering a conjectural history of money, we shall investigate a conjectural evolution of this money creation power. (It is conjectural in that it is not an exact history of one place but what we believe to have been the logical and approximate development in most places.)

A CONJECTURAL HISTORY OF MONEY

Money is defined as any widely accepted medium of exchange. A commodity that is used as money does not necessarily have any intrinsic value aside from its general acceptability in exchange and for the settlement of debt. If the law requires that it be accepted in the settlement of debt, it is also *legal tender*.

Among the most primitive tribes exchange was conducted by the barter sys-

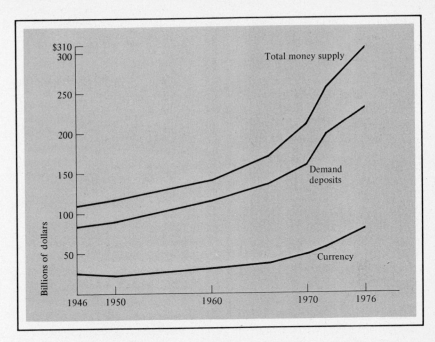

Figure 30.1 **The money supply and its component parts. Total money supply = demand deposits + currency.** (Source: *Federal Reserve Bulletin*, May 1974 and October 1976.)

tem. *Barter* means that one commodity is directly traded for another in the market without the use of money. For example, we may find trade in this form:

$$1 \text{ coat} = 2 \text{ hats}$$

If this exchange ratio persists for some time, people may come to think of one coat as worth two hats, or they may think of one hat as worth half a coat.

The second evolutionary step was to the crudest kind of money, a stage in which some particular commodity was used as money. Any convenient or often-used commodity might eventually attain the status of money if it were relatively scarce and therefore valuable. For example, in a community in which the number of cows owned was a status symbol, we might find that cows played the role of money. Thus

$$2 \text{ coats} = 1 \text{ cow} \qquad 1 \text{ cow} = 4 \text{ hats}$$

People in this society would calculate all their production and wealth in terms of cows. They might also actually sell or trade coats for cows and then use the "cow money" to buy hats, or vice versa.

Cows, however, are not a very convenient money commodity. They are perishable and not easily divisible, problems that could be solved by using precious metals or stones. The need to have large numbers of pieces of money that are of equal value led to the third step of the evolution, the development of *metallic money*. Precious metals have several virtues as a medium of exchange: (1) They are valuable; one need carry only a small amount to buy other commodities. (2) They are easily divisible. Uniform coins of various values can be made by melting, and thus the exact amount necessary for any purchase can be used. (3) They are nonperishable and hence can be stored indefinitely.

The durability and portability of metallic money means it may be used not only for calculating value ratios but also in every exchange. Thus trade takes this form:

$$1 \text{ coat} = 1 \text{ oz. gold} \qquad 1 \text{ oz. gold} = 2 \text{ hats}$$

Any commodity (e.g., a coat) may be sold for metallic money. Then the metallic money is put away until its holder wishes to buy another commodity (e.g., a hat).

The next step in the evolution came when paper claims were substituted for metallic money such as gold, but they were still payable in gold. These claims were originally issued by goldsmiths, private bankers, and merchants. Governments soon followed suit, issuing their own paper money, which consisted of IOUs, or promises by the government to pay in gold on demand. Of course it was possible to issue more paper money than gold because not everyone demanded gold at the same time.

The modern issue of *inconvertible paper money* is the fifth step in the evolution of money. Paper money looks the same as before, but a government declares that it will no longer convert, or pay its paper IOUs in gold on demand. This method of money creation financed the American and French Revolutions and the U.S. Civil War. Almost all governments had recourse to this expedient in the monetary chaos following World War I and during the Great Depression. At the same time they usually prohibited private institutions from issuing paper money. One way governments made their paper money more acceptable to the populace was to accept it themselves for tax payments and to declare it legal tender. Of course the value of inconvertible paper money today has no direct connection with gold reserves.

The most recently evolved form of money is the checking account. Sums of money in checking accounts are bookkeeping entries called *deposits*. They are actually promises to pay—that is, they are debts of the bank. Checks written against these accounts are orders to transfer deposit funds to others' accounts or to convert some of the deposit account into currency. The owner of such an account may have brought currency to the bank or may have deposited a check. He may have signed a note and borrowed the money. In such a case the bank and the individual merely exchange IOUs. But the bank's IOU, the demand deposit, serves all the functions of money. Checks drawn against the balance make payment without the use of currency or coin. Although a check is not legal tender, the deposit is convertible into legal tender, and the deposit account is money. It is apparent that the distinguishing characteristic of a bank is that, unlike any other private enterprise, the evidence of its debt to an individual is accepted as money.

A CONJECTURAL EVOLUTION OF MODERN BANKING

Perhaps we can illustrate the role of the modern banker by returning to conjectural history. Centuries ago, when the market system was evolving, goldsmiths had large quantities of precious metals. To protect them, secure storage facilities had to be constructed. Other individuals sought the same security for their money but did not have enough money to justify the expense of constructing such facilities. The local goldsmith began to accept their coin (the sole form of money at this time) and precious metals. As evidence of these deposits the depositor was provided with a receipt. The goldsmith earned income by demanding payment from the individual depositor for the safekeeping function performed.

In time, goldsmiths who had developed reputations for honesty found that these deposit receipts began to circulate and could be used by the individuals holding them in payment of debt. For example, merchants, instead of carrying coin on business trips, would deposit it with a reputable and renowned goldsmith. The receipt could then be used to settle accounts in distant lands. Hence as long as the goldsmith was willing and able to redeem these deposit receipts, or paper claims, on demand for coin, they performed the function of money. Here we see the initial stages in the development of both the banking system and paper claims as money. The validity of the paper claims as money was premised on their general acceptability as money, which depended on the confidence that the public had in the goldsmith's ability to convert the paper claims into coin on demand.

Thus far, however, goldsmith's have not performed the primary distinguishing function of bankers, the money creation function. All they have done is to match their metallic assets with paper claims. Their balance sheets probably would resemble this:

Assets		Liabilities	
Coin in vault	$1000	Deposits	$1000
Total assets	$1000	Total liabilities	$1000

Sooner or later goldsmiths realize that they can create debt (demand deposits and notes payable on demand) in excess of the coin they hold in their vaults. Why can they do this? First, because the people have confidence in their ability to redeem their paper claims into coin on demand. Second, this confidence leads other people to accept the paper claims in settlement of their debts. Therefore at any given time only a small portion of the paper claims need to be converted into coin.

As long as goldsmith-bankers can readily meet this small portion of claims for coin, they are in a position to increase their total liabilities beyond the actual amount of coin they have in their vaults. In other words, they are able to create money. And the total of coin, bank notes, and deposit receipts now in circulation exceeds the amount of coin that has been minted by the government authority. The bank notes (issued by the goldsmith-bankers to those who borrow from them) and the deposit receipts are *money,* the same way coin is money, because people are willing to accept them in payment for any debt. If an individual receives payments in the form of either coin or bank note or a deposit receipt, it makes no difference to that person at all as long as he or she can use these equally for making his or her own payments.

Goldsmiths (who are now bankers because they create money) will then keep in their vaults an amount of coin large enough to meet the demands for coin that will be made upon them. Of course they can roughly estimate these demands from their experience. The banker-goldsmiths' balance sheets probably would resemble this.

Assets		Liabilities	
Coins in vault	$ 800	Notes payable	$ 600
Loans	800	Deposits	1000
Total assets	$1600	Total liabilities	$1600

The bankers' liabilities in this example clearly exceed the coin in their vaults. What they have done is lend money to individuals, of which $200 has had to be paid out in the form of coin (reducing their coin from $1000 to $800). However, people are willing to hold the other $600 of loans in the form of bank notes. Thus the bankers have created new liabilities while holding only half of their total liabilities ($800) in the form of coin. They now have an additional form of income: the interest they earn from the loans they make. The banker has created money in excess of the coin in their vaults to the amount of $800.

The bankers' ability to create money is limited by the portion of notes and deposits they are forced to hold in the form of coin because of institutional or other considerations. In this case, because they have to hold 50 percent of their deposits and note liabilities in the form of coin, they can expand the money supply by only twice the amount of coin in their vaults.

Here we see the development, in its initial stages, of the modern banking system. The bankers now create debts that circulate freely as money and that slowly come to form an increasing part of the total money supply. They have succeeded in converting their idle coins, which earn no interest, into loans for which they charge a rate of interest. The borrowing-lending function, formerly performed by moneylenders, is now performed by bankers. The uniqueness of bankers, however, lies in the fact that, unlike the moneylender, they can make loans in excess of the actual coin in their vaults.

OPERATION OF MODERN COMMERCIAL BANKS

The bankers' business consists of taking the money deposited with them, on some of which they pay interest, and lending it out at higher rates of interest. Money deposited in time or savings accounts pays interest to depositors, but it must stay frozen, or on deposit, for some definite time before the interest is paid (thus it is counted only as *near money*). Money deposited in checking accounts available on demand (and therefore counted as part of the *money supply*) pays no interest. In order to pay the interest on savings accounts, bankers must get higher interest rates on the money they lend to others.

Bankers are torn between two objectives. On the one hand, they want to make as much profit as possible by lending out as much as they can (and the riskiest loans pay the highest interest rates). On the other hand, they want safety; they want to be able to pay off easily any depositor who demands his or her money. Technically the banker is said to seek *liquidity*. The most liquid assets are those most easily available in cash to pay off depositors. Thus the most liquid asset is money in paper currency and coins (or even gold), which pay no interest to the banker. The next most liquid assets are government notes and bonds, sometimes called near money, which pay low interest but can be cashed immediately (although at variable prices if cashed before maturity). Least liquid are risky private loans, which may pay high interest but cannot be cashed for a long time and may never be paid back if the individual goes bankrupt. The precise way in which the entire American banking system holds its assets is indicated in Table 30.1.

Bank liabilities consist mainly of deposits, or the amount that is owed to their depositors. The assets of the whole banking system include gold (held only by the government's Federal Reserve Bank), currency (a very small item), and U.S. Government bonds. By far their largest assets, however, are the loans that banks will some day collect back from individuals and businesses. For purposes of analysis we shall often classify all assets merely as *reserves* of money and near money or as *loans* to businesses, individuals, and governments. We shall soon discover that modern banks are required by the government to keep a certain ratio of their deposits in the form of reserves, which limits their power to make loans.

THE FEDERAL RESERVE SYSTEM

On December 23, 1913, President Woodrow Wilson signed the Federal Reserve Act establishing the Federal Reserve System (Fed). It was the government's answer to the banking failures and monetary panics of the early 1900s. The Fed is

---

Table 30.1   **Consolidated Balance Sheet for the Banking System of the United States on October 27, 1971**

Assets (in Millions)		Liabilities and Capital (in Millions)	
Gold Certificates (Held by Federal Reserve)	$ 10,500	Total Deposits	$571,000
Treasury Currency	7,600	Capital Owned by Stockholders	70,200
Loans	489,300		
U.S. Government Bonds	133,800	Total Liabilities	
Total Assets	$641,200	and Capital	$641,200

Source: *Federal Reserve Bulletin*, November 1971, p. A19.

the central bank of the United States, corresponding to the Bank of England or the Bank of France. Its original purposes were to give the country a currency flexible enough to meet its needs and to improve the supervision of banking. Today, however, these form only a part of broader and more important objectives, which include maintaining price stability, fostering a high rate of economic growth, and promoting a high level of employment.

Federal Reserve functions are carried out through 12 Federal Reserve banks and their 24 branches, but there is also central coordination by the Board of Governors in Washington. The Board of Governors consists of seven members appointed by the President and confirmed by the Senate. One of the Board's duties is to supervise all Fed operations. The Board participates in all of the principal monetary actions of the Fed. It has full authority over changes in the legal reserve requirements of banks (within the limits prescribed by Congress). The Board "reviews and determines" interest rates of the individual Federal Reserve banks, and it has the authority to establish the maximum rates of interest member banks may pay on savings and other time deposits. In addition, the Board is responsible for the regulation of stock market credit.

The Presidents of the 12 regional Federal Reserve banks are *not* publically elected or appointed; they are usually conservative bankers.[1] The President of each Federal Reserve Bank is appointed by the Board of Directors of that bank. Each Board of Directors has nine members, *six of whom (Class A and Class B) are elected directly by the member banks* (usually on the advice of the state bankers' association, their lobbying group). The other three directors (Class C)

are supposed to be representative of a broader public. In fact, they represent the same narrow interests as the others: twenty-nine of the thirty-six current Class C directors are executives or directors of corporations, mostly large.[2]

The House Banking Committee of the U.S. Congress surveyed all of the 108 directors (12 Federal Reserve banks times 9 directors) and concluded that the directors are "representative of a small elite group which dominates much of the economic life of this nation."[3] These directors of the regional Federal Reserve banks include *no* women, *no* labor union members or worker representatives, *no* consumer organization members, *no* small farmers, and only two blacks. What is more incredible is that the Federal Reserve has existed 63 years and has had 1088 persons on its regional boards of directors, but *none* have been women, *none* have been workers or consumer representatives, and only four have been blacks.

There is also a Federal Open Market Committee (FOMC), which has the important function of buying and selling government bonds on the open market. The FOMC is composed of the seven members of the Board of Governors of the Federal Reserve (mostly conservative economists and big business representatives) plus five Presidents of the regional Federal Reserve banks (the 12 Presidents take turns on the FOMC, but they are all bankers). These are the people who determine the major part of U.S. monetary policy.

---

[1] All facts in this and the next paragraph from Congressman Henry Reuss (Chairman of House Committee on Banking, Currency, and Housing), "A Private Club for Public Policy," *The Nation*, October 16, 1976, pp. 370–372.

[2] Ibid., p. 371.

[3] Quoted in ibid., p. 371.

The Federal Reserve system controls the money supply in order to achieve its purposes. The real bases of the value of the nation's money supply are the goods produced and confidence in the government. Until recently, however, the money supply of the United States had as its legal base the country's gold stock, which stood at $11.8 billion on August 26, 1970. Congress had required the Federal Reserve to hold an amount equal to 25 percent of its liabilities in the form of gold, but this was purely a congressional whim. The requirement was removed in 1968 with no significant effect on the efficiency with which money has performed its functions.

Although the Federal Reserve banks still hold gold certificates, this is merely one of several types of assets. Gold certificates need bear no necessary relationship to Federal Reserve liabilities (i.e., they bear no necessary connection to the U.S. money supply). The other principal types of assets are government securities and loans to the member banks. The principal liabilities are Federal Reserve note currency, which constitutes most of the paper currency held by the public, and member bank reserves, which, as will be seen, form the basis for the creation of credit money by the banking system.

The Fed specifies exactly how much reserves each member bank must hold in relation to its deposits. Congress has set the following limits on reserve ratios that the Fed may require: for the demand deposits of big city banks, a minimum of 10 percent to a maximum of 22 percent; for demand deposits of country banks, a minimum of 7 percent to a maximum of 14 percent; and for saving deposits in all banks, a minimum of 3 percent to a maximum of 10 percent. Actual reserve requirements set by the Fed are at 18.5 percent for city bank demand deposits, between 8 and 13 percent for country bank demand deposits (increasing with the size of bank), and 3 percent on all saving deposits.[4]

Banking reserves of money or "checking accounts at the Fed" may be kept either in the bank vault or in the nearest Federal Reserve Bank. If it is kept as a deposit in a Federal Reserve Bank, the member bank may even earn a small interest on its money reserves. Country banks are given a lower required reserve ratio, apparently on the theory that they may also use loans from the larger city banks as part of their emergency reserves.

The first purpose of the reserve system is, of course, to ensure that the bank has sufficient funds to meet its depositors' withdrawals. Yet in the Great Depression thousands of banks failed because runs on the banks by depositors exhausted their reserves. This purpose is now more fully met by the Federal Deposit Insurance Corporation (FDIC), which guarantees all deposits up to $40,000. The more important purpose that the Fed now serves is to control the money supply as a tool of general economic control.

MONETARY POLICY

One of the longstanding ways in which government has influenced the economy has been through the use of policies designed to expand or diminish the flow of money and credit. The main idea is that in a depression, an increased flow of

---

[4] See *Federal Reserve Bulletin*, August 1976, p. A9.

money and credit will combat unemployment by increasing purchases of both consumer and investment goods. In times of prosperity, restriction of money and credit will reduce inflationary pressures by reducing the flow of demand. Monetary policy works mainly through its effects on the price for renting the commodity called money—that is, the rate of interest on loans. If the government can increase or reduce the supply of money while the demand for it remains constant, then interest rates may be lowered or raised. And if spending plans are financed by borrowed funds and if these plans react in any way to changes in the rate of interest, it follows that changes in the supply of money for loans will have some effect on total spending.

In an inflationary situation exactly how should monetary policy be applied and how effective is it? The supply of money and credit may be restricted by monetary policy through three major controls: (1) raising the required Federal Reserve ratio, (2) raising the interest rate the Federal Reserve charges banks, and (3) sale of government bonds by the Federal Reserve. Let us see how each of these controls is supposed to work.

First, in order to restrict credit the Federal Reserve may raise the ratio of reserves banks are required to hold against their deposits. Furthermore, as soon as one bank decreases its loans, the effect on all banks may be several times as great by virtue of the money multiplier (see Appendix to this chapter). Thus in theory the raising of the Federal Reserve ratio from 10 to 20 percent would lower the multiplication of money by banks from tenfold to only fivefold. If all banks were fully loaned out, this would cause a great decrease of loans. A reduction in the volume of loans may then mean less money available for consumer and investor spending, thus reducing inflationary pressures.

Second, the Federal Reserve may also raise the interest rate that banks must pay if they wish to borrow from the Federal Reserve Banks. Then a bank will either have to charge higher interest rates on loans to its customers or reduce the amount it lends in order to avoid borrowing reserves from the Fed. Either way, less money may be available for further consumption and investment spending, which may reduce demand and thus lead to a lower rate of price inflation.

Finally, the Federal Reserve may sell more government bonds to banks or rich individuals. The money to pay for the bonds must come from bank reserves or from individual bank deposits. In either case the ability of banks to make loans is reduced (manyfold, according to the money multiplier—see Appendix to this chapter). Thus again consumer and investment spending may be decreased and inflationary pressures reduced.

These methods of reducing money spending in an inflation may encounter certain obstacles. First, each assumes banks had already made loans up to their maximum ratio of deposits to reserves. But banks often keep extra reserves above even the highest possible required reserve ratio and thus can keep lending until these reserves are exhausted. Second, these monetary controls assume that corporations must borrow from banks all the money they need for new investments. But corporations often keep their own internal savings, which they may decide to use regardless of bank policies. Third, in cases in which the government succeeds only in getting banks to raise their interest rates (by lowering money supply), there may be little effect on demand. If expected profit rates are rising even faster than interest rates, corporations may still be willing to borrow and invest more rapidly. In all of these cases the government may be able to restrict the money supply, but the velocity, or speed, of spending of the present money supply may increase even more rapidly.

Despite these weaknesses, monetary policy, if applied strongly enough (and rapidly enough because time is required for it to take effect), can choke off a general inflation. Of course too severe a remedy may cause instability in the bond and stock markets, loss of confidence by domestic and foreign investors, and eventually a business downturn. There is, indeed, considerable evidence that Federal Reserve attempts to reduce inflation were part of the causes of the downturns of 1969–1970 and 1973–1975.[5]

In a depression exactly the opposite monetary policy may be applied. The supply of money and credit may be expanded by (1) lowering the required Federal Reserve ratio, (2) lowering the interest rate the Federal Reserve charges banks, or (3) purchase by the Federal Reserve of government bonds in the open market to put more cash into the hands of individuals and banks. These measures are designed to increase the volume of borrowing and thus the volume of spending by increasing the supply of money for loans and lowering interest rates.

Obstacles to monetary policies intended to combat depression include most of those met by counterinflationary policies and a few that are different and more difficult to surmount. First, the interest rate cannot go below zero, and in actual practice lenders will not go below a floor that is somewhat above a zero rate. Yet during a depression it may require a zero or even negative interest rate to stimulate borrowing. Second, neither consumers nor most investors seem much stimulated to borrow by slightly lower interest rates. Businesspeople apparently consider the pessimistic outlook that foresees smaller profits or even losses to be quantitatively much more important than interest rates in investment decisions. Moreover, most businesses prefer to invest from internal funds; when their profits fall drastically in a depression, they are not much attracted by any kind of loan.

You can lead a businessperson to the river of loans, but you cannot force him or her to drink. The government may increase the banks' supply of money, but consumers and businesses may reduce the amount of their borrowing and spending even more rapidly. In short, monetary policies may have some effect in minor recessions, but when pessimistic expectations become general in a depression, monetary policy may be able to do little or nothing to expand the volume of spending.

MONEY AND CREDIT IN BUSINESS CYCLES

Business cycles are intensified by the use of money and credit in a capitalist economy. Monetary panics have often closed and bankrupted hundreds of banks, as in 1907 and 1932. In every contraction the flow of credit is disrupted to some extent, further restricting both consumer and investor demand. The stock market crash of 1929 also drastically contracted the funds available for investment.

[5] See ibid., p. 370.

A closely related factor is the credit policies of financial institutions. They charge high interest rates at the peak of the crisis, pushing many small businesses to the wall. On the other hand, they are free and easy with credit during expansion, encouraging much speculation, which usually goes beyond reasonable sales prospects. Therefore, expansion of money and credit supplies during expansion intensifies the boom, while collapse of money and credit in crises worsens depressions. So money and credit, like other factors already discussed, do not cause depression by themselves, but their reactions can turn mild downturns into awful depressions.

In spite of government regulations and controls on the monetary system, as well as use of the Federal Reserve to stabilize money flow, this problem is not ancient history. In 1975 two radical economists wrote,

> The specter haunting today's capitalist world is the possible collapse of its financial institutions and an associated world economic crisis. . . . The banking and credit community is showing increasing signs of weakness. Thus, in the span of one year the United States witnessed the two largest bank failures in its history (U.S. National Bank in San Diego and Franklin National Bank in New York). In addition, . . . more than a dozen European banks reported big losses or failed in 1974.[6]

Of course, 1974 was a recession year, but data on long-run trends indicate an increasing problem of weakness in the credit area that is likely to exacerbate any future U.S. crisis. There is a trend toward more and more corporate borrowing from banks. This results from the constant drive of corporations to increase their profits by borrowing capital (say, at 6 percent interest) to invest it and get a return higher than the interest rate (say, a profit rate of 15 percent). This long-run trend is quite clear in Table 30.2.

By the first half of 1974 nonfinancial corporations owed banks an amount equal to 25 percent of the GNP originated by these corporations. In addition, they owed other financial institutions an amount equal to 5 percent of their product. This means an enormous burden of interest payments. It is easy to meet these payments during a profitable business expansion. In a depression, however, these interest payments (and return of principal, since loans will not be extended) may lead to disaster.

On the other side, banks make the most profits themselves by expanding loans as far as possible; if the bank pays depositors 5 percent but lends the money for 10 percent, the profit is considerable. The trick is not to let deposits sit idle but to lend as much as possible. In an expansion, when corporations look like very safe bets to return both principal and interest on time, banks rush to lend them money. The long-run trends toward less safe lending positions are visible in Table 30.3.

The long-run trend in large commercial U.S. banks has been to lend out a larger and larger percentage of deposits. At the same time, their liquid reserves of cash and U.S. treasury bonds and notes are becoming a smaller and smaller percentage of their deposits. This makes them big profits in a boom, when most loans are repaid with interest. In a depression, however, many corporations and

---

[6] Harry Magdoff and Paul Sweezy, "Banks: Skating on Thin Ice," *Monthly Review*, February 1975, p. 1.

Table 30.2 **Borrowing by U.S. Corporations**

| | All Corporations | | All Nonfinancial Corporations | |
Year	Long term debt bonds and mortgages (in $billions)	Long term debt as percent of stock investment	Bank loans (in $billions)	Bank loans as percent of GNP originating in nonfinancial corporations
1950	$ 66	70%	$ 18	12%
1955	98	87	26	12
1960	154	110	38	14
1965	210	130	61	16
1970	$363	181%	$103	20%

Source: Various U.S. government publications, reported in Harry Magdoff and Paul Sweezy, "Banks, Skating on Thin Ice," *Monthly Review*, (February 1975), pp. 3–4, reprinted in the excellent collection by David Mermelstein, *The Economic Crisis Reader* (New York: Vintage Books, 1975).

many consumers cannot repay their loans let alone pay interest. The banks, therefore, are faced with falling profits and are caught in a bind for cash. They may not be able to meet withdrawal demands of depositors (which usually increase in a depression), so some banks will fail and go bankrupt, thereby intensifying the depression.

Table 30.3 **Lending by Large Commercial U.S. Banks**

Year	Loans ($billions)	Deposits ($billions)	Loans as Percent of Deposits	Cash plus U.S. Treasury Bonds and Notes as Percent of Deposits
1950	$ 32	$ 88	36%	54%
1955	48	105	46	43
1960	72	127	56	35
1965	120	182	66	22
1970	189	267	71	18
1974	$319	$389	82%	14%

Source: Various U.S. government publications, reported in Harry Magdoff and Paul Sweezy, "Banks, Skating on Thin Ice," *Monthly Review,* February 1975, pp. 3–4; reprinted in the excellent collection by David Mermelstein, *The Economic Crisis Reader* (New York: Vintage Books, 1975).

SUMMARY

In this chapter we examined the money supply and its probable evolution from barter to paper money to credit. Today the most important component of the money supply is the demand, or checking, deposits and credit granted by the banks. The Federal Reserve System was established to regulate banks and stabilize the money supply. The Fed is controlled by big business and bankers, so it may sometimes act to control inflation, but its policies often increase unemployment. When corporations borrow too much, the risky credit structure may collapse for some corporations and some banks; the collapse may be too quick for the Federal Reserve to help them.

APPENDIX

HOW BANKS MULTIPLY MONEY

Exactly how much new money can banks create with a given amount of new deposits? Obviously, this depends in large part on what reserve ratio the Federal Reserve requires them to hold. Part of each new deposit must be held in reserve, and part may be lent out. For convenience assume that the Federal Reserve ratio is set at 20 percent for all kinds of deposits in all kinds of banks. Then if a bank receives a $1000 deposit, it deposits the $1000 at the Federal Reserve Bank, thus increasing its reserves by $1000. It would seem that, with only 20 percent required in reserve, the new reserve of $1000 would permit the bank to make new loans totaling $4000 and thereby create $4000 in new money. Its new reserves of $1000 would be 20 percent of the original $1000 deposit and the $4000 in new deposits created by the loans. It might thus appear that a single bank could expand the money supply by a multiple of each new deposit it receives.

This is not the case, however. Something called *adverse clearing balances* prevents this. Assume that recipients of the $4000 in new loans write checks, totaling $4000, drawn on their newly created demand deposits. Now, assume (for simplicity of analysis) that these checks are all deposited with another bank. This second bank will immediately deposit these checks in the account it maintains at the Federal Reserve Bank, which increases the reserves of the second bank by $4000 but simultaneously charges these checks against the reserve account of the original bank. This reduces the original bank's reserves by $4000.

The Federal Reserve Bank then sends the checks back to the original bank on which they are drawn. The bank reduces by $4000 the demand deposits of the writers of the checks. Thus the bank finds its reserves reduced by $4000 and its demand deposits reduced by $4000. Because it had reserves equal to 20 percent of its demand deposits and because it is required to maintain this ratio of reserves to demand deposits, it can afford to lose only 20 percent as much in reserves as it loses in demand deposits.

When the bank lost $4000 in demand deposits, this permitted it to lose only $800 (20 percent of $4000) in reserves. Thus it has lost $3200 in reserves that it could not afford to lose. Obviously it overextended its loans by $3200. If the bank had lent only $800 instead of $4000, it would not have experienced this difficulty.

To avoid these adverse clearing balances with the Federal Reserve Bank, a bank must restrict its loans to its *excess reserves.* When the bank received its new deposit of $1000, it was required to hold only $200 of it in reserves. This means it had excess reserves of $800 (the original $1000 it received minus the $200 it must hold as reserves). Thus it can be concluded that if a single bank received a new $1000 deposit, it must keep $200 in reserve but could lend out

$800. It lends money by giving its customers a new demand deposit of $800, thus creating money.

Yet a single bank may reasonably claim it adds nothing to the money supply. When the customer actually uses the loan, he or she draws his or her deposit down to zero, while the bank merely pays out the $800 in cash. It is when the whole banking system is considered that a new deposit will generally lead to a multiple expansion of the money supply. How this expansion works can be seen in Figure 30A.1 and in Table 30A.1.

When the $800 loan from Bank A (in Figure 30A.1) is spent, it becomes new deposits in Bank B, which are the basis for new reserves of $160 and new loans of $640. In the case of the whole banking system, the process will continue until all of the original new deposit ($1000) becomes required reserves in various banks. Because the new required reserves are then $1000 (or 20 percent of all new deposits), the new loans are $4000 (or 80 percent of all new deposits). Based on an initial new deposit of $1000 in money, the banking system has thus created

---

Table 30A.1 How the Money Multiplier Works

1. Assume an initial increase in deposits of $1000.
2. Assume a required Federal Reserve ratio of 20 percent.
3. Assume that banks are always fully loaned out.

Bank	Increase in Loans	Increase in Deposits (or Money Supply)	Increase in Reserves (Required)
Bank A	$ 800	$1000	$ 200
Bank B	$ 640	$ 800	$ 160
Bank C	$ 512	$ 640	$ 128
Bank D	$ 410	$ 512	$ 102
Bank E	$ 328	$ 410	$ 82
Bank F	$ 262	$ 328	$ 66
	—	$ 262	—
—	—	—	—
—	—	—	—
—	—	—	—
—	—	—	—
All Banks	Total Increase in Loans	Total Increase in Deposits (or money supply)	Total Increase in Reserves (required)
	$4000	$5000	$1000

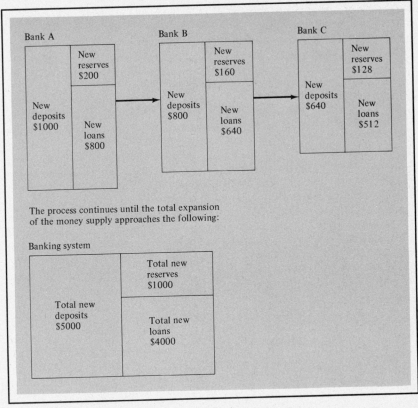

Figure 30A.1 **How the money multiplier works (with Federal Reserve ratio of 20%)**

a total increase in deposits of $5000 (assumed to be demand deposits and therefore counted as money).

For our analysis we use the concept of the money multiplier, which is analogous to, but not to be confused with, the investment multiplier of income determination. The *money multiplier* may be defined as follows:

$$\text{Money multiplier} = \frac{\text{total increase in deposits}}{\text{initial new deposit}}$$

A simple formula for deriving the money multiplier is

$$\text{Multiplier} = \frac{1}{\text{required Federal Reserve ratio}}$$

Assuming that each banker has to keep 20 percent of his or her deposit liabilities in the form of cash, the money supply can be expanded to five times the amount of cash that the banking system holds:

$$\text{Multiplier} = \frac{1}{0.20} = 5$$

Thus the initial new deposit of $1000 is multiplied by 5 to get a $5000 total increase in deposits (or in the money supply).

The analysis does not yet take into account several kinds of leakage that may occur in varying degrees over time. The assumption that banks are always fully loaned up is not consistent with the facts. There are often some excess reserves—that is, reserves above the legal requirement. Therefore the volume of expansion of deposits does depend on the degree to which bankers decide to make the maximum loans on their reserves. It also depends on the degree to which businesspeople wish to accept these loans. Finally, the whole process takes time, and only a certain amount of the predicted expansion will occur in any given period. It is nevertheless generally true that banks lend in some multiple of their reserves and that total expansion of the money supply will be greater, the smaller the required Federal Reserve ratio.

CHAPTER 31

INFLATION AND STAGFLATION

The Keynesian explanation of inflation boils down to the idea that inflation results when aggregate demand is greater than the aggregate supply provided by a fully employed labor force. It must also be understood that the aggregate monetary or effective demand includes, not just coins and paper money and demand deposits, but all the forms of credit in the economy—in short, demand includes anything that allows an individual or business or government to purchase goods and services now, whether they pay now or later. This has the important effect that demand may be expanded to some extent by banks and financial institutions and/or by government manipulation of the financial system.

We shall find that this Keynesian explanation of inflation by excess aggregate demand, including credit, is adequate to explain most of the inflation of past U.S. capitalist history up through the 1940s. In the 1950s, however, traces of a new kind of inflation emerged that were confusing in Keynesian terms. Moreover, the inflation of the late 1960s and early 1970s is definitely a new variety that the usual Keynesian model cannot explain; it is inflation at a time of deficient aggregate demand. We begin this chapter with a look at those types of inflation that a simple Keynesian model can explain; then we turn to the present type, which it cannot explain. The possibilities and the inadequacies of present governmental policy are also examined.

NORMAL INFLATION IN BUSINESS EXPANSIONS

In most, but not all, business expansions in the United States prices have risen. In most, but not all, U.S. business contractions prices have fallen. The best index of U.S. wholesale prices reveals that in 23 of the 26 cyclical expansions and contractions between 1890 and 1938, prices moved in the same direction as business activity and production.[1]

In Keynesian terms prices usually moved up in expansions because effective demand for all products was moving upward faster than the physical supply of products. In contractions, prices usually moved down (e.g., by about 50 percent in the Great Depression) because effective demand for all products was moving downward faster than the physical supply of products was decreasing. Higher

[1] See Frederick Mills, *Price-Quantity Interactions in Business Cycles* (New York: National Bureau of Economic Research, 1946).

prices took up part of the increased demand in expansion, while lower prices were part of the reaction to decreased demand in contraction.

Why does the flow of aggregate demand in money terms rise so rapidly during a period of expansion? On the one hand, the money supply expands because banks give credit (in the form of demand deposits). Businesses want to borrow in order to take advantage of profitable opportunities, and banks want to lend because it appears that businesses can easily repay the loans with interest. Therefore, the money supply in circulation will increase rapidly.

Not only is there more money in circulation, but it turns over faster because consumers and businesses both spend more rapidly. In Keynesian terms the level of consumption and investment both rise. Consumers wish to get bargains before prices rise further and also because they feel assured of future income. Businesses likewise dig into their hoarded savings—and borrow more on credit—to make the investments that appear attractive. In times of expansion everyone wishes to spend in order to buy goods rather than to hoard money.

In a depression, on the other hand, the flow of money demand usually decreases even faster than the transactions with the national product. Banks call in their loans and businesses do not want to make new loans; therefore, the money supply rapidly declines. Furthermore, individuals and businesses hoard their savings for the rainy days ahead, especially because there are no attractive opportunities for investment. As a result, money circulates more slowly and hoarding increases considerably in a depression. For these reasons, during most of U.S. history, depression was normally a time of price inflation.

INFLATION IN WARTIME

The usual inflation experienced during peacetime prosperity has been very slow and very slight compared with the rapid and spectacular inflation stimulated by wartime spending. Just how closely price inflation is correlated with war may be seen in Figure 31.1. Very rapid price inflation accompanied the Revolutionary War, the War of 1812, the Civil War, and World War I. We shall see later that there was also rapid price inflation in World War II, the Korean War, and the Vietnam War.

During wartime there is little production of consumer goods or private producer goods. At the same time there is full employment, with high wages and profits. All of the increased goods and services are in the military sphere and are all bought by the government—which finances most of its purchases by printing money or by borrowing, with only limited tax increases. Therefore, civilians have relatively high incomes and high monetary demand, but the amount of available civilian goods and services is very limited. Furthermore, as prices begin to rise rapidly, people rush to buy goods before prices rise further, thus increasing the spending flow even faster than income rises because their propensities to consume and invest are rising.

INFLATION IN THE MIDST OF UNEMPLOYMENT

We must examine the recent course of inflation and begin to ask how it has been caused. Figure 31.2 records an intial large drop in prices during the Great De-

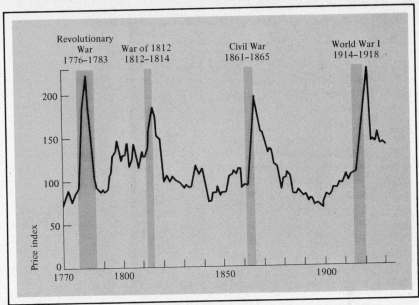

Figure 31.1 **War and inflation in U.S. history (wholesale price index, 1770–1929).**
(Source: U.S. Department of Commerce, Historical Statistics of the United
States, 1789–1945, Washington, D.C.: GPO, 1949.)

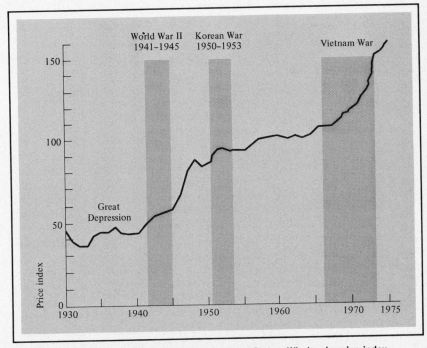

Figure 31.2 **Recent price movements in the United States. Wholesale price index,
1929–1975; base: 1957–1959 = 100.** (Source: U.S. Department of
Commerce, *Statistical Abstracts of the United States, 1964;* p. 351; and
Federal Reserve Bulletin, August 1973, p. A-66.)

pression of 1929–1933. Then, with the recovery of demand, there was a price rise until 1937. The recession of 1938 caused a price drop, which was followed by the slow rise of prices during World War II. This rise would have been much more rapid except that price control held down inflationary pressures. Immediately following World War II, however, the vast demand for consumer and investment goods burst the dam and flooded the market with purchasing power, resulting in the rapid price rises of 1946–1948. A recession lowered prices in 1949, then the Korean War caused a second major round of inflation in 1950–1951. Another recession kept prices steady at the end of the Korean War, after which they rose steadily until 1960. Prices remained fairly stable in the early 1960s but rose sharply from 1965 to 1971 because of the Vietnam War.

The surprising point is that the price index rose rather than declined in the recessions of 1958, 1969, and 1974; and prices remained approximately stable in the recessions of 1954 and 1961. During all these recessions the prices of industries with monopolistic power actually rose in the face of declining aggregate demand.

It is such evidence that forces us to distinguish the inflations of the late 1950s, 1969, and 1974 from the ordinary *demand-pull inflation,* which is caused by the upward pull of aggregate demand. Here, instead, prices apparently are pushed upward by individual firms and industries. It is called *cost-push inflation* to indicate the belief that prices are pushed upward by either higher profit margins or higher wage costs. Many conservative economists argue that monopoly or oligopoly power of firms is *not* responsible for spiraling prices. On the contrary, conservatives argue that the bargaining power of labor unions pushes wages upward and that prices only follow wages. The opposite view, held by most radicals, is that prices are pushed up by monopolies to make higher profits, that wages mostly lag behind prices, and that wage increases are merely bemoaned as an excuse for higher prices.

STAGFLATION

Stagflation is defined as the condition of price inflation in the midst of stagnant or falling production and heavy unemployment. This is a new phenomenon in the United States. As mentioned earlier, in most cycles till the 1950s, prices rose in the expansion and fell in the contraction. In all of these cyles, of course, unemployment declined in the expansion phases and rose during the contractions.

On the basis of such data, traditional economists found a relation between prices and unemployment. These economists argued that wages and prices always rise in periods of falling unemployment, that is, in economic expansion; while wages and prices always fall when unemployment rises, that is, in economic contraction. This assumed relationship of unemployment to inflation was first graphed by Professor Phillips and is therefore called the *Phillips curve.* He used the actual statistics from history. For simplicity we present in Figure 31.3 a curve of the same variety, based on imaginary data (of roughly the same order as the real data). The Phillips curve says that unemployment and inflation can and do exist together in the U.S. economy. It says that as unemployment decreases, inflation increases—or as unemployment increases, inflation decreases.

The Phillips relationship has held true in most recent *expansions,* that is, unemployment falls and prices rise. It does *not* seem, however, that it still holds

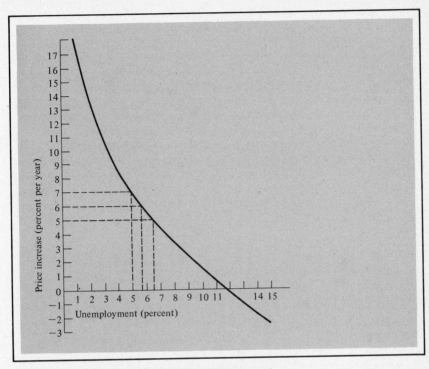

Figure 31.3 **Unemployment and inflation (Philips curve)**

true for contractions. In a Great Depression like the 1930s, vast unemployment *might* bring lower prices. In our recent experience, however, in the recessions and depressions of the 1950s, 1960s, and 1970s, unemployment and prices have *both* increased.

Unemployment has increased drastically in every one of the last five contractions, though least in the mild recession of 1961. Consumer prices, however, did not fall in any of these five contractions. They rose very slightly in the 1961 recession, rose more in the 1958 recession, still more in the 1970 recession, and rose most in the 1973–1975 depression! Wholesale prices stayed almost constant in the 1954 and 1961 recessions, rose a little in 1958, a little more in 1970, and showed an astounding rise in the 1973–1975 depression!

Of course, Phillips did not say that prices would fall in recessions, only that the *rate* of inflation (or price increase) would be less as unemployment rose. In the recessions of the 1950s and 1960s, prices were stable or rose a little, but the *rate* of inflation did decline as unemployment increased. In the 1973–1975 depression, it appears that not only did prices keep rising, but the *rate* of inflation (or price increase) became even stronger! The behavior of prices and unemployment over the whole 1970–1975 cycle is shown in Figures 31.4.

LABOR UNIONS AND INFLATION

There is no evidence that labor unions obtain such high wages as to cause inflation. The most important fact to stress is that real wages decline in each

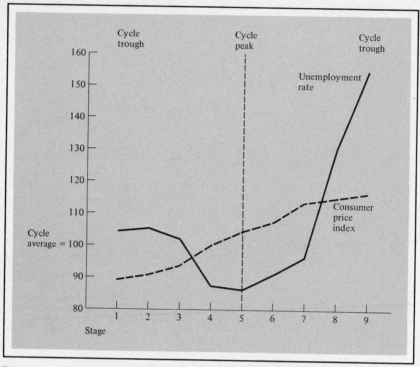

Figure 31.4   **Unemployment and consumer prices, United States, 1970–1975. Average value for each variable over whole period, November 1970 to May 1975, is set at 100. Average rate of unemployment was 5.9 percent. Average level of consumer price index (1967 = 100) was 134. All data is monthly. See Appendix for data on several cycles.** (Source: Derived from data in U.S. Department of Commerce, *Survey of Current Business,* August of 1971, 1972, 1973, 1974, and 1975.)

depression or recession. In other words, although money wages have risen somewhat in recent contractions, they have risen much less than prices. We saw in Chapter 26 that aggregate wages rose less than total revenue. We saw in Chapter 27 that wages per hour rose less than prices. This means that inflation during the contraction periods cannot be blamed on wages because they lag behind prices. In human terms the worker's standard of living declines in each depression-plus-inflation.

Nor can price inflation in expansions be blamed on high wages. In Chapter 27 it was shown that labor cost per unit actually declines in most of the expansion. Therefore, the cost of paying wages cannot possibly be the cause—though it may be the excuse—for higher prices in most of the expansion period. The slight rise in labor costs in the later expansion period is not enough for wages to catch up with the earlier productivity rises. Again, these wage increases are only an excuse for price increases and are not the determining factor.

Finally, it was shown in Chapter 17 that union strength in most industries has been declining. The percentage of workers unionized reached a peak in 1945 and has declined drastically since then. Declining labor unions can hardly be used to explain more rapid inflation (especially in contractions with high unemployment)—except that the weakness of unions has helped business monopolies in their economic and political domination. Of course, it is true that the industries with business monopolies also have the strongest unions. The reason is that the large size of most of the monopoly corporations means that more workers are concentrated in one place and are therefore easier to organize. Yet even in the concentrated industries the percentage of union membership has declined, so it is hard to believe that unions have had much to do with inflation in these industries.

To the extent that unions may contribute to inflation in the concentrated industries, two facts are worth noting. First, in the aggregate for all workers in all industries, labor costs per unit still decline in expansions and real wages still decline in the contractions. Second, to the extent that the monopolies do more easily grant wage increases, and then use them as excuses to raise prices even further, these increases go to a rather small, select group of workers. There is a great deal of data showing that the more concentrated, high wage, more unionized industries mainly use a white male labor force.[2] The more competitive, low wage, less unionized industries exploit a labor force that has a very high percentage of minority workers and women workers. So any wage increases in the concentrated industries have only resulted in a little redistribution of income to the better-off workers, while workers as a whole have definitely lost from the inflation process. Moreover, it is worth repeating that the degree of unionization has declined even in the more concentrated industries.

MONOPOLY POWER AND ADMINISTERED PRICES

In the Great Depression of the 1930s (and in the smaller depression of 1938), Gardiner Means found what he called *Administered prices* in the monopoly sector.[3] In these more concentrated industries, Means found that prices were not set in a competitive market but were carefully administered or set in the best interests of the monopolies. He found that the competitive prices changed frequently, but the administered or monopoly prices changed very seldom.

More specifically, Means found that the prices in the competitive sector registered large declines in the depression contractions; but the administered prices in the monopoly sector declined very little. Means defines the competitive sector as the 20 percent least concentrated industries, while the monopoly sector is defined as the 20 percent most concentrated industries. From 1929 to 1932, prices in the more competitive sector fell 60 percent, but prices in the monopoly sector fell only 10 percent.[4] A few prices in the monopoly sector even rose a little in the face of the Great Depression.

In the expansion of 1933–1937 competitive prices rose by 46 percent, while

[2] See Barbara Deckard and Howard Sherman, "Monopoly Power and Sex Discrimination," *Politics and Society*, vol. 4, Fall 1974, pp. 475–482.

[3] Gardiner Means, "Inflation and Unemployment," in John Blair, ed., *The Roots of Inflation* (New York: Franklin, 1975), pp. 1–15. Also see the summary of Means' findings in John Blair, *Economic Concentration* (New York: Harcourt Brace Jovanovich, 1972), part 4.

[4] Means, op. cit., pp. 8–9.

monopoly prices rose only 10 percent. In the depression of 1937–1938 competitive prices fell again by 27 percent, while monopoly prices fell only 3 percent! Monopoly prices are clearly more stable and very resistant to the decline of demand in depressions. It will be shown that the stability (or increase) of monopoly prices is achieved at the expense of large price declines for small and competitive business, lower purchasing power for consumers, and high unemployment of workers.

Table 31.1 shows that the industries with great monopoly power lowered their prices very little; but they kept prices from going down more only by reducing their production by very large percentages. The more competitive sectors had no choice but to let their prices be forced down by lack of demand, while their production declined less because of greater demand at the lower prices. The monopoly sector thus held up its prices and profit per unit at the expense of great decreases in production and large-scale unemployment. The competitive sector lowered production less, fired fewer workers, but suffered much greater declines in prices and profits per unit. A highly monopolized economy is thus more apt to produce high rates of unemployment in every decline.

Data for more recent contractions show similar patterns, becoming only more dramatic in the latest depression. The competitive sector is defined in Table 31.2 as all those industries where concentration of sales by eight firms is under 50 percent. The monopoly sector is defined as all those industries where concentration of sales by eight firms is over 50 percent. This table on the behavior of prices in the monopoly sector and prices in the competitive sector is perhaps the most important in this book.

Table 31.2 reveals that the pattern for the 1948 recession was the same as in the 1929 and 1937 depressions. In all three cases, monopoly prices declined a

Table 31.1 **Price and Production Behavior in Depression, 1929–1932**

	Decline (in percent of 1929)	
	Prices	Production
Motor vehicles	12	74
Agricultural implements	14	84
Iron and steel	16	76
Cement	16	55
Automobile tires	25	42
Leather & leather products	33	18
Petroleum products	36	17
Textile products	39	28
Food products	39	10
Agricultural commodities	54	1

Source: U.S. National Resources Committee (under the direction of Gardiner Means), *The Structure of the American Economy*, (Washington, D.C.: 1939), p. 386.

Table 31.2   **Competitive and Monopoly Prices (changes in price indexes from cyclical peak to trough, i.e., in contractions)**

Dates of Cycle Peaks and Troughs	Changes in Competitive Prices	Changes in Monopoly Prices
Nov. 1948–Oct. 1949	−7.8%	−1.9%
July 1953 –Aug. 1954	−1.5	+1.9
July 1957 –Apr. 1958	−0.3	+0.5
May 1960 –Feb. 1961	−4.0	+0.1
Nov. 1969–Nov. 1970	−3.0	+5.9
Nov. 1973–March 1975	+1.8%	+27.0%

Sources: Price changes for 1948–1949, 1953–1954, and 1957–1958 from Robert Lanzillotti, Hearings before the Joint Economic Committee of the U.S. Congress, *Employment, Growth and Price Levels* (Washington, D.C.: U.S. GPO, 1959), p. 2238. Price changes for 1969–1970 from John Blair, "Market Power and Inflation," *Journal of Economic Issues,* June 1974. Price changes for 1960–1961 and 1973–1975 calculated by author from U.S. Department of Labor, *Wholesale Prices and Price Index* (Washington, D.C.: U.S. GPO, Government Printing Office, April 1961 and August 1975).

little, while competitive prices declined an enormous amount. In the 1954 and 1958 recessions, we see the first indications of the new stagflation behavior. Competitive prices decline as usual, though by a small amount. But monopoly prices actually rose in the recessions, though again by a small amount. The new situation is very clear in the 1970 recession, in which competitive prices decline by a significant amount, while monopoly prices reveal a considerable rise. A finer division indicates still stronger price declines in the more competitive industries. Whereas prices in all industries under 50 percent concentration fell 3.0 percent, prices in industries under 25 percent concentration fell by 6.1 percent.

Price data on the 1973–1975 depression indicate that monopoly prices rose in the depression by an astounding percentage. This very large price increase throughout the now-dominant monopoly sector caused even competitive prices to show a slight rise in the depression for the first time on record. This undoubtedly caused great disruption in the competitive sector, decreased production, increased bankruptcies, and increased unemployment.

PRICES OF AUTOS, OIL, AND FOOD

Before giving a systematic analysis of such price behavior, it is worth looking at three of the most important examples of monopoly pricing and restriction of production. The most obvious is the auto industry, in which the big three control over 90 percent of U.S. domestic production. The largest, General Motors (GM), is usually the price leader. In the early part of the 1973–1975 depression, from the third quarter of 1973 to the third quarter of 1974, demand for autos fell rapidly and GM sales were down 22 percent. Yet GM did not lower its prices as traditional economics would predict. Rather, GM raised its prices by $900 to $1000; the lower sales were met by further restriction of production and firing thousands of GM workers.[5]

Oil prices rose dramatically during the 1973–1975 depression. The companies blamed the price rises on the Arab oil producers. But the fact is that the U.S. companies artificially restricted oil production for many years before that time. Internationally, almost all oil in the Arab countries was owned by Anglo-U.S. companies, who carefully controlled the flow (and made profit rates that were over 100 percent every year from 1950 to 1970 on the oil from that region).[6] In the United States, with immense oil deposits of its own, the oil companies have not built a new refinery since 1965 and they have cut back exploratory drilling by 60 percent since 1956.[7] Even during the so-called shortage, the U.S. oil companies held immense amounts of oil off the market in reserve holding areas. So it is the U.S. oil companies who caused the shortage, who raised U.S. prices, and who made enormous profits from it.

Finally, U.S. consumers have been badly hurt by rising food prices and restricted food production. Yet myth has it that food production is a purely competitive area, so the high prices could not possibly be the result of monopoly. Thus, the argument is that high food prices must be due to Russian wheat deals (a very small percentage of the crop) or to a bad anchovy harvest off Peru or some other random factor, but not to monopoly because there is none. The fact is that the number of small farmers is shrinking while the number of giant agribusiness corporations is rising. On the supply side, farmers must buy most of their implements and fertilizers from monopolies, such as International Harvester. On the selling side, Campbell sells 90 percent of soups, four firms sell 90 percent of breakfast cereals, Gerber sells most baby food, Del Monte sells most canned fruits and vegetables, and just 20 supermarket chains sell 40 percent of all food.[8]

The power of the monopolies in food sales was accurately summed up by one investigator of the high prices of our Thanksgiving meals: "The Smithfield ham comes from ITT, the turkey is a product of Greyhound Corporation, the lettuce comes from Dow Chemical Company, the potatoes are provided by the Boeing Company, and Tenneco brought the fresh fruits and vegetables. The applesauce is made available by American Brands, while both Coca Cola and Royal Crown Cola have provided the fruit juices."[9] In the 1973–1975 depression, prices received by farmers dropped, but these middlemen (canners, packers, and distributors controlled by conglomerates) increased their share of the food dollar to 60 cents, so retail prices actually rose!

EXPLANATION OF PRICE BEHAVIOR

In all recessions before the 1950s, prices fell. That behavior was predictable and easily explained by traditional economic theory. Neoclassical theory leads us to

[5] See Richard Edwards, "The Impact of Industrial Concentration on the Economic Crisis," in David Mermelstein, ed., *The Economic Crisis Reader* (New York: Random House, 1975), pp. 217–218.

[6] See Farouk Akhdar, "Multinational Firms and Developing Countries (Ph.D. dissertation, University of California, Riverside, 1975), pp. 85–95.

[7] See Bennett Harrison, "Inflation by Oligopoly: Two Case Histories," *The Nation*, August 30, 1975, pp. 145–148.

[8] See William Robbins, "The American Food Scandal," in Mermelstein, op. cit., p. 326.

[9] William Robbins, "The American Food Scandal," in Mermelstein, op. cit., p. 325.

expect that falling demand will cause both output and prices to decline. By reducing supply and also reducing prices to sell more of the supply, the amount of output supplied is brought back into equilibrium with the demand in each industry.

Similarly, in the aggregate, Keynesian theory predicts that an excess supply will lead to falling production, unemployment, and falling prices. If there are institutional rigidities or monopoly power, then there will be stable prices. Keynesian theory predicts price inflation only when there is an excess demand above the supply at full employment.

Neither neoclassical nor Keynesian theory predicts price inflation in the face of falling demand and unemployment. Yet that has been the fact in the monopoly sector in the recessions of 1954, 1958, 1970, and 1975. Of course, traditional theory would admit that firms with monopoly power can always set prices higher if they wish to restrict their supply enough to do so. But why, in the face of falling demand, should monopolies find it profitable to reduce their production so drastically as to actually increase prices?

Only a few economists, mostly in the Marxist and institutionalist tradition, have provided some answers to this question. In most of the monopoly sector a single large firm in each industry sets prices; other firms just follow this price leader. These large firms mostly follow a policy of setting the price as a certain margin of profit added on to their cost level. This procedure of *cost-plus pricing* by the large corporations has been confirmed by a large number of empirical investigations.[10]

The giant corporations do *not* maximize their short-run profit by setting prices as high as possible at any given moment. Rather, they set prices with a profit margin that will insure their maximum long-run growth—and maximum long-run profits. This profit margin must, therefore, be enough to meet fully their expected needs for growth and expansion. Each corporation sets a *target profit level* based on its previous earning record and the record of the leaders in its industry.

What happens if a giant corporation finds its sales revenue falling in a recession or depression? The firm will try to regain enough revenue to reach its target profit by higher price markups on the remaining sales. This process has been illustrated very well in an arithmetic example in an excellent article by Wachtel and Adelsheim, who write,

> For example, say a firm operating in a concentrated industry has direct costs (raw material and labor) of $200 per unit of output and sets its profit markup above direct costs of 20 percent, therefore selling the product for $240 per unit and making a profit of $40 per unit. Let us say the firm has a target level of profits of $40,000; to realize this profit level it will have to sell 1,000 units at $240 per unit. Now we have unemployment and a recession which causes the volume of sales to fall, say, to 950 units. But if the firm still has a traget profit level of $40,000, which it wants to attain, it will have to raise its prices to slightly over $242 per unit from the previous level of $240 per unit. It does this by raising its percentage markup over costs to 21 percent compared to the previous 20 percent. Having increased their profit per unit, the firm now achieves its target profit level, but the resultant manifestation in the economy is the simultaneous occurrence of inflation and unemployment.[11]

[10] See Alfred Eichner, "A Theory of the Determination of the Mark-up Under Oligopoly," *Economic Journal*, vol. 83, December 1973, pp. 1184–1199.

[11] Howard Wachtel and Peter Adelsheim, "The Inflationary Impact of Unemployment: Price Markups During Postwar Recessions, 1947–1970," U.S. Congress Joint Economic Committee, *Hearings* (Washington, D.C.: GPO, November 1976).

This illustration assumes little or no further decrease in demand when the price is marked up. But Wachtel and Adelsheim point out that their conclusion—that monopolies will raise prices in a recession by implementing these policies—holds true even if the price increases cause some further decline in demand. Of course, even the tightest monopoly, in reality, will lose a few customers from any price rise, but most of them have a strong enough market control—and a strong enough image from advertising—that they won't lose many customers. Just how high a price they can set is a function of their degree of monopoly power—a power that is roughly reflected in their high degrees of industrial concentration.

More specifically, their degree of monopoly power over price has three main constraints. First, if the industry raises its price (led by the price leader), how many customers are willing or able to switch to a substitute product? Second, if the price is raised and if this leads to a higher profit margin, how many new firms will be able to enter the industry, or how high are the barriers to such new entrants? Third, what is the realistic likelihood of any government intervention if the price gouging becomes too obvious to be overlooked?

It follows from this cost-plus behavior that such oligopoly firms do not change their prices as frequently as competitive firms. Even if there is rapid inflation of prices and costs, these firms usually keep one price for quite a while, then raise it to the new level dictated by their usual profit margin above costs. Thus there is considerable evidence that in periods of business expansion and rapid inflation, it is the prices of the more competitive firms that rise more rapidly and change from day to day.

In a recession, however, the small, competitive firms are immediately forced to drop their prices as demand falls (since no one of them can restrict the industry supply), regardless of the effect on their profit rates. Not so the large, oligopoly firms. In the recession, if their costs per unit remain the same (as they do in physical terms over a wide range of output), then they can and will adjust their prices, so as to maintain total profits as near constant as possible. Of course, that entails extra reduction of production and unemployment of many more workers than in a similar competitive industry, but that is not their worry.

If, as in recent recessions, costs per unit actually rose in the early part of recessions (with declining productivity), they will actually raise prices as far as they believe necessary to maintain profit rates. Productivity per unit declines at first because the corporations hesitate to fire excess workers (at the lower production levels) since the decline may be only temporary. When the recession deepens and they realize it may be lengthy, the large corporations make very drastic employment cuts to be efficient at a much lower output.

MONOPOLY AND STABILITY OF PROFIT RATES

According to this cost-plus explanation of monopoly price and output behavior, the monopoly sector should show much more stable profit rates than the competitive sector. And indeed they do. Profit rates rise almost twice as fast in the competitive sector as profit rates in the monopoly sector in the average expansion. But profit rates in the competitive sector also fall almost twice as fast as profit rates in the monopoly sector in the average contraction. Specifically, in the eleven most concentrated industry groups in the cycles of the 1950s and early

1960s, the profit rate (on sales for all U.S. manufacturing corporations) rose an average of 27 points in expansions and fell an average of 30 points in contractions. In the same period in the nine most competitive industry groups, the profit rate rose an average of 52 points in expansions and fell by 58 points in contractions.[12] The conclusion is that monopoly profit rates are far more stable than competitive profit rates.

Table 31.3 presents similar data on cyclical fluctuations in corporate profit rates according to the size of the corporation. These data on profit rate fluctuations by size are interesting because most large corporations have monopoly power, and most monopolized industries contain very large corporations. The extent of monopoly power is reflected in the table in the fact that average profit rate increases with size. Table 31.3 also shows that the profit rates of the larger corporations rise less in expansions and fall less in contractions than the profit rates of the smaller corporations. Therefore, it may be concluded that the profit rates of large monopoly corporations are far more stable than those of small competitive corporations.

Why do the large monopoly corporations have more stable profit rates in boom and bust? First, they attempt to set their prices so as to maintain a stable profit rate. Second, their monopoly power allows them to set their prices at those levels. They maintain those prices in contractions by restricting their production and employment. In expansion they raise prices only slowly while rapidly increasing their production and employment to obtain or keep a high share of the expanding market. Third, the costs of the largest corporations may rise a little at lower output levels but nowhere near the cost increase per unit of the small

Table 31.3 **Corporate Size and Profit Rate on Sales, 1970–1975**

Asset Size	Change in Expansion	Change in Contraction	Average Value of Profit Rate Over Whole Cycle
0–$1 million	+87	−22	4%
1–5 million	+36	−24	5
5–10 million	+22	−13	6
10–50 million	+27	−18	7
50–100 million	+29	−10	7
100–250 million	+12	− 5	7
250–1 billion	+13	− 8	8
over $1 billion	+22	− 5	9

Source: Federal Trade Commission, *Quarterly Financial Reports of Manufacturing Corporations* (4th quarter 1970 through 2nd quarter 1975).

Notes: Expansion from 4th quarter 1970 to 4th quarter 1973; contraction from 4th quarter 1973 to 2nd quarter 1975. Quarterly data, all U.S. manufacturing corporations. Average value set equal to 100 points. Expansion change measures rise in point standing from initial trough to cycle peak. Contraction change measures fall in point standing from cycle peak to final trough.

[12] See Howard Sherman, *Profits in the United States* (Ithaca, N.Y.: Cornell University Press, 1968), p. 171.

corporations in each contraction. The unit costs of small corporations rise rapidly when they go below optimum capacity. Fourth, the effective interest burden of small corporations is greater than in large corporations both because they pay higher interest rates and because they borrow a higher percentage of their capital. Fifth, and very important, the small corporations have all their eggs in one basket (with no reserves), while the large conglomerates are very diversified with some investments in industries that may happen to grow in spite of a contraction. The conglomerates can shift reserve capital from strong to weak areas.

There is also some evidence that crises hit the small competitive firms long before they hit the large monopoly firms. In the business expansions in the period from 1947 to 1963, the profit margins of the nine most competitive industry groups turned down 6.7 months before the expansion peak on the average. Yet the profit margins of the monopoly industries (the eleven most concentrated groups) did not feel the squeeze for another 4 months, turning down on the average only 2.2 months before the expansion peak. It appears that the increased monopolization of the economy produces a more stable sector of high monopoly power but further destabilizes the competitive sector. And the instability of the competitive sector is the prime factor setting off each new crisis of overproduction and contraction.

GOVERNMENT POLICY IN STAGFLATION

Since World War II the American economy has experienced a first in the nation's history: simultaneous unemployment and inflation. This situation appears impossible, according to elementary Keynesian analysis, because inflation implies an excess of demand over supply, while unemployment implies an excess of supply over demand. The answer to the riddle, as demonstrated above, lies in the monopoly power of American capitalism. In spite of a certain amount of unemployment, the largest corporations actually still have the power to continue to raise their prices, which might be called *profit-push* inflation.

No aggregate monetary or fiscal policy can remedy or prevent both inflation and unemployment in these circumstances. To end unemployment by increasing aggregate demand sufficiently to affect output in all sectors allows the monopoly sector to set off another inflation spiral. To end inflation by reducing aggregate demand sufficiently to affect monopoly prices causes catastrophic unemployment in the whole economy. The capitalist governments of America and Europe have generally chosen to combat inflation at the expense of more unemployment. Yet even high levels of unemployment have failed to end inflation; only truly catastrophic levels of unemployment would end inflation given the present monopoly structure of the economy.

WAGE-PRICE CONTROLS

Since neither monetary nor fiscal policy is much good against stagflation, even the conservative Nixon administration was forced to try the drastic solution of direct wage-price controls. On August 15, 1971, Nixon announced a new economic policy designed to save America and increase corporate profits.

Phase 1 ran for 90 days from August to November 1971. All wages, prices, and rents were frozen. Profits were not frozen. In actuality all wage increases were prevented, but some prices continued to creep upward. Nixon explained that the controls were necessary because we had combined inflation and unemployment, and all other monetary and fiscal policies had failed.

Phase 2 lasted from November 1971 until January 1973. The freeze was ended, but there were mandatory controls of wages, prices, and rents, though not of profits. Under this system inflation continued, though at a reduced rate of "only" about 4 percent per year. Unemployment fell from its highest level (in the official data) of about 6 percent in the 1971 recession down to about 5 percent. When one realizes that the official data leave out many people and do not even try to count part-time unemployment, this is still a very high level. Wages were successfully kept to a very, very slow increase in this period, but profits rose spectacularly (as we shall see in detail).

Phase 3 was supposed to "phase out the economic stabilization program back to the free market, since the price target was being achieved," according to administration spokespersons. It removed all controls over prices in all industries except food, health, and construction, and substituted voluntary controls. The voluntary controls were no controls at all because they had no enforcement procedure; therefore business paid no attention to them, so prices skyrocketed, rising at about 8 percent a year. In the end even the administration admitted failure in holding down prices and had to institute a new freeze. Phase 3 lasted only from January to June 1973. A striking feature of it was the pressure kept on the unions to abide by voluntary controls and the extent to which the unions did restrain workers from asking for wage raises. Thus there was a very, very slight rise in money wages, and a drastic decline in the earning power of workers. Again there were no controls on profits, which continued to soar.

Phase 3½ was a second freeze. All prices were frozen, but there were no controls on unprocessed food or on rents. Neither wages nor profits were frozen, but wages remained under Phase 3 controls. This phase lasted only 60 days, from June to August 1973.

Phase 4 began in August 1973 and ended in April 1974. It was again a mandatory system of controls over prices, wages, and rents, but not over profits. It was very effective in holding down wages, but prices continued to rise at about 10 percent per year. The lack of enforcement on the price side was apparent in the case of the oil industry. The Cost of Living Council allowed the price of "old oil" (from existing wells, averaging less than $1 a barrel to produce) to rise from $4.25 to $5.25 a barrel. The council allowed the price of "new oil" (which costs no more than $2 a barrel to produce) to rise to $10.50. Then during the (phony) shortage winter of 1974, the Federal Energy Office allowed the retailers' profit margin to rise from 7.25 cents a gallon to 11 cents—and this increase was not rescinded in the later period of surplus.[13]

In all of 1973 the actual buying power of workers declined by 4 percent, while profits rose rapidly. In the first half of 1974, unemployment rose to 6 percent, real gross national product declined, and the rate of inflation rose to 12 percent. According to the usual definitions, the U.S. economy was in a recession in the midst of an unprecedented inflation. Nixon, however, denied it was a recession,

[13] See Bennett Harrison, "Inflation by Oligopoly," *The Nation,* August 30, 1975, p. 147.

preferring to call it a slight readjustment. Much later, President Ford finally admitted it was a recession, but not a depression, even though unemployment was over 9 percent. Ford still resisted any attempts to cure unemployment until late 1974; even in October 1974, he was still talking about *raising* taxes.

We have seen that 1975 was a year of depression, high unemployment, and declining real wages owing to inflation. In late 1975 and 1976, the economy recovered somewhat, corporate profits rose, *but* unemployment continued very high, while inflation also continued at a slower pace. Because of the wage-price controls and the continued inflation and unemployment, the actual buying power of workers (real wages in constant 1967 dollars) reached a peak in 1972 and have been declining ever since. Thus the real weekly wages of an urban worker with three dependents (after adjustments for higher prices and after Federal Income taxes) were $96.64 in 1972, $95.73 in 1973, $90.97 in 1974, $90.53 in 1975, and $90.36 in April 1976.[14] This 1976 level of real wages was actually *below* the 1965 level (which was $91.32)!

CONTROLS, INEFFICIENCY, AND CORRUPTION

Economists of all ideological views criticized the controls but for different reasons. The conservatives, such as Milton Friedman, were horrified at the violation of the First Commandment of laissez-faire economics: Thou shalt not interfere with the market process of setting wages and prices.[15] They have always argued that resources, including capital and labor, cannot be efficiently allocated if prices are not set by competition in the market. If the government arbitrarily sets prices, how can a businessperson calculate most efficiently what to produce or what technology to use? If a businessperson does follow the arbitrary prices set by the government, then industry will not produce what consumers desire, nor will industry produce it in the cheapest possible way. It will not be produced as cheaply as possible because those prices do not correctly reflect the true scarcities of resources, and it will not be the combination of goods that consumers desire because those prices do not correctly reflect true consumer preferences. Thus wage-price controls doom a capitalist economy to inefficiency.

Radicals agree with the truth of this insight. Radicals—and some conservatives—go further along these lines to point out that a huge bureaucracy would be needed to really enforce these controls. Not only would that bureaucracy have enormous repressive power, but it would also be wide open to corruption. After all, if businesspeople cannot freely raise their prices when opportunity arises, then they are better off spending their time and money bribing bureaucrats to raise their prices than worrying about producing a better quality product. At the same time, the controls do not end the money-grubbing aspect of capitalism. If capitalists cannot freely raise prices, then they will either bribe the bureaucrats as described or else evade the controls by selling illegally (that is, on a black market, the way much gasoline was sold during the crisis). In this sense comprehensive wage-price controls in a capitalist system combine the worst

[14] U.S. Labor Department data, reported in Fred Burton, "The Economic Squeeze on the Worker, 1976," *AFL-CIO American Federationist,* June 1976, p. 1.
[15] See Milton Friedman, *Newsweek,* August 30, 1971, p. 45.

aspects of capitalism and Soviet-style socialism: a huge and inefficient bureau-cracy plus private greed.

Controls and Income Distribution

When the conservatives, such as Friedman, argued against the controls, their own solution was an unregulated private capitalism. The liberals, such as Paul Samuelson, pointed out politely that Nixon had already tried that solution and that it was private capitalism that had resulted in our present unpleasant mixture of inflation and unemployment.[16] Moreover, they pointed out that even the usual monetary and fiscal policies could not cope with inflation and unemployment at the same time. In fact, it was the liberals who first advocated the controls; they expected controls to hold down prices, while welfare spending would increase demand to eliminate unemployment. At first the liberals applauded Nixon's con-trols. Even in their naiveté, though, their initial reactions were a little doubtful on two points: Would Nixon actually hold down prices or just wages? And would he actually spend enough on welfare programs to end unemployment?

They were right to worry and wrong to applaud at all. Nixon actually (1) held down wages, (2) allowed prices to continue to rise, and (3) did nothing to cure unemployment, except some military spending. The important thing to under-stand is that this was not accidental, nor would Nixon be the only President to do such a thing. It was shown above that all U.S. governments have been strongly pro-business, for the very good reason that business money elects them (and many other reasons). Any wage-price controls under a business-dominated gov-ernment can be expected to favor business.

The only difference with Nixon is that there was a great deal of evidence in his case that he accepted business bribes (such as those of ITT and the dairy indus-try) beyond the usual legal election campaign contributions, and he was much more blunt about his probusiness biases than most Presidents have been. For example, in his speech announcing the wage-price controls, Nixon said, "All Americans will benefit from more profits. More profits fuel the expansion. . . . More profits means more investment. . . . And more profits mean there will be more tax revenues. . . . That's why higher profits in the American economy would be good for every person in America."[17] Vice-President Agnew repeated the theory, saying, "Rising corporate profits are needed more than ever by the poor."[18] Can you think of some things the poor might need more than rising corporate profits?

Nixon and Agnew were really telling the truth this time. They succeeded quite well in their objectives of limiting wages and raising profits. Thus in all of Phase 1 and Phase 3½ wages didn't rise at all. During all of the longer Phases 2 and 3, average hourly earnings rose only 5.9 percent a year. At the same time the cost of living rose by about 4 percent yearly in Phase 2, and 8 percent yearly in Phase 3, and about 10 percent yearly in Phase 4. Since the cost of living rose faster than wages in 1973, for the first time on record in a year of economic expansion, the buying power of workers declined. In 1973, during Phases 3 and 4, wages rose

[16] See Paul Samuelson, *Newsweek*, August 30, 1971, p. 46.
[17] President Richard Nixon, in TV speech, August 15, 1971.
[18] Vice-President Agnew, at National Governors' Conference, 1971.

by about 5 percent and retail prices by about 9 percent, so real wages (that is, what the worker can buy) declined by 4 percent.

One way Nixon achieved these results was by appointing a probusiness Pay Board to make wage decisions. The big unions first joined it, hoping to salvage some crumbs, then withdrew when they found they were to be allowed nothing. The AFL-CIO said, "We joined the Pay Board in good faith, desiring—despite our misgivings—to give it a fair chance. . . . The so-called public members are neither neutral nor independent. They are tools of the Administration, and inbued with its viewpoint that all of the nation's economic ills are caused by high wages. As a result, the Pay Board has been completely dominated and run, from the very start, by a coalition of the business and so-called public members. . . . The trade union movement's representatives on the board have been treated as outsiders—merely as a facade to maintain the pretense of a tripartite body."[19]

While real wages were declining in Phases 3 and 4, profit rates were actually climbing. Profit rates on investor's equity (before taxes) in all of manufacturing were "only" 16.5 percent in 1971, but rose to 18.4 percent in 1972; then—under Phase 3—rose to 21.6 percent in 1973; then—under Phase 4—rose to 23.4 percent in 1974 in the first year of the depression.[20] A strange depression!

Finally, in the first quarter of 1975, the profit rate fell to 15.0 percent (not seasonally adjusted). When this fall in the profit rate occurred, Congress and President Ford took immediate action to stimulate the economy by lower taxes, and the profit rate jumped back up to 19.2 percent in the second quarter of 1975.

One must conclude that the inevitable results of wage-price controls under a capitalist government are additional corruption and inefficiency, as well as a shift in income distribution away from wages and toward profits. The meaning of the political business cycle is also clarified. At the peak of expansion, when workers are pushing for higher wages, the U.S. government talks about inflation; and it uses restrictive monetary or fiscal or direct controls to lower wages and even promote a little unemployment. At the bottom of the depression, the U.S. government is moved by corporate pleas to stimulate the economy. The capitalist system would generate boom and bust cycles without government interference, but the government does reinforce them and may often serve as the catalyst setting off the downswing as well as the upswing (at such times as the economy was ripe for a change in direction anyway).

STAGFLATION POLICY AND THE IDEOLOGY OF ECONOMISTS

It was noted earlier that most traditional economists see high wages as the cause of economic downturns. According to Leftwich and Sharp, "The general solution to involuntary unemployment is a reduction in real wage rates until the amount of labor demanded equals the amount supplied. In a competitive market, the reduction in real wage rates would take place automatically."[21] In their view, the prob-

[19] AFL-CIO Executive Committee, in *The National Economy* (AFL-CIO, 1973), p. 7.
[20] Federal Trade Commission, *Quarterly Financial Report for Manufacturing Corporations*, 1st Quarter 1974 and 1st Quarter 1975, pp. 12–16.
[21] Richard Leftwich and Ansel Sharp, *Economics of Social Issues* (Homewood, Ill.: Irwin, 1974), p. 249.

lem is that unions use monopoly power to prevent workers' wages from falling, since competition among workers would force wages to drop when unemployment exists. So they imply that government should control wages. Of course, it is true that lower labor costs would induce capitalists to hire more workers if demand for products remains the same. But demand is the fly in the ointment. Wage income is the largest component of consumer demand, so lower wages mean less demand for products, which means less demand for workers.

When conservatives tire of discussing unions, they discuss government. Thus Milton Friedman and the monetarist school explain depressions in this way:

> Most of the blame is assigned to misguided policies of the government. . . . For example, a considerable amount of government activity was generated in an effort to combat the [Great] Depression, which is usually blamed on instability of the private sector. However, monetarists contend that the Depression was caused by improper monetary policies. . . . The government is seen as using intervention as a cure for problems which are actually caused by intervention. . . . The [private] economy can restore equilibrium through appropriate changes in prices with relatively little instability in output, employment, or other real factors.[22]

Friedman's monetarist views involve a whole catalogue of errors, which can only be briefly listed here. First, as was proven in Chapters 23 to 28, the Great Depression and most other depressions were created by the normal workings of the private capitalist system. Government policies may worsen, or sometimes set off, depressions but they are not the basic cause of capitalist systemic instability and its proclivity to cycles of boom and bust. Second, monetary policy played a very small role in the 1930s, and Roosevelt's fiscal policy did help somewhat in the mid-1930s (but it was too little and too late). Moreover, it was the conservative Republican Hoover who let the depression intensify; just as the recent depression was at first encouraged by the Nixon-Ford administration. How much more conservative and noninterventionist than Hoover could a President be? Earlier in this chapter we saw that the U.S. government is not an independent factor above the battle but the servant of private capitalism, so it can only do as private capitalism desires.

Third, the modern monetarists repeat the ancient advice of Say's law: that the private economy left to itself will automatically restore full employment. As a main mechanism, they rely on prices dropping under competitive pressures as demand drops; this would sell more goods and keep a high level of production and employment. Unfortunately, as shown in this chapter, the competitive process now operates only in one small sector where prices and profits drop drastically. In the larger monopoly sector, prices do not fall and even rise in the recession, while production and employment fall rapidly. Moreover, as shown above, even if wages and prices moved downward with alacrity, this would more likely result (as it often did in earlier depressions) in a downward spiral of falling demand than in an immediate cure.

Faced with simultaneous inflation and unemployment, the liberal Paul Samuelson saw a dilemma with no obvious way out of it. Milton Friedman and his friends see it simply as a case requiring the sacrifice of heavy unemployment (by

---

[22] William Mitchell, John Hand, and Ingo Walter, *Readings in Macroeconomics* (New York: McGraw-Hill, 1975), pp. 271-272.

workers, not by Friedman) to keep stable prices. He claims that in any given situation there is a *natural rate* of unemployment, which is the level of unemployment that will prevent further inflation. "This unemployment rate is thus consistent with any rate of inflation, and they argue that attempts to move the unemployment rate permanently below . . . this 'natural rate' by use of aggregate demand policies will result in an *acceleration* of the rate of inflation."[23] Since it is natural, nothing can be done about it, and any attempt to reduce the natural unemployment will only make things worse. Perhaps high unemployment with stable or rising monopoly prices *is* natural in the monopoly stage of capitalism; but then why stick with capitalism?

ANTITRUST POLICY

There are many liberal economists, and even many U.S. senators, who agree that monetary and fiscal policy are inadequate to stop an inflation generated by monopoly power. In fact, they perceive monopoly power as the prime cause of many U.S. political and economic problems. Their solution is to break up the monopolies through stronger antitrust laws. For several reasons, the trust-busting solution is not a good one, though any radical can sympathize with it.

The liberals see monopoly as an accident, a temporary aberration. Chapter 18 proved, however, that the monopolies are the very heart of U.S. capitalism. Giant monopoly corporations produce and sell the majority of American goods. Therefore, to break up all the monopolies is not a simple reform but would constitute a major revolution.

It must also be emphasized that breaking up a monopoly into just four or five parts does little good. Most of our so-called monopoly industries are right now technically oligopolies, with four to eight major firms dominating them. They all play follow-the-price-leader, however, so they all act exactly like a single monopoly firm. To achieve something approaching pure competition requires many thousands of small firms in each industry, so each monopoly must be broken into thousands of parts. Would it make technological sense to break up the auto, oil, or steel industries into thousands of tiny firms?

Even if Americans were willing to sacrifice that much efficiency and extra effort in production, is it politically feasible? As long as U.S. capitalism is to be preserved, how could there be the political and economic power to cut up its very heart into thousands of pieces? To make a major revolution without disturbing the basic system is not feasible. At present, as we saw above, the antitrust laws are much too mild to be any barrier to increasing economic concentration. But even if stronger laws were passed, that would not be enough because the antitrust laws are never enforced. The antitrust division of the Justice Department always operates on a shoestring, with a budget far less than the legal department of any of the giant corporations. And if the laws are totally rewritten, and the enforcement budget multiplied a thousand times, the conservative Supreme Court always narrowly restricts the antitrust laws (and might declare a sweeping one unconstitutional). There is thus no feasible political hope within

[23] David Ott, Attiat Ott, and Jang Yoo, *Macroeconomic Theory* (New York: McGraw-Hill, 1975), p. 260.

the capitalist system for substituting millions of competitive firms for the present monopolies.

Suppose, however, such a political revolution within capitalist boundaries were successful. A country of all small, competitive firms would presumably resemble the present competitive sector. This sector is characterized by (1) sweat shops, low wages, more exploitation of workers; (2) self-exploitation of the small business owner and his or her family, with long hours and little rewards; (3) little or no research and very little efficiency; and (4) violent swings downward in depression, with big losses and thousands of bankruptcies. Is this what one wants as an ideal situation resulting from the vast effort of a political revolution?

SUMMARY

Chapters 22 through 28 proved that the cycle of boom and bust, with periodic high levels of unemployment, is inherent in capitalism. In every expansion demand is limited by the poverty of the masses of worker-consumers, while costs of new equipment and raw materials rise as capitalists in these areas find supply always below the rising demand. In every contraction the excess supply, or overproduction relative to effective demand, is cured by wiping out many smaller capitalists, with the monopolies buying their capital cheaply; by drastic reduction of all supply; by unemployment lowering labor costs; and by stagnation lowering the costs of raw materials and equipment.

This chapter showed that the phenomenon of inflation now appears in recessions because of the vast increase in concentrated monopoly power. In several recessions of the 1950s and 1960s, while competitive prices dropped in each contraction, monopoly prices rose. In the depression of 1973–1975 general inflation increased competitive prices a little, while monopoly prices soared. As a result of the monopolists' control over prices—as well as some other factors associated with absolute size—the monopoly profit rates are relatively stable, declining very little in recession or depression. The small competitive firms, however, bear the full burden of the depression profit decline, though workers shoulder an even bigger burden through reduced real wages. Hence, increasing monopoly has caused greater declines of production and unemployment, while raising prices through that very restriction of supply.

Monopoly, however, is not the only factor whose increase has led to both more inflation and greater unemployment, First, the capitalist government of the United States is influencing the economy more strongly than ever before and is in part responsible for the current stagflation. We showed that, in addition to the inherent business cycle of private capitalism, there is a political business cycle. The government helps choke off expansion to keep wages down, but the government also helps stimulate the economy in a depression to restore profitability by more sales.

Since aggregate monetary and fiscal policy will not cure simultaneous inflation and unemployment, the Nixon-Ford administration was forced to try direct wage-price controls to restrict cost-push inflation. Its problems are (1) inefficiency as prices no longer reflect demand and supply conditions; (2) probusiness

bias, allowing for reduction of real wages through price loopholes and little attention to unemployment; and (3) continued monopoly profits based on old money
grubbing, new loopholes, and new black markets.

The second factor intensifying the U.S. economic problem is the international
scene. In Chapter 34 we shall find that the U.S. economy has, to some extent, lost
its totally dominant position of the 1950s.

APPENDIX

PRICE AND UNEMPLOYMENT DATA

Table 31A.1 **Price Movements in the United States, 1929–1975**
(wholesale price index for all commodities, 1967 = 100)

Year	Index	Year	Index
1929	49	1953	87
1930	45	1954	88
1931	38	1955	88
1932	34	1956	91
1933	34	1957	93
1934	39	1958	95
1935	41	1959	95
1936	42	1960	95
1937	45	1961	95
1938	41	1962	95
1939	40	1963	95
1940	41	1964	95
1941	45	1965	97
1942	51	1966	100
1943	53	1967	100
1944	54	1968	103
1945	55	1969	107
1946	62	1970	110
1947	77	1971	114
1948	83	1972	119
1949	79	1973	135
1950	82	1974	160
1951	91	1975	175
1952	89		

Sources: U.S. Bureau of Labor Statistics, *Handbook of Labor Statistics 1974* (Washington, D.C.: Government Printing Office, GPO, 1975), p. 325, and U.S. Bureau of Labor Statistics, *Monthly Labor Review*, March 1976, p. 85.

Table 31A.2 **Unemployment and Prices, U.S., 1970–1975**

Stages of Cycle	Trough Nov. 1970	Expansion			Peak Nov. 1973	Contraction			Trough March 1975
	1	2	3	4	5	6	7	8	9
Unemployment	104	105	102	88	86	91	96	129	154
Consumer price index	89	91	94	99	104	107	112	117	119
Wholesale price index	83	82	89	101	106	113	122	130	130
Implicit price deflator	90	92	95	99	104	107	111	116	118

Source: Derived from monthly data in U.S. Department of Commerce, *Survey of Current Business* (August 1971, August 1972, August 1973, August 1974, August 1975). Level in each stage is set so that cycle average = 100.

Table 31A.3 **Unemployment and Prices in Cyclical Expansions**

Expansion	Changes in Unemployment Rate	Changes in Consumer Price Index	Changes in Wholesale Price Index
Oct. 1949–July 1953	−109	+12	+11
Aug. 1954–July 1957	− 39	+ 5	+18
Apr. 1958–May 1960	− 32	+ 2	+ 1
Feb. 1961–Nov. 1969	− 69	+23	+13
Nov. 1970–Nov. 1973	− 18	+15	+23

Source: Derived from monthly data in U.S. Department of Commerce, *Survey of Current Business* (August 1971, August 1972, August 1973, August 1974, August 1975). Change is from Stage 1 to Stage 5 of cycle, where level at each stage is set so that cycle average = 100.

Table 31A.4 **Unemployment and Prices in Cyclical Contractions**

Contraction	Change in Unemployment Rate	Change in Consumer Price Index	Change in Wholesale Price Index
July 1953–Aug. 1954	+84	0	0
July 1957–Apr. 1958	+65	+ 2	+ 1
May 1960–Feb. 1961	+27	+ 1	0
Nov. 1969–Nov. 1970	+49	+ 6	+ 3
Nov. 1973–March 1975	+68	+15	+24

Source: Derived from data in U.S. Department of Commerce, *Survey of Current Business* (August 1971, August 1972, August 1973, August 1974, August 1975). Change is from Stage 5 to Stage 9 of cycle, where level at each stage is set so that cycle average = 100.

CHAPTER 32

ECONOMIC GROWTH

For the sake of simplicity it is assumed in this chapter that aggregate effective demand rises as rapidly as aggregate supply, that Say's law holds and that there are no depressions caused by lack of demand. Here we ask, How fast is it technically possible for the economy to grow? What is the maximum *potential* rate of growth of output obtainable by the economy? Because all problems of demand are assumed away, the remaining problem may be resolved into two questions: (1) How much of each input (land, labor, capital) can be procured under existing circumstances for use in production? (2) How much output can be obtained from these inputs in the production process?

PRODUCTION IS DETERMINED BY LABOR, CAPITAL, NATURAL RESOURCES, AND TECHNOLOGY

Many different physical inputs constitute an economy's production base. For convenience these may be grouped into three categories: capital, labor, and natural resources. *Capital* includes inventories of raw materials and goods in process as well as all plant and equipment. *Labor* means the number of man-hours available as well as the degree of skill of the available labor force. *Natural resources* include all useful materials (including land) known to be in the territory of the economy. Resources may be depleted by use or natural erosion but may be increased by new geological discoveries. *Technology* is the knowledge that determines how much output can be produced by a given combination of inputs. Therefore the level of potential output is a function of the currently available technology, natural resources, capital, and labor. A thorough analysis of the growth potential of any existing economy should consider each of these inputs in turn as well as the interrelations between them.

The actual long-run economic growth of the United States is summarized in a government report as follows:

> It has been estimated that real gross national product grew 4.3 percent per year from 1839 to 1879; 3.7 percent per year from 1879 to 1919; and 3 percent from 1919 to 1959. . . . The growth of the labor force and of the capital stock partly explains our economic growth. In addition, more than half the growth is accounted for by improvement in the factors of production and technology.[1]

No one would deny the importance of improvements in technology or the quality of labor or capital; therefore no one denies the urgent need for such

---

[1] U.S. Congress, Joint Economic Committee, 86th Cong., 1st sess., *Employment, Growth, and Price Levels* (Washington, D.C.: GPO, 1959), p. xxiii.

things as research, education, and public health measures. Recent studies, however, have shown that it is very difficult to get exact quantitative estimates of just how important the respective contributions resulting from the growth in the different factors of technology have been.[2]

Here we may leave aside the intricate factual questions involved in separating out the behavior and influence of each of the components of growth. The level of potential output may always be considered to be determined solely by the amount of any one factor (e.g., labor) and by the amount of output produced by a given level of that input (e.g., output per worker). Of course the amount produced by any one factor is influenced by the levels of all the others and by improvements in technology.

FULL-EMPLOYMENT GROWTH

In this section the labor force is assumed to be always fully employed. Potential growth of output is then determined by the growth of the labor force and by the amount produced per unit of labor.

Productivity of Labor

The law of diminishing returns states that each additional worker adds less output than the worker hired before him. It holds true only if capital, natural resources, and technology remain unchanged and if some minimum scale of employment is reached. Given these assumptions, the law of diminishing returns is a truism; it cannot be other than true. All other things remaining the same, it is obvious that if enough workers are crowded onto a single plot of land or even the entire world, the crowding alone will eventually cause the product of an additional worker to decline. But many of the classical economists—Malthus, for example—went much further than the truism embodied in the law of diminishing returns. They predicted that diminishing returns per worker in the economy as a whole *would* come about in actual fact. Malthus reached this dismal conclusion on the grounds that population increase would be very rapid and would far outweigh the slow increase of capital, technology, and natural resources.

The gloomy long-run prediction based on this interpretation of the law of diminishing returns has not been borne out by the facts of historical progress. First, it is not even clear that the world population is at the minimum level at which further additions to the working force would bring diminishing returns, even if natural resources, capital, and technology were to remain constant. Second, labor itself improves in quality as scientific and technical education advance, although this may properly be classed as an aspect of technological improvement. Third, it was usual to argue that the earth is only so large and that its natural resources are slowly being depleted. The supply of *known* natural resources, however, is steadily expanding as a result of continual discoveries of new reserves. Furthermore, there have been important discoveries of new uses for previously neglected materials—for example, coal was once merely a hard

[2] See, for example, E. D. Domar, "On the Measurement of Technological Change," *Economic Journal,* December 1961, pp. 709–729.

black stone of no use for fuel or heating purposes. Moreover, better ways have been found to use available resources—for example, power production by atomic fission or fusion, or food production by hydroponic farming. Of course the last two means of resource expansion are also aspects of technological improvement.

Another reason why there have not been diminishing returns per worker in the economy as a whole is the increasing use of capital per worker, which allows a single worker to produce far more than previously. The final and most important reason for the defeat of diminishing returns is that development of technology in the past century has meant a much more efficient use of the available capital, natural resources, and labor. At the early date when Malthus wrote, it was still possible largely to ignore technological progress. Today even the blindest economist is forced to consider the starting advances continually made in productive know-how.

Empirically the evidence shows that population in the developed countries has not outraced technology, natural resources, and capital but that, on the contrary, product per person has grown enormously. In U.S. agriculture increase of output has far outrun increase of employment. In fact, between 1870 and 1940 employment in agriculture rose by only 34 percent, while output rose by 279 percent.[3] The United States thus has no problem of lack of food but rather a surplus relative to effective cash demand.

It may be concluded that *in the industrialized private enterprise economies slowed progress or retrogression is caused not by natural and technical problems but by man-made economic institutions that give rise to recurrent economic catastrophes.* The advent of atomic energy makes it especially clear that the natural sciences have given us ample power to obtain in the future fantastic levels of abundance or to blow to pieces the entire world.

Increase of Labor

The increase of the labor force is determined primarily by population growth, but it is also governed by changes in the age composition of the population and by the sociological attitudes and labor laws that determine the ages of beginning and retiring from work as well as the maximum hours of work. Many Malthusian-minded theorists mechanically project the present world rate of population growth into the near future and easily arrive at quite astronomical figures for total population. But it was demonstrated earlier that, to date at least, capital and technology have had no trouble keeping ahead of population growth; they probably could keep pace with even massive population growth in the coming years.

The mechanical prognostications of vast population growth, however, do not seem to have taken into account the best present knowledge of population growth patterns. Malthus described people breeding like animals and population exploding with only a few kinds of checks to its expansion. He spoke of "preventative checks" as those that cause lower birthrates. He recognized only abstention from sex or vice and sexual deviation and did not consider voluntary birth control through family planning and contraceptive methods. When preventative

[3] See Arthur Burns, *Frontiers of Economic Knowledge* (Princeton, N.J.: Princeton University Press, 1954), p. 4.

checks fail, according to Malthus, the result will be "positive checks" to population, where "positive" means a higher death rate. Thus positive checks include wars, famine, and disease.

It is true that in many primitive economies at a low level of productivity, we often find very high birthrates. At this stage, however, population may be constant for centuries because it is held in check by equally high death rates, caused indeed by wars, disease, and starvation. A second stage of rapid population growth usually follows the beginnings of industrialization and the introduction of modern methods of public health sanitation. With better control of disease and enough food production, death rates decline. As long as birthrates remain high, the population soars. (This problem is examined in Chapter 35.)

At the third stage, however, as the economy matures, we find culture and education spreading to all the population. Knowledge of contraceptive devices for birth control also spreads, as well as the desire to use these means in order to keep the family to a manageable size. Thus all of the more industrialized countries have shown some tendency toward lower and lower birthrates during the past 100 years, although there have been some upward spurts in the rate for short periods.

FULL-CAPACITY GROWTH

So far we have concentrated on the increase of the labor force and output per worker. It is more convenient for our purposes, however, to estimate the potential growth of output in relation to the increase of capital and the output per unit of capital. Of course the output per unit of capital will reflect changes in technology, natural resources, and the labor supply.[4]

We may state a very simple relationship between output and capital at any given moment. The national product, or output, must equal the output per unit of capital times the amount of capital in use. Thus a simple formula may be written

$$\text{Output} = \frac{\text{output}}{\text{capital}} \times \text{capital}$$

Of course this formula is always true by definition, and the only question is whether it is fruitful to think in these terms.

In the United States about \$3 of capital goods are in use for each \$1 of annual national product. So the ratio of output to capital is about 1:3. Therefore when the value of capital stock, including all machines and factories, was about \$1500 billion, the economy produced annually an output of about \$500 billion.

Now we may extend this analysis to a growing economy. The rate of growth of output is determined by the growth of capital and the changes in output per unit of capital. More precisely, the rate of *growth* of output is equal to the *increase* in output per *increase* in capital multiplied by the ratio of the *increase* in capital to output. Thus, we may write the equation of growth

$$\frac{\text{Increase in output}}{\text{Output}} = \frac{\text{increase in output}}{\text{increase in capital}} \times \frac{\text{increase in capital}}{\text{output}}$$

[4] This approach is detailed in E. D. Domar, "Expansion and Employment," *American Economic Review*, March 1947, pp. 34–35.

This equation is true by definition, so it is always true. Notice that the formula is true not only for increases but also for decreases in output; we could substitute the word *change* for the word *increase* to obtain a more general formula.

The change (increase or decrease) in output as a ratio to present output is how we define the *rate of growth* of output. For example, if we produced $100 last year and we now produce $103, then the rate of growth is 3/100, or 3 percent per year.

The change in output as a ratio to the change in capital is defined as the *marginal* output/capital ratio. For example, if we invest $9 in additional capital and this results in a $3 increase in our output of national product, then we may say that the marginal output/capital ratio is 1:3. Finally, recall that an increase in capital is our definition of *investment*. Moreover, in this chapter it is assumed (for the sake of simplicity) that the amount of investment is just equal to the amount of saving. Therefore we may say that the *increase in capital* means the same thing as *investment*, or the same thing as *saving*. Then the ratio of increase in capital to output might be written as investment to output or saving to output.

If the equation of growth is put into these new terms, it may be written as follows:

$$\text{Rate of growth} = \frac{\text{change in output}}{\text{change in capital}} \times \frac{\text{saving}}{\text{output}}$$

We are merely affirming that how fast the economy grows depends on how much is saved and invested *and* how much is produced by new investments.

Consider an example of the use of this equation of growth. If the average ratio of saving to output is 9 percent and if the marginal output/capital ratio is 1:3, then we find that

$$\text{Rate of growth} = \tfrac{1}{3} \times 0.09 = 0.03, \text{ or 3 percent per year}$$

This has been approximately the performance of the U.S. economy over a long period.

The mechanics of the growth process may also be examined year by year. Table 32.1 assumes the same proportions as in the example just given of U.S. economic growth.

In Table 32.1 we have illustrated the arithmetic of a growing economy for a few years' time. The table begins at an arbitrary level of $100 for convenience in calculation. The table is purposely incomplete so the reader may finish it. Start with the output of the latest year. First, divide this output into 9 percent saving and 91 percent consumption (or a propensity to consume of 91 percent). Second, having found the amount saved or invested (the increase of capital), we can then find the increase of output for the next year by applying a marginal output/capital ratio of 1:3. For example, because saving or increase of capital was $9 in Year 1, the increase of output in Year 2 is one-third of that, or $3. The table is completed by merely repeating these two steps year after year. As long as the propensity to save and the marginal output/capital ratio remain unchanged, this economy will continue to grow at a steady 3 percent per year.

It is important to emphasize as many recent studies have done, that the most important factors in determining how much output will be produced by a given

Table 32.1 **Example of Economic Growth**

Assume $\dfrac{\text{increase in output}}{\text{increase in capital}} = \dfrac{1}{3}$ and $\dfrac{\text{saving}}{\text{output}} = 0.09$.

Year	Output (or National Product)	Saving = Investment = Increase In Capital	Increase in Output
1	$100.00	$9.00	$3.00
2	103.00	9.30	3.10
3	106.10	9.55	3.18
4	109.28	—	—
5	—	—	—
6	—	—	—
7	—	—	—

capital investment are the level of technology and the level of education of the labor force. It has been shown repeatedly that *the most profitable social use of resources* is in education—or production of *human capital,* as some cold fishes call it. Education not only raises the skills of workers in using physical capital but also leads to more research and creates higher levels of technology. Countries with a high level of resources in education have grown most rapidly.

AMERICAN GROWTH EXPERIENCE

What has been the actual long-run trend of the output/capital ratio in U.S. history? According to the best estimates, it has fluctuated around the level of $1 of annual national product to every $3 of the stock of capital.[5] There was a declining trend of product per unit of capital from the 1880s to World War I, but this was just about balanced by a rising trend in productivity from then until the 1940s. Other conflicting studies have shown as much as a one-third rise in capital productivity since the 1880s.[6] Because the data are very poor and there are very difficult problems of definition of *output* and *capital,* the recorded changes may not be very significant; therefore it makes some sense to treat the marginal output per unit of capital as roughly constant in the simplest approximation to a long-run projection.

At first glance this seems a strange result because we might expect the product per unit of capital to rise as a result of great technological advances. However, that is not at all necessary because output per unit of capital is determined

[5] Fully discussed in Nicholas Kaldor, *Essays on Economic Stability and Growth* (New York: Free Press, 1960), p. 260.

[6] See, for example, Moses Abromovitz, "Resources and Output Trends in the U.S. Since 1870," *American Economic Review,* May 1956, p. 8.

by two opposed trends. On the one hand, vast technological improvement has meant rapid growth in the output *per worker.* On the other hand, U.S. technology has been embodied in huge amounts of machinery per worker, and thus the growth of capital has been almost as rapid as the growth of output. Of course, it must be remembered that even if the ratio of output to capital in the U.S. economy has stayed roughly constant over a very long period, there are very wide differences among industries and also very wide differences between prosperity and depression when much capital may remain unused.

What has been the actual course of saving (and investment) behavior in the United States? We saw in Chapter 26 that the ratio of saving to national product has remained remarkably stable over a very long period. Thus in the United States the long-run propensity to save remains roughly between 9 and 11 percent.[7] Furthermore, the evidence indicates that the marginal output/capital ratio has fluctuated in about the neighborhood of 1:3. Assuming that these two ratios hold for the future, we may predict growth according to the growth formula. Taking one-third of 9 percent, we have a 3 percent rate of growth. This is approximately the rate of growth American GNP has achieved over a long period.

SAVING AND GROWTH

There are two quite distinct points of view about saving. The classical economists, concerned as they were about economic growth, called for as much thriftiness and saving as possible. In early nineteenth-century England they observed that the savings of businesspeople were being used to build more capital. They drew the moral that more thrift and saving lead to more rapid increase of capital and, consequently, to more rapid economic growth.

Keynes pointed out that this conclusion is true only if we assume full employment and the rule of Say's law, which claims that demand is always enough for any supply of goods and that all saving is automatically invested. Indeed, we made this simplifying assumption when we asked how fast the economy would grow *if* there were always enough demand and *if* all saving were always invested. This assumption, however, is *not* true. During each depression it is painfully obvious to all Americans that there is not full employment. In each depression most saving is *not* being invested (except in the statistical sense of investment in unplanned and unwanted inventory pileups).

Keynes showed that, with unemployment and lack of investment opportunities, more saving may actually lead to *less* production rather than any economic growth. This finding constitutes the Alice-in-Wonderland theme of the *paradox of thrift,* which says that greater thrift and saving may sometimes lead to less investment, not more. If the economy is faced with a lack of money demand, then a higher propensity to save may simply lower consumer demand still further. The lower consumer demand may then lead to still less output and income and therefore less aggregate saving and investment than there was before individuals tried to save more of their income. Thrift may always be an individual virtue, as Ben Franklin preached, but it is not always a social virtue when there is a lack of paying customers in a private enterprise economy.

---

[7] See Simon S. Kuznets, *National Product Since 1869* (New York: National Bureau of Economic Research, 1946), p. 119.

More saving at a given income level is a benefit to the economy if, and only if, there is an equal increase in investment. In other words, more saving, which could supply more capital to produce more output, is helpful only if businesspeople expect demand to rise by an equal amount. Otherwise they will hoard the increased saving and precipitate a depression.

In the modern world we cannot afford to ignore either side of the problem. The U.S. rate of growth has not been as fast as desired. Setting aside more saving to invest in more capital makes it *possible* to raise the rate of growth. But this happy possibility cannot become a reality as long as significant numbers of unemployed persons and unused capacity continue. Such conditions show that all of the savings now available are not being invested. More saving would only cause more unemployment in this case. First one must guarantee a solution to the Keynesian problem of finding profitable investment outlets for all existing savings. Then one can worry about the classical problem of generating a higher rate of saving to allow the possibility of more investment.

SUMMARY

This chapter began by discussing the quantity of output that may be produced. The quantity of output is determined by (1) the known natural resources, (2) the amount of capital available, (3) the level of technology, and (4) most of all, the labor force and its level of training and education. The potential rate of growth of output depends on the growth of these four factors. It was also seen that this potential is not realized to the extent that the capitalist system creates unemployment.

Let us repeat that economic growth is necessary if many social ills are to be solved. With the widespread existence of poverty here and abroad, no one can deny that a larger output of goods and services is needed if everyone is to enjoy a high standard of living. Yet excessive concern with growth for its own sake has often obscured many significant economic and social problems. In the next chapter we will see that human welfare could be improved even with no further growth if various kinds of waste were eliminated—and if more of the product went to the average person than to the few rich individuals. It will also be shown that the quality of economic growth (with a minimum of waste and pollution) is at least as important as the *quantity* of growth.

CHAPTER 33

WASTE AND POLLUTION

This chapter explores all the wasteful aspects of production in the United States as well as the sources of pollution and environmental destruction. The wasteful products should not be included in a calculation of social welfare because they do not provide social benefit, even though they are included in the government's accounting of GNP. The pollution and other harm caused by some products should actually be *subtracted* from GNP as a social cost if we wish to compute the total national welfare from economic growth.

MILITARY PRODUCTION AND WASTE

We saw in Chapter 29 that most military "goods and services" (or evils and disservices) are not needed by the people of the United States. We saw that they serve the interests of the big businesses that produce for the military or have investments abroad that the military protect from foreign revolutions. We also noted that a dollar of military expenditure not only generates demand to that amount but also generates further spending by the workers and profit makers who receive the military spending. In other words, *if the system cannot reach full employment any other way, then military spending can produce full employment.* On the other hand, if military spending takes place when there is already full employment, then it competes with private spending for labor and resources and can only cause inflation.

It is a fact, however, that the U.S. capitalist system normally operates far below full employment. It is also a political fact of life—as we saw in Chapter 29—that no other kind of government spending can possibly be done on the scale needed to produce full employment. Therefore, within the present system's political and economic constraints, it is true that vast military spending is "necessary" to maintain full employment. Moreover, we have noted that such spending not only puts people to work producing military destruction but also has secondary effects of raising consumer and investor spending.

Obviously, however, military spending and wars also result in more taxes, inflation, wounds, deaths, and alienation and deterioration of life for millions. So whether or not it is wasteful to have military spending—$1.7 trillion from 1947 to 1971—depends on whether we could have a system in which it was possible to have full employment at peaceful pursuits without any military spending. Radicals believe that such a system is possible—that democratic socialism is such a system. Therefore radicals argue that all military spending is wasteful. If we had had as much employment as we did from 1947 to 1971, but all of the military spending had been put into productive plant and equipment for peaceful products, then in our present state of technology, or ratio of productive facilities to output, the United States could be producing *every year* about $600 billion more in goods and services—or more than half again as much as we are now producing.

MONOPOLY AND WASTE

Production does not reach optimal efficiency below some crucial size. Thus the increase in importance of large firms does mean that most of the economy has the ability to produce at lower costs than ever before. The data on both costs and profit rates reveal the possibility of high efficiency at a fairly constant level beyond the minimum-size firm.[1] In addition, the very large firms also have disproportionately larger research facilities and hold a very large portion of all unexpired patents. Therefore they have the greatest potential for efficiency improvement. Moreover, many investment projects are simply too large for small firms.

But the large, entrenched firm stands to lose most by the obsolescence of present machinery. It also loses most from product improvements that will reduce the number of units the customer needs to buy. Therefore if the large firm has a monopoly position and faces no serious competitive pressure for improvement, it *may* hide away and not use many important new inventions. Monopoly power may also be used to restrict supply in order to maintain prices. Monopolies will expand production as rapidly as possible only in the unusual periods of unlimited demand, such as World War II. Therefore although large monopolies have the potential to produce better goods more cheaply than small competitive firms, in many cases they do not use that potential but produce less useful goods sold at high prices.

Finally, we have seen that the existence of economic concentration may have increased the severity and possibly the number of depressions because of its destabilizing effects on the remaining small businesses. If this is so, then unless it has had a fully offsetting effect in increasing growth during prosperity, it would seem that this is another reason why the net effect of monopoly may be to lower the rate of economic growth. This is not to say, of course, that breaking up large firms into smaller units would increase economic growth; this would certainly cause a major decrease of economic efficiency in addition to probable negative effects on investment.

What should be done about monopoly waste? Conservatives argue that there is very little waste and nothing should be done. Liberals wish to break up monopolies in spite of the inefficiency of small firms. Radicals argue for democratic control of monopolies by workers and the public.

WASTEFUL SALES EXPENSES

In the United States a very large amount of human effort is put into the peculiar occupation of getting people to buy products they may not want. Obviously every

[1] See J. S. Bain, "Price and Production Policies," in Howard S. Ellis, ed., *A Survey of Contemporary Economics* New York: McGraw-Hill, 1948), p. 140.

society needs to distribute its goods from the factories to the consumers, but the U.S. economy goes far beyond that. It spends billions of dollars and millions of hours of labor time for sales workers to go around from door to door or to stand in a store and persuade other people to buy things. A huge percentage of this effort is not technically necessary and so may be called wasteful.

A second aspect of selling is advertising. Again, some small amount of advertising is needed in any society to supply useful information to consumers. Studies of the U.S. economy, however, indicate that more than 90 percent of all our advertising is not information but an attempt to persuade consumers that each of several identical products is better than the others. Therefore $15–20 billion a year (or more) is spent on advertising that should be described as wasteful.

A third aspect of selling is the giving of estimates. In many industries, such as construction, a tremendous amount of highly skilled effort by highly paid engineers consists in providing estimates on which their company may bid for a new job (e.g., a public school or road or military facility). In each of these cases the buyer of the construction has already had its own engineers furnish an estimate; in addition, another ten or twelve sets of engineers may do this difficult work of cost estimation all over again.

A fourth aspect of selling reaches back into production. It is the designing of new products or changes in existing products—not to make them better and sometimes even to make them worse—in such a way that they will be more attractive to consumers. One example is women's skirts, in which the hemline is regularly raised or lowered so that women wishing to keep in style will have to buy new skirts or dresses. Another example is the yearly change of automobile models. One year tails were put on cars, another year they were taken off. In some years it has been estimated that these automobile model changes took up to 2.5 percent of the entire GNP in totally wasted effort.[2]

Last but not least, sales efforts take the even more despicable form of "planned obsolescence." This means engineers are put to work designing a product that will fall apart quicker than previous ones so that the consumer will have to buy a new one.

ENVIRONMENTAL DESTRUCTION

One poetic observer writes, "America was once a paradise of timberland and streams but it is dying because of the greed and money lust of a thousand little kings who slashed the timber all to hell and would not be controlled."[3] It is not, however, just a matter for poets and far-off forests. Anyone flying to Los Angeles will notice a large, brownish cloud covering much of Southern California. And this cloud—called smog—does not merely look bad and cut visibility but also menaces the people's health. Ironically, many people in the 1930s and 1940s came to Southern California because they had respiratory problems, because it was a place where the air was crystal clear, warm, dry, and healthy. It seems almost incredible that in such a short time it could become a place where a few

[2] Franklin Fisher, Zvi Grilliches, and Carl Kayson, "The Costs of Automobile Changes Since 1949," *Journal of Political Economy,* October 1962.

[3] Garret De Bell, ed., *The Environmental Handbook* (New York: Ballantine, 1970), p. 3.

minutes of outside work in the afternoon is exhausting and the air itself causes thousands of cases of respiratory diseases among children.

Let us list systematically the major forms of pollution.[4] First, there are visible objects such as cans and waste paper, and smoke. Businesses spew over 25 billion tons of pollutants into the air and water and land every year. This includes about 150 million tons of smoke and fumes that blacken the skies and poison the air, 22 million tons of waste paper products, and 3 million tons of mill tailings. This is not a new phenomenon but has increased with economic growth. It creates problems particularly in slums in central-city areas that get much of the smoke and act as dumping grounds for garbage; it has also gone to the extent of blocking some rivers with solid wastes.

Second, there are organic wastes, detergents, and fertilizers, including human and animal wastes, and materials such as nitrates and phosphates that lead to rapid growth of algae. Altogether, about 50 *trillion* gallons of heated and polluted liquids are dumped into our streams, rivers, and lakes each year. This amount has been rapidly increasing in recent years. When the organic wastes and algae cause exhaustion of the oxygen in the water, other life is unable to survive, and septic decay by anaerobic bacteria causes terrible odors and incubates many diseases.

Third, there is local air pollution, including smoke, carbon monoxide from auto exhausts, nitrogen oxides and sulfur oxides, and photochemical smog produced by hydrocarbons reacting chemically in the air. Automobiles are the worst offender, producing 86 million tons of pollutants a year, but industry and power plants produce another 43 million tons. Altogether, all sources in the U.S. economy introduce 72 million tons of carbon monoxide, 26 million tons of sulfur oxides, 13 million tons of nitrogen oxides, 19 million tons of hydrocarbons, and 12 million tons of particulate matter into the air each year. This pollution causes property damage, local weather changes, lung diseases, and many other diseases; in some temporary emergency situations (caused by local air inversions) even deaths have been caused.

Fourth, there is worldwide atmospheric pollution, including carbon dioxide and dust clouds, which may affect the climate. Increasing carbon dioxide in the atmosphere tends to trap heat and warm the earth, while dust reflects the sun's rays, so that it tends to cool the earth. If either trend become dominant, our climate would change drastically.

Fifth, there are persistent poisonous materials, including DDT and the heavy metals (lead, mercury, and cadmium), that threaten health. DDT remains in each animal until it is eaten by another, right up the chain to humans, causing various health effects. The heavy metals tend to attack the central nervous system of any animal.

Sixth, there is increasing stray energy, including sonic booms and high-decibel sounds. Of increasing importance is the fact that nuclear power plants pro-

---

[4] The following list and most of the data in the rest of this chapter come from Mathew Edel, *Economies and the Environment* (Englewood Cliffs, N.J.: Prentice-Hall, 1973). This slender book is by far the clearest, best-written, most careful, and most revealing study of the political economy of ecology published to date. We highly recommend it as the best introduction to the field.

duce heat, atomic contamination, and radioactive fallout. Increased heat can disturb the whole animal and plant environment; noise can do both psychological and physical damage; and radioactivity not only hurts the present body but carries over through genetic defects to the next generation.

Finally, there is the mere fact of congestion, which increases other forms of pollution and also does direct damage. Crowding not only has very bad effects on human psychology but also increases the probabilities of epidemic diseases.

CAUSES AND CURES OF POLLUTION

The diagnosis of what causes pollution leads each different theory to a different prescription of how to cure it. Each of these diagnoses and prescriptions is associated with a general political outlook: conservative, liberal, or radical.

The Conservative View

Many conservatives deny that the picture is as grim as we have painted. Thus Presidents Nixon and Ford acknowledged that there is some environmental problem, but gave it very low priority and vetoed most bills designed to do something about it. (Profits come first.)

The conservative economists who do take the problem seriously begin, as usual, with Adam Smith's analysis—that the "invisible hand" of competitive private enterprise will balance all costs and benefits to consumers and producers and will finally give the optimal social result. They acknowledge that to some extent the market does not seem to be working well enough to prevent pollution. They argue that the reason is that pollution costs constitute a slight exception to Adam Smith's rule (that competition results in an optimal social result).

The reason that Adam Smith's rule is partially violated in this area, they say, is that some costs—like pollution—are costs to all of society but are not costs to individual firms. Moreover, the benefits of nonpollution go to all of society rather than to individual firms. Thus the costs of pollution do not lower their profits, nor do the benefits of nonpollution raise their profits. Therefore since the behavior of individual firms is determined solely by their expected profits, they ignore the fact of the pollution they create. This is the view of serious conservative economists, though they use slightly different rhetoric to describe the problem.

Since the problem is "merely" that pollution does not affect the competitive market producer, the solution is to make pollution marketable. One conservative approach is to make air and water into private property so owners could sell or rent them. Then we could have competition between those who wish to buy air to pollute and those who wish to buy air to breathe. Of course if someone got a monopoly of air, we might not be able to afford breathing. And how much a person could breathe or drink would depend on one's income.

To avoid a monopoly on air and water, the slightly less fanatic conservatives suggest that the government could auction off the "right to pollute" certain areas, or firms could pay for pollution damage, or we could all pay firms not to pollute by giving subsidies from local governments!

The Liberal View

Liberals argue that it could make capitalism slightly ridiculous and be highly inequitable to buy and sell air and water in this way. Mainly they argue that the problem is much broader than the conservatives acknowledge, so such minor patching could not work. They argue that these costs of pollution—which are external to private accounting and are therefore called *externalities*—pervade the whole system. They are not simply a minor exception to Adam Smith's model but are involved in almost all production of goods and services. Furthermore, they point out that many of the benefits of nonpollution of air or water are collective or public goods by nature—that is, there is no way to divide up clean air for sale to some people but not to others.

Therefore the liberals conclude that private enterprise cannot solve this problem by tinkering with new "property rights" in air and water but that the government must exercise its power to stop pollution. Thus the liberal Samuelson says, "Is reliance on spontaneous business efforts futile in the solution of a problem like this? Experience gives a pessimistic answer. . . . Since no one profit maker has the incentive, or indeed, the power, to solve problems involving 'externalities,' here is a clear case for some kind of public intervention."[5] So liberals advocate various laws to control the polluters.

POWER AND POLLUTION: A CRITIQUE OF THE LIBERAL VIEW

The liberal view asserts that the capitalist state can pass and enforce laws controlling pollution while preserving capitalism. They fail to see that the "right to pollute" is deeply imbedded in our present economic system and that all efforts to control it must meet the fiercest opposition. Thus even the *New York Times* (in an editorial on February 9, 1971) admits that "a corporate manager has his attention focused on the profit targets and production schedules. He has a *natural resistance* to taking into account environmental costs. . . . What is involved is a conflict of values. Nixon proposes many excellent environmental measures but he often talks the old fashioned language of the profit-first businessman."

We saw in Chapter 20 that the entire governmental apparatus always tends to put the interests of private property ahead of human values. Therefore the "natural resistance" of businesspeople to pollution controls tends to be passed on to the government that it dominates. This is true of liberal as well as conservative governments but is perhaps more obvious in the case of a directly business-subservient government like Nixon's or Ford's. There is no conflict of values but a conflict of interests; just enough must be said about the environment to get Nixon and Ford elected by the public that demands controls. Yet they must also make sure that no such controls are put into effect so as to satisfy all the businesspeople who give them their campaign funds.

[5] Paul Samuelson, *Economics*, 9th ed. (New York: McGraw-Hill, 1973), pp. 816–817. For a more thorough statement of the same view, see A. Freeman, R. Haveman, and A. Kneese, *The Economics of Environmental Policy* (New York: Wiley, 1973).

For these reasons the Nixon-Ford administration emphasized ecology in various State of the Union addresses. But when it came to proposing laws, the administration always argued for the words "taking into account the practicability of compliance." These words mean that no pollution control is "practical" or legal if it cuts down profits in any way! Since almost all controls do cut into profits, no controls would be practical in the Nixon-Ford administration's view. There is no evidence so far that the Carter administration will do anything more substantial about pollution in any case where pollution control is seriously opposed by big business.

When he opposed any increase of public transportation to replace the polluting automobile, the Ford administration's Undersecretary of Commerce J. Herbert Hollomon revealed their true concerns, saying: "The automobile contributes directly or indirectly to a substantial portion of our Gross National Product. It is a significant item in our trade relations with the rest of the free world. It involves a large segment of our work force and is a major factor in the production of some of our largest industries."

Indeed, the automobile and related industries are very important interests in our economy. When we add together auto production (the big three especially), plus gas and oil production (including 15 of the 60 largest corporations), plus highway builders, plus tire companies, and so on, they produce more than 12 percent of GNP and pack a tremendous political clout. When we ask why there is not more public investment in rapid transit systems or more public research into alternatives to the internal combustion engine, the answer seems to be the raw political-economic power of the auto, gas, and highway industries. In fact, private opposition and political constraints have reduced rides on public transit from 23 billion in 1945 to only 8 billion a year in 1967.

The highway lobby is probably second in power only to the military-industrial complex. There are lobbyists at Congress from the American Road Builders Association, the Associated General Contractors of America, the National Highway Users Conference, American Trucking Associations, the American Association of State Highway Officials, and the American Automobile Association—as well as representatives of many individual firms. So far this lobby has been able to prevent much use of the immense highway funds for public transit. (The same lobbyists have also been successful in preserving the oil depletion tax loophole.)

In addition to preventing the passage of pollution control laws (or better rapid transit or research for better cars), the same forces have been quite successful in preventing effective use of the laws that have been passed. For example, there are antipollution boards in many states, but most of them are totally dominated by the very polluting firms they are supposed to control. In Chapter 20 the Federal Power Commission was found to be similarly controlled by the gas and electric power interests. Even brand new commissions suffer the same fate. For example, in California the construction industry spent millions of dollars to defeat a law for the preservation of the seashore; but when the law was passed anyway, the Governor (Reagan) and local governments both appointed mostly representatives of the same polluting interests to the new boards designed to oversee the protection of the seacoast.

Since autos are the most important source of smog, we would expect many legal procedures to force the auto companies to institute controls. Their tremendous power, however, has been used to emasculate such law enforcement. For example, "throughout 1969, the Department of Justice in Washington held a secret hearing to discuss with industry lawyers its charge that automobile manufacturers have conspired to stifle the introduction of smog-control devices on automobiles. On September 11, the department announced that it had entered into a consent decree allowing the companies to escape federal sanctions by promising that they would not conspire any more."[6] Furthermore, in the general atmosphere of big business influence in the Nixon-Ford administration, it was easy for the auto companies to exert pressure on the Environmental Protection Agency. As a result, the EPA has postponed the enforcement of the standards set by the Clean Air Act passed by Congress. Finally, the auto lobby has forced Congress itself to postpone enforcement of the Clean Air Act.

Even if the laws are enforced, the existence of the capitalist system brings about a clash between the environmental and economic interests of most people. For example, under the Clear Air Act a cement factory in the little town of San Juan Batista has been found guilty of terrible pollution of the air. The company admits this but says that it will "cost too much"—that is, it will lower profits—to install the proper purification machinery. Therefore the entire cement factory is closing and will move elsewhere. In this way the burden of environmental protection is made to fall on local workers and on the local people and governments.

This strategy is known as *divide and rule*. It has been very effectively used by polluting businesses to split the opposition to pollution. Thus in the case of the California shoreline protection law, the construction industry bosses got the construction unions to oppose it as well—for the alleged reason that more of them would be unemployed if there were less construction. Similarly in the case of funds for highways the Teamsters union always supports these funds and new road building against community wishes—again because they wish to protect their jobs. "Because America does not guarantee workers jobs in their own communities, people must be concerned that investment take place near where they live."[7] So the conflict between jobs and ecology is built into our present capitalist system.

Another conflict utilized by the big polluters is that between the interests of different states. Given this conflict, the oil companies wanted the individual states to control "tidelands oil" rather than the federal government. Each state is relatively weak by itself compared to the industrial giants, so they can always threaten to take their business elsewhere. It is thus easier to take resources, such as oil, away from individual states or to be allowed to pollute individual states.

The same kind of conflict and threats can be utilized at the national level. Already many small countries have capitulated to a vast amount of pollution rather than losing business and jobs to other countries. Even the powerful United States is not immune. Since the environmental protection laws have been

[6] De Bell, op. cit., p. 269.
[7] Edel, op. cit., p. 130.

tightened, many of our own powerful multinational corporations have moved or threatened to move whole enterprises to less well-protected countries.

THE REVIVAL OF MALTHUSIANISM

In the early nineteenth century the Reverend Malthus studied population and poverty. He decided that population always increases in geometric progression—2, 4, 8, 16, etc.—because people breed like rabbits. He also decided that production could increase only arithmetically—1, 2, 3, 4, etc.—because of our limited land and resources. Therefore from this mechanical exercise he concluded that poverty is caused by too much population and that there is nothing we can do about it. The only alternatives are to abstain from sex altogether or to wait until famine and disease remove the excess population. Malthus overlooked technology, which allows us always to produce more per worker. He also overlooked the fact that after industrialization more educated and sophisticated men and women would decide to have less children per family by practicing birth control. Therefore instead of ever-decreasing product per person, the developed countries have experienced ever-increasing product per person. Furthermore, we shall see in Chapter 35 that the less-developed countries are kept that way not by population pressure but mainly by foreign imperialism.

In recent years many conservatives, some liberals, and even some radicals have brought back to life the old Malthusian argument: They conclude that rising population and rising production together doom us to ecological catastrophe and to eventual poverty as our resources are eventually depleted. The only way out, they tell us, is to have a zero rate of population growth and a zero rate of economic growth. Partly they are concerned with the very real problems inherent in growth under capitalism. The well-known liberal economist John K. Galbraith makes this perfectly correct point, saying, "I am not quite sure what the advantage is in having a few more dollars to spend if the air is too dirty to breathe, the water too polluted to drink, the commuters are losing out in the struggle to get in and out of the city, the streets are filthy, and the schools so bad that the young perhaps wisely stay away, and hoodlums roll citizens for some of the dollars they saved in tax."[8]

The problem comes when this correct point is pushed much too far. One commentator in the *New York Times* wrote, "There are, alas, a few 'iron laws' . . . The hard fact is: growth of production is the basic cause of pollution growth."[9] Even stronger are the doomsday statements made by the Club of Rome, a group of businessmen and management experts. On the basis of certain arbitrary assumptions about resource and waste disposal variables, they "scientifically prove"—by putting everything into a computer—that in just a certain number of years hundreds of millions of people will die from either pollution or lack of food. On this basis some conservatives conclude that we can do nothing but live—and die—with pollution and poverty, while many liberals and some radicals argue that

[8] J. K. Galbraith, in congressional testimony, quoted in Michael Harrington, "Reactionary Keynesianism," *Encounter* 16, March 1966, p. 51.
[9] Edwin Dale, *New York Times Magazine*, April 19, 1970, p. 27.

the only hope is to limit absolutely to present or lower levels the amount of economic growth and the amount of population.

We certainly agree that there is an enormous problem here. It is not true, however, that this fate is inevitable or that limiting growth and population are the only or even the best answers. In the first place, the link between pollution and GNP growth is not a simple one-to-one relationship. If we spend $10 for an evening at the theater, the accountants record $10 GNP growth; but very little pollution is created. If, on the other hand, we spend $10 for gas for pleasure driving, a great deal of pollution is created. It turns out that much of the worst pollution is associated with petroleum products, certain heavy industries, and military industry. If we eliminated the automobile and military production, most pollution would be gone.

The problem is not merely the fact that some GNP growth involves much more pollution than other growth; it is also the fact that much of this spending is on unnecessary or even harmful goods that could be eliminated—without reducing food, clothing, and shelter. Furthermore, some activities *should* grow—for example, growth of services combatting pollution—even though these will be treated as GNP growth by the accountants. Finally, much more of the GNP can be recycled.

In the second place, no-growth policies cannot be considered apart from income redistribution policies. Under the present capitalist system poor people rightly suspect that "no growth" means they would be frozen into poverty forever.

In the third place, international redistribution must be considered. At United Nations conferences, when affluent American delegates have argued for no-growth policies, the poor countries have rightly suspected that this means their whole countries would be frozen into poverty forever. In addition, when birth control is advocated by the U.S. government for these countries, they are rightly suspicious of nationalist and racist motives for reducing their populations but not the U.S. population. It is also a fact that the best way to get birth control and less population growth is by achieving an urban and industrialized society (which means more growth for these countries), since people then have the knowledge of birth control and the desire for fewer children.

In the fourth place, the theorists of no growth never consider whether a different political economic system could achieve much less pollution even with the same growth. Yet we have seen that, while some pollution is caused by any massive economic growth under present technology, it is capitalist greed for profits that causes many additional problems. It is a government dominated by capitalist economic power that is slow to legislate and slow to enforce pollution controls. It is a capitalist system that cannot guarantee workers other jobs when some jobs are prohibited because of pollution effects. It is capitalist systems that cannot willingly redistribute to poor people and poor countries the existing goods and services. It is the capitalist system that makes poor people and poor countries suspicious of birth control—though birth control would make very good sense under a non-profit-oriented system. Finally, it is impossible to conceive of a no-growth rule imposed on capitalism; how could private enterprise exist if it is prevented from growing? It would mean monopolies for existing industries, ever-higher prices, and no new competitors allowed—plus a very extensive government bureaucracy to give detailed instructions to prevent growth.

THE RADICAL VIEW

Obviously radicals agree that some pollution is likely in any highly industrialized and densely populated economy. But a very large part of pollution in the U.S. economy is due to the capitalist economic system for all the reasons given previously. "Look at the values which galvanize energies and allocate resources in the business system: pursuit of money, enrichment of self, the exploitation of man—and of nature—to generate still more money. Is it surprising that a system seeking to turn everything into gold ends up turning everything into garbage?"[10]

Radicals argue that the correct solution is a new economic system, one in which the people decide democratically how to run it, rather than having the decisions being made by a few people. Note that this is a classic definition of "socialism." It excludes the Soviet Union, however, because they also have an economic system dominated by a few undemocratically selected rulers.

Under a democratically run socialist economy, wasteful goods and services— such as vast military production, oversized private automobiles, and advertising signs by the millions—would be eliminated. Under a democratically run socialist economy, the national income would be shared much more equally than today, so most people could live better at any level of GNP than under our present system of unequal distribution. Under a democratically run socialist economy, there would be no private enterprises to push frantically for more growth to make more profits. Finally, birth control information and devices would be freely available to all.

THE ENERGY "CRISIS"

Is there a crisis? The available data are very poor because the oil, gas, and electric companies have tried very hard to keep them secret. It seems, however, that the U.S. economy does have plenty of energy reserves for the next few decades. For the short run the question is only what the companies are willing to produce. For the long run, there undoubtedly will be shortages if the system continues as it has.

If there is a shortage at present, who is to blame? In the first place, the energy companies are to blame because they have purposely restricted production. The oil companies have plenty of crude oil but have not built enough refineries. The electric companies have also not built enough generating plants. Why not? Because these are monopolies or oligopolies. By the exercise of their monopoly power, they can restrict production. Restricted production means less supply to the market, which causes a "shortage" that allows them to charge higher prices. These higher prices result in greater profits per unit. Of course if the companies reduced supply too far, their total profits would fall; but they are very careful to reduce supply only far enough to optimize profits for the whole industry.

This is quite apparent in the profit rate data. While consumers were told to cut their heat and freeze a little to conserve energy—while paying higher prices— the companies had zooming profits in 1973. The profits of Exxon alone rose from $1.5 billion in 1972 to $2.5 billion in 1973. The profits of the nine largest compa-

[10] Editorial, *Ramparts*, May 1970, p. 2.

nies rose by 45 percent in the first 9 months of 1973[11] and still further in the last quarter.

While their profits rose, they created a smoke screen of very extensive advertising propaganda—and all their advertising is tax deductible. First, they argued that they couldn't expand faster because environmental groups harassed them. Yet the data show that they did not want to expand faster because they wanted a "shortage." There is even some evidence that the oil companies asked the Arab countries to hold back some of their oil.

Second, the oil companies argued that the one to blame is really the consumer. Exxon sponsors ads to say that housewives should do their errands all in one trip to save gas. It sponsors other ads to say that we should all drive slower. The companies even tell us to lower our house temperatures to save heating oil. But it is wrong to blame the people or to ask them to make voluntary sacrifices. It is the companies who caused the shortage and are profiting from it.

Yet it is *not* the case that the companies are run by evil men who beat their mothers. They are simply part of the capitalist system acting the only way they can within that system. The system is planless. Thus the companies can restrict their production with no one to tell them no. At the same time, it is only good business practice to tell consumers to use more of their product. There have been gigantic advertising campaigns to tell us to use more gas in the home, more gadgets of every kind in the home, and larger energy-eating autos. Their profits are maximized, which is their duty to stockholders, only by restricting production while increasing demand. If a corporate executive did not follow these policies, either the executive would be fired by the stockholders or the whole company would go bankrupt.

Moreover, the system is characterized by monopoly in almost every industry. Monopoly means, according to all economists, restricted production, more advertising, and higher profits. This same system tends to squander all our resources, both by urging consumers to spend more money on everything and by its own wasteful advertising—and by all-out support for ever-larger military spending.

Finally, the system tends to oppose really basic research to find new, cheaper, and more plentiful sources of energy. Such research might destroy the cozy monopoly power of the large energy corporations. At any rate it is a risk because they might have to scrap a large amount of existing equipment and might not be able to establish monopolies over the new sources of energy. They are thus very conservative about fundamental new ideas and try to prevent the government from doing much basic research either. For all of these reasons, the business system is not only responsible for the present limited "shortages" but is likely to create very real shortages of every kind of energy in the future if we allow it to keep working as it has always done.

The blame must also be placed on the government. Besides the normal inefficiency, the real problem is that the government is on the side of the energy companies. Its highest goal is to create more profit for the companies. The main reason for this attitude is that the politicians get most of their large contributions from the large corporations; in return, they are expected to do favors for those

---

[11] These data are from an excellent article by Frank Ackerman and Arthur MacEwan, "Energy and Power," *Monthly Review 25*, January 1974, pp. 1–14.

corporations. Thus the Federal Power Commission is filled by the President with commissioners who are all representatives of the oil, gas, and electric companies. That is normal for all political administrations in a society dominated by big business.

We noted earlier that the big oil and electric companies benefited from the "crisis" through higher profits. Moreover, the administration and the companies have used the occasion to try to push through Congress various legislation they have always wanted. They have argued for a delay in the Clean Air standards to save on energy—and, incidentally, to protect the auto companies' profits. They have argued for loosening the antitrust laws so the government and all the companies could collaborate to save oil and gas—and to allow more profits by the companies. They have used the "crisis" as an excuse for pushing the Alaska oil pipeline, for keeping oil depletion allowances, and for numerous other probusiness measures.

Who has been hurt by the energy "crisis"? We noted that the large corporations have actually benefited from it. Yet most people have been hurt. Tenants have had to pay higher rents while receiving less heat. Workers have been fired with energy shortages as an excuse. All consumers have had to do with less oil and gas. Moreover, most cutbacks to businesses have hurt small businesses because their quotas have not been enough to stay in business. Also hurt have been the small, independent oil companies. The shortage has thus resulted in further economic concentration.

What is a reasonable solution? It seems obvious that the resources of the United States should belong to all Americans. Yet it seems that the corporations have used their control of those resources to exploit their workers, restrict production, and charge high prices to consumers. Therefore it seems only just that we the people should take over the large monopolized energy companies. The public and the workers in these enterprises should each elect representatives to directing boards that would run the companies. This way we could extend our political democracy to democratic control over the energy industry. A democratically controlled industry could expand production and sponsor basic research while cutting some prices and reducing the profit margin.

SUMMARY

There are various kinds of economic waste: military production, monopoly misallocation, most advertising and sales expenses, planned obsolescence, lack of conservation, and pollution. There is pollution of land, air, and water. Extreme conservatives argue that nonpollution (such as clean air) could be given a price and bought and sold in the market, thus automatically solving the problem. Liberals believe that is insufficient; legal controls are needed to prevent pollution by private enterprise. Radicals don't believe controls will work under capitalism; a democratic socialist society is a necessary condition for an end to waste and pollution.

CHAPTER 34

INTERNATIONAL CAPITALIST TRADE AND FINANCE

Stagflation, that is, inflation in the midst of stagnation, has engulfed all the leading capitalist countries. In Western Europe and Japan, depressions in the United States did *not* cause major downturns in the 1950s and 1960s. In the 1973–1975 depression, however, these countries joined the U.S. economic contraction. In Table 34.1 we see that this was a lengthy depression in all of the leading capitalist countries, and the decline in production (and rise in unemployment) was very considerable in all of them. Contrary to many predictions, the rate of inflation remained high in all of these countries throughout the depression. In fact, the inflation rate was lowest in West Germany where the unemployment rate was also relatively low.

Table 34.1 **Stagflation in International Capitalism, 1973–1975**

	Number of Months of Decline	Percentage Decline in Industrial Production	Inflation Rate in Depression (mid-1975)
France	18 months	15%	11%
West Germany	22	10	6
Italy	16	19	17
Japan	18	17	13
United Kingdom	19	9	20
United States	16	14	9

Sources: Number of months from National Bureau of Economic Research, reported in *Riverside Press-Enterprise,* (Sept. 5, 1976), p. F-7. Industrial production from Organization for Economic Cooperation and Development, reported in Newsweek, (Sept. 15, 1975), p. 57. European Inflation rates from "Worldwide Depression Policies," *Riverside Press-Enterprise,* (Sept. 14, 1975), p. A-2. Japanese inflation rate from *Japan Economic Journal* (October 7, 1975, and February 4, 1975), both at p. 13. U.S. inflation rate from U.S. Bureau of Labor Statistics, *Monthly Labor Review,* (March, 1976), p. 85.

MONOPOLY POWER IN OTHER CAPITALIST COUNTRIES

By the 1950s all the leading capitalist countries showed high levels of concentration of output and sales by a few firms in each industry. In Great Britain in the 1950s, for example, the top four firms had the following percentages of total sales in various industries: 91 in explosives, 56 in electric lamps, 73 in distilled liquors, 47 in aircraft, 93 in petroleum refining, and 90 in cement. In Japan the top four firms had the following percentages of total sales in various industries: 65 in electric lamps, 52 in steel ingots, 49 in cement, 98 in beer and ale, 42 in petroleum refining, and 56 in pharmaceutical products. In France the top four firms had the following percentages of total sales in various industries: 57 in aircraft, 76 in shipbuilding, 72 in petroleum refining, and 53 in cement.[1]

Since the 1950s concentration has increased in each of the leading capitalist countries. The share of the one hundred largest manufacturing firms in all manufacturing ouput in the United Kingdom rose from 21 percent in 1948 to 38 percent in 1963 to 51 percent in 1970![2] Similarly, in France by 1962 in 56 industrial groups, just four firms had over 50 percent of the sales in 21 of these groups. "French industry, since 1962, appears to have a market structure more concentrated than American industry itself."[3] Finally, in the entire European economic community (excluding the United Kingdom) the share of total output produced by the 50 largest firms was 35 percent in 1960, 35 percent in 1965, and 46 percent in 1970.[4] During the process of integrating several economies in the early 1960s, concentration held steady. When integration was completed in the mid-1960s, however, there were a large number of mergers and the share of the largest 50 rose rapidly.

Similar industrial structures lead to similar economic behavior and performance. For example, an important study in Japan finds that monopoly prices fluctuate much less than competitive prices, so that in recessions monopoly prices in Japan have fallen less (or risen more) than competitive prices.[5] It is, therefore, no surprise that increasing monopoly power in Europe and Japan has helped produce—as in the U.S. economy—the strange phenomenon of inflation in the midst of depression. Of course, this is not the only reason for the new phenomenon, but it is an important one.

There are also plenty of defenders of big business who put the whole blame for Japanese and European stagflation on the workers. One economist makes his class viewpoint very clear: "To put the case bluntly, the British labor movement has been independent, parochial, generally oblivious to modern economic thinking, and, moreover, apparently unaware of what policies will serve its own long-run interest, much less that of the general economy."[6] Isn't it surprising that

[1] Joe Bain, *International Differences in Industrial Structure* (New Haven: Yale University Press, 1966), p. 130.

[2] P. Sargent Florence, "Stagflation in Great Britain," in John Blair, ed., *Roots of Inflation* (New York: Franklin, 1975), p. 88.

[3] Data and quote from French National Institute of Statistical and Economic Studies, reported in Joel Dirlam, "The Process of Inflation in France," in Blair, op. cit., p. 114.

[4] See H. W. de Jong, "Experience Within the European Economic Community," in Blair, op. cit., p. 187.

[5] Yoshihiro Kobayashi, "Movements of Price and Profit in the Periods of Rapid Growth in the Japanese Economy," *Economic Studies Quarterly*, August 1971, in Japanese.

[6] Florence, op. cit., p. 76.

British labor, like American labor, is oblivious to that "modern economic thinking" that tells it to lower its own wages in its own interest? And since workers are 80 percent to 90 percent of the population, what is the interest of "the general economy" that is different from labor's interest? Yet some economists seem to think that the interest of the "general economy" means the interest of big business.

There is no evidence that high wages in Britain—rather than low wages and low demand—have led to Britain's current unemployment and inflation. Moreover, one serious research study shows that a long-run falling profit share in England is a myth, that the profit share (after taxes) in national income has been constant from 1950 to 1973.[7] On the contrary, there is plenty of evidence that business monopoly power *has* increased in England.

The increase of business monopoly power in western Europe is the first factor explaining stagflation there. The second factor is the policy pursued by European governments. In England it is called the *stop-and-go policy*. At the peak of the cycle, the government tries to stop the rise of wages by direct controls or even by general restrictive policies. In the trough of the depression, the government tries to stimulate the economy, to make profits go upward by various means. These policies, which constitute a political business cycle of capitalism, are likewise pursued by all the other western European governments.[8]

The third factor explaining stagflation is the international situation. In the following sections we examine (1) the degree of international concentration of the multinational corporations, (2) the changing power of the U.S. economy vis-à-vis western Europe and Japan, (3) the problems of trade balances and supposed shortages caused by these changes, and (4) how international problems worsen stagflation in each country.

CONCENTRATION BY MULTINATIONAL (GLOBAL) FIRMS

The present degree of economic concentration in the entire capitalist world by a few enormous multinational corporations constitutes a new structural stage for international capitalism. The term *multinational* suggests management from many countries, whereas the truth is that each firm is governed mostly by the nationals of one developed capitalist country. The term *global corporation* may be less misleading. The one proposition uniting all these corporations is the notion that the whole globe is their oyster, that vast profits may be made by control of markets in several countries.

In pursuit of profit, U.S. based global corporations have been rapidly expanding abroad. In terms of total assets of U.S. industries, by 1974 about 40 percent of all consumer goods industries, about 75 percent of the electrical industry, about 33 percent of the chemical industry, about 33 percent of the pharmaceutical industry, and over half of the $100 billion petroleum industry was located outside

---

[7] M. A. King, "The United Kingdom Profits Crisis: Myth or Reality," *The Economic Journal,* vol. 85, March 1975, pp. 33–54.

[8] See the description of the depression policies country by country in "World-wide Depression Policies," *Riverside Press-Enterprise,* September 14, 1975, pp. A2, A4.

the United States![9] Moreover, this expansion trend has increased and perhaps accelerated in recent years. In 1957 investment in plant and equipment by U.S. firms abroad was already 9 percent of total U.S. domestic investment in plant and equipment; but by 1970 that investment abroad rose to 25 percent of domestic investment. In 1961 sales of U.S. manufacturing abroad were only 7 percent of total sales by all U.S. manufacturing corporations, but that figure rose to 13 percent by 1970. In 1960 the foreign dollar deposits of the largest U.S. banks were only 8.5 percent of domestic deposits, but by 1970 foreign deposits rose to 65 percent of domestic deposits.[10]

The pattern of ownership by foreign-owned global corporations is most striking in the less developed countries. In Chile, before Allende's socialist government, global corporations controlled at least 51 percent of the 160 largest firms. In Argentina, global corporations control more than 50 percent of the total sales of the 50 largest firms. In Mexico, global corporations control 100 percent of rubber, electrical machinery, and transportation industries. Moreover, in Mexico foreign ownership in the metal industry rose from 42 percent in 1962 to 68 percent in 1970, while foreign ownership in tobacco rose from 17 percent in 1962 to 100 percent in 1970. In Brazil, global corporations own 100 percent of automobile and tire production, while their share of machinery rose from 59 percent in 1961 to 67 percent in 1971, and their share of electrical equipment rose from 50 percent in 1961 to 68 percent in 1971.[11]

It is also important to note that many transactions within and between capitalist countries are conducted solely between subsidiaries of the same parent corporation. A large-scale sample found over 50 percent of total foreign trade transactions in the capitalist world are of this nonmarket intracorporate variety between subsidiaries of the same company.[12] This means that taxes can be shifted to those countries where the rates are lowest. It also means that fiscal policies may not operate—or may operate mainly to the benefit of the global giants. Several studies show that the largest corporations in the United States absorb a disproportionate part of all government spending and tax reductions designed to stimulate the economy.[13]

The global manufacturing corporations are serviced by global banks with tenacles almost everywhere. At their urging additional credit has been created as a new currency, the $110 billion dollar pool of Euro-dollars (and the Special Drawing Rights, which acts as currency). Since there are no reserve deposit requirements on the Euro-dollars, they are particularly unstable and contribute a strong impetus, by further credit creation, to inflationary pressures. This international credit expansion, plus rapid monetary flows between corporate subsidiaries across borders, makes it less possible than ever for any capitalist nation to control its money supply by any conceivable monetary policies.

It should also be noted that union bargaining power has been further weakened by the power of the global corporations to shift production rapidly from areas of high wages to low wage areas. For example, if the United States has

[9] See Richard Barnet and Ronald Muller, *Global Reach* (New York: Simon & Schuster, 1974), p. 17
[10] Ronald Muller, "Global Corporations and National Stabilization Policy," *Journal of Economic Issues*, vol. 9, June 1975, pp. 183–184.
[11] Barnet and Muller, op. cit., p. 147.
[12] See Muller, op. cit., p. 194.
[13] See ibid., p. 188 and his footnote 6.

high wages, they shift to Mexico, and if even Mexican wages are considered too high, they shift to Hong Kong.[14]

Finally, the international concentration of investment decisionmaking in a relatively small number of corporations, plus the very intimate ties of international trade and investment among all the capitalist countries, bind these economies closely together. Therefore, a contraction begun in one country, or in just a few global corporations, spreads at lightning speed to the others. If investor demand declines in several countries at once, then their import trade in raw materials declines, lowering demand for exports in several other countries. If unemployment rises in several countries at once, then their demand for consumer goods from abroad also declines. Thus the entire capitalist world tends to move in the same direction in its investment decisions as well as its demands from trading partners. This encourages explosive expansion amidst spiraling optimistic speculations, or universal contraction amidst a downward spiral of lower profits and pessimism.

THE CASE OF CANADIAN-AMERICAN ECONOMIC RELATIONS

Canada invests hundreds of millions of dollars annually in less developed countries. With these investment dollars goes a large measure of Canadian economic power within many of these countries. However, a Canadian government report in 1968 showed that foreigners owned $33 billion of Canadian assets. The principal owners of these assets were the United States (approximately 80 percent) and the United Kingdom (approximately 12 percent). The bulk of this foreign ownership was direct or equity ownership (about 60 percent).[15]

The composition of this foreign ownership conformed perfectly with the time-honored explanation of economic expansionism: the securing of sources of raw materials and markets for manufactured goods. Fifty-four percent of all Canadian manufacturing industries were owned by foreigners, and 60 percent were controlled by foreigners. Foreign ownership of mining and smelting stood at 62 percent. The petroleum and natural gas industry was 64 percent foreign owned and 74 percent foreign controlled.

Within the manufacturing sector the industries that were oligopolistically organized were almost completely foreign owned. These figures are 97 percent of the automobile industry, 97 percent of the rubber industry, 78 percent in chemicals, and 77 percent in electrical apparatus. These industries were controlled almost exclusively by U.S. interests.

This control of oligopolistic industries was reflected in the fact that of the 414 corporations with assets above $25 million, 53 percent of these assets were in firms that were more than 50 percent owned by nonresidents; the figure for firms with assets below $25 million was 32 percent.

The immense profitability of American subsidiaries in Canada is grossly un-

---

[14] See Barnet and Muller, op. cit., chaps. 10 and 11.
[15] *Canadian Privy Council Report of the Task Force on the Structure of Canadian Industry* (Ottawa: Queen's Printer, January 1968). These data and those that follow were taken from various pages of the report.

derestimated if one looks simply at the more than $1 billion a year in interest and dividends received from Canadian firms. Payments for management fees, royalties, franchises, advertising, rent, professional services, and so forth probably amount to nearly $500 million a year, although accurate statistics on these do not exist.

Very possibly an even larger source of profits (for which no statistics would be available) lies in the buying-and-selling policies of parents and subsidiaries. Thus an American company controlling Canadian natural resources can pay a high price for these resources and show a large profit on the books of the subsidiary—or it may pay a low price and show the profits on its own books. Similarly, an American manufacturing firm that requires its Canadian subsidiary to purchase manufactured components from the parent company can follow pricing policies that can make the profits appear on either side of the border. This permits the company to use an optimum combination of tax loopholes in both countries.

It appears probable, however, that the greatest pressures exist for American corporate managers to maximize the parent company's profits. It is generally the profits of the parent on which these managers' personal careers depend. Thus a study of the National Industrial Conference Board showed that while manufactured component parts represented 35 percent of material costs for Canadian industries, they represented only 23 percent of material costs for American industries.

The results of this economic takeover have manifested themselves in the decreasing degree of independence both externally and internally in Canada's economic and political policies. Over the past ten years Canada has been under constant pressure to follow the U.S. "line" on Vietnam more closely. U.S. subsidiaries have openly refused employment to U.S. immigrants who appear to be draft dodgers; Canada has not refused American nuclear weapons; U.S. subsidiaries, by taking orders from the parent company, follow U.S. State Department guidelines and partially subvert the Canadian government's attempts to increase trade with certain communist states.

Moreover, American control of the composition of Canadian investment results in a far less than optimally arranged industrial structure. American firms have literally made a "little America" of Canada's economy. The result in many industries is a large number of units each producing at a smaller-than-optimum scale. Canada, with a population equivalent to roughly 10 percent of that of the United States, gives its consumers an array of brand names virtually identical to that faced by the American consumer.

Perhaps in the long run the worst evil of American ownership will be the complete elimination of the possibility for Canadians to achieve a more equitable distribution of wealth. Within a capitalist society the primary means of redistributing wealth (at least in theory, if not in deed) have been the use or potential use of death duties, inheritance taxes, taxes on gifts and bequests, and capital gains taxes. Because almost all Canadian assets owned by foreigners are owned by foreign corporations and because the foreign corporations almost never die or divest themselves of their Canadian holdings, these methods can never substantially redistribute wealth.

RISE AND DECLINE OF THE U.S. EMPIRE

Until the Civil War American capitalism was far behind European capitalism. It had the advantage, however, of having no feudal or semifeudal encumbrances. After the Civil War it also abolished slavery and opened the whole country to capitalism. Moreover, the U.S. economy was relatively short of labor, so it was forced to use the most advanced technology. As a result, U.S. industrialization proceeded very rapidly after 1870, and it eventually overtook and passed British and other European industry. Finally, the two world wars devastated much of Europe but stimulated the U.S. economy. By 1945 the United States emerged completely dominant in the capitalist world.

Between 1945 and 1950 the U.S. gross domestic product (GDP) was equal to that of the whole rest of the world combined. Thus in 1950 the French GDP was only 10 percent of the American, West Germany's only 8 percent, Italy's only 5 percent, Japan's only 4 percent, the United Kingdom's only 13 percent—and all five only 39 percent of the American GDP. In 1950 the United States produced 82 percent of all the world's passenger vehicles, produced 55 percent of the world's steel production, and consumed 50 percent of the world's energy consumption.[16]

Throughout this period U.S. firms also extended their control over much of European industry. By 1965 American firms or their subsidiaries owned 80 percent of computer production, 24 percent of the motor industry, 15 percent of the synthetic rubber industry, and 10 percent of the production of petrochemicals *within* the entire European Common Market. Furthermore, it is well to remember how concentrated this ownership is. About 40 percent of all U.S. direct investment in Britain, France, and Germany is owned by Ford, General Motors, and Standard Oil of New Jersey.[17]

American firms have maintained a relative superiority over western European firms because of (1) greater size of capital assets and (2) greater technological advances. The size advantage of U.S. corporations is indicated by the fact that, of the hundred largest global corporations, 65 are based in the United States, 11 in the United Kingdom, 18 in other Common Market nations, and 5 in Japan. Because they have greater size and financial power, U.S. firms are able to do more technological research. Furthermore, the continued enormous U.S. military spending has subsidized much technological research for U.S. firms. U.S. spending on research per capita is still three to four times that of European research spending. Finally, the United States has drained away many of the best brains in Europe (after they were trained in Europe). Between 1959 and 1967 about 100,000 of the best doctors, scientists, and technicians left western Europe for the United States.[18]

In spite of all these initial and continuing advantages, the absolute superiority of the U.S. economy in world production has slowly faded away. It was restricted and then reduced by three main factors. First, the Soviet Union broke away from the capitalist world in 1917 and has steadily gained on the U.S. economy since

[16] See Albert Syzmanski, "The Decline and Fall of the U.S. Eagle," in David Mermelstein, *The Economic Crisis Reader* (New York: Random House, 1975), pp. 65–70.

[17] See Ernest Mandel, *Europe vs. America: Contradictions of Imperialism* (New York: Monthly Review Press, 1970), pp. 22–23.

[18] See ibid., pp. 30–43, an excellent presentation.

the late 1920s. Despite the one awful hiatus of the Second World War, Soviet production now rivals the U.S. total.

Second, the old colonial empires were overthrown at the end of World War II. At first, the new "independent" neocolonial countries turned to the U.S. economy for aid and investment, so U.S. power expanded further. Later, however, wars of liberation (as in Vietnam) spread and were focused against the United States as the main policeman of imperialism.

Lastly, as a counterweight to the Communist countries and the increasing resistance of the Third World, the United States was forced to give strong support to the rebuilding of the capitalist economies of Japan and western Europe. These economies began in 1945 with a skilled labor force but devastated factories. As their industry was rebuilt from scratch, they used the latest technology and began the long march to catch up with the U.S. economy. Whereas the data show that the United States ruled supreme in the early 1950s, it was being challenged by the growing power and competition of Japan and western Europe in every market by the early 1970s.

The United States was still the largest, but it no longer was far larger than the combination of all the rest. Thus by 1972 the French gross domestic product (GDP) had risen to 17 percent of American GDP, West Germany's rose to 22 percent, Italy's rose to 10 percent, Japan's rose incredibly to 24 percent, the United Kingdom's to 14 percent—all five of these together now had a GDP equal to 86 percent of American GDP. In specific areas of basic production, the U.S. share of the world total fell between 1950 and 1972 from 82 to 29 percent of passenger vehicles, from 55 to 20 percent of steel production, and from 50 to 33 percent of world energy production. The competitive position of Japan and western Europe was also strengthened by the fact that their productivity per labor-hour, especially Japanese productivity, rose much faster than U.S. productivity. On the other hand, Japanese and west European wage levels also rose faster than U.S. wage levels, which hurt their competitive position a little, but they are still somewhat lower than U.S. wage levels.[19]

BALANCE OF PAYMENTS PROBLEM

Problems with the U.S. balance of payments have arisen largely because of the resistance of the Third World and the increasing competition of Japanese and west European capitalists. To demonstrate this we must understand what the balance of payments is and how it works.

Suppose a U.S. firm exports $1000 worth of Coca Cola to Germany. Then the German importer sells the Coca Cola for deutschemarks (DMs), say for DM 4000. If the exchange rate is $1 = 4 DM, then the importer buys 1000 U.S. dollars with the 4000 DMs, and pays the U.S. exporter 1000 dollars. Suppose at the same time a U.S. importer imports beer worth 4000 DM from Germany. The U.S. importer sells the beer for 1000 dollars (or more). Then the U.S. importer buys 4000 DM for 1000 dollars and pays 4000 DM to the German beer firm. In this case both sides are satisfied, the trade between the two countries is in balance, and the monetary exchanges balance.

[19] See Syzmanski, op. cit., pp. 66–69.

There are two reasons why this example worked out so neatly. First, the demand for *foreign exchange* (which is generally what foreign currencies are called) was exactly equal to the supply of foreign exchange. The demand for foreign exchange, it should be noted, arose from the import of foreign goods, while the supply of foreign exchange arose from the export of domestic goods. Second, the supply of and demand for foreign exchange were equal because the *exchange rate* at which dollars could be converted was $1 = 4 DM. There are, then, two important considerations in the financing of foreign transactions: (1) the number and magnitude of transactions giving rise to a demand for and supply of foreign exchange and (2) the rate at which dollars can be converted to foreign exchange, or the exchange rate between American dollars and the various foreign currencies. Each of these must be considered.

We begin by taking the exchange rate as given and examining the international transactions that give rise to a demand for and supply of foreign exchange. The *balance of payments* is a systematic accounting of all such transactions for one country for a given period, usually one year. Transactions are aggregated into different categories. The *current account* records all sales and purchases of goods and services between Americans and foreigners.

Table 34.2 summarizes the U.S. current account for 1975. All items on the left side of the table are transactions that created a supply of foreign exchange. The transactions listed on the right side created a demand for foreign exchange. From the current account transactions in 1975, the United States earned $12.7 billion dollars more foreign exchange than it spent. How did the U.S. economy achieve this favorable balance in its current account? We can examine the various entries in the current account to find out.

In 1975 the United States exported more than it imported, a favorable situation (for money flowing in) that has existed in nearly every year in the twentieth century. The favorable trade gap, however, was much smaller in the 1970s than it had been in the 1950s. In fact, in some recent years the United States has actu-

---

Table 34.2 **Current Account of U.S. Balance of Payments for 1975 (in billions of dollars)**

Transactions that created a supply of foreign exchange		Transactions that created a demand for foreign exchange	
U.S. exports of merchandise	$107.1	U.S. imports of merchandise	$ 98.1
Purchases of transportation, insurance and other private services (net)	2.2	Pensions, gifts, and other transfers (net)	1.8
Income from foreign investments	17.9	Foreigners' income from U.S. investments	11.8
		U.S. government grants to foreigners	2.8
Totals	$127.2		$114.5
Net Balance	12.7		

Source: *Federal Reserve Bulletin*, April 1976, p. A58.

ally had an unfavorable balance of trade; that is, U.S. imports exceeded U.S. exports. In 1974, U.S. imports exceeded U.S. exports by $5.4 billion! In the latest available data U.S. imports exceeded our exports by $1.8 billion in the one month of February 1977 (partly due to unusually cold weather)!

In the 1950s the U.S. economy had done most of the exporting and little importing; and all other countries complained of dollar shortages needed to pay for their imports. By 1970 the flows of merchandise were more equal. Thus Japanese exports were only 2 percent of U.S. exports in 1948 but rose to 58 percent in 1972. Exports of the European economic community rose from 53 percent of U.S. exports in 1948 to 254 percent in 1972. Even exports of the Communist countries rose from 30 percent of U.S. exports in 1948 to 79 percent in 1969.[20]

Secondly, U.S. firms supplied slightly more transport and other services to foreigners than vice versa. The gap here has also narrowed, but it is a smaller item. Finally, U.S. income from private investments abroad—profits and interest—is far higher than the income of foreigners from investments in the U.S. economy. The figures in Table 34.2 show only the net amounts by which transportation and other services created a supply of foreign exchange.

Unfortunately, as Table 34.3 shows, there are other transactions influencing the balance of payments. For one thing, the outflow of money into U.S. investments abroad is a much higher than the inflow of foreign investments to the United States (but remember the offsetting profit flows). In most recent years the military items have been very important. U.S. firms bring in money by selling military supplies to other countries. In general, however, the outflow of U.S. government money for military purchases abroad and military and economic aid to an assortment of dictators abroad has been much larger. In 1975 the deficit was only about $800 million. In each of the two previous years, however, it had been over $2 billion.

This outflow of money for military purposes is obviously linked to U.S. opposi-

---

Table 34.3   **Remainder of U.S. Balance of Payments for 1975 (in billions of dollars)**

Transactions that created a supply of foreign exchange		Transactions that created a demand for foreign exchange	
Net balance carried forward from current account	$12.7	Military purchases (net over sales)	$ .8
Foreigners' investments in the U.S.	5.9	U.S. Government investments abroad	1.7
		U.S. private investments abroad	14.7
Totals	$18.6		$17.2
Overall Balance	1.4		

Source: *Federal Reserve Bulletin*, April 1976, p. A58.

---

[20] Ibid., p. 70.

tion to the liberation movements of the Third World. The United States has spent $1.4 trillion on militarism since 1945 at home and abroad.[21] This staggering burden has been a major factor in causing both inflation at home and balance of payments difficulties abroad.

The balance of payments for 1975 shows a surplus of $1.4 billion. This was a most unusual year. In nearly every year since the 1950s the U.S. has had a deficit in its balance of payments. In 1974, for example, the deficit was $10.7 billion and preliminary figures show a sizable deficit in 1976 (the 1976 final figures were not available when this was written).

THE INTERNATIONAL MONETARY CRISIS

Because the United States spends more abroad nearly every year than it takes in, this payment deficit must somehow be balanced in the foreign area. The deficit was actually made up in two ways. The United States paid out gold and foreigners were forced to extend low-cost loans to Americans.

The first way, the drain of U.S. gold stock to foreign countries, is easy to understand. When U.S. corporations and the U.S. government spend more abroad than they earn from trade and investments, then some of the difference is paid in gold. In 1945 the United States had 75 percent of the world's gold reserves. But two-thirds of that gold stock has now fled abroad. By 1968 American reserves had fallen to only $15 billion, or less than the $24 billion of the European Economic Community alone.[22]

The second source for financing excess foreign investments has been cheap foreign loans. To understand why foreigners must make these loans, consider the role of the American dollar in the financing of international transactions. Since every country has a different currency and some of the currencies have unstable values, it is necessary to have a currency with which to conduct international business. The American dollar is used far more extensively than any other currency for this purpose. The American dollar is, then, the currency of which other countries must keep a balance in order to facilitate their foreign financial transactions, just as the individual must keep a small balance of currency to finance his day-to-day transactions.

But the worldwide volume of international transactions has grown rapidly and continuously since World War II. This means other countries have been forced continuously to build up their American dollar bank balances. If U.S. currency were not the international medium of exchange, foreigners would immediately demand that the dollars be taken back in exchange for more U.S. exports or for gold. These commodity exports or gold exports would represent the *real* payment for the foreign resources U.S. corporations have taken over. But because foreign countries must continuously build up American dollar balances if they are to continue to engage in international transactions, they are forced to keep them. This means they get no real payment for the resources they hand over to U.S. corporations. They are in effect extending low-cost loans that need never be repaid as long as the American dollar is the international medium of exchange.

[21] Sidney Lens, "The Shortage Economy," in Mermelstein, op. cit., p. 107.
[22] Ibid., p. 107.

By 1972 foreigners in the rest of the world held 82 billion U.S. dollars.[23] They were accepted because the dollar is used in international trade and was allegedly as good as gold. But the strength of the dollar was declining, both because of the gold and dollar drain outward and because of U.S. inflation. Fewer U.S. goods could be bought with a dollar, so there was pressure for a lower exchange rate of dollars to other currency.

Although U.S. business and the U.S. government had spent too many dollars abroad, the United States tried to maintain a fixed rate of exchange and to force foreigners to hold on to large reserves of dollars. In 1968 and again in early 1971, attempts by foreigners to convert their dollar holdings into gold or into other currencies created minor crises. Throughout the 1960s and early 1970s, it had been obvious that the size of the recurring American balance-of-payments deficit was too large. This meant U.S. currency was *overvalued*—that is, in order to make the deficit manageable, the value of the U.S. dollar should be decreased. Otherwise, the value of undervalued currencies such as the German DM or the Japanese yen should be increased.

The problem with removing the fixed exchange rate for dollars was that in 1970 foreigners held $43.3 billion in American dollars.[24] If the value of the American dollar were decreased by 10 percent, these foreigners would suddenly lose the equivalent of about $4.33 billion. This large amount of wealth would simply evaporate. Consequently, if foreigners received the slightest hint that the American dollar was about to be devalued, they immediately sought to exchange their dollars for gold or other currencies before the devaluation could take place.

In the 1968 and early 1971 crises, the governments of the United States and the western European countries succeeded in convincing dollar holders that the exchange value of the dollar would be maintained. This averted a major crisis, but the problem remained. If the United States continued to spend lavishly on a worldwide military empire and continued to attempt to extend its worldwide economic hegemony, then the pressure of foreigners attempting to convert unwanted dollar balances into gold or other currencies would constantly present the threat of a worldwide run on the dollar any time the fear of devaluation became widespread. Most economists agreed that if such a run on American dollars were to develop, the international monetary structure would collapse. If this were to occur, foreign trade would undoubtedly be drastically reduced, as it was after the international financial crisis of the early 1930s.

In the face of these dangers President Nixon took drastic action on August 15, 1971. The fact that America's exports were substantially less than its imports for the first time in many years precipitated extreme policy measures. In order to end America's persistent balance-of-payments deficit, the President did three things. First, he imposed a 10 percent tariff surcharge. In order to reduce demand for imports, Americans were forced to pay 10 percent more for all imported foreign goods. Second, the President announced a 90-day wage-price freeze (with wages frozen but leaving profits free to increase). This was designed mainly for domestic effects, but its foreign effect was to make American exports more competititive in foreign markets.

The third and most extreme measure taken by the President was to sever the

---

[23] Ibid, p. 107.
[24] *Federal Reserve Bulletin*, April 1971, p. 270.

direct link between the American dollar and gold. The American dollar had maintained a fixed exchange rate with other currencies by maintaining a fixed price of gold. Since the value of gold in terms of other currencies was also fixed, this fixed the exchange rates between any two currencies. For example, if gold costs 35 American dollars per ounce and also 15 British pounds per ounce, then the price (in American dollars) of one British pound would be fixed at $2.33.

When the President cut the tie between gold and the American dollar, the United States no longer had a fixed exchange rate. The value of the dollar in relation to other currencies was allowed to fluctuate according to supply and demand.

It soon became apparent, however, that other countries were unwilling to allow their currencies to appreciate substantially in relation to the American dollar. The entire capitalist world was experiencing a recession during this period, and a decline in the value of the American dollar would stimulate demand for American exports because they would now cost foreigners less of their own currency. This increased export demand would add to aggregate demand in the United States and help us pull out of our recession. But by the same reasoning, an upward revaluation of foreign currencies in relation to the American dollar would decrease the exports of these countries to the United States because they would cost Americans more dollars than before. The decreased demand for their exports would decrease aggregate demand in these countries, worsening the problems of recession and unemployment.

By December 18, 1971, the American dollar had depreciated by over 10 percent. That meant, of course, that holders of American dollars had lost nearly $4 billion because of the dollar's depreciated value. Resistance to further depreciation had stiffened appreciably, so the United States returned to a fixed exchange rate on that date.

Over the next year and a half, it required extensive intervention in the foreign exchange market by various governments and central banks to maintain that fixed exchange rate. It became increasingly obvious that some fundamental realignment of currency values was needed. By early 1973 the economic situation in the capitalist world had changed from one in which recession and unemployment were the principal problems to one in which rapid inflation was the main concern. The United States took advantage of this economic change and in March 1973 announced that once again the dollar was to be allowed to fluctuate according to supply and demand.

Since that time the dollar has dropped in value in a number of periods. Yet the U.S. government and other governments have also worked to stabilize it. Moreover, when the European economies themselves weakened in the stagflation of 1974–1975, their currencies did not remain stronger than the dollar.

It is important to understand the domestic impact of these international payments and monetary problems. When different capitalist countries wish to help their firms compete for the export market, they traditionally do this by lowering wage costs. Wages may be held down by direct controls a la Nixon, or by increasing unemployment through restrictive monetary and fiscal controls. Real wages may also be reduced by lowering the exchange value of the dollar or by higher tariffs, in either case causing higher prices for imported goods. The idea of the Nixon-Ford administration was to end the international U.S. payments deficit by selling U.S. goods more cheaply on the basis of lower wages, or by forcing U.S. consumers to buy fewer imports (German beer or small foreign cars) through higher prices for these goods. Thus the international problems were seen as constraints or excuses for greater burdens on American workers in the shape of lower wages and unemployment as well as more inflation. The inflationary policy is particularly evident in President Ford's efforts to increase oil prices. So far, the Carter administration seems to be following similar policies under energy Tsar, James Schlesinger.

SHORTAGES

International shortages—that is, supply less than demand at present prices— certainly played a part in the inflationary spiral. These shortages, however, were not natural accidents (except in a few minor cases) nor were they acts of God; they were clearly contrived by human actors. In the case of food and fuels, the two most important categories, conservatives have blamed Soviet wheat buyers and Arab oil sheiks.

The evidence, however, indicates that the blame for the oil "shortage" must be placed much closer to home than Arabia. One careful investigator writes indignantly that it is hypocritical to blame the raw material producing countries for inflation. He stresses the fact that

> the major imperialist powers control the marketing of raw materials—so that even when nationalizations are undertaken, profits are not seriously threatened. But most of the world's raw materials continue to be owned by the major imperialist monopolies, above all by U.S. firms.[25]

For many decades U.S. and western European based global corporations controlled all the oil production and made astonishingly high rates of profit. In the late 1960s and early 1970s, it was those global corporations that decided to restrict the expansion of supply—by reducing oil exploration or the building of new refineries, as discussed in Chapter 33—and thereby created an artificial shortage designed to raise prices. The Arab oil embargo was used as an excuse to make rapid price increases.

It is true that in recent years some of the oil-producing countries have taken larger shares of revenue by taxes or even by nationalization. They were able to do this by the increased power of the whole Third World and the Communist countries, so this does represent a shift of power that accounts for some small part of the U.S. and western European inflation. It has meant the rise of a new ruling class in the Arab countries, Iran, and Venezuela that is a peculiar combination of semifeudal attitudes, capitalist production, and some financial capitalist power—though they still act closely in coordination with the global corporations to the benefit of both parties.

Nor have the global corporations lost much, if anything; they are simply getting some new stockholders and new forms. Most of the production and financing companies in the oil-producing countries are not publicly owned even today (and most other raw materials are purely private). For example, in Kuwait one

[25] Dick Roberts, "Ripening Conditions for Worldwide Depression," in Mermelstein, op. cit., p. 97.

investment company is 25 percent privately owned and the other is 50 percent privately owned, with about half the private stock being foreign owned.[26] But even if production is all nationalized, the fact—as pointed out in the quotation above—is that the global corporations continue to control all the distribution and marketing of oil. Therefore, it is the global corporations who set the market prices, determine their profit margins, and continue to make enormous profits.

There are several facts indicating that the Arab oil boycott was nothing more than an excuse for the monopolies to raise prices. First, 60 percent of U.S. oil is produced at home and is unaffected by Arab production costs, yet the price of U.S. crude oil rose from $3.50 to $7.00 a barrel. Second, from March 1973 to March 1974 Arab oil producers raised their taxes by 17 cents a barrel, but U.S. gasoline prices rose almost 30 cents a gallon for all gas, regardless of origin. Third, the U.S. government allows the oil companies to deduct all payments to foreign governments from their U.S. taxes, so this cost was passed on to all other U.S. taxpayers (in addition to passing it on to consumers at the pump). Finally, the minute the embargo was over, the companies suddenly found large reserves of oil on hand, so they didn't need to buy any more but did not lower the prices.[27]

The high price of U.S. food was blamed on a shortage created by sales to the Soviet Union. Yet the main blame seems to fall on agribusiness and the U.S. government. First of all, for many years the U.S. government paid large farm subsidies to get farmers *not* to plant food over large areas of the best farmland. "As late as 1973, after the shortages of 1972, the government was still paying over $3 billion to keep roughly 50 million productive acres out of farming use."[28] Then, when deficits in the balance of payments became a problem the U.S. government reversed itself and tried to stimulate production, not for domestic consumption but for exports. The government encouraged the export of food as fast and as fully as possible in order to get foreign currency to pay for U.S. investment and military spending abroad. Thus, exports of U.S. food on the world market tripled between 1969 and 1973 as a result of careful planning by agribusiness and the government.[29] Of this enormous planned outflow of food for profit, the Soviet wheat deal formed a very minor part even of the sales of wheat.

In conclusion, the inflation and the so-called shortages have several not surprising bases. The inflation was not caused by accidental natural calamities because these tend to even out over a few years time. The inflation, however, has not evened out but has picked up over some years. A small part was caused by a shift in power toward the Arab ruling classes away from the oil companies. But this was fairly minor and cannot account for the long inflation. Most of the inflation and "shortages" were caused by the global monopolies in collusion with the U.S. government, begun by the Vietnam War spending and always made worse by the continued excessive outflow of money for military purchases and military aid abroad.

[26] Ernest Mandel, "The Emergence of Arab and Iranian Finance Capital," in Mermelstein, op. cit., p. 316.

[27] David Pugh and Mitch Zimmerman, "The 'Energy Crisis' And the Real Crisis Behind It," in Mermelstein, op. cit., pp. 278–279.

[28] Union for Radical Political Economics, National Food Collective, "The Capitalist Food System," in Mermelstein, op. cit., p. 357.

[29] Ibid., p. 359.

SUMMARY

International economic transactions differ from those within national boundaries. The two main differences are (1) different currencies are involved and must be exchanged and (2) differing economic and political relations exist among nations, with some dominant, others subordinate, and others in intermediate positions.

The balance of payments is an accounting of all transactions between the residents of one country and the rest of the world. It summarizes the country's sources of foreign exchange and the uses to which the foreign exchange is put. The fact that the American dollar has been widely used as an international currency has helped finance a worldwide military network as well as an ever-increasing private economic empire acquired through American investment abroad. However, recurring deficits in the American balance of payments forced President Nixon to take steps on August 15, 1971, that led to a devaluation of the American dollar in relation to other major currencies. This is likely to reduce the acceptability of the American dollar as an international medium of exchange.

APPENDIX

THE GAINS FROM INTERNATIONAL TRADE

The most obvious reason why nations engage in foreign trade is that many commodities cannot be grown or produced in certain regions of the world. Without foreign trade Americans would be unable to purchase coffee, cocoa, tea, coconuts, bananas, or any of a large number of commodities that cannot be produced in the United States. In addition to these consumer commodities, the United States depends heavily on imports for many of the most important minerals. In the late 1960s, for example, imports of iron ore were equivalent to 43 percent of the amount mined domestically; for copper, the figure was 18 percent; for lead, 131 percent; for zinc, 140 percent; for bauxite, 638 percent; and for petroleum, 31 percent. This partial listing alone indicates how crucial imports of agricultural products and minerals are to the American economy.

The United States can also gain from importing manufactured commodities if the *relative* costs of producing two commodities differ between the United States and some other country. To illustrate this, let us return to the example of beer and Coca-Cola.

Assume that the United States and Germany each produce all the beer and Coca-Cola they consume domestically. Assume further that in the United States the average annual production per worker of beer is 5000 gallons and of Coca-Cola is 7500 gallons. Assume further that in Germany the figures are 4000 gallons (beer) and 3000 gallons (Coca-Cola). Table 34A.1 shows hypothetical prices for the two commodities (German prices are given in dollars for easier comparison) in the two countries. These prices reflect ratios of labor productivity.

From these figures we see that the United States is more efficient in the production of both beer and Coca-Cola. Economists would say that the United States has an *absolute advantage* in the production of both commodities. It might seem that the United States would be better off not to import either beer or Coca-

Table 34A.1 **Price Per Gallon of Beer and Coca-Cola in the United States and Germany Before Trade (in dollars)**

	United States		Germany	
Beer	$0.60	Beer		$0.75
Coca-Cola	0.40	Coca-Cola		1.00

Cola from Germany because it can produce both more efficiently. This is not true, however. It would pay the United States to import beer and export Coca-Cola because the United States has a comparative advantage in the production of Coca-Cola and Germany has a comparative advantage in the production of beer.

The existence of a comparative advantage depends on the *relative* costs of the two commodities, not the absolute efficiency in producing them. In the United States beer costs 50 percent more to produce than Coca-Cola, whereas in Germany, beer costs 25 percent less to produce than Coca-Cola. Therefore relative to the cost of producing Coca-Cola, Germany is more efficient in producing beer. Similarly, in the United States, Coca-Cola costs 33 percent less to produce than beer, whereas in Germany, Coca-Cola costs 33 percent more to produce than beer. Therefore relative to the cost of producing beer, the United States is more efficient in producing Coca-Cola.

Assume that the United States persuades Germany to exchange beer for American Coca-Cola at the prices prevailing in Germany. Some American workers will be shifted from beer production to Coca-Cola production. For each worker transferred from producing beer to producing Coca-Cola, the United States will lose 5000 gallons of beer (which the worker will no longer produce) and gain 7500 gallons of Coca-Cola (which the workers will begin to produce). This Coca-Cola can be sold in Germany for $7500 (because the price of Coca-Cola is $1 per gallon in Germany). Then, paying the German price of 75 cents per gallon for beer, the United States can use the proceeds to purchase 10,000 gallons of beer.

The final result of this series of events will be that for every worker in the United States shifted from beer production to Coca-Cola production, the United States will lose 5000 gallons of domestically produced beer but gain 10,000 gallons of German-produced beer. Obviously the United States will be better off after the trade. But the prices at which the two countries traded are identical to the German prices before trade. This means that the United States received all of the gains from trade and Germany received no gains at all.

Assume now that Germany persuades the United States to trade at the prices prevailing in the United States. Then Germany will receive all of the gains from trade. When the Germans shift a worker from production of Coca-Cola to production of beer, the worker will produce 4000 gallons of beer (rather than 3000 gallons of the Coca-Cola). This beer will be sold in the United States (at 60 cents per gallon) for $2400. With the proceeds of this sale the Germans can purchase 6000 gallons of Coca-Cola (at the rate of 40 cents per gallon). Thus if trade occurs at the U.S. prices, the Germans will shift workers from production of Coca-Cola to production of beer, which they will export to the United States. In doing so they will lose 3000 gallons of domestically produced Coca-Cola for every worker so shifted, but they will gain 6000 gallons of American-produced Coca-Cola. Obviously this situation benefits the Germans.

From these examples two conclusions can be drawn: (1) If the relative costs of producing two commodities in two countries differ, then trade can benefit one or both of the countries, and (2) if the prices at which trade takes place are the same as those prevailing in one country before trade began, then that country receives none of the gains from trade and the other receives all of the gains.

We can draw a third conclusion, which is undoubtedly obvious from the preceding discussion: If the ratio of prices at which trade takes place lies somewhere between the price ratios in the two countries, then both countries will share in the gains from trade. If, in the beer-Coca-Cola example, the United States and Germany traded at the rate of one gallon of beer equals one gallon of Coca-Cola, then both countries would benefit from trade. The reader can calculate the gains in each country as workers are shifted to export production. Such a calculation will verify the fact that both countries would benefit from trade at a price ratio that lies between the two domestic price ratios.

When two countries engage in trade, the one that is able to exert the greater bargaining power will succeed in pushing the trade prices closer to the ratio of prices and production costs of the other country. In doing this the more powerful country will reap most of the gains from trade. Many economists have collected evidence to show that in the trade that takes place between advanced, industrialized countries and less developed agricultural countries, the industrialized countries reap nearly all of the benefits.[1]

THE CASE FOR FREE TRADE

To what extent ought a country to engage in international trade? Nearly 200 years ago the classical economists (particularly David Ricardo) developed the analysis of comparative advantage and correctly identified the economic gains that two trading partners can secure. On the basis of this analysis they concluded that as long as anyone in either of the two countries desired to engage in further trade, then it was possible to reap more gains from trade. In practice this meant the government ought to place no restrictions on trade. People should be free to trade to any extent they wished. This conclusion was an integral part of the general laissez-faire policy advocated by the classical economists.[2]

Over the past 200 years most orthodox economists have advocated free trade. They have extended and refined their analyses of comparative advantage and the gains from trade, but they have not altered the essential argument. They have consistently contended that any restrictions on international trade will reduce the volume of trade and that any reduction of volume will reduce the gains from trade. Therefore most economists have concluded that restrictions on international trade reduce a nation's economic welfare.

The consistent advocacy of free trade might seem surprising in view of the fact that only rarely during the past 200 years have the governments of the major capitalist countries pursued such a policy. Most of the time they have erected a wall of tariffs to keep out foreign goods. A tariff is a tax on an import that forces the importer to charge a higher price to the general public in order to pay the tariff. Thus the tariff is really a tax paid by the consumer of the import.

Tariffs have usually been imposed for two reasons. First, in the nineteenth century the American government used the tariff as its chief source of tax rev-

---

[1] See, for example, U.N. Economic Commission for Latin America, *The Economic Development of Latin America and Some of Its Problems* (New York, 1949); Raoul Prebisch, "The Role of Commercial Policies in Underdeveloped Countries," *American Economic Review*, May 1959; and Hans Singer, "The Distribution of Gains Between Investing and Borrowing Countries," *American Economic Review*, May 1950.

[2] See Chapter 4.

enue. Second, industries that must compete with foreign producers for the domestic market have lobbied for tariffs to protect their monopoly power from foreign competition. Because neither of these reasons would be particularly appealing to the general public, many arguments with greater popularity have been put forward. Historically there have been three very common arguments for tariffs in the United States. Economists consider them all fallacious. We shall examine each.

1. It is often argued that tariffs protect American workers from competition from foreign workers who are paid very low wages. This argument concludes that tariffs maintain higher wage rates for American workers. While free trade may hurt the workers in industries that are undersold by foreign competitors (the workers will probably have to transfer to new occupations), it should raise the overall wage level. This is because, as we have seen, the total output available for consumption increases after trade. It seems unlikely that workers would not share in this increase.

2. It is sometimes proposed that tariffs are ideal taxes because the foreign exporter pays the tax. As we have already noted, however, the American importer is forced to raise the price that is charged to the American customers. Therefore the American public pays most of the tax in the form of higher prices for the commodities it consumes.

3. Finally, there are the campaigns to "buy American products" to "keep money in the United States." This simplistic argument assumes that when imports are purchased, money leaves the country, and that if they had not been purchased, consumers would have bought American-produced commodities. It is argued that purchasing foreign products deprives American business people of sales and American workers of jobs. The problem with this argument is that it ignores the fact that when the United States engages in foreign trade commodities are *exported* as well as imported. The foreign demand for U.S. exports increases the sales of American business people and creates jobs for American workers.

There are other arguments for tariffs, some not so obviously fallacious as those we have discussed. Most economists agree, however, that in a powerful, industrialized economy like the United States, there are really no convincing arguments for tariffs. The few problems tariffs might help solve (e.g., industrial relocations or regional economic depressions) could certainly be solved more efficaciously by other, more direct government policies.

What is true for industrialized countries, however, is not necessarily true for less developed countries. Many less developed countries have become suppliers of raw materials and agricultural products for industrial countries. They generally receive such low prices for their exports that their standard of living remains abysmally low. If they engage in free trade, small local manufacturing industries cannot hope to compete with foreign giants. As a consequence, industrialization takes place very slowly, if at all. These countries would certainly be justified in placing some kind of restrictions on imports as an aid to industrialization. The issues involved in the relationship between advanced, industrialized countries and less developed ones will be considered in the next chapter.

CHAPTER 35

ECONOMIC UNDERDEVELOPMENT:

Natural Causes or Imperialism?

In Chapter 32 the problems of economic growth in developed industrial economies were considered. In economies that have not industrialized, the problems of economic growth are substantially and qualitatively different from those examined in Chapter 32. Before meaningful growth in per capita output and income can take place in these economies, they must undertake industrialization.

The economic, social, and political obstacles to industrialization are different from the problems of advanced industrial countries. Economic growth in the developed countries means mere incremental additions to output within an established structure. Development of the less developed countries means basic social, political, and structural economic changes to lay the foundations for growth.

It is therefore necessary to devote an additional chapter to the question of economic development. The countries of the world are commonly divided into three groups: (1) socialist countries, (2) industrially developed capitalist countries, and (3) underdeveloped capitalist countries, or the *Third World*. It is with this third group that we shall be concerned in this chapter.

FACTS OF ECONOMIC UNDERDEVELOPMENT

There are at least two generally accepted definitions of a *less developed* country, one based on an economic index and the other based on certain distinguishing characteristics. The economic index generally employed is average income per person (GNP divided by population). According to this criterion, a country with an average income per person of less than some amount—say, $200 or $300 per year—is classified as less developed.

The phrase *less developed,* it must be emphasized, has misleading sociological connotations. For example, there is no correlation between level of income and level of cultural or social development. Obviously ancient Greece or Egypt or China had very highly developed cultures and very low average income levels. Further, an average may hide wide disparities in individual incomes. For example, Kuwait has one of the highest levels of average income per head; but most of the income is concentrated in the hands of a few very rich people, and there is an enormous gulf between the very rich and the very poor (despite Kuwait's much-publicized welfare handouts). The high average income per Kuwaiti is solely the result of this little country's oil resources, and therefore one cannot assume that it is highly developed in an overall sense.

Dissatisfaction with the use of a single, purely economic measure of underdevelopment has led some students of the subject to suggest a definition based on several distinguishing characteristics of less developed countries: (1) low income per person, (2) the existence of a very high portion (often 80 percent or more) of the population engaged in agriculture, (3) a low level of techniques used in production, (4) a low level of education, and (5) a low level of capital formation.

According to any definition of developed and less developed, the fact is that more than 50 percent of the population of the capitalist, or private enterprise, world live in countries that can be classified as less developed. The enormity of the problem is indicated by the estimate that to raise the incomes of the portion of the world's population living in these countries to an average of only $200 per person per year (less than one-tenth of the average American income), about $85 billion of aid per year would be needed.[1]

Among private enterprise, or capitalist, countries in the lowest category, with income per person less than $100 per year (and mostly agrarian and lacking in technology, education, or capital) fall India, most of Asia, and most of Africa. In the second category, with income per person between $100 and $300 a year (and still very underdeveloped in all other indexes), are most of Latin America, North Africa, Indonesia, and the Philippines. In the third category ($300–600; still very poor, but slightly developed in some aspects) are a few Latin American countries, the Union of South Africa, Greece, and Spain. The fourth category ($600–1500; well developed in many aspects) includes Israel, Australia and New Zealand, Japan, and most of western Europe. In a category by themselves are Canada and the United States with over $2500 of income per person per year. (Kuwait and Qatar are also listed in this category, but these are tiny areas sitting on top of oil wells, with most of the income going to a few sheiks.)

In the advanced capitalist countries workers' wages have grown greatly in the past 100 years. But conditions in most of the capitalist world, its less developed part, have shown little or no improvement, and incomes remain at incredibly low levels. Most African and Asian incomes are less than one-tenth, and most Latin American incomes are about one-fifth, of the average income in the advanced capitalist countries. In fact, many of them are not only below poverty but also below subsistence levels. "Two-thirds of the inhabitants of the underdeveloped countries of the Third World do not get the essential minimum of 2,500 calories per day; the expectation of life for many of them is less than half that in the highly developed countries."[2]

The gap between rich and poor is reflected in the fact that in 1964 two-thirds of the world's population produced only about 25 percent of world output. At the

[1] See Frederic Benham, *Economic Aid to Underdeveloped Countries* (London: Oxford University Press, 1961); all figures given here are in terms of the worth of the U.S. dollar in 1960.

[2] Perre Jalee, *The Pillage of the Third World* (New York: Monthly Review Press, 1965), p. 8.

same time, the United States alone (with only 6 percent of world population) produced about 30 percent of world output.

And the gap is widening.

In the whole period 1953–1964 the advanced capitalist countries showed rates of growth twice as rapid as those of the less developed capitalist countries.[3] Thus the advanced capitalist countries outproduced the less developed ones (in product per person) by 10:1 in 1950 but by 11:1 in 1960 and almost 12:1 in 1969.[4]

COLONIALISM AND NEOCOLONIALISM

It will help us to understand the current economic, social, and political conditions of less developed countries if we briefly examine some aspects of their history. In particular, we are interested in their relationships with the economically more advanced countries over the last several centuries.

From the fifteenth century onward, the developing capitalist economies of Europe grew economically and militarily at a rate then unparalleled in human history. From the fifteenth to the nineteenth centuries, they slowly came to dominate much of the rest of the world. They plundered, enslaved, and ruled so as to extract the maximum from their subjects.

Such havoc was created that ancient and culturally advanced civilizations disappeared, as in Peru and West Africa, and progress was set back hundreds of years by the destruction of native industries, as in India. On the other side, the plunder was so great that it constituted the main element in the formation of European capital and provided the foundation for prosperous trade and eventual industrialization.

By the end of the nineteenth century, almost all of the present less developed countries were under the colonial rule of the more advanced countries. The imperialist countries invested in the colonial countries at astoundingly high profit rates, primarily because of a cheap labor supply and enforced lack of competition. The capital was invested mainly in extractive industries, which exported raw materials to the imperial country. In the imperial country, the cheap raw materials were profitably turned into manufactured goods, part of which were exported back (tariff free) to the colonial country.

The tariff-free imported finished goods generally completed through competition the destruction (often begun by plunder) of the colonial country's manufacturing industries. An example of this may be seen in colonial India, especially in its textile industry:

> India, still an exporter of manufactured products at the end of the eighteenth century, becomes an importer. From 1815 to 1832, India's cotton exports dropped by 92 percent. In 1850, India was buying one quarter of Britain's cotton exports. All industrial products shared this fate. The ruin of the traditional trades and crafts was the result of British commerical policy.[5]

The development of the colonial areas was thus held back by the imperialist

---

[3] Ibid., p. 11.

[4] Jalee, loc. cit., and current UN data.

[5] Charles Bettleheim, *India Independent* (New York: Monthly Review Press, 1968), p. 47. Also see Romesh Dutt, *The Economic History of England* (7th ed., London: Routledge & Kegan Paul, 1950), pp. viii–x.

countries, while the development of the imperialist countries was greatly speeded by the flow of plunder and profits from the colonies. The exception that proves the rule is Japan. Japan escaped colonialism as a result of several more or less accidental factors. Thus it was able independently to industrialize and develop its own advanced capitalist economy. Japan achieved this alone among the countries of Asia, Africa, and Latin America because the others had all been reduced to colonies and had their futher development prevented.

The half-century from 1890 to World War II was the peak period of colonialism, when all the world was divided among the western European and North American powers. In the late 1940s and 1950s, a new era began, with formal independence achieved by hundreds of millions of people throughout Asia and Africa as a result of struggles fomented by the impact of two world wars, the Russian and Chinese revolutions, and long-pent-up pressures for liberation. The day of open colonialism is over, but the pattern still holds by which the ex-colonial countries export food or raw materials. In fact, the less developed countries are often dependent mainly on exports of just one product, and they still import most of their finished goods. Foreign investment still dominates their industries. Because of the continuance of the underlying colonial economic patter, we are justified in describing this situation as *neocolonialism,* in spite of formal political independence.

In fact, formal independence has changed the essential economic relationships very little. On the one side are all the less developed, newly independent countries, still under foreign economic domination, still facing all the old obstacles to development. On the other side are the advanced capitalist countries, still extracting large profits from the dependent Third World. The imperialist group includes all the countries that extract profits by trade and investment. Thus it includes most of western Europe, Japan, and the United States. Neocolonial profits from the less developed countries flow even to countries like Switzerland that never held colonial power over any less developed country.

Although there are still cases of direct occupation (e.g., the Panama Canal), most neocolonial control comes through economic and monetary penetration. This ranges from blatant forms such as subsidies and military supplies to highly complex monetary agreements. It also seems to be characteristic to grant independence to small territories, tiny divisions of former colonial domains. Thus they have no political or economic power with which to resist continued domination.

It should also be noted that the economic control often is not direct but built up in a complex pyramid. For example, some American companies directly invest in northeast Brazil. More control of that area, however, is achieved through American domination of major southern Brazilian companies, which, in turn, buy controlling interests in companies in the northeast. Still more control is achieved through American domination of some western European companies, which, in turn, own some major Brazilian firms or directly own some of the local firms in the northeast.

OBSTACLES TO DEVELOPMENT

Is overpopulation the primary obstacle to economic development? This view is widely held by the average man in the street, many newspaper reporters, even some university professors. Little systematic evidence is presented to substantiate it. Generally proponents merely point to the vast number of poor and starving people in India as an example. Even such an eminent "economist" as Robert S. McNamara (former president of Ford Motor Company and former U.S. secretary of defense) asserts that "the greatest single obstacle to the economic and social advancement of the majority of the peoples in the underdeveloped world is rampant population growth."[6]

The important point to note about McNamara's ideology is that it tells the hungry people that the "greatest single obstacle" to their development is their own animal sexual desires. The function of this ideology is thus identical to that of the theory that underdevelopment is due to racial inferiority, the laziness and/or stupidity of "the natives." It provides the perfect defense to the suspicion of these peoples that their problems are due to antiquated social systems, rapacious ruling classes, and above all, foreign domination and exploitation.

If one turns to the facts, there is no evidence that high population density is the prime cause of underdevelopment. More precisely, there is no statistically significant correlation between high population density and low income per person. On the contrary, many countries with high incomes per person also have high population densities. For example, Belgium has 816 people per square mile, West Germany has 624, and the United Kingdom has 588. India has only 406 people per square mile, and most of the less developed countries have much lower population densities.

In fact, we find many cases of concomitant successful development with rapid population increase. The highest recorded rate of population growth over a long period occurred in the United States during the years 1850–1950; but because U.S. production also grew at record rates, America not only became a developed country but also had record growth rates of output *per person,* and thus individual welfare improved.

Of course if a country is standing still economically, any growth of population is a terrible problem. We do not deny that overpopulation can be a problem; we only maintain that it is always *relative* to growth of output. The basic problems are seen when we try to explain why output is rising so slowly in less developed countries. Although population is a problem, it is secondary to these larger problems, and exclusive focus on it tends to hide the more important problems.

Moreover, it turns out that the key to reducing population growth is development of industrialization and urbanization. A rural family with a primitive technology finds young children useful for many tasks. An urban family in an industrialized country sees children as an economic burden until they have undergone a long education. Furthermore, birth control information is much more effective in an urban setting in which a woman may find cultural interests outside the home and needs family planning to develop her own independent life. Thus all the developed areas from the United States to the Soviet Union have witnessed rapid declines in birth rates as the agrarian sector has shrunk and education and culture have spread as a result of economic development.

Another theory of underdevelopment claims that the less developed nations

---

[6] Robert S. McNamara, "Introduction" to H. Gray and Shanti Tangri, eds., *Economic Development and Population Growth, A Conflict?* (Lexington, Mass.: Raytheon/Heath, 1970). All of the Western experts in the collection simply assume (or present inadequate proofs of) McNamara's ideology.

are all those that by accident have relatively few natural resources on their territories. Yet the less developed countries in 1965 provided 37.5 percent of the total output of raw materials in the capitalist world, including the bulk of many strategic materials. This is certainly a large enough absolute amount for a solid industrial base. But the less developed countries do not produce anything like 37.5 percent of manufactured goods. In fact, most of their raw materials are taken away to the advanced capitalist countries and are there manufactured into finished goods (some of them being sold back at a high profit to the less developed countries).

It appears, therefore, that the main obstacles to development are *not* natural or biological factors inherent in the less developed countries. The main obstacles are *not* sexual desires and procreation, laziness, low intelligence, or lack of natural resources. The obstacles reside in the present social relationships of human to human: the fact that all of the peasants' and workers' surplus over immediate needs is extracted from them by the landlords, moneylenders, tax collectors, and foreign corporations. We shall show that the native ruling classes use their high incomes for luxury consumption and that most of the foreign corporations' enormous profits are removed from the country.

As a result, there is a lack of capital for investment in development. The lack of capital (and lack of nonhuman power per person) *is* correlated with low income per person.[7] Lack of capital means not only little construction but also little new equipment and little technological improvement. It also means few funds available for education and training, let alone research. Lack of capital also means that millions of workers cannot be employed at a sufficient rate of profit and thus are left unemployed or underemployed. Thus it is the social relationships (and their consequences) that are the real obstacles to development.

As an example, consider the present revolution in agriculture in several less developed countries. In this "green revolution," new types of grains have been introduced, especially in India and Pakistan. They have brought much higher yields, and thus one of the technical barriers to feeding the population seems to be falling. To make efficient use of the new processes and output, however, requires large mechanized farms. Indeed, small peasants are being evicted in growing numbers to make way for large agricultural enterprises. The dispossessed peasants are swelling the ranks of the unemployed in the cities. At the same time, complaints are heard from the large farm owners that there is overproduction of grain relative to the small money demand of the poor. Thus the social relationships form a barrier to technological development.

It is a mere truism to say growth would be faster if the less developed countries had more capital, more technology, and more education and training. In fact, for many less developed capitalist countries, the problem is not a low rate of growth of income per person but no growth at all. Aggregate income does not grow much faster than (and maybe not as fast as) the population. Moreover, a complete change is needed from a rural, agrarian economy to an urban, industrialized economy. The issue, then, is how to *begin* to develop, how to start from little or no growth at all, and how to change the whole economic structure.

We shall argue that the obstacles are mainly institutional: (1) an internal ruling class that spends much of its income on luxuries and government revenues on

[7] See David Landes, *The Unbound Prometheus* (Cambridge, England: Cambridge University Press, 1969).

unnecessary public monuments or military expenditures, (2) foreign trade on very poor terms, which creates an exploitative economic dependence and imports the wrong items for development, and (3) foreign investment in low-priority areas with high profits sent abroad. Notice that this view is quite opposite to the views of most traditional economists.

INTERNAL OBSTACLES TO DEVELOPMENT

Let us begin with the internal obstacles to development created by the less developed countries' social systems. The typical situation finds millions of peasants engaged in subsistence farming, obligated to pay high rents to landlords, high interest to moneylenders, and high taxes to local and national governments. From their original small net products, peasants usually pay more than half to meet these obligations, thus retaining hardly enough for their bare subsistence and none for major improvement or investment.

The landlords and moneylenders take much of the surplus from the peasant and spend it on conspicuous luxury consumption. If they reinvest any, their extreme conservatism prompts them to invest in more land or to send it to some safe foreign country; little, if any, is invested in industry. The governments are mostly dominated by a small elite of wealthy landlords and merchants (in turn, often dominated by foreign elements), who have little motivation to invest government funds in constructive projects; in fact, the advent of industrial capitalism would undermine their power. Most government revenues are spent on military goods and services for the purpose of internal repression. Governments spend some on showcase projects (e.g., sports arenas) or, as in Venezuela, in beautification of the capital city. The little that is invested constructively is usually for roads or ports to serve the needs of foreign investors.

The reactionary ruling groups in the less developed capitalist countries are generally supported by the advanced capitalist countries (including the U.S. State Department). It is not that the U.S. State Department *wants* backwardness and governments dominated by reactionary landlords and military cliques. On the contrary, it would undoubtedly be happier with rapidly developing liberal capitalist countries (with American firms having most of the development investments). The problem is that these areas have only very few and very weak native capitalists who are linked by blood and marriage to the landlords and militarists. The countries are very much a part of the international commercialized capitalist market, but they have no steam to develop their own dynamic capitalism and thus remain appendages of the advanced capitalist countries.

Not only is there no strong group willing to build a liberal capitalism in these countries, but also the real political alternative is usually a left-leaning socialist government. Plans for rapid development have been an essential part of socialist programs, as with the socialist government of Cuba. But these socialist development programs have been violently attacked by the U.S. State Department. In Brazil and Greece and several other countries, very mild socialist governments (whose practical measures only *helped* native small capitalists and were not yet even contemplating socialism) were overthrown by military coups supported by the CIA. Thus the real choice in the less developed countries has not been between landlords and militarists versus liberal capitalists but between landlords and militarists (and a few native capitalists) versus socialist movements (composed of workers and peasants and students). In every case so far the United States has chosen to support reactionary landlords and militarists such as Franco or Ky or Thieu.

THE EFFECTS OF FOREIGN TRADE
ON LESS DEVELOPED COUNTRIES

The colonial era left the economies of the Third World countries very dependent on foreign demand and consequently very sensitive to the foreign business cycle of expansion and depression. It is also a fact that international investments and trade in primary products (i.e., raw materials, both agricultural and mineral) show the greatest fluctuations. "It follows that any country whose economy is intimately dependent on foreign investment or whose trade is greatly dependent on primary commodities will be seriously affected by swings of business arising outside its own borders."[8]

This dependence is recognized in the less developed countries. The government of Ceylon states, "The economy of Ceylon depends almost entirely on its export in tea, rubber and coconut products. . . . About 80 percent of the people are employed directly or indirectly in the production and handling of these exports."[9] The government of Burma says explicitly: ". . . the most important source of unemployment in Burma is a decline in prices of raw materials caused by the depression generated elsewhere."[10]

The statistics for many countries, both developed and less developed, show that (1) a high portion of the demand for their national product is the demand for exports, and (2) exports to the United States constitute a high portion of the total export demand. Thus the United States often absorbs more than half, and always more than one-third, of the exports of Canada, Brazil, Chile, Mexico, the Philippines, and others.[11]

In addition to the special place of dominance of the United States vis-à-vis the less developed Third World, there are some data bearing on the trade relations of all the developed capitalist countries with the Third World.[12] First, in the less developed countries there is rapid growth in production *only* of the raw materials and food products exported to the imperialist countries. Production of goods for internal use in the Third World grows very slowly, if at all.

Second, 73.5 percent of the total trade of the developed capitalist countries is with each other. The continued dependence of the less developed countries, however, is reflected in the fact that fully 74 percent of *their* total trade is with the developed countries. Between 1948 and 1964 there were three important trends: "(1) The commercial growth of the imperialist countries was much greater in value than that of the Third World . . ., (2) the imperialist countries have come to

[8] League of Nations, *Economic Stability in the Post-war World* (Geneva: League of Nations, 1945), p. 103.

[9] United Nations, Department of Economic Affairs, *National and International Measures for Full Employment* (New York: United Nations, 1949), p. 42.

[10] Ibid., p. 21.

[11] See annual reports for all countries in International Monetary Fund, *International Financial Statistics* (Washington, D.C., published annually).

[12] Jalee, op. cit., pp. 25–55.

depend less on the Third World for their exports, and (3) the latter has become more dependent on the countries of the capitalist group."[13]

These data also confirm the picture of the less developed countries as raw material exporters and finished-goods importers. Detailed examination "shows that the trade of the Third World is wildly out of balance: 85 percent of its exports consists of raw materials and another 5 percent of common metals, products of the first state of smelting. Only 10 percent of the total consists of manufactured goods, most of which are textiles. Imports, on the other hand, are predominantly manufactured goods (60 percent of the total)."[14] Because most of the manufactured imports are consumer goods, such a pattern can never lead to development but only to continued dependence.

The situation of dependence is still more exaggerated for each less developed country taken by itself. Each tends to export only one or two goods and to trade with only one or two buyers (so that the buyers can easily exert monopoly power). "For the vast majority of Third World countries the range of products is as narrow as possible; one, or two, or three products often providing three-quarters, or even more, of the trade of a country. The number of countries selling and buying is also very restricted; a single imperialist country usually occupies such a dominant position that it can exercise every kind of pressure."[15] It should be emphasized that the only cases where the former colonial master has not retained control of the Third World countries are cases where control has shifted to the United States—for example, all of Latin America, and parts of Africa and Asia.

In contrast, in recent years the developed capitalist countries' exports have consisted of only 30 percent of raw materials and 70 percent of manufactured goods.[16] In fact, the international division of labor is becoming more and more pronounced rather than equalized. That is to say, the developed countries are producing a larger and larger percentage of the manufactured goods of the capitalist world, and the less developed Third World countries are producing a larger and larger percentage of the raw materials.

There is also a trend toward a worsening balance of trade for the Third World. This trend results from the fact that in the last 15 to 20 years international prices of most products have risen, but prices of most primary products have fallen. Because Third World countries export mainly primary goods, they are receiving lower prices, or less and less in each exchange of goods. The developed capitalist countries are receiving higher prices for their finished goods, or more and more in each exchange. Hence the foreign exchange of the less developed countries is drained off, their development is retarded, and their balance-of-trade positions deteriorate further.

Another aspect of the worsening international payments situation arises from Western control of so-called invisible trade, or services. Over 90 percent of world shipping is controlled by the developed capitalist countries. Between 1951 and 1961 they increased the shipping rates paid by less developed countries by about 60 percent. The countries of Asia, Africa, and Latin America pay over $2

[13] Ibid., p. 32.
[14] Ibid., p. 33.
[15] Ibid., p. 43.
[16] United Nations, *Statistical Yearbook* (New York, published annually).

billion a year in shipping costs and insurance payments. Most of this money accrues to the developed capitalist countries.

We have noted that in recent years the value of the trade among the industrialized capitalist countries has grown much more rapidly than their trade with the Third World. As a result, the Third World's share in the trade of the developed capitalist countries fell from 32 percent in 1948 to 23 percent in 1964.[17]

Do the developed capitalist countries really need the trade of the less developed world as much today as previously? The percentage decline in trade suggests reduced importance. This was a period, however, of rapidly rising world trade; the absolute amount of trade between the two groups *rose* from $12 billion in 1948 to more than $25 billion in 1964. Furthermore, almost all of the increase in trade among countries in the industrialized capitalist bloc was in manufactured goods. While some of these exchanges are urgent, most of them merely increase efficiency; more expensive substitutes could easily be arranged (and, of course there is a heavy flow of luxury consumer goods, which could be ended without causing permanent damage).

The situation is quite different in the trade of the industrialized capitalist bloc with the less developed Third World. This trade is vital and irreplaceable. When developed capitalist countries import major food products and raw materials, they realize that these imports are very important. The food products are essential parts of the diets of Westerners, and the raw materials are indispensable for their factories. The manufactured goods that the underdeveloped countries buy are needed desperately because these countries do very little manufacturing themselves.

FOREIGN INVESTMENT

Much the same picture emerges if we look at American foreign investment. It is often argued that this investment channels American dollars into less developed countries. These dollars, it is claimed, can then be used to finance industrialization in the less developed countries. The data, however, do not confirm this argument. On the contrary, the data reveal that the rates of profit of U.S. firms in the Third World areas are so high that they extract more in profit each year than they put into the area in investment.

The multinational or global firms are the present instrument whereby enormous profits are extracted from the neocolonial countries and sent back to the imperialist countries. U.S. firms' profits from abroad were only 7 percent of total U.S. corporate profits in 1960 but rose to 30 percent by 1974.[18] The top 298 U.S.-based global corporations earn 40 percent of their entire net profits overseas, and their rate of profit from abroad is much higher than their domestic profit rate. In office equipment, for example, the overseas rate was 26 percent and domestic only 9 percent. There is dramatic evidence for specific companies: In 1972, the

[17] Jalee, op. cit., p. 53.
[18] See Ronald Muller, "Global Corporations and National Stabilization Policy," *Journal of Economic Issues,* vol. 9, June 1975, p. 183.

overseas profit rate was 72 percent for United Brands, 51 percent for Parker Pen, and 53 percent for Exxon.[19]

In the neocolonial countries, the global corporations skim off a very large percentage of all profits for themselves. For example, in 1971 in Brazil the global corporations grabbed 70 percent of the total net profits of the five important sectors of rubber, motor vehicles, machinery, household appliances, and mining. Moreover, much of these corporate investments are not U.S. funds at all but are provided by local capitalists. In all of the Latin American manufacturing operations of U.S.-based global corporations from 1960 to 1970, about 78 percent of the investments were financed by local funds. Yet the same corporations, between 1965 and 1968, sent 52 percent of all their profits back to the United States.[20]

As a result of the use of local funds for investment, plus high profit rates and the sending of most profits to the United States, the neocolonial or Third World countries actually have a net outflow of capital to the United States. This surprising fact has been documented by the U.S. Department of Commerce for the period 1950–1970, in which there were striking differences in the flow pattern to and from the advanced capitalist countries and to and from the less developed Third World.

Table 35.1 shows that U.S. firms invested much more in the advanced capitalist countries of Western Europe than they extracted in profits. In Canada the profit and investment flows to and from the U.S. firms were about even. But in Latin America, Asia, and Africa, the United States—acting through multinational firms—extracted in profits $26 billion more than it invested in the same period!

In Latin America alone, in the shorter period from 1950 to 1965, there was a net flow of 7.5 billion U.S. dollars from that area to the United States ($11.3 billion profit minus $3.8 billion new investment). Yet profit rates were so great that at the same time the value of U.S. direct investments in Latin America rose from $4.5

Table 35.1 **Profit and Direct Foreign Investment, U.S., 1950–1970 (in billions of dollars)**

	Western Europe	Canada	Latin America	Asia and Africa
Investment from United States	15.5	10.6	6.0	9.5
Profit to United States	−10.4	−10.0	−17.1	−24.6
Net Gain of capital in Foreign Region	5.1	0.6	−11.1	−15.1

Source: U.S. Department of Commerce, *U.S. Business Investments in Foreign Countries* (Washington, D.C.: GPO, 1970), p. 85. Later data from Department of Commerce collected in Linda Majka, *The Military Industrial Complex Reconsidered* (unpublished M.A. thesis, University of California, Santa Barbara, 1973).

[19] See Richard Barnett and Ronald Muller, *Global Reach* (New York: Simon and Schuster, 1974), pp. 16–17.
[20] See ibid., pp. 147 and 153.

billion to $10.3 billion. In fact, in the period 1957–1964 only 12 percent of direct U.S. investment in Latin America came from the United States; 74 percent was reinvestment of profits or depreciation funds from Latin American operations. Similarly, in Africa and Asia in the period 1950–1965 American corporations invested only $5 billion but transferred to the United States $14 billion in profits, for a net flow of $9 billion to the United States. Yet enough profit remained for reinvestment so that U.S. direct investments in Africa and Asia rose from $1.3 to $4.7 billion.[21]

Two facts are blatantly obvious from these data: (1) The rate of profit in U.S. investments abroad is several times higher in the less developed than in the advanced capitalist countries, and (2) the less developed neocolonial countries generously make a good-sized contribution to U.S. capital accumulation.

STAGFLATION AND IMPERIALISM

What is the impact on the U.S. economy of the extraordinarily high profits that flow in from the neocolonial countries? When each U.S.-based global firm finds and grabs a new market, its excess investment funds can now be invested abroad. Moreover, the new investment can be expected to yield high profits year after year. The problem is that for the economy as a whole, these new profits pour in from overseas faster than new investment areas can be found for the mounting funds. This capital accumulation is in excess of the investment opportunities domestically or abroad. Therefore, in a depression the situation is worsened by adding to savings when there is already a surplus of saving beyond what can be invested profitably.

For the less developed Third World countries, the outflow of immense amounts of capital (in the form of profits) is disastrous for their growth and feeds their own peculiar type of stagflation. These neocolonial countries have long suffered the odious combination of inflation and unemployment. In September 1974 inflation rates in the advanced capitalist world averaged a high 12.6 percent, but inflation rates in the less developed capitalist countries averaged 19.1 percent.[22] The rates of unemployment in the less developed capitalist countries have been scandalous for many years, often over 30 or 40 percent of the urban labor force.

To understand their type of stagflation, it must be stressed that the less developed neocolonial countries suffer from a tremendous lack of capital. This is quite unlike the advanced capitalist countries, who usually suffer from a surplus of capital far beyond the profitable investment opportunities. Lack of capital means not only a small amount of new factory construction but also little new equipment, very little in research funds, and very slow technological improvement. Lack of capital also means few funds for the education and training of human beings, the most important lack in the long run.

The Third World countries lack capital because of the institutional-structural arrangements within most of them and vis-à-vis the capitalist world. First, most

---

[21] U.S. Department of Commerce, *United States Business Investment in Foreign Countries* (Washington, D.C.: GPO, 1970), p. 85.

[22] See First National City Bank of New York, *Monthly Economic Letter*, September 1974.

have an internal ruling class that spends much of its income on luxuries, spends government revenues on unnecessary public monuments or on vast military establishments, and banks much of its wealth in Switzerland or the United States. Second, most of them have very poor terms of trade for large parts of each business cycle because prices of raw materials from the Third World fall much faster in depressions than prices of finished goods from the advanced capitalist world. Thus in the 1973–1975 depression prices of most raw materials remained constant (with the partial exception of oil prices), while prices of finished goods went sky high.

Finally, as shown above, the outflow of profits and interest from the Third World countries is much, much larger than the flow of foreign investment into them. For all these reasons there is a horrendous lack of plant and equipment, a lack of technological progress, and a lack of highly trained workers.

The lack of plant and equipment means that millions and millions of workers have little or nothing with which to work. Therefore, these millions cannot be profitably employed. Since the rate of profit would be insufficient, these millions of human beings are left unemployed. Because it is due to lack of capital, this unemployment continues even in the face of demand for products and severe shortages leading to inflation.

The stagflation in the less developed capitalist world is thus characterized by lack of capital, while stagflation in the advanced capitalist world is characterized by surplus capital. This difference is reflected in the fact that mass unemployment of workers in the advanced capitalist countries is accompanied by high rates of nonutilization of capital (idle machines and factories). Mass unemployment of workers in the less developed capitalist countries, on the contrary, often coexists with full utilization of their tiny supply of capital plant and equipment.

Of course, stagflation in the neocolonial countries is worsened by their dependent position. The global corporations generally have little competition and exercise their monopoly power to keep prices of goods within these countries high even during global depressions. Moreover, the global corporations often reduce all their investments during a depression (though not as much as competitive firms must do), but they continue to extract and return to their home countries as much profit as possible throughout the depression, thus intensifying the lack of capital. Finally, it is worth repeating that the raw material products of the Third World suffer the greatest price declines or the smallest price rises in depression periods, so they bear a considerable part of the international burden of the slump.

TYPES OF INVESTMENT

In addition to the basic fact that high profit rates squeeze more capital out of the less developed countries than foreign investment puts in, there is the problem that most foreign investment goes into areas that are least helpful to industrial development. We saw that in trade the less developed countries mainly export raw materials and import manufactured goods. This trade pattern is supported by the pattern of foreign investment.

On the whole the investment is mainly in the primary industries producing raw materials. But the materials are then shipped back to the developed capitalist countries for manufacture. On the one side, this discourages real industrial development. On the other side, it means the less developed countries are limited to production of the least valuable types of goods in international trade (since the relative price of raw materials has been declining). The fact is that the foreign capitalist firms in the less developed countries are located largely in the export sectors of the economy, exporting the goods that are easiest to sell in the international markets.

The International Monetary Fund report for 1963 states that "much of the foreign product capital investment in the underdeveloped countries takes the form of direct investment in primary production for export, especially in the oil industry."[23] The U.S. Department of Commerce figures show that in Latin America, Asia, and Africa a large majority of all U.S. investment is in the extractive industries, especially petroleum. Only in Europe and Canada is the majority of U.S. investment in the nonextractive industries, mostly in manufacturing.

It is true that in the past decade there has apparently been a strong shift in this pattern in some less developed countries. In several countries, such as Peru, there has been a sharp rise in the percentage of foreign investment going into manufacturing rather than agriculture or extraction of raw materials. These investments take advantage of the extraordinarily cheap labor to move part of U.S. and other foreign firms' operations within the less developed countries themselves (thus the "multinational" firms, to be discussed). Some economists—even radicals—argue that the trend toward more manufacturing investment is a fundamental change, an aid to development, and an attempt to integrate the less developed countries into the capitalist world.

Unfortunately, this change in the statistics has so far not been much of a help to development of the less developed countries (although it has meant that the foreign-directed multinational firms control ever more of their economies). There are three reasons for this. First, although it has increased, manufacturing is still a much smaller percent of all foreign investment than agriculture and extractive industries. Second, almost all the manufacturing investment is in light or consumer goods rather than heavy, basic, producer goods. Third, most of the investment in consumer goods industries is not in production but only in assembly. Thus a U.S. firm may produce refrigerators or cars, ship the parts to Brazil, and have its subsidiary there assemble and sell them. This does not seem much of an aid to Brazilian industrial development.

INVESTMENT BY GLOBAL (MULTINATIONAL) FIRMS

The ways in which American firms extract profits from less developed countries have changed since World War II. It used to be that most investment was in the form of loans or stock purchases in existing companies or the setting up of brand new companies (with or without native participation). Today such purely financial movements are less important. Rather, the capitalist corporation simply establishes branches of its own firm or completely subordinate satellite firms. The day of the global firm is here.

[23] International Monetary Fund, op. cit., 1963 report.

Not only does the giant global firm operate equally well in the United States and abroad, but also its board of directors, and its sphere of influence, usually reflect an inseparable mixture of financial and industrial interests. In the fantastic size and complexity of their structure, which includes both finance and industrial capital, and the multiplicity of their interests, which include both domestic and foreign sales, the giant corporations of today are very different from earlier banking or industrial interests.

As we saw in Chapter 34, through their global corporations, American capital thus directly owns a large chunk of western European industry, and the capitalists of all the developed countries together own the major industrial enterprises of the less developed capitalist countries. "There are no reliable figures for the Third World as a whole which measure the extent of foreign economic intervention, but it is certain that many, perhaps even most, of the industrial undertakings of the underdeveloped countries are foreign-owned or controlled."[24] A careful investigation of one important neocolony concludes: "Foreign capital can . . . be said to share the control of the Indian economy with domestic capital on what is very nearly a fifty-fifty basis."[25]

It should also be stressed that most of these global or multinational firms are none other than our old friends, the few largest American corporations. In the last official survey by size of firm (using data for 1957), it was found that 45 giants (each investing over $100 million abroad) had 57 percent of total American direct foreign investment, that 163 firms had 80 percent, and that 455 firms had 93 percent.[26] Certainly any survey today would show increased concentration.

The concentration of profits is much greater. In 1966 more than half of American profits from abroad went to only 16 firms (all among the top 30 according to the *Fortune* listing). Moreover, these profits were not a small sum, even in terms of total American profits. From 1950 through 1959 profits from foreign investments were about 15 percent of total American corporate profits, so half of that was still a tidy sum for a handful of giant corporations.[27]

It was also noted in Chapter 34 that foreign sales were and are growing much more rapidly than domestic sales. Moreover, in 1961 only 460 of the thousand largest U.S. companies had a subsidiary branch in Europe, but by 1965 over 700 of them had a branch in Europe. This means, of course, that there is amazing concentration of capital in the few largest American firms, not only the capital of the United States but also that of the entire capitalist world.

All of the largest American firms are on the road to being truly global, thinking from a viewpoint based on their worldwide investments. Therefore they are not merely interested, as was the earlier industrialist, in the export of commodities or, as was the earlier banker, in the export of capital. Rather, many have some of their major assembly plants in foreign countries and export a great deal from those subsidiaries. In fact, many foreign subsidiaries are large-scale exporters to the U.S. market. For example, in 1967 sales of all U.S. enterprises abroad totaled $32 billion, of which 11 percent was exported to the United States. That 11 per-

[24] Jalee, op. cit., p. 22.

[25] Bettleheim, op. cit.

[26] U.S. Department of Commerce, *United States Business Investments in Foreign Countries* (Washington, D.C.: GPO, 1960), p. 144.

[27] Arthur MacEwan, "Comment on Imperialism," *American Economic Review*, May 1970, p. 246.

cent constituted a total of $3.5 billion of goods, or 25 percent of total U.S. imports that year.

As noted earlier, this especially means that profits can be transferred around within the corporation, from a subsidiary in one country to a subsidiary in another. Therefore the reports of total profit remittances from the colonial areas to the United States can no longer be trusted as more than a general indicator. An entire corporation's total profits are the crucial point, and they often include hidden profits in one sibsidiary by reason of another selling to it more cheaply, or hidden losses in one subsidiary by reason of another selling to it at prices above the market price. For example, it appears that in 1961 bauxite production in Jamaica, Surinam, and Guyana yielded to American corporations a rate of profit of from 26 to 34 percent. Yet this does not really give the total picture. Much of their costs "on materials and services" turn out to be exceedingly high payments to American corporations, also subsidiaries of the same major corporate group. On top of that, between 1939 and 1959 the price of bauxite in the United States almost doubled, but the price of bauxite exported from Surinam and Guyana remained almost the same throughout the whole period. Thus these firms' West Indian subsidiaries overpaid greatly for their materials and services and were underpaid for their finished product. (Notice that this also means more corporate taxes going to the United States but much less going to the West Indies.)

It follows that the multinational companies may have conflicting interests when it comes to terms, export subsidies, foreign investment, and so forth. They are absolutely united, however, in desiring there to be as many nations as possible whose laws and institutions are favorable to the unhampered development of private enterprise. Thus there is much intracorporate conflict over economic details, but there is no conflict over the main political and strategic issues concerning the defense of imperialism.

The United States, of course, is not alone in making foreign investments, yet its role has changed tremendously and is certainly dominant at present. Thus in 1914 the United States had only 6.3 percent of the capital-exporting countries' foreign investments; in 1960, it controlled 59.1 percent of all foreign investments. Canada's share has also increased, but most major Canadian industries are owned or controlled by American firms.

At the same time, the investments of the United Kingdom fell from 50.3 percent to 24.5 percent of the total (although Britain remains the largest foreign investor on a per capita basis). France's fell from 22.2 percent to only 4.7 percent, and Germany's, from 17.3 percent to 1.1 percent. Clearly total western European control of foreign investments has fallen drastically while American and Canadian investments have risen sharply.

What are the consequences of global firms? On the political side there is an important and expected change. Under the old system, there was conflict, direct and inevitable, between each of the investing countries. Under the new system at least some of that conflict is eliminated. Thus a global or multinational firm has the interests of many different countries and many different investment bases to consider. Still, most global firms have their home offices in the United States. This, of course, greatly increases the dominance of the United States in the world scene.

NEOCOLONIAL "AID"

From 1951 to 1959 average annual donations from the advanced countries to the less developed ones amounted to $1.304 billion per year. The long-term public loans of capital amounted to $748 million per year. This gives a total of $2.052 billion per year.[28] Since these data include some aid and loans from the socialist countries, they overstate the amount provided by the advanced capitalist countries. For the year 1965 the Organization for Economic Cooperation and Development calculates that public aid from advanced capitalist (imperialist) countries to the less developed countries totaled $6.270 billion. Even including private investments and loan funds, which amounted to only $3.879 billion, the total comes to $10.149 billion for the whole year 1965. This is only 0.99 percent of the national income of the imperialist countries.[29] Furthermore this is a very generous estimate using extremely exaggerated figures. Such a small amount, certainly less than 1 percent of the national income of the countries giving the aid, could not be considered much of a burden. And also, unfortunately, it is not much of a help.

As we saw, the private investment part is itself more than offset by the profit and interest return on the investments. The small public aid does not even offset the capital extracted by imperialism. The public aid that is (1) nonmilitary and (2) in the form of official donations or grants may be some help, but it is not a large total amount. Even this "help" has extreme qualifications in that it is often used to bolster repressive governments, to subsidize foreign investments "to subsidize foreign imports which compete with national products, to introduce technology not adapted to the needs of less developed countries, and to invest in low-priority sectors of the national economies."[30] The long-term public loans for nonmilitary purposes may also be some help, but the necessity to return principle and interest is rapidly becoming a main worry of the less developed areas. Thus the United States officially admits that for all less developed countries receiving U.S. aid, "the cost of maintaining such large indebtedness is at present eating up approximately 30 percent of all new assistance."[31]

It is the declared policy of all of the American agencies, such as the Agency for International Development, that the countries that receive the aid shall use it primarily to beef up the private enterprise sectors of their economies and shall not use it for public investment, which is often the most necessary in these countries for rapid development. Obviously it goes without saying that the aid of the United States is directed to shore up these countries against communism and is not given for any pure idealistic reason. In fact, the American aid agencies often point out that "(1) Foreign aid provides a substantial and immediate market for U.S. goods and services. (2) Foreign aid stimulates the development of new overseas markets for U.S. companies. (3) Foreign aid orients national economies toward a free-enterprise system in which U.S. firms can prosper."[32]

[28] United Nations, *The International Flow of Long-Term Capital and Official Donations, 1951–1959* (Table 7).

[29] Jalee, op. cit.

[30] Theotino Dos Santos, "The Structure of Dependence," *American Economic Review* 60, May 1970; 233.

[31] U.S. Congress, Senate, Committee on Foreign Relations, *Some Important Issues in Foreign Aid* (Washington, D.C., 1966), p. 15. Also see Magdoff, op. cit., pp. 52–57.

[32] Magdoff, op. cit., p. 13.

The U.S. Agency for International Development boasts that "Private enterprise has greater opportunities in India than it did a few years ago . . . fertilizer is an example of a field which is now open to the private sector, and was not in the past. This is largely a result of the efforts which we have made, the persuasion that we along with other members of the consortium have exerted on the Indian government."[33] A more blatant case of political pressure occurred in Brazil, where American aid fell from $81.8 million to $15.1 million from 1962 to 1964 because the United States disliked the Goulart government. When "good" reactionary military officers overthrew Goulart, American aid jumped to $122.1 million in 1965 and $129.3 million in 1966.[34]

Nor are all the rewards of foreign aid purely ideological and in overseas areas. Just as the aid agencies claim, large parts of U.S. business benefit directly from the foreign aid program. Thus 24.4 percent of U.S. exports of iron and steel products are financed by the U.S. Agency for International Development. Similarly financed are 30.4 percent of the fertilizer exports, 29.5 percent of railroad equipment exports, 11.5 percent of nonferrous metal exports, and 5 to 10 percent of the U.S. exports of machinery and equipment, chemicals, motor vehicles and parts, rubber and rubber products, and textiles.[35]

IMPACT OF IMPERIALISM ON THE UNITED STATES

The impact of military spending on the United States was discussed in Chapter 29. Most U.S. military expenditures at home and abroad serve the aims of imperialism: protecting raw materials, foreign markets, commercial routes, spheres of influence of U.S. business, and U.S. investment opportunities (as well as capitalism in general). The profits from U.S. foreign trade and U.S. foreign investment, and from the military production to defend U.S. interests amount to about 25 to 30 percent of all profits. And recalling that most military and foreign profits go to the same few giant corporations, we begin to have some idea of the importance of American imperialism.

Conservative economists would object to lumping military profits with the profits from imperialism, but we believe it is impossible to separate the two. By 1969 the United States had a total of 1,517,000 military personnel in 1,400 foreign bases of all types, in 70 or 80 foreign countries (not including Korea and Vietnam).[36] The major reason for this multibillion-dollar allocation of resources is the need to maintain control over the vast American overseas investment empire. Note also that the decision to fight for a given area depends not only on the profits to be made from that area but even more on its military-strategic impor-

[33] Reported in U.S. Congress, House, Committee on Foreign Affairs, *Hearing on Foreign Assistance Act of 1968*, p. 185.

[34] Agency for International Development, Statistics and Reports Division, *U.S. Economic Assistance Programs, 1943–1966* (Washington, D.C., March 30, 1967), p. 28. Also see Magdoff, op. cit., pp. 39–47.

[35] Charles Hyson and Alan Stout, "Impact of Foreign Aid on U.S. Exports," *Harvard Business Review*, January-February 1968, p. 71. For a more recent and more complete analysis of foreign aid see Steve Weissman et al., *The Trojan Horse: A Radical Look at Foreign Aid* (San Francisco: Ramparts Press, 1974).

[36] Data from Harry Magdoff, "Militarism and Imperialism," *American Economic Review*, May 1970, pp. 237–242.

tance to the structure of imperialism in a wider area. "Understood in these terms, the killing and destruction in Vietnam and the expenditure of vast sums of money that are not balanced in the eyes of U.S. policy-makers against profitable business opportunities in Vietnam; rather they are weighed according to the judgment of military and political leaders on what is necessary to control and influence Asia, and especially Southeast Asia, in order to keep the entire area within the imperialist system in general, and within the United States sphere of influence in particular."[37]

We may now make an evaluation of the costs and benefits of imperialism and militarism to the United States. On the benefit side, military production and military service do increase employment, assuming that the nation begins from a position of major unemployment. On the harmful side, the flow of capital to the United States (profits and interest from foreign investment less current investment) must have a negative effect on domestic profit rates and employment through the competition of more capital. Still, the net effect on employment is probably positive.

The public at large, the taxpayer, pays the direct costs, including $115 billion for six years of fighting in Vietnam.[38] Non-Vietnam military expenditures continued throughout the period at about $50 billion a year. Because America entered the war with a low level of unemployment, unemployment was not reduced (although *perhaps* a major depression was avoided at some point); but employment and demand remained high enough so that monopoly power brought about price inflation, which lowered the public's real income.

More than 45,000 Americans have been killed in Indochina and more than five times that many wounded. (About 1 million Vietnamese civilians have been killed, but that is presumably not a cost to America.)

The necessary climate of racism against the "inferior" Indochinese has also worsened racism at home (as racism learned and practiced by the soldiers in Vietnam is brought back to the United States). The need to limit opposition to the war has increased repression and denial of civil liberties and has especially undermined academic freedom in the colleges. The attempt to curb inflation by cutting all welfare spending increases the costs to the poor. For the public as a whole, therefore, the costs in blood and money are vast, and outweigh any slight employment benefits.

For the largest corporations, however, the balance is very different. They do pay some added taxes for the war, but they are able to pass on most of these to consumers and workers. They do have some higher costs from inflation, but their own prices rise faster. We speak here of the whole military-imperialist effort, not just the war in Vietnam. Some sections of big business found that the Vietnam War overheated the economy too much or was a tactically "bad" (that is, losing) war, and so opposed it. Aside from that specific tactical situation, their interests are clear: Profits from military production and from foreign investment represent about 25 to 30 percent of all corporate profits.

Furthermore, the largest 100 corporations receive more than half of that very large amount, or the difference between depression and very high profit rates. Therefore for the giant corporations the benefits of the military-imperialist effort

[37] Magdoff, op. cit., pp. 14–15.
[38] U.S. Bureau of the Budget.

clearly outweigh the costs (although whether some of these benefits dribble down to the very top strata of labor in order to keep labor content is still highly controversial). Because the same corporate interests are dominant in the capitalist state, it is no wonder that militarism and imperialism continue to be American policy, regardless of the tremendous cost to the American people.

SUMMARY

The less developed capitalist countries are not only poor but also are growing more slowly than the developed ones; the gap is increasing. While too much population is obviously a problem for less developed countries, the question is, What holds back their development? The most important barriers seem to be (1) reactionary ruling classes that waste much of the product in unproductive ways, (2) a trade pattern in which the less developed countries export mainly raw materials and import most of their finished goods, and (3) imperialist investment at such high profit rates that the profit outflow is greater than the current investment inflow.

Imperialism and militarism have both benefits and costs for the United States. Imperialist wars (as in Vietnam) and military spending for them do create some jobs, but they also create inflation, high taxation, reduction in welfare services, more racism, and thousands of dead and wounded Americans (and there are more rational and constructive ways of creating employment). On the other side, there are vast benefits for a small number of giant corporations that make very high profit rates on foreign investment and on military production.

PART FOUR

SOCIALIST ECONOMIC SYSTEMS:

An Introduction to Comparative Economics

CHAPTER 36

VARIETIES OF SOCIALISM

The word *socialism* has been used to mean a great many different things. To begin with, it refers to (1) a system of ideas, (2) a political movement, and (3) an economic system of actual institutions. In Chapters 5 and 6 the early socialist ideologies and the Marxist socialist theories were discussed. These were systems of ideas. To complicate matters, there are now many varieties of Marxist socialist ideas alone, not to speak of other socialist ideas. Different views within the general set of Marxist ideas are currently expressed by the Russians, the Chinese Maoists, the outlook of Cuba's Castro, and many others. We shall not develop each of these but shall refer to them from time to time when relevant.

In the second category, political movements, there is also a wide variety. In fact, most systems of socialist thought have generated socialist political movements. Today there are many parties calling themselves Socialist or Labor parties. Many of these, such as the Social Democratic party of West Germany specifically do *not* advocate a fully socialized economy but urge a mixture of capitalist and socialist economic forms (mostly the status quo, as it now exists in West Germany). The other main political branch of the socialist movement is tenanted by the parties calling themselves Communist. These parties do claim to advocate socialist economic systems. Finally, there are many radicals in the United States and elsewhere who advocate socialism but do not belong to any of the Socialist or Communist parties.

Socialist *ideas* are ideas put forth by the various socialist movements. Socialist *movements* include all the Socialist, Communist, and radical parties and individuals who favor some variety of socialist system. What is a socialist economic *system?* A capitalist economic system is one in which there is private ownership for private profit of all the means of production (factories, equipment, land). *A socialist economic system is one in which there is public (or social) ownership for the public good of all the means of production.*

The words *public ownership*, however, are very ambiguous. We must ask three very basic questions to clarify this definition: (1) What is the political form (or system) of public decision making? (2) At what level, national or factory or other, are decisions made by the "public"? (3) Who owns the product of this "public" production?

DEMOCRACY AND SOCIALISM

Who is the "public"? The classical socialist vision assumed that public ownership meant extension of political democracy into the economic sphere. Under capitalism, a few powerful individuals own and control the economy. Under socialism, the public, through its democratically elected representatives, would own and control the economy. This control by the masses of the people—by the multitudes of working men and women rather than the few plutocrats—was seen as the heart of socialism.

Unfortunately, the end of private ownership of productive facilities came first in the less developed countries of eastern Europe, the Soviet Union, and China. In these countries there was little or no democratic tradition or institutions; their socialist governments were born in the midst of civil and world wars; and survival and rapid growth were their main problems. Therefore, contrary to every socialist dream, they emerged as one-party dictatorships. Political and economic power are held by tiny, self-appointed elites.

Can this be called socialism? There is, by law, only "public" and not private ownership of the productive facilities. But the "public" decisions are made by a small, nonelective elite. Communists claim that this is socialism, but most other socialists claim that it is not. In the next two chapters we shall discuss the development and functioning of the Soviet Union (and to a lesser extent, China) as an example of an economy with government ownership with decisions made by a one-party political dictatorship. For convenience we shall call this economy socialist, but readers must decide for themselves whether it really meets the definition of socialism as public or social control of the economy.

CENTRAL PLANNING AND SOCIALISM

As we shall see, during the period of Stalin's control of the Soviet Union, it was taken for granted by most people that socialism means central planning. Indeed in the Soviet Union Stalin and a small elite around him decided on the economic direction, and a small group of economic planners in Moscow developed a plan to carry out his decisions. That plan was law, and it governed all Soviet enterprises in considerable detail. In Chapter 38, however, we shall see that even in the Soviet Union there has been a considerable loosening and decentralization since the late 1960s wherein individual managers have been given more decision-making power on the day-to-day operation of their enterprises.

In eastern Europe this process has been carried much further with individual enterprises acting as independent units in the market in several countries. It has gone furthest in Yugoslavia, where the manager of the enterprise is no longer appointed by the government but by a council elected by all the workers in the enterprise. The Yugoslavs claim that this is an essential feature of "real" socialism, but others claim that this is a retreat from public or national ownership back toward capitalism. Again, the reader will have to decide.

SOCIALISM AND COMMUNISM

To explain the definition of socialism, we first asked whether it implies a democratic political system. Next, we asked whether it means national control by the "public" or local control by workers in each enterprise (or by regions or even by local communes). Our third question is, Who should own the public product? In other words, how do individuals acquire consumer goods and services? As a matter of definition it is generally agreed that *socialism* means public ownership plus the payment of wages according to work done, which wages are used to buy consumer goods and services. But a pure *communist* economy would be one in which there was public ownership plus distribution according to need. In other words, there would be no wages or prices, and people would take goods and services without paying as they needed them.

No present government or major political party advocates complete and immediate communism. But the Chinese Communists have gone much further than anyone else in moving toward equal wages and in expanding the sector of free goods and services. The Soviet Union continues to have a very wide range of wages, but it does have a considerable sector of free goods and services; mainly, all medical and educational services are free to the public. Even the United States has a few free goods and services, such as our public parks and highways. We shall return to this issue in our evaluation of socialism in the last chapter of the book.

SUMMARY

Socialism refers to a set of ideas, a political movement, or an economic system. A socialist economic system is usually defined as one having "public" ownership of the means of production. But several questions about this definition are very controversial. Is it socialism if decisions are made by a small group rather than democratically by all the people in a free election process? Does socialism mean central planning by the federal government, or does it mean decentralized decision making by each local group of workers? Does socialism mean continuing differential prices and wages according to ability, or does socialism mean communal ownership of the product with individuals taking what they need?

CHAPTER 37

SOCIALIST DEVELOPMENT IN RUSSIA AND CHINA

Marx and most of his nineteenth-century disciples believed the end of capitalism was near, at least within the next several decades. The capitalist system proved to have considerably more staying power than they imagined. Lenin attributed much of this prolonged viability to the gains made through imperialism. Ironically, the same imperialism led, indirectly, to the demise of a great European power, Russia. A socialist revolution overtook the fallen giant, and power was seized, in the name of Marxism, led by Lenin and the Bolsheviks.

THE BOLSHEVIK REVOLUTION AND THE CIVIL WAR

The general competitiveness of nineteenth-century imperialism created an international climate of tensions and distrust. With the crumbling of the once powerful Ottoman Empire, the major European powers scrambled to seize territory over which the Turks were no longer able to maintain hegemony. The predictable result was open armed conflict: World War I. The war so weakened the economic and political structure of Russia that the tsarist government collapsed in 1917. It was replaced by a provisional government, which also proved unable to cope with the chaotic situation.

Finally, in October 1917, the Russian Bolsheviks seized power in an almost bloodless coup. For the first time socialists had the reins of power and could attempt to create a society without the many evils of capitalism they had consistently denounced. The problems that had overcome the tsar and the provisional government, however, were of an overwhelmingly magnitude, so the Bolsheviks, who were mostly political activists without experience in governing, had no easy road to tread.

The new government found itself in the midst of a war that had devastated the foundations of the economy, slowed transportation and communication almost to a halt, and created something approximating social anarchy. One of the chief sources of Bolshevik power was the support of the mass of peasants who were revolting against centuries of ruthless exploitation. In an elemental revolutionary thrust, the peasants seized the holdings of wealthy landlords and rich peasants. They divided the land up into millions of tiny plots. When, as one of their first acts after taking power, the Bolsheviks announced a land reform, they were merely putting an official stamp of approval on an event that was a *fait accompli,* about which they could have done nothing even if they so desired. Nevertheless, the new, small and inefficient peasant holding made it exceedingly difficult for the Bolsheviks to secure the food to feed their armies and urban dwellers. Moreover, the newly independent peasants wanted to consume the little they produced.

In the cities, most important enterprises and industries were in the hands of capitalists who were hostile to and distrusted the Bolsheviks. A very large percentage of the physical capital of these enterprises had been destroyed, and the allocation of raw materials and supplies had been severely disrupted. The Soviets had hardly begun to extricate themselves from the war with Germany when a group of reactionary protsarist and procapitalist generals launched a military drive to destroy the new government.

The reactionary forces were supported by the major capitalist powers. Not only did their army (called the *White Army*) receive financial and material aid, but also most of the major capitalist governments sent armed troops to destroy the Soviet government. Few Americans realized it at the time, but President Wilson sent thousands of American soldiers and spent millions of tax dollars on a war that, like the Vietnam War nearly a half-century later, was undeclared.

WAR COMMUNISM

Thus in a period of bitter and extensive warfare, while the economy and whole society were approaching a state of total anarchy, the Bolsheviks were forced to take extreme measures in order to survive. The policies followed during the period from 1918 to 1921 were called *war communism.* The Communist government was driven under the exigencies of war, hunger, and chaos to attempt to impose centralized control on all economic processes. (The Bolshevik Party changed its name to Communist at this time.)

In May 1918 the government gave one of its agencies the power to obtain and distribute food. It became necessary to use brute coercion to wrest food from some of the richer peasants. Workers' detachments were sent to find and confiscate hoards of grain. Poorer peasants also attacked the richer ones and confiscated their hoards. The richer peasants resisted bitterly, and the result was almost a second civil war. Ultimately, however, the threat of a triumph of the White Army and a return of the old landlord class kept most peasants loyal to the Communists; their support was instrumental in the Communist victory in the civil war.

Being unable directly to secure sufficient resources to keep the economy going and fight the civil war, the government created large sums of money with which to buy resources in the market. The result was an inflation so drastic that money became almost worthless. Many state enterprises ceased using money in transactions among themselves. In 1919 and 1920 most workers' wages were no longer paid in money but rather in products or services. Many essential commodities, including municipal services such as public trains and tramcars, were free to workers.

The government was forced to nationalize almost all industry, from the largest factories down to enterprises employing only a few people. This was the only way in which they could gain the required amount of control over industry. It was made necessary not only because of the confusion but also because most capitalists and managers had a deeply ingrained hostility toward the Communists, and many actively attempted to sabotage the government's efforts. The nationalization drive ultimately became an attempt to eliminate all privately owned manufacturing enterprises.

There was also a drive to ban all private trade. Middlemen and tradespeople were said to be parasitic and to depend on exploitation of both producers and consumers for their profits. All trade and selling was to be transacted by governmental agencies. The government was never very effective at enforcing this ban especially in a number of critical areas in which severe shortages existed.

By 1920, when it became obvious that the White Army would be defeated, many more peasants began to resist the government's confiscation of their surpluses. Other pressures against the total regimentation of economic life began to assert themselves. In early 1921 the sailors at the Kronstadt Naval Station revolted against the miserable conditions of their life. (Ironically it had been a revolt of the sailors at the same naval station that had helped the Bolsheviks seize power three and a half years earlier.)

THE NEW ECONOMIC POLICY

Under these pressures the government abruptly abandoned many of the policies of war communism and inaugurated what was called the *new economic policy* (NEP). The government continued to own and operate heavy industry, power, transportation, banking, and some wholesale trade. Many small businesses and most retail and wholesale trade, however, were returned to private ownership and private profit making. Peasants were allowed to sell their goods in the market, and confiscation was ended.

The economy responded very rapidly to NEP policies. By 1928 the crises were over and the economy had been restored to its prewar levels of output in most industries. But the prewar levels were woefully inadequate. The USSR was still primitive and backward by Western standards. Furthermore, "instructed" by the earlier armed intervention by the great Western powers and the continuing barrage of anticommunist pronouncements and propaganda from most Western governments, the Communists felt threatened by the West. Believing that the USSR would eventually be attacked by hostile Western powers unless it achieved such strength that they would be reluctant to do so, the Communists accepted the fact that rapid industrilization would be absolutely necessary. Moreover, their socialist goals also required an industrialized economy.

THE INDUSTRIALIZATION DEBATE

With all Communists accepting the necessity of rapid industrialization, a debate raged in the late 1920s over the most efficient method of financing this industrialization. In order to feed and clothe the workers producing capital goods and to spare the material resources necessary for the construction of factories and machinery, large surpluses had to be appropriated by the government. Foreign capital goods could also be purchased if the surpluses could be marketed in the West. With the overwhelming majority of the Soviet work force employed in agriculture (and a large percent of these in subsistence agriculture), it was obvious that most of the surplus would have to come from agriculture. But Soviet economists and political leaders were divided on the question of how best to appropriate this agricultural surplus.

One group of conservative Communists (or *right-wing deviationists*, as Stalin called them) was led by the economist Nikolai Bukharin. He believed industrial planning should emphasize increased production of agricultural machinery and consumer goods to be sold to the peasants. The peasants should be paid high prices for their grain and should be offered consumer goods and agricultural machinery at low prices to induce them to expand output and market a continually larger surplus. Industrial development, Bukharin believed, was limited by the rate of expansion of agricultural production.

A second group, consisting of *left-wing* Communists, was led by Leon Trotsky, ex-commander of the Red Army and Lenin's chief lieutenant during the civil war, and Eugene Preobrazhensky, the leading Marxist economist of the period. They favored extracting a maximum surplus from agriculture by paying peasants low prices for produce (with heavy taxes) charging them high prices for manufactured goods. Agriculture should be more efficiently organized, they believed, by the formation of large-scale collective farms. Many sectors of the economy should be purposely neglected or short-changed in order to devote a maximum of resources and manpower to the rapid expansion of heavy industry, which, when fully operational, would efficiently produce the capital necessary to catch up in the industries neglected in the initial phases of industrialization.

Joseph Stalin used the antagonisms created in the debates as a means of achieving power for himself. At first he aligned himself with the conservatives to form a coalition that ousted Trotsky and his left-wing sympathizers. He then turned on Bukharin and his followers and successfully stripped them of their power, leaving himself in full control. Having thus gained power, he began to move along lines that had been advocated by Trotsky and Preobrazhensky, although he moved more rapidly and more harshly than they had ever advised.

COLLECTIVIZATION

In November 1929 the government announced a policy of promoting collectives as a means of increasing agricultural production. At first the collectivization was to have been voluntary. Suddenly, however, in early 1930 the government decided to force collectivization as widely as possible and eliminate the richer peasants *as a class* by turning their holdings over to collectives. The resulting change was so profound that a careful expert could say: ". . . The events of 1929–34 constitute one of the great dramas of history."[1]

Only the poor peasants could be persuaded to join the collectives voluntarily; but they owned so few animals and so little capital that collectives could not succeed with them alone. The middle-income and rich peasants resisted forced

[1] Alec Nove, *An Economic History of the USSR* (Baltimore: Penguin, 1969), p. 160.

collectivization with bitterness and ferocity. At times this resistance was so wide-spread as to constitute what could almost be called a second civil war. When the richer peasants realized they could not defeat the government directly, they began to burn buildings, destroy equipment, and slaughter animals. By 1931 one-third of Russia's cattle, half of its sheep and goats, and one-fourth of its horses had been slaughtered.

The drama of the battle over collectivization was one about which many books have been written. Here it will suffice to say that an immense social cost was incurred but that it did bring about the revolution in Soviet agriculture that made industrialization possible. Collectivization succeeded in drastically increasing the government's collections of grain. The 22,100,00 tons from the 1930–1931 harvest amounted to more than twice the tonnage collected by the government in 1928–1929.

INDUSTRIALIZATION

When collectivization placed a large economic surplus in government hands, Soviet industrialization proceeded at a striking rate on the basis of successive Five-Year Plans during the 1930s. Industrial growth at such a rapid pace was unprecedented in history. Official Soviet figures for the 1930s show an average annual growth rate in industrial production of about 16 percent. Studies by Western economists using different methods of arriving at indexes of industrial production show somewhat lower rates (ranging from about 9 percent to about 14 percent), but by any of these estimates the performance was without historical precedent.[2]

The major Soviet achievement was not simply a higher rate of industrial growth; it was a significant transformation of the whole society so that industrial growth could begin and continue. Before 1928 the USSR was overwhelmingly agricultural with tiny islands of industry; by 1938 it was a major industrial power with agriculture playing a secondary role. Before 1928 the USSR was mostly rural; by 1938 the urban population had tripled—there was a constant flow of people from country to city and a flow of ideas from city to country. Before 1928 there was 80 percent illiteracy; by 1938 over 90 percent could do some reading and writing, there was a very large adult education movement, and all young people were in school. In other words, the Soviet Union changed from a less developed country in 1928 to one of the main developed countries in 1938.

This spectacular rate of growth was interrupted by World War II, during which the Soviet Union suffered unparalleled losses. Estimates of the number of Soviet citizens killed in World War II are generally around the 20 million figure, although some experts place the figure at 30 million. Early in the war, Hitler rapidly conquered an area that contained over half of the USSR's prewar productive capacity. The German-occupied territory had accounted for 70 percent of Soviet coal mining, 60 percent of iron ore production, 50 percent of steel capacity, and 33 percent of the area sown in grain.

When the Soviet army retreated, it destroyed many productive facilities to

[2] For a short discussion of various estimates of Soviet industrial production, see Howard J. Sherman, *The Soviet Economy* (Boston: Little, Brown, 1969), pp. 79–99.

prevent their use by the Germans. When the Germans were subsequently pushed back, they also pursued a scorched-earth policy, destroying everything of value as they retreated. Especially hard hit were factories and houses. In addition to killing more than 20 million Soviet people, the Germans destroyed the homes of another 25 million, totally razing about 2,000 towns and 70,000 villages.

The destruction of these millions of people, homes, factories, untold millions of animals, and railroads, transportation, and communications systems left the USSR an almost totally devastated "victor" in World War II. The economic progress of the 1930s, which had been purchased at a high social and human cost, was in large measure erased by the fascist attempt to conquer the Soviet Union.

Despite these losses, however, the Soviets retained their economic organization and general skills, and with their experience with economic planning gained during the 1930s they recovered with miraculous speed. By 1950 gross industrial production was actually substantially higher than it had been in 1940, and agricultural production had recovered almost to its prewar level.

THE POST-WORLD WAR II SITUATION

During the 1950s, the Soviet economy continued to grow at an impressive rate. From 1950 through 1958, its average growth rate was over 3.5 times that of the United States, according to official Soviet estimates, and nearly 2.5 times the U.S. rate, according to most American estimates.[3] The growth rate slowed during the late 1950s and early 1960s, but the Soviet economy still appears to have done better in its leanest years than the American economy did in the booming prosperity of the early and middle 1960s. This Soviet slow-down led to a series of reforms launched in 1965 and improved performance in the late 1960s.

The Soviet experience has proved that their model of central planning can achieve industrialization at a very rapid pace. But has their record led to any conclusions about the ability of a socialist economy to overcome the difficulties socialists have traditionally attributed to capitalism? The question is very difficult to answer because most socialist criticisms of capitalism have assumed that socialism, when it came, would be superimposed on the productive structure of an industrial capitalist economy. Many of the worst evils found in the USSR during the past 50 years represent the social costs of industrialization and should not be compared with conditions under capitalism during the same period. A more appropriate comparison would be with England during the Industrial Revolution.[4]

Conditions of work were harsh and the worker's standard of living was low throughout the 1930s. After the first Five-Year Plan had provided the impetus toward industrialization, many leading Communists argued that more attention should be given to the working and living conditions of the laborers. Increasingly as the decade passed, the regime became less and less tolerant of such requests. Protests against prevailing conditions were often met with repression and terror.

The Stalinist purges of the late 1930s constitute one of the bleakest chapters

---

[3] See Sherman, op. cit., p. 105.
[4] See Chapter 5.

in Russian history. They are certainly the nadir in the history of the Soviet Union. Stalin's paranoid excesses were barbarously harsh. Framing any real or imaginary opponent as a traitor, Stalin eliminated three-quarters of the men who had been elected to the Party Central Committee in 1934, 90 percent of the Soviet Army's generals, and many others of lesser status. In all, probably 500,000 persons were jailed or executed in the purges, in addition to the recalcitrant peasants who were dislocated and often sent to forced-labor camps in the collectivization drive.

In 1953 Stalin died. By that time economic progress had made political liberalization possible. Since the execution in late 1953 of Stalin's chief executioner, Beria, violence has not been used to settle political issues in the Soviet Union. Leaders have come and gone, but no one has been executed as a consequence of political differences. Accompanying this decrease in coercive force has been a general increase in political and intellectual freedom. The increase has been very uneven and sporadic, however, and the Soviet society remains a substantial distance from the traditional ideals of socialism.

RECENT ECONOMIC REFORMS

In the more liberal atmosphere that has prevailed since the mid-1950s, Soviet literature on the problems of economic planning under socialism has increased immensely. The basic problem under investigation has been the question of evaluating various output mixes and input costs. One of the most important issues with which the Soviets have been dealing is that of the relationship between the market and the plan. Specifically, the economists have debated the issue of the appropriate extent of centralized versus decentralized economic decision making. In 1962 the economist Evsei G. Liberman published an article in *Pravda* that initiated a debate on decentralization. This "great debate" eventually led to a series of economic reforms beginning in 1965.

The *Kharkov incentive system* (which was what Liberman named his plan) called for important changes in the planning process only at the level of the firm. For the entire economy, "the basic levels of centralized planning—prices, finances, budget account, large capital investments . . . all the value, labor and natural indices of rates and proportions of production, distribution and consumption will be determined entirely at the center."[5]

Liberman proposed that enterprises be assigned only their final output mix. The appropriate technology was to be determined by each firm. The more efficiently a firm used its inputs, the lower would be its costs. The lower its costs, the higher would be its net revenue, or profits (total sales revenues minus total costs). Therefore the size of a firm's profits would be an index of its efficiency. Bonus payments were to be given to firms that made profits above some profitability norm established for the industrial sector in which the firm was a part.

From 1962 to 1965 the Kharkov system was supported and attacked in a lively and penetrating debate. Critics pointed out that cost and profit calculations do

[5] E. G. Liberman, "Plan, Profits and Bonuses," in M. E. Sharpe, ed., *The Liberman Discussion: A New Phase in Soviet Economic Thought* (White Plains, N.Y.: International Arts and Sciences Press, 1965), p. 79.

not mean a thing if prices and costs do not accurately reflect a normative, or ethical, evaluation of social values and social costs. The Liberman proposal did not contain any new insights into the solution of this problem. Supporters argued that giving the individual firms more autonomy and responsibility would result in greater economic maneuverability and stronger individual initiatives. These, they asserted, would lead to greater efficiency regardless of whether prices accurately reflected social values. The greater individual freedom in making production decisions and the lure of profit bonuses would lead to more enthusiastic and conscientious application of productive effort.

Critics countered by pointing out the long socialist tradition that rejects, on moral grounds, any economic system that depends on acquisitive, greedy, pecuniary motives. They insisted that Marx's analysis of alienation proved that the root cause of alienation was the use of human beings by other human beings as mere objects to be utilized in the quest for more profits. What, these critics wondered, would differentiate a socialist factory manager, who hired laborers solely to maximize the factory's profits, from his capitalist counterparts?

In September 1965, however, it became obvious that, for the time at least, the Liberman supporters had won the day. The Soviet government proposed a major organizational reform, which was adopted as law by the Supreme Soviet on October 2 of that year. Although the reform did not make profits the only criterion of productive efficiency (as Liberman had proposed), profits did become the principal one among several criteria. Firms were given much more autonomy in purchasing and organizing inputs in the productive process. And bonuses were paid out of profits to managers who were successful under the new system. (The debate and the reforms are considered in more detail in Chapter 39.)

SUMMARY OF THE SOVIET EXPERIENCE

The Soviet Union industrialized with truly phenomenal speed, despite obstacles many economic and political systems probably could not have surmounted. Judged strictly from the goal of rapid industrialization, Soviet socialism has been a spectacular success.

But most socialists, in the nineteenth and early twentieth centuries at least, envisioned a socialist society that would be superimposed on the productive base of an advanced, industrialized capitalist economy. Capitalism was objectionable in their eyes because production was undertaken for profits and not for human welfare. Prices in a market economy merely reflected, for them, an index of the capitalists' ability to exploit workers and consumers in order to maximize profits. Such a system was, in their opinion, thoroughly irrational from top to bottom. They wanted it to be replaced by a socialist system in which human beings would live to their fullest potential in a decent environment. The problems involved in assessing social values and social costs in order to plan rationally were hardly touched upon by these socialists. Their goal was the replacement of capitalism with a humanist socialism. The problems of rational planning they left to be solved after socialism was achieved.

During the reign of Stalin, the goal of rapid industrialization overrode all others. The harsh intellectual repression, commencing with the purges of the late 1930s and lasting until Stalin's death in 1953, resulted in a nearly total eclipse of meaningful intellectual endeavors to solve the economic and philosophical problems of humanistically oriented socialist planning.

In 1956, after this long period of intellectual stagnation, Soviet economic thought came to life. The problems of social evaluation, rational planning, and decentralization of economic decision making have all received thoughtful, penetrating analyses since then. No definitive answers to these problems have emerged from the Soviet debates, but the fact that official dogma has not precluded a broad and thorough intellectual campaign to come to grips with these issues is cause for optimism. The Soviet Union has certainly not achieved anything resembling the socialist system envisioned by the great thinkers in the socialist tradition. But with industrialization successfully behind them, and having initiated some beginnings of political and intellectual freedom, they may well be starting on the path to such a socialist system. Only time will tell.

SOCIALIST DEVELOPMENT IN CHINA

Since World War II socialism has been established in several countries. In some it has developed along lines quite different from the Soviet Union's version. China is the largest country in which socialists have triumphed. The Chinese experience differs from that of the Soviet Union in many ways. For these reasons, we shall briefly examine some of the main features of Chinese economic development since 1949.

In 1911 the fall of the Manchu dynasty marked the beginning of a period of rapid social change in China. Between 1911 and 1949, the Chinese economy had been ravaged by revolution, civil war, foreign invasion and exploitation, and flood and famine. When the Communists took over in 1949, they inherited an extremely poor and backward economy.

The industrial sector was very small and mostly foreign owned. In the major urban centers most industry and commerce had come almost to a standstill. Dams, canals, and irrigation systems were in a dilapidated condition. The fighting had destroyed most of the railroad lines. Inflation had nearly ruined the money system. And worst of all, the population that had survived the preceding disasters were abysmally poor, half-starved, and exhausted.

The Chinese economy was basically feudal, with about 80 percent of the population employed in agriculture. The coastal cities had become enclaves of foreign capitalist industry, but in 1949 there was less industry in China than existed in Russia in 1914 or in India when it became independent in 1947.

The first step taken by the new government was to begin a massive land reform. In 1949 landlords and rich peasants, who constituted less than 10 percent of the population, owned 70 percent of the land.[6] By 1952 the land reform had been completed, and over 300 million poor peasants had benefited.

Other policies undertaken between 1949 and 1952 were designed to restore the economy to its prewar level and to create the necessary economic, political, and social prerequisites for a successful planned economy. Accomplishments during this period were impressive. The government suppressed the banditry

[6] E.L. Wheelwright and Bruce McFarlane, *The Chinese Road to Socialism* (New York: Monthly Review Press, 1970), p. 32. Most of the statistics in this section are from this source.

that had been rife during the period of social turmoil, restored the dilapidated railroad system, and repaired and extended the irrigation systems. An extensive system of public health, preventive medicine, and sanitation was initiated. Perhaps most significant of all, it undertook to provide a relatively equal distribution of the available food and clothing.

By 1952 the government believed conditions justified launching its first Five-Year Plan, to cover the years 1953–1957. The slogan was "Learn from the Soviet Union." Ministries, each responsible for an industry, were established in Peking. Planning was centralized, with the ministries fixing prices and output targets. A high priority was given to the major capital goods industries.

In education, public health, and industry, most of the plan's targets were achieved. By 1958 the educational system had graduated 431,000 students, including 130,000 engineers, more than twice the number produced in the previous 20 years. The public health program virtually eliminated such diseases as cholera, typhoid, and plague, which previously had regularly decimated the Chinese population.

Considerable increases in the output of heavy industry were also achieved: "Crude steel output increased from 1.5 million metric tons to 5.35 million; coal from 66.5 to 130.7 million; petroleum from 0.44 to 1.46 million; cement from 2.9 to 6.9 million; sulphuric acid from 190 thousand metric tons to 632 thousand; and electric power from 7.3 billion kilowatt hours to 19.3 billion."[7]

There were also failures during the first Five-Year Plan. The size and complexity of the Chinese economy made it extremely difficult to plan everything from the center. Inevitably there were inefficiencies, wastes, dislocations. Light industry was growing very slowly. And there were problems in the agricultural sector remarkably similar to those the Soviet Union had encountered in the 1920s. As a consequence, in 1956–1957 the Chinese stepped up the process of agricultural collectivization. By the end of 1957, almost all peasant households were in collectives.

The second Five-Year Plan was never undertaken, for in 1958 the Chinese launched their *Great Leap Forward,* an all-out effort to transform radically the most basic social and economic institutions. This transformation involved a complete rejection of the planning model of the Soviet Union and ultimately an almost complete break with the Soviet Union.

The first and most basic change was the establishment of *people's communes.* China's 752,000 collective farms were reorganized into 26,500 communes. The collectives had included an average of 158 households; in the new communes, the average was 5,000 households. The new organizations were designed to permit effective mobilization of the massive rural labor force to facilitate the construction of many labor intensive capital projects and to increase the production in small-scale industries. These functions were, of course, in addition to the households' more basic role as producers of agricultural products.

The communes undertook such important projects as construction of new irrigation systems and water conservation systems and afforestation programs. They also organized small-scale production in several industries, including cloth weaving, machinery repair, simple tool making, and the manufacture of many other industrial products. (The "backyard" smelting of pig iron that was widely

[7] Ibid., p. 36.

ridiculed in the Western press never did have the importance attributed to it in the West.)

The communes established schools for technical training, research institutes, and spare-time facilities for general education. They also served to ration and distribute food and other consumer goods, and maintained communal kitchens, laundries, and children's nurseries. In general, they were integrated social units performing many social, political, and cultural functions for the people.

In late 1957 and early 1958, there was a widespread attempt to decentralize industrial decision making. The central authorities continued to control the capital goods industries, but consumer goods industries were put under the control of provincial authorities.

The years 1959–1961 were years of crisis. Innumerable problems were encountered in the communes, where radical social reorganization was occurring simultaneously with the introduction of new systems of production and education. The primary cause of the crisis, however, was disastrous harvests. Many Western observers believed China was on the brink of social collapse.

Gradually, however, as Western scholars gathered more information, they realized that along with the failures the Chinese had achieved many successes. The Great Leap Forward

> familiarized millions of backward peasants with industrial techniques at great immediate cost, but at an equally great potential benefit. It liberated China from excessive reliance on the Soviet developmental model which, whatever its strengths, was not suitable to a populous Asian land. . . . It achieved a strategically and economically significant dispersion of industry and an increase in the number of home-made scientists and technicians. . . . By 1962 China's meager army of scientific and technical personnel had almost doubled; important inroads had been made on illiteracy; and the number of types of steel, rolled steel, and nonferrous metals had increased by 200 percent, and those of machine tools by 150 percent. . . . Contrary to the oft-repeated assertions in the West, the commune system of socio-economic organization was not jettisoned, merely made more rational.[8]

During the 1960s several changes were made in Chinese economic priorities. First, increased emphasis was given agricultural production and light industries in the national investment program. A larger share of the output of heavy industry was devoted to agricultural machinery, chemical fertilizers, insecticides, fuel, electric power, irrigation equipment, and building materials. Second, much greater stress was placed on improving the quality of all goods produced. Third, there was a general reorganization of the communes aimed at increasing their effectiveness. Between 1958 and the late 1960s, the average number of households per commune fell from 5000 to about 1600.

ACCOMPLISHMENTS OF CHINESE SOCIALISM

Since the Great Leap Forward the Chinese have not made general production statistics available to the West. Thus we lack quantitative evidence with which to

---

[8] Jan S. Prybyla, "Red China in Motion: A Non-Marxist View," in Harry G. Shaffer, ed., *The Communist World* (New York: Appleton, 1967), p. 176.

evaluate their economic performance since 1958. Judgments about China's progress must be made from firsthand observations of the general conditions under which the people are living. Many contemporary economists have visited China. When an economist visits China and wants to evaluate its performance, he or she

> studies the official statistics and publications put out by the government and other institutions. He talks to the country's economists. He moves around as much as he can, visiting various units of production over as wide a field as possible. In his travels, . . . he utilizes his previous experiences and observes the condition of the people—whether they appear well fed and healthy, whether there appears to be substantial unemployment (real or disguised), the absence or presence of beggars, standards of cleanliness and hygiene, the quality and range of consumer goods in the shops, other products exhibited in trade fairs and elsewhere, the standard of public housing, the clothing of the people, the leisure habits of the people, and so on.[9]

Before making such judgments, the economist should keep in mind the conditions prevailing in China after World War II. Over the previous several decades, approximately 100 million people had perished in floods, famines, war, and revolutions. The overwhelming majority of those remaining were starving, poverty-stricken, demoralized people. Intestinal and lung diseases were endemic; the country was regularly devastated by epidemics of various communicable diseases.

Economically, China was much more backward than Russia had been before the Revolution. Russia's petroleum production in 1913, for example, was over 27 times as great as China's was in 1943. Steel production in prerevolutionary Russia was 3½ times that of China. On the eve of collectivization, the Soviets had 210,900 tractors; in 1949 the Chinese had 400. Russia's 1913 railroad mileage was approximately 45,600; China had 13,600 in 1949, and most of its railroads went inland only far enough for foreign capitalist powers to bring its raw materials to the seaports to be shipped abroad.

In agriculture, chemical fertilizers had virtually never been used before 1949. Reckless deforestation and soil erosion had made a large percentage of cultivable farmland subject to periodic devastating floods. Agricultural techniques were abysmally backward. It is only against this background that we can evaluate the Chinese economic performance since 1949.

Agricultural accomplishments are perhaps most important because of the massive, starving population that existed in 1949. The Chinese reorganized their agriculture. They increased the degree of mechanization, produced and used substantially more chemical fertilizers, and greatly expanded the supplies of eggs, vegetables, fruits, poultry, fish, and meat. Today, China feeds her entire population and exports more food than she imports. One American economist has gone so far as to state that "it would not be farfetched to claim that there has been less malnutrition due to maldistribution of food in China over the past twenty years than there has been in the United States."[10]

In education there have also been important achievements. Virtually all urban children and most rural children attend school. Illiteracy, which before the Revo-

[9] Wheelwright and McFarlane, op. cit., p. 13.
[10] John W. Gurley, "Maoist Economic Development: The New Man in the New China," *The Review of Radical Political Economics,* Fall 1970, pp. 34–35.

lution was almost universal, has been nearly eliminated. A wide variety of schools and technical training centers exists at all levels throughout China.

The gains in the medical and public health fields are very impressive. A Canadian doctor recently reported on his visits to Chinese medical colleges, hospitals, and research institutes. He reported that they had high medical standards, used high-quality equipment, and dispensed excellent medical care, which was almost all comparable to Canadian standards.[11] A member of the U.S. Public Health Service has written that "the prevention and control of many infectious and parasitic diseases which have ravaged [China] for generations [was a] most startling accomplishment." He also asserted that "the improvement of general environmental sanitation and the practice of personal hygiene, both in the cities and in the rural areas, were also phenomenal."[12]

In the area of industrial production, China is definitely still a backward nation. Nevertheless, its achievements have been much more impressive than those of other comparably situated less developed countries, and this despite the extremely low starting point, which precluded successful industrialization within a period comparable to that of the Soviet Union.

Considering all of the facts, we can conclude:

> The truth is that China over the past two decades has made very remarkable economic advances (though not steadily) on all fronts. The basic overriding economic fact about China is that for twenty years she has fed, clothed, and housed everyone, has kept them healthy, and has educated most. Millions have not starved; sidewalks and streets have not been covered with multitudes of sleeping, begging, hungry, and illiterate human beings; millions are not disease ridden. To find such deplorable conditions, one does not look to China these days, but, rather to India, Pakistan, and almost anywhere else in the underdeveloped world. These facts are so basic, so fundamentally important, that they completely dominate China's economic picture, even if one grants all of the erratic and irrational policies alleged by her numerous critics.[13]

CHINESE ECONOMIC PHILOSOPHY

Any country undergoing industrialization must devote massive amounts of resources to the building of industrial capacity. This means, of necessity, that the average worker must remain relatively poor for a long period. While the low standard of average consumption must remain for some time, the incentives for labor during industrialization can be achieved in either of two ways.

The first method is the one used by the Soviet Union. There, although the average worker's wage remained very low, the few skilled technicians, engineers, and managers were offered high material incentives. Thus egotistic drive for more material benefits was manipulated to achieve industrialization, just as it had been during capitalist industrialization.

The second method, used by the Chinese, attempts to develop other types of incentives. Materialistic incentives are discouraged. Ideological propaganda emphasizes the importance of overcoming selfish, egotistic behavior. The well-

---

[11] G. Leslie Wilcox, "Observations on Medical Practices," *Bulletin of the Atomic Scientists,* June 1966.
[12] Quoted in Gurley, op. cit., p. 35.
[13] Ibid., p. 34.

being of everyone and the development of socialism and other social, nonindividualistic motives are stressed.

Many Western observers have noted that the income differential in China between factory worker and factory manager is quite small. Futhermore, the factory manager is expected to take his or her turn at tedious or menial labor such as sweeping the factory floor. As a consequence, workers and managers have much closer and more amiable personal ties in China than they do in most other countries.[14]

Education and training are less specialized. Each person is trained to do a number of jobs and may rotate from manual to mental labor, from urban to rural employment, and from rank-and-file positions to leadership positions. The Chinese emphasize the notion that narrow specialization prevents an individual from achieving his or her mental, emotional, and creative potential.

Some economists have criticized this policy. They assert that it is inefficient and retards the training of the large number of highly skilled technicians desperately needed for industrialization to be successful.

The Chinese reject this criticism on two grounds. First, they argue that they consider the making of well-rounded, intelligent, and creative human beings to be the final goal of industrialization. Rigid specialization, they assert, treats the individual as a *means* and not as an *end* because it stunts his or her development in the interest of greater productive output. Second, they believe that even though rigid specialization may bring short-run advantages in production, in the long run it is disadvantageous. Over the longer period a broadly educated, creative, and happy population, whose motives are social rather than individualistic, will be much more productive. Further, they assert that this is the only concept of human development that is consistent with traditional ideals of socialism.[15]

The Soviet and Chinese models of socialist industrialization are certainly strikingly different. At present, rigorous attempts to compare and evaluate the effectiveness of the two models would be premature. The two countries have so many differences in their histories, cultures, and general economic circumstances that one cannot generalize from the experience of the one to evaluate the other. Nevertheless, they do present contrasting approaches for any less developed country that might wish simultaneously to industrialize and to build a socialist society.

SUMMARY

The first revolution calling itself socialist occurred in 1917, in Russia. Against incredible odds the Russian Communists ended the tsarist autocracy; won a civil war in which 14 foreign countries intervened against them; socialized industry; collectivized agriculture; carried through a successful change from a rural, illiterate, and less developed economy to a predominately urban, highly educated,

---

[14] See, for example, Barry M. Richman, *Industrial Society in Communist China* (New York: Random House, 1969), chap. 9.

[15] For a good discussion of Chinese economic philosophy, see Gurley, op. cit., pp. 29–38; Wheelwright and McFarlane, op. cit., pp. 197–240; and Edgar Snow, "Mao's Attributes," *The Listener*, May 29, 1969.

and advanced economy; and defeated the onslaught of Hitler's fascist armies. Income is distributed more equally than in the United States, and the Soviet rate of production growth exceeds the U.S. rate. Unfortunately, the Soviet Union paid for all of this not only in decades of hard work and postponed consumption, not only in blood and millions of lives lost, but also in political dictatorship that formerly executed its enemies and often represses intellectual life even today.

In 1949 the Chinese Revolution ousted the old, corrupt regime of Chiang Kai-shek after decades of fighting against Chiang's forces and resisting Japanese imperialism. In less than a quarter of a century, the Chinese have had remarkable success in raising living standards and hopes in what was once the most backward of all large countries. Their industrialization drive apparently has appealed even more than the Soviets' to social consciousness and less to immediate individual money incomes. It is still too early to undertake a detailed evaluation of their performance (although some other less developed countries are already very much influenced by the Chinese model of development). Thus in the next two chapters we turn to the Soviet experience and examine it in detail.

CHAPTER 38

PROBLEMS OF SOCIALIST PLANNING

We assume for the time being that the centralized, dictatorial Soviet model represents a kind of socialism. Although many socialists would argue that the Soviet Union is not really socialist, the Soviet case is considered here simply because it holds the record of the longest experience with some kind of planning under some kind of socialism.

THE SOVIET ECONOMIC MODEL

In the capitalist United States most land and factories are privately owned. In the socialist Soviet Union, most land and factories are publicly owned, with the government claiming to represent the public. Public ownership, of course, tends to mean public direction and therefore usually means planning. The principal type of household income in the Soviet Union is wage income for labor. In the United States, income consists not only of wages but also of profits, rent, dividends, and interest. The latter incomes are derived basically from private property; thus most U.S. planning is necessarily limited in scope to the confines of single enterprises in which decisions reflect the search for private profit.

In the Soviet Union the only exceptions to public ownership are a small percentage of cooperative industrial enterprises composed mainly of handicraft workers. There are also many collective farms that are supposed to be cooperatives but are subject to considerable central control (but each farmer also has a small private plot of land).

In the publicly owned enterprises, the Soviet government, or some agency of the government, appoints a manager, who is solely responsible for the performance of the factory and whose bonus is based on how well the factory performs. The manager's performance and conduct are checked by numerous agencies, and he or she may be promoted, transferred, or fired at any time. In turn, the manager hires and fires all the other workers at the enterprise.

The government grants the enterprise its plant and equipment and initial working capital, although it is now beginning to charge interest on capital. After the initial grant of capital, however, the enterprise is made financially independent. It must meet all costs of wages and materials out of revenue from sales and must also replace or repair depreciated and broken capital out of revenues from sales. And it is normally expected to show a profit above all of its costs.

The Soviet economy is centrally planned. The most important economic orders originate from the USSR Council of Ministers, but additional orders to the enterprise may come from regional or local governmental bodies. Further orders may originate or be transmitted through the agency directly supervising the enterprise, whether that agency is associated with a regional governing body or with the ministry directing some industrial area. Finally, all of these orders from governmental or supervisory bodies are supposed to be in accord with the plan, which emanates from the Central Planning Commission or its subordinate agencies. The enterprise manager is solely responsible for the performance of the factory, then, only in the sense that all orders received must be executed within the constraint of the resources allocated.

The Central Planning Commission first collects information up the ladder, from enterprise through agencies, in order to evaluate the last year's performance and the present conditions and possibilities. Then the Commission is told by the Council of Ministers what goals it must strive to meet. On these bases it draws up a general plan for the whole economy, although production and allocation details are provided for only, say, 2000 commodities. The draft plan is then shown to all agencies on down the ladder to the enterprise. After all these units have added their detailed modifications and suggestions, the Central Planning Commission draws up the final draft.

The plan is supposed to provide sufficient investment for the desired rate of growth, guarantee balance among all the industrial needs and outputs, and choose the best assortment of goods. At any rate the Central Planning Commission hands the plan over to appropriate government bodies to enact into law. It is then passed on with detailed commands, expanded at each intermediate level, until the enterprise receives a formidable document that is supposed to tell it exactly what to produce for a year (or some other period), how to produce it, what prices to charge, and what funds it may use. Again, the manager is judged on how well these commands are followed, though he or she has always had some decision-making power over details. The economic reforms of 1965 augmented the manager's decision-making power (discussed below).

PLANNING FOR GROWTH

In the case of a centrally planned economy such as the Soviet Union's, it may be assumed that *aggregate* effective demand always rises as rapidly as aggregate supply, although *particular* goods may be unsalable for various reasons. Thus there are no retardations or depressions caused by lack of demand. If the problems of demand are thus eliminated, then growth will depend simply on how fast output can be expanded. The supply problem may be resolved into two questions: (1) How much of each input (labor, capital, natural resources, and technology) can be procured under existing circumstances for use in production? (2) How much output can be obtained from these inputs in the production process?

Long-term growth in the American economy has averaged about 3 percent per year. For the years 1950–1970 conservative U.S. estimates place Soviet GNP growth at 6 percent per year; official Soviet figures indicate 9 percent per year.[1] (It is worth noting that China, in spite of political upheavals, also achieved a 6 percent growth rate each year from 1949 to 1966.[2]) Even the conservative American estimate is still high enough to call for an explanation.

[1] The data used in this paragraph are discussed in detail in Howard J. Sherman, *The Soviet Economy* (Boston: Little, Brown, 1969), chap. 5.

[2] See the testimony by John Gurley in U.S. Congress, Joint Economic Committee, *Mainland China in the World Economy* (Washington, D.C.: GPO, 1967), p. 188.

One reason for the high Soviet growth rate is that there is always sufficient aggregate demand in the Soviet Union for full employment of labor and full use of capacity. Therefore all Soviet saving is used for investment because the planners can always find a use for new capital. In fact, Soviet planners usually complain of a *scarcity* of capital because they attempt to invest more than the entire available amount of savings. In the United States, however, when business owners cannot find a profitable investment for all of their savings, some planned saving does not become investment in new capital. American economists often complain of *too much* planned saving, while planned investment in additional capital is less than it could be, sometimes causing depressions.

Another reason for the high rate of Soviet growth is the enormous amount of resources invested in education and scientific research. By this means the Soviets' output per unit of capital has been greatly increased. First, education has given them a highly trained work force capable of very productive labor. Second, education and science have given them a rapidly rising level of technology.

It is obvious, however, that the Soviet people have to pay a price for their high rate of growth of output. It is impossible to have both higher consumption and higher investment out of the same output (assuming we began with full employment); the Soviets have sacrificed some present consumption for more investment. Furthermore, in reality total Soviet output is still far below the U.S. level, and thus the Soviet consumption level is even lower. In purely human terms, moreover, we must stress that when the Soviets began their rapid industrial expansion, their consumption was at a miserably low level. Therefore each percent of national product taken from consumption in order to make investments meant a very great amount of present human misery accepted as the cost of future growth.

However, the simple growth formula also indicates that if the Soviet Union continues to grow twice as fast as the United States, after some years both their total output *and* their consumption will be larger than those of the United States. That is true, however, only if they continue to build new capital at the same rate and maintain the same increase of output per unit of new investment (through more education and more scientific research). It is no wonder that a major *political* issue in the Soviet Union has been and coninues to be how much of national output should be devoted to present consumption. Conversely, how much should be taken away from present consumption and put into investment in order to increase future consumption?

AGGREGATE BALANCE VERSUS INFLATION

The question of aggregate balance in the Soviet economy is mostly a reflection of the growth problem already discussed. Basically the resources supplied for investment must just equal the amount required or demanded for investment, while the amount supplied to consumers must just equal the amount they will demand at present incomes and prices. The capitalist economy of the United States has frequently been plagued by lack of adequate demand for the products of private enterprise. In the planned economy of the USSR, there has *always* been sufficient aggregate demand since the planning period began in 1928, and there has never been general or aggregate unemployment. In the USSR, however, the problem has usually been that the government has demanded much more for investment than could be supplied and has failed to provide enough consumer goods to satisfy household demand.

Because aggregate demand has always more than equaled the amount of available resources and manpower, aggregate unemployment has been nonexistent since 1928. Of course the Soviet Union does have a considerable amount of frictional and structural unemployment. *Frictional* unemployment may be defined as ordinary labor turnover. *Structural* unemployment occurs when the structure of industry and technology changes, so that millions of workers must change jobs from one place to another, from one industry to another, or from one skill to another. These changes require large amounts of retraining and moving expenses. Many observers recently have reported significant unemployment from this source. The Soviet Union may also have some seasonal unemployment, which occurs because in certain industries, especially agriculture, demand for labor varies during the year. It may not be profitable for a society to transfer these workers to another job for only a few months, although the Chinese now use them to build dams and roads.

As implied earlier, the main problem of aggregate balance in the Soviet economy has not been unemployment created by lack of demand but rather inflation caused by excessive demand for labor and all goods. The main reason for the inflation of the 1930s and 1940s was the excessvie increase in government demand for investment goods, military supplies, and free, or nonpriced, welfare services, which created an excess demand for all inputs, including labor. The excess demand for labor pushed up wage rates much faster than productivity, and thus workers' demand for consumer goods rose faster than total production and much faster than the output of consumer goods.

The excessive wage payments (which resulted in inflation) occurred as a result of decisions both at the national level and at the level of the firm. In the initial industrialization and wartime periods, the planners called for much larger increases in investment and military goods than in consumer goods; the discrepancy was usually even greater in the fulfillment of plans. Related to the high level of investment and military spending was the practice of over-full-employment planning mentioned earlier. At the enterprise level, over-full-employment planning meant managers were given output targets that, for most firms, were essentially unachievable with the amount of labor and other inputs legally available to them.

In order to meet their production plans, therefore, Soviet managers found themselves competing strenuously for materials and labor. Prices of material goods going to enterprises were effectively controlled, and most deliveries of goods were ordered by direct central priorities and rationing. Workers, however, did move from job to job according to the incentive of higher wages, and thus this was the path followed by managers competing for labor inputs. In the 1930s and 1940s managers were able to overspend their payrolls with few if any penalties but were under extreme pressure to meet output targets. They would bid notoriously high to obtain the scarce supply of workers, and even hoarded unneeded workers against future needs.

As a final result of this process, the workers attemtped to spend their rapidly increasing wages on the much smaller increase in consumer goods. The consequence was too much money chasing too few goods in the consumer goods market, and steadily rising prices until 1947. This is the basic pattern of prewar and wartime inflation: excess demand for labor as a joint result of the high rate of investment and over-full-employment planning, and excess demand for consumer goods as a result of wages rising faster than productivity and faster than the output of consumer goods.

In the face of these extreme inflationary pressures, Soviet policy was always to maintain constant or declining prices by administrative fiat. In practice, the pressures forced them to raise prices for long periods in the 1930s and 1940s. These reluctantly imposed increases did not soak up the full demand, however, and the result was *repressed inflation,* or regulation of prices below the free-market level. Repressed inflation showed up in shortages and long queues for many goods. Because their wages often could not be spent for any goods (because none were available at any price), workers' incentives to labor declined.

Only since 1947 has the problem been brought under some control (although a smaller degree of repressed inflation still exists). Since that time, (1) the State Bank allows enterprises to pay wages above the planned amount *only to the extent* that they increase output above plan, and (2) the degree of over-full-employment planning appears to have been sharply reduced (because the most urgent investment and military demands have lessened).

RELATIONS BETWEEN INDUSTRIES: MICROBALANCES

We have examined the aggregate (or macro) balances between the major parts of the economy, such as consumption and wages or saving and investment. Now the analysis must turn to the individual (micro) balances required between different industries. In this context each *industry* is defined as a collection of enterprises producing a single product for which no close substitute exists.

Soviet planners have been using a fairly simple approach called the *method of balances* to state macro- and microbalances. The following example at least roughly approximates how they would record all the sources from which one product—say, iron—is obtained, and all the uses to which it is put—that is, the total need for iron in the economy.

The balance of sources (or intake) and uses (or outgo) for the iron industry would appear as follows:

Iron industry	
1. Imports	1. Exports
2. Reduction in inventory	2. Increase in inventory
+ 3. Production listed by plants or regions	+ 3. Uses by other industries, usually listed by region
e.g., a. Iron from Ukraine b. Iron from Latvia	e.g., a. Iron needed in Ukraine b. Iron needed in Latvia
Total Sources	Total Uses

Of course it is only the totals that must balance. But somehow enough iron must be available to meet each use or need in each area of the country.

This method runs into many problems. It is very difficult to achieve such a balance among all the conflicting needs and available materials in any one industry. Moreover, the balances are all related because each industry relies on others for supplies. For example, more steel is needed to produce more blast furnaces, but more blast furnaces are needed to make more steel. Recently consideration has been given to adopting the input-output method developed in the West (by which a computer can estimate all the balances *if* it is given the correct information).

PRICES AND ECONOMIC PLANNING

One of the most important issues in Soviet planning is the question of how the planners are to decide which outputs society should produce. A related question is which technology is the cheapest for society to use in production.

Under capitalism, the search for profits dictates what is produced. Socialists have been persistent in pointing out that this method of deciding what to produce gives a higher social priority to trinkets, useless gadgets, and other trivia for the wealthy than it does to the necessities of life for the poor. Socialists have always rejected the notion that market prices reflect meaningful social values.

Yet price offers a convenient basis for comparing goods and services that are not directly comparable. If capitalists determined that they could produce several alternative "bundles" of commodities with, say, the $1 million of resources at their disposal, deciding which bundle to produce would be relatively simple for them. Given the resources at their disposal, they would produce the bundle of commodities that had the highest dollar value. They do not claim to be making a philosophical or moral judgment. They are merely maximizing their profits.

But when socialist planners are faced with the same situation—a fixed group of resources from which several possible combinations of outputs can be attained—theirs is a far more difficult task. They are not attempting to maximize profits. It is the general social welfare that they wish to maximize. In order to choose the combination of commodities that maximizes social welfare, the prices used for calculations must reflect perfectly the goals of a socialist society.

Until the 1950s this was not a terribly important problem for Soviet planners. The USSR was still a backward economy in the 1930s, and therefore rapid industrialization could be achieved simply by copying the product mix and technologies of the most advanced capitalist countries.

During the 1940s the war and the necessities of reconstruction dictated the product mix to the socialist planners. By the mid-1950s they had achieved a reconstructed industrial economy with immense productive capacity. Many more possibilities were technologically feasible. Furthermore, although rapid growth was still important, it had lost much of its urgency, while the goal of increasing the general welfare and providing more comforts for consumers had assumed much more importance. Under these circumstances the question of how to evaluate the different possible commodity mixes became a central issue of socialist controversy in the Soviet Union.

USE OF THE MARKET UNDER SOCIALISM

In the modern world socialism has usually meant central planning. We shall now examine the Soviet debate and reforms, which decreased the degree of centralized power over economic decision making, and also the Yugoslav experience with extreme decentralization of economic decision making.

Marx himself wrote very little about the details of socialist planning; he always emphasized that it would be utopian to discuss such details before the advent of an actual socialist economy. But clearly Marx and Engels disapproved of the planlessness of capitalism. In addition, they felt it to be an important cause of the periodic crises of depression or inflation. Nevertheless, this does not indicate that they would necessarily disapprove of the market device under socialism since socialism provides a very different economic environment in which markets can be controlled in accordance with the general welfare of the public.

RECENT SOVIET EXPERIENCE

Soviet planning reforms may have been generated partly by the increasing complexity of the economy. The argument is that rational planning is more difficult and more necessary in relatively advanced than in less developed countries. Technical innovation, which is now one of the most important Soviet goals, depends mainly on continuous local initiative at the production point. By contrast, throughout the 1920s and 1930s the main problem was putting to work in industry the resources that were unemployed or less profitably employed in agriculture. For this purpose central control was very efficacious.

In the atmosphere of increased freedom for scientific inquiry after 1956, there arose a faction of economists whose approach was pragmatic. They analyzed organizational matters and very concrete policy issues; through experimentation they hoped to develop solutions for limited problems. During the 1950s criticism of the malfunctions of the enterprise incentive system flowed largely from their evidence and conclusions.

Kharkov Professor Evsei G. Liberman was one of these critics. In fact, he was not the most important critic but was chosen by the political leaders to spark the public debate. Liberman published three papers in Soviet journals during the 1950s. He argued that specific problems created by existing success indicators could be overcome by appropriate changes in the operational constraints on enterprises. The reforms he advocated in 1959 were essentially those that touched off a major controversy in 1962. However, until 1962 both the man and his recommendations were ignored by other writers as well as by the general public.

The debate was given urgency when the Soviet political leadership became alarmed over the retardation in growth rates apparent in the early 1960s. In addition to temporary problems (such as increased military spending), these difficulties and the need for reform may have been due to the growing complexity and interdependence of Soviet allocations, which made it increasingly difficult to devise priority rankings and balance the plan.

In 1964 public discussion was again requested by the editors of *Pravda*. The inference is that desires for economic reform from within the party had significantly grown in the interim. The party was probably influenced by the intensification of the Soviet economy's problems between 1962 and 1964, including the rapidly mounting inventories of consumer goods, the grain crop failures in 1963, and the declining growth rate. The Soviet party was surely also influenced by the virtual stagnation of the Czech economy in 1963, the inception in 1964 of profit sharing and a charge on capital in Hungary, and the continued success of the decentralized Yugoslav system.

OFFICIAL REFORMS

Although "economic experiments" were given varied trials during 1964 and 1965, it was not until September 1967 that the government responded with a major organizational reform in industry, which moved somewhat in the direction of the Liberman proposals. Adopted as law by the Supreme Soviet on October 2, the stipulations of the Kosygin Reform were conservative and tentative, yet they did begin the process of reform. The section pertaining to the individual enterprise contains four significant new policies. First and most important, managers' bonuses are paid for fulfillment of planned targets for sales, profit or profitability, and physical output. The scale of bonuses was designed to provide relatively higher rewards for fulfillment of targets. Moreover, to evaluate the amount of sales, the *gross value of output* indicator was replaced by *output sold*, which implies the necessity to produce what the consumers desire. Numerous detailed target directives were eliminated, including the norms for labor productivity, number of workers and employees, and average wages.

Second, the enterprise can now retain and utilize a large portion of profits (and some portion of depreciation allowances) for bonuses, welfare purposes, and decentralized investment. This turned out to be a very significant measure giving financial muscle to the decentralization reforms. Third, half of decentralized investment is financed by repayable and interest-bearing loans from banks, and interest charges are levied (in the form of a tax) on all fixed and working capital put at the enterprise's disposal. Fourth, contracts between enterprises are more strictly enforced, prohibiting superiors from changing enterprise plans at will during the plan period.

The new economic system, however, continues to maintain the method of direct material allocation (there are recent reports of some attempts to replace or modify it through the introduction of large wholesale-warehouse-like establishments in which enterprises can buy anything they need). The reformed system also keeps the central limits on total payrolls and allows managers to choose the labor mix only within those limits. At the same time the more decentralized investments have resulted in a significant decrease in central control over the determination of future output.

It must be admitted that even these limited reforms have run into bureaucratic obstruction and sabotage. Thus there have been numerous reports of continued extralegal interference by government and party organs in the day-to-day operations of enterprises, including those on the new system. The undoubted difficulties of the new system will be resolved eventually either by renewed centralization or by further reform (toward greater use of the market in socialism). Which direction is taken will depend on many factors, including external ones such as a peaceful world atmosphere.

THE YUGOSLAV MODEL

The Yugoslav experience revealed to the whole world that a socialist economy could be largely decentralized and directed mainly by the market. Although at first it was denounced with the usual Stalinist unanimity, later, when the anti-Stalinist tide began to rise, the Yugoslav economy became a model to investigate.

The Cominform (or Communist Information Bureau) was established in 1947 by Stalin primarily as a means of keeping eastern Europe, and perhaps especially Yugoslavia, on a tight leash. In 1948, however, Yugoslavia broke with the USSR and advocated complete independence and equality for all socialist nations. The Yugoslavs complained that the Russians had attempted to dominate their army, to exploit their economy through joint companies, to use secret agents to investigate and blackmail important Yugoslavs, and to threaten the cutting off of all trade should Yugoslavia take any independent action. In reply the Cominform excommunicated Yugoslavia, charging that it had slandered the USSR and was no longer Marxist because it had stopped pushing collectivization.

The Yugoslavs eventually answered that the USSR had deviated further and further from socialist democracy toward bureaucratic overcentralization. By 1950, as a concrete reaction, the Yugoslavs had begun to decentralize their economy and create their own socialist democracy, focused on *workers' councils* in each factory. During this period the Yugoslavs advanced the economic theory that central or administrative planning may at first greatly help the progress of a less developed or war-torn socialist economy. As the economy becomes more built up, complex, and interrelated, however, such extreme central direction "turns into its opposite" and becomes a barrier to further progress. Some variant of this theory has become the basis for reforms in much of eastern Europe and even the Soviet Union.

FRAMEWORK OF THE YUGOSLAV ECONOMIC SYSTEM

After 1950 farming in Yugoslavia reverted to private ownership (as it did in Poland after 1957). There are few Yugoslav collectives today, although the goal of collectivization supposedly remains. In fact, the government is very, very gradually buying up individual pieces of land as farmers retire. There is also a private business sector, mostly in the areas of trade and handicrafts. Private businesses and farms may hire up to 5 people, but this limit apparently has been exceeded in practice. Farmers may acquire up to 10 hectares of land. The private sector thus plays a very small role in industry but constitutes almost the whole of the farming sector. Private enterprise also plays an increasing role in the catering and service sector.

In the socialist sector of industry each factory is run as a producer's cooperative under the control of its own workers' council. The workers' councils are a feature unique in Yugoslav socialism. Many other eastern European countries are slowly directing their economies toward fully independent activity by each enterprise. Yet at present none of them intends to institute workers' councils as a basic feature, preferring control by government-appointed managers. (When revolutionary tides ran strong, workers' councils were temporarily introduced in Poland [in 1956–1957] and Czechoslovakia [in 1968–1969].) Today only the Yugoslavs consider workers' councils the most vital part of their economic structure. They not only praise their allegedly democratic aspects but also claim that they motivate workers and managers to the highest efficiency. Some Yugoslavs even assert that the workers' councils are responsible for their high rate of growth, which skeptics attribute primarily to a high rate of investment.

How does the system of workers' councils operate? The workers elect a council. The manager is then appointed by the local government, but the workers' council has veto power over the appointment of the manager. The council can also fire the manager; set wages, within limits established by the central government; set prices, also within limits defined by the central agencies; set production targets and determine technology; and dispose of its profits after taxes through additions to wages, collective welfare projects, or reinvestment. Taxes collected by the national government are used to finance major investment projects as well as defense and welfare.

Because all firms compete in the market, the prices set will be rational from the viewpoint of neoclassical economics, provided that there is pure and perfect competition. Nevertheless, because a large percentage of investment is still under central control, capital cannot freely flow to areas of higher profits. This constitutes a barrier to entry of other firms and may allow monopoly or oligopoly to arise in any area in which the central government sets an optimum firm size that is very high in relation to the total market. Because Yugoslavia is a relatively small country and the total market for many commodities is limited, there are many industries in which optimum firm size demands only one or a few producers. As the result of such monopolies, (1) price relationships are distorted away from the socially "rational" price, (2) resources are therefore allocated wrongly from the social viewpoint, and (3) consumers are exploited in the sense of paying higher prices to these particular firms.

Expansion and new investment by a particular firm also have some peculiar aspects under this system. If an entirely new firm is organized, it has its own council to look after the benefits of its own workers. New firms are often, but not always, set up by old ones. However, a new workers' council does not return any profits to the firm that set it up, although it is obligated to pay interest to the government on the capital it has been given. Some of the "sponsored" new enterprises are treated legally as mere subsidiaries of the old firms and the additional profits are divided among the workers of both the old and new firms. In either case the way a council evaluates a new investment project outside its own plant is far more complicated than the usual profit calculus of a capitalistic competitive firm. One would expect some tendency to limit projects to those that might be considered a legitimate part of the old firm.

In addition to these microeconomic aspects of investment, there is something new in this system with respect to the question of aggregate investment. What is to keep a particular firm's workers from deciding that all of their profits should go into current wages or welfare projects rather than reinvestment and expansion of the productive base? Legally the only constraint is that the firm must first pay its taxes to the central government. The central government does take a very large tax bite, and much of this revenue has been used for investment, which has contributed singificantly to Yugoslavia's impressive rate of economic growth. Yugoslavs also claim that the workers are generally very willing to make many large reinvestments, supposedly being content to wait for the large future returns.

The Communist party group within each enterprise also strongly encourages collective welfare projects and reinvestment for expansion of the productive base. And the manager of the enterprise exerts a somewhat independent pressure, in most cases advocating expansion of the enterprise's capital. Actually it appears that the balance of power over the distribution of income between workers and managers and higher authorities varies from plant to plant as well as from year to year. At present the ratio of investment to national income is very high. Therefore a large percentage of all investment, especially that going into new enterprises, must be and is still done by the central government, but an increasing percentage is coming under the control of existing firms and local governments.

It should be noted that the revenue of the enterprise must pay (1) interest on loans from the banking system, (2) depreciation allowances, (3) interest to the central government on the initial capital investment, (4) the turnover tax on sales, (5) miscellaneous taxes and fees, and (6) the income tax on profits. After the firm has paid these expenses, it is free to divide the rest of the revenue between wages and new investment. Yet the workers still must pay an additional social insurance tax on their wages. It is also required that at least 24 percent of investment funds go to a housing fund and to communal investment projects such as recreation centers. One further restriction lies in the fact that the government enforces a minimum wage for each worker.

For some time the total of all taxes, including profit tax, turnover tax, and interest on initial capital, amounted to about one-third of GNP. In the 1960s about 50 percent of government revenues were spent on defense, 35 percent on welfare, and 15 percent on investment. But allocations by enterprises pushed gross investment up to the 35 percent of GNP.

In other areas, too, decisions are not made by the enterprise-level worker's councils. Central planning is responsible for (1) all of the most important investment projects, (2) most research and development, and (3) the education of skilled and professional workers.

SOME PROBLEMS OF THE YUGOSLAV SYSTEM

Prices or products in Yugoslavia are set by the enterprises (to the extent allowed by government price control), and the enterpises have every reason for increasing prices at every opportunity. If output demanded does not fall proportionately, then higher prices give the workers' council an opportunity to pay higher wages. Furthermore, as already noted, a small country such as Yugoslavia inevitably has many monopoly producers because a single large-scale, optimum size enterprise takes such a huge slice of an industry. This problem is mitigated in part by foreign trade because foreign competition helps keep the monopolies in line. The result of the strong wage position and monopoly structure has been a chronic tendency toward price inflation. One interesting consequence of the monopoly pricing is that socialist Yugoslavia has passed an antimonopoly law against combinations in restraint of trade or conspiracies to raise prices.

In addition, the natural reaction of a central government with a planning tradition was the imposition of a large number of price controls. It was noted earlier that by 1967 a large percentage of Yugoslavia's industrial sales were of price-controlled goods. (This was supposed to be a temporary situation, but is still in effect.) Firms either may set prices only within certain limits, or they must get agency approval for any price change. Bureaucracy thus returns to the price-setting stage via the back door, although the enterprises are still the formal sources of all prices.

Another Yugoslav problem has been the continuing importance of regional or national rivalries. This is especially significant in the investment process, in which the allocation is achieved partly by local and regional agencies. Some of the allocation is by central planners, but they themselves may be afflicted by regional biases. Moreover, it is not just a matter of regional rivalries; the regions are in vastly different stages of economic development. To achieve equality in the level of development, it still is necessary to invest, say, in Macedonia, despite the fact that the project could do much better in a more advanced region. This is a profound problem; in the short run at least, it causes a great loss from investment allocation that is inefficient in terms of what might be done were there no extraeconomic regional considerations.

Another problem arises from the attempt to give real power to workers' councils over the specific plants and enterprises. This tends to result in the splitting up of industries into units small enough for democratic participation. But the political objective may conflict with the economic goal of achieving enterprises large enough to utilize all possible economies of scale. Thus the railways of Yugoslavia have been divided into a rather loose association of more than 160 autonomous enterprises, far too many competing firms in an industry that requires integration. Similarly, Yugoslavia has five factories producing entire radios; considerable economics of scale might be obtained by having each factory specialize in a single radio component. In recent years there has been a strong trend in some industries toward merger of enterprises, in spite of the obstacles presented by entrenched workers' councils.

Another problem that socialism was supposed to have avoided but that is found in Yugoslavia today is a certain degree of job insecurity and unemployment. It is theoretically possible that a system of market socialism such as Yugoslavia's might be subject to a certain degree of aggregate unemployment. In the past this has generally been overcome by a sufficient amount of central investment and by exportation of about 400,000 workers, mostly to West Germany. Nevertheless, there is a continuing problem of frictional unemployment, to the degree that inefficient enterprises are allowed to go bankrupt although there is some noneconomic pressure against this. Moreover, there actually was a significant amount of aggregate unemployment in 1966 and 1967.

In addition to the regional biases mentioned earlier, investment allocation under the Yugoslav system is subject to certain distortions owing to the limited outlook of individual enterprises operating on purely profit criteria. Because workers are attached to the firm only for a limited time (at most during their lifetime), the workers' councils tend to neglect many long-run considerations in favor of short-run rapid returns. Furthermore, some individual Yugoslav firms, like those under a private enterprise system, tend to overlook the possible social benefits the damages of their investments. For example, each firm does not consider fully the effects on the community of the smog they create.

A quite different problem is posed by the private nature of Yugoslav farming. Because it is not only private but also of generally low productivity, with low yields per worker, this sector tends to conflict with the socialized and rapidly modernizing industries. The official Yugoslav remedy is that farming itself will eventually be socialized, but the lack of significant movement in this direction may leave one skeptical about the political feasibility of the move at any time.

Finally, consider the left-wing Chinese criticism that the Yugoslav system will eventually revert to capitalism. This is based on the notion that workers and managers in particular plants are coming to have a vested economic interest in those plants. It is hard to see, though, how the workers of a given plant in the Yugoslav system can ever use their possession of the plant either to exploit other workers or to pass on their position as an inheritance to their children.

Related to the allegation just described is the charge that the Yugoslav economic psychology is reverting to a bourgeois obsession with profit-making activity. Both Yugoslav workers and managers concentrate on their own individual moneymaking with no care for social needs, and some social welfare projects have actually been reduced to promote "private initiative." While this backward psychological movement certainly is the case to some extent, it is not easy to see that the central-planning alternative produces less of a moneymaking psychology on the part of workers and managers. Moving in a different direction, the Chinese have retained central planning but have drastically reduced the income differentials between unskilled workers, skilled workers, and managers. Thus while the Yugoslavs are relying more and more on individual material incentives, the Chinese claim to be relying more on collective moral incentives.

SUMMARY

Soviet economic planning faces various economic problems, although they are very different from American economic problems. The Soviets have full employment because their planners can always use excess funds for more projects. However, they have had inflation problems because they have tried to produce even beyond their physical capacities and have paid out more wages than there were consumer goods available at current prices.

There is also a constant political fight over producing more consumer goods versus producer goods (for growth) versus military goods versus welfare goods (including education, which also contributes to growth).

Moreover, there is need for balances between individual products; each industry must produce enough to meet the need for its product from every other industry. Finally, the planners must decide how much of each product to produce and how to produce it.

For several years in the 1960s, a debate raged in the Soviet Union over how far to decentralize the economy. In 1965 the government passed limited reforms that increased the freedom of action of the plant manager in several areas and made the manager's bonus dependent more on maximizing profits than on following a detailed output plan. The central plan is still very important, and the profits still go to the public rather than to any individual.

Since 1950 Yugoslavia has pursued an extreme form of decentralization and use of the market, leading many observers to question whether it has retained any planning or any socialism. All major decisions in the enterprise are made by a workers' council directly elected by the workers in each factory. It appoints the manager (jointly with the local government) and decides how much income is to be reinvested, how much is to be distributed, and who shall get the income distributed. Thus ownership is no longer really public in Yugoslavia; rather, the ownership resides with all the workers in each enterprise as a collective or cooperative venture. A basic criticism leveled by some radicals has been that this wide use of the market and money incentives instills a more bourgeois psychology and leads back toward capitalism.

CHAPTER 39

POLITICAL AND SOCIAL PROBLEMS UNDER SOCIALISM

So far only the core of purely economic problems under socialism has been discussed. Socialist countries, it has been demonstrated, can plan in a rational manner for the whole economy; they do achieve the necessary balance for full employment (although with some inflation problems); and by using a high rate of saving and investment, they have usually achieved very high rates of growth. Further, there are attempts to overcome some of the problems of overcentralized planning, partly through the application of better economic theory and advanced computer analysis and partly through some decentralization of decision making.

Now we must examine the impact of socialism on the more general problems of equitable income distribution, free social services, racism, sexism, pollution, dictatorship, imperialism, and alienation. Obviously a book could be devoted to each of these problems, so in this brief chapter we shall do no more than pose some problems and note some trends in the socialist countries.

EXPLOITATION OR EQUITABLE INCOME DISTRIBUTION

The distribution of income in the Soviet Union is very similar to the distribution of wage income in the United States. The difference is that there is no upper end to the distribution; there is no private profit income, no rent income, no interest income (except on savings lent to the government). To the extent that only wage income is given to Soviet citizens, we may say that there is no exploitation in Marx's sense of the term.

However, some Soviet income that is supposedly wages paid for labor may be exploitive income in disguise. The incomes of the top government officials, top Communist party officials, and top military men are known to be very high but are state secrets. Officially they are paid labor income; but because they set their own wages, these "wages" may be considerably above an income based on labor alone. To the extent that this is so, it is fair to question just how socialist is the Soviet Union. It may be added that most observers believe the income distribution in China (and Cuba) to be much more egalitarian, as was Soviet income distribution immediately after the 1917 Revolution.

FREE SOCIAL SERVICES

In any event it is a long way to the complete equality, or payment according to "need," that is promised for communism. Still, the highly differential wages paid in the Soviet Union are made considerably more equal by the very large sector of free goods and services available to everyone. Of course all goods and services are produced by human effort and therefore are not free in that sense. But the Soviet government chooses to give many goods and services to its citizens without payment.

The Soviets are particularly proud of their very extensive, excellent, and free medical services. They are also proud of their completely free educational system, from elementary school to graduate school. Good students are also given scholarships large enough to live on without outside work. Their retirement system is comprehensive, as is the right to a paid vacation each year. Paid maternity leaves with job security are also mandatory under the law. The area of free goods and services provided by the public is clearly far larger than in the United States, although just how large is controversial. One careful estimate says that the United States currently spends about 8 percent of its Gross National Product (GNP) on nonmilitary publicly-financed free goods and services, including 4 percent of GNP on education and 1 percent on health services. The same estimate finds that the Soviet Union spends about 28 percent of its GNP on nonmilitary publicly-financed free goods and services, including 9 percent of GNP for education, 7 percent for health, and 6 percent for public housing.[1] Presumably, under full communism all goods and services will be free, but the present Soviet leadership is certainly not rushing in that direction—partly because the leadership, with high incomes, have a vested interest in the present system.

RACISM

The Soviet government has always propagandized against racism, and there is little or no prejudice against black people in the Soviet Union (but there are very few blacks there). It does appear that some racial prejudice has been used as a political weapon to get popular support in the verbal struggle between the Russians and the Chinese (and it has apparently been used on both sides). There also used to be much propaganda against anti-Semitism, but Stalin used anti-Semitism as a weapon against his political opponents, and Hitler brought propaganda against the Jews with him when he invaded Russia. As a result of these two sources of prejudice, and because the Jew continues to be a convenient target for prejudice, some Soviet writers still make anti-Semitic statements. (Many racist statements are made under the guise of anti-Zionism, a perfectly legitimate political position that is grossly misused in this case.)

One should not overestimate Soviet use of anti-Semitism. Many Soviet authors are allowed to attack it, if they do not criticize top leadership. Moreover, Soviet Jews have much *higher than proportional* numbers of students and faculty in

---

[1] See the interesting and useful little book by Burnham P. Beckwith, *Free Goods, The Theory of Free or Communist Distribution* (published in 1976 by B. P. Beckwith, 656 Lytton Avenue, Palo Alto, Calif. 94301), p. 200.

higher education, as well as scientists, actors, concert artists, and journalists. This by no means results from discrimination in their favor, but it does indicate lack of discrimination in certain educational and economic areas; their high proportions result simply from an urbanized, education-oriented tradition. Only in political positions are Jews almost completely unrepresented.

SEXISM

In combatting sexism the Soviet system has shown its most striking successes. Women are close to equality in number of college students and have a rapidly rising number of Ph.D.'s (now over one-third of the total). They constitute about 20 percent of Russia's associate professors. More than 50 percent of all doctors and lawyers are women, and in the sciences and all other professions the percentages are very high (even including one-third of all engineers). Women account for more than 50 percent of the total Soviet labor force.

On the negative side, it must be admitted that the attitudes of Soviet men have changed very little since pre-Revolutionary days. Or more precisely, the social situation of Russian women was so low that, even with fantastic upgrading, it still appears poor by the standards of the U.S. women's liberation movement. Men and women do take it for granted that the average Soviet woman has a job appropriate to her abilities and *at equal pay*. They also assume that she is entitled to a lengthy maternity leave while being paid and retaining her job. Moreover, most children are given good care each day in child care centers, a service that is well developed in the Soviet Union and is free to all. But men still assume that when a woman returns from a hard day's work she is exclusively responsible for the children in the evening. She is also expected to cook and clean the house while the man, who worked the same number of hours in the day, relaxes and does nothing. This situation has not changed at all in the countryside; it is beginning to change very slowly among educated urban men and women.

POLLUTION

The Soviet Union has much less pollution than the United States, but that is partly a consequence of less economic development—particularly because there are vastly fewer automobiles. Yet the reduction of pollution is also due to the fact that private profit has been replaced by social control. All new facilities, including whole cities, are carefully approved by a sanitation inspector who is pledged to strict protection of the environment. There were also a new set of very strict antipollution laws passed in the late 1960s.

Nevertheless, many cases of environmental destruction have been reported, in loud and agonized voices, by Soviet newspapers and journals. The reasons for the pollution, in spite of social planning and laws, can be traced to the continued private interests of Soviet managers and some bureaucrats. The manager's bonus depends on how much is produced and how low the costs are, but the manager can produce more at lower costs by paying no attention to pollution. As a countermeasure, fines are beginning to be applied to polluting managers. Yet some managers are protected by higher bureaucrats because their performance too is judged on the basis of how much their district produces and at how low a monetary cost. Under Stalin *production* was the sole goal *at any cost*—monetary, human, or environmental.

And that is natural. People at very low income levels need to increase their food, clothing, and shelter for survival; worry over polluting the environment is a luxury they cannot afford. With economic development and affluence, pollution becomes a major problem, which can and must be solved.

DICTATORSHIP

One reason for the Soviet disregard of human feelings and environmental destruction during the period of rapid industrialization was the lack of democratic control over the leadership. Stalin ruled as a sole and arbitrary dictator. Even at present, decision making is only partially shared with the Central Committee, which consists of a few hundred individuals. A considerable amount of freedom of discussion and criticism does exist now, but it is still very much limited to safe subjects and the criticism of local leaders. Thus there was vast public discussion of educational reforms and new marriage and divorce laws, but no dissent at all was allowed on the invasion of Czechoslovakia, and intellectuals are still carted off to jail for criticizing basic policies of the top leadership.

The Soviet trend to dictatorship over the working class (rather than democratic representation of it) began during the emergency situations of civil war and foreign intervention. The new Soviet government not only was menaced by a violent uprising of the old reactionary forces (tsarist military men, landlords, and so forth) but also was invaded in 1918 by troops from 14 foreign countries, including the United States. All this in a country with very little democratic tradition, grinding poverty, and 70 percent or 80 percent illiteracy. Still, there was considerable revival of free speech and debate in the 1920s. This was stifled, and Stalin became absolute dictator only later when the all out industrialization program was launched.

Rapid industrialization implies, as we have seen in previous chapters, a vast concentration of the country's resources in investment in new factories and machinery. These resources for investment could come only (because there was no foreign help) from the effort and sweat of a population provided with very few consumer goods. Because over 70 percent of the population were peasants in agriculture, this meant squeezing out every bit of agricultural product from them above their minimum survival needs (and sometimes, in the early years, even that was taken). The food was given to the industrial workers or exported to buy foreign machinery. Thus most of the population was hostile to the government and would not have backed this drastic program in any democratic vote. Hence it was the attempt to overcome economic backwardness rapidly by heroic means at the expense of the present generation that led inevitably to the terrorist Stalinist dictatorship. In the recent period, with greater affluence, a reduced industrial pace, and the spread of general education, it is possible to see a long-run trend toward political liberalization. (But the trend often gives way to very regressive steps.)

. IMPERIALISM

We saw in an earlier chapter that imperialism has tended to flourish under capitalism because it has brought vast gains to the owners of a few large corporations, even though it has meant taxes and inflation and deaths and wounds in wars for most of the population of the imperialist countries. The Soviet Union has no private owners of large corporations, nor can anyone make private profit from an overseas investment or from a military contract. In fact, Soviet planners recognize military spending for what it is, a drain on their ability to produce more consumer and producer goods for the society.

Still, it is a fact that the Soviet Union has taken aggressive actions against Czechoslovakia and Hungary and has subjected them to involuntary military occupation. It is a fact that the Soviet Union and China have clashed on their borders. What are the ultimate causes of these actions if they are not related to private profits? Partly, at least, the causes would seem to be related to the continuing undemocratic character of the Soviet government, and to the fact that top leaders make high salaries and have vested interests in maintaining their positions. It is often easier to keep political power at home by putting people's minds on foreign adventures and always reminding them of the possibilities of foreign intervention. It also means further extension of the Soviet leaders' personal political control over eastern Europe.

The most succinct analysis of Soviet foreign policy has been provided by Andreas Papandreou, a man whose country (Greece) was taken away from him by a military coup known to be backed by the CIA.[2] Professor Papandreou says, "While the expansionist-capitalist dynamic is absent in the Soviet Union, the bureaucratic-militarist dynamic is very present indeed. . . . Thus, while the Soviet Union lacks an imperialist dynamic that springs from its economic organization, it does not lack an expansionist dynamic which reflects the needs of its establishment to consolidate its world position. . . ."[3]

ALIENATION

Legally speaking, the Soviet worker is one of the owners of all the factories in his and her land. Nevertheless, in the workers' own factory they must still take orders from the supervisor, arrive on time, and often do tedious routine work for many hours. Thus although one kind of alienation has been eliminated or reduced by socialism, other kinds still persist because of the needs of any modern industry.

The alienation in the factory is reinforced by the lack of democratic control over national political and economic policies. The Soviet worker is ordered about by the supervisor, by the manager above, by the higher economic agencies, by the police and secret police, by several layers of bureaucracy, and ultimately by the top political leaders, who are self-perpetuating. Thus the worker still has the

[2] Professor Papandreou was chairperson of the Department of Economics at University of California, Berkeley, before he returned to join the cabinet in the Greek government. The military coup resulted in his imprisonment and then exile. Now he is head of a socialist party.
[3] Andreas Papandreou, *Man's Freedom* (New York: Columbia University Press, 1970), p. 49.

feeling of facing a huge faceless machine. Undoubtedly, greater democratic participation in national decision making would reduce some of this alienated feeling.

Perhaps some greater feeling of control over one's life would also be contributed by a wide area of workers' control in the factory. In Yugoslavia, where workers' councils do have full legal control over the manager and the enterprise, some of this type of alienation may have been eliminated. Still, we noted that the Yugoslavs achieved this control at the expense of other kinds of alienation. Specifically, elimination of centralized bureaucracy means substitution of the marketplace as the arena of economic decision making. It thus means even more reliance on purely material motivations, on local gain (sometimes by monopoly profit) at the expense of the rest of society, and on highly differentiated individual incomes.

Both the Soviet Union and Yugoslavia (and to a lesser extent China) retain highly unequal income distributions. The Soviet income distribution is, however, many times less unequal than the American, mainly because the Soviets have no private income from ownership of capital. And the Soviets do have a much wider area of free public goods and services. Nevertheless, they are far from the communist principle of "payment according to need." In a society with this range of income distribution, even though it has socialist ownership of production, there are workers with relatively low incomes who feel left out of the growing affluence. And there are top leaders with very large individual incomes (only vaguely associated with their labor contribution) who have a vested interest in preserving their economic and political privileges. Hopefully, if and when the socialist countries achieve 70 percent or 80 percent of their distribution in free goods and services, workers will feel less alienated, the political structure will give up its coercive powers, and the whole attitude of people toward work and power will change. But for the present that is only speculation.

SUMMARY

From the viewpoint of most American radicals, the Soviet Union has been much more successful in solving economic problems (such as full employment, growth, and income distribution) than social and political problems (such as the elimination of alienation and dictatorship). The other countries calling themselves socialist are still too new to make any definite evaluation, except to point out that they have evolved a remarkable variety of social, political, and economic models, many of which are strikingly different from the Soviet model. All of these countries are still very, very far from the utopian communist ideal of people working for the social good without wages or prices—and with no coercive government. Moreover, since the U.S. economy has already finished the rough road of industrialization, a radical change here can begin with both socialism and democracy. These goals, plus peace and an end to discrimination, are the ideals for which radicals must struggle.

SUGGESTED FURTHER READINGS

Two journals contain numerous very useful and very interesting articles on every subject mentioned in this book. One is the *Review of Radical Political Economics* (Union for Radical Political Economics, Room 201, 41 Union Square West, New York, NY 10003). The other is *Monthly Review* (62 West 14th Street, New York, New York 10011).

For Part One on economic history, the best overall work is Maurice Dobb, *Studies in the Development of Capitalism* (International Publishers). A moving biography and explanation of Marx's ideas is Franz Mehring, *Karl Marx* (Ann Arbor Paperbacks). A good statement of Marx's theory of history is in Michael Harrington, *The Twilight of Capitalism* (Simon and Schuster).

For Part Two, the clearest exposition of different theories of value is Maurice Dobb, *Theories of Value and Distribution Since Adam Smith* (Cambridge University Press). The fullest data on monopoly power are in John Blair, *Economic Concentration* (Harcourt Brace Jovanovich). A moving history of the labor movement is in Richard Boyer and Herbert Morais, *Labor's Untold Story* (United Electrical, Radio and Machine Workers of America). The radical theory of government is stated in Ralph Miliband, *The State in Capitalist Society* (Basic Books). A good empirical description of the U.S. government is William Domhoff, *Who Rules America?* (Prentice-Hall). The socioeconomic role of education is explained in a potent fashion in Samuel Bowles and Herbert Gintis, *Schooling in Capitalist America* (Basic Books).

The nature of the labor process and labor markets is revealed in Richard Edwards, Michael Reich, and David Gordon, editors, *Labor Market Segmentation* (D. C. Heath). An excellent study of the economics of discrimination is Raymond Franklin and Solomon Resnik, *The Political Economy of Racism* (Holt, Rinehart & Winston). A comprehensive book on sex discrimination is Barbara Deckard, *The Women's Movement: Political, Socioeconomic, and Psychological Issues* (Harper & Row).

For Part Three, a powerful little book on pollution and ecological problems is Mathew Edel, *Economics and the Environment* (Prentice-Hall). On imperialism, the best single thing is Harry Magdoff, *The Age of Imperialism* (Monthly Review Press). A fascinating case study of imperialism, written as an autobiography, is Cheddi Jagan, *The West on Trial* (International Publishers). The relation of U.S. monopoly to private waste and government waste is explored in Paul Sweezy and Paul Baran, *Monopoly Capital* (Monthly Review Press).

For Part Four, the classic study of the Chinese Communists is by the journalist Edgar Snow, *Red Star Over China* (Grove). A more up-to-date and very exciting book is Jack Belden, *China Shakes the World* (Monthly Review Press). On the Soviet Union, the best analyses are found in the works of Isaac Deutscher. He gives a comprehensive political history in his biography *Stalin* (Oxford University Press). He is a superb writer and is at his best in his beautiful political biography *Trotsky* (Vintage Books, three volumes). The economy of Yugoslavia is carefully described by Howard Wachtel, *Workers Management and Workers Wages in Yugoslavia* (Cornell University Press).

Three excellent collections of radical readings covering all areas of economics are: (1) Richard Edwards, Michael Reich, and Thomas Weisskopf, editors, *The Capitalist System* (Prentice-Hall); (2) David Mermelstein, editor, *Economics: Mainstream Readings and Radical Critiques* (Random House); and (3) David Gordon, *Problems in Political Economy: An Urban Perspective* (D. C. Heath).

INDEX

77 78 79 80 9 8 7 6 5 4 3 2 1